T0155249

Programming in ILE RPG

Fifth Edition

Bryan Meyers

Jim Buck

MC|PRESS

MC Press Online, LLC
Boise, ID 83703 USA

Programming in ILE RPG

Bryan Meyers and Jim Buck

Fifth Edition

MC Press offers excellent discounts on this book when ordered in quantity for bulk purchases or special sales, which may include custom covers and content particular to your business, training goals, marketing focus, and branding interest.

MC Press Online, LLC

Corporate Offices: 3695 W. Quail Heights Court, Boise, ID 83703-3861 USA

Sales and Customer Service: (208) 629-7275 ext. 500;

service@mcpressonline.com

Permissions and Bulk/Special Orders: mcbooks@mcpressonline.com

www.mcpressonline.com • www.mc-store.com

ISBN: 978-1-58347-379-5

WB201509

Dedication

For my greatest accomplishments, Jason and Lindsey.

—B.D.M.

For my son Shannon, who I am very proud of!

—J.E.B.

About the Authors

Bryan Meyers is well known to IBM i technicians as the author of a number of books and magazine articles about the IBM i operating system and languages. His programming, management, and consulting career has spanned most of the IBM midrange history from the System/360 through the AS/400, and now IBM i. For much of that time, Bryan was the IT director for an international hospitality franchisor. He has also managed computer operations for municipal government, international construction, and broadcasting industries. Bryan's company, Enskill.com, provides onsite and online IBM i training to organizations worldwide.

Jim Buck's career in IT has spanned more than 30 years, primarily in the manufacturing and healthcare industries. Jim is an 11-year president of the Wisconsin Midrange Computer Professional Association (www.WMCPA.org) and has served on a number of teams developing IBM and COMMON certification tests. Jim is also a recipient of the 2007 IBM System i Innovation – Education Excellence Award, 2013 IBM Champion award, and the 2014 COMMON Presidents Award. Jim is a programming instructor at Gateway Technical College and is active in the IBM i community working to help students, colleges, and companies develop the next generation of IBM i professionals.

Acknowledgments

Editing the work of a single author can be a daunting task; working with two authors may seem like an impossible challenge. Cindy Bushong was up to the call, patiently working through our individual grammatical quirks with never a whisper of frustration. Anne Grubb at MC Press took over the publishing process in midstream, and kept us to a semblance of a schedule. Dan DiPinto created an eye-catching cover, and the skilled production team at Wordstop deftly performed layout duties. Finally, thanks to Barbara Morris at IBM, who graciously provided clarification when we were confused, and who rerouted us when we were on the wrong track.

The following Gateway Technical College graduates lent their programming skills to produce the databases, programming examples, and other ancillary materials for instructors: Ajay Gomez, Michelle Lyons, Kelly Mason, Steven Rusch, and Karyl Ruiz. Additional expertise developing the COMMON Associate RPG Developer exam was provided by the following Gateway Technical College graduates: Nick Arndt, Ajay Gomez, Mike Lamere, Brian Lannoye, and Jackie Zampanti, These young people are the next generation of IBM i professionals, and they should be proud of their accomplishments and efforts.

Contents

Supplemental materials for this book are available for download at
www.mc-store.com/Programming-ILE-RPG-Fifth-Edition/dp/1583473793.

Or scan the QR code to access this book's supplemental materials:

Preface

ILE RPG, the version of the RPG language that participates in IBM's Integrated Language Environment (ILE), represents a dramatic step forward in RPG's evolution. ILE RPG (also known generically as RPG IV) diverges from its predecessor, RPG/400 (aka RPG III), in significant ways. In many ways, though, ILE RPG maintains backward compatibility with older versions of RPG. Programs written using earlier RPG syntax can be readily converted to the new syntax. Although such backward compatibility is a practical solution for language developers and programmers, it means that the language must retain some components that, in fact, the new features make obsolete.

Writing a textbook about a new version of a language presents authors with a difficult decision: How much emphasis to give to those features that, although still available in the language, really represent an outmoded approach to programming? Giving obsolete syntax equal importance with the language's more modern features might inappropriately encourage students to write outdated code; at the very least, equal coverage can unnecessarily complicate the learning process. However, ignoring those obsolete features completely would give students an incomplete understanding of the language and would ill prepare them for program-maintenance tasks. With the introduction of free-format specifications, the challenge becomes even more problematic than before. The free-format syntax represents a much more dramatic departure from traditional columnar RPG than did previous releases.

This textbook tries to solve the dilemma by initially presenting students with the most suitable, modern techniques that ILE RPG offers for solving typical programming problems. As ILE RPG becomes widespread, it's important to present students with the language in its most current form, using the style and techniques that will serve them for the long term. Thus, the bulk of the book features the appropriate methods and strategies that contemporary programmers use, relegating much of the older style, operations, and fixed-format techniques to a special section in many chapters: "Navigating Legacy Code." This section still discusses ILE RPG, but it points out older coding styles that may appear in programs that programmers may have to maintain.

Programming in ILE RPG tries to bridge the gap between academia and the business world by presenting all the facets of RPG that a professional programmer needs. The material is introduced incrementally, and the book is organized so that students quickly begin writing complete, although simple, programs. Each successive chapter introduces additional information about RPG syntax and fundamental programming methods so that students become increasingly proficient at developing RPG programs—programs that grow in complexity as students progress through the book.

Each chapter includes a brief overview, which orients students to the material contained in the chapter, and a chapter summary, which reviews the chapter's major points. The end-of-chapter sections include discussion and review questions and exercises designed to help students develop their analytical and problem-solving skills, as well as their proficiency with RPG syntax.

Improved Structure Makes Learning Easier

The structure and order of this edition of *Programming in ILE RPG* have dramatically changed from previous editions of *Programming in RPG IV*. The new sequence of topics is the result of actual experience using the existing materials in both corporate training and academic institutional environments. We think you'll find that the new order and the new topics work better than previous editions to methodically introduce students to RPG. This edition also places much more emphasis on ILE and on Structured Query Language (SQL) than did previous editions. It enhances earlier coverage of procedures, service programs, binding, and APIs. The material uses Release 7.2 as a baseline and is current at that release and later.

Appendix A and the downloadable "ILE RPG Style Guide" (download information is provided at the end of this section) are intended to be reference material not only for students but also for working RPG programmers. Appendix A serves as a reference digest of RPG specifications, keywords, and miscellaneous entries. The style guide suggests style guidelines for writing programs that will be easy to read, understand, and maintain.

Although a complete introduction to using IBM i programmer tools is beyond the scope of this text, Appendix B introduces students to working on the system by using Rational Developer for i (RDi) as well as the older, but still widely used, Programming Development Manager (PDM). This appendix also acquaints students with RDi's LPEX editor and PDM's Source Entry Utility (SEU). Appendix C provides some insights into program testing and debugging, often bewildering processes for beginning programmers.

Depending on the length of the school term and the pace of the course, some instructors may choose to present this material over two terms. Instructor materials are available to those instructors adopting this text for classroom use. The materials provide answers to the review questions and solutions to the exercises. The instructor materials also include the source code for the solutions to the programming assignments and copies of the output produced by the solutions. The materials contain two versions of the databases used in the text. One is based on traditional files developed using DDS, and the other is an SQL schema.

Supplemental Materials Online

Supplemental materials offer students further opportunity to hone their programming skills. These programming assignments, their accompanying data files, and an ILE RPG style guide, are available for download at *www.mc-store.com/Programming-ILE-RPG-Fifth-Edition/dp/1583473793*. Or simply scan the QR code at the end of this section to access the download links on the book's Web page.

The programming exercises for each chapter are arranged roughly in order of difficulty, so that instructors can assign programs appropriate to their time schedules and their students' abilities. Although none of the program solutions are long by commercial standards, some of the necessary algorithms are quite difficult; the assignments require time and effort on the students' part to develop correct solutions. Unfortunately, there is no easy road to becoming a good programmer, nor can students learn to deal with program complexity by merely reading or talking it about it. Programming, as much as any other activity we know, is truly a matter of learning by doing. Those students interested in becoming IT professionals must recognize that they have chosen a rewarding—but demanding and challenging—profession, and they need to realize that they must be willing to work hard to succeed in this profession.

To give students experience developing application systems, rather than programming in a vacuum, most of the programming assignments relate to three fictitious organizations and their application needs. By working on these assignments, students should gain a sense of how a company's data files are repeatedly used by numerous applications for different, related purposes. To find supplemental information about each of these entities, including database files, visit the following sites:

- Pyxis Global Airlines: www.pyxisair.net
- Cloud Services 24x7: www.cloudservices24x7.net
- Wibaux University: www.wibaux.net

(This supplemental information is also available at the previously mentioned *mc-store.com* link.)

The following supplemental materials for this book are available for download at *www.mc-store.com/Programming-ILE-RPG-Fifth-Edition/dp/1583473793*.

- Programming Assignments
- ILE RPG Style Guide
- Data Files for Programming Exercises

Or scan the QR code to access this book's supplemental materials:

CHAPTER 1

Introduction to Programming and RPG

1.1. Chapter Overview

This chapter introduces you to RPG and describes its history and evolution from punched cards to a modern business programming language. It also explains general programming and computer-related concepts that you need to know as you begin to program in ILE RPG.

1.2. Programming

Computer programming involves writing instructions for a computer that tell it how to process, or manipulate, data. No matter how complex a computer application is, its actions are ultimately directed by individual lines of code that operate on input information and generate a result. When you organize and group those individual instructions together, they typically represent a step-by-step process that results in a specific product, such as a sales report. It is a computer programmer's job to design, organize, write, and test those individual lines of code, creating a working computer program as the end result.

The computer is a binary device with electronic components that can depict only two states: on and off, or flow of current and no flow. To represent those states, computers internally store and manipulate instructions (and data) as patterns of **bits**, or binary digits, with values of 1 or 0. Programmers originally were forced to write computer instructions as strings of 1s and 0s, using machine language. Humans, however, do not function as well at this low representation level. Fortunately, advances in computer science soon led to the development of high-level languages (HLLs).

A **high-level language** allows a programmer to write computer instructions in a format and syntax that is more easily recognizable than long strings of 1s and 0s. This HLL **source code** is stored in a file on the computer. But before the computer can actually execute the instructions, they must be translated into the bit patterns that the computer can recognize. The computer itself can accomplish this translation by using a special program called a **compiler**. A compiler reads the source code and translates it into machine language that the computer can understand.

1.3. History of RPG

IBM introduced the **Report Program Generator** (RPG) programming language in the early 1960s. RPG was one of the first HLLs. It filled a niche for providing quick solutions to a common business task: generating reports needed within the business. RPG was unique among computer languages in several respects.

RPG is a procedural language. **Procedural languages** typically require that you explicitly code each processing step or instruction, in the correct sequence, to define the procedure or process necessary for the computer to produce the end result. Unlike other procedural languages, RPG did not require the programmer to detail each processing step. Instead, the language included a fixed-logic cycle that automatically executed the normal read-calculate-write process in most report programs.

The RPG programmer's job was to accurately describe the files, record layouts, calculations, and output desired for a specific program. RPG required that these descriptive specifications appear in a specific sequence within a program and that entries within each specification line appear in fixed locations, or columns. The programmer typically coded these specifications onto paper hole-punch cards, a deck of which formed the source code for a program. The RPG compiler read that card deck and, through its logic cycle, supplied the needed missing steps to provide a standard machine language program for the computer to execute.

Another unique characteristic of RPG was its use of a special class of built-in variables called **indicators**. These variables, many of which simply had numbers for names, were predefined to the computer and could have only one of two values: '1' or '0' (corresponding to *on* or *off*). A programmer could set the indicators to on or off in one part of the program and then reference their status in another part of the program to specify what processing was to occur.

1.3.1. RPG II

By the late 1960s, RPG had gained popularity, especially in small and midsize data processing departments. Programmers were stretching the language beyond its original intended use, using RPG for complex computations and complicated file updating as well as for report generation.

Accordingly, IBM introduced an enhanced version of the language, RPG II, when it released its System/3 computer. A few other computer vendors observed the popularity of RPG and developed RPG II compilers for their minicomputers, but for the most part, RPG remained a language associated with IBM installations.

1.3.2. RPG III

During the 1970s, several trends in data processing became apparent. First, as computers became less expensive and more powerful, and as operating systems became more sophisticated, interest in interactive programs began to mushroom. In **interactive applications**, a user interacts directly with the computer through a terminal or workstation to control the actions of a computer program as it is running. Previously, programs had involved only **batch processing**, in which the computer processes a *batch* of data (typically representing business transactions) without user intervention.

A second emerging trend was a growing interest in a database approach to data management. With a database approach, programmers define data independently of programs by using a database design tool, such as **Structured Query Language (SQL)**. The files storing the data are rigorously designed and organized to minimize redundancy and to facilitate accessing data stored in separate files. Any program can use these database files without having to explicitly define the details of the data within the program itself.

Finally, a third trend during that decade was an increasing concern with program design. This trend resulted in a methodology called **structured design**. As companies' libraries of developed programs continued to grow, the need to revise those programs to fit evolving business requirements grew as well. It became apparent that computer professionals had paid too little attention to the initial design of programs. Poorly designed programs were causing inefficiencies in program maintenance. Experts attributed much of this inefficiency to *spaghetti code* (i.e., programs that included undisciplined, haphazard transfer of control from one part of a program to another).

Advocates of structured design recommended restricting indiscriminate flow of control within a program and using only those operations that kept tight controls on that flow. With this emphasis on structured design, concepts of modular programming and code reusability also began to emerge.

IBM addressed all these trends when it introduced the System/38 minicomputer in 1979. This computer's architecture was unique in that the design of the computer and its operating system featured a built-in database. The S/38 required data files to be predefined at a system level before a program could reference or use those files. This requirement alone forced IBM to release a new version of RPG to allow external file definition. IBM called this version RPG III.

At this time, IBM also made several other major changes to RPG. First, it added features that made it easier for programmers to develop interactive applications. Second, to address structured design issues, IBM included structured operations for looping and decision logic. Finally, to support modular code and reusability, IBM revamped the language to include the capability to perform calls to other programs and to pass data between programs.

1.3.3. RPG/400

In 1988, IBM announced its successor computer to the S/38: the Application System/400, or AS/400. With the new computer came a new version of RPG—RPG/400.

Despite its name, RPG/400 was really just a compiler that read the existing RPG III syntax, with a few new operations and enhancements. Following RPG/400's initial release, IBM periodically added more features to the language, but these changes were relatively minor as well.

1.3.4. ILE RPG

Meanwhile, a growing number of critics accused RPG of being difficult to understand because of its short data names, abbreviated operation codes, and rigidly fixed format. The critics contended that the language was showing its age in its limited choice of data types (e.g., no direct support for date data types), its inability to handle multidimensional arrays, and its patchwork approach to data definition.

To address some of these criticisms, in 1994, concurrent with the release of Version 3 of the AS/400's operating system (called OS/400), IBM introduced a version of RPG sufficiently unlike earlier versions that it warranted a name change: ILE RPG, informally known as RPG IV. In addition to trying to address the criticisms previously mentioned, IBM included RPG as part of its newly introduced **Integrated Language Environment (ILE)**, a programming model that allows program modules to be first compiled and then bound together into executable programs. This change supported the growing interest in developing reusable units of code and improving system performance. Moreover, it let programmers develop a program by using modules written in different languages and then bind these modules into a single program.

ILE RPG relaxes many of the strict fixed-format requirements previous RPG versions imposed, allowing free-format expressions and keyword notation in its specifications. Data-naming limits have been extended, and many other artificial limits have been effectively removed from the language. In addition, ILE RPG adds several new organizational constructs, including a central data-definition specification and procedure prototyping, which lets many program modules efficiently share information with each other. ILE RPG borrows many of the best features of other programming languages, incorporating those features into its own new syntax.

IBM has rebranded the AS/400 hardware several times over its lifetime to conform to current marketing strategies. It has been known by various combinations of AS/400, eServer, iSeries, and System i. Recently, IBM has consolidated its enterprise hardware into the Power Systems server line. The OS/400 operating system software has also been rebranded, first as i5/OS and now IBM i, which is the name we use in this text. Despite the system's various names, though, the ILE RPG syntax remains intact.

Note
Today, IBM Power Systems servers can run with a choice of operating systems, including Linux, AIX (an IBM-branded flavor of UNIX), and IBM i. ILE RPG is exclusive to IBM i and will not compile programs for Linux or AIX environments.

Recent releases of ILE RPG have focused on enabling the RPG architecture to coexist with Internet-based applications and objected-oriented languages, including Java. Modern e-business applications usually incorporate several hardware platforms (most notably, Intel-based computers) and software standards. As RPG evolves, it strives to maintain compatibility with these platforms and standards.

These changes have quieted, but not suppressed, RPG's critics. However, given the large base of existing RPG applications and IBM's present willingness to support RPG, it is likely that the language will continue to evolve and will remain the primary language for application development on IBM i for many years to come.

Comparing RPG programs written 20 years ago with those written by RPG professionals today reveals their great design differences. These differences are not due solely to the use of operations unavailable in the past, although the new operations enabled the changes. The biggest change is that RPG, originally a language that emphasized specification instead of procedure, has been transformed by programming practices into a largely free-format procedural language. Today's programmers virtually ignore RPG's fixed-logic cycle—the feature that made the language unique in the 1960s. And most modern programmers use RPG's indicators only in those instances in which the language absolutely requires their use.

Note
Though this book refers to Power Systems hardware throughout, most ILE RPG concepts also apply to older AS/400 and iSeries hardware. The IBM i operating system concepts apply to the operating system under its old names, OS/400 and i5/OS, as well.

1.3.5. Learning the RPG Language

Many RPG texts start by instructing students in RPG II and introduce RPG III or ILE RPG only after thoroughly indoctrinating the students in the fixed-logic cycle and the use of indicators. This book begins by teaching RPG as today's programmers use it.

The newest releases of the ILE RPG compiler allow free-format specifications, which provide many advantages, including better readability, improved reliability, the ability to indent code, and a similarity to other languages you may already know. Generally, this book presents free-format illustrations. Because free format is a relatively new feature of RPG, however, it's likely that you will encounter many older fixed-format RPG programs. To support those programs, we also include examples of fixed-format ILE RPG entries and compare them with their preferred free-format alternatives.

Now that you have an understanding of RPG's evolution, we can turn to some basic programming concepts that you need to know before you begin to learn ILE RPG programming.

Tip
For better or worse, most companies still use some programs that were written 20 or more years ago. Because your first job in the computer profession is likely to involve maintenance programming, you no doubt will be working with some programs based on RPG III, or even RPG II. You therefore need to understand the features of these language versions so that you can modify such programs when you encounter them.

1.4. Program Variables

Computer programs would be of little worth if you needed a different program each time you wanted to change the values of the data to be processed. For example, assume you are developing a payroll program and one processing step is to multiply the number of hours worked by pay rate. If you must rewrite this step to explicitly state the number of hours worked and the hourly pay rate for each employee, you are better off calculating wages manually or with a calculator. The power and value of computer programming rests in the concept of variables.

A program **variable** is a named data item within a program that represents a location in the computer's memory that can store data. When a programming instruction involves the manipulation of a variable, the computer checks the value stored at that memory location and uses that value in the calculation. Thus, you can instruct the computer to multiply the value stored in variable Hours by the value stored in variable Rate and then store the answer in variable GrossPay. If Hours contains 35 and Rate 6, GrossPay becomes 210; if Hours contains 40 and Rate 5, GrossPay becomes 200; and so on. In a program, you might represent this process by using variable names in this expression:

```
GrossPay = Hours * Rate;
```

RPG has traditionally used the term *field* rather than *variable*. Modern usage tends to restrict the term **field** to those variables defined within a database file and uses **variable** for other data items defined in the program, but the terms are generally interchangeable. RPG is a strictly typed language that requires you to define all variables by naming them, assigning each one a fixed length that determines the amount of memory allocated for storing the variable's values, and declaring what type of data (e.g., character, numeric, date) the variable contains. A program variable's name has meaning only within the context of the program where it is defined, even if it is a field in a database file. Subsequent chapters of this book examine the methods RPG uses to define variables and the data types it allows.

1.5. Libraries, Objects, and Data Files

An important IBM i architectural concept is that of objects. Almost every named entity is an **object**, and every object is categorized by type. The object type identifies the purpose of the object and how it is used by the computer. The following are some common object types:

- Libraries (designated as object type *LIB), which are containers for other objects
- Files (*FILE), which hold formatted data records
- Programs (*PGM), which contain executable machine instructions
- Commands (*CMD), which are shortcuts to executing programs
- Data areas (*DTAARA), which are spaces that store brief unformatted information
- User profiles (*USRPRF), which contain user IDs, passwords, and authorization and configuration information

RPG programs typically center on processing sets of data in files stored on disk or removable storage. Like other objects, files are stored within libraries. You can refer to an object by its **simple object name** (e.g., CUSTOMERS) without referring to a specific library. Or you can refer to an object by using its **qualified name**, which specifies the library where the object is stored (e.g., FLIGHTPROJ/CUSTOMERS). The qualified name includes the library name first, a slash (/) separator character, and then the object name. When you use the simple name, the system searches a path called the **library list** to locate the object to process. However, when you use the qualified name, the system processes the object in the specified library without regard to the library list.

The IBM i database—officially known as DB2 for IBM i—supports two major types of database files: physical files and logical files. A **physical file** contains physical data, whereas a **logical file** contains a customized view of the data in a physical file. Logical files do not hold actual data records. Instead, they provide sorting and selection criteria for processing the records in the physical file. Logical files are typically maintained dynamically. That means when you change a record in a physical file, the view of that data changes in every logical file related to the physical file. Changing a record in a logical file also alters the physical record in the related physical file. RPG does not distinguish between physical files and logical files; it uses the same coding and techniques to process either one.

Generally, the information in a physical file falls into one of two conceptual categories: transaction or master. Files containing details of transactions, generated during the course of the day's business, are transaction files. **Transaction files** might include individual sales transactions, orders, hours worked, journal entries, or similar information. Once you have processed a transaction file, you typically have no further use for it except for archival purposes. In contrast, most companies have sets of data that are of long-term importance to the company. These files, called **master files**, contain vital information about customers, products, accounts, and so on. Although you can update or change master files, companies regard master files as permanent files of data. The IBM i database does not specifically identify files as master files or transaction files. Instead, it stores all the data in physical files (within libraries) in arrival sequence order. Your RPG application determines how you will use the data in the file.

Files contain one or more members. **Members** are individual groups, or sets, of data within the file, each with the same format. The data in a file exists inside a member. Typically, an RPG program processes the data in only one member, usually the first (or only) member in a file. Figure 1.1 shows a typical library-file-member hierarchy.

1.5.1. Files, Records, and Fields

All files are organized into a data hierarchy of file-member-record-field. A file is a collection of data about a given kind of entity or object. For example, a business might have a customer master file that contains information about its customers. In the IBM i architecture, a file is a distinct object, which you can create, move, copy, rename, delete, save, and restore as a unit. Files encompass one or more members, or subsets, of the file object. A member is not an object; it is a component of the file object—most files have only one member.

A file member, in turn, is split into **records** that contain data about one specific instance of the entity. Data about customer number 032145698 is stored in a record within the customer file, and data about customer number 195241055 is stored in a separate record within that same file.

Figure 1.1: Libraries, files, and members

Finally, each record holds several discrete pieces of data about each entity instance. For example, a customer record might contain the customer's account number, name, postal code, email address, and so on. Each of these items is a field. A field generally represents the smallest unit of data that you want to manipulate within a program.

The components of this data hierarchy are similar to a spreadsheet's rows and columns, which correspond to a file's records and fields. Figure 1.2 illustrates the data in a file as a spreadsheet.

CUSTNO	CFNAME	CLNAME	CADDR	CZIP	CPHONE	CEMAIL	CDOB	CGENDER
032145698	MEGAN	JOHNSON	310 ORANGE ST.	54911	9202091547	meganj2@gmail.com	11,071,993	F
032214521	JILLIAN	BAZION	7118 TULIP AVE.	71674	6233104568	jbazion3234@mail.com	5,161,991	F
101456320	KATHY	KOONTZ	8762 TAILS AVE	99529	9202861454	koontzk@sleep.com	5,301,987	F
110161975	JULIA	ROBINS	434 BISON VALLEY ROAD	53105	2629855695	JROBINS@YAHOO.COM	10,161,975	F
111121958	JON	THOMPSON	124 MAIN BLVD	53104	2625385599	JTHOMPSON@GMAIL.COM	11,121,958	M
125478545	SUSAN	ANTHONY	7867 NORTH AVE.	89123	9876543217	anthonys@gmail.com	9,091,999	F
191482511	NARIZA	ABDUL HALIM	5652 N. 46TH ST.	49008	6161254115	narizaah@verizon.net	2,111,955	M
191775858	Jental	ABDUL HALIM	5652 N. 46TH ST.	49008	6161254115	jentalah@verizon.net	12,122,012	F

Figure 1.2: Data file organization

All records within a file have the same fields of data. The file's **record format**, or record layout, describes the fields within a record. Physical files (i.e., files that have data) have only one record format. Because you define these fields to be fixed in length, if an alphanumeric value—for example, a person's last name—is shorter than the space allocated for it, blanks, or spaces, occupy the unused positions to the right of the value. For a numeric value that is smaller than the space allocated for it, the system stores zeros in the unused positions. If the Loyalty Points field, for example, is nine positions long and has a value of 25897, the value is stored in the file as 000025897. Note that numeric values are stored as *pure* numbers, without **currency symbols** (e.g., dollar signs); **thousands separators** (e.g., commas); or **radix characters** (decimal marks, e.g., period). A numeric field that includes decimal places is described with a total length, including the decimal places. For example, a numeric field described as seven digits with two decimal places can contain a value up to 99,999.99, which it stores as 9999999.

Note
Different countries use different notations for numeric representation using currency symbols, thousands separators, and radix characters. This text uses the United States convention: $123,456.78. Your installation might use other formats.

1.6. Programming Specifications

In many installations, programmers work from specifications they receive from systems analysts. These specifications detail the desired output of a program, the required input, and a general statement of the necessary processing. The programmer must then develop the instructions needed to generate the appropriate output from the given input, ensuring that the correct data manipulations occur.

Analysts can provide record layouts to describe the record formats of input files that a program is to use. One common method of presenting a record layout, called **length notation**, lists fields in the order in which they appear and gives the length of each field. The other common method, **positional notation**, explicitly shows the beginning and ending position of each field. As Figure 1.3 shows, these methods include information about the data type of each field, along with the number of decimal positions for numeric data. Generally, length notation is preferred.

Programmers use several tools to retrieve and document the record layout for a file. Rational Developer for i (RDi) features a Field Table view, as Figure 1.4 shows. IBM i includes the **DSPFFD (Display File Field Description)** command, which displays or prints the record layout. This command can also put the record layout information into another database file. Figure 1.5 illustrates the typical DSPFFD output.

Customer Number	First Name	Last Name	Address	Postal Code	Phone	Email	Birth Date (0 decimals)	Gender
1-9	10-24	25-44	45-74	75-79	80-89	90-139	140-144	145-145

Length Notation

Field	Data Type	Length	Decimal Positions
Customer Number	Alphanumeric	9	-
First Name	Alphanumeric	15	-
Last Name	Alphanumeric	20	-
Address	Alphanumeric	30	-
Postal Code	Alphanumeric	5	-
Phone	Alphanumeric	10	-
Email	Alphanumeric	50	-
Birth Date	Packed Numeric	8	0
Gender	Alphanumeric	1	-

Positional Notation

Field	Data Type	From/To	Decimal Positions
First Name	Alphanumeric	10-24	-
Last Name	Alphanumeric	25-44	-
Address	Alphanumeric	45-74	-
Postal Code	Alphanumeric	75-79	-
Phone	Alphanumeric	80-89	-
Email	Alphanumeric	90-139	-
Birth Date	Packed Numeric	140-144	0
Gender	Alphanumeric	145-145	-

Figure 1.3: Alternative methods of describing record layouts

	Properties	Source Prompter	Field Table ⊠	Commands Log	Data Table

: File FLIGHTPROJ/CUSTOMERS (9 Fields)

Name	Record	Type	Length	Text
CUSTNO	CUSTSREC	Character	9	CUSTOMER NUMBER
CFNAME	CUSTSREC	Character	15	CUSTOMER FIRST NAME
CLNAME	CUSTSREC	Character	20	CUSTOMER LAST NAME
CADDR	CUSTSREC	Character	30	CUSTOMER STREET ADDRESS
CZIP	CUSTSREC	Character	5	ZIP CODE
CPHONE	CUSTSREC	Character	10	CUSTOMER PHONE
CEMAIL	CUSTSREC	Character	50	CUSTOMER EMAIL
CDOB	CUSTSREC	Packed Decimal	8.0	CUSTOMER DATE OF BIRTH
CGENDER	CUSTSREC	Character	1	F=FEMALE M=MALE

Figure 1.4: RDi Field Table

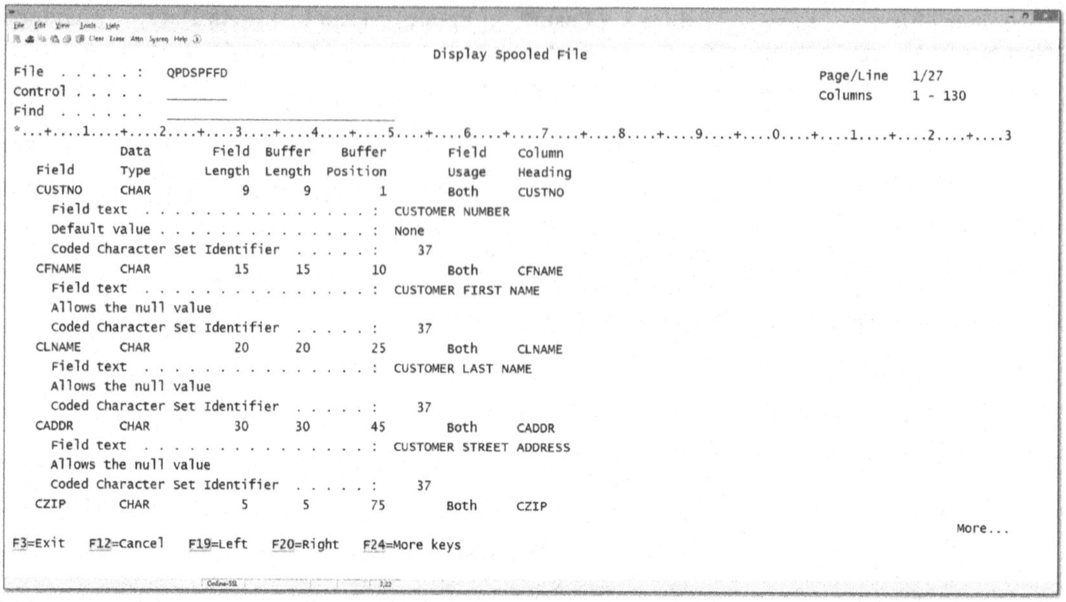

```
                                    Display Spooled File
File . . . . . :   QPDSPFFD                                              Page/Line   1/27
Control . . . . .  ________                                              Columns     1 - 130
Find  . . . . . .  ______________________________
*...+....1....+....2....+....3....+....4....+....5....+....6....+....7....+....8....+....9....+....0....+....1....+....2....+....3
               Data          Field  Buffer   Buffer        Field    Column
   Field       Type          Length Length   Position      Usage    Heading
   CUSTNO      CHAR             9       9        1         Both     CUSTNO
     Field text  . . . . . . . . . . . . . . . :  CUSTOMER NUMBER
     Default value . . . . . . . . . . . . . . :  None
     Coded Character Set Identifier  . . . . . :     37
   CFNAME      CHAR            15      15       10         Both     CFNAME
     Field text  . . . . . . . . . . . . . . . :  CUSTOMER FIRST NAME
     Allows the null value
     Coded Character Set Identifier  . . . . . :     37
   CLNAME      CHAR            20      20       25         Both     CLNAME
     Field text  . . . . . . . . . . . . . . . :  CUSTOMER LAST NAME
     Allows the null value
     Coded Character Set Identifier  . . . . . :     37
   CADDR       CHAR            30      30       45         Both     CADDR
     Field text  . . . . . . . . . . . . . . . :  CUSTOMER STREET ADDRESS
     Allows the null value
     Coded Character Set Identifier  . . . . . :     37
   CZIP        CHAR             5       5       75         Both     CZIP
                                                                                          More...
F3=Exit   F12=Cancel   F19=Left   F20=Right   F24=More keys
```

Figure 1.5: DSPFFD command output

Notice that the record format has a name (CUSTSREC in Figure 1.4). RPG programs can generally refer to the filename or the record format name, depending upon the operation being performed.

1.6.1. Designing the Report

When the desired output includes a report, most programmers design the details of the report with an online development tool, such as Report Designer, a component of the RDi software product described in Appendix B. **Report Designer** is a visual tool you use to design the desired report layout. Figure 1.6 illustrates the Report Designer user interface (refer to Appendix B to learn how to use this valuable tool).

The position of lines on the display indicates the desired line spacing on the report layout. The display also shows all constants (e.g., report headings or titles, column headings) that the report is to include and where on the report they are to appear. The Report Designer display generally represents variable information by using Os for characters or 6s for numbers, with each O or 6 representing one character or number.

You often want numeric data presented with special formats to facilitate comprehension. The Report Designer display can depict the desired formatting, or **output editing**. Currency symbols, thousands separators, radix characters, and other insertion characters included on the display specify that these characters are to appear in the printed output. For example, in Figure 1.4, the display indicates to insert slashes within the date, to place asterisks to the right of totals, and to include a currency symbol with the grand total amount.

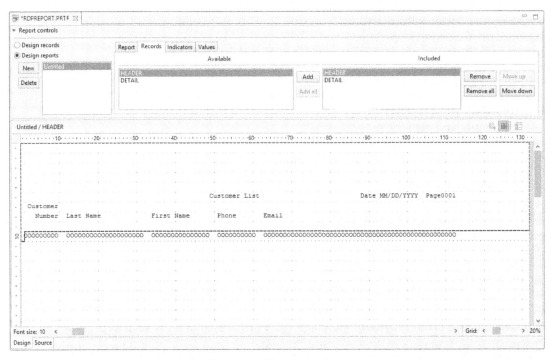

Figure 1.6: Report Designer

You can print some data on the report by using zero suppression. **Zero suppression** means simply that leading, nonsignificant zeros are not printed. Thus, 000123 prints as bbb123 (where b = blank) if zero suppression is in effect.

Currency symbols (e.g., $) can appear two ways in output: as fixed or as floating symbols. A **fixed currency symbol** is positioned in a set column of the output, regardless of the number of significant digits in the number following the sign. A **floating currency symbol** is printed next to the leftmost significant digit of the number—its position varies, or *floats*, depending upon the value of the number with which it is associated.

You may also need to consider whether negative numeric values should print in a fixed position or float either to the left or right of the numeric value. Another common notation is to print the characters CR to the right of a negative numeric value to indicate a credit notation.

1.7. The Program Development Cycle

The programmer's job is to develop a solution to a data processing problem represented by the program specifications. To achieve this solution, the programmer generally uses a method called the **program development cycle**.

This process, which summarizes the sequence of activities required in programming, includes the following steps:

1. Define the problem.
2. Design the solution.
3. Write/code the program.
4. Compile and bind the program.
5. Test and debug the program.
6. Document the program.
7. Maintain the program.

The cycle starts with problem definition. It should be obvious that unless you understand the problem, as described in the programming specifications, you have little chance of devising a correct solution.

Once you understand the problem, you need to design a solution. **Program design** requires working out the process, or **algorithm**, to reach the solution to the problem before expressing it in a given programming language. Formal design tools such as program flow charts or pseudocode can help clarify and illustrate program logic. Some programmers develop their own methods of sketching out a program solution.

Regardless of the method you use, the importance of designing a solution before writing the program cannot be overemphasized. Developing a correct, well-structured design for a program represents the challenge of programming. This is the stage where most of your thinking should occur. Time spent at the design stage results in time saved fixing problems later in the cycle.

Writing the program involves translating the design into a program by using a particular programming language. This stage is often called **coding**. Beginning programmers may find this task difficult because they are unfamiliar with the rules of the language. Once you have mastered the syntax of a language, however, coding becomes almost a mechanical process that requires relatively little thought. The challenge of programming lies in design.

Years ago, coding consisted of keypunching program statements onto cards. Today, most program entry is done interactively on a terminal by using a system utility called an **editor**. Many tools, known as **integrated development environments (IDEs)**, exist to help with this step of the program development cycle. For IBM i, the two most common IDEs are **Program Development Manager (PDM)** and a more current product, **RDi**. PDM includes an editor called **Source Entry Utility (SEU)**, which Figure 1.7 illustrates. Figure 1.8 shows RDi's editor—**LPEX (Live Parsing Extensible Editor)**. A special type of physical file, the **source physical file**, is specifically formatted to hold program source statements. When you use an editor to code a program, you are typically changing records in the source physical file.

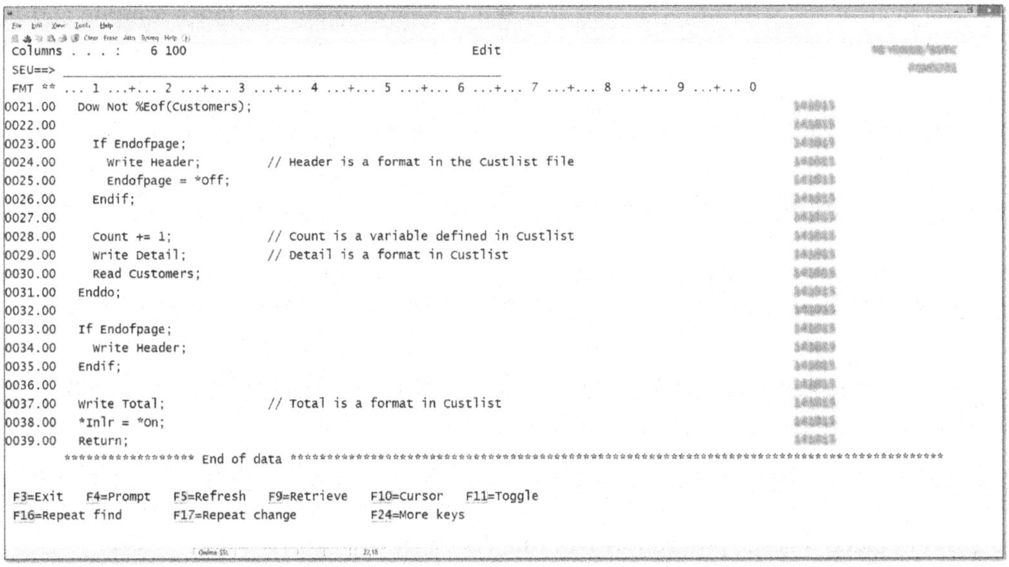

Figure 1.7: Source Entry Utility (SEU)

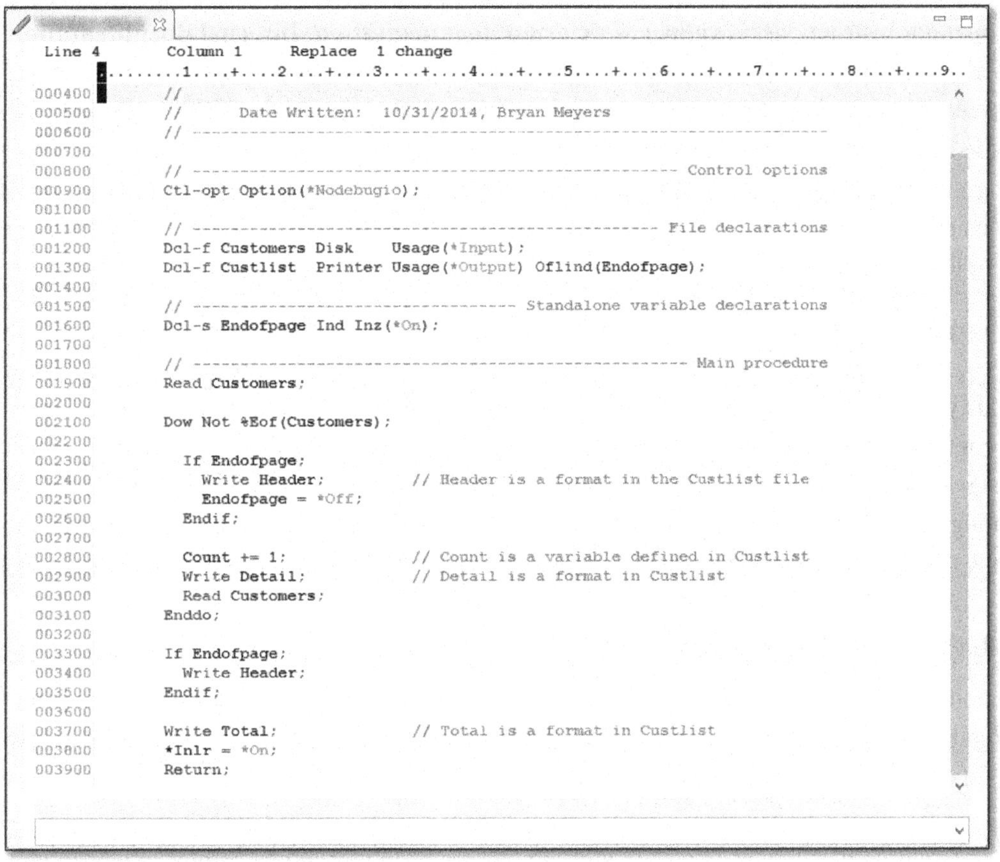

```
Line 4        Column 1     Replace  1 change
       .........1....+....2....+....3....+....4....+....5....+....6....+....7....+....8....+....9..
000400     //
000500     //     Date Written:  10/31/2014, Bryan Meyers
000600     // ----------------------------------------------------------------
000700
000800     // -------------------------------------------------- Control options
000900     Ctl-opt Option(*Nodebugio);
001000
001100     // -------------------------------------------------- File declarations
001200     Dcl-f Customers Disk    Usage(*Input);
001300     Dcl-f Custlist  Printer Usage(*Output) Oflind(Endofpage);
001400
001500     // --------------------------------- Standalone variable declarations
001600     Dcl-s Endofpage Ind Inz(*On);
001700
001800     // -------------------------------------------------- Main procedure
001900     Read Customers;
002000
002100     Dow Not %Eof(Customers);
002200
002300       If Endofpage;
002400         Write Header;        // Header is a format in the Custlist file
002500         Endofpage = *Off;
002600       Endif;
002700
002800       Count += 1;            // Count is a variable defined in Custlist
002900       Write Detail;          // Detail is a format in Custlist
003000       Read Customers;
003100     Enddo;
003200
003300     If Endofpage;
003400       Write Header;
003500     Endif;
003600
003700     Write Total;             // Total is a format in Custlist
003800     *Inlr = *On;
003900     Return;
```

Figure 1.8: Live Parsing Extensible Editor (LPEX)

After you have coded your program and stored it as source code, you must compile and bind it to translate the RPG source code into machine language and prepare it for execution. The compiler translates the source code, and the **binding process** copies the compiled code into a program object (in a library, of course), which the computer can then execute. The compile and bind steps are two distinct processes, but for many programs, you can combine the steps with a single command to the computer.

Testing the program is required to determine the existence of syntax or logic errors in your solution. **Syntax errors** are errors in your use of the rules of the language. The computer flags these errors either as you enter the statements or later when the compiler tries to translate your statements into machine language. **Logic errors** are errors of design. It is up to you, as the programmer, to detect such errors through rigorous program testing by running the program with sets of test data and carefully checking the accuracy of the program's output. **Debugging** means discovering and correcting errors. Testing should continue until you are convinced that the program is working correctly.

Program documentation provides material useful for understanding, using, or changing the program. Some documentation, such as system and program flow charts, user manuals, or operator instructions, is known as **external documentation**. **Internal documentation** refers to comments included within the code itself. Such comments make the program more understandable to other programmers. Although documentation appears as one of the final stages in the program development cycle, it is best to develop documentation as you progress through the stages of the cycle. For example, providing comments within a program is easiest as you are actually entering the program, rather than waiting until the program is completely tested and running.

Program maintenance is the process of making changes once the program is actually being used, or *in production*. Estimates are that up to 70 percent of a programmer's time is spent modifying existing programs. The need for maintenance can arise from a *bug* discovered in a program or from changing user needs. Because maintenance is a way of life, you should design all programs you develop with ease of future maintenance in mind. This means, among other things, ensuring that your code's logic and organization are clear, that variable names are unambiguous, and that internal comments are appropriate and sufficient.

1.8. Program Entry and Testing

To complete the program entry and testing stages, you must eliminate all program errors. As indicated earlier, these errors fall into two general classes: syntax errors and logic errors. Syntax errors represent violations of the rules of the language itself and are relatively easy to identify and correct. Logic errors occur in your program and cause the program to produce incorrect results. You detect these problems by extensively testing the program with sets of test data and correcting program statements that are causing incorrect processing.

As mentioned earlier, you typically enter a program by interacting with the system's editor. Your program statements, called *source code*, are stored in a source physical file. The set of statements for one program module constitutes a **source member** (often called a **compile unit**). Members containing code for ILE RPG source have a **member type** property of **RPGLE** to distinguish them from members containing source for other languages. The editor specifies the member type when it first creates the source member.

The editor detects some syntax errors as you enter your program and lets you correct them immediately. Other syntax errors become apparent when you attempt to compile your program. To **compile** means to translate the source code into machine language, or **object code**. A program called a **compiler** accomplishes this translation, provided you have not violated any rules of ILE RPG in writing your program. The IBM i command **CRTRPGMOD (Create RPG Module)** executes the ILE RPG compiler, which translates RPGLE source members. If syntax errors prevent the translation from being completed, the compiler provides you with a list of the syntax errors it encountered. You must fix all such errors before you can progress to the next stage of testing.

When your program is free of syntax errors, the compiler creates a module object. The **module** is an intermediate building block for a program. You must, in turn, bind the module (with other modules, if appropriate) to produce an executable program that can be run on the server. The **CRTPGM (Create Program)** command accomplishes this binding step. If your source code represents an entire program in one module, the **CRTBNDRPG (Create Bound RPG Program)** command lets you combine compiling and binding into a single step.

After you have successfully compiled and bound your program, you need to run it with test data to determine whether it is working correctly. Note that the computer executes the bound program object (i.e., the translated version of your program). Errors discovered at this stage require you to back up, make changes to the program by using the editor, and then recompile the program and bind it again before conducting additional testing. Figure 1.9 illustrates this iterative process.

If you forget to recompile and rebind your program after making changes to the source code, the computer will run your old version of the program because you have not created a new object incorporating those changes.

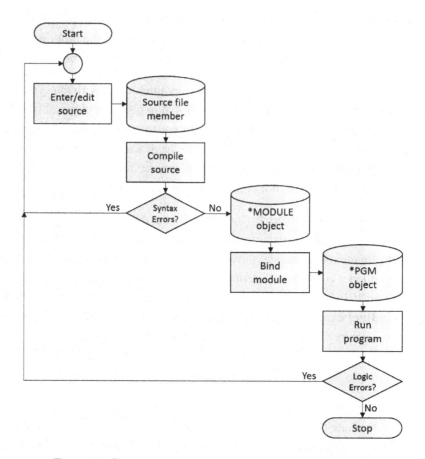

Figure 1.9: Steps required to enter, test, and debug a program

1.9. Chapter Summary

Report Program Generator, or RPG, is a high-level programming language introduced by IBM in the early 1960s to provide an easy way to produce commonly needed business reports. Since introducing RPG, IBM has added enhancements to expand the language's functionality. Programmers originally used RPG's fixed-logic cycle and built-in indicators to minimize the need for explicit procedural instructions within their programs. As processing requirements have grown more complex and concerns about program understandability have increased, programmers have moved away from the fixed-logic cycle and now tend to explicitly include all processing instructions within their programs.

Variables enable programs to process different sets of data. RPG provides this flexibility through fixed-length named fields that generally represent character or numeric data (although other types of data are supported).

The IBM i object architecture uses libraries to store named entities for specific purposes. A prominent type of object is the file, which stores data records. Data is typically organized in a hierarchy of files, records, and fields. Physical files contain actual data records, whereas logical files allow for sorting and selecting records in a physical file. Relatively temporary data files that often need to be processed only once are called *transaction files*, and files of data of lasting importance to the company are known as *master files*.

The process of developing a program is frequently described as the program development cycle. The cycle begins with problem definition. The problem often is presented through programming specifications, which include record layouts of files the program is to use, utilities that describe the layout of desired reports and displays, and an overview of needed processing.

In addition to defining the problem, the program development cycle includes designing the solution, writing the program, compiling and binding the program, testing and debugging, documenting, and—eventually—maintaining the program once it is in production. Too often, programmers shortcut the design stage and try to develop their logic as they write the program. This approach often leads to programs that are poorly designed or full of errors that must be corrected.

You enter an RPG program as source code by using an editor provided for that purpose. The program is stored as a source member within a source physical file on the system. Because computers execute machine language instructions, your source program must be translated into a machine language program object before the computer can run it. A special program known as a *compiler* performs this translation.

As part of its translation, the compiler flags all entries in your source program that it cannot understand. These kinds of errors are called *syntax errors* because they occur from your misuse of the rules of the language. Syntax errors prevent the creation of an object program.

After your source code has successfully been compiled, you need to bind the resulting module into an executable program and then test the program by running it with input data. You must correct logic errors in the program that are preventing the program from working correctly to produce the desired results. Each time you use the editor to correct a problem in your program, you must recompile the source member and bind the module again before running it to incorporate the changes into the executable program.

1.10. Key Terms

algorithm

batch processing

binding process

compile

compile unit

compiler

CRTBNDRPG (Create Bound
RPG Program)

CRTPGM (Create Program)

CRTRPGMOD (Create RPG
Module)

currency symbol

debugging

DSPFFD (Display File Field
Description)

editor

external documentation

field

file

fixed currency symbol

floating currency symbol

high-level language (HLL)

indicators

integrated development
environment (IDE)

Integrated Language
Environment (ILE)

interactive applications

internal documentation

length notation

library list

Live Parsing Extensible
Editor (LPEX)

logic errors

logical files

master files

member

member type

module

object

object code

output editing

physical file

positional notation

procedural languages

program design

program development cycle

Program Development
Manager (PDM)

program maintenance

qualified name

radix character

Rational Developer for i
(RDi)

record format (layout)

records

Report Designer

Report Program Generator
(RPG)

RPGLE

simple object name

source code

Source Entry Utility (SEU)

source member

source physical file

structured design

Structured Query Language
(SQL)

syntax errors

thousands separator

transaction files

variable

zero suppression

1.11. Discussion/Review Questions

1. What was the original purpose of RPG?
2. What are indicators? Are they still used?
3. What trends emerged in the 1970s to influence the enhancements included in RPG III?
4. What criticisms influenced IBM's enhancements to RPG in RPG IV? What computer-industry developments have contributed to the evolution of RPG IV?
5. Do you think that a programming language that requires revisions over time is poorly designed in the first place? Why or why not?
6. Give an example of a syntax error and a logic error in your native language (e.g., English). This question will have many responses. List some representative answers.
7. Would it make sense to describe a person's complete address (street address, city, state, and zip code) as one field? Why or why not?

8.   Would you define each letter in a person's last name as a separate field? Why or why not?

9.   Keeping in mind the fact that all records within a file generally have the same fixed number of fields, how do you think your school handles the problem of storing information about the courses you've taken?

10. Differentiate between source code and object code.

11. When you are compiling programs, binding refers to what step in the process? Why is this necessary?

12. Would you build a house without a blueprint? Is this a good analogy to writing a program without first designing it? Why or why not?

13. Explain why the Integrated Language Environment is important to RPG programmers.

14. Why is it important to use external documentation like pseudocode and flow charts in developing your programs?

15. Why is it important for students of RPG to learn about the older versions of the language?

16. Why is the fixed-logic cycle not (or rarely) used in RPG today?

17. Explain the difference between length notation and positional notation. Why is one preferred over the other?

18. What are the benefits of using IDEs such as Rational Developer for i (RDi) instead of traditional development tools like SEU, SDA, and PDM?

19. Describe the differences between CRTPGM and CRTBNDPRG. Can you use these two commands interchangeably?

20. Why is program maintenance part of the program development cycle? What portion of a programmer's time is consumed performing this function?

1.12. Exercises

Note: You might need your instructor's help with the location of the tables used in these exercises.

1.   Develop a list of data fields you think your school might store in its student master file. Then, design a record layout for this file that includes the length you need for each field, an indication of the data type (character or numeric), and the number of decimal positions of numeric fields.

2.   Research the history and development of the IBM Power System platform. How has this system and its software changed over the years?

3.   Using the DSPFFD command, display and/or print the record for the GTCSTP and the GTCSTP tables.

4.   Using RDi and the Field Table view, display the record layout for the WUINSTP table and the data from the WUSTDP table.

Notes

CHAPTER **2**

Getting Started

2.1. Chapter Overview

This chapter introduces you to the sections of an ILE RPG program. It also illustrates how to write a simple file read/write program by using a procedural approach, as well as how to include comments within your programs as documentation.

2.2. The Sections of an ILE RPG Program

ILE RPG programs consist of four main sections:

- **Control options** section—provides default options for the program
- **Declarations** section—identifies and defines the files, variables, and other data items a program is to use
- **Main procedure** section—details the processes, calculations, and procedures the program is to perform
- **Subprocedure** section—includes declarations and processes for optional distinct functions (subprocedures) of the RPG program that either the main procedure section or other subprocedures can execute once or many times

Not every program includes each section. Within your source code, though, these sections must appear in the order above with all program lines in the same section grouped together. Additionally, within the declarations section, good programming style dictates that you group certain types of declarations (e.g., file declarations) and code them in a consistent order.

Note

RPG is a rapidly evolving language. This textbook reflects ILE RPG's capabilities at Release 7.2. This release introduced significant changes to the language, including greatly expanded free-format syntax.

Wherever practical, the text is applicable to all officially supported release levels, including future ones. But if a feature requires a specific level, we try to mention that requirement.

The ILE RPG compiler processes source member entries in columns 6–80 of each line. Columns 1–5 and those beyond column 80 are not used. You code free-format RPG statements in columns 8–80 of each line in a source member. Column 6–7 *must* be blank. If a source line contains an entry in columns 6–7, the compiler assumes that the line uses an older fixed-format specification. Free-format statements generally consist of an instruction that indicates the purpose of the statement, followed by zero or more **keywords** and values that further refine the instruction. For example, the following statement defines a variable named Today:

```
Dcl-s Today Date(*Iso) Inz(*Sys);     // Today's date
```

This statement uses the Dcl-s (Declare Standalone Variable) instruction to indicate the purpose of the statement. It then names the variable (Today) and uses the Date keyword to designate the data type of the variable, along with the display format of the date (*ISO). The Inz(*Sys) keyword initializes the variable with the current system date when the program starts; that is, the starting value of the Today variable is the current system date.

It's important to notice the semicolon (;) at the end of the statement. Free-format RPG uses the semicolon as a **terminator character** (similar to the way a period ends a sentence). A single statement can span multiple lines of code, but only one statement can appear on any single line.

You can add **comments** to a program to document it for other programmers who might maintain the program later, or to explain it to yourself. A comment begins with two slashes (//). When the compiler encounters two slashes, it treats the rest of the line as a comment. A line can also consist solely of a comment with no other instructions.

Tip
As you begin to work with RPG statements, don't be overwhelmed by what
appear to be hundreds of entries with multiple options. Fortunately, many
entries are optional, and you use them only for complex processing or
to achieve specific effects. This book introduces these entries gradually,
initially showing you just those entries needed to write simple programs.
As your mastery of the language grows, you will learn how to use additional
entries required for more complex programs.

2.3. A Sample ILE RPG Program

Let's start with the minimal entries needed to procedurally code a simple read/write
program. To help you understand how to write such a program, we walk you through the
process of writing an RPG program to solve the following problem.

You have a file, Customers, with records (rows) laid out, as in Figure 2.1. This layout,
called a **record format**, is stored in the Customers file itself when the file is created. The
record format describes the **fields** (columns) in a record. Every record format has a name
(CUSTSREC in Figure 2.1). ILE RPG requires that the record format name be distinct from the
filename. When the RPG program refers to the Custrec format, it uses the layout in Figure
2.1. Chapter 3 further explains how to create the Customers file by using SQL.

▤ Properties	☑ Source Prompter	▦ Field Table ⊠	⬚ Commands Log	▨ Data Table

: File FLIGHTPROJ/CUSTOMERS (9 Fields)

Name	Record	Type	Length	Text
CUSTNO	CUSTSREC	Character	9	CUSTOMER NUMBER
CFNAME	CUSTSREC	Character	15	CUSTOMER FIRST NAME
CLNAME	CUSTSREC	Character	20	CUSTOMER LAST NAME
CADDR	CUSTSREC	Character	30	CUSTOMER STREET ADDRESS
CZIP	CUSTSREC	Character	5	ZIP CODE
CPHONE	CUSTSREC	Character	10	CUSTOMER PHONE
CEMAIL	CUSTSREC	Character	50	CUSTOMER EMAIL
CDOB	CUSTSREC	Packed Decimal	8.0	CUSTOMER DATE OF BIRTH
CGENDER	CUSTSREC	Character	1	F=FEMALE M=MALE

Figure 2.1: Record layout for Customers file

You want to produce a report laid out according to the example in Figure 2.2. This report
layout is also represented in a special kind of file called a **printer file**. For this example, you
call the printer file Custlist. Like the Customers file, the Custlist file contains record formats
that describe the lines to print on the report. When the output is a printed report rather than a
data file, *record* roughly translates to one or more related *report lines*. Most reports include
several different report-line formats. In the example, name the record formats Header,
Detail, and Total. The Header format describes lines 1–9 in Figure 2.2, and the Detail format

describes line 10 and subsequent lines until the Total format, which prints at the end of the report. Chapter 3 details how to create the printer file and its formats by using a utility called *Data Description Specifications (DDS)*.

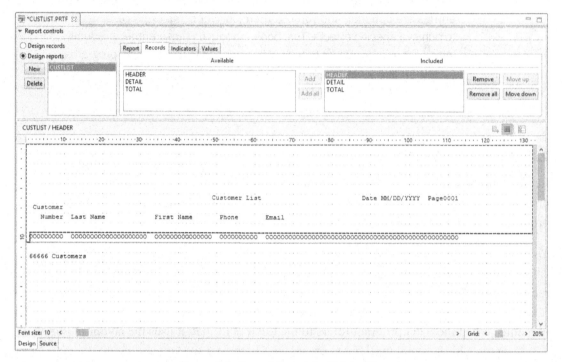

Figure 2.2: Report layout for Printer file

When you compare the desired output with the Custsrec record layout, you can see that the Detail format's output fields are present on the input records, but not all input fields in Customers are used in the report. The processing consists of reading each record from the input file, counting it, writing that data to the report with appropriate headings, and formatting the variable data. Finally, at the end of the report, the Total format prints the record count.

The following is the completed sample ILE RPG program. Note that the order of the program statements is control options, declarations, and main procedure. (This program does not include subprocedures.) RPG requires this order. Also note that you can use blank comment lines or comment lines of dashes to visually break the program into logical units and that using lowercase lettering within internal documentation helps it stand out from program code.

```
// ----------------------------------------------------------------
// This program produces a customer listing report. The report data
// comes directly from input file Customers.
//
                                                         Continued
```

```
//      Date Written:  10/31/2013, Bryan Meyers
// ----------------------------------------------------------------


// -------------------------------------------------- Control options
Ctl-opt Option(*Nodebugio);


// ---------------------------------------------------- File declarations
Dcl-f Customers Disk    Usage(*Input);
Dcl-f Custlist  Printer Usage(*Output) Oflind(Endofpage);


// ------------------------------ Standalone variable declarations
Dcl-s Endofpage Ind Inz(*On);


// ---------------------------------------------------- Main procedure
Read Customers;


Dow Not %Eof(Customers);


  If Endofpage;
    Write Header;        // Header is a format in the Custlist file
    Endofpage = *Off;
  Endif;


  Count += 1;            // Count is a variable defined in Custlist
  Write Detail;          // Detail is a format in Custlist
  Read Customers;
Enddo;


If Endofpage;
  Write Header;
Endif;


Write Total;             // Total is a format in Custlist
*Inlr = *On;
Return;
```

ILE RPG lets you use both uppercase and lowercase alphabetic characters, but the language is not **case sensitive**. Thus, any lowercase letter you use within a file or variable name is interpreted as its uppercase equivalent by the compiler. To aid in the program's readability, use **title case**, wherein each word in the source code is capitalized.

Let's examine the program, line by line, to understand its basic syntax and purpose. As we examine the program in detail, you can refer back to it to get a complete picture of the entire program. The comments each begin with // characters and require no further explanation.

Tip

It's a good idea to designate the various sections of the program with comment *divider lines*, as the example shows, to make the program easier to read and analyze.

2.3.1. Control Options

The first section, control options, is useful for controlling the program's behavior and for specifying certain compiler options. Control specifications provide the following functions:

- default formats (e.g., date formats) for the program
- changes to normal processing modes (e.g., changing the internal method the program uses to evaluate expressions)
- special options to use when compiling the program
- language enhancements that affect the entire program

A **Ctl-opt (Control option)** instruction can include more than one keyword (with at least one space between each one), and a program can have multiple Ctl-opt statements. Appendix A includes a complete list of Control option keywords and their usage. Not all programs require Ctl-opt statements, but if they are present, control options must appear as the first statements in a program.

In this example, the following instruction informs the compiler that the debugger facility (described in Appendix C) is to ignore all input and output specifications, improving the debugger's performance:

```
Ctl-opt Option(*Nodebugio);
```

Control options might also dictate the date and time formats to use, as in the following example:

```
Ctl-opt Datfmt(*USA) Timfmt(*HMS);
```

2.3.2. Declarations

Next is the declarations section. RPG uses this section to declare (define) all the data items that the program needs to do its job. Every data item the program requires must be defined to the program. The example program includes two types of declarations: file declarations and standalone variable declarations. The declarations can be in any order, but it's a good idea to group similar declarations and organize them in a logical fashion. Let's start with file declarations.

2.3.2.1. File Declarations

File declarations describe the files your program uses and define how to use the files within the program. Each file a program uses requires its own file declaration, which begins with a **Dcl-f (Declare File)** instruction. Although you can declare the files in any order, it is customary to declare the input files first:

```
Dcl-f Customers Disk    Usage(*Input);
Dcl-f Custlist  Printer Usage(*Output) Oflind(Endofpage);
```

When a program declares a file, all the record formats and fields in that file become available to the program. No further declarations are necessary for the program to use those items. Let's examine each of the entries for the sample program. As you continue in subsequent chapters, we'll explain the entries not described here. (Appendix A includes a complete summary of all the ILE RPG instructions.)

In the illustrative problem, file Customers contains the data you want to process. The program's output is a printed report. Although you usually think of a report as hardcopy, rather than as a file per se, in RPG you produce a report through a printer file. This file then resides as a spooled file in an output queue, where it waits until you release it to a printer. Your administrator or instructor will tell you which output queue to use for your programs and explain how to work with spooled files in the output queue.

2.3.2.1.1. Filename

The first entry following the Dcl-f instruction names the file. In ILE RPG, filenames can be a maximum of 10 characters. They must begin with an alphabetic character or one of the special characters $, #, or @. The remaining characters can be alphabetic characters, numbers, or any of the four special characters _, $, #, and @. A filename cannot contain blanks embedded within the permissible characters.

The practice problem's input file is called Customers. The report file is Custlist.

2.3.2.1.2. Device

The entry following the filename indicates the device associated with a file. Database files are stored on disk. Accordingly, Disk is the appropriate device entry for the Customers file. The device associated with printer files is Printer.

2.3.2.1.3. File Usage

The Usage keyword specifies how the program is to use the file. The two types in this program are *Input and *Output. An **input file** contains data to be read by the program, and an **output file** is the destination for writing output results from the program. In the example, Customers is an input file, and Custlist is an output file.

2.3.2.1.4. Overflow Indicator

RPG supports many other file keywords (discussed in Chapter 4, and listed in Appendix A) to give you an opportunity to amplify and specialize the basic file description. Typically, you code them with one or more values (arguments) in parentheses immediately following the keyword itself. You can code more than one keyword on a declaration line. If a declaration requires more than one line, you can simply continue coding keywords on subsequent lines, ending the last line with a semicolon (;).

In the sample program, the printer file uses one such keyword: **Oflind** (Overflow indicator). **Overflow** is the name given to the condition that happens when a printed report reaches the bottom of a page. Usually, when overflow occurs, you eject the printer to the next page and print a new set of heading lines before printing the next detail line. Your program can automatically detect overflow through the use of a variable called an *overflow indicator*. The Oflind keyword associates the printer device with the overflow indicator for that file. In the example, the overflow indicator is named Endofpage (you can name it anything you choose). If the Custlist file signals overflow, the Endofpage indicator is automatically set to *On. You can then test that indicator just before printing a detail line to determine whether you want to print headings first. After printing the headings, the program should set Endofpage to *Off and then wait for the printer file to turn it *On again.

No other Dcl-f entries are required to describe the files the sample program used. In this introductory explanation, we skip some of the entries that are not needed in this program (we'll cover them later).

2.3.2.2. Standalone Variable Declarations

Variable declarations describe those variables that do not originate from a file and that do not depend upon a specific structure or format. They *stand alone* in the program and are often referred to as **standalone variables**. For these data items, the program needs to know, at a minimum, the name of the variable and its data type (e.g., character or numeric). Additional keywords can amplify or specialize the variable's properties. The example program declares one variable by using the **Dcl-s (Declare Standalone Variable)** instruction:

```
Dcl-s Endofpage Ind Inz(*On);
```

2.3.2.2.1. Variable Name

The first entry following the Dcl-s instruction names the variable. In ILE RPG, variable names can be up to 4,096 characters (although the practical limit is much lower). They must begin with an alphabetic character or one of the special character $, #, or @. The remaining characters can be alphabetic characters, numbers, or any of the four special characters _, #, $, and @. A variable name cannot contain blanks embedded within the permissible characters.

The example declaration describes the Endofpage variable, which you are using as the overflow indicator for the Custlist file. Because this variable isn't defined anywhere else, you must declare it here.

Tip

Although RPG allows them, avoid the use of special characters $, #, or @ in RPG names. These special characters may not exist in all languages and character sets within which your program may attempt to compile. When the language or character set cannot recognize the character, the compiler cannot successfully translate the code. Also avoid the underscore (_) in an RPG name; it's a *noisy* character and doesn't significantly aid the readability of your program.

Although not an RPG requirement, it is good programming practice to choose field names that reflect the data they represent. For example, Loannumber is far superior to X for the name of a field that stores loan numbers. Choosing descriptive field names can prevent your accidental use of the wrong field as you write your program, and it can help clarify your program's processing to others who may have to modify the program.

If the name won't fit on a single line, consider renaming the data item. You can, however, use an ellipsis (…, three periods across three positions) as a special continuation character within the name to allow a longer name. On the following lines, you simply continue the definition.

2.3.2.2.2. Data Type

Following the variable name, you use a keyword to indicate the general type of data the variable represents (e.g., character, numeric, date) as well as how the program is to store it internally. Chapter 4 examines the various data types that RPG supports. In the example, the Ind data type designates the variable as an indicator. An **indicator** (which many other computer languages refer to as a **Boolean data type)** is a single-byte variable that can contain only two logical values: '1' or '0'. You can also refer to these values by using the figurative constants *On and *Off, respectively. Indicator data is usually used within an RPG program to signal a true/false condition.

In the example, Endofpage is an indicator that the program uses to signal printer overflow.

2.3.2.2.3. Initialize Keyword

You can enter the remaining keywords in a variable declaration in any order. In the example, you have only one additional keyword: **Inz (Initialize)**. The purpose of a variable is to hold a value. Once you've defined a standalone variable, you can assign it a value, use it with operations, or print it. The Inz keyword supplies an **initial value** for a variable. This is the value the variable has when the program first starts. In the example, you initialize Endofpage to have a value of *On.

2.3.3. Main Procedure Section

You have now defined the files and variables your application is to use. Next, you need to describe the processing steps to obtain the input and write the report. That is the purpose of the **main procedure**. The main procedure is the main body of your program—the part that outlines the processes, calculations, and procedures that your program executes. In many cases (as in the example), the program does all the work in the main procedure. The main procedure is the first part of your program that is executed when you initially call it.

In the example, the main procedure is coded with no special designation and without an explicit name. It simply consists of a number of instructions that the program executes to do its work. When the program is called, an internal sequence of preset events known as the **RPG cycle** starts the program, initializes its storage, and executes the main procedure. When the main procedure is finished, the cycle shuts down the program, deallocates all objects it is using, and cleans up its storage. Because the built-in cycle controls the execution of the main procedure, this type of program is termed a **cycle main program**. Unlike with some other computer languages, an RPG cycle main program does not require that you explicitly name the main procedure. Most of the programs you encounter will be cycle main programs. Another ILE RPG program model, the linear main program, which Chapter 14 covers, does allow you to explicitly name the main procedure.

Before coding the main procedure, you need to develop the logic to produce the desired output. Generally, you complete this stage of the program development cycle—designing the solution—before doing any program coding, but we delayed program design to give you a taste of the language.

You can sketch out the processing of your program by using **pseudocode**, which is simply stylized English that details the underlying logic needed for a program. Although no single standard exists for the format used with pseudocode, it consists of key control words and indentation to show the logic structures' scope of control. It is always a good idea to work out the design of your program before actually coding it in RPG (or in any other language).

Pseudocode is language independent and lets you focus on what needs to be done, rather than on the specific syntax requirements of a programming language.

The program exemplifies a simple read/write program in which you want to read a record, increment the record count, process that record, and repeat the process until no more records exist in the file (a condition called **end-of-file**). This kind of application is termed **batch processing** because once the program begins, a *batch* of data (accumulated in a file) directs its execution. Batch programs can run unattended because they do not need control or instructions from a user.

The logic the read/write program requires is quite simple:

Correct algorithm

Read a record

While there are records

    Print headings if necessary

    Increment the record count

    Write a detail line

    Read the next record

Endwhile

Print last report total line

End program

Note that While indicates a repeated process, or loop. Within the loop, the processing requirements for a single record (in this case, simply writing a report line) are detailed and then the next record is read.

You may wonder why the pseudocode contains two read statements. Why can't there be just a single read, as in the first step within the following While loop?

Incorrect algorithm

While there are records

    Read the next record

    Print headings if necessary

Increment the record count

Write a detail line

Endwhile

Print last report total line

End program

The preceding algorithm works fine as long as each read operation retrieves a data record from the file. The problem is that eventually the system tries to read an input record and fails because no more records exist in the file to read. When a program reaches end-of-file, it should not attempt to process more input data. The preceding incorrect algorithm will inappropriately write a detail line after reaching end-of-file.

The correct algorithm places the read statement as the last step within the While loop so that as soon as end-of-file is detected, no further writing occurs. However, if that is the only read, your algorithm will try to write the first detail line before reading any data. That's why the algorithm also requires an initial read (often called a **priming read**) just before the While loop to *prime* the processing cycle.

After you have designed the program, it is a simple matter to express that logic in a programming language—once you have learned the language's syntax. The following main procedure shows the correct algorithm expressed in ILE RPG. Notice the striking similarity to the pseudocode you sketched out earlier.

```
Read Customers;

Dow Not %Eof(Customers);

  If Endofpage;
    Write Header;
    Endofpage = *Off;
  Endif;

  Count += 1;
  Write Detail;
  Read Customers;
Enddo;
```

Continued

```
If Endofpage;
   Write Header;
Enddo;


Write Total;
*Inlr = *On;
Return;
```

The instructions usually begin with an operation that specifies an action to take. RPG supports numerous reserved words, called **operation codes,** to identify valid operations. Many of these operations are followed by operand values, which RPG calls **factors,** to provide the compiler with the details necessary to perform an operation. Other operation codes (Dow and If in this example) are followed by expressions that the program is to evaluate. Finally, each instruction must end with a semicolon (;). Spacing is not usually critical. You can code the specification in any position from 8 to 80, but positions 6 and 7 *must* be blank. You can also indent operations to clarify the flow of the program.

2.3.3.1. RPG Operations

The RPG program executes the main procedure sequentially from beginning to end, unless the computer encounters an operation that redirects flow of control. The program uses eight operation codes: Read, Dow, Enddo, If, Endif, Write, Eval, and Return. Let's look at the specific operations within the main procedure of the program. The intent here is to provide you with sufficient information to understand the basic program and to write similar programs. Several of the operations described in the following section are discussed in more detail in subsequent chapters of this book.

2.3.3.1.1. Read (Read Sequentially)

Read is an input operation that instructs the computer to retrieve the next sequential record from the named input file—in this case, your Customers file. To use the Read operation with a file, you must have defined that file as Usage(*Input). Reading a record makes all the field values in that record available to the program for processing.

2.3.3.1.2. Dow (Do While), Enddo

The Dow operation establishes a loop in RPG. An Enddo operation signals the end of the loop. Note that this Dow and Enddo correspond to the While and Endwhile statements in your pseudocode. The Dow operation repetitively executes the block of code in the loop as long as the condition associated with the Dow operation is true. Because the program's Dow condition is preceded by the word Not, this line reads, "Do while the end-of-file condition is not true." It is the direct equivalent of the pseudocode statement "While there are more records...," because the end-of-file condition turns on only when your Read operation runs out of records.

The %Eof entry in this statement is an ILE RPG **built-in function**, which returns a true ('1' or *On) or false ('0' or *Off) value to indicate whether or not the file operation encountered end-of-file. Built-in functions (or BIFs) perform specific operations and then return a value to the expression in which they are coded. Most BIFs let you enter values called **arguments** in parentheses immediately following the BIF to govern the function. In this case, %Eof(Customers) means that you want your program to check the end-of-file condition specifically for the Customers file.

The **Enddo** operation marks the end of the scope of a Do operation, such as Dow. All the program statements between the Dow operation and its associated Enddo are repeated as long as the Dow condition is true. Every Dow operation requires a corresponding Enddo operation to close the loop.

2.3.3.1.3. If

RPG's primary decision operation is the **If** operation. When the relationship expressed in the conditional expression coded with the If operation is true, all the calculations between the If and its associated Endif operation are executed. However, when the relationship is not true, those statements are bypassed. By coding

```
If Endofpage = *On;
```

or simply (because Endofpage is an indicator)

```
If Endofpage;
```

you are instructing the program to execute the subsequent lines of code only if the overflow indicator Endofpage is *On:

```
Write Header;
Endofpage = *Off;
```

The **Endif** operation marks the end of an If operation's scope. All the program statements between the If operation and its associated Endif are executed as long as the If condition is true. Every If operation requires a corresponding Endif operation to close the block.

Tip

It is common practice to indent blocks of code that appear between Dow or If and their associated Enddo or Endif operations. By indenting the blocks, you can easily see which code is associated with the Dow or If operation. Don't overdo it, though. Indenting a couple of spaces is enough.

2.3.3.1.4. Write (Write a Record)

A **Write** operation directs the program to output a record to an output file. In the example, because the output file is a printer file, writing a record to the file has the effect of printing the format, consisting of one or more lines. The first Write operation specifies Header as the record format to print if Endofpage has been reached. As a result, the three heading lines of your report are printed. Later, a second Write specifies the Detail format. When the program executes this line of code, the record format Detail is printed, using the values of the fields from the currently retrieved Customers record. The last Write operation prints the Total record format. Header, Detail, and Total are record formats that reside in the Custlist file (Figure 2.2). All the information you need to format the printed report is in the file, not in the RPG program.

```
Write Header;
Write Detail;
Write Total;
```

2.3.3.1.5. Eval (Evaluate Expression)

The **Eval** operation assigns a value to a variable. In the sample program, coding

```
Eval Endofpage = *Off;
```

assigns the value *Off to the overflow indicator Endofpage. You do this after printing the heading lines so that the program knows that it is no longer necessary to print the headings until Endofpage is reset to *On automatically. (Endofpage is initially set to *On to ensure that the program prints headings on the first page of the report.)

In most cases, specifying Eval is optional. You can simply code the assignment expression without explicitly coding the Eval operation:

```
Endofpage = *Off;
```

Later in the program, you use the line

```
*Inlr = *On;
```

to assign the value *On to a special reserved indicator variable called **Last Record** (coded as *Inlr, read as indicator LR). *Inlr (commonly referred to simply as LR) performs a special function within ILE RPG. If LR is on when the program ends, it signals the computer to close the files and free the memory associated with the program. If LR is not on, the program continues to tie up some of the system's resources even though the program is no longer running.

You may have also noticed this implied Eval statement in the example:

```
Count += 1;
```

This statement uses the += operator, one of several **concise operators** that RPG supports. This statement simply adds 1 to the current value of the Count variable. It is equivalent to coding the following:

```
Count = Count + (1);
```

RPG's concise operators are simply shortcut coding techniques you can use when the result of an expression (Count, in this case) is also the first operand in the expression. RPG supports the following concise operators:

- += to increment a variable
- -= to decrement a variable
- *= for multiplication
- /= for division
- **= for exponentiation

2.3.3.1.6. Return (Return to Caller)

The **Return** operation returns control to the program that called it—either the computer's operating system or perhaps another program. Program execution stops when a Return is encountered. Although your program ends correctly without this instruction (provided you have turned on LR), including it is a good practice. Return clearly signals the endpoint of your program and lets the program become part of an application system of called programs. (Chapter 13 deals with called programs in detail.)

2.4. Building the Program

To create this program, you use an editor, such as SEU or LPEX, to enter the ILE RPG code into a source file member with a member type of RPGLE. A source file **member** is a set of data within a source file. Usually, a source file contains more than one member, each of which holds the source code for a single program. Once the source member contains all the necessary code, you then use the **CRTBNDRPG (Create Bound RPG Program)** command to compile the source and create the program. Figure 2.3 shows the prompted CRTBNDRPG command. The compiler generates a listing, which you use to verify the creation of the program or to find errors. Appendix B describes the tools you might use to edit and compile a program.

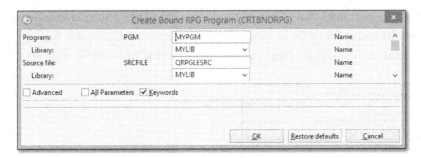

Figure 2.3: CRTBNDRPG command

Once the program is successfully created, execute it by using the CALL command. The output of your program is a spooled file, CUSTLIST, in an output queue. You can view the report by using the WRKSPLF (Work with Spooled Files) command, or you can release it to a printer.

2.5. Navigating Legacy Code

Earlier releases of RPG (Release 7.1 and earlier) identify the sections of a program by using different kinds of lines, called **fixed-format** specifications. Fixed format means that the location of an entry within a program line is critical to the entry's interpretation by the RPG compiler. Although you can write most modern programs by using **free-format** coding, which does not have significant positional restrictions, you may encounter fixed format when you are maintaining existing programs. Good programming style prefers free-format coding, but you can freely mix fixed format and free format within the same program.

Each type of fixed-format specification has a particular purpose. Following are the specification types:

- Header (Control) specifications—provide default options for the source
- File specifications—identify the files a program is to use
- Definition specifications—define variables and other data items the program is to use
- Input specifications—depict the record layout for program-described input files

- Calculation specifications—detail the procedure the program is to perform
- Output specifications—describe the program output (results)
- Procedure boundary specifications—segment the source into units of work, called *procedures*

Not all programs need every kind of fixed-format specification. Fixed-format specification types require a different identifier, or form type, which must appear in position 6 of each program line. A File specification line of code, for example, must include an F in position 6. For this reason, File specifications are commonly called **F-specs**.

Fixed-format specifications must appear in a specific order, or sequence, within your source code, with all program lines that represent the same kind of specification grouped together. The following list illustrates the order in which the specifications are grouped. Notice that the fixed-format specifications generally follow the same order as the free-format sections of a program.

H	Header (control) specifications
F	File specifications*
D	Definition specifications*
I	Input specifications
C	Calculation specifications
O	Output specifications
P	Procedure boundary
F	File specifications for procedure*
D	Definition specifications for procedure*
C	Calculation specifications for procedure
P	Procedure boundary

* Beginning with Release 7.2, you can mix File specifications and Definition specifications in any order.

Most specifications require fixed-position entries in at least part of the specification. The editor you use to enter your source code can provide you with prompts to facilitate making your entries in the proper location. (Appendix B provides more information about editors.)

Even though specifications are primarily fixed format, some also support a free-form area, where you can code keywords and values with little or no regard to their specific location within the free-form portion of the specification. Beginning with Version 5, RPG supports free-format calculation specifications, but—until Release 7.2—all other specifications must be fixed format.

Note

The fixed-format code samples in this book use two (or more) ruler lines to help you determine where to insert your fixed-format entries. The first ruler line indicates column position, and the following line (or lines) contains *prompts* similar to those an editor supplies. Most editors also provide a similar ruler line near the top of the editing window. These ruler lines should not appear in your source code; they are provided to help you understand where entries should appear.

When you begin maintaining a fixed-format program, notice that an entry does not always occupy all the positions allocated for it within a specification. When that happens, a good rule is that alphabetic entries start at the leftmost position of the allocated space, and unused positions are to the right. Numeric entries, however, are usually right-adjusted, and unused positions are to the left.

2.5.1. Fixed-Format Specifications for a Sample Program

Let's look at a fixed-format version of the example program and compare it with the free-format version shown earlier.

```
*.. 1 ...+... 2 ...+... 3 ...+... 4 ...+... 5 ...+... 6 ...+... 7 ...+ ... 8
* --------------------------------------------------------------------
* This program produces a customer listing report. The report data
* comes directly from input file Customers.
*     Date Written:  10/31/2013, Bryan Meyers
* --------------------------------------------------------------------


* ------------------------------------------------------- Control options
H Option(*Nodebugio)


* ------------------------------------------------------- File declarations
FCustomers IF   E             Disk
FCustlist  O    E             Printer Oflind(Endofpage)


* ------------------------------------ Standalone variable declarations
D Endofpage      S            N   Inz(*On)


                                                        Continued
```

```
*  ------------------------------------------------------ Main procedure
C                    Read       Customers

C                    Dow        Not %Eof(Customers)

C                    If         Endofpage
C                    Write      Header
C                    Eval       Endofpage = *Off
C                    Endif

C                    Eval       Count += 1
C                    Write      Detail
C                    Read       Customers
C                    Enddo

C                    If         Endofpage
C                    Write      Header
C                    Enddo

C                    Write      Total
C                    Eval       *Inlr = *On
C                    Return
```

Notice that fixed-format RPG specifications do not require a semicolon delimiter. Fixed format traditionally uses an asterisk (*) in position 7 to denote a comment. You can also use slashes (//) to begin a comment in fixed-format code, but the comment cannot be on the same line as other code; it must be on a separate line.

2.5.2. Control Specifications

Control specifications (Control options) require an H in position 6. The remaining positions, 7–80, consist of reserved **keywords**, which have special values and meanings associated with them. Fixed-format control specifications mimic the function of the Ctl-opt instruction in free-format code. The keywords have no strict positional requirements—they can appear in any order and in any position 7–80. The following header shows the layout of a Control specification for the fixed-format variation of your program:

```
*.. 1 ...+... 2 ...+... 3 ...+... 4 ...+... 5 ...+... 6 ...+... 7 ...+... 8
HKeywords++++++++++++++++++++++++++++++++++++++++++++++++++++++++++++++++++
H Option(*Nodebugio)
```

2.5.3. *File Description Specifications*

The fixed-format File specification (F-spec) is comparable to the Dcl-f (Declare File) instruction covered earlier. All File specifications include an F in position 6. Each file a program uses requires its own File specification line. The following header shows the layout of a File specification and the completed File specifications for your program. Note that in addition to column positions, the ruler lines include prompts to help you remember where to insert required entries.

```
*.. 1 ...+... 2 ...+... 3 ...+... 4 ...+... 5 ...+... 6 ...+... 7 ...+... 8
FFilename++IPEASFRlen+LKlen+AIDevice+.Keywords++++++++++++++++++++++++++++++++
FCustomers IF   E            Disk
FCustlist  O    E            Printer Oflind(Endofpage)
```

2.5.3.1. Filename (Positions 7–16)

In positions 7–16 (labeled Filename++ on the ruler line), you enter the name of the file. Note that you code filenames, like other alphabetic entries, beginning in the leftmost position allowed for that entry—in this case, position 7. Simply leave blank all unneeded positions to the right of the name.

2.5.3.2. File Type (Position 17)

Position 17 (labeled I on the ruler line) specifies the file usage. It is the fixed-format equivalent of the Usage keyword used by the Dcl-f free-format instruction. The two types in this program are input (type I) and output (type O).

2.5.3.3. File Designation (Position 18 Input Files Only)

Every input file requires a file designation entry (position 18, labeled P). File designation refers to the way the program accesses, or retrieves, the data in the file. In the example, you retrieve data by explicitly reading records within your program, rather than by using the built-in retrieval of RPG's fixed-logic cycle. In RPG terminology, that makes the file **full procedural**, so F is the appropriate entry for position 18. Because this designation applies only to input files, you leave it blank for the Custlist specification line. The Dcl-f free-format instruction has no entry for a file designation. All files that Dcl-f declares are assumed to be full procedural files.

2.5.3.4. File Format (Position 22)

The next required entry is file format. An E in position 22 (labeled F) stands for external format, which means that the file's record formats are implicitly contained in the file itself. Chapter 3 explains externally described files in further detail. The Dcl-f free-format instruction uses externally described files as the default entry, so no entry is necessary when you use Dcl-f to declare an externally described file.

2.5.3.5. Device (Positions 36–42)

The Device entry indicates the device associated with a file. You enter the device names left-adjusted in positions 36–42 (labeled Device+). This entry corresponds to the Disk and Printer keywords used earlier in the free-format Dcl-f example.

2.5.3.6. Keywords (Positions 44–80)

The Keywords area of the File specification gives you an opportunity to amplify and specialize the basic file description in the positional area (positions 6–43) of the F-spec. RPG allows many reserved keywords (listed in Appendix A) in this area of the specification. These are the same keywords that the Dcl-f instruction uses. You can code more than one keyword on a specification line, in positions 44–80, without being too concerned about other positional requirements. Most RPG programmers, however, prefer to limit their code to one keyword per line. If a specification requires more than one keyword, you can simply continue coding them in the Keywords area on subsequent F-spec lines.

No other File specification entries are required to describe the files the sample program uses. In this introductory explanation, we've skipped some of the entries that are not needed in this program (we'll cover them later).

2.5.4. Definition Specifications

Definition specifications, identified by a D in position 6, follow the File specifications in the fixed-format example. D-specs define to your program those data items that do not originate as fields in a file's record layout. In the example, Endofpage is one such data item. The following shows the general layout of the Definition specification as well as the example code:

```
*.. 1 ...+... 2 ...+... 3 ...+... 4 ...+... 5 ...+... 6 ...+... 7 ...+... 8
DName++++++++++ETDsFrom+++To/Len+IDc.Keywords++++++++++++++++++++++++++++++
D Endofpage       S              N    Inz(*On)
```

This definition corresponds to the Dcl-s instruction in the earlier free-format example.

2.5.4.1. Data Item Name (Positions 7–21)

To define a standalone variable, you first name the variable anywhere in positions 7–21 (Name+++++++++++) of the line. The name need not begin in position 7. In fact, to aid readability, many programmers always leave position 7 blank to separate the data item name from the D in column 6.

2.5.4.2. Definition Type (Positions 24–25)

Definition specifications use positions 24–25 (Ds) to indicate the type of data item the line is defining. For a standalone variable, enter an S (for standalone) *left-adjusted* in these positions. In the free-format example earlier, the Dcl-s instruction serves the same purpose. Chapter 4 covers the other entries for other definition types.

2.5.4.3. Data Type (Position 40)

Position 40 (I) indicates what data type RPG uses to internally store a variable. For an indicator variable, enter an N (iNdicator) in position 40. Chapter 4 describes other possible entries for this position. Data type N corresponds to the Ind keyword used by the Dcl-s free-format instruction.

2.5.4.4. Keywords (Positions 44–80)

The Keywords area of the Definition specification provides an opportunity to further define the simple definition in positions 7–43. In this case, the example uses the Inz (Initialize) keyword to set Endofpage *On when the program starts.

2.5.5. Calculation Specifications

In the fixed-format example, the program's main procedure is written using Calculation specifications. C-specs are identified by a C in position 6. The following shows the general layout of Calculation specifications:

```
*.. 1 ...+... 2 ...+... 3 ...+... 4 ...+... 5 ...+... 6 ...+... 7 ...+... 8
CLON01Factor1+++++++Opcode(E)+Factor2+++++++Result++++++++Len++D+HiLoEq....
CLON01Factor1+++++++Opcode(E)+Extended-Factor2+++++++++++++++++++++++++++++
```

Notice that there are two general layouts. Most RPG operations use the first, traditional format (e.g., Factor 2, Result), and some use the second (Extended-Factor 2). You can freely intermix the two layouts. For the example, you need not be overly concerned about the differences between the two layouts; in fact, it may not even be obvious which operations are using which layout. The completed C-specs for the example program's main procedure are as follows:

```
*.. 1 ...+... 2 ...+... 3 ...+... 4 ...+... 5 ...+... 6 ...+... 7 ...+... 8
CLON01Factor1+++++++Opcode(E)+Factor2+++++++Result++++++++Len++D+HiLoEq....
CLON01Factor1+++++++Opcode(E)+Extended-Factor2+++++++++++++++++++++++++++++
C                   Read      Customers
                                                               Continued
```

```
C                   Dow       Not %Eof(Customers)

C                   If        Endofpage
C                   Write     Header
C                   Eval      Endofpage = *Off
C                   Endif

C                   Eval      Count += 1
C                   Write     Detail
C                   Read      Customers
C                   Enddo

C                   If        Endofpage
C                   Write     Header
C                   Enddo

C                   Write     Total
C                   Eval      *Inlr = *On
C                   Return
```

Let's compare the fixed-format C-specs with the free-format main procedure shown earlier.

2.5.5.1. Operation Code (Positions 26–35)

Positions 26–35 (Opcode(E)++) contain the operation code, left-adjusted. In general, these are the same operation codes the free-format example used, although fixed-format C-specs also support several obsolete operation codes that are no longer commonly used. Notice that the operation code must begin in position 26. Fixed-format calculations do not allow indenting.

2.5.5.2. Factor 2 (Positions 36–49)

Many operation codes use operand values (factors) to provide the compiler with the details necessary to perform the operation. In the example, the following lines specify a Factor 2 operand, left-adjusted, in positions 36–49:

```
C                   Read      Customers
C                   Write     Header
C                   Write     Detail
```

Some operation codes (though none in the example) also use a Factor 1 operand in positions 12–25 and a Result factor in positions 50–63.

2.5.5.3. Extended-Factor 2 (Positions 36–80)

Some operation codes, most notably Eval, support an Extended-Factor 2 in positions 36–80 as an alternative to the earlier shorter Factor 2. You can use the extended layout to code expressions instead of using simple operands. Operation codes that use the Extended-Factor 2 layout do not use Factor 1. In the example, these lines use the Extended-Factor 2:

```
C                   Dow       Not %Eof(Customers)
C                   If        Endofpage
C                   Eval      Endofpage = *Off
C                   Eval      Count += 1
C                   Eval      *Inlr = *On
```

Notice that the Eval operation, usually optional in free-format code, is *required* when you are using fixed-format C-specs.

2.6. Free vs. Fixed

As you can see, RPG's free-format instructions have a more consistent, modern layout than do the fixed-format equivalents. If you are using free format, you'll probably find it easier to concentrate on your program's logic instead of its exact positional syntax. In addition, free-format operations allow you to use indentation to visually explain blocks of related code. You don't need to remember which operation codes support which C-spec layout if you are using free format.

Version 5 supported free-format calculations, but it retained fixed format for other specifications. Release 7.2 introduced the remaining free-format instructions, such as Dcl-f (to replace F-specs) and Dcl-s (to replace some D-specs). Although you should use free format wherever possible, you can intermix free-format code with fixed-format code.

Before Release 7.2, it was necessary to code free-format calculations between /Free and /End-free instructions. These instructions, called **compiler directives**, direct the ILE RPG compiler to use free-format syntax rules for all the instructions within the block of code between the directives. This requirement became especially onerous if you mixed free-format code with fixed-format code, because RPG required that you constantly switch between modes. The following example shows how to use the /Free and /End-free directives. You must code them exactly as follows, beginning with a slash (/) character in position 7.

```
*.. 1 ...+... 2 ...+... 3 ...+... 4 ...+... 5 ...+... 6 ...+... 7 ...+... 8
 /Free
  Regpay = Reghours * Rate;
  Ovtpay = Ovthours * Rate * 1.5;
 /End-free
C     Taxable      Mult      Rate         Tax
 /Free
  Total = Taxable + Tax;
 /End-free
```

As you can see, mixing free format and fixed format makes the code unnecessarily jumbled and difficult to understand. Starting with Release 7.2, the /Free and /End-free directives are no longer required, but you should still avoid mixing the two syntax options unless it's absolutely necessary:

```
*.. 1 ...+... 2 ...+... 3 ...+... 4 ...+... 5 ...+... 6 ...+... 7 ...+... 8
  Regpay = Reghours * Rate;
  Ovtpay = Ovthours * Rate * 1.5;
C     Taxable      Mult      Rate         Tax
  Total = Taxable + Tax;
```

2.7. Internal Documentation

You might think that after you have a program written and running, you are done with it forever and can move forward, developing new programs. However, a majority of all programming is maintenance programming rather than new application development. **Maintenance programming** involves modifying existing programs to fix problems, addressing changing business needs, or satisfying user requests for modifications.

Because the programs you write will most likely be revised sometime in the future, either by yourself or by another programmer in your company, it is your responsibility to make your programs as understandable as possible to facilitate these future revisions. RPG programmers use several techniques to document their programs.

2.7.1. Program Overview

Most companies require overview documentation at the beginning of each program. This documentation, coded as a block of comments, states the function or purpose of the program, all special instructions or peculiarities of the program that those working with it should know, the program's author, and the date the program was written.

If the program is revised, entries detailing the revisions, including the author and the date of the revisions, usually are added to that initial documentation. For a program that uses several indicators, many programmers provide an indicator *dictionary* as part of their initial set of comments to state the function or role of each indicator used within the program.

2.7.2. Comments

Another good way to help others understand what your program does is to include explanatory documentation internal to your program through the use of comment lines. ILE RPG comments begin with double slashes (//) entered anywhere in position 8–80. In free-format specifications, these comments can comprise an entire line or a portion of the line. Once the compiler encounters the // characters, it ignores the rest of the line, treating the remainder as a comment. In fixed-format specifications, the comments make up an entire line and cannot include compilable code.

Comments exist within the program at a source code level only (not in the compiled object) for the benefit of programmers who may have to work with the program later. Include comments throughout your program as needed to help explain specific processing steps that are not obvious. In adding such comments, you can assume that anyone looking at your program has at least a basic proficiency with RPG; your documentation should help clarify your program to such a person. Documenting trivial, obvious aspects of your program is a waste of time. However, failing to document difficult-to-grasp processing can cost others valuable time. Inaccurate documentation is worse than no documentation at all because it supplies false clues that can mislead the person responsible for program modification.

Appropriately documenting a program is an important learned skill. If you are uncertain about what to document, ask yourself, "What would I want to know about this program if I were looking at it for the first time?"

2.7.3. Blank Lines

In addition to the use of comments, many programmers find that a program's structure is easier to understand when blank lines break the code into logical units. To facilitate using blank lines within your code, ILE RPG treats two types of lines as blank: First, any line that is completely blank between positions 6 and 80 can appear anywhere within your program. Second, if position 6 contains a valid specification type, and positions 7–80 are blank, the line is treated as a blank line; however, the line must be located in that portion of the program appropriate for its designated specification type.

2.8. Chapter Summary

ILE RPG programs are written as fixed-format specifications or free-format instructions or a combination of both. Different specification forms convey different kinds of information to the RPG compiler, which translates the program into machine language.

The control options section provides default options for the program. The declarations section identifies the files and other data items the program uses. The main procedure section details the processes the program performs.

File declarations contain descriptions of all files used within a program. The file object contains a record format that describes the fields comprising the record. Printer files also contain record formats that depict the layouts of the printed lines on a report. Other declaration instructions describe data items that do not originate in a file, such as standalone variables.

The main procedure section contains instructions, or processing steps, to be accomplished by the computer. When RPG's built-in cycle controls the execution of the main procedure, the program is known as a *cycle main program*. Each instruction includes an RPG operation code (by coding it either explicitly or, in the case of the Eval operation, implicitly in an expression) and can include additional operand entries, depending upon the specific operation. The computer executes operations in the order they are given in the program source, unless the computer encounters an operation that specifically alters this flow of control.

RPG source code is stored in a source file member with a member type of RPGLE. The CRTBNDRPG command compiles the source and creates the program object. The CALL command executes the program.

Early releases of RPG used fixed-format specification lines instead of free-format instructions. Although free format is now preferred, you can freely intermix free format and fixed format in the same program.

An important part of programming is documenting the program. Comment lines, signaled by double slashes (//) in nearly any position of a specification line, can appear anywhere within a program. You code most comments on a separate line, but in free-format specifications, you can include them on the same line as executable RPG statements, after the RPG statements. The ILE RPG compiler ignores such comments.

Within your code, you can insert completely blank lines and lines that are blank except for the specification type to visually break the code into sections.

The following table summarizes the operation codes and BIFs discussed in this chapter. Optional entries appear within curly braces ({}):

Function or Operation	Description	Syntax
Ctl-opt	Control options	Ctl-opt {keywords};
Dcl-f	Declare file	Dcl-f file-name device {keywords};
Dcl-s	Declare standalone variable	Dcl-s name data-type {keywords};
Dow	Do while	Dow logical-expression;
Enddo Endif	End a structured group	Endxx;
%Eof	End-of-file	%Eof{(file-name)}
Eval	Evaluate expression	{Eval} result = expression;
If	If	If logical-expression;
Read	Read a record	Read file-name;
Return	Return to caller	Return;
Write	Write a record	Write record-format;

2.9. Key Terms

arguments
batch processing
Boolean data type
built-in function (BIF)
case sensitive
comments
compiler directives
concise operators
control options
CRTBNDRPG (Create Bound RPG Program)
Ctl-opt
cycle main program
Dcl-f
Dcl-s
declarations
Dow
Enddo

Endif
end-of-file
Eval
Factor
fields
fixed format
free format
full procedural
If
indicator
initial value
input file
Inz
keywords
Last record
main procedure
maintenance programming
member

Oflind
operation code
output file
overflow
positional
priming read
printer file
pseudocode
Read
record format
records
Return
RPG cycle
standalone variables
subprocedure
terminator character
title case
Write

2.10. Discussion/Review Questions

1. Explain the use of the Dcl-s instruction.
2. List the sections of an RPG program and describe the use of these sections.
3. Explain the use of the Dcl-opt instruction.
4. Which of the following are invalid RPG IV variable names? Why?

   X
   ABC
   @end
   _YTD_Sales
   YR END
   InvoiceNumber
   1STQTR
   QTY-OH
   SALES
   CUST#
   YR_END
   avg.sales
   #3
   CustNo
   $AMT
   Day1
   Yearend
   cusTnbR

5. What is an indicator? What specific methods of turning on indicators were introduced in this chapter? How can you use indicators to control processing? What alternative ILE RPG feature can you use to reduce or eliminate indicators in a program?
6. How can you obtain five blank lines between detail lines of a report?
7. RPG automatically initializes all the fields used in a program when it starts. Why would the language need the Initialize keyword?
8. List some fields that ILE RPG automatically provides for your use.
9. Why do you often need two read statements within a program?
10. Explain the use of the Oflind keyword.
11. List and explain the different options available when using the Dcl-f declaration.
12. What is LR? Why is it used?
13. What is maintenance programming? What programming techniques can you adopt to facilitate maintenance programming?

14.   Why does ILE RPG include both edit codes and edit words? What exceptions are there to the rule that an edit code and an edit word or constant should never appear together on the same Output specification line?

15.   What are the programming implications of the fact that ILE RPG is not case sensitive?

16.   Describe internal and external documentation. Why is so much importance placed on correctly documenting a program?

17.   Research and list the advantages and disadvantages of using Control specifications.

18.   Research and list the data types that are supported in RPG.

19.   Explain what the RPG cycle is. Is the RPG cycle still in use today?

2.11. Exercises

1. A customer listing program uses data from the GTCSTP table to generate a report that reflects all the data in the file. The table layout is as follows:

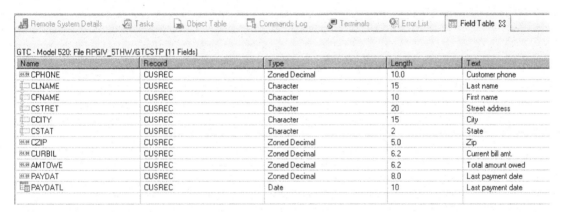

GTC - Model 520: File RPGIV_5THW/GTCSTP (11 Fields)

Name	Record	Type	Length	Text
CPHONE	CUSREC	Zoned Decimal	10.0	Customer phone
CLNAME	CUSREC	Character	15	Last name
CFNAME	CUSREC	Character	10	First name
CSTRET	CUSREC	Character	20	Street address
CCITY	CUSREC	Character	15	City
CSTAT	CUSREC	Character	2	State
CZIP	CUSREC	Zoned Decimal	5.0	Zip
CURBIL	CUSREC	Zoned Decimal	6.2	Current bill amt.
AMTOWE	CUSREC	Zoned Decimal	6.2	Total amount owed
PAYDAT	CUSREC	Zoned Decimal	8.0	Last payment date
PAYDATL	CUSREC	Date	10	Last payment date

Write the pseudocode and flow chart to produce the report.

2. Design a report for the application in exercise 1.

Notes

3

Creating and Using Files

3.1. Chapter Overview

In this chapter, you learn how IBM i handles database files. You also discover the differences between tables and views and between physical and logical files. This chapter examines field reference files and introduces you to the IBM i data types and the storage implications of numeric, character, and date data types. It also covers how to use SQL or DDS to define database files and how to access these files from within RPG programs. In addition, this chapter compares externally described files with program-described files, and it explains externally described device files and how to use DDS to define them.

3.2. IBM i Database Concepts

The IBM i operating system is unique in the way it handles data. Unlike other systems, which require additional, costly software to provide them with database capabilities, IBM i was designed with database applications in mind, and the database is tightly integrated into the operating system. The operating system automatically treats all data files as part of a large relational database system. One consequence of this approach is that all data files must be defined to the system independently of application programs. Even those applications that on the surface seem to be creating files are actually creating records and storing them in a file that must have been defined to the operating system before program execution.

You can define these files to the system at a record level (i.e., not divided into individual fields) or at a field level. If you define a file only at the record level, RPG programs that use that file must subdivide that record into the appropriate fields by using fixed-format Input or Output specifications. This type of file is called a **program-described file** because you explicitly code the field descriptions in the RPG programs that are to use the file. However, if you break down the file to the field level—outside the programs that use it—you do not need to code those field definitions within every program that uses the file, as the compiler automatically retrieves the definitions into the program. This type of file is called an **externally described file** because the field definitions are external to the programs that use the file (the field definitions are a part of the file object itself). ILE RPG programmers almost universally prefer externally described files over program-described files.

Externally described files can reduce the need for duplication of data (redundancy) across files, following well-established database design principles. Externally described files impose standardization among programmers and across applications, because all programs using a given file use the same field definitions and names. And externally described files increase programmer efficiency and reduce errors, as programmers don't need to duplicate the file definition effort each time they need to use a file within a program.

Externally described files also simplify system maintenance. For example, if it is necessary to add a field to a record layout or to change a field's definition (e.g., expand postal code to 10 characters), you make these changes in only one place (in the external file definition), rather than in every program that uses that file. Simply recompiling the programs that use the file lets them use the new layout and, in many cases, without changes to their coding—under certain conditions, even recompiling is unnecessary.

3.3. Physical and Logical Files

IBM i lets you define two kinds of database files: physical files and logical files. **Physical files** store data records in arrival sequence (i.e., the order in which they are written to the file). If you define a physical file at a field level and one or more of those fields are designated as a **key field**, you can subsequently access records stored in that file in either **key sequence** or **arrival sequence** (first in, first out). If you do not define a key field, access is limited to arrival sequence.

Logical files describe how data appears to be stored in the database. Logical files do not actually contain data records. Instead, they store **access paths**, or pointers, to records in physical files. A logical file is always based on one or more physical files. The three most common uses for a logical file are to provide these capabilities:

- Sorting the records in a physical file
- Selecting certain records from a physical file
- Selecting certain fields from a physical file's record layout

RPG does not distinguish between physical files and logical files. It uses the same coding and techniques to process either one.

A third type of file, the **device file**, associates a layout with a hardware device, such as a printer or a workstation. For example, a printer file contains a description of a printed report's appearance, and a workstation file describes the layout of one or more display screens. RPG processes device files by using techniques similar to those it uses to process database files.

3.4. SQL Database Concepts

You may already be familiar with **Structured Query Language (SQL)**, an industry-standard language for defining, accessing, and manipulating a database. The IBM i operating system uses SQL to create database objects, and ILE RPG programs can incorporate SQL statements to access and update data. The IBM i database principles correspond to SQL standards, but they predate SQL. Consequently, the system also uses an alternative tool, **Data Description Specifications (DDS)**, to define and create database objects. Additionally, IBM i employs DDS to create device files, which SQL does not address.

ILE RPG can process data objects originally created by SQL as well as DDS. SQL can also access and manipulate physical files and logical files that were originally created using DDS. Today, SQL is the preferred tool for creating database objects, and DDS remains the sole means of creating device files. Accordingly, you must learn both SQL and DDS to effectively create all the objects you'll use in your RPG programs. IBM i and SQL sometimes use different terms for the same or similar things. Figure 3.1 compares the SQL terminology with the equivalent IBM i system names.

SQL Name	IBM i System Name
Schema (or Collection)	Library (*LIB)
Table	Physical file (*FILE PF-DTA)
View	Unkeyed logical file (*FILE LF)
Index	Keyed logical file (*FILE LF)
Row	Record
Column	Field

Figure 3.1: SQL terminology vs. system terminology

Note
SQL and RPG are two separate topics. Because SQL is an industry standard, information about SQL is available from numerous resources, including the online IBM Knowledge Center. This text covers basic SQL concepts—enough to get you started using it with ILE RPG—but advanced coverage of SQL goes beyond its scope.

SQL groups statements into four major categories:

- **Data Definition Language (DDL)** statements
- **Data Manipulation Language (DML)** statements
- **Embedded SQL Host Language** statements
- **SQL Procedural Language (SPL)** statements

You use DDL statements to create new objects, such as tables, and to alter the structure or properties of existing database objects (this chapter primarily discusses DDL statements). Some common DDL statements are as follows:

- CREATE TABLE
- CREATE VIEW
- CREATE INDEX
- ALTER TABLE

DML statements retrieve and manipulate the contents of existing database objects (i.e., the data in the tables). The following are regularly used DML statements:

- SELECT
- INSERT
- UPDATE
- DELETE

Embedded SQL statements are SQL instructions that you can incorporate—along with DDL and DML statements—into an RPG program. Chapter 10 deals with some basic DML statements as well as embedded SQL. Here are some regularly used embedded SQL statements:

- DECLARE CURSOR
- FETCH
- SELECT INTO

SPL is a separate SQL-based programming language used to create programs and functions that can be executed from within an SQL environment. Coverage of SPL statements is available from many other sources and goes beyond the scope of this text.

3.5. SQL Development Tools

Programmers use a variety of utilities to generate and process SQL statements, but the three primary ones are as follows:

- Interactive SQL
- RUNSQLSTM (Run SQL Statements) command
- IBM Data Studio

The **Interactive SQL** facility provides you with an SQL *command line* for directly entering SQL statements into the system. This utility is probably the most commonly used means of executing SQL statements. You can use it to create and alter database objects as well as to retrieve data from existing objects. The **STRSQL (Start SQL Interactive Session)** command presents a display, as Figure 3.2 illustrates, for entering free-format SQL statements one at a time. Function keys help to enter SQL statements effectively, and a prompting feature allows you to enter just part of an SQL statement and then prompts you for the remaining entries. Interactive SQL retains a history of the SQL statements you enter during a session. If you wish, you can save those statements to a source member for documentation or for later use as a script.

```
                               Enter SQL Statements

Type SQL statement, press Enter.
===> CREATE TABLE CUSTOMERS (CUSTNO CHAR(9) NOT NULL PRIMARY KEY,
                             CFNAME CHAR(15) DEFAULT ,
                             CLNAME CHAR(20) DEFAULT ,
                             CADDR CHAR(30) DEFAULT ,
                             CZIP CHAR(5) DEFAULT ,
                             CPHONE CHAR(10) NOT NULL,
                             CEMAIL CHAR(50) NOT NULL,
                             CDOB DECIMAL(8 , 0) NOT NULL,
                             CGENDER CHAR(1) NOT NULL)
                 RCDFMT CUSTSREC




                                                                          Bottom
 F3=Exit    F4=Prompt    F6=Insert line    F9=Retrieve    F10=Copy line
 F12=Cancel              F13=Services      F24=More keys
```

Figure 3.2: Interactive SQL display

The **RUNSQLSTM (Run SQL Statements)** command provides a scripting facility for executing SQL statements stored in a source file member. Unlike Interactive SQL, which executes single statements individually, an SQL script can execute a series of statements. Not all SQL statements are valid in a script; for example, a script cannot include a simple SELECT statement. But scripts are especially useful for DDL statements to create and alter database objects, and for documenting those statements in a source member. To code the script, you use the same editor (LPEX or SEU) that you use for coding RPG programs. Figure 3.3 shows a typical SQL script. Notice that statements can span several source lines and that every SQL statement ends with a semicolon (;).

```
QSQLSESS.MBR ✕
   Line 1        Column 1      Insert
   ---+----1----+----2----+----3----+----4----+----5----+----6----+----7----+----8----+----9----+---10·
   000100 CREATE TABLE CUSTOMERS (CUSTNO CHAR(9) NOT NULL PRIMARY KEY,
   000200                         CFNAME CHAR(15) DEFAULT ,
   000300                         CLNAME CHAR(20) DEFAULT ,
   000400                         CADDR CHAR(30) DEFAULT ,
   000500                         CZIP CHAR(5) DEFAULT ,
   000600                         CPHONE CHAR(10) NOT NULL,
   000700                         CEMAIL CHAR(50) NOT NULL,
   000800                         CDOB DECIMAL(8 , 0) NOT NULL,
   000900                         CGENDER CHAR(1) NOT NULL)
   001000             RCDFMT CUSTSREC;
   001100
   001200 LABEL ON COLUMN CUSTOMERS.CUSTNO
   001300        TEXT IS 'CUSTOMER NUMBER';
   001400
   001500 LABEL ON COLUMN CUSTOMERS.CFNAME
   001600        TEXT IS 'CUSTOMER FIRST NAME';
   001700
   001800 LABEL ON COLUMN CUSTOMERS.CLNAME
   001900        TEXT IS 'CUSTOMER LAST NAME';
   002000
   002100 LABEL ON COLUMN CUSTOMERS.CADDR
   002200        TEXT IS 'CUSTOMER STREET ADDRESS';
   002300
   002400 LABEL ON COLUMN CUSTOMERS.CZIP
   002500        TEXT IS 'ZIP CODE';
   002600
   002700 LABEL ON COLUMN CUSTOMERS.CPHONE
   002800        TEXT IS 'CUSTOMER PHONE';
```

Figure 3.3: SQL script for RUNSQLSTM command

IBM **Data Studio client** is part of the IBM Data Studio software suite, which provides the graphical tools that you need for developing and administering databases. The Data Studio client can be installed alongside the RDi development environment so that the two products can share common features. (RDi also includes a Data perspective with many of the same capabilities as Data Studio.) In Figure 3.4, Data Studio uses a form-fill approach to create and alter data objects. It then generates an SQL script, which you can save and run.

Properties ✕

<Table> CUSTOMERS

	Name	Primary ...	Domain	Data Type	Length	Scale	Not Null	Generated	Default Value/Generate ...
General									
Columns	CUSTNO	☑		CHAR	9		☑	☐	
Relationships	CFNAME	☐		CHAR	15		☐	☐	SYSTEM_DEFAULT
Documentation	CLNAME	☐		CHAR	20		☐	☐	SYSTEM_DEFAULT
	CADDR	☐		CHAR	30		☐	☐	SYSTEM_DEFAULT
	CZIP	☐		CHAR	5		☐	☐	SYSTEM_DEFAULT
	CPHONE	☐		CHAR	10		☑	☐	
	CEMAIL	☐		CHAR	50		☑	☐	
	CDOB	☐		DECIMAL	8	0	☑	☐	
	CGENDER	☐		CHAR	1		☑	☐	

Figure 3.4: IBM Data Studio Properties view

3.6. Creating Tables with SQL

SQL **tables** contain the actual data in a database. When SQL creates a new table, the database creates a single-member physical file object in a library. Tables are arranged into **rows** (records) and **columns** (fields). Appropriately enough, SQL uses the **Create Table** statement to produce a table:

```
Create Table Customers
            (Custno  Char(9)       Not Null Default Primary Key,
             Cfname  Char(15)      Default,
             Clname  Char(20)      Default,
             Caddr   Char(30)      Default,
             Czip    Char(5)       Default,
             Cphone  Char(10)      Not Null Default,
             Cemail  Char(50)      Not Null Default,
             Cdob    Decimal(8,0)  Not Null Default,
             Cgender Char(1)       Not Null Default)
            Rcdfmt Custsrec
```

Character spacing and alignment are generally not important, as SQL is a free-format language, but it's useful—especially when you are writing SQL scripts—to align the various components and clauses of the statement to make them easier to read and edit. Although the following statement accomplishes the same result as the preceding statement, it is much more difficult to read and analyze:

```
Create Table Customers (Custno Char(9) Not Null Default Primary Key, Cfname
Char(15) Default, Clname Char(20) Default, Caddr Char(30) Default, Czip
Char(5) Default, Cphone Char(10) Not Null Default, Cemail Char(50) Not
Null Default, Cdob Decimal(8,0) Not Null Default, Cgender Char(1) Not Null
Default) Rcdfmt Custsrec
```

Both of these Create Table statements contain three major clauses: 1) the name of the table, 2) its column structure (i.e., its fields), and 3) the name of the record format.

3.6.1. Table Name

The first clause names the table to create. The table identifier must begin with an alphabetic character or one of the special characters $, #, or @. In addition to those characters, the remaining characters can be numbers or an underscore (_). A table identifier cannot include embedded blanks.

IBM i object names are limited to 10 characters, and you should limit the table name to 10 characters as well. Specifying a table name longer than 10 characters causes SQL to generate a system object name. For example, if you create an SQL table called LOCALCUSTOMERS, SQL produces an object called LOCAL00001, or some similar nondescript name. In this case, you can use the SQL Rename statement to give the table a more useful object name:

```
Rename Table Localcustomers To System Name Localcusts
```

3.6.2. Column Definitions

The second clause in the Create Table statement lists all the columns that make up the table layout. The columns are listed individually inside a single set of parentheses. Each column definition includes at least the column name and a data type. If you specify a column name longer than 10 characters, or with invalid characters, SQL generates a system name.

The following are the most common built-in data types used with IBM i:

- CHAR (fixed-length character)
- VARCHAR (variable-length character)
- DECIMAL (packed numeric)
- NUMERIC (zoned numeric)
- SMALLINT (two-byte integer)
- INTEGER (four-byte integer)
- BIGINT (eight-byte integer)
- DATE
- TIME
- TIMESTAMP

We examine each of the data types in detail later in this chapter.

In addition to the name and data type, each column definition can include optional constraint clauses to further define the column. A **constraint** specifies a rule for the data in a table. Commonly used constraint clauses include the following:

- NOT NULL
- DEFAULT
- UNIQUE
- PRIMARY KEY

The **NOT NULL constraint** prevents the column from containing null values. A **null value** represents the absence of data for a column. You can set a null-capable column to null instead of an actual value. Most IBM i tables specify NOT NULL for each column, forcing that column to always have a value.

The **DEFAULT constraint** indicates that the column is to contain a **default value**. The default value is provided for that column to all new rows (records) if no other value is specified. You can specify a constant default value for a column. For example, for a column that includes the constraint DEFAULT 99999, SQL assigns a value of 99999 to that column unless the SQL statement specifically indicates another value. If the constraint doesn't specify a constant default value, numeric columns default to zero, character columns default to blanks, and date-related columns use the current value. A column, regardless of data type, that is null capable has a default value of null. Column definitions that omit both NOT NULL and DEFAULT clauses are implicitly null capable with a default.

As you might expect, the **UNIQUE constraint** guarantees that every row in the table has a unique value for that column. A related rule, **PRIMARY KEY**, combines the NOT NULL and UNIQUE constraints. PRIMARY KEY ensures that a column (or combination of two or more columns) contains a unique value that identifies a specific row in the table. A table can have only one primary key. If the primary key consists of only one column, you can specify the primary key constraint with that column definition:

```
Create Table Customers
        (Custno Char(9) Primary Key,

        ...

        Cgender Char(1))
```

If the primary key is a combination of two or more columns, you must specify the primary key constraint separately at the end of the column definitions:

```
Create Table Customers
        (Company Char(3),
        Custno  Char(9),

        ...

        Cgender Char(1),
        Primary Key (Company, Custno))
```

3.6.3. Record Format Names

A unique feature of the IBM i database is the requirement that a record format (layout) have a name. Moreover, RPG requires that the record format name be distinct from the table name. To accommodate this requirement, the IBM i version of SQL enhances industry-standard SQL by including a **RCDFMT clause** to name the format:

```
Create Table Customers (…) Rcdfmt Custsrec
```

When the Create Table statement does not include RCDFMT, the format name is the same as the table name. In that case, the RPG program must rename the format when it declares the file:

```
Dcl-f Customers Rename(Customers:Custrec);
```

(This declaration appears in the RPG program. It is *not* an SQL statement.)

3.6.4. Qualified Names and Naming Conventions

You can refer to objects either by a simple name, such as Customers, or by a **qualified name**. An object's qualified name includes the name of the **schema** (library) in which the object is stored. Depending upon the naming convention you use, a qualified name might be either Flightproj/Customers or Flightproj.Customers for an object stored in a schema called Flightproj. You can also write the Create Table statement shown earlier as

```
Create Table Flightproj/Customers …
```

or

```
Create Table Flightproj.Customers …
```

to explicitly place the table in the Flightproj schema.

Generally, the IBM i operating system uses a slash (/) as a separator character for qualified objects. SQL supports this **system naming convention**, but *only for IBM i* objects. The industry-standard **SQL naming convention** uses a period (.) as the separator character for SQL statements on platforms other than IBM i. The default is the system naming convention. The SQL **Set Option** statement can change the naming convention for an SQL session:

```
Set Option Naming = *Sql
```

or

```
Set Option Naming = *Sys (Default)
```

Specifying qualified names is always unambiguous, regardless of which naming convention you use. But when an SQL statement refers instead to simple names, the naming convention determines how the system finds objects and where it places newly created objects. SQL implicitly qualifies all simple object names with a value contained in a variable called the **current schema**. The current schema is the default location for creating new objects. The default value of the current schema differs depending upon the naming convention you use. If you use the system naming convention, SQL will search the job's library list (*LIBL) when it resolves objects with simple names. The SQL naming convention, however, implicitly qualifies simple object names with your user profile name (which SQL calls the authorization identifier).

To summarize:

- *SYS naming uses the library list (*LIBL).
- *SQL naming uses the user profile name.

The SQL naming convention is more portable, but the system naming convention may be more familiar and convenient.

You can change the value of the current schema to use a specific schema with the SQL **Set Schema** statement:

```
Set Schema = Flightproj
```

or

```
Set Schema = Default (to use defaults)
```

3.7. Data Types and Data Storage

You must assign a **data type** to each column in a table. The column's data type determines how its values are stored, how much storage the column occupies, and what kinds of operations can be performed on the column when it is used within a program. Commonly used data types fall into three general categories:

- Character
- Numeric
- Date

To understand the various data types, let's first examine how the computer stores data. You probably know that any numeric value can be converted from its familiar decimal, or base 10, value to a corresponding value in binary, or base 2, notation. The computer stores all data in this binary format, with all data represented as a combination of 1s and 0s. At first glance, data representation should be a simple matter of converting values from one base to another. Many characters and values that you want to represent to the computer are not numbers, though—instead, they are letters of the alphabet, for example, or special characters such as $ and {.

A **bit** is a binary digit that can have a value of 1 or 0 (sometimes called *on* or *off*). A string of eight bits is called a **byte**. A byte can have up to 256 different possible combinations of bit states; the system can use these combinations to represent up to 256 different characters.

IBM developed a coding scheme to allow a data character—numeric or non-numeric—to be represented to the computer. This coding scheme, based on the English alphabet, is called **Extended Binary Coded Decimal Interchange Code**, or **EBCDIC** (generally pronounced as eb-si-dik). EBCDIC assigns a unique eight-bit binary pattern to each representable character. Capital A, for example, is 11000001 in EBCDIC, and the digit 1 is represented as 11110001. The leftmost four bits are often called zone or **high-order bits**, and the rightmost four bits are digit or **low-order bits**. Because eight bits constitute a byte, it takes one byte of storage to store each character in EBCDIC. IBM i stores all non-numeric, or character, data values this way: one byte represents a character.

Instead of reading long strings of 1s and 0s, most programmers find it easier to represent byte values by using **hexadecimal** (base 16) **notation** for the high and low order bits, according to the following table:

Hexadecimal	Bit Pattern
0	0000
1	0001
2	0010
3	0011
4	0100
5	0101
6	0110
7	0111
8	1000
9	1001
A	1010
B	1011
C	1100
D	1101
E	1110
F	1111

Using this table, you can see that the bit pattern 11000001 can be referred to as hex character C1 (usually noted as X'C1').

All computers use some kind of an encoding system to represent characters as bit patterns, but not all systems use EBCDIC, which is unique to some IBM systems. You may already be familiar with the encoding system called **ASCII** (American Standard Code for Information Interchange), generally pronounced as as-kee. EBCDIC was developed separately from ASCII. Consequently, the bit patterns in ASCII are not the same as those in EBCDIC. For example, the letter A in EBCDIC is represented by a hex C1, but in ASCII it is a hex 41. In addition, the two schemes use different collating sequences; that is, they do not sort all the characters in the same sequence. In EBCDIC, lowercase characters sort before uppercase characters, and letters sort before numbers (e.g., a, b, c, ... A, B, C, ... 7, 8, 9). In ASCII, the opposite is true (e.g., 1, 2, 3, ... A, B, C, ... x, y, z). Figure 3.5 shows some commonly used characters and their equivalent EBCDIC and ASCII encoding (in EBCDIC sequence).

Character	EBCDIC Bits	Hex	ASCII Bits	Hex	Character	EBCDIC Bits	Hex	ASCII Bits	Hex	Character	EBCDIC Bits	Hex	ASCII Bits	Hex
(space)	0100 0000	40	0010 0000	20	u	1010 0100	A4	0111 0101	75	P	1101 0111	D7	0101 0000	50
a	1000 0001	81	0110 0001	61	v	1010 0101	A5	0111 0110	76	Q	1101 1000	D8	0101 0001	51
b	1000 0010	82	0110 0010	62	w	1010 0110	A6	0111 0111	77	R	1101 1001	D9	0101 0010	52
c	1000 0011	83	0110 0011	63	x	1010 0111	A7	0111 1000	78	S	1110 0010	E2	0101 0011	53
d	1000 0100	84	0110 0100	64	y	1010 1000	A8	0111 1001	79	T	1110 0011	E3	0101 0100	54
e	1000 0101	85	0110 0101	65	z	1010 1001	A9	0111 1010	7A	U	1110 0100	E4	0101 0101	55
f	1000 0110	86	0110 0110	66	A	1100 0001	C1	0100 0001	41	V	1110 0101	E5	0101 0110	56
g	1000 0111	87	0110 0111	67	B	1100 0010	C2	0100 0010	42	W	1110 0110	E6	0101 0111	57
h	1000 1000	88	0110 1000	68	C	1100 0011	C3	0100 0011	43	X	1110 0111	E7	0101 1000	58
i	1000 1001	89	0110 1001	69	D	1100 0100	C4	0100 0100	44	Y	1110 1000	E8	0101 1001	59
j	1001 0001	91	0110 1010	6A	E	1100 0101	C5	0100 0101	45	Z	1110 1001	E9	0101 1010	5A
k	1001 0010	92	0110 1011	6B	F	1100 0110	C6	0100 0110	46	0	1111 0000	F0	0011 0000	30
l	1001 0011	93	0110 1100	6C	G	1100 0111	C7	0100 0111	47	1	1111 0001	F1	0011 0001	31
m	1001 0100	94	0110 1101	6D	H	1100 1000	C8	0100 1000	48	2	1111 0010	F2	0011 0010	32
n	1001 0101	95	0110 1110	6E	I	1100 1001	C9	0100 1001	49	3	1111 0011	F3	0011 0011	33
o	1001 0110	96	0110 1111	6F	J	1101 0001	D1	0100 1010	4A	4	1111 0100	F4	0011 0100	34
p	1001 0111	97	0111 0000	70	K	1101 0010	D2	0100 1011	4B	5	1111 0101	F5	0011 0101	35
q	1001 1000	98	0111 0001	71	L	1101 0011	D3	0100 1100	4C	6	1111 0110	F6	0011 0110	36
r	1001 1001	99	0111 0010	72	M	1101 0100	D4	0100 1101	4D	7	1111 0111	F7	0011 0111	37
s	1010 0010	A2	0111 0011	73	N	1101 0101	D5	0100 1110	4E	8	1111 1000	F8	0011 1000	38
t	1010 0011	A3	0111 0100	74	O	1101 0110	D6	0100 1111	4F	9	1111 1001	F9	0011 1001	39

Figure 3.5: EBCDIC and ASCII coding

3.7.1. Character Data Types

Character data can be any symbol that the system supports. Alphabetic letters, numbers, and special characters (e.g., punctuation marks, currency symbols) are all character data. A **character string** is a sequence of characters. An RPG program typically processes character data by assigning values from one character variable to another, by concatenating (joining) character strings, or by converting character data to another data type.

Note

Typically, each character occupies a single byte in storage. But some character sets use two bytes to store each character. These are known as *double-byte character sets* and are most commonly used by languages such as Japanese or Chinese that have more symbols than one byte can represent.

Extended versions of ASCII, called Unicode and UCS (Universal Character Set) also have become widely accepted. These newer character sets, which extend beyond the English alphabet, are also double-byte character sets, and have a much wider array of available characters than either EBCDIC or ASCII.

3.7.1.1. CHAR

When SQL defines a column as CHAR (or CHARACTER), it is defining a **fixed-length character string**. You specify the length attribute in parentheses. All values in the column have the same length in storage. Values that don't fill the entire length are padded with blanks. The following column definition defines Address, a fixed-length character column 35 characters (bytes) long:

```
Create Table Customers (... Address Char(35), ...)
```

Most character columns in an IBM i database are fixed length. When you don't specify a length, the column is one byte—the maximum length is 32,766.

3.7.1.2. VARCHAR

Specifying a data type of VARCHAR (or CHAR VARYING or CHARACTER VARYING) defines a column as a **variable-length character string**. You specify the maximum size (up to 32,740) in parentheses. The following column definition defines Email, a variable-length character column 1–256 characters long:

```
Create Table ... (... Email Varchar(256), ...)
```

You use a variable-length character string when the length is uncertain. Typically, the value in a variable-length column is not padded with blanks to fill the entire allotted storage space. Instead, the same column in different rows contains different lengths, depending upon the column value. Use CHAR when most values in a column are likely to be the same size, and use VARCHAR when you anticipate the values will vary considerably in size.

3.7.2. Numeric Data Types

Numeric data is limited to numeric digits 0–9. Numeric variables also incorporate a sign embedded in the rightmost position of the variable. An RPG program typically processes numeric data by assigning values from one numeric variable to another, by evaluating arithmetic expressions, or by converting numeric data to another data type.

SQL defines numeric data with a precision and a scale. **Precision** refers to the total number of digits available in the number without regard to any sign. **Scale** indicates how many of those digits are fractional (i.e., to the right of the decimal point).

Numeric data types that SQL supports include numeric, decimal, and integer (as well as other less-frequently used types). Why are there different data types for the same class of values? RPG does not differentiate among numeric data types in determining the kinds of operations that you can perform on a field or the kinds of output editing that are possible; however, the data type of a numeric field—zoned numeric, packed decimal, or integer—determines how that field is represented and stored within the database.

To understand the various data representations, recall the EBCDIC coding scheme used to represent characters, in this case, numbers. The following table shows the EBCDIC codes for the digits 0–9:

Digit	EBCDIC Bits	Hex
0	1111 0000	F0
1	1111 0001	F1
2	1111 0010	F2
3	1111 0011	F3
4	1111 0100	F4
5	1111 0101	F5
6	1111 0110	F6
7	1111 0111	F7
8	1111 1000	F8
9	1111 1001	F9

Notice that the high-order bits (zone) of all digits are identical: 1111. This means that the zone portion is redundant for numeric data; that is, if the database already knows that the data is numeric, it knows that the zones of the data are all 1111, or F. The database can take advantage of this knowledge to store numeric data efficiently.

3.7.2.1. NUMERIC

Specifying a data type of NUMERIC (or NUM) defines a column as a **zoned** (or signed) **decimal** number. Zoned decimal numbers take a full byte to store each digit of a numeric value. Thus, a three-digit number occupies three bytes. The zone of the rightmost digit stores the sign of the data: 1111 (F) represents a positive value, whereas 1101 (D) represents a negative value. Zoned representation, then, is nearly identical to character representation except that the sign is embedded in the rightmost digit's byte:

Value to Represent	Bits (3 bytes)	Hex	Characters
+136	11110001 11110011 11110110	F1 F3 F6	136
-136	11110001 11110011 11010110	F1 F3 D6	13O

The following column definition defines CredLimit, a zoned decimal numeric column with a precision (total length) of nine digits and a scale (number of decimal places) of two digits:

```
Create Table ... (... CredLimit Numeric(9,2), ...)
```

Accordingly, CredLimit can hold a value up to 9,999,999.99. The maximum precision for a numeric column is 63 digits, and the scale can be any number from 0 to the precision of the number. If you omit scale, it is assumed to be 0; if you omit both precision and scale—specifying simply NUMERIC—SQL assumes NUMERIC(5,0).

Zoned decimal values can be useful when a program needs to present numeric values as text. For positive numeric values, the zoned numbers render as the correct characters (136, in the preceding example). For negative numbers, however, the last digit renders as an alphabetic character J–R (X'D1'-X'D9').

3.7.2.2. DECIMAL

Specifying a data type of DECIMAL (or DEC) defines a column as a **packed decimal** number. Packed numbers take advantage of the redundancy built into digit representation by simply not bothering to store the zones of numbers. In packed format, only the digit, or low order, bits of a number are stored, with the sign of the number represented by an additional four bits. These sign bits always occupy a packed decimal value's last four bit positions:

Value to Represent	Bits (2 bytes)	Hex	Characters
+136	00010011 01101111	13 6F	■?
-136	00010011 01101101	13 6D	■_

Data in packed format takes just over half the amount of storage necessary to store the same number in zoned decimal format. A three-digit number occupies two bytes. This may not seem like a great difference, but larger numbers generate larger storage savings: a 63-digit number in packed format occupies only 32 bytes.

The following column definition defines the same CredLimit column in the earlier example, but this time it is a packed decimal number:

```
Create Table ... (... CredLimit Decimal(9,2), ...)
```

If you omit scale, it is assumed to be 0; if you exclude both precision and scale—specifying simply DECIMAL—SQL assumes DECIMAL(5,0). Because of the method packed numbers use to store numeric values, programmers usually define packed decimal columns with an odd precision so that the complete value (with the sign added) occupies whole bytes.

Notice that the character representation for packed numbers is not generally easily translatable to the numeric value. The hexadecimal representation usually makes sense, but the bit patterns for packed numbers render as nondisplayable or unrelated EBCDIC characters.

Most numeric columns in the typical IBM i database are packed decimal numbers. Although some programmers prefer to define numeric columns as zoned—because it's easier to print or view the raw data in this format—the computer works more efficiently with numbers stored in packed decimal format. For most numeric processes, RPG implicitly converts numeric values to packed decimal format before processing them.

3.7.2.3. INTEGER, SMALLINT, BIGINT

You've seen that packed decimal numbers are more compact than zoned decimal numbers. Integer representation is even more compact than packed decimal representation. Integers store numeric values in a binary format. Each bit in a string is assigned a decimal value, and the values of the *on* bits are simply added together to determine the number's signed value. SQL supports three integer-related data types. Which one you use will depend upon the range of values that the numbers must hold:

Data Type	Bytes	Digits	Lowest Value	Highest Value
SMALLINT	2	5	-32,768	32,767
INT (or INTEGER)	4	10	-2,147,483,648	2,147,483,647
BIGINT	8	19	-9,223,372,036,854,775,808	9,223,372,036,854,775,807

The following column definition defines the column Terms, an integer:

```
Create Table ... (... Terms Int, ...)
```

Notice that there is no need to indicate a precision or scale. The precision (10) is set by the INT data type, and the scale for all integers is 0.

Although the use of integers is common in RPG programs, its use in database objects is less so. Most numeric database columns are DECIMAL or NUMERIC data types, which have more flexible precision and scale options than Integer data types. If, however, the anticipated data values fit into the allowed range and scale for any of the Integer data types, they are an efficient and useful data type for numeric data.

3.7.3. Date and Time Data Types

IBM i supports several **date and time data types**, which represent dates, times, and time-stamps. An RPG program typically processes dates by assigning one date variable to another, by perform date arithmetic and comparisons, or by converting a date to another data type. The date and time data types are neither character nor numeric data types; they are distinct data types that the computer can easily recognize, process, and manipulate as dates without requiring special coding or conversion. They are sometimes called *native dates*, as opposed to *legacy dates*, which are character strings or numbers that have valid date or time values. Legacy dates require special processing to convert them to dates or to use them as dates.

3.7.3.1. DATE

Specifying a data type of DATE defines a column as a date. A date is a three-part value, incorporating a month, day, and year between 0001–9999. When defining a date, you do not need to specify a length because the system determines the length automatically. The following column definition defines the column Renewal, a date:

```
Create Table ... (... Renewal Date, ...)
```

An ILE RPG program can retrieve a date value and process it. The presentation of the date in the program conforms to any of eight different formats in use by the program. Chapter 8 covers the date data type in more detail.

3.7.3.2. TIME

Specifying a data type of TIME defines a column as a time of day, integrating hours, minutes, and seconds. Time data follows many of the same principles as the date data type. When defining a time, you do not need to specify a length. The following column definition defines the column CallTime, a time:

```
Create Table ... (... CallTime Time, ...)
```

An ILE RPG program can retrieve a time value and process it. As with dates, the presentation of the time in the program conforms to any of five different time formats in use by the program, which Chapter 8 details.

3.7.3.3. TIMESTAMP

A **timestamp** is a combination of a date and time in a single variable. Specifying a data type of TIMESTAMP defines a timestamp column. Timestamps have six or seven parts: year, month, day, hour, minute, second, and optionally fractional seconds. The following column definition defines the column LastUpdate, a timestamp with microseconds included:

```
Create Table ... (... LastUpdate Timestamp, ...)
```

By default, timestamps contain microseconds (six digits to represent fractional seconds):

```
2015-06-30-12.34.56.789012
```

If you need a different scale, the column definition can include a length 0–12 to represent the desired number of fractional seconds' digits. For example,

```
Create Table ... (... LastUpdate Timestamp(0), ...)
```

omits all fractional seconds:

```
2015-06-30-12.34.56
```

3.8. Creating Views with SQL

SQL **views** provide alternative ways of accessing the data in a table. Although a program can retrieve and process virtual rows from a view, the view does not actually contain data. Instead, it stores an access path, a sequence of pointers to the actual data in one or more tables. When SQL creates a new view, the database constructs an unkeyed logical file based on a physical file. An RPG program does not make a distinction between a table and a view when it is processing the file—the program can read and generally update the file whether it is a table or a view.

The most common uses for a view are to select certain rows (a subset) from a table, select a subset of columns from a table, or select a combination of both functions. The SQL **Create View** statement produces a view. The access path is built from an SQL Select statement integrated within the Create View statement:

```
Create View Custmales
          As Select * From Customers Where Cgender = 'M'
          Rcdfmt Custmrec
```

or

```
Create View Custdir
        As Select Clname, Cfname, Cphone, Cemail >From Customers
        Rcdfmt Custdrec
```

or

```
Create View Custusa
        As Select Clname, Cfname, Cphone, Cemail >From Customers
                Where Country = 'USA'
        Rcdfmt Custurec
```

These Create View statements contain three major clauses: 1) the name of the view, 2) a Select statement—more accurately called a *fullselect*—to designate the rows and columns to be in the view, and 3) the name of the view's record format.

A **fullselect** is a component of the Create View statement. It specifies the rows and columns from one or more tables that make up the view. The fullselect names the columns to retrieve, the table from which to retrieve them, and optionally a Where clause to specify criteria for row selection.

In the following fullselect,

```
Select * From Customers Where Cgender = 'M'
```

the view includes only those rows from the Customers table that represent male (Cgender = 'M') customers. The view has all the same columns as the original table (Select *). Although the Customers table contains all the possible rows, if a program processes this view instead, the view will have access only to male customers.

When the view is to have only certain columns from the table, the fullselect names those columns to use:

```
Select Clname, Cfname, Cphone, Cemail From Customers
```

In this example, the fullselect specifies only four columns from the table to include in the view. Every row from the table is also in the view because the fullselect has no Where clause to filter out rows. You can, however, combine a column list and a Where clause in the same fullselect:

```
Select Clname, Cfname, Cphone, Cemail From Customers
        Where Country = 'USA'
```

Note that you cannot sort a view, nor can the fullselect contain an SQL Order By clause.

3.9. Creating Indexes with SQL

An SQL **index** is a database object whose primary purpose is to improve the performance of SQL statements. An index does not contain data, and SQL cannot retrieve rows from an index. The IBM i database implements an index as a keyed logical file. As you might expect, the SQL **Create Index** statement creates an index:

```
Create Index Custidx
            On Customers (Czip, Clname)
            Rcdfmt Custxrec
```

This Create Index statement contains four major clauses: 1) the name of the index, 2) the name of the table on which to create the index, 3) a list of the key fields in the index, and 4) an optional record format name. The statement might also include a Where clause to cause the index to select only those rows that fulfill specific criteria:

```
Create Index Custidx
            On Customers Where Cstate = 'FL' (Czip, Clname)
            Rcdfmt Custxrec
```

Although SQL does not retrieve data from an index, an ILE RPG program can declare the index in its file declarations, enabling it to read and write records in the Custidx logical file.

3.10. DDS Database Concepts

While most recent database objects are created by using SQL, many files are still defined by using DDS. The procedure for creating database file definitions with DDS is similar to that of creating an RPG program. The first step is to use an editor, such as the RDi LPEX editor, to create a source member of definition statements. Most installations use a file named QDDSSRC to store members representing externally described files. The source member type of a physical file member is PF, and the type of a logical file member is LF. The editor automatically provides prompts appropriate to the member type you specify.

Data Description Specifications (DDS) comprise a fixed-format language that you can use to code the source definitions for physical and logical database files as well as for display and printer files. All DDS lines include an A in position 6. An asterisk (*) in position 7 of a DDS source line signals a comment line. You can use comment lines throughout the file definition. At a minimum, you should include a few comment lines at the beginning of each file definition to identify the nature of the file.

In addition to comment lines, DDS includes record format descriptions, which name each record layout (format) within the file; field definition lines, which describe fields within records; and perhaps key specifications to designate which fields are to serve as keys to the file. The particular nature of these specifications depends upon whether you are defining a physical file or a logical file.

DDS extensively uses a variety of keywords, each with a special meaning. Keywords that apply to the file as a whole are called **file-level keywords**, those that apply to a specific record format within the file are known as **record-level keywords**, and those that associate only with a specific field are termed **field-level keywords**.

Although all externally defined files share those general features previously mentioned, the details of a DDS definition depend upon the type of file you are defining. Accordingly, let's first look at using DDS to define physical files.

3.10.1. DDS for Physical Files

The concept of a physical file object parallels that of an SQL table. In fact, SQL tables are implemented as physical files. When you use DDS to describe the file, the physical file's source statements define the record format of the file. Physical files can contain only one record format. That means that every record within a physical file must have an identical record layout. The record format is signaled by an R in position 17, and you enter a name for the record format in positions 19–28 (Name++++++).

Following the record format specification, you must enter lines to define each field the record contains. After the field definitions, you optionally can designate a key for the file. A K in position 17 denotes a key field. When you list a key field, its contents determine a sequence in which you can retrieve records from the file. Figure 3.6 shows the DDS code for the Customers file discussed earlier.

```
*CUSTOMERS.PF 23
   Line 4        Column 1      Replace  18 changes
            ....A...........Name+++++RLen++TDpB......Functions++++++++++++++++++++++++++++
   000101    A* Customers physical file
   000102    A                                        UNIQUE
   000103    A            R CUSTSREC
   000104    A              CUSTNO        9A           TEXT('Customer Number')
   000105    A              CFNAME       15A           TEXT('Customer First Name')
   000106    A              CLNAME       20A           TEXT('Customer Last Name')
   000107    A              CADDR        30A           TEXT('Customer Street Address')
   000108    A              CZIP          5A           TEXT('ZIP Code')
   000109    A              CPHONE       10A           TEXT('Customer Phone')
   000110    A              CEMAIL       50A           TEXT('Customer Email')
   000111    A              CDOB          8P 0         TEXT('Customer Date of Birth')
   000112    A              CGENDER       1A           TEXT('F=Female M=Male')
   000113    A            K CUSTNO
```

Figure 3.6: Physical file DDS

Let's look at the details of this definition. First, UNIQUE is a file-level keyword. (All file-level keywords appear at the beginning of the DDS, before any record format specification line.)

UNIQUE stipulates that the file cannot contain records with duplicate key values. When you include this keyword, attempts to write a record to the file with a key value identical to a record already in the file causes the system to generate an error message. Use of UNIQUE is optional—without its use, the system permits records with duplicate key values.

The record format line is next. Note the R in position 17 and the format name, CUSTSREC, left-aligned in positions 19–28. DDS allows record format names (and field names, for that matter) up to 10 characters. DDS source code cannot contain lowercase alphabetic characters, except in a string enclosed in double quotation marks, so you must enter all record format and field names in DDS source as uppercase.

You define the fields of a record on successive lines below the record format line. The field name begins in position 19 (Name++++++). Next, you specify the length of the field, right-adjusted in positions 30–34 (Len++). Numeric field definitions must include a decimal entry (Dc, positions 36–37) to indicate how many decimal places the field includes. You use position 35 to specify the data type. DDS supports the following commonly used data types, discussed earlier:

- A = Character
- S = Zoned (signed) numeric
- P = Packed numeric
- L = Date
- T = Time
- Z = Timestamp

DDS recognizes other data types as well, but these character, numeric, and date data types satisfy most common requirements. When you do not specify a data type in position 35, DDS defaults to A for character fields or P for numeric fields (i.e., those with a decimal positions entry in positions 36–37).

Following the definition of all the fields to appear within the record, you can designate one or more fields as the record key by coding a K in position 17 and specifying the name of the key field in positions 19–28. In the example, CUSTNO is named as the file's key field. Notice that you must define the key field as part of the record before naming it in the K specification. If you list more than one key line, you are specifying a composite (concatenated) key. For a **composite key**, list the key fields in order from major to minor. Note that fields need not be adjacent to each other within the record to be key components.

The TEXT keyword entries are optional ways to provide documentation. In the example, TEXT is used with each field to explain what the field represents. You must enclose text comments with apostrophes (') and surround them with parentheses. Although text comments are not required, it makes good sense to include them, especially if your field names are somewhat cryptic. TEXT also can appear as a record-level keyword to document the record format.

Programmers new to DDS are sometimes confused by the fact that the filename is not included within the DDS (except perhaps within a comment line). The filename is determined when you actually compile the DDS. By default, the name of the source member becomes the name of the compiled object, or database file.

3.10.2. DDS for Logical Files

Although you can, in theory, *get by* using only physical files to define your data, you are just scratching the surface of the IBM i database capabilities until you begin to use logical files. The concepts behind logical files correspond to those of SQL views and indexes.

Recall from the introduction to this chapter that logical files define access paths to data stored in physical files. You can use a logical file to change the retrieval order of records from a file (by changing the designated key field), to restrict user views to a subset of fields or records contained in a physical file, or to combine data stored in two or more separate physical files into one logical file. Although the data is stored in physical files, after you have defined logical files to the system, you can refer to these logical files in RPG programs as though the logical files themselves actually contained records. The advantage of using logical files is that they can provide alternative ways to look at data, including different orders of record access, without redundantly storing the actual data on the system.

A logical file based on a single physical file is called a **simple logical file**. The method of defining simple logical files is similar to that of defining physical files. You first specify a record format, then stipulate a list of fields (optional), and follow that with one or more (optional) key fields. Because logical files provide views of physical files, you must include the **PFILE** keyword beginning in position 45 of the Keywords area on the record format line, followed, in parentheses, by the name of the physical file upon which the logical record format is based.

The easiest way to code a simple logical file is to use the same record format name within the logical file as the record format name in the physical file on which the logical file is based. With this method, the system assumes the record layouts of the files are identical. As a result, you do not need to include fields within your logical record description. However, you can still designate one or more fields as a key, and this key does not have to match the key of the physical file. The example in Figure 3.7 shows a logical file based on customer file Customers.

Notice that this DDS contains no field-level entries. With this definition, all the fields defined within the physical file are implicitly included within the logical file. Because the logical file is keyed on last name and then first name, keyed sequential access of this logical file retrieves the customer records in alphabetic order by last name then by first name. Programmers widely use this kind of logical file definition to change the retrieval order of records in a file. Its effects are identical to that of physically sorting file records into a different order, but without the system overhead that a physical sort requires. This logical file is similar to an SQL index, and indeed, SQL can use this logical file as an index to improve the performance of some SQL statements.

```
/ *CUSTL1.LF 
   Line 3          Column 1     Insert    7 changes
        .....A.........T.Name++++++...............Functions++++++++++++++++++++++++++++++
   000100       A* CUSTL1 logical file
   000101       A* Customers keyed by last name, first name
   000102       A          R CUSTSREC              PFILE(CUSTOMERS)
   000103       A            K CLNAME
   000104       A            K CFNAME
```

Figure 3.7: Logical file DDS based on Customers file

To restrict the logical file so that it includes only some of the fields from the physical file, give the logical file a record format name different from that of the record format name in the physical file, and then list just those fields to include in the logical file. Only the fields listed are accessible through the logical file. Again, you can designate one or more of these fields to serve as the key to the file. Figure 3.8 illustrates the DDS for such a logical file.

```
/ *CUSTDIR.LF 
   Line 3          Column 1     Insert    9 changes
        .....A.........T.Name++++++...............Functions++++++++++++++++++++++++++++++
   000100       A* Logical file CUSTDIR
   000101       A* Customers file with directory fields only
   000102       A          R CUSTDREC              PFILE(CUSTOMERS)
   000103       A            CLNAME
   000104       A            CFNAME
   000105       A            CPHONE
   000106       A            CEMAIL
   000107       A          K CLNAME
   000108       A          K CFNAME
```

Figure 3.8: Logical file DDS displaying accessible fields

Notice that you do not need to specify length, type, and decimal positions for the fields in a logical file. These field attributes are already given in the physical file on which the logical file is based.

You can define logical files to include only a subset of the records contained in the physical file by using Select and Omit specifications. You use this feature only if the logical file first contains a key specification. Your specifications base the record inclusion or exclusion on actual data values present in selected fields of the physical file records.

For example, assume you want to include only the male customers from the Customers file. You'd simply designate Cgender as a select field (S in position 17) and then, in position 45, provide the basis for the selection. One way to do this is with the COMP keyword. COMP specifies a comparison between a field's value and a single given value to serve as the basis of selection or omission. You specify the nature of the comparison by using one of eight relational operators:

- EQ (equal to)
- GT (greater than)
- GE (greater than or equal to)
- LT (less than)
- LE (less than or equal to)
- NE (not equal to)
- NG (not greater than)
- NL (not less than)

Figure 3.9 shows DDS using Select/Omit to create a logical file consisting of a subset of the records in the Customers file. The S in position 17 indicates a Select specification, and the O in position 17 of the next line indicates an optional Omit specification. The DDS simply indicates that the file should select all records with Cgender equal to 'M' and omit all other records.

```
*CUSTMALES.LF
   Line 3        Column 1      Insert    9 changes
        .....A.........T.Name++++++...............Functions++++++++++++++++++++++++++++
   000100      A* Logical file CUSTMALES
   000101      A* Customers file - male customers only
   000102      A          R CUSTSREC              PFILE(CUSTOMERS)
   000103      A            K CUSTNO
   000104      A          S CGENDER               COMP(EQ 'M')
   000105      A          O                       ALL
```

Figure 3.9: Logical file DDS using Select and Omit specifications

In addition to COMP, DDS often uses two other keywords to identify selection criteria. The VALUES keyword is similar to COMP, but it allows comparison with multiple values. The RANGE keyword lets you set a range of values to select or omit.

DDS offers many other database capabilities beyond the physical and logical file constructs that you've examined here. Variants on logical files, for instance, can be much more complex than the simple examples we've illustrated. For example, you can create logical files based on two or more physical files with multiple record formats—with each format based upon a different physical file. The logical file then gives the appearance that the physical files have been merged together.

Another feature, join logical files, joins fields from different physical files into a single record, using a matching field common to the physical files upon which to base the join. The logical file then appears as if the data exists in one file, with one format, when in reality, it has been brought together from several different physical files. You can, however, accomplish many of these same results with an SQL statement, or within an RPG program, without using complex logical files. Most programmers prefer to stick with simple logical files and avoid these more complex constructs. In addition to the keywords in this chapter, the DDS can use several dozen other keywords used with data file definitions. For additional details about these capabilities, see IBM's online Knowledge Center.

3.10.3. *Creating Database Files with DDS*

The first step in creating a physical or logical file is to enter the DDS statements into a source member by using an editor. As previously mentioned, it is standard practice to use source file QDDSSRC to store database source members. Also recall that the source type is PF for physical file and LF for logical file.

After you've entered your DDS code, you must compile it to create the file as an object on the system. If you are working from a development platform, such as RDi, follow the same procedure to compile a database object that you use to create a program module object. To compile by directly entering a command at a command line, rather than by working through menus or other tools, use commands **CRTPF (Create Physical File)** and **CRTLF (Create Logical File)**.

If the system encounters syntax errors while trying to create your file, it sends a message indicating that the creation was unsuccessful. Otherwise, the system informs you that the job completed normally and that the database object now exists.

Once the file object exists, you can use it to store data. You can enter data into physical files by using system utilities, by writing values to the file through a program, by copying records to the file from another file, or by using SQL statements.

You must create a physical file before you can create logical files based on that physical file, as failure to do so results in error messages. Also, you must delete all the logical files associated with a physical file before you can delete the physical file.

Be aware of one additional caveat: if you want to change a physical file's definition after you have stored data in the file, *deleting the file deletes the data in the file as well*. You can avoid such data loss by using the **CHGPF (Change Physical File)** command. This command also can accomplish changes to a physical file without deleting the data or dependent logical files.

When you compile an RPG program that uses an externally described file, the file must exist before your program can be compiled successfully. If you change the definition of a physical or logical file after you have compiled a program that uses that file, you must recompile the program before the system will let the program run. This feature, called **level checking**, prevents you from running a program based on an obsolete or inaccurate definition of a database file.

3.11. Externally Described Printer Files

In addition to allowing the external definition of database files, ILE RPG lets you define reports externally. Externally describing printer files offers many of the same benefits as externally describing database files. In particular, this method lets you change a report format without changing the source code of the program that produces the report—a wise approach to application maintenance. Also, if you externally define printer files, you can use a system utility, such as RDi's **Report Designer**, to help you design the report's layout visually on your workstation. The utility then generates the DDS required to describe the report so you don't have to do the grunt work of figuring out line position and spacing entries. (Appendix B covers Report Designer in more detail.)

You use DDS to define printer files in a source file, the same as you do for database files. The source members of printer files, like those of database files, are generally stored in QDDSSRC. A printer file's type, however, is **PRTF**.

After you have generated the source code by using an editor or another utility, you compile the source to create a printer file object. The compiler command for printer files is **CRTPRTF (Create Printer File)**. Once the object exists, it can receive output from a program for printing. The DDS code for a printer file is analogous to that of a database file, except that its focus is the definition of record formats of information to be sent to a printer. A record format in a printer file represents one or more printed lines on the report. Printer files can contain multiple record formats, each defining a different set of output lines. The DDS can also include keyword entries at the file level, the record level, and the field level to define the output's position or appearance or both.

To illustrate how to externally define a printer file, let's reconsider the customer listing report from Chapter 2. Recall that the desired report includes headings and detail lines. The Report Designer layout for the report is reproduced in Figure 3.10. The ILE RPG program in Chapter 2 wrote data to three report lines (grouped as Header, Detail, and Total) to generate this output. These lines are defined in the externally described report by using DDS.

The code in Figure 3.11 shows the DDS for the customer list. If you use RDi Report Designer to create the report, you can easily use tabs to switch between the Design View in Figure 3.10 and the Source View in Figure 3.11. By comparing the design in Figure 3.10 with the DDS code in Figure 3.11, you can understand how the DDS code renders the report.

First, you must define one record format for each line or group of lines to print in a single output operation. Then, for each of those record formats, you need to specify the fields and literals you want to print as part of that format, the vertical line spacing each format should follow, where the variable or constant data should appear horizontally on a line, and the editing (if any) to associate with the numeric fields.

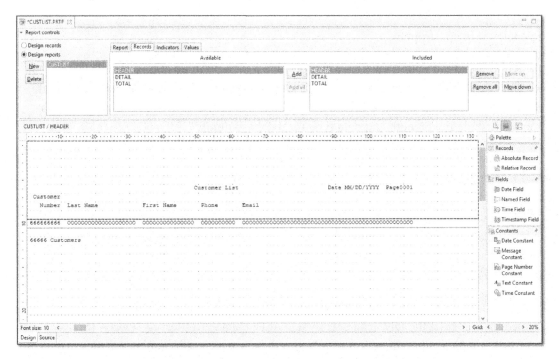

Figure 3.10: Layout for customer listing report

```
*CUSTLIST.PRTF
   Line 26        Column 1     Insert    3 changes
        .....+A*..1....+....2....+....3....+....4....+....5....+....6....+....7....+....8....+..
000001     A           R HEADER                        SPACEA(2)
000002     A                                      6 50'Customer List'
000003     A                                      6 89'Date'
000004     A                                      6 94DATE(*YY) EDTCDE(Y)
000006     A                                      6106'Page'
000007     A                                      6110PAGNBR EDTCDE(Z)
000008     A                                      7  3'Customer'
000009     A                                      8  5'Number'
000011     A                                      8 13'Last Name'
000012     A                                      8 35'First Name'
000013     A                                      8 52'Phone'
000014     A                                      8 64'Email'
000015     A           R DETAIL                        SPACEA(1)
000016     A             CUSTNO         9          2
000018     A             CLNAME        20         13
000020     A             CFNAME        15         35
000022     A             CPHONE        10         52
000025     A             CEMAIL        50         64
000027     A           R TOTAL                         SPACEB(1)
000028     A             COUNT          5    0     2EDTCDE(Z)
000030     A                                      8'Customers'
000032
```

Figure 3.11: DDS for printer file

Each record format begins with an R in position 17, followed by the format's name in positions 19–28 (Name++++++). Next, for each record format, you need to define all the information that is to print as part of that format. Specify fields in positions 19–28, just as for database files. Constants and literals are coded in positions 45–80 (Functions) and must be enclosed in apostrophes.

To define each field within the DDS, you provide its length in positions 30–34 (Len++), and for numeric fields, you indicate the number of decimal positions in positions 36–37 (Dp). Blanks in the decimal position columns signal a character field. This is similar to the way you defined the field length and data type for database fields.

You also need to specify where each piece of information is to appear on the report. When the data is to print on an exact vertical line number, positions 39–41 (Lin) indicate the line. The entry in positions 42–44 (Pos) specifies the field's or constant's horizontal position (where it starts within the line). Thus, in the example, Customer List prints on vertical line 6, beginning in horizontal position 50. The report skips to that line when the program writes the record format. When the report is already past the specific lines to be printed, it skips to that line on the next page. The Header format in the example DDS uses absolute lines (6, 7, and 8).

Sometimes, though, the vertical position of a line is relative to the previous line already printed. In that case, the DDS can specify a SPACEB (Space Before) or SPACEA (Space After) keyword to indicate that the report should simply space a certain number of lines from the current vertical position. The Detail and Total formats in the example use relative spacing, rather than absolute skipping, to determine the vertical position. Each time the report prints the Detail format, it spaces a single line—SPACEA(1)—afterward, similar to a carriage return. Before the report prints the Total format, it spaces one more line—SPACEB(1)—so that an extra blank line exists before the total prints.

You can code the SPACEB and SPACEA keywords (as well as the SKIPB and SKIPA keywords, which indicate absolute skipping) at either the **record-format level**, if they apply to the entire format, or at the **field level**, if they apply to a single field. The example specifies them at the record level for each format, before any fields are specified in the DDS. Depending upon the report's requirements, you can stipulate them at the field level instead (for example, on the same line as CEMAIL). The Header format uses a SPACEA keyword, in addition to specific line numbers. After the last literal (Email) prints on the heading, the report spaces down two lines in preparation for printing the next Detail format.

DDS prints the system date and the report page numbers by using DDS-reserved keywords DATE and PAGNBR. When you specify DATE(*YY), the report uses four digits to represent the year; however, when you indicate DATE(*Y) or simply DATE, the report prints only two digits. These fields, as well as the Count field, also use the EDTCDE (Edit Code) keyword to make the values more readable.

Other optional features of externally described printer files (e.g., changing fonts, printing bar codes, using indicators, defining fields by reference) are beyond the scope of this text. But with this introduction, you should be able to use DDS to externally describe most common types of printed output.

3.12. Output Editing

Output editing refers to formatting output values by suppressing leading zeros and adding special characters—such as decimal radix characters, thousands separators, and currency symbols—to make the values easier for people looking at the output to comprehend. RPG and DDS allow you to edit numeric fields (but not character fields). Editing is used in part because of the way numbers are stored in the computer. For example, if Amount, a six-byte field with two decimal positions, is assigned the value 31.24, the computer stores that value as 003124. Although the computer keeps track of the decimal position, a radix character is not actually stored as part of the numeric value. If you print Amount without editing, the number prints as 003124—the nonsignificant zeros appears, and there is no indication of where the decimal should be.

3.12.1. Edit Codes

To make it easier to specify the most commonly desired kinds of editing, DDS includes several built-in **edit codes** you can use to indicate how you want to print a field's value. You associate an edit code with a field by entering the code in parentheses immediately following the EDTCDE keyword at the field level for each field you want to edit. All commonly used edit codes automatically result in **zero suppression** (i.e., printing blanks in place of nonsignificant leading zeros) because that is a standard desired format.

Some editing decisions vary with the application. Do you want numbers to print with thousands separators (e.g., commas) inserted? How do you want to handle negative values—ignore them and omit any sign, print CR immediately after a negative value, print a minus sign (-) after the value, or print a floating negative sign to the left of the value? And when a field has a value of zero, do you want to print zeros or leave that spot on the report blank? A set of 16 edit codes (1 through 4, A through D, and J through Q) cover all combinations of these three options. The table in Figure 3.12 details the effects of the 16 edit codes. Thus, if you want commas, zero balances to print, and a floating negative sign, you use edit code N. If you do not want commas or a sign but do want zero balances to print, use edit code 3.

Edit Code	Positive	Negative	Zero		Edit Code	Positive	Negative	Zero
1	9,999,999.99	9,999,999.99	.00		J	9,999,999.99	9,999,999.99-	.00
2	9,999,999.99	9,999,999.99			K	9,999,999.99	9,999,999.99-	
3	9999999.99	9999999.99	.00		L	9999999.99	9999999.99-	.00
4	9999999.99	9999999.99			M	9999999.99	9999999.99-	
A	9,999,999.99	9,999,999.99CR	.00		N	9,999,999.99	-9,999,999.99	.00
B	9,999,999.99	9,999,999.99CR			O	9,999,999.99	-9,999,999.99	
C	9999999.99	9999999.99CR	.00		P	9999999.99	-9999999.99	.00
D	9999999.99	9999999.99CR			Q	9999999.99	-9999999.99	

Figure 3.12: Edit codes

DDS provides four additional useful edit codes: W, X, Y, and Z. Edit codes W and Y result in slashes being printed as part of a number representing a date. Using edit code Y renders the value 12252015 as 12/25/2015, and the value 122515 prints as 12/25/15. Edit code W prints 20151225 as 2015/12/25, and 151225 displays as 15/12/25. Although edit codes W and Y are normally used to edit dates, you can also use them with any field for which slash insertion is appropriate.

Edit code Z simply zero-suppresses leading nonsignificant zeros. Z does *not* enable the printing of a decimal point or a negative sign. So if a field contains a value of -234.56, the Z edit code causes the field to print as 23456. The use of Z is usually limited to whole number fields.

With one exception, all the edit codes suppress leading zeros. Edit code X, however, retains them. For this reason, the X edit code is useful when you want to convert a numeric value to a character string and retain the leading zeros.

You can include a floating currency symbol immediately to the left of a numeric value if you are using an edit code (except for W–Z). For example, specifying EDTCDE('$') prints a number as $12,345.67. Or, you can specify asterisk fill to print an asterisk in place of each suppressed zero; for example, EDTCDE(*) might print ***12,345.67.

3.12.2. Edit Words

Given the variety of edit codes built into DDS, you might expect find a code to fit your every need. Unfortunately, that is not the case. Telephone numbers and tax identification numbers represent good examples of values that we are used to seeing in a format that an edit code cannot supply. DDS includes an alternative to edit codes, called **edit words**, which can help in this kind of situation.

You code an edit word (EDTWRD) in the Functions area of the DDS at the field level for the field you want to edit. Edit words and edit codes are never used together for the same field because they perform the same function. An edit word supplies a template, or mask, into which you insert a number, and you enclose the template with apostrophes. Within the template, a blank position indicates where a digit should appear, and a 0 indicates where zero suppression should occur. With no zero in the edit word, the default is to zero suppress to the first significant digit.

You can use any characters as insertion characters within the template. The insertion characters print in the specified place, provided they are to the right of a significant digit. A currency symbol at the left of the edit word signals a fixed currency symbol, and a currency symbol adjacent to a zero denotes a floating currency symbol. To indicate a blank as an insertion character, use an ampersand (&).

Examine the following table to see how edit words work. You can duplicate the effects of edit codes with an edit word. Generally, RPG programmers use edit words only when no edit code is available that provides the format they want for their output.

EDTWRD(' - - ')	999-99-9999
EDTWRD(' & & ')	999 99 9999
EDTWRD('0( ) - ')	(999)999-9999
EDTWRD(' , **DOLLARS* *CENTS')	*9,999*DOLLARS*99*CENTS

3.13. Using a Field Reference File

To create a record format for a database file or a printer file, DDS needs to know the data attributes of each field in the format; that is, it needs the field length, data type, number of decimal positions, and so on. In the previous examples (Figures 3.6 and 3.11), you provided the length in positions 30–34, and for numeric fields, you specified the number of decimal positions in positions 36–37. The REF (Reference) feature of DDS gives it the capability to copy field definitions from one file to another, thus eliminating the need to duplicate field definitions in every externally described file that has the same fields as another one. In essence, fields in one externally described file can *inherit* the data attributes of the fields in another externally described file, called the **field reference file**. The DDS code in Figure 3.13 modifies the similar code from Figure 3.11.

```
*CUSTLIST.PRTF

 Line 25      Column 1     Insert    20 changes
    .....+A*..1....+....2....+....3....+....4....+....5....+....6....+....7....+....8....+..
000001   A                                       REF(CUSTOMERS)
000002   A              R HEADER                  SPACEA(2)
000003   A                                     6 50'Customer List'
000004   A                                     6 89'Date'
000005   A                                     6 94DATE(*YY) EDTCDE(Y)
000006   A                                     6106'Page'
000007   A                                     6110PAGNBR EDTCDE(Z)
000008   A                                     7  3'Customer'
000009   A                                     8  5'Number'
000011   A                                     8 13'Last Name'
000012   A                                     8 35'First Name'
000013   A                                     8 52'Phone'
000014   A                                     8 64'Email'
000015   A              R DETAIL                  SPACEA(1)
000016   A                CUSTNO    R          2
000018   A                CLNAME    R          13
000020   A                CFNAME    R          35
000022   A                CPHONE    R          52
000025   A                CEMAIL    R          64
000027   A              R TOTAL                   SPACEB(1)
000028   A                COUNT        5  0     2EDTCDE(Z)
000030   A                                     8'Customers'
000032
```

Figure 3.13: DDS code with reference file

In the first code line, notice the **REF** keyword at the file level preceding the record formats. This keyword names a *parent* file that the DDS is to use whenever a field definition *inherits* a field. In this case, the Customers file is the field reference file. Then, in the Detail format, notice that no data attributes are listed for the Custno, Clname, Cfname, Cphone, and Cemail fields. Instead, the R in column 29 instructs DDS to obtain the properties for these fields from the already existing Customers file. This DDS principle is similar to the RPG concept of externally described files. When you compile the printer file, the compiler automatically copies the definitions into the printer file. (The Count field, which does not exist in the Customers file, must still have complete data attributes explicitly coded.)

You can use this ability to create a physical file that serves as a centralized **data dictionary** of fields used within an application system. You might never actually use this kind of file for data storage. Its sole purpose is to provide field definitions for use in subsequent physical file creation. After you have created a field reference file, you can define the fields that comprise your physical files simply by referring to the definitions contained in the field reference file.

Field reference files can enforce a uniformity and consistency throughout an application system that facilitates program development and maintenance. Using such files, however, requires a thoughtful, structured approach to application system development. Thus, you should determine your data needs before file creation or application development.

3.14. Navigating Legacy Code

3.14.1. Program-Described files

Many ILE RPG programs have a history that dates back to earlier RPG syntax rules and features. Externally described files discussed in this chapter were first introduced to the language with the RPG III syntax, which preceded today's RPG. Before then, programs were written using program-described files. As the name suggests, **program-described files** are described entirely inside the RPG program; that is, the record layout must be detailed in the program source itself. Declaring a file as a program-described file prevents the compiler from retrieving the record layout or other file attributes from an external file description. Instead, the program uses two fixed-format specification types to provide the record layout: Input specifications and Output specifications.

Most programmers prefer to use externally described files, but if you must maintain a program written before that feature was available, you need to understand how the program works. Even today, it's possible that a program-described file is appropriate; for example, if you are processing a *flat file* (i.e., one that is not parsed into individual fields), you will probably declare it as a program-described file. Let's look at a version of the example program that uses program-described files. In addition to including Input and Output specifications, this program also makes some necessary changes to the File specifications and Calculation specifications. You can compare this variation with the one in Chapter 2, which uses externally described files.

```
*.. 1 ...+... 2 ...+... 3 ...+... 4 ...+... 5 ...+... 6 ...+... 7 ...+ ... 8
 * -----------------------------------------------------------------------
 * This program produces a customer listing report. The report data
 * comes directly from input file Customers.
 *     Date Written:  10/31/2013, Bryan Meyers
 * -----------------------------------------------------------------------


 * ---------------------------------------------------------- Control options
H Option(*Nodebugio)


 * --------------------------------------------------------- File declarations
FCustomers IF   F  145        Disk
FQprint    O    F  132        Printer Oflind(*Inof)


 * ---------------------------------------- Standalone variable declarations
D Count          S              5U 0


 * -------------------------------------------------------------- Input layouts
ICustomers NS
I                              1    9  Custno
I                             10   24  Cfname
I                             25   44  Clname
I                             80   89  Cphone
I                             90  139  Cemail


 * ------------------------------------------------------------- Main procedure
C                   Eval      *Inof = *On
C                   Read      Customers

C                   Dow       Not %Eof(Customers)

C                   If        *Inof
C                   Except    Header
```

Continued

```
C                    Eval      *Inof = *Off
C                    Endif

C                    Eval      Count += 1
C                    Except    Detail
C                    Read      Customers
C                    Enddo

C                    If        *Inof
C                    Except    Header
C                    Endif

C                    Except    Total
C                    Eval      *Inlr = *On
C                    Return

*  ------------------------------------------------------------ Output layouts
OQprint    E          Header        1  6
O                                           62 'Customer List'
O                                           92 'Date'
O                     *Date       Y   103
O                                           109 'Page'
O                     Page        Z   113

O          E          Header        1
O                                           10 'Customer'

O          E          Header        2
O                                           10 'Number'
O                                           13 'Last Name'
O                                           44 'First Name'
O                                           56 'Phone'
O                                           68 'Email'

O          E          Detail        1
O                     Custno            10
O                     Clname            32
```

Continued

```
O                          Cfname              49
O                          Cphone              61
O                          Cemail             113

O          E               Total       1
O                          Count       Z    6
O                                           16 'Customers'
```

3.14.2. File Specifications

To use program-described files in an RPG program, you must first make a few changes to the File specification:

```
*.. 1 ...+... 2 ...+... 3 ...+... 4 ...+... 5 ...+... 6 ...+... 7 ...+... 8
FFilename++IPEASFRlen+LKlen+AIDevice+.Keywords++++++++++++++++++++++++++++++++
FCustomers IF   F  145         Disk
FQprint    O    F  132         Printer Oflind(*Inof)
```

The first significant change is in position 22 (labeled F on the ruler line); this entry designates the file format. An F in position 22 stands for fixed format, which means that this is a program-described file and that each record has the same fixed length. This entry is the *trigger* that signals a program-described file. All files, regardless of type, require an entry for file format—either an F for program-described files or an E for externally described files.

You define the record length in positions 23–27 (Rlen+) for each program-described file. Data file records can be any length from 1 to 99,999 bytes, but it is important that you code the correct value for this specification. When you compute the lengths of all the fields in Customers, you get a length of 145 bytes, so you enter 145, right-adjusted in positions 23–27. Most printers support a line of 132 characters. As a result, records of printer files (which correspond to lines of report output) are usually 132 positions long. Accordingly, output file Qprint is assigned a record length of 132 on its File specification. Qprint is an IBM-supplied printer file, one of several that are typically used for program-described reports. Externally described files do not require—indeed, do not allow—a record length entry because the compiler retrieves the correct length.

The other change you may notice in the F-spec for Qprint is the use of an IBM-supplied indicator for overflow. You could have used a named indicator (e.g., Endofpage) as in the earlier program. But most programs that use program-described printer files tend to use any of eight indicators built into RPG: OA, OB, OC, OD, OE, OF, OG, and OV. You code these indicators as *INOA, *INOB, and so on. Because these indicators are already a part of RPG, you need not further define them. These indicators work only with program-described files. For externally described files, use a named indicator or one of the reserved numbered indicators *IN01–*IN99. In the sample, you name indicator OF as the overflow indicator for Qprint by coding Oflind(*Inof) in the Keywords area of the appropriate F-spec.

3.14.3. Definition Specifications

Definition specifications define those variables that do not otherwise appear in a database file (see Chapter 2 for details about definition specifications). In this version of the program, you must use a D-spec to define the Count variable, which you use in the report. The U in position 40 (labeled I in the ruler line) indicates that Count is an unsigned integer. Entries in positions 33–39 (To/Len+) and 41–42 (Dc) specify that Count is five digits with no decimal places. Chapter 4 describes other possible entries for these positions.

```
*.. 1 ...+... 2 ...+... 3 ...+... 4 ...+... 5 ...+... 6 ...+... 7 ...+... 8
DName++++++++++ETDsFrom+++To/Len+IDc.Keywords+++++++++++++++++++++++++++++++
D Count          S              5U 0
```

3.14.4. Input Specifications

Fixed-format **Input specifications** (I-specs) describe the record layout for a program-described file. The layout includes the name of each field the program is to use, its relative location in each record, and its data attributes. Every Input specification has an I on column 6. The I-spec has no free-format equivalent:

```
*.. 1 ...+... 2 ...+... 3 ...+... 4 ...+... 5 ...+... 6 ...+... 7 ...+... 8
IFilename++SqNORiPos1+NCCPos2+NCCPos3+NCC..............................
I......................Fmt+SPFrom+To+++DcField++++++++++L1M1FrP1MnZr......
ICustomers NS
I                              1   9  Custno
I                             10  24  Cfname
I                             25  44  Clname
I                             80  89  Cphone
I                             90 139  Cemail
```

Input specifications use two types of lines:

record identification entries, which describe the input records at a general level
field description entries, which identify the specific fields within the records

Together, these two types of lines describe the structure of the record layout for each program-described input file in the program. Each record identification line must precede the field entries for that record.

3.14.4.1. Record Identification Entries

Every record layout begins with a record identification entry containing the name of the input file in positions 7–16 (labeled Filename++ on the specification line). This name must match the entry on the File specification—in this case, Customers. The filename is a left-adjusted entry. Next, in positions 17–18 (labeled Sq), enter a Sequence code. This entry signals whether the system should check the order of records in the file as the records are read during program execution. Sequence checking is relevant only when a file contains multiple record formats (i.e., records with different field layouts). When sequence checking is inappropriate (which is usually the case), code any two alphabetic characters in positions 17–18 to indicate that sequence checking is not required. Many programmers use NS to signal *no sequence*. Because the Customers file contains a single record format, enter NS in positions 17–18.

Field description entries immediately follow the record identification entry. You define each field within the record by giving the field a valid name, specifying its length, and declaring its data type. Although you can define the fields of a record in any order, convention dictates that fields be described in order from the record's beginning to its end.

3.14.4.2. Field Location (Positions 37–46)

You define a field's length by specifying the beginning byte position and ending byte position of the field within the input record. The beginning position is coded as the *from* location (positions 37–41, labeled From+). The ending position is the *to* location (positions 42–46, labeled To+++). If the field is one-byte, the *from* and *to* entries are identical because the field begins and ends in the same location of the record.

Program-described character fields can be up to 32,766 bytes. Numeric fields can be up to 63 digits. Remember that for packed numeric fields, the number of bytes the field occupies is not the same as the number of digits; the I-specs indicate the number of bytes. The beginning and ending positions are right-adjusted within the positions allocated for these entries. You do not need to enter leading, nonsignificant zeros.

3.14.4.3. Decimal Positions (Position 47–48)

Numeric fields require a decimal position entry in positions 47–48 (labeled Dc), indicating the number of decimal positions to the right of the decimal point. A field must be numeric to use in arithmetic calculations or to edit for output, so it is important not to overlook the decimal position entry. When a numeric field represents whole numbers, the appropriate entry for its decimal positions is 0 (zero). Numeric fields can contain up to 63 positions to the right of the decimal point. Remember that the total length of the numeric field includes any decimal places (but not the decimal point itself or comma separators). To define a field as a character field, simply leave the decimal position entry blank.

3.14.4.4. Field Name (Positions 49–62)

The last required entry for a field description specification is a name for the field being described. This name, which you enter left-adjusted in positions 49–62 (labeled Field++++++++++), must adhere to the rules for valid field names in RPG. Within a record, a valid field name

- uses alphabetic letters, digits, or the special characters _, #, @, and $
- does not begin with a digit or an underscore
- does not include embedded blanks

In addition, a field name generally is 14 characters or fewer. This is a practical limit, imposed by the fixed-format nature of the Input specification.

The alphabetic characters can be upper case, lower case, or both. ILE RPG does not distinguish between letters on the basis of their case, but using a combination of uppercase and lowercase characters (e.g., capitalizing each word in the source code) makes your field names easier for others to understand.

Although not an ILE RPG requirement, it is good programming practice to choose field names that reflect the data they represent by making full use of the 14-character name limit. For example, Loannumber is far superior to X for the name of a field that stores loan numbers. Choosing descriptive field names can prevent your accidental use of the wrong field as you write your program and can help clarify your program's processing to others who may have to modify the program.

3.14.4.5. Data Type (Position 36)

For most alphanumeric (character) or numeric fields, you can leave position 36 (labeled P) blank. But for fields that represent other types of data, you must make an entry in position 36 to tell the compiler the external data type of the field. Chapter 4 provides a complete examination of RPG data types. The sample program uses only character or numeric fields, so it does not require any entries here.

One more thing before we leave Input specifications: you may have noticed that the record layout described in the I-specs does not include all the fields from the Customers file. When the program does not use a field, that field need not appear in the Input specifications, but the remaining entries must reflect their correct position in the record layout. When a program does not use all the fields coded in the Input specifications, the compiler issues a warning, but this is not necessarily an error condition that prevents a successful compile. The following Input specifications, which include *all* the fields from the layout, also work:

```
*.. 1 ...+... 2 ...+... 3 ...+... 4 ...+... 5 ...+... 6 ...+... 7 ...+... 8
IFilename++SqNORiPos1+NCCPos2+NCCPos3+NCC.................................
I......................Fmt+SPFrom+To+++DcField+++++++++L1M1FrPlMnZr......
ICustomers NS
I                             1    9   Custno
I                            10   24   Cfname
I                            25   44   Clname
I                            45   74   Caddr
I                            75   79   Czip
I                            80   89   Cphone
I                            90  139   Cemail
I                    P      140  144   0Cdob
I                           145  145   Cgender
```

3.14.5. Defining Output Layouts

Although Calculation specifications follow immediately after Input specifications in RPG programs, we discuss **Output specifications** next because their required entries parallel those needed on Input specifications in many ways. Every program-described output file named on the File specifications needs a set of Output specifications that provide details about the required output. All Output specification lines must have an O in position 6.

Output specifications, like Input specifications, include two kinds of lines: record identification lines, which deal with the output at the record level, and field description lines, which describe the content of a given output record. When the output is a report rather than a data file, *record* roughly translates to *report line*. Most reports include several different report-line formats, and each needs a separate definition on the Output specifications.

```
*.. 1 ...+... 2 ...+... 3 ...+... 4 ...+... 5 ...+... 6 ...+... 7 ...+... 8
OFilename++DF..N01N02N03Excnam++++B++A++Sb+Sa+............................
O.............N01N02N03Field+++++++++YB.End++PConstant/editword/DTformat++
OQprint    E           Header       1  6
O                                      62 'Customer List'
O                                      92 'Date'
                                                              Continued
```

```
O                          *Date        Y   103
O                                           109 'Page'
O                           Page         Z   113

O          E                Header       1
O                                            10 'Customer'

O          E                Header       2
O                                            10 'Number'
O                                            13 'Last Name'
O                                            44 'First Name'
O                                            56 'Phone'
O                                            68 'Email'

O          E                Detail       1
O                           Custno            10
O                           Clname            32
O                           Cfname            49
O                           Cphone            61
O                           Cemail           113

O          E                Total     1
O                           Count         Z    6
O                                            16 'Customers'
```

Output specifications require a record identification entry for each different line of the report. You must follow each of these lines, representing a record format, with detailed information about what that record format (or report line) contains. The report includes five record formats. Three of the lines are headings (called Header in the code), which should appear at the top of the report page, and the final two formats are detail lines of variable information (called Detail and Total).

3.14.5.1. Record Identification Entries

The first record identification entry requires a filename entry in positions 7–16 (labeled Filename++). This filename serves to associate the record being described with the output file described on the File specifications. Thus Qprint, your output file, appears as the filename entered on the first record identification line of the preceding Output specifications. Although the Output specifications include five record format descriptions, because each describes a format to be written to the same file (Qprint), you do not have to repeat the filename entry on subsequent record identification entry lines.

Each record format description must have an entry in position 17 (labeled D) to indicate the type of line being described. In this context, *type* refers to the way ILE RPG is to handle printing the line. Because you are using procedural techniques to generate the report instead of relying on RPG's fixed-logic cycle, all the record format lines are **Exception lines**. As a consequence, enter an E in position 17 of each record format line.

In ILE RPG, it is common practice to provide a name in positions 30–39 (labeled Excnam++++) for each exception line. Although not required, such names let you control printing without the use of indicators. By using **exception names**, you can easily refer to lines you want to print from within your Calculation specifications. Moreover, you can assign the same name to lines that need to be printed as a group simultaneously. Because the report has three lines that should be printed together at the top of the page, each line has the name Header. You identify the fourth line, which contains the variable information from the data file, as Detail and the fifth line as Total. Note that Headings, Detail, and Total are arbitrarily assigned names, not RPG-reserved terms.

You need one more set of entries to complete the record format line definitions. These entries describe the vertical alignment of a given line within a report page or relative to other report lines. Two kinds of entries control this vertical alignment: space entries and skip entries. Each variant offers *before* and *after* options.

It is important to understand the differences between space and skip entries. **Space entries** specify vertical printer positioning *relative to the current line*. Space is analogous to the carriage return on a typewriter or the Enter key on a computer. Each space is the equivalent of pressing the Return (or Enter) key. Space before (positions 40–42, labeled B++) is similar to pressing the Return key before you type a line, and space after (positions 43–45, labeled A++) is comparable to pressing Return after you type a line.

The same record format line can include both a space before and a space after entry. When both the space before and the space after entries are left blank within a record format description, the system defaults to space 1 after printing—the equivalent of single-spacing. If you have either a space before or a space after entry explicitly coded and the other entry is blank, the blank entry defaults to 0. The maximum value you can specify for any space entry is 255.

In contrast to space entries, **skip entries** instruct the printer to *skip to* the designated line on a page. Skip entries specify an *absolute vertical position on the page*. Skip 6 before printing causes the printer to advance to the sixth line on a page before printing; skip 20 after printing causes the printer to advance to the twentieth line on the page after printing a line. When the printer is already past that position on a given page, a skip entry causes the paper to advance to the designated position on the next page. Most often, you specify a skip before entry only for the first heading line of a report. Programmers most often use skip entries to advance to the top of each new report page. Skip entries are also useful when you are printing information on a preprinted form, such as a check or an invoice.

You code a skip before entry in positions 46–48 (labeled Sb+) and specify skip after entries in positions 49–51 (labeled Sa+). If you do not code any skip entries, the system assumes that you do not want any skipping to occur. The maximum value you can specify for any skip entry is 255.

The following record format lines show the spacing and skipping entries for the sample program:

```
*.. 1 ...+... 2 ...+... 3 ...+... 4 ...+... 5 ...+... 6 ...+... 7 ...+... 8
OFilename++DF..N01N02N03Excnam++++B++A++Sb+Sa+.............................

OQprint   E            Header        1  6

   ...

O         E            Header        1

   ...

O         E            Header        2

   ...

O         E            Detail        1

   ...

O         E            Total      1
```

Because you want the first heading of the report to print on the sixth line of a page, code a skip 6 before entry in positions 46–48 of the record format line describing that line. The space 1 after entry (positions 43–45) for that same heading line advances the printer head to the correct position for the second Header line (i.e., line 7).

The second Header line, with its space 1 after entry, positions the printer head for the third Header line, which in turn, with its space 2 after entry, positions the printer head for the first Detail line of data to print. Because the report detail lines are to be single spaced, exception line Detail contains a space 1 after entry. The Total line spaces an additional line before printing to create a blank line before the totals print.

Although the record format lines of the Output specifications deal primarily with the vertical positioning of each line, the subsequent field description entries describe the content of the lines. Each record format line of the Output specifications is followed by field description entries. Each field description specification does the following:

- identifies an item to display on the line
- indicates where the item is to appear horizontally on the line
- specifies all special output formatting for that item

The item to print is either a variable (field) or a constant (literal). You can enter field-level items to include within a record format in any order, although by convention programmers enter them in the order in which they are to appear in the output.

3.14.5.2. Field Name (Positions 30–43)

You code the name of each field whose value is to display as part of the output record in positions 30–43 (labeled Field+++++++++). Any field appearing as part of the Output specifications must have been defined earlier in the program, either as part of a file layout in the Input specifications or as a defined data item in the Definition specifications.

In the sample program, most of the fields to be printed are part of the Detail record format. These are the same fields—Clname, Cfname, Cphone, and Cemail—that you defined as part of your input record (though not necessarily in the same order as they appear in the record layout). When you include these field names in the output, each time your program processes a successive record from the input file, each Detail line printed contains the data values present in those fields of the input record.

In addition to the input fields, two RPG reserved words, which function as built-in, predefined fields, appear as part of the report headings. In the first Header line, notice the field name Page. RPG supplies this field to automatically provide the correct page numbers for a report. Page, a four-digit numeric field, has an initial value of 1. This value is automatically incremented by 1 each time the report begins a new page.

The *Date field, also displaying as part of the first Header line, is another RPG reserved word. *Date, an eight-digit numeric field, stores the current date, typically in mmddyyyy format. Any time your program needs to access the date on which the program is running, you can simply use *Date as a field. RPG also stores a six-digit version of the date in reserved word Udate.

Finally, the Total line includes a field called Count. You defined this variable in the Definition specifications earlier.

3.14.5.3. Constants (Positions 53–80)

In addition to fields, whose values change through the course of a program's execution, Output specifications typically contain **constants**, or **literals**, characters that do not change and instead represent the actual values that are to appear on the report. You enter each constant, enclosed within apostrophes ('), in positions 53–80 (labeled Constant/editword/

DTformat++) of the Output specifications. The left apostrophe should appear in position 53; that is, you enter constants left-adjusted within positions 53–80. A constant cannot appear on the same Output specification line as a field—each needs its own line.

In the sample program, the first heading is to contain the word *Date* as well as the actual date value. Accordingly, you code 'Date' as a constant within the first Header line and code the word *Page* similarly. Also, part of this first heading is the title *Customer List*. Although two words make up this constant, you enter the group of words as a single constant, enclosed in apostrophes. The spaces between the words form part of the constant.

The second and third report lines, or record formats, consist of column headings for the report. You handle these as constants as well and enter the appropriate values in positions 53–80. Notice in the sample program that the column heading lines are divided into conveniently sized logical units and that each unit is then coded as a separate constant. The Total line also includes a constant, 'Customers'.

3.14.5.4. End Position in Output Record (Positions 47–51)

You denote where a field or constant appears horizontally within a line by coding its *end position* (the position of its rightmost character) within the line. To specify an end position, enter a numeric value that represents the actual position desired for the rightmost character of the field or constant. You right-adjust such an entry within positions 47–51 (labeled End++).

For example, because you want the *e* in constant 'Page' to appear in column 109 of the first heading line of the sample report, you code a 109 in positions 50–51. The Output specifications include an end position for each field or constant that is part of your report.

Note
O-specs specify the *ending* position of an entry for a program described output file, whereas DDS signals the *beginning* position of an entry for an externally described output file.

3.14.5.5. Edit Codes (Position 44)

Three of the fields appearing in the output—Page, Count, and *Date—have an entry in position 44, Edit codes (labeled Y). As you'll recall, an edit code formats numeric values to make them more readable. Output specifications use the same edit codes discussed earlier in this chapter.

3.14.6. Processing Program-Described files

Most of the Calculation specification entries in the sample program should look familiar to you by now. There are two differences: 1) the use of *Inof instead of Endofpage for handling overflow and 2) the use of the Except operation code instead of Write.

Remember that a Write operation directs the program to output a record to an output file, or print a line on a report. You typically use the Write operation to process externally described files. The more common operation code when processing program-described files is called **Except (Exception Output)**. The Except operation, like Write, prints a report line or write a record to a file. But Except always writes one or more record formats defined in Output specifications. So, when the program encounters this operation

```
Except Header;
```

it prints the three Output specification lines named Header in the order they appear in the O-specs.

3.15. Chapter Summary

You can define IBM i database files at a record level or at a field level. If you define a file only to the record level, RPG programs that use that program-described file must define the record layout in the program by using fixed-format Input specifications and Output specifications. If, instead, you define the record layout outside the programs that are to use it (i.e., in the file itself), the compiler automatically retrieves the definitions from the externally described file into the program.

Externally described files offer several advantages over program-described files. Using externally described files shortens your program's code and eliminates redundant code across an entire application. If you use externally described files to define report formats, you can use utilities, such as Report Designer, to design the reports and generate the necessary code to create them.

Physical files contain data records, whereas logical files provide access paths, or pointers, to the physical file records. A logical file is always associated with one or more physical files. Both physical and logical files can contain a key that lets you retrieve records based on the key's value. The key can consist of one or several data fields. A physical file can contain only a single record format or type. Logical files can provide an alternative key sequence for accessing the data in a physical file. Logical file record formats may or may not include all the fields from their associated physical file. Within logical files, you can also specify records for selection or omission based on data values of the records in the physical file to which the logical file is related.

You can use industry-standard SQL or IBM-proprietary DDS to define externally described data files. SQL is the preferred tool for creating database objects, and DDS remains the sole means of creating device files, such as printer files. Often the differences between SQL and DDS are a matter of terminology. An SQL table is a physical file, and an SQL view is an unkeyed logical file.

Before you can compile an RPG program that uses externally described files, the files must exist as compiled objects. The SQL Create Table statement creates an externally described physical file, and the SQL Create View or Create Index statement creates a logical file. If you use DDS instead to create externally described files, you must first store specifications in a source member, then compile the source. The command for compiling physical file (PF) source is CRTPF (Create Physical File); for logical file (LF) source, use CRTLF (Create Logical File). To compile an externally described printer file (PRTF) source member, the command is CRTPRTF (Create Printer File). No SQL statement exists to create a printer file.

You must assign a data type to each column (field) in a table. The column's data type determines the kinds of operations that can be performed on the column. Three data classes IBM i recognizes are character (or alphanumeric), numeric, and date. Character fields occupy one byte for each character in the field.

The three most common numeric data formats are zoned decimal, packed decimal, and integer. Zoned decimal is easiest to view but consumes the most room on disk. Packed decimal eliminates redundant high-order bits in storing digit values. Integer data types are the most compact data type.

Native date fields are not the same as numeric fields that store date information. The date, time, and timestamp data types make it easy to deal with date validation and arithmetic.

The IBM i database requires that a record format (layout) have a name, and RPG requires that the record format name be distinct from the table name.

DDS and RPG support edit codes and edit words to format the presentation of numeric values on reports and displays.

An RPG program that uses a program-described file must define the record layout for the file. When the file is an input file, RPG uses fixed-format Input specifications to define the record format. When the file is an output file, such as a printer file, Output specifications describe the layouts. The Except operation writes a record to an output file, naming an Output specification to write.

The following table shows the syntax for the Except operation examined in this chapter. Optional entries appear within curly braces ({}):

Function or Operation	Description	Syntax
Except	Exception output	**Except {except-name};**

3.16. Key Terms

access path
arrival sequence
ASCII
bit
byte
character data
character string
CHGPF (Change Physical File)
column
composite key
constants
constraint
Create Index
Create Table
Create View
CRTLF (Create Logical File)
CRTPF (Create Physical File)
CRTPRTF (Create Printer File)
current schema
Data Definition Language (DDL)
Data Description Specifications (DDS)
data dictionary
Data Manipulation Language (DML)
Data Studio client
data type
*Date
date and time data
DEFAULT constraint
default value
device file

EBCDIC
edit codes
edit words
embedded SQL
Except operation
exception line
exception name
externally described file
field description entries
field-level keywords
field reference file
file-level keywords
fixed-length character string
fullselect
hexadecimal notation
high-order bits
index
Input specification
integer
Interactive SQL
key field
key sequence
level checking
LF
literals
logical file
low order bits
null value
numeric data
output editing
Output specifications
packed decimal
PF
PFILE
physical file

precision
PRIMARY KEY
program-described file
PRTF
qualified name
RCDFMT clause
record identification entries
record-level keywords
REF
Report Designer
row
RUNSQLSTM (Run SQL Statements)
scale
schema
Set Option
Set Schema
simple logical file
skip entry
space entry
SQL naming convention
STRSQL (Start SQL Interactive Session)
Structured Query Language (SQL)
system naming convention
table
timestamp
UNIQUE constraint
variable-length character string
view
zero suppression
zoned decimal

3.17. Discussion/Review Questions

1. Explain the advantages of externally describing database files. Do externally described printer files share the same advantages?
2. Explain the difference between a logical file and a physical file.
3. What is a composite key, and why is it used?
4. What are the advantages of logical files? Why not just create lots of physical files to store records in different orders or to present different combinations of data fields?
5. How does the system know whether you intend a keyword to be file level, record level, or field level?
6. Why might you use UNIQUE as a keyword in the DDS for a physical file? Would you use the UNIQUE constraint for the same reason in an SQL defined table?
7. What are the naming rules when you create tables with SQL?
8. List the commonly used constraints and their meanings.
9. Provide three practical examples of using logical files.
10. Explain the differences among keywords COMP, RANGE, and VALUES.
11. If Select and Omit specifications were not available in logical file definitions, how could you produce a report that included only the employees of the ACT and MIS departments and excluded other employees?
12. What is a join logical file? Why is it used?
13. Explain the difference between arrival sequence and key sequence of sequential record retrieval.
14. Assume you want to write a program that uses an externally described logical file that is based on a physical file. What order would you use to create the three objects required to execute the program? Why?
15. Some programmers argue that standards in file and field naming and the use of features such as field reference files reduce their opportunities to be creative and should not be enforced. How would you respond to these people?
16. Explain the difference between *SYS and *SQL naming conventions.
17. Explain the difference between SKIPA, SKIPB, SPACEA, and SPACEB.
18. Explain the difference between an SQL index and an SQL view.
19. What is the purpose of the PFILE keyword in a logical file?
20. What are the advantages of using field reference files? Are there any disadvantages?
21. Describe the difference between a skip entry and a space entry on the Output specifications.

3.18. Exercises

1. A library wants a database file to store book title; author's last name, first name, and middle initial; catalog number; publisher; date published; number of pages; and number of copies owned.

a. Code a physical file definition to store this data after determining what you believe to be the appropriate fields and the length and type for each field. Consider what the key field (if any) should be and whether use of keyword UNIQUE is appropriate.

b. Code the SQL Create statement to create an SQL table with the same fields.

2. The library wants to be able to access the catalog information described in exercise 1 based on author's last name, first name, and middle initial. Among other things, staff members want to be able to print listings by author so that all books by the same author appear together.

a. Define a logical file that enables this type of access.

b. Code the SQL Index statement that enables this type of access.

3. The library also wants to store a description of each book. Because the books' descriptions vary greatly in length, from a few words to a long paragraph, the person designing the library's database has suggested storing the descriptions in a separate physical file, in which each record contains the catalog number, a description line number, and 40 characters of description.

a. Define this physical file. Using DDS, how would you define the keys for this file?

b. Code the SQL Create statement to create an SQL table with the same fields.

4. Define a field reference file for the library based on the data requirements of exercises 1 and 3, and then rewrite the physical file definitions to exploit the field reference file.

5. The library has decided that it is also necessary to store the first date this book was purchased in the file described in exercise 1. What steps are required to add this field to the file? How will this affect the logical files that you have created? Is it possible for you to *lose* the data that you have collected?

Notes

CHAPTER 4

Using Declarations

4.1. Chapter Overview

Now that you can write simple read/write programs in ILE RPG, this chapter demonstrates how to define the files and data items—work variables, data structures, and constants—your program might need to perform its tasks. You also learn how to identify the database files and device files your program uses, and how it will use them. ILE RPG supports a rich set of data types, so this chapter explains which ones are appropriate for most business programming. It also examines how to set the initial value for a data item and how to distinguish among program variables, literals, and constants.

4.2. Introducing Declarations

ILE RPG requires that you **declare** (define) all the files, variables, and other data items used in your program. You must name all the files and instruct the compiler how the program is to use them. In addition, you must name all the other data items and specify their attributes. The declarations section must appear in your source code, following control options (if present), before any processing takes place. Declarations define these items to your program:

- Files
- Named constants
- Standalone variables
- Data structures
- Prototypes
- Procedure interfaces

Depending upon the type of data item you are declaring, RPG uses the following instructions:

- Dcl-f (Declare file)
- Dcl-c (Declare constant)
- Dcl-s (Declare standalone variable)
- Dcl-ds (Declare data structure)
- Dcl-pr (Declare prototype)
- Dcl-pi (Declare procedure interface)

This chapter explains how to define files, named constants, standalone variables, and data structures. Chapter 13 covers prototypes and procedure interfaces.

Declarations can appear in any order, although it is useful for maintenance purposes to group the declaration types together and to arrange them in alphabetic order. Because declarations concentrate data definitions into a single group of consecutive statements near the beginning of your program, they facilitate later program maintenance.

4.3. Declaring Files

Chapter 2 introduced the **Dcl-f (Declare file)** instruction, which describes each file the program uses and defines how to use that file. The general format of the Dcl-f instruction is as follows:

```
Dcl-f file-name {device} {optional-keywords};
```

When a program declares a file, all the record formats and fields in that file become available to the program. No further declarations are necessary for the program to use those items. In the following code, file Customers contains the data you want to process. The output of your program is a printer file.

```
Dcl-f Customers Disk    Usage(*Input);
Dcl-f Custlist  Printer Usage(*Output) Oflind(Endofpage);
```

4.3.1. Filename

The first entry following the Dcl-f instruction names the file. The filename is the only required entry for the Dcl-f instruction. An externally described file must exist at the time you compile the program. A program-described file need not exist at compile time because the compiler contains all the information it needs to compile the program. But when you eventually run the program, the file must be available.

4.3.2. Device

The entry following the filename indicates the device associated with a file. The three most frequently used device keywords are as follows:

- Disk—for database files
- Printer—for reports
- Workstn—for interactive displays (discussed in Chapter 12)

RPG assumes the file is an externally described file. You can, however, specify *EXT for an externally described file:

```
Dcl-f Customers Disk(*Ext)    Usage(*Input);
Dcl-f Custlist  Printer(*Ext) Usage(*Output) Oflind(Endofpage);
```

But if the file is a program-described file, you must indicate the record length with the device keyword:

```
Dcl-f Customers Disk(145)    Usage(*Input);
Dcl-f Qprint    Printer(132) Usage(*Output) Oflind(Endofpage);
```

The record length for a program-described file can be from 1 to 32,766 bytes.

The filename and device entries are **positional**; that is, they must be entered in the correct order on the Dcl-f line: filename, then device. You can enter the remaining file keywords in any order. If no device entry exists, the compiler assumes that the device is Disk and that the file is externally described. The following file declarations are equivalent:

```
Dcl-f Customers Usage(*Input);
Dcl-f Customers Disk Usage(*Input);
Dcl-f Customers Disk(*Ext) Usage(*Input);
```

4.3.3. File Usage

The Usage keyword specifies how the program is to use the file. For example, an input file contains data to be read by the program, whereas an output file is the destination for writing results from the program. A program can use a file many ways, so several values are necessary for the same Usage keyword. The following Usage entries are valid:

- Usage(*Input)—the program can read existing records from a file.
- Usage(*Output)—the program can write new records to a file.
- Usage(*Input:*Output)—the program can read records and add new ones.

- Usage(*Update)—the program can change (but not delete) existing records in a file.
- Usage(*Delete)—the program can delete existing records from a file.
- Usage(*Update:*Delete)—the program can change or delete existing records.
- Usage(*Update:*Delete:*Output)—the program can change, delete, or add new records.

Which entry you use will depend upon the program's purpose. Chapter 9 details how to access and update database files.

If you don't specify a Usage keyword, the usage depends upon the device. When the device is Disk, RPG assumes Usage(*Input), and when the device is Printer, RPG assumes Usage(*Output). For device Workstn, RPG defaults to Usage(*Input:*Output). The following lines are equivalent:

```
Dcl-f Customers Disk    Usage(*Input);
Dcl-f Custlist  Printer Usage(*Output) Oflind(Endofpage);
Dcl-f Display   Workstn Usage(*Input:*Output);
```

or (omitting Usage):

```
Dcl-f Customers Disk;
Dcl-f Custlist  Printer Oflind(Endofpage);
Dcl-f Display   Workstn;
```

or even (omitting Disk device):

```
Dcl-f Customers;
Dcl-f Custlist Printer Oflind(Endofpage);
Dcl-f Display  Workstn;
```

Tip

As a general rule, the Usage keyword is required only for Disk files that have capabilities beyond simple input. The other Usage defaults, for Printer and Workstn files, are appropriate assumptions.

4.3.4. File Keywords

In addition to Device and Usage, the Dcl-f instruction supports a number of other keywords to expand on the basic file declaration. Following are some frequently used file keywords:

- Oflind
- Keyed, Keyloc
- Rename, Prefix
- Extdesc, Extfile, Extmbr

Previous chapters have already covered the Oflind (Overflow indicator) keyword, which associates an indicator with a printer file's page overflow condition.

4.3.4.1. Keyed, Keyloc

The **Keyed** keyword specifies to process the file by key instead of using arrival sequence. To manage an externally described file by key, simply include the Keyed keyword with no additional values:

```
Dcl-f Customers Keyed;
```

For a program-described file processed by key, you must include some additional information, as the following example shows:

```
Dcl-f Customers Disk(145)
              Keyed(*Char:5) Keyloc(2);
```

This specification names the Customers file as a program-described file processed by key. The Keyed(*Char:5) entry indicates that the key is alphanumeric (the only type of key Dcl-f allows for a program-described file) and five bytes long. The Keyloc(2) entry informs the compiler that the key begins in position 2 of the record layout. If the Keyloc keyword is missing for a program-described file, RPG assumes the key begins at the first position in the format.

4.3.4.2. Rename, Prefix

Recall from Chapter 3 that SQL supports the RCDFMT clause to name a record format for a file. If, however, you create a file without using that clause, the SQL Create Table statement creates a record layout with the same name as the table name. RPG requires that the record format name be distinct from the filename. In this case, the Dcl-f instruction can rename the record format within the program:

```
Dcl-f Customers Rename(Customers:Custrec);
```

In this example, the Customers file also has a record format named Customers. However, the RPG program will rename the format Custrec.

The **Rename** keyword might also be useful when two files used by a program have the same record format. For example, if the two files Customers and Custnames both have record layouts called Custrec, you can rename one or both of the record formats to differentiate them:

```
Dcl-f Customers;
Dcl-f Custnames Rename(Custrec:Custrec2);
```

A related keyword, **Prefix**, facilitates renaming individual fields in an externally described file. For example, in the preceding Rename example, if both Customers and Custnames have identically named fields, you can prefix one or both of the files by adding the Prefix keyword:

```
Dcl-f Customers;
Dcl-f Custnames Rename(Custrec:Custrec2)
                Prefix(C2);
```

The RPG program then knows all the fields in the Custnames file as C2Custno, C2Clname, C2Cfname, and so on. Fields in the Customers file retain their original names.

If the files already use a prefix as part of a database naming convention, Prefix can replace the existing prefix (or a part of it):

```
Dcl-f Customers;
Dcl-f Custnames Rename(Custrec:Custrec2)
                Prefix(C2:2);
```

Let's assume here that both Customers and Custnames have fields named CuCustn, CuName, CuAddr, and so forth. In this program, the fields in Custnames are referred to as C2Custn, C2Name, C2Addr, replacing the first two characters of the original field names.

It's important to note that the Rename and Prefix keywords apply only to the RPG program within which they are coded. They do not affect the naming conventions used in the actual database. These keywords are simply a means of accommodating RPG requirements to differentiate record formats and field names.

4.3.4.3. Extdesc, Extfile, Extmbr

The Extdesc, Extfile, and Extmbr keywords serve to redirect the compiler or the program (or both) to a file other than the one named in the Dcl-f instruction, or to redirect the program to a specific member in a multiple-member file. This redirection is commonly called an

override. The **Extdesc** keyword, which is valid only for externally described files, names a file that the compiler is to use to retrieve the record layouts for the file named in the Dcl-f instruction. For example, you can instruct the compiler to retrieve the record layout from a specific library that might not be in the compiler job's library list:

```
Dcl-f Customers Extdesc('DEVLIB/CUSTOMERS');
```

The Extdesc override only occurs when you compile the program, not when you execute it. The **Extfile** keyword, though, overrides the filename at runtime, when the program executes it:

```
Dcl-f Customers Extfile('PRDLIB/CUSTOMERS');
```

To override the file at compile time *and* at runtime, use both Extdesc and Extfile keywords:

```
Dcl-f Customers Extdesc('DEVLIB/CUSTOMERS')
                Extfile('PRDLIB/CUSTOMERS');
```

Or, if the overrides are to the same file at both compile time and runtime, use the following:

```
Dcl-f Customers Extdesc('DEVLIB/CUSTOMERS')
                Extfile(*EXTDESC);
```

Recall that a file member is a set of data within a database file and that source members store RPG code in a source file. Other database files also have members, though most database files are single-member files. But occasionally, an RPG application may need to process one or more members of a multiple-member file. By default, RPG processes only the first member it encounters in a file. You can use the **Extmbr** keyword on a Dcl-f instruction to override the file to a specific member instead:

```
Dcl-f Customers Extfile('PRDLIB/CUSTOMERS')
                Extmbr('DOMESTIC');
```

4.4. Declaring Named Constants

The concept of the named constant is closely associated with the concept of a literal. A **literal** is a means of noting a fixed value (e.g., a number, a character string, or a date). For example, the number 789 is a literal, as is the character string 'September'. ILE RPG lets you associate a data name with a literal so that you can reference the literal by its name throughout your program. The resulting data item is a **named constant**.

Once you've defined a named constant, you can use it with any processing appropriate to its type. The value of a named constant is fixed. You cannot change it during the course of program execution.

Named constants let you define constants in one place near the beginning of your program rather than coding them as literals throughout your calculations. This practice is a standard of good programming because it facilitates maintenance programming. If a programmer needs to change a value, such as Taxrate, it is much easier and less error-prone to locate the named constant and change its value in that one place rather than having to search through an entire program looking for and examining the purpose of every calculation in which the literal value .0765 occurs.

Before we examine how to declare named constants, let's dig a little deeper into literals.

4.4.1. Numeric Literals

A **numeric literal** is a number, and its value remains fixed throughout the program (unlike a variable, whose value can change throughout the program). A literal can contain a radix character or a sign, or both. If the numeric literal includes a sign, the sign must be the leftmost character of the literal. If the numeric literal does not include a sign, the computer assumes that the literal represents a positive number.

Other than a radix character and a sign, a literal can contain only the digits 0 through 9. Never use blanks, currency symbols, percent signs, or thousands separators in numeric literals, and do not enclose them in apostrophes ('). The numeric value can be as long as 63 digits, with up to 63 decimal positions. Some examples of valid numeric literals follow:

```
-401230.12
0.0715
102
1
+3
-1
3.1416
.123456789
```

4.4.2. Character Literals

Often, you will want to work with character values as well with as numeric values. RPG lets you use character literals for that purpose. **Character literals** are character strings. Like numeric literals, character literals maintain a constant value during the execution of the program. To indicate that a value is a character literal (and not a variable name), simply enclose it within apostrophes. No restriction applies on what characters can make up the literal. Any character that you can represent via the keyboard—including a blank— is acceptable. If the literal is to include an apostrophe character, use two apostrophes to represent it. Character literals can be up to 16,380 bytes. Some examples of character literals follow:

```
'John Doe'
'Abc 246 #18w'
'321444'
'Jane Dough''s Pizza''45%'
```

Tip
You cannot use a character literal enclosed in apostrophes with an arithmetic operation even if all the characters of the literal are digits. Numeric literals are not enclosed within apostrophes.

4.4.3. Typed Literals

In addition to numeric and character literals, you can express other data values, such as dates and times, by using **typed literals**. To code a typed literal, enclose the value within apostrophes and precede it with a data type code to indicate which data type the literal represents. To refer to a value of January 1, 2018, for example, you'd code D'2018-01-01' as the literal. Other common data type codes for literals are T (for times), Z (for timestamps), and X (for hexadecimal literals). Here are more examples of typed literals:

Data Type	Typed Literal
Date	D'2008-03-15'
Time	T'08.56.20'
Timestamp	Z'2008-03-15-08.56.20.000000'
Hexadecimal	X'F0F0F0'

4.4.4. Defining Constants

A **named constant** assigns a name to a literal so that you can reference the literal by its name throughout your program. The named constant's value never changes during processing. The **Dcl-c (Declare Constant)** instruction defines the named constant:

```
Dcl-c name value;
```

The Dcl-c instruction requires only the name of the constant and its value. The constant is defined with no specific length or type; those attributes are implicit in the value. The data item name must begin with an alphabetic character or the special character $, #, or @. The remaining characters can be alphabetic characters, numbers, or any of the four special characters _, #, $, and @. A data item name cannot contain blanks embedded within the permissible characters.

You enter the literal value of the constant following the name. Enter numeric constant values with a radix character or sign if appropriate, but never with thousands separators. Enclose character constant values within apostrophes. Constants of other data types should follow the rules indicated earlier for typed literals. Here are some valid constants:

```
Dcl-c Taxrate     .0765;
Dcl-c Pi          3.142;
Dcl-c Country     'United States';
Dcl-c Longestword 'floccinaucinihilipilification';
Dcl-c Disclaimer  'This report is proprietary, +
                   and may contain confidential information, +
                   not to be disclosed.';
Dcl-c Phoneedit   '0(   )   -    ';
Dcl-c Millennium  D'2001-01-01';
```

You might occasionally see the value for a named constant coded within parentheses following the Const keyword. This notation is valid but optional, and most programmers prefer simply to code the value without the Const keyword. The following two constant declarations are equivalent:

```
Dcl-c Taxrate Const(.0765);
Dcl-c Taxrate .0765;
```

A character constant can be at most 16,380 bytes, and a numeric constant can contain up to 63 digits, with up to 63 decimal positions. To enter a named constant too long to fit on a single line, continue the value onto the next line, using a plus sign (+) to signal that the constant resumes with the first nonblank character on the next line.

Tip

Always use a named constant instead of a literal in your program, unless the use of the literal is obvious. Using named constants makes your programs much easier to read, understand, and maintain than if you use literals. For example, it's easier to immediately understand the use of the term Taxrate than the literal .0765. It's also easier to change the program later if the rate changes.

One exception to this rule might be the use of the literals '1' and '0', which have generally accepted meanings of *On and *Off, respectively.

4.4.5. Using Figurative Constants

ILE RPG includes a special set of reserved words called **figurative constants**, which are implied literals that can be used without a specified length. Figurative constants assume the length and decimal positions of the variables with which they are associated. Some of RPG's figurative constants are as follows:

- *Blank (or *Blanks)
- *Zero (or *Zeros)
- *Off
- *On
- *Hival
- *Loval
- *All
- *Null

RPG lets you assign *Blank or *Blanks to cause a character variable to be filled with blanks. Assigning *Zero or *Zeros to both numeric and character variables fills the variables with 0s.

Figurative constants *Off and *On represent '0' and '1' character values. *Off is the equivalent of '0', and *On equates to '1'. Although you can use *Off and *On with any character variable of any length, programmers most often use *Off and *On to either change or compare an indicator's value.

Assigning *Hival fills a variable with the highest possible collating value appropriate to its data type. Setting a character variable to *Hival sets all the bytes to hexadecimal FF (all bits on). For a numeric variable, *Hival is the maximum positive value allowed for the data representation, usually all 9s and a plus sign (+). Assigning *Loval fills a variable with the lowest possible collating value appropriate to its data type—for example, hexadecimal 00 (all bits off) for character variables and the minimum negative value for numeric variables. Programmers often assign *Hival or *Loval to a variable to ensure that the variable's value is the maximum or minimum possible.

Assigning figurative constant *All immediately followed by one or more characters within apostrophes repeats the string within the apostrophes cyclically through the entire length of the result variable. For example, assigning *All'Z' to a character variable fills the variable with Zs, and assigning *All'7' to a numeric variable fills the variable with 7s.

The constant *Null represents a null value. You generally use *Null to represent the absence of any value—which is not the same as using blanks or zeros. Usually, ILE RPG uses *Null only in unusual situations, which we examine later.

4.5. Defining Standalone Variables

Standalone variables (sometimes called *work fields*) are not part of a database record or any other kind of data structure. They *stand alone* in the program, without depending upon any other kind of data item. A typical use for a standalone variable might be as a counter to count the number of transactions being processed, as an intermediate variable to temporarily hold a value for later processing, as an accumulator to keep running track of year-to-date sales amounts, or as an indicator to represent whether a condition is true. Unlike a named constant, the value stored in a standalone variable might change often while the program is running. The **Dcl-s (Declare Standalone Variable)** instruction defines a variable:

```
Dcl-s name {data-type} {optional-keywords};
```

Here are a few examples of definitions for standalone variables:

```
Dcl-s Citystatezip        Char(40);
Dcl-s Taxexempt           Ind;
Dcl-s Totaldue            Packed(7:2);
Dcl-s Yeartodatetotalsales Packed(11:2);
Dcl-s Counter             Uns(10);
Dcl-s Basedate            Date;
```

4.5.1. Data Item Name

The name must conform to the rules governing data item names, the same rules used for named constants. The name should reflect the contents of the variable. Data item names can be up to 4,096 characters, but it's best to restrict them to a manageable length. If the variable is to be used in an externally described file, its name should be 10 or fewer characters.

4.5.2. Data Type

The attributes for a variable are described in a data type keyword, following the variable's name. You'll recall from Chapter 3 that the three basic classes of data used in most business programming are numeric, character, and date data. RPG supports several variations of these data classes, along with a few others that have special uses. The following are most frequently used data type keywords:

- Char, Varchar, Ind
- Zoned, Packed, Int, Uns
- Date, Time, Timestamp
- Pointer

Most of these data types were discussed in Chapter 3, but ILE RPG supports several others as well. This chapter expands on some of the additional data types that are not directly related to SQL or DDS. Chapter 18 covers the Pointer data type.

4.5.2.1. Char, Varchar, Ind

When a declaration defines a variable as Char, it is defining a **fixed-length character string**. You specify the length attribute in parentheses. All values in the column have the same length in storage. A value that doesn't fill the entire length is padded with blanks. The following definition defines Address, a fixed-length character variable 35 characters (bytes) long:

```
Dcl-s Address Char(35);
```

The length can be between 1 and 16,773,104 bytes. You can specify either a literal or a named constant (but not another variable) for the length. If you stipulate a named constant, you must define the constant in the program source before defining the variable:

```
Dcl-c Labelwidth 35;
Dcl-s Address Char(Labelwidth);
```

If the variable is defined with a Varchar data type, it is a variable-length character string. Recall from Chapter 3 that this data type is appropriate when the length is uncertain. You specify the maximum size (up to 16,773,100 bytes) in parentheses. As with a fixed-length character string, the length can be a literal or a named constant (which you define before the variable). The following declaration defines Email, a variable-length character column 1 that is 256 characters long:

```
Dcl-s Email Varchar(256);
```

Chapter 7 examines variable-length character strings in more detail.

Note
You may have noticed that the maximum sizes for RPG variables are larger than the limits for fields defined by SQL or DDS. Although the database might not support some very large fields, character data items defined in an ILE RPG program generally have higher limits, up to about 16 MB.

A third character data type, Ind, defines an **indicator**. A program uses an indicator, sometimes called a flag or a **Boolean data type**, to signal a true/false state. An indicator is a single-byte character field that can have only two possible values: *On ('1') or *Off ('0'). The program can set indicators on or off, and then subsequent processing can be conditioned by the state of the indicator. The following declaration defines an indicator that should be familiar to you by now, Endofpage:

```
Dcl-s Endofpage Ind;
```

Because all indicators are one byte, you do not specify a length for an indicator.

4.5.2.2. Zoned, Packed, Int, Uns

Recall from Chapter 3 that zoned (or signed) variables store numeric data, with each digit occupying a single byte, and that packed variables use only a half byte for each digit. RPG supports both numeric data types:

```
Dcl-s Daynumber Zoned(2:0);
Dcl-s Totaldue  Packed(7:2);
```

The parameter values inside the parentheses specify the precision (total digits) and scale (decimal digits), respectively. Maximum precision and scale are both 63 digits; the precision must be at least as large as the scale. Either or both of the values can be a literal or a named constant (which you define before the variable). If you do not specify a scale, it defaults to zero. The following declarations are equivalent:

```
Dcl-s Daynumber Zoned(2:0);
Dcl-s Daynumber Zoned(2);
```

Zoned numbers are equivalent to SQL's NUMERIC data type, and Packed numbers are the same as DECIMAL in SQL.

A numeric variable defined with Int is a signed integer. Recall from Chapter 3 that integers are the most compact means of storing numeric values. The following declaration defines a five-digit signed integer, Counter:

```
Dcl-s Counter Int(5);
```

The length in parentheses (which can be a literal or constant) must be 3, 5, 10, or 20 digits:

Digits	Bytes	Lowest Value	Highest Value
3	1	-128	127
5	2	-32,768	32,767
10	4	-2,147,483,648	2,147,483,647
20	8	-9,223,372,036,854,775,808	9,223,372,036,854,775,807

Integers have no decimal places and have limited ranges. If, however, the anticipated data values fit into the allowed range and scale for any of the integer sizes, they are an efficient and useful data type for numeric data. A five-digit integer is equivalent to SQL's SMALLINT, a 10-digit integer is equivalent to INT in SQL, and a 20-digit integer corresponds to BIGINT.

A variation on signed integers—Uns—defines an unsigned integer. Unsigned integers follow the same principles as do signed integers except that their values are always positive. The following declaration defines Counter, a five-digit unsigned integer:

```
Dcl-s Counter Uns(5);
```

Unsigned integers have a range of values different from signed integers:

Digits	Bytes	Lowest Value	Highest Value
3	1	0	255
5	2	0	65,535
10	4	0	4,294,967,295
20	8	0	18,446,744,073,709,551,615

4.5.2.3. Date, Time, Timestamp

The RPG date-related data types correspond to the SQL types. The following declarations define date and time variables called Today and Now:

```
Dcl-s Today Date;
Dcl-s Now Time;
```

By default, timestamps include microseconds (six digits to represent fractional seconds):

```
Dcl-s Lastupdate Timestamp;      // 2015-06-30-12.34.56.789012
```

If you need a different scale, the variable definition can include a length parameter 0–12 to represent the desired number of fractional seconds' digits:

```
Dcl-s Lastupdate Timestamp(0);   // 2015-06-30-12.34.56
```

4.6. Assigning Initial Values to Data

In addition to defining data items, such as standalone variables, you can assign an **initial value** to those data items. If the data item is a variable, its value can change during program execution, but its initial value is the one the variable contains when the program starts.

To initialize (i.e., assign an initial value to) a standalone variable, specify the value by using the **Inz (Initialize)** keyword in the variable's definition. You indicate the initial value by using a literal, a named constant, or a figurative constant. The following definitions all provide initial values to the variables:

```
Dcl-s Maxlimit Packed(7:2) Inz(10500.00);  // Same as next statement
Dcl-s Maxlimit Packed(7:2) Inz(10500);


Dcl-s Compname Char(40) Inz('Kay Elmnop Enterprises');


Dcl-s Highlimit Packed(7:2) Inz(99999.99); // Same as next statement
Dcl-s Highlimit Packed(7:2) Inz(*Hival);


Dcl-s Check Char(9) Inz(X'000000000000000000'); // Same as next
Dcl-s Check Char(9) Inz(*Allx'00');                 // Same as next
                                                    Continued
```

```
Dcl-s Check Char(9) Inz(*Loval);


Dcl-s Basedate Date Inz(D'1899-12-30');
```

You can use some special reserved values to initialize date-related definitions. To initialize a date field to the job date (the same as *Date in the previous examples), code Inz(*Job) in the keyword area of the field's definition. You can also initialize a date, time, or timestamp field to the current system date at runtime by coding Inz(*Sys). What's the difference between the job date and the system date? You can think of the job date as being an *as of* date that is assigned to a job when you run a program, although it may or may not be the actual date that the program is running. The system date, however, is always the current date:

```
Dcl-s Today Date Inz(*Sys);
```

One other useful initialization value, *User, can be used with character fields if they are at least 10 bytes. Coding Inz(*User) for a character field assigns the name of the current user profile to the character field:

```
Dcl-s Username Char(10) Inz(*User);
```

Know that it is not always necessary to assign an initial value to a data item. RPG automatically initializes data items to default values when the program starts unless you use the Inz keyword to initialize the variable. The default values are typically blanks for character variables and zeros for numeric variables. If the default values are sufficient, you need not initialize the data item, as the following examples show:

```
// The following definitions for Totaldue would result in identical
// initial values
Dcl-s Totaldue Packed(7:2) Inz(0);
Dcl-s Totaldue Packed(7:2) Inz(*Zeros);
Dcl-s Totaldue Packed(7:2) Inz;
Dcl-s Totaldue Packed(7:2);


// The following definitions for Title are equivalent
Dcl-s Title Char(25) Inz(' ');
Dcl-s Title Char(25) Inz(*Blanks);
Dcl-s Title Char(25) Inz;
Dcl-s Title Char(25);
```

Remember that the Inz keyword assigns only a variable's initial value. In subsequent chapters, we discuss how you can assign new values to a variable once a program is running.

4.7. Defining Data Structures

In addition to named constants and standalone variables, you can define **data structures**, which are simply a means of organizing multiple variables within a single section of contiguous portions of memory. Data structures can provide flexibility in your handling of data by letting you group variables into a logical structure, subdivide variables into **subfields**, and redefine variables with different data types or names. An RPG program can process the entire data structure as a unit or its subfields individually.

RPG uses three instructions to declare data structures:

- Dcl-ds (Declare data structure)
- Dcl-subf (Declare subfield)
- End-ds (End data structure)

These instructions take the following form:

```
Dcl-ds ds-name {optional-keywords};
   {Dcl-subf} name {data-type} {optional-keywords};
End-ds {ds-name};
```

The following code illustrates a simple data structure definition:

```
Dcl-ds Customer;
   Company   Zoned(2:0);
   Id        Zoned(5:0);
   Name      Char(35);
   Address   Char(35);
   City      Char(21);
   State     Char(2);
   Postcode  Char(10);
   Credlimit Zoned(11:2);
End-ds;
```

The **Dcl-ds (Declare data structure)** instruction signals the beginning of a data structure. Following Dcl-ds, you can enter a name for the data structure, or you can use *N if the data structure is to be unnamed. The name is optional unless you plan to refer to the data structure as a whole elsewhere in your program. RPG treats named data structures as character strings, encompassing all their subfields. Data structure names follow the same rules as variable names.

Although you can enter the length of the entire data structure with the Dcl-ds instruction by using the Len keyword, Len is generally optional. If you omit it, the system derives the length of the structure as a whole from the lengths of its subfields. The maximum total length for a data structure is 16,773,104 bytes. You can also use the following Dcl-s instruction in the preceding example:

```
Dcl-ds Customer Len(121);
```

4.7.1. Defining Data Structure Subfields

The lines to describe subfields constituting the data structure follow the line with the Dcl-ds instruction. You define each subfield entry by giving it a name. It's normal practice to indent the subfield definition to make the hierarchical layout of the data structure easily visible. The order of the subfields should represent their actual relative positions in the data structure. Following the subfield name, specify a data type keyword. Any data type allowed for standalone variables is also allowed for data structure subfields.

Note
Numeric subfields that appear in data structures are usually Zoned, not Packed. Because a data structure is fundamentally considered a character variable, zoned numbers are generally more flexible because each digit is also a character. Packed, Int, and Uns data types are valid for numeric subfields if the program has no need to process the data structure or its subfields as character data.

In the unlikely event that the subfield's name is the same as an RPG operation code (e.g., Dow, Read, Write, Return), you must code a Dcl-subf (Declare subfield) instruction preceding the subfield name. Otherwise, you need not use Dcl-subf for a subfield declaration.

The data structure definition must accurately represent the locations of its subfields. Normally, each subfield immediately follows the preceding subfield in the data structure. Occasionally, your program will encounter a data structure that does not use all the locations in the data structure and will skip those unneeded locations. Usually, this occurs only with data structures that are predefined by an application or by IBM. In that case, use the **Pos (Position)** keyword to specify the beginning location for a subfield:

```
Dcl-ds Indicators Len(99);
  Exit   Ind Pos(3);
  Cancel Ind Pos(12);
  Error  Ind Pos(50);
  Sflclr Ind Pos(90);
  Sfldsp Ind Pos(91);
  Sflend Ind Pos(92);
End-ds;
```

The position must be between 1 and the length of the data structure. This data structure is 99 bytes, but only positions, 3, 12, 50, 90, 91, and 92 are used—as named indicators in specific positions.

4.7.2. Initializing Data Structures

Once you have defined the data structure subfields, you can initialize them by using the Inz keyword. The Inz keyword initializes entire data structures or data structure subfields. If you code Inz (with no value following it) on the Dcl-ds instruction, the program initializes all the subfields in the data structure with initial values appropriate to the subfields' data types. If you do not code Inz on the Dcl-ds instruction, the entire data structure, including all its subfields, is initialized with blanks—unless you code individual Inz keywords for specific subfields.

Data structures are considered character variables regardless of the data types of their subfields. As a result, they contain blanks at the start of your program unless you explicitly initialize their subfields. You initialize a data structure globally when you include the Inz keyword in the data structure header line. This use of Inz automatically initializes all subfields in the entire data structure.

Specifying Inz on the Dcl-ds instruction initializes all subfields to the default value appropriate for their data types (e.g., all numeric subfields are set to zero, all character fields to spaces):

```
Dcl-ds Phone Inz;
  Areacode Zoned(3:0);
  Exchange Zoned(3:0);
  Localnbr Zoned(4:0);
  Name     Char(35);
End-ds;
```

Without the Inz keyword, all the subfields are initially blank. The program ends abnormally if you try to perform arithmetic operations on Areacode, Exchange, or Localnbr without first initializing them.

Alternatively, you can initialize specific subfields of a data structure by including the Inz keyword as part of their definitions. To initialize a subfield to a value other than the default, you can include the desired value within parentheses following Inz. Although you can express this value as a literal or a named constant, it must fit the subfield's data type. Moreover, it cannot be longer than the subfield nor have more decimal positions than the subfield (if the type is numeric).

```
Dcl-ds Phone;
   Areacode Zoned(3:0) Inz;
   Exchange Zoned(3:0) Inz(555);
   Localnbr Zoned(4:0) Inz;
   Name     Char(35);
End-ds;
```

In this example, Areacode and Localnbr are initially zero, Exchange is 555, and Name is blank. You can also combine data structure initialization with individual subfield initialization to obtain the same result:

```
Dcl-ds Phone Inz;
   Areacode Zoned(3:0);
   Exchange Zoned(3:0) Inz(555);
   Localnbr Zoned(4:0);
   Name     Char(35);
End-ds;
```

4.7.3. Overlapping Subfields

The locations of subfields within a data structure can overlap, and the same position within a data structure can fall within the location of several subfields. A data structure declaration can use two keywords, Pos (Position) and **Overlay**, for these purposes.

To illustrate the concept of overlapping, or defining subfields within subfields, the following example assumes your program contains variables Firstname (15 bytes) and Phone (10 digits). The program needs to work with just the initial of the first name and with the area code, exchange, and local portions of the phone number as separate data items. Data structures let you easily access the data that way.

```
Dcl-ds *N;
  Firstname Char(15);
    Initial Char(1) Overlay(Firstname);
End-ds;


Dcl-ds *N Inz;
  Phone      Zoned(10:0);
    Areacode Zoned(3:0) Overlay(Phone);
    Exchange Zoned(3:0) Overlay(Phone:4);
    Localnbr Zoned(4:0) Overlay(Phone:7);
End-ds;
```

The Overlay keyword indicates that Initial is to be a part of Firstname rather than a subfield adjacent to it. In the preceding code, subfield Initial contains the first letter of the value of Firstname. If you code a position with the Overlay keyword, the position signals the location in the subfield where the overlay should begin. Phone is divided into three pieces accessible through subfields Areacode, Exchange, and Localnbr. Because Areacode, Exchange, and Localnbr share common space with Phone in the unnamed data structure, if your program alters the value of any one subfield, the overlapping subfields reflect that change. You can also use the Pos keyword to indicate the starting position of each subfield relative to the data structure itself:

```
Dcl-ds *N Inz;
  Phone      Zoned(10:0);
    Areacode Zoned(3:0) Pos(1);
    Exchange Zoned(3:0) Pos(4);
    Localnbr Zoned(4:0) Pos(7);
End-ds;
```

The Overlay keyword also supports the special value *Next. Specifying *Next instead of a position begins a subfield at the next available position of the overlaid subfield field. The following code reworks the Phone example by using *Next:

```
Dcl-ds *N Inz;
  Phone      Zoned(10:0);
    Areacode Zoned(3:0) Overlay(Phone);
    Exchange Zoned(3:0) Overlay(Phone:*Next);
    Localnbr Zoned(4:0) Overlay(Phone:*Next);
End-ds;
```

When you use the Overlay keyword, the data name within the parentheses must be a subfield already defined within the current data structure. The subfield being defined must be completely contained within the subfield.

You can use Overlay to redefine subfields in a data structure with different names or data types, or both. In the following example, subfield Basedate is a native date, but Basechar is a character subfield. Both subfields occupy the same location in the data structure. If your program changes the value of one subfield, it also changes the value of the other one.

```
Dcl-ds *N Inz;
  Basedate Date;
  Basechar Char(10) Overlay(Basedate);
End-ds;
```

4.7.4. Externally Described Data Structures

The data structures discussed up to now are program-described data structures. The entire data structure description (i.e., all the subfields) is explicitly described in the program. RPG also supports externally described data structures similar to the way it handles externally described data files. The subfields in an externally described data structure follow the layout of an existing file—the subfields in the data structure have the same names, locations, and data attributes as the record format. Externally described data structures might be useful when you want to use a data structure in several different programs, when your company's standards dictate the use of specific data structures, or when you need a data structure to mimic the layout of an existing file's record format.

Recall from previous chapters the record layout for the example Customers file (see Figure 4.1). Here's an example of an externally described data structure based on that file's layout:

```
Dcl-ds Customers Ext End-ds;
```

Often, the name of an externally described data structure is the same as the file upon which the data structure is based. The **Ext (External)** keyword tells the compiler that this data structure is externally described. Ext must be the first keyword following the data structure name. Because the compiler automatically acquires the subfields from the Employees file, it is not necessary to code any subfields for the data structure—all the fields in the file become subfields in the data structure. Notice that, because you need not explicitly list any subfields, the End-ds instruction can appear on the same line as the Dcl-ds instruction.

Properties	Source Prompter	Field Table 🔀	Commands Log	Data Table

: File FLIGHTPROJ/CUSTOMERS (9 Fields)

Name	Record	Type	Length	Text
CUSTNO	CUSTSREC	Character	9	CUSTOMER NUMBER
CFNAME	CUSTSREC	Character	15	CUSTOMER FIRST NAME
CLNAME	CUSTSREC	Character	20	CUSTOMER LAST NAME
CADDR	CUSTSREC	Character	30	CUSTOMER STREET ADDRESS
CZIP	CUSTSREC	Character	5	ZIP CODE
CPHONE	CUSTSREC	Character	10	CUSTOMER PHONE
CEMAIL	CUSTSREC	Character	50	CUSTOMER EMAIL
CDOB	CUSTSREC	Packed Decimal	8.0	CUSTOMER DATE OF BIRTH
CGENDER	CUSTSREC	Character	1	F=FEMALE M=MALE

Figure 4.1: Customers file record layout

If the name of the data structure does not match the name of the file upon which it is based, the data structure definition requires the **Extname (External name)** keyword to explicitly name the file:

```
Dcl-ds Custds Ext Extname('CUSTOMERS') End-ds;
```

or (omitting Ext):

```
Dcl-ds Custds Extname('CUSTOMERS') End-ds;
```

You can code additional program-described subfields following the data structure header, and you can use Overlay to describe subfields that overlap existing subfields in the data structure:

```
Dcl-ds Custds Extname('CUSTOMERS');
  Lastdate Date;
  Rating   Char(1);
End-ds;
```

If you want the name of a subfield to be different from the name of the field in the external file, you can use the **Extfld (External Field)** keyword to associate the subfield name with the file's field name:

```
Dcl-ds Custds Extname('CUSTOMERS');
  Address Extfld('CADDR');
End-ds;
```

To initialize an externally described data structure, use the Inz keyword. To initialize the subfields to their default values as indicated in the external file's definition, specify Inz(*Extdft):

```
Dcl-ds Customers Ext Inz(*Extdft) End-ds;
```

You can override the external default for one or more subfields by listing them with their own Inz keyword:

```
Dcl-ds Custds Extname('CUSTOMERS') Inz(*Fxtdft);
  Custno    Extfld  Inz('999999999');
  Lastdate  Date    Inz(*Sys);
  Rating    Char(1) Inz('5');
End-ds;
```

4.7.5. Qualified Data Structures

Normally, an RPG program can refer to the individual subfields in a data structure by their simple names. Those names must be unique; that is, you cannot typically have multiple data structures with identically named subfields. A **qualified data structure** lets you ignore that rule. When you include the Qualified keyword on a data structure header line, you create a qualified data structure.

The Qualified keyword indicates to the compiler that you will refer to the subfields in the data structure by their qualified name (i.e., the data structure name followed by a period and the subfield name). If the Qualified keyword is not used, you will refer to the subfields by their simple name, and that name must be unique. Qualified data structures can be program described or externally described, and they must be named data structures. The following examples illustrate how to define qualified data structures:

```
Dcl-ds Customer Qualified;
  Company   Zoned(2:0);
  Id        Zoned(5:0);
  Name      Char(35);
  Address   Char(35);
  City      Char(21);
  State     Char(2);
  Postcode  Char(10);
  Credlimit Zoned(11:2);
End-ds;
```

Continued

```
Dcl-ds Vendor Qualified;
  Company   Zoned(2:0);
  Id        Char(7);
  Name      Char(35);
  Address   Char(35);
  City      Char(21);
  State     Char(2);
  Postcode  Char(10);
End-ds;
```

In these examples, the RPG program must refer to subfields Customer.Name or Vendor. Name to refer to the Name subfield in either the Customer data structure or the Vendor data structure. Notice that the subfields can have identical names even if they don't have identical data attributes. In the previous examples, Customer.Id is a five-digit zoned numeric field and Vendor.Id is a seven-character field. The data structures need not have identical subfields, and the subfields need not be in the same order in each data structure. You can use qualified subfield names almost anywhere in the program that allows a variable name.

Tip
Use qualified data structures extensively to help document the origins of a data structure subfield. They are especially useful in large complex programs, and in those programs that comprise many modular programming devices, such as subroutines and procedures (discussed later).

4.8. Using Like, Likeds, and Likerec

Several Definition specification keywords let you define data structures, data structure subfields, and standalone variables that *inherit* certain characteristics of other data items in the program. RPG uses the **Like, Likeds, and Likerec keywords** to define a new data item like an already-defined *parent* data item.

The Like keyword defines a standalone variable or data structure subfield that adopts the length and the data type of another data item. When you define a data item with the Like keyword, the data type, decimal positions, and, usually, the length are left blank because the compiler retrieves those attributes from the referenced parent. Here are some examples of using Like:

```
// Variables Firstname and Lastname are both character fields,
// 20 bytes long
Dcl-s Firstname Char(20);
Dcl-s Lastname  Like(Firstname);

// Variables Statetax and Fedtax are both zoned numeric fields, with
// 7 digits and 7 decimals
Dcl-s Statetax Zoned(7:7);
Dcl-s Fedtax    Like(Statetax);

// Data structure Customer is a data structure, totaling 90 bytes.
// Variable Label is a character standalone variable, 90 bytes long.
Dcl-ds Customer;
  Name     Like(Lastname);
  Address  Char(35);
  City     Char(21);
  *N       Char(1);
  State    Char(2);
  *N       Char(1);
  Postcode Char(10);
End-ds;

Dcl-s Label Like(Customer);
```

In these examples, the newly defined data item uses the existing parent data item (another standalone variable, data structure, or data structure subfield) as a reference when assigning data attributes. You can also adjust the size of the new character or numeric data item, based on the parent, by including a second parameter for the Like keyword, along with a plus sign (+) to add length or a minus sign (-) to subtract length:

```
// Variables Name and Longname are both character fields.
// Name is 20 bytes long, Longname is 35 bytes long.
Dcl-s Name     Char(20);
Dcl-s Longname Like(Firstname:+15);
```

Continued

```
// Variable Unitsales is a packed number, 9 digits, 2 decimals.
// Variable Totalsales is also packed, 11 digits, 2 decimals.
Dcl-s Unitsales  Packed(9:2);
Dcl-s Totalsales Like(Unitsales:+2);
```

The Like keyword is useful in documenting data dependencies in your program and in ensuring the reliability of future program maintenance. In the preceding example, if you were to change UnitSales to, say, 13 digits, the RPG compiler would automatically define Totalsales as 15 digits without any additional coding.

Another keyword, Likeds (Like Data Structure), defines one data structure (or a data structure subfield) to be like another data structure, with the same subfields:

```
// Data structure Vendor will have the same subfield structure as
// data structure Customer
Dcl-ds Customer Qualified;
  Name       Char(35);
  Address    Char(35);
  City       Char(21);
  *N         Char(1);
  State      Char(2);
  *N         Char(1);
  Postalcode Char(10);
  Origdate   Date Inz(*Sys);
End-ds;


Dcl-ds Vendor Likeds(Customer);
```

The subfields in the new data item are identical to the parent data structure. The new data structure is implicitly qualified, even if the parent data structure is not qualified. This means that you must refer to the subfields in the new data structure by their qualified name (e.g., Vendor.Name, Vendor.Address), even though you do not explicitly code the Qualified keyword. The preceding example also qualifies the Customer data structure, for the sake of consistency. Notice that End-ds is not used when the data structure is defined with Likeds because no additional subfields are allowed.

Also in the preceding example, subfield Vendor.Origdate is *not* automatically initialized to the current system date, even though Customer.Origdate is coded with the Inz keyword.

Using the Like and Likeds keywords copies only the data attributes of the parent, not its values. You can, however, initialize a data structure with the same values as its parent by adding a special Inz value:

```
Dcl-ds Vendor Likeds(Customer) Inz(*Likeds);
```

Coding Inz(*Likeds) initializes all the subfields in the new data structure with the same values as the parent's initial values.

Similar to Likeds, the Likerec (Like Record Format) keyword defines a data structure (or a subfield) to be like a record format defined in a Dcl-f file declaration instruction. In the following example, both data structures, Before and After, have the same layout as the Custsrec format in the Customers file:

```
Dcl-f Customers Keyed;

Dcl-ds Before Likerec(Custsrec);
Dcl-ds After  Likerec(Custsrec);
```

Data structures using Likerec are similar to externally described data structures, but Likerec must refer to a record format that exists in a file declared in the program. Data structures with Likerec are implicitly qualified, so this program refers to Before.Caddr, After.Caddr, and so on. Notice that you do not use End-ds when defining the data structure with Likerec because no additional subfields are allowed.

An additional Likerec feature (also available with externally described data structures) allows you to restrict the subfields in the data structure to the key fields only. The following example uses the Custdir logical file (from Chapter 3 and in Figure 4.2) to define a data structure that consists of two subfields—Custkeys.Clname and Custkeys.Cfname—the two key fields from the record format:

```
Dcl-f Custdir Keyed;

Dcl-ds Custkeys Likerec(Custdrec:*Key);
```

Specifying the figurative constant *Key as the second argument for the Likerec keyword restricts the data structure to using only the key field definitions from the record format.

```
/ *CUSTDIR.LF ⛶                                                              ▭  ⊟
   Line 3        Column 1     Insert    9 changes
        ▪....A..........T.Name+++++...............Functions++++++++++++++++++++++++++++
   000100       A* Logical file CUSTDIR
   000101       A* Customers file with directory fields only
   ⃒000102      A          R CUSTDREC                  PFILE(CUSTOMERS)
   000103       A            CLNAME
   000104       A            CFNAME
   000105       A            CPHONE
   000106       A            CEMAIL
   000107       A          K CLNAME
   000108       A          K CFNAME
```

Figure 4.2: Logical file DDS, showing key fields

4.9. Navigating Legacy Code

In programs written before IBM i Release 7.2, the task of declaring files and other data items fell to two fixed-format specifications:

- File specifications (F-specs)
- Definition specifications (D-specs)

Previous chapters introduced these specifications. Now, we summarize the possible entries.

4.9.1. File Specifications

The following header shows the layout of a File specification and the completed File specifications for your program. Note that in addition to column positions, the ruler lines include prompts to help you remember where to insert required entries.

```
*.. 1 ...+... 2 ...+... 3 ...+... 4 ...+... 5 ...+... 6 ...+... 7 ...+... 8
FFilename++IPEASFRlen+LKlen+AIDevice+.Keywords++++++++++++++++++++++++++++++++
FCustomers IF   E              Disk
FCustlist  O    E              Printer Oflind(Endofpage)
```

4.9.1.1. Filename (Positions 7–16)

Enter the filename, left-adjusted, in positions 7–16.

4.9.1.2. File Type (Position 17)

Position 17 (labeled I on the ruler line), specifies the file usage. It is the fixed-format equivalent of the Usage keyword that the Dcl-f free-format instruction uses. Here are the possible entries:

- I = Usage(*Input)
- O = Usage(*Output)

- U = Usage(*Update:*Delete)
- C = Usage(*Input:*Output)

4.9.1.3. File Designation (Position 18 Input Files Only)

Every input file requires a file designation entry (position 18, labeled P). Nearly all files are full procedural files; that is, their processing is explicitly coded in the program and not controlled by the RPG cycle. All files declared by the Dcl-f instruction are assumed to be full procedural, so no other entry is allowed. For fixed-format F-specs, the commonly used entries are as follows:

- F = full procedural
- P = Primary file (RPG cycle)
- S = Secondary file (RPG cycle)

4.9.1.4. End-of-File (Position 19 Primary and Second Files Only)

For primary or secondary files, position 19 (labeled E on the ruler line) indicates whether the program can end before processing all records from the file. If the program must process all records from all files before it ends, leave position 19 blank; otherwise, enter E in position 19 for the files that require full processing before the program can end. Position 19 has no effect on full procedural files, so leave it blank.

4.9.1.5. File Addition (Position 20)

For input and update files, this position (labeled A) specifies whether records can be added to the file. You can always add records to output files, whether or not an entry is in position 20. For input and update files, however, you must code an A in position 20 to allow the addition of records. The equivalent entries on the Dcl-f instruction are Usage(*Output), Usage (*Input:*Output), or Usage (*Update:*Ouput).

A fixed-format F-spec always allows you to delete records from an update file. But the Dcl-f instruction requires that you explicitly specify Usage(*Update:*Delete), Usage(*Output:*Delete), or Usage(*Delete) if you intend to delete records from the file.

4.9.1.6. File Format (Position 22)

The two possible entries for file format are E for an externally described file or F for a program-described file.

4.9.1.7. Record Length (Positions 23–27 Program-Described Files Only)

For program-described files, enter the record length, right-adjusted, in positions 23–27. The Dcl-f instruction specifies the record length on the Device keyword—for example, Device(132). For externally described files, do not enter a record length.

4.9.1.8. Key Length (Positions 29–33 Program-Described Files Only)

For program-described files processed by key, enter the key length, right-adjusted, in positions 29–33. The Dcl-f instruction specifies the key length on the Keyed keyword. For externally described files, or if the file is not being processed by key, do not enter a key length.

For a program-described file, if the key begins in a position other than the first one, use the Keyloc keyword to specify the beginning location.

4.9.1.9. Key Type (Position 34)

This position indicates whether the file is processed by key. The normal entries are as follows:

- (blank) = Sequential processing, not by key
- K = Externally described file, processed by key
- A = Program-described file, processed by alphanumeric key

4.9.1.10. File Organization (Position 35 Program-Described Files Only)

For program-described files processed by key, enter I in this position; otherwise, leave it blank.

4.9.1.11. Device (Positions 36–42)

The Device entry indicates the device associated with a file. Here are the common entries:

- Disk
- Printer
- Workstn

4.9.1.12. Keywords (Positions 44–80)

The Keywords area of the File specification augments the basic file description in the positional area (positions 6–43) of the F-spec. We covered the most regularly used keywords earlier.

4.9.2. Definition Specifications

Definition specifications, identified by a D in position 6, follow the File specifications in traditional fixed-format RPG. D-specs define to your program those data items that do not originate as fields in a file's record layout. They are equivalent to the Dcl-c, Dcl-s, and Dcl-ds instructions as well as a few others we discuss later. Chapter 2 introduced D-specs, but now we examine them in further detail to help you understand any legacy code you might encounter during your career. The following shows the general layout of the Definition specification and a few examples:

```
*.. 1 ...+... 2 ...+... 3 ...+... 4 ...+... 5 ...+... 6 ...+... 7 ...+... 8
DName++++++++++ETDsFrom+++To/Len+IDc.Keywords+++++++++++++++++++++++++++++++
D Taxrate        C                 .0765
D Country        C                       'United States'

D Totaldue       S            7P 2

D Customer       DS
D   Company                   2S 0
D   Id                        5S 0
D   Name                     35A
D   Address                  35A
D   City                     21A
D   State                     2A
D   Postcode                 10A
D   Credlimit                11S 2
```

4.9.2.1. Data Item Name (Positions 7–21)

You specify the name of the data item in positions 7–21. You can indent data item names within this area to visually clarify a structure.

4.9.2.2. External Description (Position 22)

For an externally described data structure, enter an E here; otherwise, leave position 22 blank.

4.9.2.3. Definition Type (Positions 24–25)

Definition specifications use positions 24–25 (Ds), left-adjusted, to indicate the type of data item that the line is defining. For data items already covered, these are the valid entries:

- C = Dcl-c (Declare constant)
- S = Dcl-s (Declare standalone variable)
- DS = Dcl-ds (Declare data structure)
- (blanks) = Dcl-subf (Declare subfield)

4.9.2.4. Length (Positions 33–39)

Enter the length of the variable, right-adjusted in positions 33–39 (To/Len+). Standalone variables defined as character data can be from 1 to 16,773,104 bytes, and numeric variables can be from 1 to 63 digits.

Leave the length blank for dates, times, timestamps, or pointers. If you enter an optional length for an indicator, the length must be 1.

For character variables, you can use the **Len (Length)** keyword as an alternative to using positions 33–39. Positions 33–39 allow for a definition length only up to 9,999,999 bytes. If the defined item is longer than that, you *must* use the Len keyword to specify the data item's length. You cannot use the Len keyword with numeric variables.

Instead of entering the length for data structure subfields, you can specify the subfields' beginning and ending byte positions within the data structure. Enter the beginning position, right-adjusted, in positions 26–32 (From) and the ending position, right-adjusted, in positions 33–39 (To/Len+).

4.9.2.5. Data Type (Position 40)

Position 40 (labeled I) indicates the data type that RPG uses to internally store a variable. The data types already covered are coded in this position:

- (blank) = Default
- A = Char
- N = Ind
- S = Zoned
- P = Packed
- I = Int
- U = Uns
- D = Date
- T = Time
- Z = Timestamp
- * = Pointer

If the decimal positions entry (positions 42–43) is blank, the default data type is A (Char). But if a decimal positions entry is present, standalone variables default to P (Packed), and data structure subfields default to S (Zoned).

To define a variable-length character string, specify A for the data type and include the Varying keyword.

4.9.2.6. Decimal Positions (Positions 42–43)

For numeric variables, enter the number of decimals in positions 42–43. A number can have 0–63 decimal positions; data types I and U must have 0 decimals. If this entry is blank, the data item is considered to be non-numeric.

4.9.2.7. Keywords (Positions 44–80)

The Keywords area of the Definition specification extends the simple definition in positions 7–43. Frequently used keywords are as follows:

- Extfld
- Extname
- Inz
- Like
- Likeds
- Likerec
- Overlay
- Qualified
- Varying

4.10. Chapter Summary

ILE RPG requires you to define all the files, variables, and other data items your program will use. The declarations section of a program includes the Dcl-f (Declare file) instruction to describe files, Dcl-c (Declare named constant) to associate a named data item with a literal, Dcl-s (Declare standalone variable) to define work fields and other variables not found in a file, and Dcl-ds (Declare data structure) to allow a program to group variables into a single entity.

The Dcl-f instruction names a file and defines how to use it. When a program declares a file, all the fields in the file are available to the program as variables. The most frequently used device types are Disk for database files, Printer for printed reports, and Workstn for interactive displays. The Usage keyword specifies how the program is to use the file. The program reads records from input files, writes records to output files, changes records in update files, and deletes records if the file is delete-capable. The Usage keyword can specify logical usage combinations appropriate to the program. A file can be program described or externally described and can be processed in arrival sequence or by key.

Once you define a named constant—using the Dcl-c instruction—you can use it in the program instead of its literal value. A named constant's value cannot change during the processing of the program. You use numeric literals and constants in arithmetic operations. Character literals are enclosed between apostrophes. No restriction applies on the characters that can make up a character constant. In addition to numeric and character literals and named constants, other data types can be represented as typed literals. RPG reserves some figurative constants as well—for example, *On, *Off, *Blanks, and *Zeros.

Standalone variables are not part of a database or data structure. The Dcl-s instruction must at a minimum name the variable and give it a data type. The common data types include character, indicator, zoned numeric, packed decimal, integers, and dates. Most data types also include the length as part of the declaration. In addition to Dcl-s defining a data item, the Inz keyword can assign an initial value to the variable.

Data structures, defined using Dcl-ds, are a means of organizing variables into a single structure that a program can process as a whole or as individual subfields. Data structures are considered to be character variables, although their subfields can include other data types. The locations of subfields are normally contiguous, but they can also overlay a portion of another subfield. Data structures can be program described or externally described by a database file record format.

The Like, Likeds, and Likerec keywords let you define variables, data structures, and subfields with the same attributes as another variable, data structure, or record format.

Legacy code uses fixed-format File specifications (F-specs) and Definition specifications (D-specs) to declare files and other data items.

The following table summarizes the operation codes discussed in this chapter. Optional entries appear within curly braces ({}):

Function or Operation	Description	Syntax
Dcl-c	Declare named constant	Dcl-c name value;
Dcl-ds	Declare data structure	Dcl-ds ds-name {optional-keywords};
Dcl-f	Declare file	Dcl-f file-name device {keywords};
Dcl-s	Declare standalone variable	Dcl-s name data-type {keywords};
Dcl-subf	Declare subfield	{Dcl-subf} name {data-type} {optional-keywords};
End-ds	End a data structure definition	End-ds {ds-name};

4.11. Key Terms

Boolean data type	Extname	override
character literal	figurative constant	Pos
data structure	indicator	positional
Dcl-c	initial value	qualified data structure
Dcl-ds	Inz	Prefix
Dcl-f	Keyed	Rename
Dcl-s	Like	standalone variable
declare	Likeds	subfield
Ext	Likrec	typed literal
Extdesc	literal	Usage(*Delete)
Extfile	named constant	Usage(*Input)
Extfld	numeric literal	Usage(*Ouput)
Extmbr	overlay	Usage(*Update)

4.12. Discussion/Review Questions

1. What is the main purpose of the Declarations section of an RPG program?
2. List the types of declare instructions discussed in this chapters and their use.
3. What is a named constant?
4. What are the advantages of using named constants in a program?
5. Compare and contrast literals, named constants, and figurative constants.
6. What is the main difference between a constant and a variable?
7. When is it important to assign an initial value to a data item?
8. Which data types are appropriate for storing money-related data? Why?
9. When would you use an indicator data type?
10. What kinds of capabilities can you gain by using data structures?
11. What is a figurative constant? What are possible uses for figurative constants? How does the figurative constant *ALL work?
12. List five uses for subfields in data structures.
13. What are the advantages of using an externally described data structure?
14. Why would you need to use the Rename keyword when declaring an SQL file by using the Dcl-f instruction?
15. Why would a programmer need to use the Prefix keyword in the Dcl-f instruction?
16. Explain the difference between the Extdesc and the Extfile keywords of the Dcl-f instruction.
17. Data structures are considered character variables by default. When the program starts, what do all of the fields contain?

18. Why would a programmer want to use the Overlay keyword when defining a data structure? Code an example of using the Overlay keyword.
19. Why would a programmer use an externally described data structure?
20. Define and describe the use of the Like, Likeds, and Likerec keywords.

4.13. Exercises

1. Code the following standalone variables by using declarations (use variable names, lengths, and data types appropriate to the variable's use):

- total sales, with 11 digits precision
- product description, 30 bytes long
- sales tax rate percent
- transaction date

2. Code the following values as named constants:

- a commission rate of 2.5 percent
- the company name Acme Explosives Company
- the FICA cutoff income of $76,400
- an edit word for editing Social Security numbers
- the date January 1, 2000

3. Code a data structure for organizing information to be printed on a label. The subfields should include name, Social Security number, phone number, two address lines, city/state/ province, postal code, and country. Variable names and lengths should be appropriate to the variables' use.

4. With the data structure you created in exercise 3, redefine the Social Security number and phone number by using the Overlay keyword.

5. Code two qualified data structures (Student and Employee). Give each of these data structures the same named fields: ID, Firstname, Lastname, Streetaddress, City, State, Phone Number, and Socialsecuritynumber. Redefine the Social Security number and phone number by using the Overlay keyword.

6. How would you reference the area code in the Student data structure from exercise 5? How would you reference the Employee area code?

CHAPTER 5

Controlling Program Workflow

5.1. Chapter Overview

This chapter focuses on program design and introduces you to ILE RPG operations that let you write well-designed programs by using a top-down, structured approach. Loops, decision logic, and subroutines receive special attention. The chapter applies these design principles by teaching you how to code control break problems.

5.2. Structured Design

You typically can solve programming problems in many different ways, each of which might produce correct output. Although an important goal, correct output should not be the programmer's only goal. Producing code that is readable and easy to change is also important to programmers who are concerned with quality.

Changes in user requirements and processing errors discovered as programs are used dictate that programmers spend a lot of their time maintaining existing programs rather than developing new code. A well-designed, well-documented program facilitates such maintenance—a poorly designed program can be a maintenance nightmare.

Structured design is a widely accepted development methodology that supports quality program design. One important aspect of structured design is limiting control structures within your program to three basic logic structures:

- sequence
- selection (also called *decision*)

- iteration (also called *repetition* or *looping*)

Sequence lets you instruct the computer to execute operations serially. **Selection** lets you establish alternative paths of instructions within a program. Which optional path the program executes depends on the results of a test or condition within the program. And **iteration** permits instructions within the program to be repeated until a condition is met or is no longer met.

Sequential control flow is inherent in RPG (and other programming languages) by default. The order in which you describe operations in the procedural sections of the program determines the order in which the computer executes them. The computer begins with the first instruction, and then it continues to execute the program statements in their order of occurrence, unless it encounters an operation that explicitly transfers control to a different location within the program.

To diverge from a sequential flow of control, your program must use an explicit operation code that invokes the desired control structure. These operation codes invoke selection (decision) structures:

- If, Else, Elseif (Else If)
- Select, When, Other (Otherwise)

And these operation codes invoke iteration (repetition) structures:

- Dow (Do While)
- Dou (Do Until)
- For

Each of these control structures has a single entry point and a single exit point. Together, the structures can serve as basic building blocks to express the complex logic required to solve complicated programming problems while maintaining the tight control over program flow that facilitates program maintenance.

5.3. Relational Comparisons

Decision and iteration operations involve testing a condition to determine the appropriate course of action. This testing entails a **relational comparison** between two values. To express the comparison, ILE RPG supports six **relational symbols** that are used with decision and iteration operations:

- > (Greater than)
- >= (Greater than or equal to)
- = (Equal to)

- <=   (Less than or equal to)
  - <   (Less than)
  - <>   (Not equal to)

The way the computer evaluates whether a comparison is true depends on the data type of the items being compared. If you are comparing two numeric values (whether variables, literals, constants, or expressions), the system compares them based on algebraic values, aligned at the decimal point. The length and number of decimal positions in the items being compared do not affect the outcome of the comparison. For example, 2.25 is equal to 00002.250000, whereas 00000002.12345 is smaller than 9. A positive value is always larger than a negative value. Only the algebraic values of the data items themselves determine the result of a relational comparison between numeric fields.

You can also perform relational tests between character values. This kind of comparison occurs somewhat differently from numeric comparisons. When you compare two character values, the system performs a character-by-character comparison, moving from left to right, until it finds an unmatched pair or finishes checking. When it encounters a character difference, the difference is interpreted in terms of the EBCDIC collating sequence, discussed in Chapter 3. In EBCDIC, A is less than B, B is less than C, and so on—lowercase letters are smaller than uppercase letters, letters are smaller than digits, and a blank is smaller than any other displayable character.

If you are comparing two character items of unequal sizes, the system pads the smaller item with blanks to the right before making the comparison. To understand character comparisons, consider the following examples (in the examples, b represents a blank within the data item):

```
ART < BART
ARTHUR = ARTHURbbbb
ARTbbbb < ARTHUR
A1 < AL
123 > ABC
```

In addition to numeric and character values, you can perform relational tests against dates, times, and timestamps. If you are comparing two date-related values (whether variables, literals, constants, or expressions), the system compares them based on their relative occurrence on the calendar or the clock (i.e., earlier dates are considered to be less than later dates). The dates or times being compared need not be in the same format because the system accurately compares them, regardless of format.

You can use numbered indicators and other RPG-reserved words in relational comparisons, provided you preface the indicator with *In. (There's no need to preface named indicators declared with Dcl-s or Dcl-ds.) You can compare one indicator with another (in which case, you're trying to determine whether their values are the same), or you can compare an indicator with the figurative constants *On and *Off (or the character literals '1' and '0'), which represent the only possible values an indicator can assume.

RPG does not let you compare incompatible data types in the same expression. For example, you cannot compare a numeric data item with a character data item, or a date with a time. You can, however, use functions discussed in later chapters to convert data items among the various data types for comparison purposes.

5.4. Selection Operations

Now that you understand how RPG makes relational comparisons, you can learn how to use relational operators with those ILE RPG operations that determine flow of program control. First, we illustrate the options for sending control to alternative statements within a program: **selection (decision) operations**.

5.4.1. IF

RPG's primary decision operator is **If**. The general format of the If operation is as follows:

```
If conditional_expression;
  ...
Endif;
```

The conditional expression must be true or false. If the conditional expression is true, all the calculations between the If statement and its corresponding Endif are executed. If the relationship is not true, those statements are bypassed. The If group has one entry point (the If statement) and one exit point (the Endif statement).

For example, to count all senior citizens, you can write the following lines:

```
If Age >= 65;
  Count += 1;
Endif;
```

This code can be read, "If Age is greater than or equal to 65, then increment Count by 1." You need not limit the comparison to simple variables or literals; it can also include expressions. Assuming Credlimit, Amtowed, and Purchamt are numeric variables, and Approval is an indicator, the following statements process a sales transaction:

```
If (Credlimit - Amtowed - Ordertot) >= 0;
  Approval = *On;
  Amtowed += Ordertot;
Endif;
```

This code can be read, "If you subtract the customer's outstanding balance (Amtowed) and the order total (Ordertot) from the customer's credit limit (Credlimit) and the result (i.e., the remaining credit) is positive or zero, then approve the order and add the order total to the outstanding balance."

Sometimes, you want to execute a series of instructions based on multiple tests or conditions. ILE RPG includes the binary operators And and Or to allow such multiple conditions. When you use And to set up a compound condition, *both* relationships must be true for the If to evaluate as true:

```
If Age >= 65 And Status = 'R';
  Count += 1;
Endif;
```

When you use Or to connect two relational tests, the If evaluates to true if one or the other (or both) of the conditions is true:

```
If Age >= 65 Or Status = 'R';
  Count += 1;
Endif;
```

You can combine And and Or to create more complex conditional tests. Note that And is evaluated before Or. However, you can use parentheses to change the order of evaluation; parentheses are always evaluated first. If a conditional expression requires more room than a single specification offers, you can extend the expression to additional lines. To illustrate how And and Or are evaluated and to demonstrate the use of parentheses, we provide the following scenario. A company wants to print a list of employees eligible for early retirement. Only salaried employees are eligible (code = 'S'). Moreover, they must have worked more than 15 years for the company or be 55 (or more) years old. The following code shows an incorrect way and a correct way to express these conditions:

```
// INCORRECT
// The code below would select any employee who was salaried and had
// worked more than 15 years; it also would incorrectly include any
// employee at least 55 years old, whether or not (s)he was salaried.

If Salarycode = 'S' And Yrsworked > 15 Or Age >= 55;
  Eligible = *On;
Endif;


// CORRECT
// The parentheses in the code below cause the correct selection of
// employees who are salaried and who have either worked more than 15
// years or are at least 55 years old.

If Salarycode = 'S' And (Yrsworked > 15 Or Age >= 55);
  Eligible = *On;
Endif;
```

5.4.2. Else

You can also include an **Else** operation within an If group to set up an alternate path of instructions to be executed should the If condition be false. For example, to calculate pay and to pay time and a half for any hours over 40, you can code the following (using the + operator for addition and the * operator for multiplication):

```
If Hours <= 40;
  Totalpay = Hours * Payrate;
Else;
  Totalpay = 40 * Payrate + (Hours - 40) * Payrate * 1.5;
Endif;
```

In this example, the first expression is executed if Hours is less than or equal to 40; otherwise, the second expression is processed. Only one Else operation is allowed in an If group. The Else operation does not require a corresponding exit point because all the statements are considered to be part of the same If group. The flow chart in Figure 5.1 illustrates the basic structure of the If group.

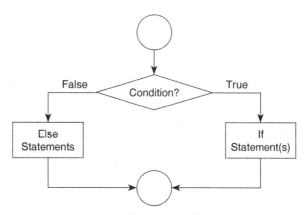

Figure 5.1: Flow chart illustrating If group

5.4.3. Nesting If Groups

You can also nest If groups. That is, you can build If groups within other If groups with or without Else operations. Each If requires an Endif in the appropriate spot to indicate the end point of that If group's influence. The following example illustrates nested If logic in ILE RPG:

```
// This code uses IF and EVAL to assign values to LifeExpect based on
// age and sex.

If Age >= 65;
  If Sex = 'F';
    Lifeexpect = 87;
  Else;
    Lifeexpect = 84;
  Endif;
Else;
  If Sex = 'F';
    Lifeexpect = 86;
  Else;
    Lifeexpect = 82;
  Endif;
Endif;
```

The flow chart in Figure 5.2 illustrates the basic structure of a nested If group.

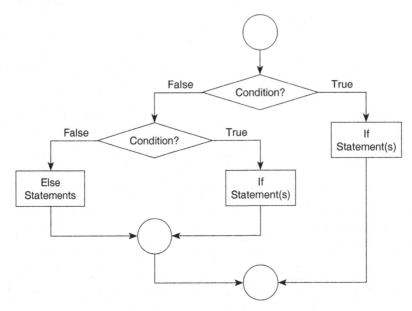

Figure 5.2: Flow chart illustrating nested If

5.4.4. Elseif (Else If)

Sometimes a program's logic requires that nesting happen only on the Else branches of the decision structure. The following example of assigning commission rates typifies this kind of construct, sometimes called **case logic**:

```
// Assign Commission Rates Based On Sales Level
If Sales <= 5000;
  Rate = .005;
Else;
  If Sales <= 10000;
    Rate = .0075;
  Else;
    If Sales <= 20000;
      Rate = .01;
    Else;
      Rate = .015;
    Endif;
  Endif;
Endif;
```

In the previous examples, each If statement requires its own corresponding Endif statement, resulting in a series of Endif statements to close individual nesting levels. As an alternative, the **Elseif** operation combines Else and If operations and requires only a single Endif at the end of the code block. The following example uses Elseif to simplify the nesting levels:

```
// Assign Commission Rates Based On Sales Level
If Sales <= 5000;
   Rate = .005;
Elseif Sales <= 10000;
   Rate = .0075;
Elseif Sales <= 20000;
   Rate = .01;
Else;
   Rate = .015;
Endif;
```

Figure 5.3 illustrates the basic structure of the Elseif operation.

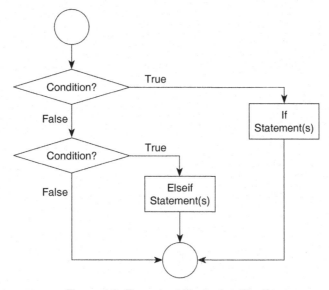

Figure 5.3: Flow chart illustrating Elseif

Notice in the examples presented so far in this chapter that the free-form syntax lets you indent code to make the logical groupings of conditions and the resulting actions more apparent.

5.4.5. Select (Conditionally Select Operations)

Although you can express even the most complex programming decisions with a series of If, Else, and Elseif operations, nested If groups can be difficult to set up and hard for others to interpret. To overcome this problem, ILE RPG uses the **Select (Conditionally Select Operations)** operation to let you simplify the coding of case logic.

The Select operation appears on a line alone to identify the start of a Select group. You follow the Select operation with one or more **When** lines, each of which specifies a condition to be tested. Next, you follow each When with one or more calculations to perform when that condition is met. When you execute the program, it checks the When conditions sequentially, starting with the first. As soon as it encounters a true condition, the computer executes the operation (or operations) following that When statement and then sends control to the end of the Select group, signaled by an EndsI (End Select) operation.

The following code uses Select to express the same logic for determining sales commission rates shown previously with nested If groups:

```
// Assign a value to rate based on level of sales
Select;
  When Sales <= 5000;
    Rate = .005;
  When Sales <= 10000;
    Rate = .0075;
  When Sales <= 20000;
    Rate = .01;
  Other;
    Rate = .015;
Endsl;
```

Notice in this example that the **Other (Otherwise)** operation code means *in all other cases*. Other, if used, should be the final *catch-all* condition listed. A Select group that includes an Other operation causes the computer to always perform one of the sets of calculations. When a Select group consists only of When conditions, no operation within the Select group is performed if no conditions are met.

Although not illustrated in the preceding example, just as in If operations, multiple operations can follow each When line—as many operations as you need to accomplish the desired processing on that branch of the Select group. You also can couple the When conditions with And and Or to create compound selection criteria, which can continue on multiple specification lines if needed.

The flow chart in Figure 5.4 illustrates the basic structure of a Select group.

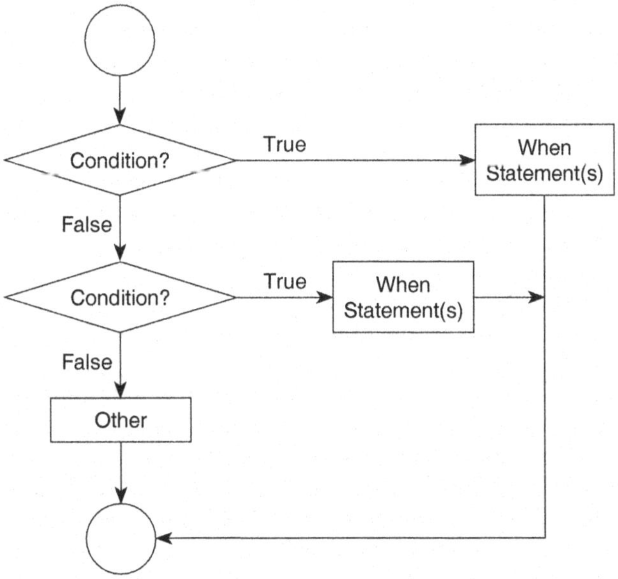

Figure 5.4: Flow chart illustrating Select

5.5. Iteration Operations

The third logical construct of structured programming is iteration. **Iteration** lets your program repeat a series of instructions—a common necessity in programming. In batch processing, for example, you want to execute a series of instructions repeatedly, once for every record in a transaction file. You have already used one ILE RPG operation that enables iteration, or looping: Dow.

5.5.1. Dow (Do While)

The **Dow (Do while)** operation establishes a loop based on a conditional test expression. All the operations coded between this operator and its corresponding end statement (Enddo) are repeated as long as the condition specified in the relational test remains true.

You have already used Dow to repeat processing while an end-of-file condition remains off. You can use Dow for other kinds of repetition as well. Assume you want to add all the numbers between 1 and 100. Using Dow lets you easily accomplish this summation, as in the following code:

```
// This routine adds all the numbers from 1 to 100.


Dow Number < 100;                   // Loop while Number is less than 100.
                                                        Continued
```

```
  Number += 1;                    // Increment Number by 1.
  Sum += Number;                  // Add Number to accumulator Sum.
Enddo;
```

Notice that we manually incremented the variable Number inside the loop. This processing is necessary so that the program can *escape* the loop when the condition is no longer true. The conditional expression is tested during each iteration before the instructions within the loop are executed. If the condition is no longer true, control falls to the first statement following the Enddo operation. If no processing takes place to change the state of the condition, the resulting *endless loop* continues forever or until an error occurs.

Like ILE RPG's decision operations, the Dow operation lets you use And and Or to form compound conditions to control the looping:

```
// Any processing specified within the loop would be repeated as long
// as both indicators 90 and 99 remain off.

Dow *In90 = *Off And *In99 = *Off;
  ...
Enddo;
```

At some point during the processing inside the Dow loop, either or both indicators must have their values changed to *On to enable the program to eventually escape the loop.

5.5.2. Dou (Do Until)

Dou (Do Until) is a structured iteration operation similar to Dow. Like Dow, Dou includes a conditional test expression. However, two major differences exist between the two operations. First, a Dow operation repeats *while* the specified condition *remains* true, whereas a Dou operation repeats *until* the condition *becomes* true. Second, Dow is a **leading-decision loop**, which means the conditional expression is tested *before* the instructions within the loop are initially executed. If the condition is false, the computer completely bypasses the instructions within the loop. Dou, in contrast, is a **trailing-decision loop.** Because the condition is tested *after* the instructions within the loop have been executed, the instructions are always executed at least once. However, instructions within a Dow loop may not be executed at all.

Figure 5.5 presents flow charts of Do While and Do Until operations to illustrate their differences.

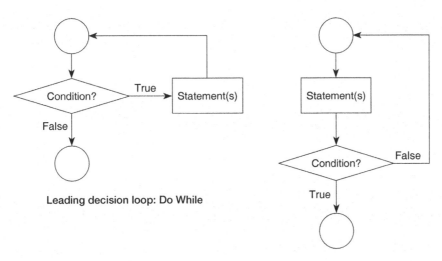

Figure 5.5: Do While vs. Do Until loops

Dow and Dou are often equally suited to setting up a looping structure. For instance, you can use Dou to solve the *add-the-numbers* problem illustrated earlier with Dow—simply change the operation and the relational test. The following code illustrates how to solve this problem by using Dou:

```
// This routine adds all the numbers from 1 to 100.
Dou Number = 100;           // Loop until Number equals 100.
  Number += 1;              // Increment Number by 1.
  Sum += Number;            // Add Number to accumulator Sum.
Enddo;
```

5.5.3. For

Often, as in the previous example, you want to execute a loop a specific number of times. To implement this kind of logic with Dou or Dow, you define a field to serve as a counter. Each time the loop repeats, you must *explicitly* increment the counter as part of your loop instructions and check the counter's value after each repetition to determine whether another iteration is needed. Dow and Dou are **condition-controlled loops**, meaning that whether the loop continues depends upon testing a condition.

ILE RPG offers the For operation designed specifically for **count-controlled loops** (i.e., for executing loops a specific number of times). Like Dow and Dou, an end operator (Endfor) signals the end of a For group. Unlike those operations, the For operation *automatically* increments its counter to ensure the repetition occurs the desired number of times.

The For operation's format is a little more intricate than that of Dow or Dou because For provides more options and defaults. The general layout of a For loop is as follows:

```
For Counter {= Start_Value} {To Limit_Value} {By Increment_Value};
```

In general, the For operation lets you specify four things:

- a variable to serve as the counter
- the starting value of the counter
- the maximum value of the counter for looping to continue
- the amount to add to the counter at the end of each repetition of the loop

Although ILE RPG lets you optionally specify these four values, you also can omit any of them except the counter field.

The counter variable must be defined as a numeric variable (preferably an integer) with zero decimal positions. You can omit the initial value for the counter, but if you do, the counter begins with the same value it had before the program entered the For loop.

In the To clause, specify a whole numeric variable, constant, or literal as a limit value. If your limit value is a variable, its value determines the number of repetitions. You can also omit the To clause, but doing so continues the loop indefinitely until the program processes a Leave operation, which we examine shortly.

The By clause specifies a whole numeric variable, constant, or literal as the increment value. If your increment value is a variable, its value determines the increment value. You can also omit the By clause. If you do, ILE RPG assumes an increment value of 1; that is, it adds 1 to the counter's value at the start of each additional pass through the loop. In the unlikely event that you need to decrement a counter instead of incrementing it, the For operation offers a variation that works in reverse, using a Downto clause.

The following examples illustrate the For loop:

```
For Idx = 1 To 50;     // Processing in this loop would be done 50 times
  ...
Endfor;

// The number of repetitions of this loop depends on the value of Iter
For Idx = 1 To Iter;
  ...
Endfor;
```

Continued

```
// This loop will repeat until the program encounters a leave operation
For Idx = 1;
  ...
  If *Inlr;
    Leave;
  Endif;
Endfor;
```

The following code shows the add-the-numbers problem implemented by using For:

```
// This routine adds all the numbers from 1 to 100.
For Number = 1 To 100;        // Loop until Number equals 100.
  Sum += Number;              // Add Number to accumulator Sum.
Endfor;
```

A For loop is a leading-decision loop, which means the value of the counter is tested against the limit value before the instructions within the loop are executed for the first time. If the counter has not exceeded the limit value, the instructions are processed repeatedly until the counter exceeds the limit. In the preceding example, after the loop is done processing, Number has a value of 101.

5.6. Loops and Early Exits

Sometimes you may want to skip the remaining instructions within a loop to begin the next iteration or cycle. In other cases, you may want to exit the loop completely before the repetition is terminated by the relational comparison. Two ILE RPG operations, **Iter (Iterate)** and **Leave**, give you these capabilities.

When the computer encounters an Iter operation, control skips past the remaining instructions in the loop and causes the next repetition to begin. Leave terminates the looping process completely and sends control to the statement immediately following the loop's End statement. You can use either or both of these statements with all the iterative operations (Dow, Dou, and For)—but not with the selection operations (e.g., If, Select).

Assume, for example, you are processing a file of customer records and printing a report line for those customers whose balance due exceeds zero. If amount due equals zero, you simply want to cycle around and read the next record from the file. The following code illustrates a solution that uses Leave and Iter:

```
// This routine processes all records in Customers and prints a detail
// line for those customers whose Amountdue is not equal to 0.

Dou %Eof(Customers);
  Read Customers;
  Select;
    When %Eof;
      Leave;                // If %Eof, pass control to Enddo
    When Amountdue = 0;
      Iter;                 // If Amountdue is zero, pass control to Dow
    Other;
      Except Detail;
  Endsl;
Enddo;
```

5.7. File Processing with Dow and Dou

Programmers often use the Dow and Dou operations in conjunction with repetitive processing of file records. The example in Chapter 2 used Dow to process the records in a file while there were records to read:

```
Read Customers;

Dow Not %Eof(Customers);
  Count += 1;
  Write Detail;
  Read Customers;
Enddo;
```

The first Read operation in this example—the one outside the loop, just before the Dow operation—is often called a **priming read**, because it *primes* the loop with data from the first record from the file (if there is one). After that record is processed, a second Read operation—inside the loop—is necessary to continue processing subsequent records.

With a few small changes to the code, the example can use Dou instead:

```
Dou %Eof(Customers);
  Read Customers;
```

Continued

```
   If %Eof(Customers);
      Leave;
   Endif;


   Count += 1;
   Write Detail;
Enddo;
```

Or:

```
Dou %Eof(Customers);
   Read Customers;

   Select;
      When %Eof(Customers);
         Leave;
      Other;
         Count += 1;
         Write Detail;
   Endsl;


Enddo;
```

This version of the file loop does not require a priming read, because the first operation inside the loop reads a record from the file. Indeed, the structure needs only a single Read. But the loop does require an early exit from the loop if that lone Read operation encounters end-of-file. Without the conditional Leave operation at end-of-file, the last record is processed twice.

Which file loop structure is better? That's a question best answered by a company's programming standards.

5.8. Top-Down Design

Up to now, this chapter has concentrated on structured design. A second design concept, top-down methodology, usually works together with a structured approach. **Top-down design** means developing your program solution starting with a broad outline and then successively dividing the big pieces into smaller and smaller units. This technique is sometimes called **hierarchical decomposition**.

Hierarchical decomposition is the method your English teacher recommended for writing research papers: work out an outline, starting with your main topics, then subdivide these into subtopics until you have decomposed to a level of sufficient detail to allow you to write the paper (or in programming terms, the individual instructions of your program).

Top-down design lets you handle problems of great complexity by permitting you to initially ignore the detailed requirements of processing. The top-down methodology works in tandem with **modular program development**, which advocates that you structure your program into logical units, or modules. In top-down design, the first, or upper-level, modules primarily control flow to and from the lower-level modules you develop later.

Each module should be as independent of the others as possible, and the statements within a module should work together to perform a single function. Structural decomposition gives you a way to deal with complexity. When used with a modular approach, structural decomposition results in programs of functionally cohesive subroutines that are easier to maintain later.

ILE RPG supports three major constructs to handle top-down design and modular development:

- Subroutines
- Called programs (discussed in Chapter 13)
- Procedures (discussed in Chapter 14)

5.9. Defining and Using Subroutines

A **subroutine** is a named block of code, inside a program, with an identifiable beginning and end. It is a set of operations invoked as a unit by referring to the subroutine's name but coded elsewhere within the program. After performing the subroutine, the program returns control to the statement immediately following the one that invoked the routine. A subroutine is an organizational technique that isolates the details of a particular task and can be invoked repeatedly from other locations in the program.

You code a subroutine between **Begsr (Begin subroutine)** and **Endsr (End subroutine)** operations. The first line contains the Begsr operation and name of the subroutine. The lines of code constituting the executable portion of the subroutine follow. The last line of a subroutine contains the Endsr operation to signal the end of that subroutine. The following code shows the skeleton of a subroutine:

```
Begsr subroutine_name;
  ...
Endsr;
```

Subroutines are coded as the last processing entries, following all other processing in the main procedure. The order in which you list the subroutines does not matter, although many programmers prefer to specify them in alphabetical order for easy reference. A program can have an unlimited number of subroutines, but each must have a unique name, based on the same rules that apply to RPG variables.

To send control to a subroutine for execution, you use the **Exsr (Execute subroutine)** operation. Enter the name of the subroutine to be performed, as follows:

```
Exsr Calctax;     // Exsr causes control to drop to subroutine Calctax.
// Control returns here when the subroutine finishes.
.
.
.
// Subroutines appear at the end of the processing.
Begsr Calctax;
  Fica =  Gross * .0765;
  Statetax = Gross * .045;

  If Gross > 5000;
    Fedtax = Gross * .31;
  Else;
    Fedtax = Gross * .25;
  Endif;

Endsr;
```

The Exsr operation simply branches to the specified Begsr operation, executes the code in that subroutine, and then returns control back to the first line following the Exsr operation. The fact that control returns to a predictable location makes it possible to maintain tight control of program flow using Exsr.

Subroutines cannot contain other subroutines. They can execute other subroutines, but a subroutine should never execute itself. This latter coding technique, called **recursion**, is not permitted for subroutines.

You sometimes may want to skip the remaining instructions within a subroutine before the program gets to the Endsr operation. The **Leavesr (Leave subroutine)** gives you that opportunity. Leavesr sends control directly to the current subroutine's Endsr operation. The following example uses Leavesr to quit the subroutine when it encounters end-of-file:

```
Begsr Calctax;
  Read Customers;
  If %Eof;
    Leavesr;
  Endif;
  Tax = Gross * Taxrate;
  Gross  += Tax;
Endsr;
```

Most RPG programs use subroutines heavily because they let a programmer first code the main processing path in broad strokes, and then they relegate the details of a discreet task to a subroutine.

5.9.1. Using the *INZSR Subroutine

*Inzsr is a specially named subroutine that automatically executes whenever a program begins, before any other user-written code. Programmers commonly use the ***Inzsr subroutine** to provide initial setup processing for a program. A program can have only one subroutine named *Inzsr. It is like any other subroutine except that it is automatically executed when the program starts. A program can also execute the *Inzsr subroutine by using the Exsr operation to reinitialize the program environment during processing. Here is an example of an *Inzsr subroutine:

```
Begsr *Inzsr;
  Default = .0751;
  Action = 'A';
Endsr;
```

In this case, the example provides initial values for program variables Default and Action. You can also accomplish this function by using the Inz keyword on the declarations for those variables. Typically, the *Inzsr subroutine is reserved for more complex initialization processing to perform before the main procedure portion of the program starts.

5.10. Control Break Logic

To see how to use top-down, structured design to help develop an easily maintained program, let's apply the techniques we have examined to solve a common business programming problem: generating a report that includes subtotals.

Assume you have a file of sales records. Each record contains a salesperson's identification number, department, the amount of a specific sale, and the date of the sale. A given salesperson may have many records in the file—depending on how successful the salesperson is—and the data file is keyed by salesperson so that all the records for that salesperson can be processed together. Figure 5.6 shows the record layout for the Salesfile.

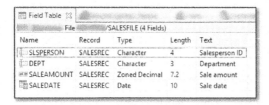

Figure 5.6: Salesfile record layout

You've been asked to write a program that includes each sales transaction's details and a subtotal of each salesperson's sales. Figures 5.7 and 5.8 illustrate the printer layout and DDS for the desired report format.

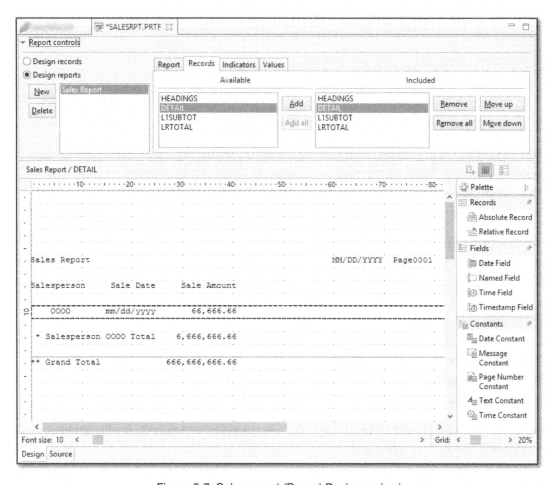

Figure 5.7: Sales report (Report Designer view)

```
                    *SALESRPT.PRTF                                                          ▭ ▢
   Line 33     Column 1    Insert
          ▮...+A*..1....+....2....+....3....+....4....+....5....+....6....+....7....+....8....+....9..
   000100        * Printer file SALESRPT, externally describing the sales report                  ᴧ
   000101       A                              REF(SALESFILE)
   000102       A          R HEADINGS          SKIPB(6)
   000105       A                             1'Sales Report'
   000106       A                            61DATE(*YY)
   000107       A                              EDTCDE(Y)
   000108       A                            73'Page'
   000109       A                            77PAGNBR
   000110       A                              EDTCDE(Z)
   000111       A                              SPACEA(2)
   000112        *
   000113       A                             1'Salesperson'
   000114       A                            17'Sale Date'
   000115       A                            31'Sale Amount'
   000116       A                              SPACEA(2)
   000117        *
   000118       A          R DETAIL           SPACEA(1)
   000119       A            SLSPERSON R       5
   000120       A            SALEDATE   R     16DATFMT(*USA)
   000121       A            SALEAMOUNTR      33EDTCDE(1)
   000122        *
   000123       A          R L1SUBTOT         SPACEB(1)
   000124       A                             2'* Salesperson'
   000125       A            L1SLSPERS R      16REFFLD(SLSPERSON)
   000126       A                            21'Total'
   000127       A            L1AMOUNT     9 2 30EDTCDE(1)
   000128       A                              SPACEA(2)
   000129        *
   000130       A          R LRTOTAL
   000131       A                             1'** Grand Total'
   000132       A            LRAMOUNT    11 2 28EDTCDE(1)
   000133
```

Figure 5.8: Sales report DDS

This kind of problem is often referred to as a **control break** problem, because the solution involves checking the input records for a change, or *break*, in the value of a control field. That occurrence signals the need for a subtotal and triggers special processing associated with printing the subtotal and preparing for the next control group.

Because the program has only one record in memory at a time, to determine when a change in the control variable's value has occurred, you need to define a standalone work variable to hold the current value of the control field. Each time a record is read, its control field's value can then be compared with the work variable. A comparison revealing that the two values are no longer equal signals that the program has just read the first record of a new group. Before continuing with the detail processing of that record, it is necessary to break away from detail processing and complete any processing that such a change requires. Typically, this processing entails printing a subtotal line, rolling over an accumulator, zeroing out the accumulator, and storing the new control field value in the work field.

With that overview of control break logic, let's develop the pseudocode for the calculations the program requires by using a top-down design strategy:

- Read first record.
- Set up hold area (L1Slspers) for first salesperson.

- While not end-of-file:
  - If Salesperson changes, execute L1Break subroutine to print subtotal.
  - Execute Detail Process subroutine.
  - Read next record.
- Execute termination subroutine.
- End program.

The preceding pseudocode outlines the program's logic. Notice that at several spots in the pseudocode, *execute* statements indicate that a number of processing steps need to be performed, but the details are not yet spelled out. This is the essence of top-down design. Once you determine that the mainline logic is correct, you can develop the logic of the additional modules, or routines:

- L1Break routine to print subtotals:
  - Print salesperson line (L1Subtot).
  - Add salesperson's subtotal (L1Amount) to grand total (LRAmount).
  - Zero out salesperson's subtotal to prepare for new salesperson.
  - Move new salesperson to hold area.
- Detail Process subroutine:
  - Print page headings, if necessary.
  - Print Detail line.
  - Add sales amount to salesperson's subtotal (L1Amount).
- Termination subroutine:
  - Execute L1Break subroutine for last salesperson.
  - Print final total line (LRTotal).

The processing in subroutine L1Break is representative of control break logic in general. Notice that L1Break is invoked from within the Termination subroutine. The break routine must be executed one last time to print the final salesperson's subtotal line before printing the grand total.

The following example shows the complete ILE RPG program, including the calculations reflecting the logic expressed in the pseudocode:

```
//  ************************************************************
//    This program produces a sales report that lists subtotals  *
//    for each salesperson.                                       *
//  ************************************************************
```

Continued

```
Dcl-f Salesfile Disk    Keyed;
Dcl-f Salesrpt  Printer Oflind(Endofpage);

Dcl-s Endofpage Ind Inz(*On);
Dcl-s L1Slspers     Like(Slsperson);


// ****************************************************************
// Mainline Logic.
// ****************************************************************

Read Salesfile;
L1Slspers = Slsperson;

Dow Not %Eof(Salesfile);

  If L1Slspers <> Slsperson;
    Exsr L1break;
  Endif;

  Exsr Detailproc;
  Read Salesfile;
Enddo;

Exsr Terminate;
*Inlr = *On;
Return;


// ****************************************************************
//  Subroutine Detailproc ... executed for each input record.
// ****************************************************************
Begsr Detailproc;
  Exsr Overflow;
  Write Detail;
  L1Amount += Saleamount;
Endsr;
```

Continued

```
// ***************************************************************
//  Subroutine L1Break ... done when salesperson changes;
//  print subtotal, roll up subtotal, zero out subtotal,
//  and reset control field value.
// ***************************************************************
Begsr L1Break;
  Exsr Overflow;
  Write L1Subtot;
  LRAmount += L1Amount;
  L1Amount = 0;
  L1Slspers = Slsperson;
Endsr;


// ***************************************************************
//  Subroutine Overflow ... print headings when necessary
// ***************************************************************
Begsr Overflow;

  If Endofpage;
    Write Headings;
    Endofpage = *Off;
  Endif;


Endsr;


// ***************************************************************
//  Subroutine Terminate ... done at end-of-file; execute
//  L1Break one last time and print grand-total line.
// ***************************************************************
Begsr Terminate;
  Exsr L1Break;
  Exsr Overflow;
  Write LRTotal;
Endsr;
```

Notice in this program that just before each line is printed, the program executes the
Overflow subroutine to ensure that heading lines print whenever the overflow indicator
(called Endofpage in this example) is on. Also notice that it is not necessary to explicitly

define fields L1Amount and LRAmount in the program, because those fields are already defined in the DDS for the printer file.

The L1 prefixes that name the variables related to the control break are a traditional naming convention meaning *level 1* break; the LR prefix notes *last record.* Any naming convention works, but L1–L9 and LR are useful prefixes to denote variables related to level breaks. Had the example contained additional control fields (perhaps department and company), you could have used additional prefixes (L2 and L3).

5.10.1. Multiple-Level Control Break Logic

Programmers often face coding solutions to multiple-level control break problems in which they must associate two or more different control fields of the input file with subtotal lines. For example, say the sample problem specified a need for department subtotals in addition to the salesperson subtotals. If you key the input file by department, and within department by salesperson, to produce the desired report requires a little more programming effort because the logic of multiple-level control break problems follows directly from that of a single-level problem.

To code a multiple-level control break program, set up a standalone work variable for each control field to hold the value of the group being processed. Code a separate break subroutine for each level. Typically, the same processing steps take place in each kind of break (e.g., printing a subtotal line, rolling up an accumulator, zeroing out the accumulator, and moving the new control field value into the work variable), but using variables appropriate to that level.

Then, before the detail processing of each record, check every control field to see whether its value has changed, verifying each one successively from major (biggest grouping) to minor (smallest grouping). The Select operation might be suitable for this purpose. If a break has occurred, execute the applicable break subroutine for the control field that triggered the break processing. Each break routine should execute the *previous* level's break routine as its first step.

Assuming that you keyed Salesfile by Department and Salesperson and made appropriate changes to the printer file, you can readily enhance the program to accommodate two control breaks:

```
Dcl-f Salesfile Disk    Keyed;
Dcl-f Salesrpt  Printer Oflind(Endofpage);


Dcl-s Endofpage Ind Inz(*On);
                                                      Continued
```

```
Dcl-s L1Slspers       Like(Slsperson);
Dcl-s L2Dept          Like(Dept);


// **************************************************************
// Mainline Logic.
// **************************************************************


Read Salesfile;
L1Slspers = Slsperson;
L2Dept = Dept;


Dow Not %Eof(Salesfile);

  Select;
    When L2Dept <> Dept;
      Exsr L2break;
    When L1Slspers <> Slsperson;
      Exsr L1break;
  Endsl;

  Exsr Detailproc;
  Read Salesfile;
Enddo;


Exsr Terminate;
*Inlr = *On;
Return;


// **************************************************************
//  Subroutine Detailproc ... done for each input record
// **************************************************************
Begsr Detailproc;
  Exsr Overflow;
  Write Detail;
  L1Amount += Saleamount;        // Roll up amount
Endsr;
```

Continued

```
// ****************************************************************
// Subroutine L1Break ... done when salesperson changes
// ****************************************************************
Begsr L1Break;
  Exsr Overflow;
  Write L1Subtot;
  L2Amount += L1Amount;       // Roll up amount
  L1Amount = 0;               // Reset subtotal
  L1Slspers = Slsperson;      // Reset control field
Endsr;


// ****************************************************************
// Subroutine L2Break ... done when department changes
// ****************************************************************
Begsr L2Break;
  Exsr L1Break;               // Process previous level break
  Exsr Overflow;
  Write L2Subtot;
  LRAmount += L2Amount;       // Roll up amount
  L2Amount = 0;               // Reset subtotal
  L2Dept = Dept;              // Reset control field
Endsr;


// ****************************************************************
// Subroutine Overflow ... print headings when necessary
// ****************************************************************
Begsr Overflow;

  If Endofpage;
    Write Headings;
    Endofpage = *Off;
  Endif;

Endsr;


// ****************************************************************
// Subroutine Terminate ... done at end-of-file
// ****************************************************************
```

Continued

```
Begsr Terminate;
  Exsr L2Break;                    // Process final level break
  Exsr Overflow;
  Write LRTotal;
Endsr;
```

Notice especially the order in which the program checks for changes in the control fields, the order in which it executes the break subroutines, and the parallels between the L1 break and L2 break routines. Once you understand the logic of a two-level break problem, you can easily write a program with any number of level breaks because you can exactly model the necessary processing steps on those required for a two-level control break.

5.11. Navigating Legacy Code

You can write all the structured operations discussed in this chapter (If, Elseif, When, Dow, Dou, and For) by using fixed-format Calculation specifications (C-specs), examined in Chapter 2. Because these operations all involve expressions, the Extended-Factor 2 format is appropriate:

```
*.. 1 ...+... 2 ...+... 3 ...+... 4 ...+... 5 ...+... 6 ...+... 7 ...+... 8
CL0N01Factor1+++++++Opcode(E)+Extended-Factor2+++++++++++++++++++++++++++++++

   // Assign Commission Rates Based On Sales Level
C                   If        Sales <= 5000
C                   Eval      Rate = .005
C                   Else
C                   If        Sales <= 10000
C                   Eval      Rate = .0075
C                   Else
C                   If        Sales <= 20000
C                   Eval      Rate = .01
C                   Else
C                   Eval      Rate = .015
C                   Endif
C                   Endif
C                   Endif
```

Notice that indentation is not allowed for the structured blocks, although you can use blank lines to help clarify the code.

5.11.1. Do, Enddo

While fixed-format code supports all the structured operation codes discussed so far, one additional operation is used *only* with fixed-format code: Do. The Do operation is a fixed-format variation of the free-format For operation for controlling a count controlled loop:

```
*.. 1 ...+... 2 ...+... 3 ...+... 4 ...+... 5 ...+... 6 ...+... 7 ...+... 8
CLON01Factor1+++++++Opcode(E)+Factor2+++++++Result++++++++Len++D+HiLoEq....

  // This routine adds all the numbers from 1 to 100.
C     1              Do        100            Number
C                    Add       Number         Sum
C                    Enddo
```

The preceding code is equivalent to the following example of the For operation, which we've already covered:

```
For Number = 1 To 100;
   Sum += Number;
Endfor;
```

The general format of the Do operation uses both Factor 1 and Factor 2:

```
*.. 1 ...+... 2 ...+... 3 ...+... 4 ...+... 5 ...+... 6 ...+... 7 ...+... 8
CLON01Factor1+++++++Opcode(E)+Factor2+++++++Result++++++++Len++D+HiLoEq....

C     start_value  DO        limit_value    counter
```

The Do operation uses principles similar to the For operation, but it fits the components into a fixed-format C-spec. You enter the iteration's starting value in Factor 1. If Factor 1 has no entry, the starting value is 1. You code the limit value in Factor 2; again, the default value is 1. In the Result, you can optionally enter the name of a counter variable. The Do group must always end with an Enddo operation. There is no fixed-format variant syntax of the For operation—you use the Do operation instead.

5.11.2. Fixed-Format Relational Comparisons

You may encounter code that uses several older structured operations and earlier forms of relational comparisons. The legacy structured operation codes generally use both Factor 1 and Factor 2:

```
*.. 1 ...+... 2 ...+... 3 ...+... 4 ...+... 5 ...+... 6 ...+... 7 ...+... 8
CLON01Factor1+++++++Opcode(E)+Factor2+++++++Result++++++++Len++D+HiLoEq....


 * Assign Commission Rates Based On Sales Level
C     Sales         Ifle      5000
C                   Z-add     .005          Rate
C                   Else
C     Sales         Ifle      10000
C                   Z-add     .0075         Rate
C                   Else
C     Sales         Ifle      20000
C                   Z-add     .01           Rate
C                   Else
C                   Z-add     .015          Rate
C                   Endif
C                   Endif
C                   Endif
```

These structured operation codes can use this fixed-format variation:

- IF*xx*
- WHEN*xx* (Used with SELECT)
- DOW*xx* (Do while)
- DOU*xx* (Do until)

When coding these operation codes, replace the *xx* with the following relational operators to compare the values of Factor 1 and Factor 2:

- GT (Factor 1 > Factor 2)
- GE (Factor 1 >= Factor 2)
- EQ (Factor 1 = Factor 2)
- LE (Factor 1 <= Factor 2)
- LT (Factor 1 < Factor 2)
- NE (Factor 1 <> Factor 2)

So the example code reads "If Sales (Factor 1) is less than or equal to 5000 (Factor 2)," and so on.

You can combine comparisons by using And*xx* or Or*xx* operations:

```
*.. 1 ...+... 2 ...+... 3 ...+... 4 ...+... 5 ...+... 6 ...+... 7 ...+... 8
CLON01Factor1+++++++Opcode(E)+Factor2+++++++Result++++++++Len++D+HiLoEq....

C      Age          Ifge      65
C      Status       Andeq     'R'
C                   Add       1              Count
C                   Endif
```

In this example, the code reads "If Age is greater than or equal to 65 and Status is equal to 'R'" to combine both lines into a single comparison.

These examples also use a C-spec Result entry (positions 50–63) as well as a couple of operation codes (Add, and Z-add), which Chapter 6 covers.

5.11.3. Conditioning Indicators

Recall from previous chapters that an indicator is a one-byte variable with only two possible values: *On ('1') or *Off ('0'). Indicators can signal whether certain conditions are true and, in turn, can control processing in the program. Early RPG programs heavily used 99 numbered indicators (01, 02, 03, …, 99), which you can use in your program. In fixed-format Calculation specifications, many operation codes can turn on indicators depending upon what happens during the execution of the operation code. When set in this manner, the indicator is known as a *resulting indicator*.

You can condition the execution of a line of code to be executed or bypassed based upon an indicator's state. When used to condition an operation, the indicator is known as a *conditioning indicator*. You can code a single conditioning indicator in positions 9–11 (labeled N01) of the fixed-format Calculation specification. The following example illustrates the use of conditioning indicators:

```
*.. 1 ...+... 2 ...+... 3 ...+... 4 ...+... 5 ...+... 6 ...+... 7 ...+... 8
CLON01Factor1+++++++Opcode(E)+Factor2+++++++Result++++++++Len++D+HiLoEq....
C                   Z-add     .10            Taxrate
C   50              Z-add     .18            Taxrate
C   51              Z-add     .25            Taxrate
C   52              Z-add     .31            Taxrate
C   N53             Add       .05            Taxrate
```

Conditioning indicators apply only to the code line on which they appear. In this example, Taxrate is set to .10 in the first line (regardless of the state of any indicators). Next, *if indicator* 50 *is* *On, Taxrate is set to .18; if indicator 51 is *On, Taxrate is subsequently set to .25; if indicator 52 is *On, Taxrate is set to .31. Finally, *if indicator* 53 *is* *Off (N53), the program adds .05 to the existing Taxrate value. The states of the indicators are presumably set as resulting indicators elsewhere in the program (we cover resulting indicators in later chapters).

Caution

Conditioning indicators are basically If operations that apply to a single line. The use of numbered indicators—whether conditioning indicators, resulting indicators, or otherwise—is strongly discouraged when you are writing new programs, but you might encounter them in older programs, especially those written before the advent of named indicators.

Free-format ILE RPG does not support the use of conditioning indicators. They appear only in fixed-format C-specs.

5.12. Chapter Summary

The goal for this chapter has been to give you a basic understanding of structured design and how it is often used with a top-down, modular approach to program development. Structured program design means developing your program logic with flow of control tightly managed by using structured operations. Top-down methodology requires you to approach designing your program hierarchically, working out its broad logic first—concentrating primarily on flow of control—and later attending to the detailed processing requirements. Both design concepts encourage a modular approach to programming, in which you design your program around subroutines of statements that form functionally cohesive units of code.

ILE RPG provides structured operations If and Select/When to implement decision logic and structured operations Dow, Dou, and For to enable looping logic. These operations let you express the conditional test associated with the operation as a free-form logical expression. All the structured operations have a single entry point and a single exit point that help maintain tight flow of control within a program.

RPG uses the subroutine as one vehicle to accommodate top-down design. A subroutine is a block of code, inside a program, that can be invoked by name. After performing the subroutine, the program returns control to the statement immediately following the one that invoked the routine.

Control break logic involves checking input records for a change in the value of one or more control fields, usually for the purpose of printing subtotals or grouping input records into subcategories.

The following table summarizes the operation codes examined in this chapter:

Function or Operation	Description	Syntax
Begsr	Begin a subroutine	Begsr subroutine-name;
Dou	Do until	Dou logical-expression;
Dow	Do while	Dow logical-expression;
Else	Else	Else;
Elseif	Else If	Elseif logical-expression;

Enddo
Endfor
Endif
Endsl
	End a structured group	Endxx;

Endsr	End of subroutine	Endsr;
Exsr	Invoke subroutine	Exsr subroutine-name;
For	For	For index {= start} {By increment} {To|Downto limit};
If	If	If logical-expression;
Iter	Reiterate a Do/For group	Iter;
Leave	Leave a Do/For group	Leave;
Leavesr	Leave a subroutine	Leavesr;
Other	Otherwise select	Other;
Select	Begin a select group	Select;
When	When true then select	When logical-expression;

5.13. Key Terms

case logic
condition-controlled loop
count-controlled loop
control break
decision operation
hierarchical decomposition
*Inzsr subroutine

iteration
leading-decision loop
modular program
    development
recursion
relational comparison
relational symbols

selection
sequence
structured design
subroutine
top-down design
trailing-decision loop

5.14. Discussion/Review Questions

1. Characterize structured design.
2. If ILE RPG did not include a relational symbol or code to check for *not equal*, what alternative way could you express the following logic in ILE RPG: "If balance due < > 0, execute the calculation routine"?
3. Why is it important to maintain a *tight* flow of control in programming?
4. Describe how ILE RPG compares numeric values.
5. Describe how ILE RPG compares character values.

6.   RPG has a Select operation. How can this construct make your programs easier to read?
7.   Can you always avoid writing nested If statements? Explain your answer.
8.   What's the difference between And and Or?
9.   Why does ILE RPG need looping operations other than For?
10.   Why are both Dow and Dou essential from a logical standpoint? Give an example of using both operations.
11.   Describe how Iter and Leave work. Are they considered structured options? Explain.
12.   Characterize a control break problem.
13.   In control break processing, why is a *hold* or work field needed to store the value of the control field?
14.   Can you think of an alternative way to handle page advance other than referencing an overflow indicator?
15.   List and describe the three control structures used in structured design.
16.   List and describe the relational operations available in RPG.
17.   What is a *priming read,* and why is it needed?
18.   Why is it important that a new programmer learn to use *hierarchical decomposition* methodology when designing a solution to a problem?
19.   List the rules that govern the use of subroutines.

5.15. Exercises

1. Use If operations to code the calculations necessary to determine property tax based on a property's value, stored in Value (six positions, zero decimal positions).

Use the information in the following table as the basis for your calculations:

Property value	Property tax
$0–$50,000	1% of value
$50,001–$75,000	$50 plus 2% of value
$75,001–$100,000	$70 plus 2.5% of value
more than $100,000	$100 plus 3% of value

2. Solve the problem described in exercise 1 using the Select operation.

3. Write a routine to determine traffic fines based on the values of two input fields: MphOver (miles over speed limit) and NbrOffense (number of offenses).

MPH over limit	Fine
1–10	$25
11–20	$40
21–30	$70
over 30	$100

Fines are determined as follows:

If the speeder is a first-time offender, there is no additional fine. However, second-time offenders are fined an additional $25 if they are no more than 20 miles over the limit and an additional $50 if they are more than 20 miles over the limit. Third-time offenders are fined an additional $50 if they are no more than 20 miles over the limit and an additional $100 if they are going more than 20 miles over the limit.

4. Use For to write the calculations you need to obtain the squares, cubes, and square roots of all numbers from 1 to 50.

5. Write four subroutines, each using a different structured operator (If, Else, Elseif, or Select) that checks an update code stored in a variable. Send control to one of three different subroutines (named AddSR, ChangeSR, DeleteSR, and ErrorSR), depending on whether the code is A, C, or D (add, change, or delete records). An invalid code should cause subroutine ErrorSR to be executed.

6. Write a Dow and a Dou that executes when the value of the variable Index is less than 100. This construct will execute a subroutine called Printline each time through the construct and will also increment the variable Index.

6

Using Arithmetic Operations and Functions

6.1. Chapter Overview

Now that you can write simple read/write programs in ILE RPG, you're ready to learn how
to perform arithmetic calculations in your programs. This chapter examines how to express
calculations by using free-form expressions and appropriate operation codes. It also introduces
you to some of RPG's built-in functions that facilitate going beyond the traditional addition,
subtraction, multiplication, and division functions used by basic arithmetic. Additionally, you learn
how to determine the correct size for fields that store the results of arithmetic operations and
how to round calculations to avoid truncation.

6.2. Simple Numeric Assignment

ILE RPG's primary assignment operation is Eval (Evaluate expression). Assigning a value
to a field simply means giving the field a value. In previous chapters, you used the Eval
operation to evaluate simple assignment expressions. Eval always works together with
an assignment expression, which consists of a result (target) variable, followed by the
assignment operator (=), followed by an expression. An Eval statement says, in effect,
"Evaluate the expression to the right of the equal sign (=) and store its value in the result
variable to the left of the equal sign." The Eval statement appears in the calculations section
of the program. Here is the general format for an Eval statement:

```
Eval Result = expression;
```

The following examples demonstrate how to use Eval for simple numeric assignment. In each case, the numeric field that appears to the left of the equal sign receives the value that appears to the right of the sign. The value to the right can be a field, literal, or named constant, but it must already be defined as numeric. You cannot define the result field within the Eval statement; you must declare it elsewhere in the program.

```
Eval Counter = 0;                  // Initialize a counter
Eval Taxrate = .045;               // Assign a value > 0
Eval Absolutezero = -273.16;       // Assign a value < 0
Eval Amtowed = Balancedue;         // Assign a field value
```

Explicitly coding the Eval operation in free-format calculations is optional unless you need to use a special feature, such as rounding (discussed later). Simply code the assignment expression, and the ILE RPG compiler assumes that it should use Eval to make the assignment. In this book, the examples will not explicitly code the Eval operation unless it is required.

6.3. Assigning Values with Figurative Constants

RPG lets you assign figurative constant *Zero (or *Zeros) to numeric variables to fill the variables with zeros. You can also assign the special values *Hival and *Loval to numeric variables. For a numeric variable, *Hival is the maximum positive value allowed for the data representation; for example, *Hival is all 9s and a plus sign (+) for a packed or zoned decimal variable. Assigning *Loval fills a numeric variable with the minimum possible value; for instance, *Loval is all 9s and a minus sign (-) for a packed or zoned decimal variable. Different numeric representations have different values for *Hival and *Loval. To find the possible range of values for integers and unsigned integers, see the table in Chapter 4.

```
Totalsales = *Zeros;
Count = *Loval;
```

6.4. Using Eval for Arithmetic

In the previous sections, you saw how to use Eval for simple numeric assignment. The Eval operation also provides a flexible and powerful method for assigning numeric fields the results of simple or complex arithmetic calculations in a single step. The expression for evaluation can contain the arithmetic operators + (addition), – (subtraction), * (multiplication), / (division), and ** (**exponentiation**, or raising a value to a power), as well as parentheses, relational symbols (e.g., <, >), logical operators (e.g., AND, OR), and built-in functions (examined later in this chapter).

A single expression can contain as many arithmetic operators, numeric literals, and numeric fields as needed to accomplish a desired calculation.

```
// Examples of calculations using the Eval operation
Withhold = Fica + Statetax + Fedtax;
Netpay = Grosspay - Withhold;
Grossprofit = Cost * .6 * Qtysold;
Avgamount = Totamount / Counter;
Numsquared = Number ** 2;
```

All values in the arithmetic expression to the right of the equal sign must, of course, be numeric fields, literals, or constants. One other restriction arises when you use division in an expression. Remember that division by zero is mathematically impossible. A runtime error occurs if, at the time of the division, the divisor (the part of an expression immediately to the right of the division sign) evaluates to zero.

When the arithmetic expression contains more than one operator, the computer uses the **rules of precedence** from mathematics to determine the order in which to perform the operations. Exponentiation has the highest precedence, followed by multiplication and division, and then addition and subtraction. When an expression contains operations of equal precedence, the system executes them in order from left to right. You can use parentheses to change the order in which the computer executes these operations—operations within parentheses are performed before any operations outside the parentheses.

```
// In this example, the multiplication will occur before the
// subtraction (because of operator precedence rules)
Answer = A * B - 1;


// In this example, the parentheses cause the subtraction to take
// place before the multiplication
Answer = A * (B - 1);
```

The expression can include as many (or as few) blanks between fields, literals, and operations as you like to make the expression readable and easy to understand. If necessary, you can simply continue the expression anywhere on subsequent lines and end it with a semicolon (;) when the expression is finished. The following code illustrates the use of a continuation line with the Eval operation:

```
Pay = Hourlyrate * 40 +
      1.5 * Hourlyrate * (Hoursworked - 40);
```

In this example, the plus sign (+) in the expression is an addition operator, not a continuation character. No special character is usually necessary to continue an expression.

Those of you who have studied algebra recognize the similarity between assignment expressions and algebraic equations. Don't be misled by this similarity, however. An algebraic equation asserts equality, whereas an assignment expression instructs the computer to perform the calculation to the right of the equal sign and then assign the result to the field left of the equal sign. In algebra, the equation $x = x + 1$ is a logical impossibility. Within an Eval operation, $x = x + 1$ is a perfectly legitimate instruction that tells the computer to add 1 to the value of field x and store the result in field x.

In fact, programmers frequently use this form of assignment expression in ILE RPG programming for counting and accumulating. For example, to count the number of customers in a file, you increment a counter field (i.e., add 1 to it) each time you process a customer record. Or, to accumulate employees' salaries, you add each salary to a field representing the grand total of the salaries:

```
Counter = Counter + 1;                    // Increment a counter
Grandtotal = Grandtotal + Empsalary;      // Accumulate a total
```

You can also decrement a counter or decrease the value of an accumulator by using subtraction:

```
Countdown = Countdown - 1;
Inventory = Inventory - Orderqty;
```

For these types of expressions, which use the result variable as the first operand in the expression, RPG offers several **compound operators**: +=, -=, *=, /=, and **=. These operators let you code this common type of expression more concisely. They perform the requested arithmetic function, using the result variable as the first operand of the operation. For example, with +=, the expression is added to the result variable. The following expressions are equivalent to the ones shown earlier:

```
Counter += 1;
Grandtotal += Empsalary;
Countdown -= 1;
Inventory -= Orderqty;
```

When you use these compound assignment operators with complex expressions, the entire expression is evaluated as a unit before the operator is processed. You can think of the entire concise expression as being enclosed in parentheses. The following expressions are equivalent:

```
Totalsale += Price + Price * Taxrate;
Totalsale = Totalsale + (Price + Price * Taxrate);
```

Of course, you can also explicitly code parentheses in the concise expression, if appropriate. To simplify code and prevent possible errors, most programmers restrict the use of the compound assignment operators to simple expressions.

6.5. Numeric Overflow, Truncation, and Field Sizes

With all arithmetic operations, one of your jobs as a programmer is to determine appropriate length and decimal position entries for result fields. It is important to allow sufficient room; otherwise, if a calculation produces an answer too big to store in the result field, a numeric overflow error or truncation occurs.

The computer stores the result of any arithmetic expression in the result field based on decimal position alignment. If the value to be stored is too large for the result field, overflow or truncation occurs, resulting in a runtime error or a loss of digits. If the overflow happens on the left side (high-order digits portion) of the result, a **numeric overflow error** occurs. Numeric overflow is a runtime error, which means your program stops and displays an error message to which the operator must respond. **Truncation** happens when the loss of digits is from the right end (the decimal portions) of the result field. Overflow or truncation occurs only when the answer has more digits (left or right of the decimal) than can fit in the result. If the answer has fewer digits, the system simply zero-fills the unneeded positions.

Overflow and truncation are important to understand because if they occur during a program's execution, the program can simply continue to run without issuing a warning that digits have been lost, or the program can end abnormally (**abend**). Losing 1/1000 of a dollar may not be the end of the world (although on a large run, it can add up), but losing $10,000 will probably cause your company some distress. Furthermore, program abends reflect poorly on the programmer.

In ILE RPG, all arithmetic expressions automatically—and without warning—truncate extra decimal positions (low-order truncation) to fit the value in the result variable's decimal positions. High-order overflow generates a runtime error that causes the program to end abnormally.

How do you determine a result field's size to ensure that truncation or abends do not inadvertently happen? Eval keeps track of any intermediate results that occur during the evaluation of its expression, maintaining full precision internally (up to limits imposed by numeric data types) until the expression is completely evaluated and ready to be stored in the result variable. However, you must analyze the expression (i.e., consider the operations it performs and whether it occurs within a loop) to estimate the size needed for the final result. Fortunately, some guidelines exist for result-variable definition to help you ensure that your result variables are large enough to store the calculated answers. The following sections present some guidelines for determining variable sizes of results occurring from two values and an operation. When in doubt, you can always manually perform some representative calculations that mirror what you want the computer to do to guide you in this matter.

6.5.1. Sizing Results for Addition

To avoid numeric overflow when adding two values, define the result variable with *one more* position *left of the decimal* than the larger of the addends' integer digit positions. Positions to the right of the decimal in the result field should equal the larger of the decimal positions of the addends. For example, if you're adding two fields, one defined as length 3.2 (i.e., one to the left and two to the right of the decimal) and one defined as length 6.3 (i.e., three to the left, three to the right of the decimal), you should define your result field as length 7.3 (four to the left, three to the right). To see why this rule eliminates the possibility of numeric overflow, simply do the addition with the largest possible values the addends can contain:

```
    999.999
+     9.99
=  1009.989
```

When you are using addition to count or accumulate, the value of the result increases each time the calculation is performed (e.g., when accumulating individuals' calculated gross pay figures to generate a grand total gross pay). In this case, to determine the necessary size of the result variable, you must have an approximate idea of how many times the calculation is to be performed (i.e., how many employees you will process). Once you have this estimate, follow the rule for multiplication, given below.

6.5.2. Sizing Results for Subtraction

To eliminate the chance of numeric overflow with subtraction, follow the rule given for addition. This advice may seem strange at first, until you realize that you must provide for the possibility of subtracting a negative number, which essentially turns the problem into one of addition.

Thus, to avoid numeric overflow when subtracting two values, define the result variable to have one more digit position to the left of the decimal position than the larger of the high-order positions of the two values. And define the result variable to have the same number of decimal positions as the larger of the number of decimal positions of the two values.

6.5.3. Sizing Results for Multiplication

When multiplying, to determine the needed number of digit positions in a result variable, add the number of positions to the left of the decimal positions of the two multipliers, and use the resulting value to determine the number of high-order digits in the result. The sum of the number of positions to the right of the decimal in the multipliers represents the number of positions your result variable must have to the right of the decimal.

For example, if you multiply 999.99 by 99.99, your result field will require five places to the left of the decimal and four to the right to store the answer without overflow. In RPG, this means a variable nine positions long with four decimal positions:

```
    999.99
*    99.99
= 99989.0001
```

6.5.4. Sizing Results for Division

When you divide by a value of 1 or greater, the maximum required positions—to the left of the decimal in the result—is the number of high-order decimal positions in the dividend (the value *being* divided). To understand this point, recognize that dividing any value by 1 yields the original value; dividing by any value greater than 1 yields a value smaller than the original value.

However, when you divide by values less than 1, computing the number of digit positions in the result becomes a more complicated process—the smaller the divisor, the more significant positions needed in the result variable. If you are working with divisors less than 1, your safest approach is to manually calculate with some representative values to get a sense of the size required to store your answer.

Because few divisions work out evenly, there is no way to guarantee you will provide enough decimal positions to avoid low-order truncation. In general, you choose the number of decimal positions for the result variable based on the degree of significance, or accuracy, that the calculation warrants. Because most business data processing deals with calculations involving currency (e.g., dollars and cents), it usually makes sense to do intermediate calculations with the maximum needed or the maximum allowable number of decimal positions (whichever is smaller) and then to reduce that to two decimal positions in the final calculation.

6.6. Rounding

When you store a value in a result variable that has fewer decimal positions than the calculated answer, common business practice dictates that you always round your answer rather than let the system truncate it. Rounding is sometimes called **half-adjusting** because of the technique computers use to accomplish this deed. The computer adds half the value of your rightmost desired decimal position to the digit immediately to the right of that decimal position before storing the answer in the result field. Because the value added is half the value of the least-significant digit position of your result, the term *half-adjust* came into being.

For example, assume the computer has calculated an answer of 3.14156 that you want to store, in rounded form, in a result field defined as length 4 with three decimal positions. The computer adds 0.0005 to the answer (i.e., 1/2 of 0.001, the lowest decimal position you are retaining in your result), yielding 3.14206. It then stores this value in the result field, truncated to three decimal positions, as 3.142. If you define the result as length 3 with two decimal positions, the computer adds 0.005 (1/2 of 0.01) to 3.14156, yielding 3.14656, and stores that answer in the result as 3.14.

Fortunately, even if you don't completely understand how the computer rounds numbers, the syntax ILE RPG uses to specify that rounding take place is simple: just enter an H (for half-adjust) within parentheses immediately following the operation code of the calculation whose result you want rounded. ILE RPG calls this entry an **operation extender** because it extends the function that the operation normally performs. The following examples show the use of the (H) operation extender:

```
// Sample calculations specifying that the result should be rounded
Eval(h) Interest = Rate * Loanamt;
Eval(h) Avgamount = Totamount / Counter;
Eval(h) Yards = Sqyards **.5;
```

Note that you must include the H in every calculation line where you want rounding to occur, even if those calculations use the same result field. The compiler does *not* warn you if you inadvertently omit an extender. Also note that you must explicitly code the Eval operation if you plan to use the H extender.

```
// In the below calcs, rounding is specified in each calculation
// that is to result in a rounded value for interest
Eval(h) Interest = Loanamt * Stdrate;
Eval(h) Interest = Altamt * Primerate;
```

Rounding occurs as the last step in evaluating the expression. If the expression is complex—encompassing several operands and several operators—the result is rounded only once, just before Eval assigns the value. In the following example, the individual clauses in the expression are *not* rounded. Instead, they are carried out to their full precision, and only the end result is rounded.

```
Eval(h) Pay = Hourlyrate * 40 + 1.5 * Hourlyrate * (Hoursworked - 40);
```

Although you most often need to round when multiplying or dividing, you can also specify rounding for addition and subtraction operations as well as for multiplication and division. Recognize that you do not always have to round when multiplying. For example, consider the following expression:

```
Inventoryvalue = Qtyonhand * Unitprice;
```

If Qtyonhand is an integer (whole number) and Unitprice is stored as dollars and cents (e.g., length 4.2), the resulting answer never contains more than two decimal positions, so you do *not* need to round the answer to store it in Inventoryvalue, defined as length 6.2.

Caution
Sometimes, out of either uncertainty or laziness, programmers decide to play it safe by rounding all arithmetic operations, regardless of whether the rounding is required. Avoid this practice. The ILE RPG compiler issues a warning message about unnecessary half-adjusting, performance may suffer, and rounding when uncalled for reflects poorly on your programming skills and style.

6.7. Improving Eval Precision

After accounting for all issues involving operator precedence, the Eval operation evaluates complex expressions from left to right, automatically allocating memory for any intermediate values the operation may need to evaluate an expression. These intermediate numeric values are limited in size to 63 total digits, including digits to the right of the decimal. Eval uses rules similar to those previously discussed to avoid size overflow within these intermediate values. In some complex expressions, or with some large operands, Eval may be forced to truncate low-order decimal positions from an intermediate result to fit the intermediate field into 63 total digits. This truncation can affect the precision of Eval's results.

To ensure the best accuracy when using Eval, instruct RPG that no intermediate value is to have fewer decimal places than the end result. This instruction, called the **result decimal positions rule** for evaluating expressions, is *not* the rule RPG uses by default. You can invoke this rule two ways:

- using the Expropts Control specification keyword
- using the (R) operation code extender

Typically, it's best to make the result decimal positions rule the default method within an RPG program by including the following Control specification keyword at the beginning of each program:

```
Ctl-opt Expropts(*Resdecpos);
```

When you include this keyword value, the RPG program uses the result decimal positions rule as its default method for evaluating *all* expressions. Using this rule helps ensure adequate decimal precision throughout the program. If you do not include this Control specification—or if you specify Expropts(*Maxdigits)—the program uses its own default rule, called the **maximum digits rule,** which can cause incorrect results for complex expressions.

If you want a *single* Eval operation to evaluate an expression with a different rule than you specified in the Control specifications, you can override the rule with an operation code extender. Specifying Eval(r) forces Eval to use the result decimal positions rule, and using Eval(m) forces the maximum digits rule. Note that you can combine several operation code extenders within the parentheses after the operation. The following example not only ensures Eval precision but also rounds (half-adjust) the result:

```
Eval(hr) Pay = Hourlyrate * 40 + 1.5 * Hourlyrate * (Hoursworked - 40);
```

6.8. Using Built-in Functions

ILE RPG supports many **built-in functions** that you use along with free-form expressions. These provide new functions that aren't available by coding simple expressions. Built-in functions always begin with a percent sign (%). You typically code built-in functions within free-format expressions in the program. You've already seen how to use the %Eof built-in function to return the end-of-file condition to a program. In addition to returning file operation results, functions can simplify complex calculations, perform string operations, and do data-type conversion. Let's examine some functions that you can use in arithmetic calculations:

- %Abs (Absolute value)
- %Div (Integer division)
- %Rem (Remainder)
- %Sqrt (Square root)

6.8.1. %Abs (Absolute Value)

The **%Abs (Absolute value)** built-in function calculates the absolute value of a numeric expression (or a numeric field or literal). This function essentially removes the sign from an expression's result. You specify the expression within parentheses immediately following the %Abs notation in the expression:

```
// In this example, Transtotal will be positive regardless of whether
// the expression results in a positive or a negative number.
Transtotal = %Abs(Debits - Credits);
```

6.8.2. %Div (Integer Division)

The **%Div (Integer division)** built-in function performs integer division of two numbers (literals, fields, or expressions) and returns the resulting integer quotient. The two numbers are passed as arguments, within parentheses—first the dividend then the divisor—and separated by a colon (:), immediately following the %Div notation. The arguments must be numeric values with no decimal places. The result of the division is also numeric with no decimal places. The division operator (/), however, performs precise division, including decimal places in the quotient if the result field is defined with decimal places.

```
// Convert total minutes to hours by dividing total minutes by 60.
// Hours is accurate to the number of decimal places defined for it.
Hours = Minutes/60;


// The %Div function will return only the integer portion of Hours,
// regardless of how many decimal places are defined for it.
Hours = %Div(Minutes:60);
```

6.8.3. %Rem (Remainder)

The **%Rem (Remainder)** built-in function returns the integer remainder when dividing two numbers (literals, fields, or expressions). The two numbers are passed as two arguments—first the dividend, then the divisor—immediately following the %Rem notation. Although programmers often use %Rem with the %Div function, it is not necessary to actually perform the division operation to obtain the remainder.

```
// Convert total minutes to hours and minutes by dividing total
// minutes by 60 to get hours and then returning the remainder as
// Minutes.
Hours = %Div(Minutes:60);
Minutes = %Rem(Minutes:60);
```

6.8.4. %Sqrt (Square Root)

The **%Sqrt (Square root)** function returns the square root of a numeric expression. The expression, which must have a positive value, is included in parentheses immediately following the %Sqrt notation. The %Sqrt function returns a value that is accurate to the number of decimal places defined for the result. You can use the (h) extender with Eval to round the result.

```
Eval(h) Hypotenuse = %Sqrt(Length**2 + Width**2);
```

6.8.5. Data-Conversion Functions

RPG requires that all the operands in an expression be of compatible data types. The program cannot mix numeric data and character variables in the same expression, even if the character variables include only numbers. Several built-in functions convert character expressions to numeric formats, or force numeric expressions into a specific numeric size. The frequently used data-conversion functions are as follows:

- %Dec (Convert to packed decimal format)
- %Dech (Convert to packed decimal format with half-adjust)
- %Int (Convert to signed integer format)
- %Inth (Convert to signed integer format with half-adjust)
- %Uns (Convert to unsigned integer format)
- %Unsh (Convert to unsigned integer format with half-adjust)

The **%Dec (Convert to packed decimal format)** function converts the result of a numeric, character, or date expression to a packed decimal format of the precision you specify. You code the numeric expression as the first parameter within parentheses following %Dec. The next two parameters indicate the number of digits and the number of decimal positions in the result.

```
Result = %Dec(Hours*Rate : 7 : 2);

// This formula calculates a monthly payment, converting it to a
// 13-digit packed number with two decimal places
Payment = %Dec(Principal * (((Interest / 12) *
                (1 + (Interest / 12)) ** Months) /
                (((1 + (Interest / 12)) ** Months) - 1))
                : 13 : 2);
```

A related function, **%Dech (Convert to packed decimal format with half-adjust)**, performs the same data conversion but rounds the result. This feature is useful for rounding individual components of a complex expression. Recall that when you code the (h) extender for Eval, the half-adjusting occurs only once, after the entire expression is evaluated. Using the (h) extender will not round the intermediate results, but by using %Dech, you can round just a portion of the expression:

```
// This formula calculates total pay, by first calculating regular pay
// and overtime pay, rounding each component (accurate to 11 digits
// with two decimal places), then adding them together
Pay = %Dech(Hourlyrate * 40 : 11 :2) +
      %Dech(1.5 * Hourlyrate * (Hoursworked - 40) : 11 : 2);

// This formula calculates a monthly payment, rounding the result,
// returning a 13-digit packed number with two decimal places
Payment = %Dech(Principal * (((Interest / 12) *
                (1 + (Interest / 12)) ** Months) /
                (((1 + (Interest / 12)) ** Months) - 1))
                : 13 : 2);
```

The integer-related functions perform functions similar to %Dec, but they return integer (signed or unsigned) results:

```
// Find the area of a circle as a rounded whole number
Result = %Inth(3.14159 * Radius**2);

// Truncate the decimal positions from a packed number
// to allow it to be used as an array element (no rounding)
X = %Uns(Hrsworked);
```

You can also use any of the conversion functions (e.g., %Dec, %Int, %Uns) to convert character expressions to numeric representation. This feature is useful when you need to use a character variable's value within an arithmetic expression. The character value must, of course, ultimately be numeric information. It can include a sign (either preceding or following the numbers) and a radix point as well as blanks anywhere in the data. The following code illustrates some examples of using these functions to convert character data:

```
Dcl-s Var1    Char(11)    Inz('123.456789-');
Dcl-s Var2    Char(11)    Inz(' + 9 . 876 ');
Dcl-s Result Packed(9:5);


Result = %Dec(Var1:5:2);          // Result =  -123.45000
Result = %Dech(Var2:5:2);         // Result =     9.88000
Result = %Dech(Var2:5:2) / 3;     // Result =     3.29333
Result = %Int(Var2:5:2);          // Result =     9.00000
Result = %Inth(Var2:5:2);         // Result =    10.00000
Result = %Uns(Var1:5:2);          // Result =   123.00000
```

ILE RPG supports many other built-in functions, and you'll learn about those functions throughout the text. Now, though, you know the key information about how to use built-in functions in your program. Built-in functions always begin with a % sign. They are coded within free-form expressions. To pass arguments to a function, pass them within parentheses immediately following the name of the function, and separate multiple arguments with colon (:) separators:

```
%function(argument1:argument2:...)
```

6.9. Navigating Legacy Code

6.9.1. Fixed-Format Numeric Operations

Free-format processing and the Extended–Factor 2 variant of Calculation specifications support the familiar operators for arithmetic operations: + for addition, - for subtraction, * for multiplication, / for division, and ** for exponentiation. Because the traditional Calculation format did not allow expressions, RPG programs written in the past may rely on several fixed-format operations to accomplish arithmetic:

- ADD
- DIV (Divide)

- MULT (Multiply)
- MVR (Move remainder)
- SQRT (Square root)
- SUB (Subtract)
- Z-ADD (Zero and add)
- Z-SUB (Zero and subtract)

All these operation codes work only with numeric Factor 1 and Factor 2 and a numeric Result. Complex expressions, requiring several computations, require several lines of code.

The Add, Sub, Mult, and Div operations are self-explanatory. They process the values in Factor 1 (positions 12–25) and Factor 2 (36–44), placing the result into the Result position (50–63):

```
*.. 1 ...+... 2 ...+... 3 ...+... 4 ...+... 5 ...+... 6 ...+... 7 ...+... 8
CLON01Factor1+++++++Opcode(E)+Factor2+++++++Result++++++++Len++D+HiLoEq....
C     {addend}     Add       addend       sum
C     {minuend}    Sub       subtrahend   difference
C     {factor}     Mult      factor       product
C     {dividend}   Div       divisor      quotient
```

If you omit Factor 1, the Result is treated as Factor 1. So the following two operations are equivalent:

```
*.. 1 ...+... 2 ...+... 3 ...+... 4 ...+... 5 ...+... 6 ...+... 7 ...+... 8
CLON01Factor1+++++++Opcode(E)+Factor2+++++++Result++++++++Len++D+HiLoEq....
C     Totalsales   Add       Orderamount   Totalsales
C                  Add       Orderamount   Totalsales
```

The Z-add and Z-sub operations zero the Result and then add or subtract Factor 2. In effect, they assign the value in Factor 2 to the Result, similar to the free-format Eval operation:

```
*.. 1 ...+... 2 ...+... 3 ...+... 4 ...+... 5 ...+... 6 ...+... 7 ...+... 8
CLON01Factor1+++++++Opcode(E)+Factor2+++++++Result++++++++Len++D+HiLoEq....
C                  Z-add     .0756         Taxrate
                   // Eval    Taxrate = .0756
```

The Mvr operation always immediately follows a Div operation. It returns to the Result the remainder from the previous Div operation. The following code divides Uyear (an RPG reserved word representing the current year) by 4, putting the quotient into variable X, and then placing the remainder into variable Y:

```
*.. 1 ...+... 2 ...+... 3 ...+... 4 ...+... 5 ...+... 6 ...+... 7 ...+... 8
CLON01Factor1+++++++Opcode(E)+Factor2+++++++Result++++++++Len++D+HiLoEq....
C     UYear       Div       4             X
C                 Mvr                     Y
                  // Eval     X = %Div(Uyear:4)
                  // Eval     Y = %Rem(Uyear:4)
```

As you might expect, the Sqrt operation assigns the square root of Factor 2 to the Result:

```
*.. 1 ...+... 2 ...+... 3 ...+... 4 ...+... 5 ...+... 6 ...+... 7 ...+... 8
CLON01Factor1+++++++Opcode(E)+Factor2+++++++Result++++++++Len++D+HiLoEq....
C                 Sqrt      X             Y
                  // Eval     Y = %Sqrt(X)
```

6.9.2. Result Field Definition

Before ILE RPG, no single place existed in the program to define the standalone variables the program would need. Instead, the fixed-format C-specs allowed you to define character or numeric variables *on the fly*, as the program used them. Positions 64–68 (Len++) specify the length in bytes or digits, and for numbers, positions 69–70 (D+) indicate the number of decimal places:

```
*.. 1 ...+... 2 ...+... 3 ...+... 4 ...+... 5 ...+... 6 ...+... 7 ...+... 8
CLON01Factor1+++++++Opcode(E)+Factor2+++++++Result++++++++Len++D+HiLoEq....
C                 Z-add     .0756        Taxrate        7 7
                  // Taxrate is defined as Packed(7:7)
C                 Move      'Y'          Taxable        1
                  // Taxable is defined as Char(1)
```

C-spec definitions make your program difficult to debug and prone to error. You should never use C-spec definitions to define variables, but you may encounter such definitions in legacy programs.

6.9.3. Resulting Indicators

Chapter 5 examined numbered indicators in the context of conditioning indicators, which fixed-format C-specs use to make the execution of a code line dependent upon a numbered indicator's state. Fixed-format C-specs also support *resulting* indicators in positions 71–76 (HiLoEq) to reflect the result of executing an operation. Numeric operation codes can set resulting indicators to signal whether the arithmetic operation's result is positive, negative, or zero. You can subsequently use resulting indicators as conditioning indicators in fixed-format Calculation specifications or Output specifications.

If the program specifies one or more resulting indicators, the appropriate indicator is set to on by an arithmetic operation. The indicator in the Hi position (71–72) is set to on if the result is positive, the indicator in the Lo position (73–74) is set to on if the result is negative, and the indicator in the Eq position (75–76) is set to on if the result is zero.

```
*.. 1 ...+... 2 ...+... 3 ...+... 4 ...+... 5 ...+... 6 ...+... 7 ...+... 8
CLON01Factor1+++++++Opcode(E)+Factor2+++++++Result+++++++Len++D+HiLoEq....
C      UYear       Div     4           X
C                  Mvr                 Y                        50
```

In this example, if no remainder is in variable Y (i.e., Y=0), indicator 50 is set to *On; otherwise, it is set to *Off. The following example sets indicator 51 to *On if the result is non-zero; otherwise, indicator 51 is *Off:

```
*.. 1 ...+... 2 ...+... 3 ...+... 4 ...+... 5 ...+... 6 ...+... 7 ...+... 8
CLON01Factor1+++++++Opcode(E)+Factor2+++++++Result+++++++Len++D+HiLoEq....
C      Taxable     Mult    Taxrate     Tax                     5151
```

6.10. Chapter Summary

ILE RPG provides the Eval operation with standard arithmetic operators to use for computations. Eval can express complex arithmetic calculations in a single, free-form expression that can continue over several lines, if necessary. Such expressions can include the arithmetic operators (+, -, *, /, and **); parentheses; numeric fields; and numeric literals. You can use numeric fields, numeric literals, and figurative constants in arithmetic calculations.

You can usually forgo explicitly coding the Eval operation. Simply code the assignment expression instead. To improve Eval's precision in complex expressions and with large operands, always specify keyword Expropts(*Resdecpos) in the program's Control specifications.

Calculations often involve creating new fields to store the results of the calculations. You must define these new fields by specifying their data type, length, and number of decimal positions (if numeric) within Dcl-s or Dcl-ds declarations. The size of result fields should be large enough to avoid numeric overflow and truncation. If an arithmetic operation's result contains more decimal positions than you want to store, you should round the calculation.

ILE RPG supports many built-in functions to simplify complex calculations and perform data-type conversion. Built-in functions always begin with a % sign, and you code them within free-form expressions. To pass values to a built-in function, enclose the values within parentheses immediately following the name of the function, and separate multiple values with colon (:) separators.

The following table summarizes the operation codes and built-in functions discussed in this chapter. Optional entries appear within curly braces ({}):

Function or Operation	Description	Syntax
%Abs	Absolute value	%Abs(numeric-expression)
%Dec%Dech	Convert to packed decimal (with optional half-adjust)	%Dec(expression {: precision : scale}) %Dech(expression : precision : scale)
%Div	Integer division	%Div(dividend : divisor)
Eval	Evaluate expression	{Eval{(hmr)}} assignment-expression;
%Int%Inth	Convert to integer (with optional half-adjust)	%Int(expression) %Inth(expression)
%Rem	Integer remainder	%Rem(dividend : divisor)
%Sqrt	Square root	%Sqrt(numeric-expression)
%Uns%Unsh	Convert to unsigned integer (with optional half-adjust)	%Uns(expression) %Unsh(expression)

6.11. Key Terms

abend
%Abs (Absolute value)
assignment operation
built-in function
compound operators
conversion functions
%Dec (Convert to packed decimal format)
%Div (Integer division)
exponentiation

Eval (Evaluate expression)
Expropts Control specification keyword
half-adjusting
*Hival
%Int (Convert to integer format)
*Loval
maximum digits rule
numeric overflow

operation extender
%Rem (Remainder)
result decimal positions rule
rules of precedence
%Sqrt (Square root)
truncation
%Uns (Convert to unsigned integer format)
*Zero

6.12. Discussion/Review Questions

1. What is the difference between assigning a value to a field by using the INZ keyword in the declarations section and assigning a value to a field in the calculations?

2. Why does it make sense that the result of a calculation or a free-form expression cannot be a literal?

3. What two mathematical impossibilities will result in a program error if your program tries to execute them?

4. Summarize the rules for determining how large to define result fields for arithmetic operations.

5. When should you round an arithmetic operation?

6. Name three uses for operation code extenders.

7. Would it be better to set EVAL precision rules to use the result decimal positions rule by using a Ctl-opt instruction or an operation code extender? Why or why not?

8. Give three examples of using data-conversion functions in ILE RPG.

9. What are some of the advantages of using built-in functions (BIFs)?

10. Why is it important for a programmer to understand how ILE RPG handles rounding?

11. How do you invoke the Expropts keyword? What effect does it have on the program?

12. Explain the use of the *Zero, *Hival, and *Loval figurative constants.

13. Why is it important for a programmer to understand overflow and truncation?

14. Several mathematical BIFs were discussed in this chapter. List these BIFs and their use.

15. Several data-conversion BIFs were discussed in this chapter. List these BIFs and their use.

6.13. Exercises

1. Write the calculations to discount field OldPrice (six digits, two decimal positions) by 10 percent to yield NewPrice.

2. Write the calculations to convert a temperature in Fahrenheit to Celsius by using the following formula:

$$C = F(F - 32) / 9$$

Assume F and C are three positions each with zero decimal positions.

3. Write the calculations to convert a measurement taken in inches (field Inches, five positions with zero decimal positions) into the same measurement expressed as yards, feet, and inches.

4. Code the calculations needed to determine the cost of wall-to-wall carpeting for a room. Field RmLength (three positions, one decimal) contains the room length in feet, field RmWidth (also three positions, one decimal) contains the room's width in feet, and field CostPerYard (four positions, two decimals) contains the cost per yard of the selected carpet.

5. Write the calculations to determine the economic order quantity (EOQ) by using the following formula:

```
EOQ = square root of (2DO / C)
```

where D (five positions, zero decimals) represents annual demand for product, O (five positions, two decimals) signifies costs to place one order, and C (six positions, two decimals) indicates carrying costs.

6. Write the formula to convert the following, and round any remainders to two decimals:

- 10.5 inches to centimeters
- 65.25 degrees Fahrenheit to Celsius
- 15.15 miles per hour to knots per hour
- 153.7 meters to feet

7. Give an example of using the %Div and %Rem BIFs to solve a problem.

8. Define the necessary standalone variables, and write the calculations to determine the total cost of ownership (TCO) by using the following formula and information:

```
TCO = P + Present Value of (O + T + SM + B - S)
```

Expense Area—5 years	System A	System B
P = Purchase costs	150,000.00	75,000.00
O = Operating costs—yearly	65,000.000	50,000.00
T = Training costs—once	30,000.00	55,000.00
SM = Software maintenance costs—yearly	62,000.00	75,000.00
B = Building—monthly	8,000.00	10,000.00
S = Salvage value	25,000.00	10,000.00

Processing Character Data

7.1. Chapter Overview

Most business programming centers around numeric information and arithmetic processes. But character data also plays a large part in many applications. In this chapter, you learn how to process, manipulate, combine, and inspect character-based information by using expressions. You'll become familiar with the rich set of built-in functions that ILE RPG uses with character data. In addition, you learn how to convert numeric data to character data so that you can use numeric data with character processing.

7.2. Simple Character Assignment

In Chapter 6, you used the Eval (Evaluate expression) operation to evaluate arithmetic expressions. Now that you know how to use Eval to assign values to numeric fields by using expressions, let's look at how to assign values to character fields. As you might guess, Eval easily handles this task as a simple assignment expression (recall that explicitly coding Eval is optional):

```
Email = 'jdoe@mydomain.com';
```

Just as in numeric assignment operations, you place the value to assign (in this case, a character literal) to the right of the equal sign and put the target variable, the result, to the left. If the literal is too long to fit on one line, or if you need to continue a long literal to another line to meet a style guideline, use a continuation character (+) to signal to the computer that the literal continues on the next line:

```
Disclaimer = 'This report contains proprietary and confidential +
                           information, and is for internal use only.'
```

Remember that when you use the + continuation character, the continuation starts with the first nonblank character in the subsequent line. The entire literal must be enclosed within a single pair of apostrophes ('). If the literal includes an apostrophe character, use two apostrophes to represent it.

The Eval operation performs the assignment by transferring the literal character by character, starting with the leftmost character. If the result variable that receives the literal is defined to be longer than the character literal, Eval pads the variable with blanks (i.e., it fills the unused positions at the right end of the variable with blanks). But if the result variable is too small to store the literal, Eval truncates the extra rightmost characters, without warning or error.

```
Dcl-s Var1 Char(7);
Dcl-s Var2 Char(12);
Dcl-s Var3 Char(12) Inz('mnopqrstuvwx');
Dcl-s Var4 Char(4);


Var1 = 'ABCDEFG';       // Var1 = 'ABCDEFG'
Var2 = 'ABCDEFG';       // Var2 = 'ABCDEFG     '
Var3 = 'ABCDEFG';       // Var3 = 'ABCDEFG     '
Var4 = 'ABCDEFG';       // Var4 = 'ABCD'
```

Notice that when the result variable is longer than the character literal, the result is padded with blanks even if it already contains other data, as the preceding example shows for the Var3 variable.

You can also use Eval to assign the contents of one character field to another. The same rules apply regarding padding and truncation.

```
Dcl-s Coursename Char(5) Inz('CS365');
Dcl-s Padcourse  Char(10);
Dcl-s Prefix     Char(2);


Padcourse = Coursename;     // Padcourse = 'CS365     '
Prefix = Coursename;        // Prefix = 'CS'
```

7.2.1. Evalr (Evaluate Expression, Right-Adjust)

The Eval operation assigns values by transferring the result of the character expression character by character, starting with the leftmost character, right padding the result with blanks if necessary. A related operation, **Evalr (Evaluate expression, right-adjust)**, works with character assignment when you want to right-adjust the result. Evalr assigns the character value starting with the *rightmost* character. If the result variable that receives the value is defined to be longer than the character value, Evalr *left pads* the variable with blanks (i.e., it fills the unused positions at the left end of the variable with blanks). Evalr does not work with numeric expressions, and unlike Eval, it must always be explicitly coded in the program. To see how Evalr works, compare the following code with the previous character assignment examples:

```
Dcl-s Var1 Char(7);
Dcl-s Var2 Char(12);
Dcl-s Var3 Char(12) Inz('mnopqrstuvwx');
Dcl-s Var4 Char(4);


Evalr Var1 = 'ABCDEFG';     // Var1 = 'ABCDEFG'
Evalr Var2 = 'ABCDEFG';     // Var2 = '     ABCDEFG'
Evalr Var3 = 'ABCDEFG';     // Var3 = '     ABCDEFG'
Evalr Var4 = 'ABCDEFG';     // Var4 = 'DEFG'
```

7.2.2. Eval-corr (Assign corresponding subfields)

The **Eval-corr (Assign corresponding subfields)** operation is a specialized version of Eval used with data structures. Eval-corr assigns subfields of one data structure to the corresponding subfields of another data structure in a single operation. To be included in an Eval-corr operation, the subfield names must be identical in both data structures and must have compatible data attributes. Their subfields need not be in the same order or have identical data attributes, but they must be compatible (i.e., Eval-corr does not assign a numeric subfield in one data structure to an identically named character subfield in another data structure). You use Eval-corr with an assignment expression:

```
Eval-corr target-ds = source-ds;
```

Both the target and the source must be data structures. At least one of the data structures must be a qualified data structure (discussed in Chapter 4); otherwise, it is impossible for them to have identically named subfields.

You may find Eval-corr a useful shortcut when your program is processing data structures. Consider the following example:

```
Dcl-ds Customer Qualified;
  Identifier  Zoned(5:0);
  Name        Char(30);
  State       Char(2);
  Zipcode     Char(10);
  Phone       Char(10);
  Creditlimit Zoned(11:2);
End-ds;

Dcl-ds Vendor Qualified;
  Identifier Uns(5);
  Name        Char(35);
  Address     Char(35);
  City        Char(21);
  State       Char(2);
  Postcode    Char(10);
  Phone       Zoned(10:0);
End-ds;

Eval-corr Customer = Vendor;
```

The single Eval-corr operation is equivalent to the following expressions:

```
Customer.Identifier = Vendor.Identifier;
Customer.Name = Vendor.Name;
Customer.State = Vendor.State;
```

The following table describes how Eval-corr processes each of the subfields:

Vendor (Source)	Customer (Target)	Action
Identifier	Identifier	Subfield assigned; both subfields are numeric, even though they are different data types
Name	Name	Subfield assigned, with truncation
Address	--	No target subfield; subfield ignored
City	--	No target subfield; subfield ignored

(Continued)

Vendor (Source)	Customer (Target)	Action
State	State	Subfield assigned
Postcode	Zipcode	Different subfield names; subfields ignored
Phone	Phone	Incompatible data types; subfields ignored
--	Creditlimit	No source subfield; subfield ignored

Each subfield's assignment follows the same rules as the Eval operation (e.g., character fields are left-adjusted, numeric subfields are aligned at the decimal). Data is assigned in the order of the subfields in the source data structure. If any subfields in the target data structure use the Overlay keyword, later assignments can overwrite earlier assignments.

7.2.3. Assigning Values with Figurative Constants

RPG lets you assign figurative constant ***Blank** (or *Blanks) to character variables to fill the variables with blanks. You can also assign the special values *Zero (or *Zeros) to fill character variables with zeros. *Hival and *Loval are also valid with character variables; *Hival is all bits on (X'FF'), and *Loval is all bits off (X'00').

Assigning figurative constant ***All** immediately followed by one or more characters in apostrophes causes the string within the apostrophes to be cyclically repeated through the entire length of the result field. A related figurative constant, *Allx, works the same as *All, except that you can specify hexadecimal character strings.

```
Dcl-s Var        Char(9);
Dcl-s Underline  Char(80);


Var = *Blanks;           // Var = '         '
Var = *Zeros;            // Var = '000000000'
Var = *Hival;            // Var is now filled with X'FF' characters
Var = *Loval;            // Var is now filled with X'00' characters
Var = *All'Z';           // Var = 'ZZZZZZZZZ'
Var = *All'Abc';         // Var = 'AbcAbcAbc'
Var = *Allx'E9'          // Var = 'ZZZZZZZZZ' (X'E9' = Z)
Var = *Allx'C18283'      // Var = 'AbcAbcAbc' (X'C18283' = Abc)
Underline = *All'-'      // Underline is now 80 hyphens
```

Figurative constants *Off and *On represent character '0' and character '1', respectively. Although you can use *Off and *On with any character variable of any length, programmers most often use these constants to assign a value to an indicator or to compare with an indicator's value. You have used *On and *Off previously in this text with Eval to set indicators on or off.

7.3. Concatenating Character Values

In the previous sections, you saw how to use Eval and Evalr for simple character assignment. These operations also provide a flexible and powerful method for joining character values together; this process is called **concatenation**. Use the + operator to concatenate two or more character values—which can be variables, literals, or constants—and assign the resulting new character value to a variable. A single concatenation expression can contain as many + operators and character operands as needed to accomplish a desired concatenation. The following examples demonstrate how to use + to concatenate strings:

```
Dcl-s Greeting   Char(12);
Dcl-s Fullname   Char(16);
Dcl-s Fullname2  Char(25);
Dcl-s Firstname  Char(5)  Inz('Susan');
Dcl-s Firstname2 Char(10) Inz('Susan');
Dcl-s Midinitial Char(1)  Inz('B');
Dcl-s Lastname   Char(7)  Inz('Anthony');
Dcl-s Lastname2  Char(10) Inz('Anthony');

Greeting = 'Hello ' + 'World';      // Greeting = 'Hello World '

Fullname = Firstname + ' ' + Midinitial + '. ' + Lastname;
                                  // Fullname = 'Susan B. Anthony'

Fullname2 = Firstname2 + ' ' + Midinitial + '. ' + Lastname2;
                                  // Fullname2 = 'Susan      B. Anthony      '
```

Notice in the last example that the new character value (Fullname2) retains all the blanks that were in the individual concatenated variables. Later, you'll examine two techniques for eliminating such unnecessary blanks.

If the concatenated string is smaller than the result variable to which it is assigned, Eval right pads the result variable with blanks. If the concatenated string is too large to fit in the result variable to which it is assigned, truncation occurs from the right end of the string. In this case, Evalr *left* pads the result and truncates from the *left*.

```
Dcl-s Firstname Char(5)  Inz('John');
Dcl-s Lastname  Char(12) Inz('Jackson III');
```

Continued

```
Dcl-s Longname  Char(25);
Dcl-s Shortname Char(10);


Longname = Firstname + Lastname;
               // Longname = 'John Jackson III          '
               // with blanks appearing in its unused rightmost positions


Shortname = Firstname + Lastname;
               // Shortname = 'John Jacks'
               // because it can store only 10 characters.


Evalr Longname = Firstname + Lastname;
               // Longname = '        John Jackson III '


Evalr Shortname = Firstname + Lastname;
               // Shortname = 'ckson III '
```

All values in the concatenation expression must, of course, be character variables, literals, or constants. You cannot use numeric values anywhere in the expression. The system executes the concatenation operations from left to right in the expression. There are no operator precedence issues to remember because the only allowed operator is the + concatenation operator.

If necessary, simply continue the expression anywhere on subsequent lines, and then use a semicolon (;) to end the expression. The following code illustrates the use of a continuation line when concatenating character values. This expression concatenates a character literal with a variable, and then it appends another literal on the end of the character string:

```
Disclaimer = 'This report is proprietary and confidential, for '
             + Companyname + ' internal use only.';
```

In this example, the plus signs (+) in the expression are concatenation operators, not continuation characters. No continuation characters are necessary unless you must continue a literal, as this chapter showed earlier.

7.4. Using Variable-Length Character Variables

All the character variables discussed so far have been **fixed-length character variables** with a specific declared length. ILE RPG also supports **variable-length character fields**. Like a fixed-length variable, a variable-length character variable has a **declared length**, which is its maximum length. But variable-length character variables also have a **current length**. The current length is generally dependent upon the variable's value, which can change while the program is running. Some character string processing is more efficient when the character string is a Varchar data type than when it is a fixed-length Char data type.

To define a variable-length character variable, use the **Varchar** keyword (or use the Like keyword to inherit the properties of an existing variable-length character variable). The variable cannot be a numeric data type. The variable's length (in parentheses) is its declared length (i.e., its maximum current length). The data item can be a standalone variable or a data structure subfield. When you define a Varchar data item, the system allocates enough memory for the entire declared length *plus either two or four additional bytes*. The computer uses this leftmost length prefix internally to store the current length of the variable. You usually never see these additional bytes, and you need not bother with them when processing the character value in the variable.

```
Dcl-s Email Varchar(256);
```

The Varchar keyword supports a second entry of either 2 or 4 to indicate how many bytes to allocate for the length prefix. Variable-length fields longer than 65,535 bytes *must* use a four-byte length prefix. For variable-length variables up to 65,535 bytes, the length prefix defaults to two bytes. For longer variables, the length prefix defaults to four bytes. Usually, you can depend on the default values and need not specify the length of the prefix. The maximum size of a variable-length character variable is 16,773,100 bytes.

```
// The following two definitions are equivalent, using two additional
// bytes to store the current length.
Dcl-s Firstvar Varchar(10);
Dcl-s Firstvar Varchar(10:2);

// This definition uses 4 additional bytes to store the current length.
Dcl-s Nextvar Varchar(10:4);

// The following two definitions are equivalent.
Dcl-s Longvar Varchar(16773100);
Dcl-s Longvar Varchar(16773100:4);
```

To initialize a variable-length character variable, you can use the Inz keyword. The initial current length, then, is the length of the initial value. The remaining allocated storage beyond the initial value is initialized to blanks, but these blanks are not part of the variable's value.

7.5. Using Built-in Functions with Character Data

The previous chapter examined several built-in functions that ILE RPG uses to simplify arithmetic expressions and to convert data to numeric data. ILE RPG also supports many built-in functions that you can use along with **character expressions**. These provide new functions that aren't available by coding simple concatenation. Most of the built-in functions that return character values return variable-length character values.

7.5.1. %Trim (Trim Characters at Edges)

The **%Trim (Trim characters)** function returns a character value after removing all leading and trailing blanks. The %Trim function has three variations: %Trim itself, %Triml, and %Trimr. %Trim removes both leading and trailing blanks, %Triml removes leading blanks only, and %Trimr removes trailing blanks only. The end result of all the %Trim functions is a **variable-length** character value (i.e., it has no defined fixed length).

```
%Trim('    New York    ') results in a value of 'New York'
%Triml('    New York    ') results in a value of 'New York    '
%Trimr('    New York    ') results in a value of '    New York'
```

Notice that the %Trim function removes only the blanks at the edges of the character value, not those inside the value. So, the preceding %Trim functions retain the blank inside 'New York' when trimming the blanks.

The %Trim functions are useful when you want to concatenate fixed-length character fields, which may contain blanks that you want to ignore in the final result. You can include the %Trim functions inside the concatenation expression to substitute the variable-length character value in the expression. The following example illustrates concatenation with and without the %Trim function:

```
Dcl-s Fullname  Char(25);
Dcl-s Firstname Char(10) Inz('Susan');
Dcl-s Midnitial Char(1)  Inz('B');
Dcl-s Lastname  Char(10) Inz('Anthony');
Dcl-s Lastname2 Char(10) Inz('  Anthony ');


Fullname = Firstname + ' ' + Midinitial + '. ' + Lastname;
                                 // Fullname = 'Susan     B. Anthony    '


                                                         Continued
```

```
Fullname = %Trim(Firstname) + ' ' + Midinitial + '. ' + Lastname;
                                  // Fullname = 'Susan B. Anthony            '

Fullname = Firstname + ' ' + Midinitial + '. ' + Lastname2;
                                  // Fullname = 'Susan       B.    Anthony '

Fullname = %Trim(Firstname) + ' ' + Midinitial + '. ' + Lastname2;
                                  // Fullname = 'Susan B.    Anthony         '

Fullname = %Trim(Firstname) + ' ' + Midinitial + '. ' + %Trim(Lastname2);
                                  // Fullname = 'Susan B. Anthony           '
```

Typically, you'll use the %Trim functions to remove blanks from a string, but you can also trim leading and trailing characters other than blanks. By coding one any of the %Trim functions with a second argument that lists one or more characters to trim, you can trim those characters from the edges of a character string:

```
Dcl-s Checkword Char(25) Inz('$*****7,654.32***');
Dcl-s Result    Char(20);

Result = Checkword;              // Result = '$*****7,654.32***    '

Result = %Trim(Checkword:'*');  // Result = '$*****7,654.32***    '
                                // Checkword contains leading $ and
                                // trailing blanks, but no edge asterisks.

Result = %Trim(Checkword:'$*'); // Result = '7,654.32***          '
                                // Checkword contains trailing blanks,
                                // so trailing asterisks are not trimmed.

Result = %Trim(Checkword:'$* '); // Result = '7,654.32             '
                                 // Edge $, * and blanks are all trimmed.
```

When you use a variable-length character variable in a character string operation, such as concatenation, you may not need to use the %Trim functions to obtain the desired results. Using Varchar data items can thereby improve the performance of your program as well as its readability. Compare the following examples:

```
Dcl-s Fullname Char(25);

Dcl-s First    Char(15)    Inz('Nelson');
Dcl-s Firstvar Varchar(15) Inz('Nelson');
Dcl-s Last     Char(10)    Inz('Mandela');

// The following lines give equivalent results.
Fullname = %Trim(First) + ' ' + Last;
Fullname = Firstvar + ' ' + Last;
```

7.5.2. %Subst (Get or Set Substring)

The **%Subst (Get or set substring)** function extracts a **substring**, or portion, of a character string. You code two or three arguments in parentheses immediately following the %Subst function:

1. the string from which the extraction is to occur
2. the position within that string where the substring is to start
3. optionally, the length of the substring

If you omit the third argument, the substring includes all the bytes from the starting position to the final, rightmost byte of the string. Thus, the format of the substring function is as follows:

```
%Subst(string:start{:length})
```

As with all functions, you use colon separators between arguments. You can represent the starting position and the optional length by using numeric variables, constants, or expressions that evaluate to integers greater than zero. If the length is too big given the starting position (i.e., the substring extends beyond the end of the string), a runtime error occurs. The following examples illustrate how to obtain a portion of a larger character string:

```
Dcl-s Phone     Char(10) Inz('9705551212');
Dcl-s Areacode  Char(3);
Dcl-s Exchange  Char(3);
Dcl-s Extension Char(4);
Dcl-s Longexten Char(7);
```

Continued

```
Areacode = %Subst(Phone:1:3);      // Areacode = '970'
Exchange = %Subst(Phone:4:3);      // Exchange = '555'
Extension = %Subst(Phone:7);       // Extension = '1212'
Longexten = %Subst(Phone:7);       // Extension = '1212   '
```

Like the other built-in functions discussed, %Subst can return a value needed within a calculation, as the preceding examples show. Unlike with most other functions, you can also use %Subst as the target (or result) of an assignment operation to change a designated substring's value. For this use, the designated string must be a variable that can be assigned a value; a constant, for example, is inappropriate. The following examples illustrate this use of %Subst:

```
Dcl-s Areacode Char(3)  Inz('406');
Dcl-s Phone    Char(10) Inz('9705551212');
Dcl-s Phone2   Char(10) Inz('9516547531');


%Subst(Phone:1:3) = '613';                    // Phone = '6135551212'
%Subst(Phone:1:3) = Areacode;                 // Phone = '4065551212'
%Subst(Phone:4:3) = %Subst(Phone2:4:3);       // Phone = '4066541212'
```

7.5.3. %Replace (Replace Character String)

The **%Replace (Replace character string)** function changes a character string value by replacing existing characters with new values. The format for the %Replace function is as follows:

```
%Replace(new-string:old-string{:start{:length}})
```

The first argument—which can be a character variable, literal, or expression—supplies the replacement string to insert into the original character string, which is the second argument—a character variable.

You can optionally specify a starting position. If you omit this third argument, the replacement occurs at the beginning of the original character variable. The fourth argument is also optional. It specifies how many characters to replace. The third and fourth optional arguments can be numeric variables, literal, or expressions. Omitting the fourth argument causes the number of characters to be the same as the length of the replacement string.

```
Dcl-s Areacode  Char(3) Inz('406');
Dcl-s Extension Char(3) Inz('690');
Dcl-s Phone     Char(10)Inz('9705551212');


Phone = %Replace('613':Phone);          // Phone = '6135551212'
Phone = %Replace(Areacode:Phone);       // Phone = '4065551212'
Phone = %Replace(Extension:Phone:4);    // Phone = '4066901212'
```

You can also specify that you want to insert a new value, without replacing any existing characters, by specifying 0 as the fourth argument:

```
Dcl-s First   Char(5)  Inz('John');
Dcl-s Initial Char(1)  Inz('J');
Dcl-s Middle  Char(7)  Inz(' Quincy');
Dcl-s Name    Char(17) Inz('B. Adams');


Name = %Replace(Initial:Name);        // Name = 'J. Adams         '
Name = %Replace(First:Name:1:2);      // Name = 'John Adams        '
Name = %Replace(Middle:Name:5:0);     // Name = 'John Quincy Adams'
```

7.5.4. %Scanrpl (Scan and Replace Characters)

The **%Scanrpl (Scan and replace characters)** function changes a character string by replacing every existing occurrence of a value in the string with a new value. The result is a new character string with the substituted values. The format for the %Scanrpl function is as follows:

```
%Scanrpl(old-value:new-value:string{:start{:length}})
```

The first argument supplies the original character value to be replaced by the new value, which is the second argument. The third argument is the character string to scan.

You can optionally specify a scan range in the fourth and fifth arguments; that is, you can indicate a starting position (fourth argument) and a number of characters to scan (fifth argument). If you omit these arguments, the entire string is scanned. Omitting the fifth argument causes the function to scan from the starting position to the end of the string. If you do specify a scan range, the result includes the parts of the original string that are outside the scan range.

The result can be larger, equal to, or smaller than the source string. The length depends on the lengths of original and resulting strings and on the number of times the replacement is performed.

The following example uses the %Scanrpl function:

```
Dcl-s String1 Char(48) Inz('SUBJECT sat on a wall. +
                           SUBJECT had a great fall.');
Dcl-s String2 Char(64);
Dcl-s Egg     Char(13) Inz('Humpty Dumpty');


String2 = %Scanrpl(Egg:'SUBJECT':String1);
  // String 2 =
  // 'Humpty Dumpty sat on a wall. Humpty Dumpty had a great fall.      '
```

7.5.5. %Xlate (Translate) Function

The **%Xlate (Translate)** function lets you translate, or convert, characters within a string to other characters. It takes following the form:

```
%Xlate(from:to:string{:start})
```

The first two arguments serve as translation tables: the first one provides the characters to translate, and the second one specifies which characters to translate them to. The third argument names a character variable containing the source string—it can also be a character literal. If you do not specify a starting location (fourth argument), the conversion begins at the first position of the source string. The function returns a translated version of the source string, which you can use in an assignment expression.

The *from* string and the *to* string must have the same number of characters, with the characters ordered so that each character in the *from* string has a corresponding character in the *to* string. The translation strings can be variables, literals, or named constants. During the %Xlate function processing, any character in the source string found in the *from* string is converted to the corresponding character in the *to* string. If a source string character does not appear in the *from* string, that character is unchanged in the return value.

If this sounds confusing, looking at some examples should help clarify how the %Xlate function works. The following examples convert uppercase letters to lowercase letters and vice versa. This kind of translation is a frequent application of %Xlate. The code sample defines the translation tables through named constants Uppercase and Lowercase:

```
Dcl-c Lowercase 'abcdefghijklmnopqrstuvwxyz';
Dcl-c Uppercase 'ABCDEFGHIJKLMNOPQRSTUVWXYZ';


Dcl-s Fielda   Char(9)  Inz('abc123ABC');
Dcl-s Lastname Char(15) Inz('BYRNE-SMITH');
Dcl-s Name     Char(15);


Name = %Xlate(Uppercase:Lowercase:Lastname);       // Name = 'byrne-smith      '
Name = %Xlate(Uppercase:Lowercase:Lastname:2);     // Name = 'Byrne-smith      '
Name = %Xlate(' ':'*':Name);                       // Name = 'Byrne-smith****'
Fielda = %Xlate(Lowercase:Uppercase:Fielda);       // Fielda = 'ABC123ABC'
```

You can also use %Xlate to strip non-numeric characters from a character variable and then convert the result to a packed decimal number by using the %Dec function. You can then use the number in arithmetic expressions.

```
Dcl-s Amount    Packed(11:2);
Dcl-s Checkword Char(17) Inz('$*****7,654.32***');


Checkword = %Xlate('$*,':'   ':Checkword); // Checkword = '      7 654.32    '
Amount = %Dec(Checkword:11:2);             // Amount = 7654.32
```

Additionally, you can combine the two functions into one statement to get the same result:

```
Amount = %Dec(%Xlate('$*,':'   ':Checkword) : 11 : 2);
```

In this example, the %Xlate function (shown in italics) is embedded as the first argument to the %Dec function. While this single statement illustrates the fact that you can include complex expressions as the arguments for many functions, you'll want to carefully weigh the brevity of this style against its readability.

7.5.6. %Scan (Scan String)

The **%Scan (Scan string)** function looks for a character or a string of characters within a character string—usually a variable, but it can also be a literal or named constant. The direction of the %Scan is left to right. %Scan takes the following form:

```
%Scan(search-arg:string{:start})
```

%Scan searches the string for the search argument, beginning with the starting position (or beginning at the first position, if you don't specify the third argument). If the string you are seeking includes blanks—whether leading, trailing, or embedded—the blanks are considered part of the pattern to find. Similarly, blanks within the searched string are not ignored. The function returns an unsigned integer value that represents the next position of the search argument in the source string. If the search argument is not found, the function returns a zero. You can include %Scan anywhere in the program where an unsigned integer expression is allowed.

The following examples illustrate some typical uses for %Scan:

```
Dcl-s Position Uns(5);

Dcl-s Fielda Char(3)  Inz('XY ');
Dcl-s Fieldb Char(10) Inz('QRSTUVWXYZ');
Dcl-s Fieldc Char(10) Inz('XY TUVWXY ');

Dcl-s Fullname Char(20) Inz('Doe/John');

Position = %Scan(Fielda:Fieldb);        // Position = 0, because 'XY ' (with a
                                        // trailing blank) is not in Fieldb
Position = %Scan(%Trim(Fielda):Fieldb);   // Position = 8

Position = %Scan(Fielda:Fieldc);          // Position = 1
Position = %Scan(Fielda:Fieldc:2);        // Position = 8

Position = %Scan('/':Fullname);           // Position = 4
```

%Scan is case sensitive (i.e., 'A' is not the same as 'a'). But you can use the %Xlate function to perform a %Scan that is not case sensitive:

```
Dcl-c Lowercase 'abcdefghijklmnopqrstuvwxyz';
Dcl-c Uppercase 'ABCDEFGHIJKLMNOPQRSTUVWXYZ';

Dcl-s Position Uns(5);
Dcl-s Fullname Char(20) Inz('Doe/John');

Position = %Scan('John':Fullname);    // Position = 5
```

Continued

```
Position = %Scan('JOHN':Fullname);      // Position = 0
Position = %Scan('JOHN' : %Xlate(Lowercase:Uppercase:Fullname));
                                        // Position = 5
```

The %Scan function is useful for inspecting text data. You can use it, for example, to scan addresses to locate all businesses or customers residing on the same street. Text-retrieval software uses operations like %Scan to index text based on the presence of keywords within the text.

7.5.7. %Check (Check Characters), %Checkr (Check Reverse)

The **%Check (Check characters)** function inspects a character string, checking whether it contains *only* the characters designated in a compare string. The first argument provides a compare string, and the second one holds the string to inspect. By coding a third argument, you can also optional specify a starting point for the inspection. The format of the %Check function is as follows:

```
%Check(comparator:string{:start})
```

You use %Check to verify the characters in a string. When all the characters in the string also appear in the compare string, %Check returns a zero. If a mismatch occurs (i.e., if any characters in the string do *not* appear in the compare string), then %Check returns an unsigned integer value that represents the leftmost position that does not match the characters in the compare string.

While both %Check and %Scan can examine character strings, there is a significant difference between the two functions. %Scan looks for the presence of the entire search argument within the string and returns the location of its occurrence. %Check verifies that each character in the string is among the valid characters in the compare string. When %Check detects a mismatch, it returns the location of the mismatch; otherwise, %Check returns a zero.

The compare string (represented in a character variable, literal, or named constant) contains a list of valid characters. The base string provides the character variable, literal, or named constant value you want checked against characters in the compare string. If %Check returns a nonzero number, that number is the first position in the string that contains a character not in the compare string.

In the following example, the %Check function verifies that the Checkword variable has only digits, blanks, or a decimal point. If any other characters are found, %Check returns the position of the first invalid character; otherwise, it returns a zero.

```
Dcl-s Checkword Char(25) Inz('      7,654.32');
Dcl-s Position  Uns(5);


Position = %Check(' .0123456789':Checkword);      // Position = 8
%Subst(Checkword:Position:1) = *Blank;             // Put a blank in position 8
Position = %Check(' .0123456789':Checkword);      // Position = 0
```

In the preceding examples, you coded the compare string as a literal. But you can also place the compare string in a variable or named constant:

```
Dcl-c Numbers ' .0123456789';
...
Position = %Check(Numbers:Checkword);     // Position = 8
```

The **%Checkr (Check reverse)** function works exactly as %Check except that it checks the string from right to left, rather than from left to right. You can use this operation to locate the rightmost invalid character in a string, or to determine the length of a string of nonblank characters in a field:

```
Dcl-s Name    Char25) Inz('Jones');
Dcl-s Length Uns(5);

Length = %Checkr(' ':Name);     // Length = 5
```

7.6. Data-Conversion Functions

All the operands in a character expression must be of a character data type; the program cannot mix numeric data and character variables in the same expression. Several built-in functions convert numeric expressions to character formats and even edit those numeric expressions by using the edit codes and edit words examined in Chapter 3. The most frequently used of these functions are as follows:

- %Char (Convert to character data)
- %Editc (Edit with an edit code)
- %Editw (Edit with an edit word)

7.6.1. %Char (Convert to Character Data)

The **%Char (Convert to character data)** function converts the result of a numeric variable, literal, named constant, or expression to a character value. %Char is especially useful when you need to include numeric data in a string expression, perhaps to concatenate a numeric value and a character string. All operands in a string expression must be in character format, so the %Char function is necessary to perform the conversion.

```
Dcl-s Message Char(45);
Dcl-s Points  Uns(10)     Inz(50273);
Dcl-s Balance Packed(9:2) Inz(-9876.54);


Message = 'You have earned ' + %Char(Points) + ' Frequent Flier Miles.';
          // Message = 'You have earned 50273 Frequent Flier Miles.  '


Message = 'Your account balance is ' + %Char(Balance);
          // Message = 'Your account balance is -9876.54              '
```

%Char always removes all leading zeros from the result. If the numeric value contains decimal places, %Char includes a decimal point at its proper alignment. If the value is negative, %Char returns a character result with a leading sign.

7.6.2. %Editc (Edit with an Edit Code)

The %Char function provides only rudimentary editing when it returns a character value, removing leading zeros and adding a decimal point and sign, if necessary. But as you saw in Chapter 3, RPG provides a rich set of editing functions through the use of edit codes. The **%Editc (Edit with an edit code)** function not only converts a number to a character value but also assigns one of those edit codes to the numeric value before converting it, optionally adding a currency symbol or asterisk leading fill (*****). The format for the %Editc function is as follows:

```
%Editc(number:edit-code{:extension})
```

The first argument is the numeric variable, literal, named constant, or expression that you want to convert. Next, enter the desired edit code as the second argument. The edit code is typically a literal enclosed in apostrophes, but it can also be a named constant. %Editc supports all the edit codes described in Chapter 3.

The optional third %Editc argument adds a currency symbol or asterisk fill to the edited value. For example,

```
%Editc(-0012.34:'J':*Astfill)
```

returns a character value of '***12.34-'. To include a floating currency symbol in the edited value, you might code the following:

```
%Editc(0012.34:'J':*Cursym)
```

This code returns a character value of ' $12.34 '. Unless you code another character, %Editc uses the program's default currency symbol. For example,

```
%Editc(0012.34:'J':'C')
```

returns a value of ' C12.34 '.

The %Editc result can include leading or trailing blanks or both, and it always returns the same length string for a given variable, regardless of its value. To eliminate the leading and trailing blanks, use the %Trim function. The following examples illustrate the use of the %Editc function:

```
Dcl-s Message     Char(45);
Dcl-s Balance     Packed(9:2) Inz(9876.54);
Dcl-s Zerobalance Packed(9:2);


Message = 'Your account balance is ' + %Editc(Balance:'J':*Cursym);
            // Message = 'Your account balance is    $9,876.54        '
Message = 'Your account balance is ' + %Trim( %Editc(Balance:'J':*Cursym) );
            // Message = 'Your account balance is $9,876.54            '

Message = 'Your account balance is ' + %Editc(Zerobalance:'J':*Cursym);
            // Message = 'Your account balance is         $.00        '
Message = 'Your account balance is ' +
                        %Trim( %Editc(Zerobalance:'J':*Cursym) );
            // Message = 'Your account balance is $.00                '
```

Recall from Chapter 3 that all but one of the edit codes remove leading zeros from the edited result. To retain the leading zeros in the character value, use the X edit code, which retains the zeros. The X edit code does not reveal the decimal point or an explicit sign. For negative numbers, the sign is embedded in the high order of the last digit—the same manner that the system uses internally to store the number. The following examples illustrate the difference in the results between the %Char and %Editc functions:

```
Dcl-s Var1    Char(15);
Dcl-s Number1 Packed(9:0) Inz(98765);
Dcl-s Number2 Packed(9:2) Inz(-98765.42);


Var1 = %Char(Number1);          // Var1 = '98765          '
Var1 = %Editc(Number1:'X');     // Var1 = '000098765      '


Var1 = %Char(Number2);          // Var1 = '-98765.42      '
Var1 = %Editc(Number2:'X');     // Var1 = '00987654K      '
```

7.6.3. %Editw (Edit with an Edit Word)

When a simple edit code won't do, the **%Editw (Edit with an edit word)** function applies an edit word to a numeric value while it converts the number to a character string. %Editw uses the same rules for creating an edit word discussed in Chapter 3. The edit word must be a literal or a named constant. The %Editw function takes this form:

```
%Editw(number:edit-word)
```

The following code illustrates some examples of using the %Editw function:

```
Dcl-c Edita '   ,   ,   **DOLLARS* *CENTS';
Dcl-c Editp '0(   )   -    ';
Dcl-c Editt '  -  -    ';


Dcl-s Var1 Char(30);


Dcl-s Amount Packed(11:2) Inz(12345.67);
Dcl-s Phone  Packed(11:0) Inz(8005551212);
Dcl-s Taxid  Packed(9:0)  Inz(987654321);


Var1 = %Editw(Amount:Edita);    // Var1 = '*****12,345*DOLLARS*67*CENTS '
Var1 = %Editw(Phone:Editp);     // Var1 = ' (800)555-1212               '
Var1 = %Editw(Taxid:Editt);     // Var1 = '987-65-4321                  '
Var1 = %Editw(Taxid:'   &   &    ');
                                // Var1 = '987 65 4321                  '
```

7.7. Retrieving Data Properties

Several functions can informally be described as *self-examination* functions. These functions let your program determine the properties of a variable, constant, or expression. Among these functions are the following:

- %Size (Byte size)
- %Len (Get/set length)
- %Decpos (Number of decimal positions)

These functions work with any data class, not just character data.

7.7.1. %Size (Byte Size)

The **%Size (Byte size)** function returns the number of bytes occupied by a variable or constant. When you use %Size to determine the length of a packed decimal or integer data item, it returns the number of *bytes* used to store the data item, not the number of digits. %Size always returns the declared byte size, regardless of variable's current value. For variable-length character variables, %Size returns the declared length plus either two or four bytes, depending upon the declaration. The following examples demonstrate how to determine %Size:

```
Dcl-s Bytes    Uns(5);
Dcl-s Company Zoned(9:0)  Inz(68600);
Dcl-s Salary  Packed(9:0) Inz(68600);
Dcl-s Name     Char(25)    Inz('John Doe');
Dcl-s Namevar Varchar(25) Inz('Al Fredo');


Bytes = %Size(Bytes);        // Bytes = 2   (integer)
Bytes = %Size(Company);      // Bytes = 9   (zoned decimal)
Bytes = %Size(Salary);       // Bytes = 5   (packed decimal)
Bytes = %Size(Name);         // Bytes = 25
Bytes = %Size(Namevar);      // Bytes = 27 (declared size + 2)
```

7.7.2. %Len (Get/Set Length)

The **%Len (Get/set length)** function returns the number of digits or characters in a variable, constant, or expression. %Len is especially useful with character expressions to determine the number of significant characters in the expression's value. For fixed-length character fields, %Len returns the declared length of the field, but for variable-length character values, %Len returns the current length of the variable or expression, which is dependent upon its value. The %Len function also supports a *Max entry to return the maximum allowed length for a variable-length field. Here are some examples of using the %Len function with character variables:

```
Dcl-s Length     Int(5);

Dcl-s Name       Char(25)    Inz('John Doe');
Dcl-s Namevar    Varchar(25) Inz('Al Fredo');
Dcl-s Firstname  VarChar(10) Inz('Frieda');
Dcl-s Lastname   Varchar(10) Inz('Slaves');

Length = %Len(Name);               // Length = 25
Length = %Len( %Trim(Name) );      // Length = 8

Length = %Size(Namevar);           // Length = 27 (declared size +2)
Length = %Len(Namevar);            // Length = 8   (current length)
Length = %Len(Namevar:*Max);       // Length = 25 (maximum length)

Length = %Len(Firstname + ' ' + Lastname);     // Length = 13

Name = '';
Length = %Len(Name);       // Length = 0
```

For numeric expressions, %Len returns the precision of the expression, not necessarily the number of significant digits in the calculated value of the expression. If you use %Len to find the decimal precision of an arithmetic expression, the system returns a length that is consistent with the sizing rules that Chapter 6 covered. For all other data types, %Len returns the number of bytes, giving the same result as the %Size function. The following examples show some ways to use the %Len function with numeric variables:

```
Dcl-s Length  Uns(5);

Dcl-s Company Zoned(5:0);
Dcl-s Salary  Packed(9:2) Inz(68600.00);
Dcl-s Tenure  Packed(3:0);

Length = %Len(Length);             // Length = 5  (integer)
Length = %Len(Company);            // Length = 5  (zoned decimal)
Length = %Len(Salary);             // Length = 9  (packed decimal)
Length = %Len(Salary * Tenure);    // Length = 12
```

Typically, you use the %Len function to obtain the length of an expression, but you can also use it to set the current length of a variable-length character field. By coding the %Len function to the *left* of the assignment operator (=), you can set the current length of the variable. Changing the current length of the variable changes the contents of the variable as well.

```
Dcl-s Length Uns(5);
Dcl-s Name   Varchar(25) Inz('John Doe');


Length = %Len(Name);       // Length = 8 (current length)
%Len(Name) = 4;            // Name = 'John'
```

7.7.3. %Decpos (Number of Decimal Positions)

The **%Decpos (Number of decimal positions)** function returns the number of decimal positions in a numeric variable or expression. %Decpos is sometimes used with the %LEN function to examine a data item or expression:

```
Dcl-s Decimals Uns(5);
Dcl-s Digits   Uns(5);
Dcl-s Salary   Packed(9:2) Inz(68600);


Digits = %Len(Salary);          // Digits = 9
Decimals = %Decpos(Salary);     // Decimals = 2
```

7.8. Navigating Legacy Code

7.8.1. Move, Movel (Move Left)

Before the introduction of Eval to the language, many RPG programs frequently used another operation code, Move, to assign a value to a variable. Move is a fixed-format operation code (not allowed in free-format RPG) that's prevalent in legacy code. Move assigns characters from Factor 2 to the Result field:

```
*.. 1 ...+... 2 ...+... 3 ...+... 4 ...+... 5 ...+... 6 ...+... 7 ...+... 8
CLON01Factor1+++++++Opcode(E)+Factor2+++++++Result++++++++Len++D+HiLoEq....
C                   Move        source-var   target-var
```

The source variable remains unchanged after the Move.

The Move operation assigns characters, starting with the *rightmost* character in the source variable and moving *left*. If the target variable is shorter than the source variable, only rightmost characters from the source are assigned to the target, enough to fill the target. If the target is longer than the source, the extra leftmost target characters are *unaffected* by the Move. The following examples illustrate the use of Move to assign character data:

```
*.. 1 ...+... 2 ...+... 3 ...+... 4 ...+... 5 ...+... 6 ...+... 7 ...+... 8
DName++++++++++ETDsFrom+++To/Len+IDc.Keywords+++++++++++++++++++++++++++++++
CLON01Factor1+++++++Opcode(E)+Factor2+++++++Result++++++++Len++D+HiLoEq....
D Source          S             10      Inz('ABCDE12345')
D Equal           S             10      Inz('67890vwxyz')
D Short           S              5      Inz('FgHiJ')
D Long            S             15      Inz('kLmNoPqRsTu9876')


C                 Move      Source        Equal
C                 Move      Source        Short
C                 Move      Source        Long
          // After Moves: Equal = 'ABCDE12345'
          //             Short = '12345'
          //              Long =  'kLmNoABCDE12345'
```

A related operation, Movel (Move left), is similar to Move, but it works from *left* to *right* (fixed-format only):

```
*.. 1 ...+... 2 ...+... 3 ...+... 4 ...+... 5 ...+... 6 ...+... 7 ...+... 8
DName++++++++++ETDsFrom+++To/Len+IDc.Keywords+++++++++++++++++++++++++++++++
CLON01Factor1+++++++Opcode(E)+Factor2+++++++Result++++++++Len++D+HiLoEq....
D Source          S             10      Inz('ABCDE12345')
D Equal           S             10      Inz('67890vwxyz')
D Short           S              5      Inz('FgHiJ')
D Long            S             15      Inz('kLmNoPqRsTu9876')


C                 Movel     Source        Equal
C                 Movel     Source        Short
C                 Movel     Source        Long
          // After Moves: Equal = 'ABCDE12345'
          //             Short = 'ABCDE'
          //              Long =  'ABCDE12345u9876'
```

Both Move and Movel support a (P) operation extender to pad extra characters in the target with blanks. Compare the following example with the earlier Move examples to see the effect of the (P) extender:

```
*.. 1 ...+... 2 ...+... 3 ...+... 4 ...+... 5 ...+... 6 ...+... 7 ...+... 8
DName++++++++++ETDsFrom+++To/Len+IDc.Keywords++++++++++++++++++++++++++++++++
CLON01Factor1+++++++Opcode(E)+Factor2+++++++Result++++++++Len++D+HiLoEq....
D Source          S              10    Inz('ABCDE12345')
D Long            S              15    Inz('kLmNoPqRsTu9876')


C                 Move(p)   Source        Long
        // After Move: Long = '      ABCDE12345'
```

When used with character data, Movel(p) is similar to Eval, whereas Move(p) is comparable to Evalr.

You can use Move and Movel with figurative constants in Factor 2 to assign a value as well:

```
*.. 1 ...+... 2 ...+... 3 ...+... 4 ...+... 5 ...+... 6 ...+... 7 ...+... 8
DName++++++++++ETDsFrom+++To/Len+IDc.Keywords++++++++++++++++++++++++++++++++
CLON01Factor1+++++++Opcode(E)+Factor2+++++++Result++++++++Len++D+HiLoEq....
                                                              Continued
D Target1         S              10    Inz('ABCDE12345')
D Target2         S              10    Inz('ABCDE12345')


C                 Move      *Blanks        Target1
C                 Move      *Zeros         Target2
        // After Moves: Target1 = '          '
        //              Target2 = '0000000000'
```

In this example, Target2 is a character variable, even though it contains all numeric zeros after the Moves.

The previous examples illustrate using Move and Movel to assign one character variable to another character variable. You can also use these operations to assign values by using other data types, including numeric values, implicitly converting the source values to the target data type, if necessary. Some restrictions apply, however.

Most important, if both the source and target are numeric variables, Move and Movel will ignore the decimal alignment of the source:

```
*.. 1 ...+... 2 ...+... 3 ...+... 4 ...+... 5 ...+... 6 ...+... 7 ...+... 8
DName++++++++++ETDsFrom+++To/Len+IDc.Keywords+++++++++++++++++++++++++++++++
CLON01Factor1+++++++Opcode(E)+Factor2+++++++Result++++++++Len++D+HiLoEq....
D Source          S             5 2 Inz(123.45')
D Target          S             5 1

C                 Move      Source        Target
            // After Move: Target = 1234.5
```

To retain the decimal alignment, the program should use an alternative, such as Z-add:

```
*.. 1 ...+... 2 ...+... 3 ...+... 4 ...+... 5 ...+... 6 ...+... 7 ...+... 8
DName++++++++++ETDsFrom+++To/Len+IDc.Keywords+++++++++++++++++++++++++++++++
CLON01Factor1+++++++Opcode(E)+Factor2+++++++Result++++++++Len++D+HiLoEq....
D Source          S             5 2 Inz(123.45')
D Target          S             5 1

C                 Z-add     Source        Target
            // After Z-add: Target = 00123.4
```

When the move operations assign a character variable to a numeric target, each character's digit portion is converted to its corresponding numeric character and then moved to the target. Blanks become zeros in the result. The rightmost character's zone portion is the sign of the target. The following example illustrates such a move:

```
*.. 1 ...+... 2 ...+... 3 ...+... 4 ...+... 5 ...+... 6 ...+... 7 ...+... 8
DName++++++++++ETDsFrom+++To/Len+IDc.Keywords+++++++++++++++++++++++++++++++
CLON01Factor1+++++++Opcode(E)+Factor2+++++++Result++++++++Len++D+HiLoEq....
D Source          S             5   Inz(' 123N')
D Target          S             5 2

C                 Move      Source        Target
            // After Move: Target = -012.34
```

7.8.2. Resulting Indicators

The move-related operations support resulting indicators in positions 71–76 (HiLoEq) to reflect the result of executing the move. If the target is numeric, the indicator in the Hi position (71–72) is set to *On for a positive result, the indicator in the Lo position (73–74) is set to *On for a negative result, and the indicator in the Eq position (75–76) is set to *On for a zero result. If the target is character data, you can code an indicator in the Eq position to be set to *On if the result is blanks:

```
*.. 1 ...+... 2 ...+... 3 ...+... 4 ...+... 5 ...+... 6 ...+... 7 ...+... 8
CLON01Factor1+++++++Opcode(E)+Factor2+++++++Result++++++++Len++D+HiLoEq....
C                   Move      Source       Target                  50
```

In this example, if Target (a character variable) is blank after the move, indicator 50 is *On; otherwise indicator 50 is *Off.

7.9. Chapter Summary

As ILE RPG's single general-purpose assignment operation, Eval supports expressions with character values as well as numeric values. The expressions can range from a simple assignment expression to more complex concatenation expressions.

For character expressions, Eval left-adjusts the result and pads to the right with blanks, if necessary. Evalr, on the other hand, right-adjusts the result and pads to the left with blanks. You can use character fields, character literals, and figurative constants in character string expressions.

Eval-corr is a specialized variation of Eval used with data structures to assign subfields of one data structure to the corresponding subfields of another data structure. The corresponding subfields must have the same name and compatible data type for Eval-corr to process them.

While fixed-length character variables always have the same declared length, variable-length data items have both a declared maximum length and a current length, which can change while the program is running, depending upon the value of the data item. Variable-length character variables can simplify coding and improve performance of complex string operations.

ILE RPG supports a rich set of built-in functions to simplify the processing of character strings. These functions can manipulate character strings, inspect their content, and convert other data types to character data. The following table summarizes the operation codes and built-in functions examined in this chapter. Optional entries appear within the curly braces ({}):

Function or Operation	Description	Syntax
%Char	Convert to character data	**%Char(expression {: format})**
%Check	Check characters	**%Check(compare-string : base-string {: start})**
%Checkr	Check characters (reversed)	**%Checkr(compare-string : base-string {: start})**
%Decpos	Number of decimal positions	**%Decpos(numeric-expression)**
%Editc	Edit with an edit code	**%Editc(numeric-expression : edit-code {: fill})**
%Editw	Edit with an edit word	**%Editw(numeric-expression :edit-word)**
Eval	Evaluate expression	**{Eval{(mr)}} Assignment-Statement**
Evalr	Evaluate expression, Right-adjust	**Evalr{(mr)} Assignment-Statement**
Eval-corr	Assign corresponding subfields from one data structure to another	**Eval-corr{(hmr)} Target = Source**
%Len	Get or set length	**%Len(expression {:*Max})**
%Replace	Replace character string	**%Replace(replacement : source {:start {: length}})**
%Scan	Scan string	**%Scan(search-arg : source {: start})**
%Scanrpl	Scan and replace characters	**%Scanrpl(newvalue : oldvalue : string {: start {: length})**
%Size	Byte size	**%Size(data-item {: *all})**
%Subst	Get or set substring	**%Subst(string : start : length)**
%Trim %Triml %Trimr	Trim characters at edges	**%Trimx(string {: characters})**
%Xlate	Translate	**%Xlate(from : to : string {: start})**

7.10. Key Terms

*All

*Blank

%Char (Convert to character data)

character expressions

%Check (Check characters)

%Checkr (Check reverse)

concatenation

current length

declared length

%Decpos (Number of decimal positions)

%Editc (Edit with an edit code)

%Editw (Edit with an edit word)

Eval (Evaluate Expression)

Evalr (Evaluate expression, right adjust)

Eval-corr (Assign corresponding subfields)

figurative constant

fixed length

%Len (Get or set length)

%Replace (Replace character string)

%Scan (Scan string)

%Scanrpl (Scan and replace characters)

%Size (Byte size)

%Subst (Get or set substring)

substring

translate

%Trim (Trim characters at edges)

Varchar

variable length

%Xlate (Translate)

7.11. Discussion/Review Questions

1. Why would an RPG programmer need to convert character data (e.g., JOHN SMITH) to upper case and lower case (e.g., John Smith)?
2. Explain the differences between the Eval and Evalr functions. Give an example of why these two functions are needed.
3. Describe the difference between the "+" and "-"continuation characters.
4. When concatenating strings, you need to avoid truncation. How would a programmer avoid truncation?
5. Are there circumstances in which a programmer might intentionally truncate data? Explain.
6. Explain how the %Trim, %Trimr, and %Triml functions work.
7. What rules apply to using the %Xlate function?
8. Explain the difference between the %Replace and %Xlate functions.
9. Under what circumstances would you use the %Scan instead of %Check function?
10. Explain the two techniques for removing unnecessary blanks when concatenating strings.
11. Give three examples in which you would use the following functions:
    a. %Len
    b. %Size
    c. %Decpos
    d. %Scan
    e. %Check
12. Give two examples in which the Eval-corr would be useful when processing data structures.
13. Given the following two data structures, would you be able to use the Eval-corr operation? If not, explain the changes required to allow the use of this function.

```
Dcl-ds Customer1;
        Studentid   Packed(5:0);
        Name        Char(30);
        State       Char(2);
        Zipcode     Packed(9:0);
        Phone       Char(10);
        Creditlimit Packed(11:2);
   End-ds;

Dcl-ds Graduate1;
        Gradid      Int(5:0);
        Name        Char(35);
        Address     Char(35);
```

Continued

```
            City        Packed(21);
            State       Char(2);
            Postcd      Char(10);
            Phone       Packed(10:0);
        End-ds;
```

7.12. Exercises

Code the following exercises by using the functions described in this chapter.

1. Write the code to convert the following data:

Before	After
JOHN SMITH	John Smith
SUSAN B. ANTHONY	Susan B. Anthony
GEORGE DAVID	David George
James Thomas Wells	J. T. WELLS

2. Write the code to convert the following data:

Before	After
2625643158	262-564-3158
262-564-3158	2625643158513465262
2625643158	513465262
985-58-9234	985-85-9234

3. Write the code to convert the following data:

Before	After
2625643158	506-564-3158
2625643158	262-999-3158
John Adams	John T. Adams

4. Write the code to convert the following data:

Before	After
JAMES CARTER THOMAS	James Thomas Carter
200 WEST STREET KENOSHA WI 53142	200 West Street Kenosha, WI 53142
Alice Susan Simmons	A. S. Simmons
938-58-7843	938-66-7843

Notes

CHAPTER **8**

Working with Dates

8.1. Chapter Overview

This chapter covers the native date-related data types. It examines how to define dates and how their format affects processing. In this chapter, you discover how to use several built-in functions to easily perform date arithmetic. You also learn how to convert among date, character, and numeric data types, and how to process legacy dates that are defined as numeric or character data.

8.2. Defining Date-Related Data

ILE RPG supports three native data types that can store and process values related to dates:

- Date
- Time
- Timestamp

Date and **time** are self-evident data types you use to store values associated with the calendar and the clock. A **timestamp** is a combination of a date and a time. Generally, ILE RPG applies the same principles and rules to all three data types. When this book refers to dates, the same concept applies to times and timestamps as well, unless we indicate otherwise.

Caution

Do not confuse the date, time, and timestamp data types with numeric or character variables that can represent date-related data. Because the native date data types are a fairly recent development in the RPG world, many applications still use numeric or character variables to deal with date-related data. With these legacy date variables, it is up to the RPG program to provide any special processing required to validate or process them as if they were dates, times, or timestamps.

8.2.1. Defining Dates with SQL

The SQL Create Table statement supports native date data types for the column definitions:

```
Create Table SalesTrans
            (...
             Saledate Date Null Default,
             Saletime Time Null Default,
             Lastupdate Timestamp(0) Not Null Default,
             ...)
```

For a timestamp, you can specify the scale (i.e., the fractional seconds) to include in the timestamp from 0 to 12 (picoseconds). If you do not indicate a scale, the timestamp defaults to a scale of 6 (microseconds). In the preceding example, Lastupdate includes no fractional seconds.

Recall from Chapter 3 that the Null or Not Null constraint controls whether the column allows null values, and that the Default **constraint** indicates that the column is to contain a **default value**. You can code a default value for any of the columns. Otherwise, for null-capable date columns, the default is null. Columns that are not null capable default to the current date, time, or timestamp.

SQL stores date-related values in a compact internal form that you cannot readily see. SQL does not normally specify an external format for date data. The values are presented to a program in a format specified in the program, typically the *ISO format discussed later in this chapter.

8.2.2. Defining Dates Using DDS

You can also define dates, times, and timestamps in externally described files by using DDS. Here is the relevant DDS for a hypothetical physical file:

```
*.. 1 ...+... 2 ...+... 3 ...+... 4 ...+... 5 ...+... 6 ...+... 7 ...+... 8
A..........T.Name++++++RLen++TDcB......Keywords++++++++++++++++++++++++++++++
 * Physical file SALESTRANS
A           R SALESREC
...
A             SALEDATE      L           TEXT('Sale Date')
A                                       DATFMT(*ISO)
A             SALETIME      T           TEXT('Sale Time')
A                                       TIMFMT(*ISO)
A             LASTUPDATE    Z           TEXT('Last Update')
...
```

Saledate is the date field in this example. DDS uses data type L in position 35 to define a native date, data type T to indictate a time, and data type Z to specify a timestamp. The digits (positions 30–34) and decimal positions (positions 36–37) entries are left blank because the system determines the length.

DDS stores date-related values in a compact internal form—the same one SQL uses—that you cannot readily see. The **Datfmt** and **Timfmt** keywords specify the default format that a program is to use to present the date or time. We examine these external formats later in this chapter. A timestamp defined with DDS has a fixed format with a microseconds scale:

```
YYYY-MM-DD-hh.mm.ss.uuuuuu
```

8.2.3. Defining Dates in ILE RPG

Within the RPG program code, standalone variables and data structure subfields can also be dates, times, or timestamps. Here are some examples:

```
Dcl-s Saledate   Date(*Iso);
Dcl-s Saletime   Time(*Iso);
Dcl-s Lastupdate Timestamp(0);

Dcl-ds Personnel;
  Birthdate Date(*Iso);
    Birthyear  Zoned(4:0) Overlay(Birthdate);
    Birthmonth Zoned(2:0) Overlay(Birthdate:6);
    Birthday   Zoned(2:0) Overlay(Birthdate:9);
End-ds;
```

These declarations use the **Date**, **Time**, and **Timestamp** keywords to indicate the data type and, optionally, the presentation format, discussed later. If the data item is a data structure subfield, you can also use the Overlay keyword (examined in Chapter 4) to redefine subfields or portions of subfields, as in the preceding example.

8.2.4. Defining Dates in Input Specifications

If a program processes program-described files, those files can contain date-related data types defined in Input specifications (I-specs):

```
*.. 1 ...+... 2 ...+... 3 ...+... 4 ...+... 5 ...+... 6 ...+... 7 ...+... 8
IFilename++SqNORiPos1+NCCPos2+NCCPos3+NCC..................................
I......................Fmt+SPFrom+To+++DcField++++++++L1M1FrP1MnZr......
ISalestransNS

   …

I                       *Iso D   21   30   Saledate
I                       *Iso T   31   38   Saletime
I                            Z   39   64   Lastupdate

   …
```

In this example, the Saledate field is a date field (indicated by the D in position 36, labeled P on the prompt), Saletime is a time (data type T), and Lastupdate is a timestamp (type Z). An entry in positions 31–35 (Fmt+S) indicates the date or time format, along with an optional separator character. The entry *ISO in positions 31–34 specifies that Saledate is in YYYY-MM-DD format, including the hyphen (-) separator characters (we discuss date formats in a moment). The field location entries (positions 37–46, From+To+++) represent the location of the field within the record format. The length of that location must correspond to the formatted length of the field. In this case, Saledate occupies 10 bytes in the record format, bytes 21–30. Dates use six, eight, or 10 bytes, depending upon their format; times (type T) occupy eight bytes; and timestamps (type Z) take up 26 bytes. Because the concept of a decimal point does not apply to native dates, positions 47–48 (Dc) are left blank.

8.3. Understanding Date Formats

Each of the date-related data types has a preset size and format, and each has a **default external format** (*ISO), based on the International Standards Organization **(ISO) standards.** The default external format for dates is a 10-byte field with format *YYYY-MM-DD*. Times have a default length of eight bytes with format *hh.mm.ss*. The default external format for timestamp (Z) has a length of 26 bytes with format *YYYY-MM-DD-hh.mm.ss.uuuuuu*.

The date and time (but not the timestamp) data types allow alternative external formats to the defaults. Date, for instance, supports eight different formats, and time supports five. The tables in Figures 8.1 and 8.2 list the valid date and time formats.

Date Format	Description	Format	Valid Separators	Edited Field Length	Example
*ISO	International Standards Organization	YYYY-MM-DD	-	10	2020-12-31
*USA	IBM US Standard	MM/DD/YYYY	/	10	12/31/2020
*EUR	IBM European Standard	DD.MM.YYYY	.	10	31.12.2020
*JIS	Japanese Industrial Standard	YYYY-MM-DD	-	10	2020-12-31
*YMD	Year/Month/Day	YY/MM/DD	/ - , . &(blank)	8	20/12/31
*MDY	Month/Day/Year	MM/DD/YY	/ - , . &(blank)	8	12/31/20
*DMY	Day/Month/Year	DD/MM/YY	/ - , . &(blank)	8	31/12/20
*JUL	Julian	YY/DDD	/ - , . &(blank)	6	20/366

Figure 8.1: Date formats

Time Format	Description	Format	Valid Separators	Example
*ISO	International Standards Organization	hh.mm.ss	.	19.30.00
*USA	IBM US Standard	hh:mm xM	:	07:30 PM
*EUR	IBM European Standard	hh.mm.ss	.	19.30.00
*JIS	Japanese Industrial Standard	hh:mm:ss	:	19:30:00
*HMS	Year/Month/Day	hh:mm:ss	: , . &(blank)	19:30:00

Figure 8.2: Time formats

Each external format includes a default **separator character**. For example, the separator character for the *ISO date format is the hyphen (-). The separator character is an intrinsic part of the format. Several of the formats let you change the separator character. Acceptable separator characters for the *DMY and *MDY date formats, for instance, are the hyphen, the slash (/), the period (.), the comma (,), and the ampersand (&), which is displayed as a blank. Acceptable separator characters for the *HMS time format are the colon (:), the period, the comma, and the ampersand for blank. To change from the default separator, simply insert the separator character you want to use after the format code (e.g., *MDY- or *HMS&).

You have several opportunities to specify an alternative format for a date field. For standalone variables or data structure subfields, code the desired format (and the alternative separator, if desired) with the Date keyword:

```
Dcl-s Duedate  Date(*USA);      // Format MM/DD/YYYY
Dcl-s Shipdate Date(*YMD&);     // Format YY MM DD
```

DDS supports a Datfmt keyword to let you indicate an alternative date format for fields in externally described files:

```
*.. 1 ...+... 2 ...+... 3 ...+... 4 ...+... 5 ...+... 6 ...+... 7 ...+... 8
A..........T.Name++++++RLen++TDcB......Keywords++++++++++++++++++++++++++++++
...
A          DUEDATE          L          DATFMT(*USA)
A          SHIPDATE         L          DATFMT(*YMD&)
```

If an RPG program uses program-described files, you can use the Datfmt keyword in a file declaration to set a default date format for that file. Or, you can set the date format individually for each date field in that file by using Input specifications:

```
*.. 1 ...+... 2 ...+... 3 ...+... 4 ...+... 5 ...+... 6 ...+... 7 ...+... 8
I......................Fmt+SPFrom+To+++DcField+++++++++L1M1FrP1MnZr......
...
I                     *Usa D  21   30  Duedate
I                     *Ymd&D  31   40  Shipdate
```

Similarly, for time fields, code the alternative format as part of the Time keyword:

```
Dcl-s Saletime   Time(*Usa);
```

Or, use the Timfmt keyword:

```
*.. 1 ...+... 2 ...+... 3 ...+... 4 ...+... 5 ...+... 6 ...+... 7 ...+... 8
A..........T.Name++++++RLen++TDcB......Keywords++++++++++++++++++++++++++++++
...
A          SALETIME         T          TIMFMT(*USA)
```

Or specify the format in I-specs:

```
*.. 1 ...+... 2 ...+... 3 ...+... 4 ...+... 5 ...+... 6 ...+... 7 ...+... 8
I......................Fmt+SPFrom+To+++DcField+++++++++L1M1FrP1MnZr......
...
I                     *Usa T  41   48  Saletime
```

You can also change the default external format of date and time fields for a program as a whole by specifying the Datfmt or Timfmt keyword (or both) within the Ctl-opt instructions.

8.4. Simple Date Assignment

In previous chapters, you used the Eval operation to evaluate numeric and character expressions. As you might guess, ILE RPG also uses Eval with dates. To assign a value to a date, time, or timestamp variable, you code a simple assignment expression:

```
Dcl-s Enrolldate Date;
Dcl-s Today      Date Inz(*Sys);


Enrolldate = Today;      // Enrolldate now contains the current system date
```

This example assigns the value in one date variable to another date variable. Just as in previous assignment operations, you place the value to assign to the right of the equal sign and the receiving variable to the left. The two date variables must both be compatible (i.e., you cannot directly assign a number to a date). But the two dates need not be in the same format, nor do both need to use the same separator characters. This example uses the Inz keyword, examined in Chapter 4, to initialize Today to the current system date. Inz(*Sys) also works to initialize times and timestamps to their current value when the program starts. To initialize a date field to the job date, you can code Inz(*Job) in the declaration.

You can also use a simple assignment expression to assign a date or a time to the relevant portion of a timestamp. The following examples assign a date and time to a timestamp:

```
Dcl-s Kdate  Date Inz(D'1963-11-22');
Dcl-s Ktime  Time Inz(T'12.34.56');
Dcl-s Kstamp Timestamp(0);
                  // Kstamp has an initial value of Z'0001-01-01-00.00.00'


Kstamp = Kdate;      // Kstamp = Z'1963-11-22-00.00.00'
Kstamp = Ktime;      // Kstamp = Z'1963-11-22-12.34.56'
```

8.4.1. Using Typed Literals

In addition to date variables, you can also assign literal values to date, time, and timestamp values by using typed literals. To code a typed literal, enclose the value within apostrophes, but precede it with a data type code to indicate which data type the literal represents. To refer to a value of January 1, 2018, for example, you'd code D'2018-01-01' as the literal. Other data type codes for date-related typed literals are T (for times) and Z (for timestamps). Here are some examples of typed literals for dates, times, and timestamps:

Data Type	Typed Literal
Date	D'2020-03-15'
Time	T'08.56.20'
Timestamp	Z'2020-03-15-08.56.20.000000' Z'2020-03-15-08.56.20'

Here's an example of using a typed literal for simple assignment:

```
Enrolldate = D'2020-12-31';
```

The format of the date or time in the typed literal can vary from one program to another. The default format is *ISO. But if you've coded a Datfmt (or Timfmt) keyword in the Ctl-opt instructions to specify a default date (or time) format for the program, the typed literal's format must match the format you code in the Ctl-opt statement. Study this example:

```
Ctl-opt Datfmt(*Usa);

Dcl-s Enrolldate Date(*Iso);

Enrolldate = D'12/31/2020';      // Enrolldate now contains 2020-12-31
```

Notice the Datfmt keyword coded in the Ctl-opt statement to indicate that the default date format for the program is *USA format. Therefore, the typed literal must show the desired date in *USA format—even though the result field, Enrolldate, is in *ISO format, as indicated in its definition. Leading and trailing zeros are required for all date, time, and timestamp typed literals.

Unlike date and time typed literals, timestamp literals must always be in the same format, regardless of any formatting keywords elsewhere in the program. The fractional seconds' portion of a timestamp literal is optional. If you indicate fewer than six fractional seconds, the timestamp is padded with zeros out to microseconds (six fractional digits).

Tip
To avoid errors when dealing with dates, avoid specifying a Datfmt or Timfmt keyword in Ctl-opt statements. Always use *ISO as your default format.

8.4.2. Assigning Values with Figurative Constants

In addition to the previously discussed options, ILE RPG lets you assign the values of named constants or figurative constants ***Hival** and ***Loval** to dates, times, and timestamps, either with the Inz keyword or during processing. *Hival and *Loval can have different values, though, depending upon which format a date is using. The formats that allow four-digit years can store any value from January 1, 0001, until December 31, 9999. Dates in the two-digit year formats are restricted to a 100-year window from January 1, 1940, until December 31, 2039. The following table displays the allowable range of values for the date and time formats. In each case, *Loval is also the default value for that format. Figures 8.3 and 8.4 show the valid range of values for dates and times.

Date Format	Format	*Loval	*Hival
*ISO	YYYY-MM-DD	0001-01-01	9999-12-31
*USA	MM/DD/YYYY	01/01/0001	12/31/9999
*EUR	DD.MM.YYYY	01.01.0001	31.12.9999
*JIS	YYYY-MM-DD	0001-01-01	9999-12-31
*YMD	YY/MM/DD	40/01/01	39/12/31
*MDY	MM/DD/YY	01/01/40	12/31/39
*DMY	DD/MM/YY	01/01/40	31/12/39
*JUL	YY/DDD	40/001	39/365

Figure 8.3: Date ranges

Time Format	Format	*Loval	*Hival
*ISO	hh.mm.ss	00.00.00	24.00.00
*USA	hh:mm xM	00:00 AM	12:00 AM
*EUR	hh.mm.ss	00.00.00	24.00.00
*JIS	hh:mm:ss	00:00:00	24:00:00
*HMS	hh:mm:ss	00:00:00	24:00:00

Figure 8.4: Time ranges

When assigning values to a date variable, you must be careful to ensure the value fits into the format that the date variable is using. For example, the following assignment generates an error:

```
Dcl-s Birthdate Date(*Mdy);


Birthdate = D'1928-07-21';      // RNQ0112 error: Invalid date
```

While July 21, 1928, is indeed a valid date, it does not fit into the 100-year window imposed by the *MDY format. Consequently, an error occurs.

Tip

To avoid errors when dealing with dates, always use one of the four-digit year formats.

8.5. Simple Date Arithmetic

In Chapter 6, you saw how to use Eval for simple numeric assignment. The Eval operation also provides a flexible and powerful method for easily performing date arithmetic by using free-format expressions. Typically, a date expression includes the arithmetic operators + (addition) and – (subtraction), as well as one or more functions that ILE RPG uses to convert a numeric value to a special internal data type called a **duration**. *Duration* is the term RPG uses to describe a unit of time between two dates, times, or timestamps. ILE RPG recognizes seven durations and provides seven corresponding functions:

- **%Years**, for dates or timestamps
- **%Months**, for dates or timestamps
- **%Days**, for dates or timestamps
- **%Hours**, for times or timestamps
- **%Minutes**, for times or timestamps
- **%Seconds**, for times or timestamps
- **%Mseconds** (microseconds), for times or timestamps

Each of these functions converts a number into a duration that can be added to (or subtracted from) a date, time, or timestamp in a familiar expression.

```
Dcl-c Terms 30;
Dcl-c Min   60;


Dcl-s Duedate     Date;
Dcl-s Invoicedate Date;
Dcl-s Endfeb      Date Inz(D'2020-02-29');
Dcl-s Endjan      Date Inz(D'2020-01-31');
Dcl-s Monthago    Date Inz(*Sys);


Duedate = Invoicedate + %Days(30);      // Add 30 days to Invoicedate
Duedate = Invoicedate + %Days(Terms);   // Add Terms (30 days) to invoice date


Endtime = Starttime + %Minutes(Min);    // Add 60 minutes to Starttime


// The following two lines are equivalent
Monthago = Monthago - %Months(1);       // Subtract 1 month from Monthago
Monthago -= %Months(1);
```

Continued

```
// The following lines illustrate leap year effects
// and the irreversibility of some date calculations
Endfeb += %Years(1);                        // Endfeb = D'2021-02-28'
Endfeb -= %Years(1);                        // Now, Endfeb = D'2020-02-28'
Endjan = Endjan + %Months(1) - %Months(1);  // Endmar = D'2020-01-28'
```

If addition or subtraction results in an invalid date, an expression uses the end of the month instead. Because of the vagaries of the calendar, addition or subtraction involving the 29th, 30th, or 31st of the month may not be reversible, as the last two examples show. The duration function must logically match the data type of the expression's result variable. For example, you cannot add a %Minutes duration if the expression's result is a date, but you can add %Minutes to a time or timestamp.

By adding a time to a date, you can assign the resulting value to a timestamp. The following example is similar to the simple assignment expression shown earlier, but it accomplishes the same end with a single expression:

```
Dcl-s Kdate  Date Inz(D'1963-11-22');
Dcl-s Ktime  Time Inz(T'12.34.56');
Dcl-s Kstamp Timestamp(0);
                    // Kstamp has an initial value of Z'0001-01-01-00.00.00'


Kstamp = Kdate + Ktime;     // Kstamp = Z'1963-11-22-12.34.56'
```

If you specify a fractional value with the %Seconds function, the value can represent any scale of fractional seconds, as small as picoseconds (12 fractional digits):

```
Dcl-s Kstamp Timestamp Inz(Z'2019-12-31-12.34.56.789000');


Kstamp += %Seconds(2.3456);      // Kstamp = Z'2019-12-31-12.34.59.134600'
                                 // Equivalent: Kstamp += %Mseconds(2345600);
```

8.6. Using Built-in Functions with Dates

In addition to the duration functions, RPG includes two functions that let you perform date processing that you cannot do with simple arithmetic-like expressions:

- %Diff, to find the difference between two dates, times, or timestamps
- %Subdt, to extract a portion of a date, time, or timestamp

8.6.1. %Diff (Difference)

The **%Diff (Difference)** function calculates the duration between two date or time values. The first two arguments must be data items of compatible types, then the third argument represents the duration code that corresponds to the duration unit you want to determine. The general format is as follows:

```
%Diff(date1:date2:duration{:scale})
```

In this format, the first date must be more recent than the second date (or time). The result is a number (not rounded, up to a 15-digit limit) with any remainder discarded. You can use the %Diff function to find the duration between

- Two dates
- Two times
- Two timestamps
- A date and the date portion of a timestamp
- A time and the time portion of a timestamp

The third argument must be a special value that corresponds to one of the seven durations:

- *Years (or *Y), for dates or timestamps
- *Months (or *M), for dates or timestamps
- *Days (or *D), for dates or timestamps
- *Hours (or *H), for times or timestamps
- *Minutes (or *Mn), for times or timestamps
- *Seconds (or *S), for times or timestamps
- *Mseconds (or *Ms), for times or timestamps

%Diff calculates the difference by subtracting the second argument from the first. The following examples show the use of the %Diff function:

```
Dcl-c Basedate    D'1899-12-30';

Dcl-s Age         Uns(5);
Dcl-s Birthdate   Date;
Dcl-s Endtime     Timestamp;
Dcl-s Fracthours  Packed(15:5);
Dcl-s Message     Char(80);
Dcl-s Starttime   Timestamp;
Dcl-s Today       Date Inz(*Sys);
Dcl-s Weeks       Uns(5);
```

Continued

```
Age = %Diff(Today:Birthdate:*Years);          // Calculate age in years


// The following two lines are equivalent
Message = 'You are currently ' + %Char(Age) + ' years old.';
Message = 'You are currently ' + %Char( %Diff(Today:BirthDate:*Years) )
          + ' years old.';


Weeks = Diff(Today:Basedate:*Days) / 7;     // Calculate difference in weeks


Eval(h) Fracthours = %Diff(Endtime:Starttime:*Seconds) / 3600;
                        // Calculate fractional hours between two timestamps
```

If the third argument is *Seconds (or *S), you can code a fourth argument specifying the scale (fractional seconds, up to 12) of the return value:

```
Dcl-s Elapsed    Packed(15:2);
Dcl-s Endtime    Timestamp;
Dcl-s Starttime Timestamp;


Eval(h) Elapsed = %Diff(Endtime:Starttime:*Seconds:3);
                    // Calculate fractional seconds between two timestamps
```

8.6.2. %Subdt (Extract from Date/Time/Timestamp)

The **%Subdt (Extract from date/time/timestamp)** function *substrings* a date; that is, it extracts a portion of a date, time, or timestamp data item. The first argument is the date, time, or timestamp variable, which is followed by a special value that specifies the portion of the value you want to extract—one of the same special values used by the %Diff function. The general format is as follows:

```
%Subdt(date:duration{:precision{:scale}})
```

Here are some examples of using %Subdt:

```
Dcl-s Birthdate Date;
Dcl-s Jdate      Date(*Jul) Inz(D'2020-02-10');
                            // Jdate is displayed in Julian format as 20/041
                                                              Continued
```

```
Dcl-s Day        Uns(5);
Dcl-s Month      Uns(5);
Dcl-s Year       Uns(5);


Year = %Subdt(Birthdate:*Years);      // Extract year from Birthdate
Month = %Subdt(Birthdate:*Months);    // Extract month from Birthdate
Day = %Subdt(Birthdate:*Days);        // Extract day from Birthdate


Year = %Subdt(Jdate:*Years);          // Year = 2020
Month = %Subdt(Jdate:*Months);        // Month = 02
Day = %Subdt(Jdate:*Days);            // Day = 10
```

The result is numeric. The %Subdt function always treats the *Days code as the day of the month (even for *Jul format dates) and always returns a four-digit year when you specify the *Years code.

For *Seconds duration, you can include a third argument to specify the precision (number of digits) of the return value and enter a fourth argument to represent the scale (fractional seconds):

```
Dcl-c Kstamp Z'1963-11-22-12.34.56.78951';


Dcl-s Secs     Packed(5:3);


Eval(h) Secs = %Subdt(Kstamp:*Seconds:6:4);    // Secs = 56.790
```

8.6.3. Data-Conversion Functions

All the operands in a date expression must be a date data type or a duration subtype—the program cannot directly mix date values with numeric or character data in the same expression. The duration functions examined earlier convert a numeric expression to a duration subtype so it can be used in a date expression. Several other functions convert numeric and character expressions to dates, times, and timestamps, and others convert date-related data back to character and numeric values. These functions are as follows:

- %Date (Convert to date)
- %Time (Convert to time)
- %Timestamp (Convert to timestamp)
- %Char (Convert to character)
- %Dec (Convert to decimal)

8.6.3.1. %Date (Convert to Date)

The primary use for the **%Date (Convert to date)** function is to convert a numeric or character value to a date data type. The value to convert can be a variable, a literal, a constant, or an expression. The format of the %Date function is as follows:

```
%Date({value{:format}})
```

The first argument is the value that you want to convert. The second argument contains the date format of the value to convert; that is, if the legacy date value were already a native date, this is the format it would be using. If you omit the second argument, %Date uses the program's default format, usually *ISO.

Recall that the separator character is an integral part of the date. The conversion function must account for the separator. If the character value contains a separator character other than the format's default, you can include a separator character with the format designation. But if the character value contains no separators, code a zero (0) following the format to indicate no separators. When converting numeric values, you need not account for a separator because numeric values do not allow a separator. Here are some examples of using %Date to convert data:

```
Dcl-s Mydate Date;


Dcl-s Var1    Char(10)    Inz('02/12/2020');
Dcl-s Var2    Char(6)     Inz('031320');


Dcl-s Num     Packed(9:0) Inz(20200414);


Dcl-s Month   Packed(3:0) Inz(6);
Dcl-s Day     Packed(3:0) Inz(16);
Dcl-s Year    Packed(5:0) Inz(2020);

Mydate = %Date(Var1:*Usa);                          // Mydate = D'2020-02-12'
Mydate = %Date(Var2:*Mdy0);                         // Mydate = D'2020-03-13'
Mydate = %Date(Num);                                // Mydate = D'2020-04-14'
Mydate = %Date( ((Year*10000) + (Month*100) + Day) );
                                                    // Mydate = D'2020-06-16'
```

%Date always returns its result in *ISO format, regardless of the format of the value you want to convert. If you omit the first argument, %Date returns the current system date:

```
Dcl-s Today Date;


Today = %Date();       // Today now contains the current system date
```

The first argument can also be a timestamp, allowing you to move the date portion of a timestamp into a date variable. Or the first argument can be the IBM-reserved word *Date or Udate to assign the current job date to a variable. *Date and Udate refer to the same value, except that *Date includes a four-digit year, and Udate includes only a two-digit year. For any of these cases—a timestamp, *Date, or Udate—you do not code a second argument because the computer already knows the format.

```
Dcl-s Asof Date;


Asof = %Date(*Date);       // Asof now contains the current job date
```

The %Date function supports several additional external formats that ILE RPG supports for backward compatibility with legacy applications (Figure 8.5). These are not valid internal date formats, but you can use them to convert character or numeric data representing dates.

External Format	Description	Format	Valid Separators	Edited Field Length	Example
*CYMD	Century/year/month/day	CYY/MM/DD	/ - , . &(blank)	9	120/12/31
*CMDY	Century/month/day/year	CMM/DD/YY	/ - , . &(blank)	9	112/31/20
*CDMY	Century/day/month/year	CDD/MM/YY	/ - , . &(blank)	9	131/12/20
*LONGJUL	Long Julian	YYYY/DDD	/ - , . &(blank)	8	2020/366
*JOBRUN	(Format and separators are determined at runtime, using the job's attributes. Valid only for two-digit year formats.)				

Figure 8.5: Legacy date formats

In Figure 8.5, the *century* portion of the date (illustrated with a C in the format column) is indicated by a single digit 0–9, with 0 representing 1900–1999, 1 representing 2000–2099, and so on, up to 9, which represents 2800–2899. So in *CYMD format, the numeric value 1171231 represents December 31, 2017. The following code illustrates the use of these external formats:

```
Dcl-s Mydate Date;


Dcl-s Var  Char(9)      Inz('120/02/12');
Dcl-s Var2 Char(7)      Inz('1200313');


Dcl-s Num  Packed(7:0) Inz(1200414);
```

Continued

```
Dcl-s Num2 Packed(7:0) Inz(2020040);

Mydate = %Date(Var:*Cymd);          // Mydate = D'2020-02-12'
Mydate = %Date(Var2:*Cymd0);        // Mydate = D'2020-03-13'
Mydate = %Date(Num:*Cymd);          // Mydate = D'2020-04-14'
Mydate = %Date(Num2:*Longjul);      // Mydate = D'2020-02-09'
```

8.6.3.2. %Time (Convert to Time)

The **%Time (Convert to time)** function is similar to %Date and uses many of the same principles. It converts a numeric or character value to a time data type. The value to convert can be a variable, literal, constant, or expression. The format of the %Time function is as follows:

```
%Time({value{:format}})
```

The first argument is the value that you want to convert. The second argument contains the time format of the value to convert. If you omit the second argument, %Time uses the program's default format, usually *ISO.

As with dates, the time separator character is an integral part of the value, and the conversion function must account for it. If the character value contains a separator character other than the format's default, you can include a separator character with the format designation. But if the character value contains no separators, code a zero (0) following the format to indicate no separators. When converting numeric values, you need not account for a separator because numeric values do not allow a separator. Here are some examples of using %Time to convert data:

```
Dcl-s Mytime Time;
Dcl-s Var    Char(10)   Inz('12:34 PM');
Dcl-s Var2   Char(6)    Inz('134500');
Dcl-s Num    Packed(7:0) Inz(145600);

Mytime = %Time(Var:*Usa);       // Mytime now contains T'12.34.00'
Mytime = %Time(Var2:*Hms0);     // Mytime now contains T'13.45.00'
Mytime = %Time(Num);            // Mytime now contains T'14.56.00'
```

%Time always returns its result in *ISO format, regardless of the format of the value you want to convert. If you omit the first argument, %Time returns the current system time:

```
Dcl-s Mytime Time;

Mytime = %Time();      // Mytime now contains the current system time
```

The first argument can also be a timestamp, allowing you to move the time portion of a timestamp into a time variable. In this case, you do not code a second argument because the computer already knows the format.

8.6.3.3. %Timestamp (Convert to Timestamp)

As you might expect, the **%Timestamp (Convert to timestamp)** function converts the value of a character or numeric expression—or a date expression—to a timestamp data type. The function takes following the form:

```
%Timestamp({value{:format}{:scale}})
```

The first argument is the value that you want to convert. The second argument is one of two special values: *ISO or *ISO0 (if there are no separators). This argument is not necessary when converting date expressions. For numeric expressions, it is required only when specifying fractional seconds—in that case, only *ISO is allowed. No other formats are permitted. The scale can be 0–12 fractional seconds, but the default scale is 6. Here are some examples of using %Timestamp:

```
Dcl-s Mystamp Timestamp(0);
Dcl-s Var     Char(14)    Inz('19631122123456');
Dcl-s Num     Packed(15:0) Inz(19991231235959);

Mystamp = %Timestamp(Char:*Iso0:0);     // Mystamp = Z'1963-11-22-12.34.56'
Mystamp = %Timestamp(Num);*Iso:0);      // Mystamp = Z'1999-12-31-23.59.59'
```

If you omit the arguments, %Timestamp returns the current system date and time in timestamp format:

```
Dcl-s Now Timestamp(0);

Now = %Timestamp();     // Now contains the current system date/time
```

The first argument can also be a date, allowing you to move the date into the date portion of a timestamp variable. In this case, you do not code a second argument because the computer already knows the format.

Caution
Before you can use %Date, %Time, or %Timestamp to convert character or
numeric data, ensure that the *legacy* format indeed contains a valid value
for the target data type. You can use the Test operation, discussed in
Chapter 16, to validate the value before you try to convert it. If you try to
convert an invalid value, a runtime error (probably RNQ0112) occurs.

8.6.3.4. %Char (Convert to Character Data)

Previously, you used the **%Char (Convert to character data)** function to convert the result
of a numeric variable, literal, named constant, or expression to a character value. %Char also
works to convert dates, times, and timestamps to character data. The %Char function can be
useful when you want to perform date-related processing but a legacy database requires that
the data be stored in character format. When you use the %Char function to convert dates,
times, or timestamps, it takes the following form:

```
%Char(value:format)
```

The first argument contains the date/time/timestamp expression to convert. The second
argument holds the format that the character result represents. You can use any of the date or
time formats discussed previously (Figures 8.1, 8.2, and 8.5). The result includes separator
characters unless you code a zero (0) after the format. Leading zeros are retained in the
character result. Here are some examples of using %Char to convert dates:

```
Dcl-s Message Char(30);
Dcl-s Expire  Date    Inz(D'2020-08-12');


Message = 'Offer expires ' + %Char(Expire:*Usa) + '.';
                         // Message = 'Offer expires 08/12/2020.      '

Message = 'It is ' + %Char( %Time() :*Usa) + ' on ' +
          %Char( %Date() :*Usa) + '.';
                         // Message contains current time and date, e.g.
                         // 'It is 12:34 PM on 08/12/2020. '
```

8.6.3.5. %Dec (Convert to Decimal Data)

Previously, you used the **%Dec (Convert to decimal data)** function to convert character
expressions to decimal format. But the %Dec function also works with dates, times, and

timestamps to convert them to numeric packed decimal format. Legacy databases most commonly use numeric formats to store date values, and the %Dec function is useful for converting native dates back to numeric formats for storage in the database. When you use the %Dec function to convert dates, times, or timestamps, it takes the following form:

```
%Dec(value{:format})
```

The first argument contains the date/time/timestamp expression to convert. Unlike with character conversion, the numeric result does not include separator characters.

The second argument contains the format that the numeric result represents. You can use most of the date or time formats examined previously (Figures 8.1, 8.2, and 8.5) except *USA when you are converting a time. The %Dec function allows you to omit the second parameter—the format. If you do, the function uses the format of the date, time, or timestamp for the numeric result. If the time format is *USA, though, you must specify another format. Here are some examples of using %Dec to convert dates:

```
Dcl-s Expiredate Date Inz(D'2020-06-30') Datfmt(*Usa);
Dcl-s Jobtime    Time Inz(T'14.25.48');


Dcl-s Nbrdate    Packed(9:0);
Dcl-s Nbrjulian  Packed(5:0);
Dcl-s Nbrjde     Packed(7:0);
Dcl-s Nbrhms     Packed(7:0);


Nbrdate = %Dec(Expiredate);           // Nbrdate = 06302020
Nbrdate = %Dec(Expiredate:*Iso);      // Nbrdate = 20200630
Nbrjulian = %Dec(Expiredate:*Jul);    // Nbrjulian = 20182
Nbrjde = %Dec(Expiredate:*Cymd);      // Nbrjde = 1200630
Nbrhms = %Dec(Jobtime:*Iso);          // Nbrhms = 142548
```

8.7. Navigating Legacy Code

Even though RPG support for native date-related data types is a relatively recent development, there are three fixed-format operation codes for processing dates:

- Adddur (Add Duration)
- Subdur (Subtract Duration)
- Extrct (Extract Date/Time/Timestamp)

These operation codes are not as flexible as the date-related functions and are restricted to the fixed-format Calculation specifications. In addition to these operations, you can use the Move and Movel operations, discussed in Chapter 7, in legacy programs to assign and convert date data types.

8.7.1. Adddur (Add Duration)

The **Adddur (Add Duration)** operation lets you add a duration coded in Factor 2 to the date specified in Factor 1, storing the answer in the date, time, or timestamp field indicated as the Result field. If Factor 1 is blank, the Factor 2 duration is simply added to the Result field. If Factor 1 is present, it can contain any data item representing one of the three date data types, but its type must match that of the Result field.

Factor 2 must contain an integer variable (or literal), which represents the number to add, and one of the seven duration codes, which indicates the kind of duration the number represents. You separate these two portions of Factor 2 with a colon (:). If the numeric portion of Factor 2 represents a negative value, the duration is subtracted rather than added. The following examples illustrate the use of Adddur. (Assume that variables Billdate, Duedate, Startdate, and Enddate are defined as date data; variables Starttime and Endtime are time data; and variable Min is numeric.)

```
*.. 1 ...+... 2 ...+... 3 ...+... 4 ...+... 5 ...+... 6 ...+... 7 ...+... 8
CLON01Factor1+++++++Opcode(E)+Factor2+++++++Result+++++++Len++D+HiLoEq....
 * Add 30 days to Billdate to determine Duedate
C     Billdate      Adddur    30:*Days      Duedate
 * Add 5 years to Duedate
C                   Adddur    5:*Years      Duedate
 * Subtract 5 months from Enddate to get Startdate
C     Enddate       Adddur    -5:*Months    Startdate
 * Add field Min, a number of minutes, to Starttime to determine Endtime
C     Starttime     Adddur    Min:*Mn       Endtime
```

8.7.2. Subdur (Subtract Duration)

The **Subdur (Subtract Duration)** operation has two uses: one is to subtract a date/time duration from a date/time value (similar to Adddur with a negative duration), and the second is to calculate the duration between two date/time units (equivalent to the %Diff function). To subtract a Factor 2 duration from a date/time data item in Factor 1 and store the answer in the Result field, code the operation the same as you would Adddur:

```
*.. 1 ...+... 2 ...+... 3 ...+... 4 ...+... 5 ...+... 6 ...+... 7 ...+... 8
CLON01Factor1+++++++Opcode(E)+Factor2+++++++Result++++++++Len++D+HiLoEq....
 * Subtract 30 days from Duedate to determine Billdate
C     Duedate        Subdur     30:*Days        Billdate
 * Subtract 5 years from DueDate
C                    Subdur     5:*Y            Duedate
```

To calculate the duration between two date/time units, place data items of compatible types in both Factor 1 and Factor 2, and place an integer result variable followed by a duration code that denotes the unit of time involved in the operation in the Result field. Again, a colon separates the two subfactors. The following fixed-format processing is accomplished with the %Diff function in free format:

```
*.. 1 ...+... 2 ...+... 3 ...+... 4 ...+... 5 ...+... 6 ...+... 7 ...+... 8
CLON01Factor1+++++++Opcode(E)+Factor2+++++++Result++++++++Len++D+HiLoEq....
 * Subtract Birthdate from Today to get Age in years
C     Todaydate      Subdur     Birthdate       Age:*Years
 * Determine the number of days left to study for a test
C     Examdate       Subdur     Todaydate       Cramtime:*D
```

8.7.3. Extrct (Extract Date/Time/Timestamp)

The third operation for manipulating dates and times, **Extrct (Extract Date/Time/Timestamp)**, extracts a portion of a date, time, or timestamp data item and stores it in the Result field, which can be any numeric or character result variable. You must couple the Factor 2 date/time data item with a duration code to signal which portion of the date/time unit to extract. Factor 1 is always blank for Extrct operations. For free-format code, the %Subdt function performs this task.

```
*.. 1 ...+... 2 ...+... 3 ...+... 4 ...+... 5 ...+... 6 ...+... 7 ...+... 8
CLON01Factor1+++++++Opcode(E)+Factor2+++++++Result++++++++Len++D+HiLoEq....
 * Determine the birth year of a birth date (Date data type)
C                    Extrct     Birthdate:*Y Birthyear
 * Extract the month of a loan (Date data type)
C                    Extrct     Loandate:*M  Loanmonth
```

8.7.4. Move, Movel (Move Left)

Recall that you can use the Move operation as an assignment operator, transferring characters from Factor 2 to the Result, moving right to left. Also recall that Movel transfers characters from left to right. If Factor 1 and Factor 2 are both dates (in any valid format), the following code accomplishes the same result as Eval:

```
*.. 1 ...+... 2 ...+... 3 ...+... 4 ...+... 5 ...+... 6 ...+... 7 ...+... 8
CLON01Factor1+++++++Opcode(E)+Factor2+++++++Result++++++++Len++D+HiLoEq....
C                   Move      DateUSA       DateISO
```

To convert a numeric or character value (literal, constant, or variable) to a date, you can specify the date format of the legacy value in Factor 1:

```
*.. 1 ...+... 2 ...+... 3 ...+... 4 ...+... 5 ...+... 6 ...+... 7 ...+... 8
CLON01Factor1+++++++Opcode(E)+Factor2+++++++Result++++++++Len++D+HiLoEq....
C     *Usa          Move      06302020      DateISO
 * DateISO = D'2020-06-30'
```

To convert the other direction—from a date to a numeric or character variable—you simply reverse the roles of Factor 2 and the Result. Again, you can use Factor 1 to specify the desired format of the legacy result:

```
*.. 1 ...+... 2 ...+... 3 ...+... 4 ...+... 5 ...+... 6 ...+... 7 ...+... 8
CLON01Factor1+++++++Opcode(E)+Factor2+++++++Result++++++++Len++D+HiLoEq....
C     *Usa          Move      D'2020-06-30' Numvar
 * Numvar = 06302020
```

8.8. Chapter Summary

ILE RPG uses the native date, time, and timestamp data types to support date-related business processing. The term *date data* covers all three data types. You can define data items as date data in SQL or DDS (for externally described files), RPG declarations, and Input specifications (for program-described files).

Although the system stores date data in a compact internal format, ILE RPG supports a number of external formats. The default format is *ISO. Each format has a default separator character, which is an integral part of the format. Four-digit year formats support any date from the year 1 through 9999, but two-digit year formats can only contain values from 1940 until 2039.

You use the Eval operation to assign values to date data and, along with duration-related functions, to perform date arithmetic. To code date-related literals, you must use a typed literal (e.g., D'2018-03-15 ').

ILE RPG provides many functions to simplify the processing of date data. The following table summarizes the operation codes and functions examined in this chapter:

Function or Operation	Description	Syntax
%Char	Convert to character data	**%Char(expression {: format})**
%Date	Convert to date	**%Date({expression {: format}})**
%Days	Number of days	**%Days(number)**
%Dec	Convert to packed decimal	**%Dec(date-expression {: format})**
%Diff	Difference between two dates/times/timestamps	**%Diff(date1 : date2 : duration-code {:scale})**
Eval	Evaluate expression	**{Eval{(mr)}} assignment-expression;**
%Hours	Number of hours	**%Hours(number)**
%Minutes	Number of minutes	**%Minutes(number)**
%Months	Number of months	**%Months(number)**
%Mseconds	Number of microseconds	**%Mseconds(number)**
%Seconds	Number of seconds	**%Seconds(number)**
%Subdt	Subset of a date, time, or timestamp	**%Subdt(date : duration-code {: precision{:scale}})**
%Time	Convert to time	**%Time({expression {: format}})**
%Timestamp	Convert to timestamp	**%Timestamp({expression {: *Iso | *Iso0} {: scale}})**
%Years	Number of years	**%Years(number)**

8.9. Key Terms

%Char function
Date
date formats
%Date function
Datfmt
%Days function
%Dec function
%Diff function
external format

duration
external format
*Hival
%Hours function
ISO standard
*Loval
%Minutes function
%Months function
%Mseconds function

%Seconds function
separator characters
%Subdt function
Time
Timfmt
%Time function
Timestamp
%Timestamp function
%Years function

8.10. Discussion/Review Questions

1. Explain the advantages of using native date, time, and timestamps. What difficulties has this caused the RPG programmer?
2. When assigning values to date variables, what should the programmer be careful of?
3. When using a Ctl-opt instruction to set a default date or time format, what is always true of typed literals?

4. When working with date expressions, can you mix date values with numeric or character data in the same expression?

5. Why would the %Date, %Time, and %Timestamp functions be important to today's RPG programmer?

6. By default in RPG, %Date always returns a date in what format? Can you change this?

7. Why would today's RPG programmer need the %Char and %Dec functions?

8. What date restrictions are placed on date fields that use two-digit formats?

9. What is the range of dates that can be stored in a four-digit native date field?

10. What is the range of dates that can be stored in a two-digit native date field?

11. Explain the *irreversibility* of adding/subtracting dates that this chapter described.

12. What are the default date and time formats and lengths?

8.11. Exercises

```
Dcl-s Startdate    Date Inz(D'1999-12-31');
Dcl-s Enddate      Date Inz(D'2001-01-01');
Dcl-s Birthdate    Date;
Dcl-s Currentdate  Date Inz(*Sys);
Dcl-s Jobstartdate Date Inz(*Job);
Dcl-s Midnight     Time Inz(T'24.00.00');
Dcl-s Birthtime    Time Inz(T'06.45.15');
Dcl-s Jobstarttime Time Inz(T'24.00.00');
Dcl-s Jobendtime   Time Inz(T'06.45.15');
```

Given the preceding date and time declarations, write the code for the following exercises. Be sure to define a variable to hold the result.

1. The number of days between Birthdate and Currentdate.

2. The number of years between Startdate and Currentdate.

3. The number of hours between Startdate and Enddate.

4. The number of minutes between Birthdate and Currentdate.

5. Add 20 years to Birthdate.

6. Add 30 months to Currentdate.

7. Add 6 hours to Jobstarttime.

8. Subtract 8 hours from Midnight.

9. Using Birthdate and Birthtime, write the code to produce the following timestamp:

Birthstamp will contain Z'1951-12-10-06.45.15.000000 '

10. Given the timestamp Z'2005-12-10-06.45.15.000000 ', write the code to break this into a native date (Startdate) and native time (Starttime).

11. Code a data structure initialized to your birth date that divides the date into three fields: BirthYear, BirthMonth, and BirthDay.

12. How old are you?

a. Define and initialize a date field called MyBirthDate with your birth date.

b. Define and initialize a date field called Today with the system date.

c. Define a zoned decimal field called DaysOld.

d. Write the code to calculate how old you are based on the previously defined fields.

13. When is New Year's Eve?

a. Define and initialize a date field called NewYearsEve with a date constant (initialize it to this year's New Year's Eve, e.g., 2015-12-31).

b. Define and initialize a date field called Today with the system date.

c. Define a zoned decimal field called DaysToNewYears.

d. Write the code to calculate the number of days until New Year's Eve based on the previously defined fields.

CHAPTER **9**

Accessing and Updating Database Files

9.1. Chapter Overview

This chapter introduces you to ILE RPG's operations for reading, writing, and updating records. It also examines both sequential and random file access techniques. In addition, the chapter discusses file maintenance—adding, deleting, and changing records in a file—and record locking considerations in update procedures.

9.2. Sequential Access

File access refers to how records can be retrieved, or read, from an input file. ILE RPG offers several alternative operations for accessing data from full procedural database files. Several of these operations are appropriate for sequential processing. You can use others for random access processing.

With **sequential access**, records are retrieved in either arrival order—first-in, first-out (FIFO)—for nonkeyed files, or in key order if the file is keyed and its file declaration (i.e., its Dcl-f instruction) indicates Keyed processing:

```
Dcl-f Customers Disk Keyed;
```

Reading generally starts with the first record in the file, with each subsequent read operation retrieving the next record in the file until eventually you reach end-of-file. This kind of sequential access is especially suited for batch processing.

ILE RPG includes several file input/output (I/O) operations that provide variations on sequential record access. Some of these operations control where in the file sequential reading next occurs, and others determine the nature of the reading itself. These operations are as follows:

- Read (Read a record)
- Setll (Set lower limit)
- Setgt (Set greater than)
- Reade (Read equal key)
- Readp (Read prior record)
- Readpe (Read prior equal)

9.2.1. Read (Read a Record)

As you know, the **Read (Read a record)** operation retrieves records sequentially from a full procedural file. The general format of the Read operation is as follows:

```
Read filename {datastructure} ;
```

A required filename designates which file the Read is to access. When the Read operation finds no additional records to read, it sets the value of the **%Eof (End-of-file)** function to *On. You should test the %Eof value after each Read operation. When you code the %Eof function, name a specific file in parentheses after the function. If you omit the filename, the %Eof function refers to the most recent file operation. The following example demonstrates the use of Read and %Eof:

```
Read Customers;
If %Eof(Customers);
  // End-of-file processing goes here
Endif;
```

If the Read operation successfully accesses a record, it positions the file at the next sequential record to be read. If the %Eof condition for a file is on, you cannot read any further records from that file unless you reposition the file, perhaps by using the Setll operation, examined next.

For externally described files, the first keyword can actually be a record format name rather than a filename. However, if the Read encounters a record format different from that named by the Read operation—as may be the case when the input file is a logical file with multiple formats—the operation ends in error. Chapter 16 discusses how to detect and handle such errors.

You can specify an additional argument for the Read operation to name a data structure to receive the record data. When you name a **result data structure**, the Read operation transfers data directly from the record to the data structure, which can improve the program's performance and give you direct control over how your program interprets the data. The following example demonstrates the use of a result data structure:

```
Dcl-f Customers Disk;

Dcl-ds Custdata Likerec(Custsrec);

Read Customers Custdata;
If %Eof(Customers);
  // End-of-file processing goes here
Endif;
```

If the Read operation is accessing an externally described file, the result data structure must use the Likerec keyword or the Extname keyword to exactly match the record format's input fields. For program-described files, the data structure's length must be the same as the file's record length in the file declarations. In the previous example, a successful Read operation transfers record data from the Customers file directly into the Custdata data structure, which reflects the layout of the Custsrec record format in file Customers.

9.2.2. SetII (Set Lower Limit)

The **SetII (Set lower limit)** operation provides flexibility related to where sequential reading occurs within a file. SetII lets you begin sequential processing at a record other than the first one in the file. You can also use it to reposition the file, for example, once end-of-file has been reached. The general format of a SetII operation is as follows:

```
Setll search-argument filename;
```

SetII positions a full procedural file at the first record whose key (or relative record number in the file) is greater than or equal to the value you specify in the search argument. The search argument can be a literal, variable name, figurative constant, or composite key (we describe composite keys later in this chapter). The second operand can be a filename or record format name (if the file is externally described).

You can use the %Equal and %Found functions with SetII. The **%Equal** function is turned on if a record is found whose key exactly matches the search argument. **%Found** is turned on if a record in the file has a key equal to or greater than the value in the search argument (i.e., if the file position was successfully set).

The Setll operation does not actually retrieve a record. It simply positions the file to determine which record the next sequential read is to access. An unsuccessful Setll causes the file to be positioned at end-of-file.

Setll has three common uses in RPG programming. The first is to reposition the file to the beginning during processing by using figurative constant *Loval as the search argument. The next sequential Read operation then retrieves the first record in the file:

```
Setll *Loval Customers;
Read Customers;              // Read first record in file
```

The second common use of Setll is to position the file to the first record of a group of records with identical key values in preparation for processing that group of records. (We examine details of this use next, when we cover the Reade operation.)

You also can use Setll to determine whether a record exists in a file without actually reading the record. If you simply need to check for the presence of a record with a given key without accessing the record's data, using Setll is more efficient than doing a Read operation:

```
Setll Custchk Customers;
If %Equal(Customers);
  Exsr Validcust;           // Record exists for Custchk key value
Else;
  Exsr Invalidcust;         // No record for Custchk key value
Endif;
```

9.2.3. Reade (Read Equal Key)

The **Reade (Read equal key)** operation sequentially reads the next record in a full procedural file if that record's key matches the search argument value. If the record's key does not match, or if the file is at end-of-file, the %Eof function is turned on. The Reade operation follows this general form:

```
Reade search-argument filename {datastructure} ;
```

The search argument can be a variable, literal, figurative constant, or composite key. The second operand can be the filename or (for externally described files) the record format name. You can specify an optional third argument for the Reade operation to name a result data structure to receive the data.

Programmers use the Reade operation within a loop to identically process sets of records with duplicate keys in a file. Often, programmers precede the first Reade with a SetII operation to position the file initially, in preparation for processing those records with keys identical to the value specified by the SetII. Assume, for example, that you want to list all orders received on a specific date and that the Orders file is keyed on date. Further assume that field Indate stores the date whose orders you want to print. The appropriate processing is as follows:

```
// Code to list all orders placed on Indate
Setll Indate Orders;


If %Equal(Orders);              // Orders placed on Indate
  Reade Indate Orders;

  Dow Not %Eof(Orders);
    Write Orderline;
    Reade Indate Orders;
  Enddo;


Else;
  Exsr Noorders;               // No orders placed on Indate
Endif;
```

This code uses the value of Indate to position the Orders file to a key value that matches that of Indate. If a match exists, the %Equal function is turned on, the program does an initial Reade of the file, and then it sets up a loop with a Dow operation. Within the loop, the program writes an order line and then reads the next record equal to Indate. The loop continues as long as the Reade is successful. If the initial SetII fails to find any order for Indate (signaled by %Equal being off), flow bypasses the loop, drops down to the Else, and executes the Noorders subroutine.

9.2.4. Setgt (Set Greater Than)

The **Setgt (Set greater than)** operation works similarly to SetII. The primary difference is that Setgt positions the file to a record whose key value is greater than the value of the search argument, rather than greater than or equal to the value of the search argument. The general form of the Setgt operation is as follows:

```
Setgt search-argument filename;
```

As with the Setll operation, the search argument can be a variable, literal, figurative constant, or composite key. The second operand can be a filename or (for an externally described file) a record format name. You can test the %Found function, which is turned on if the positioning is successful, or code Not %Found to detect unsuccessful positioning (in which case, the file is positioned at end-of-file). The %Equal function does not apply to Setgt.

```
Setgt Custin Customers;
If %Found(Customers);
  Exsr Success;
Else;
  Exsr Valuetoohi;
Endif;
```

Following a successful Setgt operation, the file is positioned so that the next record to be read is one whose key is greater than the search argument. You can also use Setgt with figurative constant *Hival to position a file to end-of-file in preparation for a Readp operation (discussed next) to read the last record in the file. Remember that Setgt, like Setll, merely positions the file; it does not actually retrieve a record from the database.

9.2.5. Readp (Read Prior Record), Readpe (Read Prior Equal)

Readp (Read prior record) and **Readpe (Read prior equal)** are sequential reading operations whose parallels are Read and Reade, respectively. The only difference between Readp and Read, and between Readpe and Reade, is directionality. The *prior* read operations move *backward* through the file. These operations follow this general format:

```
Readp filename {datastructure} ;

Readpe search-argument filename {datastructure) ;
```

Both prior read operations require a filename or a record format name. Like Reade, Readpe must have a search argument entry. Both operations also support an optional result data structure.

Like Read and Reade, both Readp and Readpe support the %Eof function. But this function is turned on at *beginning-of-file* (not end-of-file) for Readp or when the prior sequential record's key does not match the search argument value for Readpe.

Although the concept of *backward* sequential access is relatively easy to grasp, it is harder to visualize why such processing might be desired. Generally, you might use the prior read operations to process files in descending key order. Ordinarily, the database organizes keyed files in sequence by ascending key value.

To get a sense of when these operations might be appropriate, let's consider an example. Imagine the following scenario. As part of an order processing application, a program is to assign order numbers sequentially. Each time the program is run, the number assigned to the order number is to be one larger than the number of the last order processed. Assume also that the order file is keyed on order number. The following code determines the appropriate value for the new order:

```
// Code using Setgt and Readp to determine the next order number to use.
// Orders file is keyed on field Ordernbr.
Setgt *Hival Orders;
Readp Orders;

If Not %Eof(Orders);
  Ordernbr += 1;
Else;
  Ordnbr = 1;
Endif;
```

In this code, Setgt positions the file at end-of-file. The Readp operation retrieves the last record in the file (e.g., the record with the highest order number). Adding 1 to Ordernbr, then, gives you the value for the new order. If %Eof is turned on, it indicates that you are at beginning-of-file, which means no records exist in the order file. In this case, Ordnbr is 1.

9.3. Random Access

All the operations we've examined so far in this chapter deal with retrieving database records sequentially. Often, however, you want to be able to read a specific record, determined by its key value, without having to read through the file sequentially to reach that record. This kind of access is called **random access**. Random access lets you *reach into* a file and extract just the record you want. ILE RPG supports random access of full procedural database files through the Chain operation.

9.3.1. Chain (Random Retrieval from a File)

The **Chain (Random retrieval from a file)** operation requires a search argument—a variable, literal, figurative constant, or composite key—that contains the key value of the record to be randomly read. The second operand, also required, specifies the name of the file (or record format) from which to randomly retrieve the record. A third, optional, operand can name a result data structure to receive the record. The Chain operation uses this general format:

```
Chain search-argument filename {datastructure} ;
```

The **%Found** function is turned on if the random retrieval is successful (i.e., a record in the file matches the specified search argument).

```
Chain Custno Customers;

If %Found(Customers);
   Exsr Validcust;
Else;
   Exsr Nocust;
Endif;
```

In the preceding example, Custno contains the key value of the Customers record you want to read. If Chain finds the record, the program executes subroutine Validcust. But if Chain fails to find the record, the program executes subroutine Nocust. When the file contains records with duplicate keys, such that more than one record qualifies as a match, the system retrieves only the first record that matches.

When Chain successfully retrieves a record (signaled by the %Found function), the system reads the data into the program and then positions the file to the record immediately following the retrieved record. Accordingly, issuing a Read or Reade to the file following a successful Chain lets you sequentially access the file starting with the record immediately following the retrieved record. Because of this feature, you can use the Chain operation to position the file in a manner similar to SetII. The primary difference between these two approaches is that a successful Chain actually reads a record, whereas a successful SetII merely repositions the file without retrieving a record.

```
// Code to list all orders placed on Indate
Chain Indate Orders;

If %Found(Orders);            // Orders placed on Indate
```

Continued

```
   Dow Not %Eof(Orders);
      Write Orderline;
      Reade Indate Orders;
   Enddo;


Else;
   Exsr Noorders;               // No orders placed on Indate
Endif;
```

If a Chain operation does not find a record, you cannot follow it with a sequential Read operation without first successfully repositioning the file with another Chain, Setll, or Setgt operation. You can, however, follow it with subsequent Chain operations—Chain does not set the %Eof function to *On.

9.4. Using Composite Keys

As Chapter 3 discussed, both physical and logical files can have keys based on more than one field. This kind of key is called a **composite key** or a **concatenated key**. The existence of composite keys raises a puzzling question: What can you use as a search argument for Chain, Setll, Reade, and so on, when the records in the file you want to access are keyed on more than one field value?

The operation codes that support a composite key (Chain, Delete, Reade, Readpe, Setgt, and Setll) let you simply code a list of values in place of the key operand for the operation code. To understand how this feature works, assume you have a database file, Customers, keyed on Company, Region, and Custno. You are writing a program that requires you to randomly access the Customers file to retrieve information about a specific customer. To retrieve a record by using a composite key, you can list the values that make up the composite key in parentheses, separated by colons:

```
Chain (Company:Region:Custno) Customers;
```

The order in which you list the values determines the order in which they are combined to form the composite key. The variable names can have, but do not require, the same names as those of the file records' composite key. In fact, the values need not be variables; they can be literals, constants, or even expressions. However, each value's base type must match the corresponding key field in the file (i.e., numeric values for numeric key fields, character values for character key fields, etc.). The compiler performs any required conversion by using the same rules that the Eval operation uses to assign values.

The following example shows how you might use expressions and literals in the list of keys:

```
Chain ('346' : Region : %Char(Lastcustno + 1)) Customers;
```

In this example, the company is *hard-coded* as character value '346', Region is a variable, and the customer number to retrieve is calculated in an expression and then converted to a character value for use as the third key value.

9.4.1. Partial Composite Keys

Composite keys offer an additional feature that simplifies processing groups of logically associated records. Let's use the previous example, but this time, instead of wanting information about a specific customer, assume you want to be able to access all the records in Customers for a particular company and region. The following code accomplishes the desired processing:

```
Chain (Company:Region) Customers;

If %Found(Customers);

  Dow Not %Eof(Customers);
    Exsr Process;
    Reade (Company:Region) Customers;
  Enddo;

Else;
  Exsr Nocustomers;
Endif;
```

First, this example chains to the Customers file, using a *partial* composite key (with fewer key values than in the actual file) to read the first customer for the given company and region. If the Chain finds a record, the program sets up a loop that continues until %Eof comes on for Customers. Within the loop, the program executes subroutine Process and then executes a Reade to obtain the next customer for that company and region. The Reade operation within the loop sets %Eof to *On when no more records are found for that company and region. If the original Chain fails, control drops to the Else, and the program executes subroutine Nocustomers to indicate that the company/region/customer record is not in the file.

Note that you can achieve the same effects by issuing a SetII to position the file and then, provided the operation is successful, using a Reade to read the first record of the set. A successful Chain reads a record *and* positions the file to the desired location in one operation.

ILE RPG lets you access a database file based on a partial key list if the portion you want to use is the major, or top-level, key field (or fields). That is, given the Customers file described here, the following partial key lists are valid:

- Company
- (Company:Region)

But the following list is *not* valid:

- Customer
- Region
- (Region:Customer)
- (Customer:Region)
- (Region:Company)
- (Customer:Region:Company)

To allow these alternative composite keys, you need to key the database file differently, perhaps using a logical file.

9.4.2. %Kds (Key Data Structure)

The **%Kds (Key data structure)** function lets you use the subfields in a data structure as the search arguments for any file operation that supports a composite key. The %Kds function follows this general form:

```
%Kds(datastructure {:numberofkeys} )
```

When you substitute the %Kds function for the list of key values, the program uses the subfields' current values in the named data structure as the composite key list for the operation. There are no special requirements for defining the data structure, but the base types of the subfields in the data structure must be compatible with the key fields in the file. If the formats or lengths differ, the subfield values are converted to the proper format and length, using the same rules that Eval uses to assign values. The following code defines a data structure called Custkeys and then uses it as a key to Chain to the Customers file:

```
Dcl-ds Custkeys;
   Company Char(3);
   Region  Char(3);
   Custno  Char(9);
End-ds;


Chain %Kds(Custkeys) Customers;
```

To specify a partial key, you can code a second argument to the %Kds function to tell it how many key fields to use (only Company and Region in the following example):

```
Chain %Kds(Custkeys:2) Customers;
```

In connection with this support, you can use a variation of the Extname or Likerec keyword to define a data structure that automatically extracts only the key fields from a record format, eliminating the need to key the subfields explicitly. The following code creates an externally described data structure with just the key fields from the Customers file:

```
Dcl-ds Custkeys Ext Extname('CUSTOMERS':*Key) End-ds;
```

The Likerec keyword also allows you to limit the data structure to key fields only:

```
Dcl-f Customers Disk;

Dcl-ds Custkeys Likerec(Custsrec:*Key);
```

The %Kds function takes the top-level subfields (i.e., those starting at the beginning) from the Custkeys data structure.

9.5. Writing to Output Files

The operations we've looked at so far are appropriate for input files. In addition to reading records, an RPG program can deal with output (i.e., writing new records to database files). Until now, the output of your programs has been reports, but you can also designate a database file as program output. The Dcl-f instruction in this case specifies Usage(*Output):

```
Dcl-f Customers Disk Usage(*Output) Keyed;
```

If the program can both read existing records and write new records in a file, you can combine the usage values:

```
Dcl-f Customers Disk Usage(*Input:*Output) Keyed;
```

Note

The Dcl-f instruction must name a file that already exists when the program executes. If the file is externally described, it must already exist when the program is compiled. The RPG program itself cannot actually create a new file object. It simply adds new records to an existing file object, which may or may not already contain records. If the file already has records, new ones are added to the end of the file. To review creating the file object, see Chapter 3.

Once you've defined a file as an output file, the **Write (Write a record to a file)** operation lets you output records to the file. You have already used Write to write to printer files, but you can also use it to write new records to a database file. The Write operation designates the record format name (or the filename, for program-described files) to be written. The operation takes the following general form:

```
Write name {datastructure} ;
```

When a program encounters a Write operation, the current program values for all the fields making up the record layout are written to the file:

```
Write Custsrec;
```

For program-described files, you must specify an additional argument for the Write operation to name a data structure to supply the record data (for externally described files, the data structure is optional). When you include a data structure, the Write operation transfers data directly from the data structure to the record. If the file is program-described, the data structure can be any data structure with the same length as the file's declared length. For externally described files, you must use the Extname or Likerec keyword, specifying *Output fields—that is, you indicate Extname(...:*Output) or Likerec(...:*Output)—as this example illustrates:

```
Dcl-f Customers Disk Usage(*Output);

Dcl-ds Custdata Likerec(Custsrec:*Output);

Write Custsrec Custdata;
```

9.6. Update Files and I/O Operations

A common data processing task is file maintenance. **File maintenance**, or updating, involves adding or deleting records from database files, or changing the information in database records to keep the information current and correct. Records that do not exist cannot be changed or deleted. If a file has unique keys, you should not add a second record with the same key to the file. Accordingly, file maintenance routines typically require first determining whether the record exists in the file (through Chain or Setll) and then determining what update option is valid, given the found record's status.

ILE RPG includes an update file type called Usage(*Update), which lets you read, change, and then rewrite records to the file. You can use any database file as an update file simply by coding it as such in the file declarations. If the maintenance procedure involves adding new records, you must signal that fact by coding Usage(*Update:*Output). Adding a *Delete option—Usage(*Update:*Output:*Delete)—allows the program to delete records in addition to updating and writing records:

```
Dcl-f Customers Disk Usage(*Update:*Output:*Delete) Keyed;
```

An update file implicitly supports input operations. If you define a file as an update full procedural file, you can use all the input operations examined so far (Chain, Read, Reade, Readp, Readpe, Setll, and Setgt) to access records in the file. Including *Output capability lets you use the Write operation to add new records to the file. Two additional I/O operations can be used for update files:

- Update (Modify existing record)
- Delete (Delete record)

9.6.1. Update (Modify Existing Record)

The **Update (Modify existing record)** operation modifies the record most recently read from an update file. The required operand names the file (for program-described files) or the record format (for externally described files) to update. Update takes the following general form:

```
Update name {datastructure} ;
```

Before your program can update a record, it must have successfully retrieved that record with a Chain, Read, Reade, Readp, or Readpe operation. Updating a record without first retrieving one generates a system error message. To cover this case, use the %Found or %Eof function to detect instances in which no record has been retrieved.

Note
You can use the %Found function with the Chain operation, but not with the various Read operations. Those operations set %Eof (or %Error, discussed in Chapter 16) to *On if they do not retrieve a record.

Update rewrites the current program values of all the record's fields to the file. The typical update procedure is to retrieve a record, change one or more of its fields' values, and then use Update to rewrite the record with its new values. You cannot issue multiple Updates for a single Read operation. Each Update must be preceded by a record retrieval.

```
Chain Custno Customers;

If %Found(Customers);
   Balancedue += Invoiceamt;
   Lastdate = Invoicedate;
   Update Custsrec;
Else;
   Exsr Nocustomer;
Endif;
```

In this snippet, the program retrieves a record from the Customers file for a given Custno. If the program finds a record for that customer, the Balancedue and Lastdate fields (presumably in the Customers file) are adjusted, and the record (which uses the Custsrec format) in the file is updated. But if the program fails to find a record for that customer, the Nocustomer subroutine is invoked.

The optional third operand names a result data structure for the Update operation. Specifying a data structure updates the record directly from the data structure, instead of field by field. The following example demonstrates the use of a data structure with the Update operation:

```
Dcl-f Customers Disk Usage(*Update);

Dcl-ds Custdata Likerec(Custsrec:*Input);

Chain Custno Customers;
If %Found(Customers);
   Balancedue += Invoiceamt;
```

Continued

```
   Lastdate = Invoicedate;
   Update Custsrec Custdata;
Else;
   Exsr Nocustomer;
Endif;
```

For program-described files, the data structure can be any data structure with the same length as the file's declared length. For externally described files, you must use the Extname or Likerec keyword, specifying *Input fields—that is, you indicate Extname(...:*Input) or Likerec(...:*Input)—as the previous example illustrates.

The Update operation rewrites all of a database record's fields to the file. In the preceding example, the Update operation updates the current values of Balancedue and Lastdate, along with every other field in Custsrec. If your program logic has changed field values that you do not want to be updated, you can use the **%Fields (Fields to update)** function to list just those fields that you want to rewrite:

```
Update Custsrec %Fields(Balancedue:Lastdate);
```

The %Fields function specifies a list of fields to update in the record (Balancedue and Lastdate in this example). The unlisted fields remain unchanged in the database file.

9.6.2. Delete (Delete Record)

The **Delete (Delete record)** operation deletes a single record from an update file. Delete takes the following general form:

```
Delete {search-argument} filename;
```

With the Delete operation, you must code a filename or, if the file is externally described, a record format name. The first search argument is optional. If you leave it blank, the system deletes the record most recently read from that file. The record must have been previously read by an input operation (e.g., Chain or Read). Using this form of Delete without first retrieving a record from the file generates a system error message. To cover this case, use the %Found function to detect instances in which the record to delete is not found in the file:

```
Chain Custno Customers;
If %Found(Customers);
   Delete Customers;
Endif;
```

The second form of Delete retrieves a record and then deletes it. If you code a search argument to specify which record to delete, you can enter a variable name, a literal, a constant, or a composite key. When duplicate records exist in the file, the system deletes only the first record that matches the search argument. If the record to delete cannot be found, the operation sets the %Found function *Off.

```
Delete Custno Customers;
```

Note

The Delete operation logically deletes records from a file rather than physically removing them. Although a deleted record is no longer accessible to programs or queries, the record actually remains on disk until the file containing the deleted record is reorganized.

9.7. File and Record Locking

Any multiuser system needs to address the problems related to simultaneous use of the same database file. Otherwise, it is possible that if two users access the same record for update, make changes in the record, and then rewrite it to the file, one of the user's changes might get lost—a condition sometimes called **phantom updates**. Two approaches you can use to deal with this type of problem are file locking and record locking.

The easiest kind of locking is to limit access to a file to one user at a time—a condition known as **file locking**. Although IBM i permits you to lock files at a system level by issuing CL commands, usually you want to allow multiple users access to the same files simultaneously. RPG includes built-in, automatic **record locking** features to momentarily limit access to a specific record while it is being updated.

If your program designates a file as an update file, RPG *automatically* places a lock on a record when it is read within your program. Updating that record or reading another record releases the record from its locked state. While the record is locked, other application programs can access the record if they have defined the file as an input file, but not if they, too, have defined the file as an update file. The other application programs wait a prescribed amount of time (usually 60 seconds) to gain access to the record. If, after the wait, a program cannot access the record in question, the program generates an error. Other application programs can access other records in the file even if they have defined the file as an update file, but two programs cannot access the same record in update mode simultaneously. This solution eliminates the problem of lost updates.

However, record locking can cause delays and access problems for users if programmers don't structure their code to avoid locks except when absolutely necessary. The nightmare scenario you should keep in mind when designing update programs is that of the user who keys in a request to update a record, pulls up the screen of data to make changes to in the record, and then realizes it's lunch time and disappears for an hour. Meanwhile, the record lock prevents all other users from accessing the record.

One solution to this problem lies with the **(N) operation extender**, which you can use with Read, Reade, Readp, Readpe, and Chain to specify that the input operation to an update file be done without locking the record. Using this feature lets you avoid unnecessary locking. Another, less common, solution is the **Unlock (Unlock a Data Area or Release a Record)** operation. If you've read a record with a lock and want to release the lock, you can use this operation along with a filename to release the most recently locked record in that file:

```
// Random read of an update file automatically locks the record.
Chain Custno Customers;


// Random read of an update file with operation extender N
// keeps the record unlocked.
Chain(n) Custno Customers;


// Release most recently read record in Customers.
Unlock Customers;
```

If you start releasing record locks in update procedures, however, be aware that you can easily code yourself back into the phantom update problem that caused systems to incorporate record locking in the first place. If you aren't including some provision that confirms that another user has not updated a record between the time you first accessed the record and the time you are about to rewrite the record with the values from your program, leave all record locking in place. With concise programming practices, you should be able to minimize the processing time that a record is locked. When you are absolutely certain that you will not be updating a record in an update file, be sure to retrieve it with the (N) extender to prevent locking the record, or unlock it with the Unlock operation.

9.8. File Open and Close Considerations

Beyond record locking considerations, generally accepted programming practice dictates that a program should not keep a file open any longer than necessary to access the required data from the file. RPG automatically opens your files at the beginning of processing and then closes them all at the end of processing. If your program needs access to a file for only a portion of its total running time, you should take control of the file opening and closing rather than letting RPG manage those tasks for you. ILE RPG includes two operations to give you this capability:

- Open (Open a file)
- Close (Close files)

You can open and close files that RPG opened automatically. To prevent the file's initial automatic open, you must add another entry within the Dcl-f instruction for the file. The **Usropn (User Open)** keyword prevents the file from being implicitly opened by RPG and signals that the opening of the file is explicitly coded within the program:

```
Dcl-f Customers Disk Usropn;

Open Customers;
  // File processing goes here...
Close Customers;
```

The Close operation can also close all the open files in a single statement:

```
Close *All;
```

You can open a given file more than once within a program, provided the file is closed before each successive open. Closing—and then subsequently reopening—a file repositions it to the beginning of the file (%Eof is off).

Trying to open a file that's already open causes an error, but trying to close a file that's already closed does not produce an error. To avoid opening an already open file, you can use the **%Open (Return open file condition)** function to check a file's open condition:

```
If Not %Open(Customers);
  Open Customers;
Endif;
```

Caution

File opens and closes have a significant performance impact on the system, and you should avoid repeatedly opening and closing the same file while a program is running. Reserve this capability for those situations where it is truly necessary.

9.9. Putting It All Together

Now that you've learned about ILE RPG's input and output operations, you might find some sample programs helpful to demonstrate how to apply these operations. Accordingly, read the scenarios that follow and study the program solutions to develop a sense of when to use the various I/O operations.

9.9.1. Example 1

In the first scenario, a company has decided to give all its employees a 5 percent pay raise. Assume that an externally described master file of employees (Empmaster) exists, that the record format within the database file is Emprecord, and that the pay field is Pay. The file is keyed on employee ID. The following code shows a solution to this problem:

```
// ********************************************************************
// This program gives each employee in the Empmaster file a 5% raise.
// ********************************************************************

Dcl-f Empmaster Disk Usage(*Update);

Read Empmaster;

Dow Not %Eof(Empmaster);
  Eval(H) Pay = Pay * 1.05;
  Update Emprecord %Fields(Pay);
  Read Empmaster;
Enddo;

*Inlr = *On;
Return;
```

In this solution, you declare the file as an update file, but because you are not asked to add new records to the file, or to delete existing ones, the program does not specify *Output or *Delete usage. Even though the master file is keyed, you are processing the records sequentially because you want to process all the records in the file, and the order of processing is not important for this solution. All employees are to receive the raise, so the calculations consist of a simple loop that sequentially reads through the file, calculates the new pay for each employee, and then updates the employee's record (just the Pay field).

9.9.2. Example 2

Now let's enhance the problem a little. Instead of giving every employee a raise, the company wants to give only selected employees a 5 percent raise. A transaction file called Raisetrans contains the IDs of these employees (in field Empid).

This problem's processing requirements vary from the first scenario because now you need to access only those employees in Empmaster who appear in file Raisetrans. Every record in Raisetrans, however, must be processed. Accordingly, you want to sequentially process Raisetrans and use the information on each record to randomly access an Empmaster record to update.

To provide for the possible error where Raisetrans contains one or more employee IDs not in the master file, you include an externally described printer file, Errlog, with a record format called Notfound. If the program cannot find an employee in the master file, it uses this format to report the error:

```
// ************************************************************************
// This program updates employees' pay by 5% based on employee IDs
// contained in file RaiseTrans.
// ************************************************************************

Dcl-f Raisetrans Disk;
Dcl-f Empmaster  Disk    Usage(*Update) Keyed;
Dcl-f Errlog     Printer Oflind(Endofpage);

Dcl-s Endofpage Ind Inz(*On);

Read RaiseTrans;

Dow Not %Eof(Raisetrans);
  Exsr Process;
  Read Raisetrans;
Enddo;

*Inlr = *On;
Return;

// ************************************************************************
//
```

Continued

```
// Subroutine to write Heading lines
//
Begsr Overflow;

  If Endofpage;
    Write Heading;
    Endofpage = *Off;
  Endif;

Endsr;


// *********************************************************************
//
// Subroutine to process Empmaster records
//
Begsr Process;
  Chain Empid Empmaster;

  If %Found(Empmaster);
    Eval(H) Pay = Pay * 1.05;
    Update Emprecord %Fields(Pay);
  Else;
    Exsr Overflow;
    Write Notfound;
  Endif;

Endsr;
```

9.9.3. Example 3

Now let's change the problem again. This time, the employer wants to give raises to all the employees in certain departments. The Depttrans file contains the names of the departments to receive the raise.

The best way to solve this problem is to define a logical file over the Empmaster file, keyed on department, and then use the logical file for updating the employees. This approach lets you use SetII to locate the appropriate departments within the file and then use Reade to process all the employees within each department. The following program shows a solution using this approach. Note that omitting the error handling lets you focus more easily on the file-accessing process used in the program.

```
// **********************************************************************
// This program updates employees' pay by 5% based on departments
// contained in file DeptTrans. EmpMasterL is a logical file of
// employees, keyed on department.
// **********************************************************************

Dcl-f Depttrans  Disk;
Dcl-f Empmasterl Disk Usage(*Update) Keyed;


Read Depttrans;

Dow Not %Eof(Depttrans);            // Loop To Process Each Department.
  Setll Dept Empmasterl;

  If %Equal(Empmasterl);
    Reade Dept Empmasterl;

    Dow Not %Eof(Empmasterl);       // Loop For All Employees In A Dept.
      Eval(H) Pay = Pay * 1.05;
      Update Emprecordl %Fields(Pay);
      Reade Dept Empmasterl;
    Enddo;

  Endif;

  Read Depttrans;
Enddo;

*Inlr = *On;
Return;
```

As you begin to write programs that require you to access several files, try to decide how to handle access to each file. Ask yourself how many records in each file you need to process. If you must access all the records in the file or a subset (or subsets) of the records based on a common value of a field, then sequential access, using Read or Reade (for subsets of sequential records), is appropriate. To select only certain records from the file, random access by using Chain is best. And remember that the facility for defining keyed logical files lets you retrieve records based on any field. Often, defining logical files goes together with developing programs.

9.10. Navigating Legacy Code

9.10.1. *File Description Specifications*

The fixed-format File specification (F-spec) is comparable to the Dcl-f (Declare File) instruction. Chapter 2 introduced the F-spec. Let's look at some of the columnar entries appropriate to this chapter. We'll primarily examine the additional entries not covered in Chapter 2. The following header shows the layout of a File specification:

```
*.. 1 ...+... 2 ...+... 3 ...+... 4 ...+... 5 ...+... 6 ...+... 7 ...+... 8
FFilename++IPEASFRlen+LKlen+AIDevice+.Keywords++++++++++++++++++++++++++++++++++
FDepttrans IF  F 128        Disk
FEmpmaster1UF A E           K Disk
FErrorlog  O   E            Printer Oflind(Endofpage)
```

9.10.1.1. Filename (Positions 7–16)

In positions 7–16 (labeled Filename++ on the ruler line), you enter the name of the file.

9.10.1.2. File Type (Position 17)

Position 17 (labeled I on the ruler line) specifies the file usage. It is the fixed-format equivalent of the Usage keyword that the Dcl-f free-format instruction uses. The valid entries are as follows:

- I = Usage(*Input)
- O = Usage(*Output)
- U = Usage(*Update:*Delete)
- C = Usage(*Input:*Output)

9.10.1.3. File Designation (Position 18 Input Files Only)

Most files in today's programs are full procedural files, letting the program explicitly execute file input/output operations instead of using the built-in RPG fixed-logic cycle to perform file I/O. All files declared by Dcl-f are assumed to be full procedural files. Older programs, those that use the RPG cycle, can have other entries for input files:

- F = Full procedural
- P = Primary input file
- S = Secondary input file
- T = Table file

9.10.1.4. End-of-File (Position 19 RPG Cycle Only)

An E in this position tells the RPG cycle that it cannot end the program until all the records in this file have been processed. This position does not apply to full procedural files.

9.10.1.5. File Addition (Position 20)

Position 20 (A) indicates whether records can be added to an input or an update file. This position does not apply to output files, as records can always be added to an output file. The valid entries are as follows:

- Blank = Usage(*Input) or Usage(*Update:Delete)
- A = Usage(*Input:*Output) or Usage(*Update:*Delete:*Output)

9.10.1.6. File Format (Position 22)

The file format specifies whether the file is externally described or program-described:

- E = Externally described
- F = Program-described (fixed length)

9.10.1.7. Record Length (Positions 23–27 Program-described Files Only)

For program-described files, enter the record length right-adjusted in positions 23–27 (Rlen+).

9.10.1.8. Key Length (Positions 29–33 Keyed Program-described Files Only)

These columns (Klen+) specify the length of the file key (in bytes) for program-described files processed by key.

9.10.1.9. Record Address Type (Position 34)

Use position 34 (A) to specify processing by key. This entry is equivalent to the Dcl-f instruction's Keyed keyword. The following are frequently used entries:

- Blank = Process file sequentially, not by key
- K = Process externally described file by key values
- A = Process program-described file by character key
- P = Process program-described file by packed key (not supported by Dcl-f instruction)

9.10.1.10. File Organization (Position 35 Program-described Files Only)

If a program-described file is processed by key, enter an I in position 35 (I). Otherwise, leave this position blank.

9.10.1.11. Device (Positions 36–42)

The Device entry indicates the device associated with a file. You enter the device names left-adjusted in positions 36–42 (labeled Device+). Frequently used entries are as follows:

- Disk = database file
- Printer = printed report
- Workstn = interactive workstation display

9.10.1.12. Keywords (Positions 44–80)

The Keywords area of the File specification gives you an opportunity to amplify and specialize the basic file description in the positional area (positions 6–43) of the F-spec.

9.10.2. Except (Calculation Time Output)

You have already used the **Except (Calculation time output)** operation to write to printer files, but you can also use Except to write new records to a database file. The form of the Except statement to write to database files is no different from the form you use for printer files. The Except operation requires that your program include fixed-format Output specifications—even for externally described output files—to configure the layout of the output records. The general format of the Except operation is as follows:

```
Except {exceptname} ;
```

Or, if the program uses fixed-format C-specs:

```
*.. 1 ...+... 2 ...+... 3 ...+... 4 ...+... 5 ...+... 6 ...+... 7 ...+... 8
CLON01Factor1+++++++Opcode(E)+Factor2+++++++Result++++++++Len++D+HiLoEq....
C                   Except    exceptname
```

The Except operation optionally can designate a named except line in the output. When the program reaches the Except operation, it writes the named except lines (if the Except includes a name) or all unnamed except lines (if the Except does not include a name) from the Output specifications.

For an externally described file, enter the record format name, rather than the filename itself, in the O-specs in positions 7–16 (Filename++). Then list all the fields comprising the record. Omitting a field or fields from the list causes default values (usually zeros or blanks) to be written to the record for that field. Rather than listing all the fields, you can simply code *All, which has the same effect as including all the field names. The following code demonstrates how you can use Except to write records to a customer file:

```
*.. 1 ...+... 2 ...+... 3 ...+... 4 ...+... 5 ...+... 6 ...+... 7 ...+... 8
OFilename++DF..N01N02N03Excnam++++B++A++Sb+Sa+............................
O.............N01N02N03Field+++++++++YB.End++PConstant/editword/DTformat++


Dcl-f Customers Usage(*Output) Disk Keyed;

...

Except Record;

...

OCustrec    E           Record
O                       *All
```

For program-described files, the O-spec record identification entry names the file. The field description entries must list all the fields as well as their ending positions in the record layout:

```
*.. 1 ...+... 2 ...+... 3 ...+... 4 ...+... 5 ...+... 6 ...+... 7 ...+... 8
OFilename++DF..N01N02N03Excnam++++B++A++Sb+Sa+............................
O.............N01N02N03Field+++++++++YB.End++PConstant/editword/DTformat++


Dcl-f Customers Usage(*Output) Disk(145) Keyed(*Char:9);

...

Except Record;

...

OCustomers   E          Record
O                       Custno       9
O                       Cfname       24
O                       Clname       44
O                       Caddr        74
O                       Czip         79
O                       Cphone       89
O                       Cemail       139
O                       Cdob         144P
O                       Cgender      145
```

The Except operation also allows you to update just certain fields, not the entire record layout. Before the %Fields function was available, programmers used the Except operation and Output specifications to designate which fields to rewrite:

```
*.. 1 ...+... 2 ...+... 3 ...+... 4 ...+... 5 ...+... 6 ...+... 7 ...+... 8
OFilename++DF..N01N02N03Excnam++++B++A++Sb+Sa+...........................
O..............N01N02N03Field+++++++++YB.End++PConstant/editword/DTformat++


Dcl-f Customers Usage(*Update) Disk(145) Keyed(*Char:9);

...

Except Record;

...

OCustomers    E         Record
O                       Caddr           74
O                       Czip            79
O                       Cphone          89
O                       Cemail         139
```

9.10.3. File I/O Resulting Indicators

When used with fixed-format C-specs, the file read operations (Read, Reade, Readp, and Readpe) can set resulting indicators to flag an error or end-of-file condition. If the program has an indicator in the Lo position (73–74), that indicator is set to *On if the read encounters an error. To indicate end-of-file, the read operations can set an indicator in the Eq position (75–76). If this indicator is *On, it is equivalent to the %Eof function being *On.

```
*.. 1 ...+... 2 ...+... 3 ...+... 4 ...+... 5 ...+... 6 ...+... 7 ...+... 8
CL0N01Factor1+++++++Opcode(E)+Factor2+++++++Result++++++++Len++D+HiLoEq....
C                   Read      Customers                            8090
```

In this example, if the program encounters an error while reading the file, indicator 80 is set to *On. If the read operation reaches end-of-file, indicator 90 (as well as the %Eof function) is set to *On. And if the read is successful, both indicators 80 and 90 are *Off.

The Chain operation supports resulting indicators in the Hi and Lo positions:

```
*.. 1 ...+... 2 ...+... 3 ...+... 4 ...+... 5 ...+... 6 ...+... 7 ...+... 8
CL0N01Factor1+++++++Opcode(E)+Factor2+++++++Result++++++++Len++D+HiLoEq....
C    Custno         Chain     Customers                            7080
```

The indicator in the Hi position is set to *On if Chain cannot find the appropriate record (indicator 70 is *On, %Found is *Off). The indicator in the Lo position is set to *On for an error condition.

The table in Figure 9.1 summarizes resulting indicator usage for the file I/O operations. This figure also refers to the %Error function, discussed in Chapter 16.

Operation Code	Hi (71-72)	Lo (73-74)	Eq (75-76)
Chain	Not %Found	%Error	–
Close	–	%Error	–
Delete	Not %Found	%Error	–
Except	–	–	–
Open	–	%Error	–
Read	–	%Error	%Eof
Reade	–	%Error	%Eof
Readp	–	%Error	%Eof (beginning of file)
Readpe	–	%Error	%Eof (beginning of file)
Setgt	Not %Found	%Error	–
Setll	Not %Found	%Error	%Equal
Unlock	–	%Error	–
Update	–	%Error	–

Figure 9.1: File I/O resulting indicators

9.11. Chapter Summary

In this chapter, you learned many I/O operations appropriate to input, output, and update files. Read, Reade, Readp, and Readpe are input operations used to access records sequentially from a full procedural file whose type is declared as input or update. You can use the Setll and Setgt operations to position the file before a sequential read operation. Chain randomly retrieves a record and also positions the file for subsequent sequential reading, if desired. These operations use the %Eof, %Found, and %Equal functions to return information to the program about the success or failure of the operation.

Several file I/O operations let you position a file or retrieve a record based on a composite key. You can either list the individual values that comprise the composite key or use the %Kds function to associate a data structure with the composite key. Using a partial composite key lets you initiate access to sets of records that share a common value on the first field (or fields) of a composite key.

You can use Write or Except to put records into an output file or an update file. Update and Delete operations are specific to update files. You cannot Update a record without having first read it. You can, however, Delete a record without first retrieving it if you indicate the key of the record to delete in the operation. The Update operation normally changes all the fields in a record. To change only specific fields, you can use the %Fields function.

The IBM i database features built-in record locking to prevent the problem of phantom updates. Techniques, including use of the (N) operation extender or the Unlock operation, exist to minimize record locking, but you should not use them if their implementation might cause lost updates to occur.

The following table summarizes the functions and operation codes examined in this chapter:

Function or Operation	Description	Syntax
Chain	Random retrieval from a file	**Chain{(hmnr)} search-arg file-name {data-struc};**
Close	Close files	**Close file-name | *All;**
Delete	Delete record	**Delete{(hmr)} {search-argument} file-name;**
%Eof	End (or beginning) of file	**%Eof{(file-name)}**
%Equal	Exact match for Setll	**%Equal{(file-name)}**
Except	Calculation time output	**Except {name};**
%Fields	Fields to update for Update	**%Fields(name {: name ...})**
%Found	Record found for Chain, Delete, Setgt, Setll	**%Found{(file-name)}**
%Kds	Key data structure	**%Kds(data-structure-name {: number-keys})**
%Open	Return open file condition	**%Open(file-name)**
Open	Open file for processing	**Open file-name;**
Read	Read a record	**Read{(n)} file-format-name {data-struc};**
Reade	Read equal key	**Reade{(hmnr)} search-argument file-name {data-struc};**
Readp	Read prior record	**Readp{(n)} file-record-name {data-struc};**
Readpe	Read prior equal key	**Readpe{(hmnr)} search-argument file-name {data-struc};**
Setgt	Set greater than	**Setgt{(hmr)} search-argument file-name;**
Setll	Set lower limit	**Setll{(hmr)} search-argument file-name;**
Unlock	Unlock a data area or release a record	**Unlock dtaara-record-file;**
Update	Modify existing record	**Update{(e)} file-name {data-struc};** **Update{(e)} file-name** **%Fields(name {: name ...});**
Write	Create new record	**Write{(e)} file-name {data-struc};**

9.12. Key Terms

Chain (Random retrieval from a file)

composite key

concatenated key

Delete (Delete record)

%Equal

%Eof (End-of-file)

%Fields (Fields to update)

file access

file locking

file maintenance

%Found

%Kds (Key data structure)

(N) operation extender

%Open (Return open file condition)

phantom updates

random access

record locking

result data structure

Read (Read a Record)

Reade (Read equal key)

Readp (Read prior record)

Readpe (Read prior equal)

record locking

sequential access

Setll (Set lower limit)

Setgt (Set greater than)

Unlock (Unlock a Data Area or Release a Record)

Update (Modify existing record)

Usropn (User Open) keyword

Write (Write a record to a file)

9.13. Discussion/Review Questions

1. Describe the difference between sequential and random record retrieval.
2. What does *position the file* mean?
3. What are the differences between the Setgt and Setll operations?
4. Because Reade and Readpe imply reading records with matching keys, would you ever use them in programs that access files with unique keys? Explain your answer.
5. When is it appropriate to use a Reade as opposed to a Read operation?
6. What does the term *file maintenance* mean? What kinds of files are likely to need maintenance?
7. Is it possible to obtain different results when you update a file by using Except rather than Update?
8. Give an example of when you would use a partial key to access a record.
9. What is the advantage of using the %Kds function?
10. Why should you use %Found before performing a Delete operation?
11. Because designating a file type as Update gives you maximum flexibility in which I/O operations you can use with that file, why don't programmers designate all their files as update files, just in case? That is, why bother with input and output files?
12. What is the difference between a file lock and a record lock? Which technique is easier for an operating system to implement? Why? Which technique is preferable from a user standpoint? Why?
13. When you use the %Eof function, why is it good programming practice to include a filename in the statement?
14. What are the benefits of using the Chain operation? Can a programmer use other operations to accomplish the same task?

9.14. Exercises

1. Assume you have a logical file of customers, CustLZip, keyed on zip code. Write the calculations that will let you print an exception line, CustLine, for every customer whose zip code matches ZipIn. If no customers have that zip code, print exception line NoCust.

2. Your company sequentially assigns a unique customer number to each new customer. Assume customer file CustMaster is keyed on customer number, field CustNbr. Write the calculations necessary to determine what number should be assigned to the next new customer.

Note
Many programmers store the last-used number in a data area or file.

---

3. Write the specifications needed to total all the sales for a given department within a specific store.

a. You have a sales file, SalesFile, keyed on a composite key of store, department, and salesperson. (Duplicate keys are present because each record represents one sale.) Field Dept contains the desired department; field Store holds the store.

b. The sales field that you want to accumulate is SalesAmt.

c. Modify your code so that it totals all the sales of the store represented in Store.

4. Write the file declarations and calculations to let you do the following:

a. Randomly retrieve a customer in file CustMast based on the customer number in CustNbr

b. Subtract Payment from BalanceDue, and rewrite the record

c. Execute subroutine NoCust if the customer is not found in the file

5. Write the file declarations and calculations that will let you appropriately process each record in the transaction file.

a. You have a transaction file, CustTrans, of records to add, delete, or change in the CustMaster master file. The transaction record's Code field contains A, D, or C, denoting whether to add, delete, or change the record; transaction field CustNo contains the number of the customers to add, delete, or change.

b. Add is a valid option if the customer does not already exist in CustMaster.

c. Change and delete are valid only if the customer does exist in CustMaster. Execute subroutine AddRecord for valid additions, ChgRecord for valid changes, and DltRecord for valid deletions. For all invalid transactions, execute subroutine TransError. (Don't code the details of these subroutines; stop at the point of coding the EXSR statements.)

10

Processing Files Using SQL

10.1. Chapter Overview

This chapter discusses the use of SQL statements embedded into an ILE RPG program, as well as how and when to use embedded SQL as a complement to native RPG file operations. It also introduces SQL's Data Manipulation Language and demonstrates how to coordinate retrieved SQL data with RPG program variables. In addition, you learn how to handle return codes from SQL statements and how to build dynamic SQL statements as the program is executed. Finally, the chapter examines the SQL RPG precompiler and its role in creating RPG programs that use SQL.

10.2. SQL Data Manipulation Language (DML)

Chapter 3 discussed SQL's Data Definition Language (DDL), which you used to create database objects—including tables and views—and to modify their properties. SQL also categorizes a number of statements as **Data Manipulation Language (DML)**. While DDL statements deal with the database objects themselves, DML statements retrieve and manage the data within the tables (physical files). The DML statements appropriate for embedded SQL are as follows:

- Select
- Insert
- Update
- Delete

Although exhaustive coverage of SQL goes beyond the scope of this text, it is useful to briefly cover some of the frequently used statements, illustrating their format and use.

10.2.1. Select

The **Select** statement is SQL's primary query statement, roughly comparable to the RPG Read operation but with several enhancements. A basic Select statement takes the following general form:

```
Select columns From table {Where conditions} {Order by sequence}
```

The following examples illustrate the Select statement:

```
Select Custno, Cfname, Clname From Customers Where Custno = 'AB0097531'
Select * From Customers Where Custno = 'AB0097531'
Select * From Customers Where Czip = '10010' Order by Custno
```

The Select clause lists the columns that the statement is to retrieve, or it specifies—with an asterisk (*)—all the columns, in order, from the record layout to be retrieved. The From clause indicates the files from which the columns are retrieved. An optional Where clause can identify a search condition to limit the query to the records that satisfy the search condition. Finally, the Select statement can use the Order by clause to sequence the **result set**—the group of retrieved records—in a specific order.

10.2.2. Insert

SQL's **Insert** statement adds a record (row) to a table or a view. It is approximately equivalent to the RPG Write operation. A simple Insert statement takes the following form:

```
Insert Into table {(columns)} Values (values)
```

This example illustrates the Insert statement:

```
Insert Into Customers
   (Custno, Cfname, Clname, Caddr, Czip, Cphone, Cemail, Cdob, Cgender)
   Values ('AB0097532', 'John', 'Smith', '123 Main St', '60606',
           '3125555432', 'johnsmith431@mail.com', 19750701, 'M')
```

The Insert Into clause names the table. Following the table name, a column list in parentheses specifies, in the Values clause, the columns for which values will be provided. The Values clause supplies values for each of the columns in the column list. You must specify the values in the same order as the columns list, and you must have the same number of values as you have columns. The columns list is optional. If you omit it, the Insert statement assumes that all the columns on the record layout have corresponding values specified in the Values clause. If a column is null capable or is created with a default value, you can omit it from the list. In that case, the default value or a null value is used.

10.2.3. Update

Using the **Update** statement lets you modify one or more rows in a table. This statement corresponds to RPG's Update operation combined with the %Fields function. The Update statement follows this general form:

```
Update table Set column = value Where conditions
```

or

```
Update table (columns) Values (values) Where conditions
```

Here are some examples:

```
Update Customers Set Czip = '61443' Where Custno = 'AB0097532'
Update Customers (Cphone, Cemail) Values ('3095559753', 'jsmith75@mail.com')
  Where Custno = 'AB0097532'
```

These examples begin to look consistent with previous Select and Insert statements, and it is this syntactic consistency that attracts many programmers to SQL. In the first example, Update is using the Set clause to assign a value to a single column, Czip. The second example uses a columns list along with a Values clause to assign values to the corresponding columns in the columns list. As before, the Where clause identifies the records to modify. Only the columns mentioned in the Update statement are modified.

10.2.4. Delete

As you might expect, the SQL **Delete** statement removes one or more records (rows) from a table, analogous to the RPG Delete operation:

```
Delete From table {Where conditions}
```

Here are some examples:

```
Delete From Customers Where Custno = 'AB0097533'
Delete From Customers Where Czip = '60606'
```

Without the Where clause, Delete removes all the rows from the table, clearing it of any data (but not deleting the table itself).

10.3. Introduction to Embedded SQL

By now, you probably realize that an RPG program depends upon several components other than the program itself to do its work, and that the tools used with those components use languages other than RPG: database files, whether created with SQL or DDS; printer files created with DDS; perhaps Control Language (CL) commands to set up the environment in which the program will run; and so on. Even within the program itself, some sections can exploit other languages' capabilities and features. In recent years, it has become common practice to embed SQL statements within an RPG program to access and manage its database processing. Generally, these statements are DML statements, but they can include DDL as well as a few SQL statements specifically designed for use in a program.

These SQL statements can complement or entirely replace *native* file operations (e.g., Read, Write, Update, Delete). You should consider inserting SQL statements into your RPG-centered applications for many reasons. Embedded SQL is especially useful for *set-at-a-time* processing, enabling an RPG program to act upon many records by using a single SQL statement instead of an iterative file loop. SQL provides database features (e.g., security at the field, or column, level) that are unavailable with DDS or through native RPG file operations. SQL has a rich set of functions (e.g., Avg, Count, Sum) that RPG operations or functions cannot readily duplicate. RPG supports the dynamic creation of SQL statements at runtime, allowing a great deal of flexibility in the way your program processes the database. As an industry standard, SQL provides consistency across software platforms, pervasive training and documentation, and organized collaboration. In some cases, SQL can offer performance benefits over native operations.

10.4. Exec SQL

To insert SQL statements into an RPG program, you must use the **Exec SQL** directive to signal that the rest of the line is an SQL statement, not an RPG operation:

```
Exec SQL sql-statement;
```

For example, the following line in an RPG program will run the SQL Delete statement:

```
Exec SQL Delete From Customers Where Czip = '60606';
```

Exec SQL is not technically an RPG operation. It is, instead, a **compiler directive**—an instruction that is executed once when the program is compiled, not each time the program runs. It controls what the compiler does, not what the program will do. In this case, the Exec SQL statement signals to automatically convert the SQL statement in the program source into appropriate RPG operations before the program is created. Essentially, though, you can consider Exec SQL to be an RPG operation. Later in this chapter, we examine the steps in creating a program with embedded SQL statements.

The Exec SQL directive must be on a single line, but the SQL statement itself can span multiple lines. Just as with other RPG operations, you end the SQL statement with a semicolon (;):

```
Exec SQL Update Customers (Cphone, Cemail)
                          Values ('3095559753', 'jsmith75@mail.com')
                          Where Custno = 'AB0097532';
```

While you can insert most SQL statements by using Exec SQL, not all statements are allowed, and some statement require modification to work. Yet other SQL statements are allowed *only* as embedded statements in a program.

Tip
If a program is to process a file by using SQL statements, you need not declare that file with a Dcl-f instruction. Explicit file declaration is required only if the program processes a file by using native operations (e.g., Read, Write).

10.5. Using Host Variables

The previous SQL Update statement specifies explicit values to use in the table update. But this form is not productive if you have to write a new program, or modify a program, every time the values for Cphone and Cemail change. To make the SQL statement more flexible, you can replace the explicit values with **host variables**. A **host variable** is a data item that an SQL statement uses as the instrument to synchronize RPG program variables with data from tables and views. So, instead of coding explicit values in the example Update statement, you can substitute host variables:

```
Exec SQL Update Customers (Cphone, Cemail) Values (:Cphone, :Cemail)
                          Where Custno = :Custno;
```

The host variable name is preceded by a colon (:). The name corresponds to an RPG program variable. You need not define the host variable separately from the RPG variable.

It is simply a means to allow the SQL statement to refer to an RPG variable. So, if the RPG variables Cphone and Cemail have respective values of 3095559753 and jsmith75@mail .com, the end result of executing either of these two Update examples is identical. You should declare the RPG variable with the same data type and size as its associated database column.

The Insert and Delete statements can also substitute host variables for explicit column values:

```
Exec SQL Insert Into Customers
              (Custno, Cfname, Clname, Caddr, Czip,
               Cphone, Cemail, Cdob, Cgender)
            Values (:Custno, :Cfname, :Clname, :Caddr, :Czip,
               :Cphone, :Cemail, :Cdob, :Cgender);


Exec SQL Delete From Customers Where Czip = :Czip;
```

Host variable names cannot begin with SQ, SQL, RDI, or DSN. Those names are reserved for database use.

10.5.1. Select Into

While the Insert, Update, and Delete statements can be inserted into an RPG program and can use host variables, largely without changes, embedded SQL requires a modified form of the Select statement to retrieve a result set into host variables. The **Select Into** variation retrieves a single row and places the result set into RPG host variables:

```
Exec SQL Select columns Into :host-variables From table {Where conditions};
```

The Into clause lists the host variables into which the result set will be placed. The result set columns and the list of host variables share a one-to-one correspondence; that is, you must list an associated host variable, in order, for each column in the result set. The result set can have only one row. Consequently, the Where clause often refers to the table's primary key. If the result set includes more than one row, SQL returns an exception code, discussed later in this chapter.

The following example illustrates the use of Select Into:

```
Dcl-s Custno Char(9);
Dcl-s Cfname Char(15);
Dcl-s Clname Char(20);
                                                        Continued
```

```
...
                          // Program will provide a value for Custno.
Exec SQL Select  Cfname, Clname
          Into   :Cfname, :Clname
          From   Customers
          Where Custno = :Custno;
                          // Cfname and Clname will contain result set values.
```

10.5.2. Using Host Structures

Instead of listing individual host variables in an SQL statement, you may find it useful to name a single host structure instead. A **host structure** is a data structure that you can use with the Into clause:

```
Dcl-s Custno Char(9);

Dcl-ds Custdata;
  Cfname Char(15);
  Clname Char(20);
End-ds;
...
                          // Program will provide a value for Custno.
Exec SQL Select  Cfname, Clname
          Into   :Custdata
          From   Customers
          Where Custno = :Custno;
                          // Custdata subfields will contain result set values.
```

As was the case before, a one-to-one correspondence must exist between the result set columns and the subfields in the host structure.

A host data structure is especially useful for retrieving all the columns from a record layout. In this case, an externally described data structure is appropriate. Examine the following example:

```
Dcl-s Custno Char(9);

Dcl-ds Customers Ext Qualified End-ds;
```
Continued

```
...
                        // Program will provide a value for Custno.
Exec SQL Select * Into  :Customers From  Customers
        Where Custno = :Custno;
                        // Customers subfields will contain result set
values.
```

Here, Customers is an externally described data structure, patterned after the record layout in the Customers file. By selecting all the columns into the :Customers host structure, this code segment has effectively accomplished the same result as the native Chain operation. The data structure is a qualified data structure. While not required, making it a qualified data structure reduces the possibility that variable names in the data structure will conflict with names elsewhere in the program. The program refers to the data structure subfields as Customers. Custno, Customers.Cfname, Customers.Clname, and so forth.

10.5.3. Handling Null Values

Recall from Chapter 3 that the Null constraint allows a column to contain a null value. A **null value** represents the absence of any data for a column; it is an unknown value—not a zero or blank. A null-capable column can be set to null instead of an actual value. Most IBM i tables specify Not Null for each column, forcing that column to always have a value. If, however, a column is null capable, your RPG program can detect a null value in a column retrieved via SQL.

```
Exec SQL Select  Cfname, Clname
        Into  :Cfname, :Clname
        From  Customers
        Where Custno = :Custno And Cfname is Not Null;
```

This statement does not retrieve any row with a null Cfname value even if the Custno value matches the condition.

If you want the program to retrieve null-capable columns, you can use an indicator variable to detect whether or not a column value is null. An **indicator variable** is similar to a host variable, except that you use an indicator variable to detect a null value in a retrieved column or to set a column to a null value. Wherever an embedded SQL statement allows a host variable, you can optionally include an indicator variable immediately following the host variable (with no comma between the host variable and the indicator variable):

```
Dcl-s Custno      Char(9);
Dcl-s Cfname      Char(15);
Dcl-s Clname      Char(20);
Dcl-s NullCfname Int(5);
Dcl-s NullClname Int(5);
...
Exec SQL Select  Cfname, Clname
          Into   :Cfname :NullCfname,
                 :Clname :NullClname
          From   Customers
          Where Custno = :Custno;
```

In this example, :NullCfname and :NullClname are indicator variables. Even though they are named the same, an SQL indicator variable is *not* the same data type as an RPG indicator variable. While RPG indicators are a *true/false* data type, SQL indicator variables are integers (five digits, signed). In the previous example, if :Cfname has a null value, then :NullCfname has a negative value (-1). But if :Cfname is not null, then :NullCfname is positive or zero.

To set a column to a null value, you can use the SQL Update statement, setting the indicator variable to -1:

```
Cfname = *Blanks
Clname = *Blanks
NullCfname = -1;
NullClname = -1;
Exec SQL Update Customers
          Set    Cfname = :Cfname :NullCfname,
                 Clname = :Clname :NullClname
          Where Custno = :Custno;
```

If you are retrieving the result set into a host structure, you can also organize indicator variables into an **indicator structure**, which is simply a data structure that uses the indicator variables as subfields:

```
Dcl-s Custno Char(9);



                                                                  Continued
```

```
Dcl-ds Custdata;
  Cfname Char(15);
  Clname Char(20);
End-ds;

Dcl-ds Custnulls;
  NullCfname Int(5);
  NullClname Int(5);
End-ds;
...
                    // Program will provide a value for Custno.
Exec SQL Select  Cfname, Clname
           Into   :Custdata :Custnulls
           From   Customers
           Where Custno = :Custno;
                    // Custdata subfields will contain result set values.
                    // Custnulls subfields will contain indicator variables.
```

The indicator structure must contain a corresponding subfield for each column in the result set even if it is not null capable.

10.6. Handling SQL Return Codes

When RPG executes an SQL statement, SQL returns to the program several feedback tools that you can use to diagnose the results of executing the statement. If the SQL statement ends in error, the program does *not* stop but continues to run with the next subsequent statement. So, it's important to check the diagnostic response before continuing with the RPG program. The **SQL Communication Area** (SQLCA) is a data structure that contains **return codes**, subfields with valuable diagnostic information. You should not explicitly code an SQLCA data structure in your program because the SQL precompiler (discussed later in this chapter) automatically inserts it:

```
Dcl-ds Sqlca;
  Sqlcaid  Char(8);        // (Null)
  Sqlcabc  Int(10);        // Length of Sqlca: 136
  Sqlcode  Int(10);        // SQL return code
  Sqlerrml Int(5);         // Length of Sqlerrmc
  Sqlerrmc Char(70);       // Message replacement text
                                                       Continued
```

```
    Sqlerrp   Char(8);              // Product identifier: "QSQ..."
    Sqlerrd   Int(10) Dim(6);       // Diagnostic information
    Sqlwarn   Char(1) Dim(11);      // Warning flags
    Sqlstate  Char(5);              // SQL standard return code
End-ds;
```

Note

The actual data structure declaration may use fixed-format Definition Specifications, examined in Chapter 4, but the subfields are in the same locations, regardless of the method the precompiler uses to declare the SQLCA. Subfields Sqlerrd and Sqlwarn are declared as arrays, which we introduce in Chapter 11. Legacy programs might shorten some of the field names (e.g., Sqlcod or Sqlstt instead of Slqcode or Sqlstate).

The SQL Communications Area is updated every time the program executes an SQL statement. Two important subfields in this data structure are Sqlcode and Sqlstate. Both **Sqlcode** and **Sqlstate** signal the success or failure of an SQL statement, and both test for specific conditions or classes of conditions. Sqlcode returns one of the following values:

- Sqlcode = 0 means the SQL statement was successfully executed (although there may be warnings).
- Sqlcode = 100 indicates no row was found (end-of-file).
- Sqlcode > 0 (but not 100) denotes the statement was successful, but warnings were issued.
- Sqlcode < 0 signifies the SQL statement was unsuccessful.

Each Sqlcode value corresponds to an IBM i message, which you can research in IBM's online Knowledge Center documentation to obtain more details. For example, Sqlcode 100 is explained in IBM i message SQL0100, Sqlcode -0313 parallels message SQL0313, and Sqlcode 23505 corresponds to message SQ23505.

Sqlstate is similar to Sqlcode, but while specific Sqlcode values can be unique to IBM i, Sqlstate values are set by industry standards. Sqlstate is five characters long; the first two characters indicate a general class of conditions:

- Sqlstate that begins with 00 means the SQL statement was successfully executed, with no errors or warnings.
- Sqlstate that begins with 01 indicates the statement was successful, but warnings were issued.

- Sqlstate that begins with 02 signifies the SQL statement found no row (end-of-file).
- Any other Sqlstate class means the SQL statement was unsuccessful.

Sqlstate values are also detailed in IBM's online documentation.

If an error occurs during an SQL statement's execution, the RPG program continues to run the next statement as if no error had occurred. You should always explicitly test either Sqlcode or Sqlstate to check the consequence of executing an SQL statement. The following code tests for all the possibilities, checking Sqlstate:

```
Exec SQL Select  Cfname, Clname
          Into   :Cfname :NullCfname,
                 :Clname :NullClname
          From   Customers
          Where Custno = :Custno;


Select;
  When Sqlstate = '00000';
    // Select was successful
  When Sqlstate = '02000';
    // End-of-file
  When %Subst(Sqlstate:1:2) = '01';
    // Select generated warnings
  Other;
    // Select was unsuccessful
Endsl;
```

Chapter 16 includes an example of SQL error checking that uses Sqlcode instead of Sqlstate.

In Chapter 4, we discussed defining named constants to represent literal values to improve program maintainability and documentation. This technique is especially useful to document frequently used Sqlcode and Sqlstate values. The following example illustrates the technique, using a few specific Sqlstate values:

```
Dcl-c Endoffile    '02000';
Dcl-c Success      '00000';
Dcl-c Warning      '01';

...
                                                              Continued
```

```
Exec SQL Select  Cfname, Clname
          Into  :Cfname :NullCfname,
                :Clname :NullClname
          From  Customers
          Where Custno = :Custno;


Select;
  When Sqlstate = Success;              // Sqlstate 00000
      // Select was successful
  When Sqlstate = Endoffile;            // Sqlstate 02000
      // End-of-file
  When %Subst(Sqlstate:1:2) = Warning;  // Sqlstate 01xxx
      // Select generated warnings
  Other;
      // Select was unsuccessful
Endsl;
```

10.7. Using SQL Cursors

Embedded SQL is an excellent choice for set-at-a-time processing (i.e., treating entire groups of rows in one statement). Other SQL statements—notably, Select Into—work well for processing a single row from a table or view. But at times, a program may need to retrieve multiple rows into a result set and then process each of those rows individually. For those cases, sometimes known as *row-at-a-time* processing, SQL provides a mechanism called a *cursor*.

A **cursor** is a named entity in a program that SQL uses to point to and process a single row from a group of rows in a result set. Using a cursor, you can loop through a group of records, fetching and processing the records individually, similar to the way the native RPG Read operation retrieves records one at a time. RPG requires four steps to use an SQL cursor:

1. Declare the cursor.
2. Open the cursor.
3. Fetch rows.
4. Close the cursor.

10.7.1. Declare Cursor

The **Declare Cursor** SQL statement names a cursor and associates it with an SQL Select statement. The basic format is as follows:

```
Exec SQL Declare name Cursor For select-statement;
```

The Declare Cursor statement can appear only in embedded SQL and roughly parallels the RPG Dcl-f instruction. It must appear in the source code before any statements that refer to the cursor. It is a nonexecutable statement, and it should be near the beginning of the program. The following example illustrates the use of Declare Cursor:

```
Exec SQL Declare Custzip Cursor For
                    Select  Cfname, Clname
                    From    Customers
                    Where Czip = :Czip
                    Order by Custno;
```

An SQL cursor is always associated with a nested Select statement to indicate the rows to retrieve. The Select statement is not actually executed until the cursor is opened. The Select statement can include host variables and indicator variables, which are substituted when the program opens the cursor.

Rows in the result set associated with the cursor in this example can be updated or deleted. Except for a few infrequent restrictions, an SQL cursor is updatable unless you indicate otherwise. You can explicitly specify that a cursor is updateable with an Update clause:

```
Exec SQL Declare Custzip Cursor For
                    Select  Cfname, Clname
                    From    Customers
                    Where Czip = :Czip
                    For     Update;
```

In this example, any columns in the Customers table can be updated, even if they do not appear in the cursor's list of columns. You can also limit updates to specific columns, similar to the native %Fields function, by including an Update clause with a column list:

```
Exec SQL Declare Custzip Cursor For
                    Select  Cfname, Clname
                    From    Customers
                    Where Czip = :Czip
                    For     Update of Cfname, Clname;
```

If the program does not update or delete records for this cursor, to improve performance, specify a **Read Only** clause in the Select statement:

```
Exec SQL Declare Custzip Cursor For
                        Select  Cfname, Clname
                        From   Customers
                        Where Czip = :Czip
                        Order by Custno
                        For    Read Only;
```

The following example specifies a Read Only cursor as **Insensitive**:

```
Exec SQL Declare Custzip Insensitive Cursor For
                            Select  Cfname, Clname
                            From   Customers
                            Where Czip = :Czip
                            Order by Custno
                            For    Read Only;
```

When an insensitive cursor is opened, the system creates a temporary copy of the result set, and the program works with that copy. An insensitive cursor does not recognize subsequent inserts, updates, or deletes by this or any other program. Using an insensitive cursor can improve performance, but the program may not always be reading the most current data.

The cursors in these examples are **serial cursors.** Navigation through the result set is sequential, from beginning to end. After the program opens the cursor, the statement can retrieve each row can only once. The cursor must be closed and reopened if it needs to access rows in the result set again. By default, cursors are serial cursors. Adding the Scroll clause creates a scrollable cursor:

```
Exec SQL Declare Custzip Scroll Cursor For
                            Select  Cfname, Clname
                            From   Customers
                            Where Czip = :Czip
                            Order by Custno
                            For    Read Only;
```

A **scrollable cursor** permits navigation in either direction through the result set and allows a row to be retrieved multiple times without closing and reopening the cursor.

10.7.2. Open

To access the rows in the result set of a cursor, the program must open the cursor:

```
Exec SQL Open Custzip;
```

Opening a cursor processes the Select statement embedded in the cursor and makes the rows in the result set available to the program. If the cursor's Select statement includes host variables or indicator variables, their values are substituted into the statement when the cursor is opened.

10.7.3. Fetch

Embedded SQL's rough equivalent of the RPG Read operation is Fetch. Recall that the Select Into statement retrieves a single row from a result set into host variables in your program. The **Fetch** statement retrieves one or more rows from a result set that contains multiple rows. Your program can then construct a loop that processes the rows, similar to the way the native file operations process a file. The row being processed is called the **current row**.

A simple Fetch statement reads the next row in a result set into host variables in the program. Here is the format:

```
Exec SQL Fetch {Next} {From} cursor-name Into :host-variables;
```

Fetch requires that you name the cursor associated with the result set that you want to retrieve, and the cursor must have been previously declared and opened. You must also name the variables and structures that is to receive the column values. Here's an example:

```
Exec SQL Fetch Custzip Into :Cfname :NullCfname,
                           :Clname :NullClname;
```

The Select statement associated with the specified cursor dictates the contents of the result set.

The Fetch statement can also refer to a host structure, using the same syntax:

```
Dcl-ds Customers Ext Qualified End-ds;
...
Exec SQL Declare Custcursor Cursor For
                          Select *
                          From  Customers
                                                      Continued
```

```
                                  Where Czip = :Czip
                                  Order by Custno
                                  For    Read Only;
   ...
Exec SQL Fetch Custcursor Into :Customers;
```

Just as RPG's Read operation has several forms (e.g., Read, Readp), the SQL Fetch statement has multiple variations:

```
Fetch {Next} {From} cursor-name Into host-variables
Fetch Prior From cursor-name Into host-variables
Fetch First From cursor-name Into host-variables
Fetch Last From cursor-name Into host-variables
Fetch Current From cursor-name Into host-variables
Fetch Relative n From cursor-name Into host-variables
```

The default option, and the only one available for a serial cursor, is Fetch Next. For scrollable cursors, Fetch Prior retrieves the previous row, Fetch First and Fetch Last process the first and last row, Fetch Current processes the current row again, and Fetch Relative reads a row that is *n* number of rows before or after the current row.

Two other Fetch variants position the cursor before the first row or after the last row in the result set:

```
Fetch Before From cursor-name
Fetch After From cursor-name
```

Fetch Before and Fetch After do not move columns into a host variable. Instead, they position the cursor at the beginning or end of the result set. To move the first or last row into host variables, you must follow the Fetch First with a Fetch Next or the Fetch After with a Fetch Prior. In this respect, these Fetch variations are similar to RPG's Setll and Setgt.

10.7.4. Close

The Close statement closes an open cursor:

```
Exec SQL Close Custzip;
```

Once a program has processed the rows in a cursor, you should explicitly close the cursor. Closing a cursor explicitly discards its result set and releases locks on tables or views. If the program neglects to close a cursor, it can remain open to subsequent programs, depending upon the Closqlcsr value, discussed later in this chapter. Closing and then reopening a serial cursor is required to reprocess the cursor.

10.7.5. Cursor Updates and Deletes

Unless an SQL cursor is a Read Only cursor, it is updatable. The Update and Delete statements support a Where Current Of clause to update or delete the current row in a cursor's result set:

```
Exec SQL Update  Customers
          Set   Cfname = :Cfname, Clname = :Clname
          Where Current of Custzip;
```

or

```
Exec SQL Delete From Customers Where Current Of Custzip;
```

The Update statement can update columns in the table whether or not those columns are in the result set, as long as the cursor allows update of those columns. To update or delete a row, you must position the cursor on that row. This type of update, with the Where clause, is a **positioned update**. After a positioned deletion, the cursor is moved to before the next row in the result set, or after the last row if there are no more rows.

10.8. Building Dynamic SQL Statements

Up to now, all the embedded SQL statements we've discussed have been static SQL. With **static SQL**, the basic structure of each SQL statement is known at the time of program compilation. The SQL statement can use host variables to substitute values at runtime, but its general purpose and construction don't change once the program is created.

Alternatively, an RPG program can build a complete SQL statement as a character string by using data in the program. The resulting **dynamic SQL** statement is prepared at runtime, rather than when the program is created. Dynamic SQL does not use host variables. Instead, the statement substitutes **parameter values** at strategic positions in the statement. Static SQL generally performs faster, but dynamic SQL may be more flexible and can overcome some limitations of static SQL. The programmer may not always know the full text of the required SQL statements, the program may accept user input to determine the nature of the SQL statement structure, or the program may require alternative actions based on conditions at runtime. In these situations, dynamic SQL is the logical choice. Embedded dynamic SQL requires two additional steps:

1.   Prepare the statement from data in the program.
2.   Execute the prepared statement.

Programmers frequently use dynamic SQL to build a cursor when the exact nature of the cursor is unknown at the time of program creation. For example, a cursor can use different tables on different days or months, or the user can enter data into the program to select the table and the columns to include.

10.8.1. Prepare

The SQL **Prepare** statement validates a text string and translates it into an executable SQL statement. The program can build the text string by using standard RPG character processing techniques, such as concatenation. The Prepare statement lets you name the prepared SQL statement. Later, the program executes the prepared statement by referring to its name. The Prepare statement takes this form:

```
Exec SQL Prepare statement-name From :text-string;
```

The text string cannot contain a simple Select statement unless the statement is used to prepare an SQL cursor.

Programmers often use dynamic SQL together with SQL cursors. In the following example code, the Prepare statement translates the contents of the SQLstring RPG variable, creating SQLcursor, which is then used to supply the embedded Select statement for the cursor Custrecord:

```
Dcl-s SQLstring   Varchar(256);
Dcl-s Whereclause Varchar(256);
...
                   // Option, Gender, Zipcode values provided by user input
If Option = 'G';
  Whereclause = 'Where Cgender = ' + Gender;
Else;
  Whereclause = 'Where Czip = ' + Zipcode;
Endif;

                                                            Continued
```

```
                    // Construct SQLstring
SQLstring = 'Select  Cfname, Clname From Customers ' +
            Whereclause + ' Order by Custno';


Exec SQL Prepare SQLcursor From :Sqlstring;


Exec SQL Declare Custrecord Cursor
            For SQLcursor;


Exec SQL Open Custrecord;
...
Exec SQL Fetch Custrecord Into :Cfname, :Clname;
...
Exec SQL Close Custrecord;
```

In this example, the RPG processing can use variables Cfname and Clname and can include Update and Delete SQL statements (Where Current of Custrecord).

The text string cannot contain host variables, but it can include **parameter markers** to designate where value substitution should occur in the SQL statement—a parameter marker is indicated by a question mark (?). The parameter marker can appear wherever a host variable might appear if the SQL statement were a static SQL statement, for example in a Where clause:

```
Delete From Customers Where Custno = ? And Czip = ?
```

When the program subsequently executes the prepared statement, it substitutes a value for each parameter marker, in order, similar to the way a static SQL statement substitutes the value of a host variable.

10.8.2. Execute

Once a statement has been prepared, the program can run that statement many times by using the SQL **Execute** statement. If the statement includes parameter markers, the program can substitute a different value each time the statement runs. The Execute statement takes this form:

```
Exec SQL Execute statement-name {Using :host-variables};
```

Examine the following example:

```
Dcl-s SQLstring Varchar(256);
...
SQLstring = 'Delete from Customers Where Custno = ?';
Exec SQL Prepare SQLdelete from :SQLstring;


Dou Custno = 0;
  // Custno and Czip values provided by user input
  If Custno <> 0;
    Exec SQL Execute SQLDelete Using :Custno;
  Endif;
Enddo;
```

In this code fragment, the prepared SQLdelete statement includes a parameter marker. Each time the program executes SQLdelete, it substitutes the current value of Custno in place of the parameter marker. The number of parameter markers in the statement must match the number of host variables used by the Execute statement's Using clause. The host variables' order and data types must accurately correspond to the substituted positions in the prepared statement. The following example illustrates the use of two parameter markers (for Custno and Cgender):

```
Dcl-s SQLstring Varchar(256);
...
SQLstring = 'Delete from Customers Where Custno = ? and Cgender = ?';
Exec SQL Prepare SQLdelete from :SQLstring;


Dou Custno = 0;
  // Custno, Gender values provided by user input
  If Custno <> 0;
    Exec SQL Execute SQLDelete Using :Custno, :Cgender;
  Endif;
Enddo;
```

10.8.3. Execute Immediate

If a dynamic statement is to be executed only once while the program is running, and if it does not include host variables or parameter markers, the **Execute Immediate** statement can combine the Prepare and Execute statements into one:

```
Exec SQL Execute Immediate :text-string;
```

Note that the syntax between the Execute statement and the Execute Immediate statement differs. Execute refers to a prepared statement name, but Execute Immediate refers to a text string in a host variable, with no need for prior preparation. The following example demonstrates the use of Execute Immediate:

```
Dcl-s SQLstring Varchar(256);

...

// Custno value provided by user input
SQLstring = 'Delete From Customers Where Custno = ' + Custno;
Exec Sql Execute Immediate :SQLstring;
```

To execute a statement several times during the program, separate Prepare and Execute as two steps; otherwise, Execute Immediate is more efficient.

10.9. Set Option

The SQL **Set Option** statement establishes processing options to use during a program that uses embedded SQL. The Set Option statement takes the following form:

```
Exec SQL Set Option option = value, ...;
```

If you use it in a program, the Set Option statement must be coded before any other SQL statements (i.e., it must be the first Exec SQL directive in the program). The following example illustrates some common options:

```
Exec SQL Set Option Alwcpydta = *Yes,
                    Closqlcsr = *Endpgm,
                    Commit    = *None;
```

10.9.1. Alwcpydta

The Alwcpydta (Allow copy of data) option indicates whether a copy of the data can be used with a Select statement to improve performance. Using a temporary copy can improve performance, but the program may risk using an obsolete result set if someone made changes while the program is running. Alwcpydta(*Optimize) lets the system decide whether using a copy will improve performance. Alwcpydta(*Yes) and Alwcpydta(*No) respectively allow or prohibit using a copy with Select statements.

10.9.2. Closqlcsr

Closqlcsr (Close SQL cursor) specifies when to close SQL cursors if your program doesn't explicitly close them with a Close statement. This option also determines the scope of prepared SQL statements and file locks. Closqlcsr(*Endpgm) closes cursors and related resources when the program ends. Closqlcsr(*Endsql) allows cursors to remain open between program instances in a job, without having to reopen them each time you call the program, until you explicitly close them. Closqlcsr(*Endjob) lets cursors remain open until the IBM i job ends. (For ILE programs, examined in Chapter 14, Closqlcsr(*Endmod) and Closqlcsr(*Endactgrp) in turn close the cursors when a module or activation group ends.)

Note
Regardless of the Closqlcsr option, a cursor can be referenced only by statements within the same program in which it is declared. A program cannot use a cursor defined in a separately compiled program.

10.9.3. Commit

Commitment control is a database feature that permits complex transactions to be processed with an *all-or-nothing* architecture (i.e., if several database updates are required for a transaction, then all the updates must occur, or none of them will). Commitment control also allows a program to *roll back* incomplete transactions, those changes that have not yet been *committed*. A complete discussion of commitment control goes beyond the scope of this text. SQL typically assumes that commitment control is in effect for any SQL statements. If your database does not use commitment control, then the program should specify Commit(*None). But if the database does use commitment control, then this option can set the level SQL is to use.

10.10. Creating SQLRPGLE Programs

To create an RPG program that embeds SQL statements, you of course use an editor, such as SEU or LPEX, to enter the code into a source file member. Unlike previous programs, however, which used a member type of RPGLE, if the program includes SQL statements, the member type should be SQLRPGLE. Once the source member contains all the required code, you use a different compiler command, **CRTSQLRPGI (Create SQL ILE RPG Object)**, to compile the source and create the program (or module or service program, discussed in Chapters 14 and 15).

The CRTSQLRPGI command employs a **precompiler** to translate the SQL portions of the source code before actually compiling it. The precompiler converts any SQL statements to equivalent RPG code that calls database functions and creates a temporary source member. If the precompiler successfully translates the SQL code, then the command compiles the temporary source member, creating the resulting object. Appendix B describes the tools you might use to edit and compile a program with embedded SQL.

Once the program is successfully created, you can execute it like any other program by using the CALL command.

Tip

The precompiler does not typically create a listing. To debug the original source, with the SQL statements, specify Output(*Print) when you execute the CRTSQLRPGI command to print a precompiler listing.

10.11. Putting It All Together

10.11.1. Example 1

Let's repeat a couple of examples from Chapter 9, but now you use SQL instead of native file processing operations. To recall, the company wants to give selected employees a 5 percent raise. A transaction file called Raisetrans contains the IDs of these employees (in field Empid).

```
//  *****************************************************************
// This program updates employees' pay by 5% based on employee IDs
// contained in table RaiseTrans.
//  *****************************************************************


Dcl-f Errlog Printer Oflind(Endofpage);


Dcl-c Endoffile '02000';
Dcl-c Success   '00000';


Dcl-s Endofpage Ind Inz(*On);


Exec SQL Declare Raises Cursor For
                        Select Empid
                          From Raisetrans
                        For Read Only;
                                                        Continued
```

```
Exec SQL Open Raises;

Dou Sqlstate = Endoffile;
  Exec SQL Fetch Raises Into :Empid;


  Select;
    When Sqlstate = Success;
      Exsr Process;
    When Sqlstate = Endoffile;
      Leave;
    Other;
      Exsr Overflow;
      Write Notfound;
  Endsl;


Enddo;

Exec SQL Close Raises;
*Inlr = *On;
Return;

// ************************************************************************
//
// Subroutine to write Heading lines
//
Begsr Overflow;

  If Endofpage;
    Write Heading;
    Endofpage = *Off;
  Endif;


Endsr;

// ************************************************************************
//
//  Subroutine to process Empmaster records
//
```

Continued

```
Begsr Process;
  Exec SQL Update Empmaster
            Set    Pay = Round(Pay * 1.05, 2)
            Where Empid = :Empid;


  If Sqlstate <> Success;
    Exsr Overflow;
    Write Notfound;
    Sqlstate = Success;                    // Reset Sqlstate for next
iteration
  Endif;


Endsr;
```

10.11.2. Example 2

Now, the employers want to give raises to all the employees in certain departments. The Depttrans file contains the names of the departments to receive the raise.

The corresponding example in Chapter 9 used a logical file for updating the employees. With SQL, that is unnecessary because you can simply update the original physical file (table). This example illustrates the use of *set-at-a-time* processing to change all the employee records in a specific department with a single Update statement. Like the example in Chapter 9, this example omits error processing to better highlight the SQL.

```
// *******************************************************************
// This program updates employees' pay by 5% based on departments
// contained in file DeptTrans.
// *******************************************************************


Dcl-c Endoffile '02000';
Dcl-c Success   '00000';


Exec SQL Declare Department Cursor For
                              Select Dept
                                From Depttrans
                              For Read Only;
Exec SQL Open Department;
                                                      Continued
```

```
Dou Sqlstate = Endoffile;
  Exec SQL Fetch Department Into :Dept;


  Select;
    When Sqlstate = Success;
      Exec SQL Update Empmaster
                Set   Pay = Round(Pay * 1.05, 2)
                Where Dept = :Dept;
      Sqlstate = Success;                  // Reset Sqlstate for next iteration
    When Sqlstate = Endoffile;
      Leave;
  Endsl;


Enddo;


Exec SQL Close Department;
*Inlr = *On;
Return;
```

10.12. Navigating Legacy Code

Earlier versions of ILE RPG (prior to IBM i Release 5.4) used an alternative compiler directive
for embedding SQL statements. Other than the alternative syntax, all the same concepts for
embedded SQL apply to those programs. The alternative syntax follows this form:

```
C/Exec SQL
C+  sql-statement
C/End-exec
```

This variant of embedded SQL requires a C in position 6 and then a compiler directive
starting with a slash character (/) in position 7. An /Exec SQL directive begins the SQL
statement, and an /End-exec directive ends it. The SQL statement can begin on the same
line as the /Exec SQL directive or on the next continuation line, which has a C+ in positions
6–7. If the SQL statement extends to additional lines, those lines must also include the C+.
Finally, instead of a semicolon, the SQL statement ends with a /End-exec directive. The
following lines in an RPG program will run the SQL Delete statement:

```
C/Exec SQL
C+  Delete From Customers
C+   Where Czip = '60606'
C/End-exec
```

or

```
C/Exec SQL Delete From Customers Where Czip = '60606'
C/End-exec
```

Only one SQL statement can appear between each set of compiler directives.

10.13. Chapter Summary

SQL Data Manipulation Language (DML) is used to manage the data within database tables. The primary DML statements are Select (to read records), Insert (to add new records), Update (to change records), and Delete (to remove records). ILE RPG programs can embed SQL statements to complement or replace native file operations.

The Exec SQL compiler directive signals to the SQL precompiler that a source line contains an SQL statement. The SQL statement can include host variables, preceded by a colon (:), to coordinate the SQL statement with RPG native variables. The Select Into statement retrieves columns from a single row in a table and places their values into the program's host variables or into a host structure. Indicator variables are similar to host variables, except their purpose is to detect columns' null values.

The SQL Communication Area is an automatically created data structure that contains diagnostic information. Two important subfields in this structure are Sqlcode and Sqlstate, which indicate the success or failure of an SQL statement. A program should always check one or both of these values after processing an SQL statement.

While Select Into works well for processing a single row, an SQL cursor is necessary to process multiple rows in a result set. With a cursor, the program can loop through a group of records, fetching and processing the records individually. The steps in using a cursor are 1) declare the cursor, 2) open the cursor, 3) fetch rows and process each one, and 4) close the cursor. A serial cursor processes rows sequentially while a scrollable cursor allows the program to navigate in either direction through a result set. Positioned updates and deletes use a Where Current Of clause to update or delete a record pointed to by a cursor.

With static SQL, the program knows the basic structure of an SQL statement at compile time. Dynamic SQL statements, however, are prepared at runtime. Before a program can use a dynamic SQL statement, it must first prepare the text statement and then execute it. The text statement can contain parameter markers in place of host variables to designate substitution values. The Execute Immediate statement combines the Prepare and Execute statements for certain SQL instructions.

To create an RPG program that includes SQL, you must first submit the SQLRPGLE source to a precompiler, which converts the SQL statements to RPG operations. The CRTSQLRPGI command invokes the precompiler and the subsequent ILE RPG compiler.

The following table summarizes the compiler directive and SQL statements examined in this chapter:

Directive or SQL	Description	Syntax
Close	Close cursor	**Exec SQL Close name;**
Declare	Declare cursor	**Exec SQL Declare name Cursor** **For select-statement;**
Delete	Delete rows	**Delete From table {Where conditions}**
Exec SQL	Execute SQL statement	**Exec SQL sql-statement;**
Execute	Execute dynamic SQL	**Exec SQL Execute statement-name** **{Using :host-variables};**
Execute Immediate	Prepare and execute dynamic SQL	**Exec SQL Execute Immediate :text-string;**
Fetch	Read row from cursor	**Exec SQL Fetch {position}** **{From} cursor-name Into :host-variables;**
Insert	Insert new row	**Insert Into table (columns) Values (values)**
Open	Open cursor	**Exec SQL Open name;**
Prepare	Prepare dynamic SQL	**Exec SQL Prepare statement-name** **From :text-string;**
Select	Select a row	**Select columns From table** **{Where conditions} {Order by sequence}** **Exec SQL Select columns** **Into :host-variables** **From table {Where conditions};**
Set Option	Set processing options	**Exec SQL Set Option option = value, ...;**
Update	Update rows	**Update table Set column = value** **{Where conditions}** **Update table (columns) Values (values)** **{Where conditions}**

10.14. Key Terms

Close	Execute Immediate	Select
compiler directive	Fetch	Select Into
CRTSQLRPGI (Create SQL ILE RPG Object)	host structure	scrollable cursor
	host variable	serial cursor
cursor	indicator structure	Set Option
Data Manipulation Language (DML)	indicator variable	SQL Communication Area (SQLCA)
	Insensitive	
Declare Cursor	Insert	Sqlcode
Delete	Open	Sqlstate
dynamic SQL	precompiler	static SQL
embedded SQL	Prepare	Update
Exec SQL	Read Only	
Execute	return codes	

10.15. Discussion/Review Questions

1. List and define the SQL statements discussed in the chapter.
2. Investigate the history and development of SQL. Write two paragraphs summarizing the history and development of SQL.
3. Describe Data Definition Language (DDL) and Data Manipulation Language (DML).
4. Using IBM's online documentation, investigate IBM's SQL Query Engine (SQE) and the Classic Query Engine (CQE). Write two paragraphs describing IBM's development of SQE and the future of CQE. What are the benefits to today's RPG programmer when using the new query engine?
5. List the reasons to consider inserting SQL statements into your RPG-centered applications.
6. What is the purpose of the Exec SQL directive in an RPG program?
7. What is a host variable? Why is it important?
8. Why is the SQL Select Into statement needed, and what rules govern its use?
9. What is the purpose of the SQL Communications Area? How would you use this data structure in a RPG program?
10. What is an SQL cursor? Why is it needed, and what rules govern its use?

10.16. Exercises

1. Using the AIRPLANE table in the FLIGHTPROD schema, write an example of using each of the SQL DML statements discussed in this chapter and that you listed in review question 1.

2. Define a host data structure, and using an Into clause, select all the fields from the GTCSTP file and insert the values into this data structure.

3. Write the code to perform an SQL Insert into the FLIGHT table in the FLIGHTPROD schema. Using a host structure and host variables, update all the fields in the table row.

4. Using the STAFFSCHED table in the FLIGHTPROD schema, write the code to insert a record into the table, and include the code to trap any SQL errors. This code must contain the constant definitions and Select block. If your solution includes subroutines, you do not need to code them, but make sure you give them descriptive names.

5. Using IBM's documentation, investigate the *run SQL scripts* features of IBM's Access for Windows. This has an F4 function that allows programmers to easily write and test SQL statements.

   a. Write the SQL script to select all the records from the GTCSTP file sorted by CLNAME and CFNAME. Display the CPHONE, CFNAME, CLNAME, AMTOWE, and PATDAT fields.

   b. Write the SQL script over the CSCSTP file to select the customers who owe more than $500.00, sorted in descending order by amount owed. Display the CUSTNO, CFNAME .CLNAME, CSTREET, CCITY, CSTATE, CZIP, ORDDAT, and BALDUE fields.

Notes

11

Using Arrays

11.1. Chapter Overview

In this chapter, you learn how to process arrays, which are data structures that can simplify repetitive processing of similar data. In addition, this chapter discusses how to define arrays, populate them with data, and access that data. It also covers the use of arrays and array data structures together with SQL.

11.2. Representing Tables of Data

In common usage, a table is a collection of data organized into columns and rows. Similar kinds of data are stored within a column, and the data elements within a row of the table are related, or belong together. Typically, the data elements in the first column of a table are organized sequentially in ascending order to facilitate finding an item. Once you find the item you want in column 1, you then read across the row to extract the data related to that item.

The following three-column table, for example, lets you look up a U.S. state code to extract the name and sales tax rate of the state associated with that state code. (Note that the full table contains 50 codes and their corresponding names and tax rates, not just the six shown here.)

State Code	State Name	Tax Rate
AK	Alaska	.00000
AL	Alabama	.04000
AR	Arkansas	.06500
AZ	Arizona	.05600

State Code	State Name	Tax Rate
CA	California	.07500
...	...	...
...	...	...
WY	Wyoming	.04000

ILE RPG provides a data construct called an *array* that you can use to represent such collections of data. Arrays are collections of data items (elements) with the same data attributes (data type, size, format, and number of decimal positions, if numeric).

11.3. Arrays

An **array** is a grouping of data that contains multiple elements, all defined with a common name. The major difference between an RPG array and the tables as we are used to thinking about them is that a typical RPG array represents only one column of data. The preceding table data might be represented in a program by three arrays:

Abbrev

AK	AL	AR	AZ	CA	...	WY

State

Alaska	Alabama	Arkansas	Arizona	California	...	Wyoming

Taxrate

.00000	.04000	.06500	.05600	.07500	...	.04000

A program can refer to an individual element in an array by the element's ordinal position—for example, State(3) to refer to Arkansas, or it can refer to the entire array by name, such as State.

An array can be a grouping of simple data items (i.e., standalone variables or data structure subfields), or it can be a grouping of identical data structures. Array elements that are simple data items all have the same data type with the same length and (if the elements are numeric) number of decimal positions. In the Abbrev array, the state codes are all two-byte character data. The state names in the State array, however, have different lengths. To use the names in an array, you have to determine the length of the longest state name (South Carolina and North Carolina both have 14 characters) and pad the names of the other states with trailing blanks to make them all 14 characters long.

You define arrays in the declaration section of the program. The required entries are similar to those necessary for other data items. The only restriction in naming the array is that the name generally cannot begin with TAB. Typically, a simple array is defined as a standalone variable, so you use the Dcl-s instruction to declare it. Unlike other standalone variables you have worked with, however, an array stores multiple values, called **elements**. You must indicate the data type and length of each array element, along with the number of decimal positions (for numeric data). To signify how many elements the array contains, you must include the **Dim (Dimension)** keyword, specifying the number of table elements within parentheses after the keyword.

Let's look at how to define the previous three arrays:

```
Dcl-s Abbrev  Char(2)    Dim(50);
Dcl-s State   Char(14)   Dim(50);
Dcl-s Taxrate Zoned(5:5) Dim(50);
```

These definitions define three arrays—Abbrev, State, and Taxrate—with 50 elements each (as the Dim keyword indicates). Each element of Abbrev is a two-byte character field, each element of State is a 14-byte character field, and each element of Taxrate is a five-digit zoned decimal number with five decimal places. The arrays are standalone variables and are not necessarily related to each other. The resulting **runtime arrays** are so called because you load them with values during the course of program execution (i.e., at runtime; the values can also change while the program is running). You can initialize the entire array with the Inz keyword, or you can assign initial values to a runtime array by assigning values during the processing, as the following code illustrates:

```
Taxrate(2) = .04;
Taxrate(3) = .065;
Taxrate(4) = .056;
Taxrate(5) = .075;
...
Taxrate(50) = .04;
```

If you do not initialize an array, its initial elemental values will be compatible with its data type—blanks for character arrays, zeros for numeric arrays, and so on.

Runtime arrays are useful for storing related values to use in calculations during the course of the program's execution. For example, it is easier to define and process a single Monthlysales array as a standalone variable in a program instead of 12 individual standalone variables to hold monthly sales totals:

```
Dcl-s Monthlysales Packed(11:2) Dim(12);
```

11.4. Runtime Arrays and Data Structures

An alternative to declaring arrays as standalone variables is to define them as data structures or data structure subfields:

```
Dcl-ds Taxes Qualified Inz;
   Abbrev   Char(2)      Dim(50);
   State    Char(14)     Dim(50);
   Taxrate  Zoned(5:5) Dim(50);
End-ds;
```

In this example, you define the arrays as part of the Taxes data structure. This type of structure might be useful when two or more arrays are related to each other. In this case, the first element in each array relates closely to the first element in each of the other arrays in the data structure—they all relate to values for Alaska. Because Taxes is a qualified data structure, to refer to the first element in each array, the program names Taxes.Abbrev(1), Taxes.State(1), and Taxes.Taxrate(1):

```
Taxes.Abbrev(1) = 'AK';
Taxes.State(1) = 'Alaska';
Taxes.Taxrate(1) = 0;
```

The Taxes data structure can itself be an **array data structure**, a data structure declared with the Dim keyword:

```
Dcl-ds Taxes Dim(50) Qualified Inz;
   Abbrev   Char(2);
   State    Char(14);
   Taxrate Zoned(5:5);
End-ds;
```

The previous example declares 50 instances of the Taxes data structure, and each instance contains the three subfields. Because you have only one array, Taxes, you refer to the elements differently:

```
Taxes(1).Abbrev = 'AK';
Taxes(1).State = 'Alaska';
Taxes(1).Taxrate = 0;
```

or

```
Taxes(1) = 'AKAlaska          00000';
```

Array data structures must be runtime arrays and must contain the Qualified keyword. The qualified name must include an index.

The array values can come from a database file. Let's assume the data is in a file called Statefile. To load the arrays, use the following SQLRPGLE code fragments:

```
Dcl-c Endoffile '02000';


Dcl-s Habbrev  Char(2);
Dcl-s Hstate   Char(14);
Dcl-s Htaxrate Zoned(5:5);
Dcl-s X        Uns(5);


Dcl-ds Taxes Dim(50) Qualified Inz;
  Abbrev  Char(2);
  State   Char(14);
  Taxrate Zoned(5:5);
End-ds;
...
Exec SQL Declare Statecursor Cursor For
                                 Select Abbrev, State, Taxrate
                                   From Statefile
                                   Order by Abbrev
                                 For Read Only;
Exec SQL Open Statecursor;


For X = 1 to %Elem(Taxes);
  Exec SQL Fetch Statecursor Into :Habbrev, :Hstate, :Htaxrate;

  Select;
    When Sqlstate = Endoffile;
      Leave;
    Other;
      Taxes(X).Abbrev = Habbrev;
      Taxes(X).State = Hstate;
      Taxes(X).Taxrate = Htaxrate;

  Endsl;
```

Continued

```
Endfor;

Exec SQL Close Statecursor;
```

Presumably, the program executes this code once, when the program first starts, perhaps in a subroutine. If the program subsequently changes the array values, it can execute the following code just before it ends to write those changes back to Statefile:

```
For X = 1 to %Elem(Taxes);
  Habbrev = Taxes(X).Abbrev;
  Hstate = Taxes(X).State;
  Htaxrate = Taxes(X).Taxrate;

  Exec SQL Update  Statefile
            Set    State = :Hstate, Taxrate = :Htaxrate
            Where Abbrev = :Habbrev;
Endfor;
```

Both of these examples use the **%Elem (Get number of elements)** function to return the number of elements in the Taxes array. This type of programming, sometimes called *soft-coding*, documents the dependency between the number of For loop iterations and the dimension of the Taxes array. Instead of your *hard-coding* a value of 50, the compiler determines the correct value for the number of For loop repetitions by checking the Dim keyword on the Taxes declaration. If the number of elements in the *parent* Taxes ever changes, recompiling the program automatically changes the number of *child* For loop iterations.

You can use a data structure overlay to provide initial values to a runtime array whose data does not come from a file:

```
Dcl-ds *N;
  *N   Char(9) Inz('Sunday');
  *N   Char(9) Inz('Monday');
  *N   Char(9) Inz('Tuesday');
  *N   Char(9) Inz('Wednesday');
  *N   Char(9) Inz('Thursday');
  *N   Char(9) Inz('Friday');
```

Continued

```
   *N   Char(9) Inz('Saturday');
   Days Char(9) Dim(7) Pos(1);
End-ds;
```

This example initializes the first 63 bytes of the unnamed data structure with values that
correspond to the names of the days of the week. Notice that you don't need to name
each data structure subfield if you do not use the name elsewhere in the program. The Inz
keyword provides the correct initial value for each nine-byte section of the data structure.
The Days subfield is an array with seven elements, each nine bytes long. Days starts in
position 1 of the data structure (overlaying the previous subfields), so its elemental values
are the days of the week.

11.5. Runtime Arrays and Externally Described Files

It is common for programmers to want to define some fields within an input record as an
array to facilitate coding repetitive operations. Although you cannot directly define fields
as array elements within an externally described file, you can use a data structure to let you
redefine separately defined input fields into elements of a single runtime array. Remember
that an array can be a data structure subfield or an entire data structure, as well as a
standalone variable.

Assume you have a file of sales records from all of a company's sales staff. Each record
contains a salesperson's identification number and that person's total sales for each month
during the past year—12 sales figures in all. Each sales figure is 11 digits with two decimal
positions. Because you plan to redefine the sales figures as an array, you have defined Sales
as one large character field, as the following DDS specifications show:

```
*.. 1 ...+... 2 ...+... 3 ...+... 4 ...+... 5 ...+... 6 ...+... 7 ...+... 8
A.........T.Name++++++RLen++TDpB......Functions++++++++++++++++++++++++++++++
 * Externally described file SalesFile with 12 sales figures defined as
 * a single field
A          R Salesrec
A            Slsnbr       5A        Text('Salesperson Number')
A            Sales        132A      Text('Twelve Months Sales')
```

You are writing a program that uses file SalesFile as input, and you want to refer to the 12
sales figures within each record as elements of an array. To do this, you must include within
the program's declarations a data structure definition that references the sales input field and
redefines it as an array. The following specifications illustrate such a data structure:

```
Dcl-ds *N;
  Sales       Char(132);
  Salesarray Zoned(11:2) Dim(12) Pos(1);
End-ds;
```

In this unnamed data structure, the character field Sales (from file SalesFile) occupies the first 132 bytes of the data structure. Next, Salesarray is declared as an array of 12 zoned decimal elements, each with two decimal positions, also occupying bytes 1–132 of the data structure. Salesarray represents a redefinition of the Sales field, dividing the Sales field into 12 array elements, each 11 bytes long.

Another way to externally describe the sales file is to define each month's sales figure separately, as the following DDS shows:

```
*.. 1 ...+... 2 ...+... 3 ...+... 4 ...+... 5 ...+... 6 ...+... 7 ...+... 8
A..........T.Name++++++RLen++TDpB......Functions++++++++++++++++++++++++++++
 * Externally described file SalesFile
A           R Salesrec
A             Slsnbr        5A          Text('Salesperson Number')
A             Sales01      11S 2        Text('January Sales')
A             Sales02      11S 2        Text('February Sales')
A             Sales03      11S 2        Text('March Sales')
A             Sales04      11S 2        Text('April Sales')
A             Sales05      11S 2        Text('May Sales')
A             Sales06      11S 2        Text('June Sales')
A             Sales07      11S 2        Text('July Sales')
A             Sales08      11S 2        Text('August Sales')
A             Sales09      11S 2        Text('September Sales')
A             Sales10      11S 2        Text('October Sales')
A             Sales11      11S 2        Text('November Sales')
A             Sales12      11S 2        Text('December Sales')
```

Given the preceding file definition, you must slightly change the data structure to manipulate the sales figures as array elements:

```
Dcl-ds *N;
  Sales01    Zoned(11:2);
                                                              Continued
```

```
    Sales02    Zoned(11:2);
    Sales03    Zoned(11:2);
    Sales04    Zoned(11:2);
    Sales05     Zoned(11:2);
    Sales06     Zoned(11:2);
    Sales07     Zoned(11:2);
    Sales08    Zoned(11:2);
    Sales09    Zoned(11:2);
    Sales10    Zoned(11:2);
    Sales11    Zoned(11:2);
    Sales12    Zoned(11:2);
    Salesarray Zoned(11:2) Dim(12) Pos(1);
End-ds;
```

This data structure defines each month's sales amount as a successive 11-byte area within the data structure. Array Salesarray, overlaying the entire 132-byte Sales data structure, redefines the 12 sales figures as its 12 elements.

With either method of defining the input file and its associated data structure, each time you read a record from Salesfile, the 12 sales figures from that record are stored in array Salesarray. When a new input record is read, the sales figures from that record replace the array's previous contents. Thus, the contents of Salesarray change as the program is running, and that's why we call Salesarray a runtime array.

11.6. Compile-Time Arrays

A **compile-time array** obtains its data from the program's source code; the data is bound to the array when you compile the program. The array data must be entered at the end of the program, following the last program entries.

ILE RPG uses a ****Ctdata record** as a delimiter (or separator line) to explicitly identify the array whose data follows. To code this delimiter, place an asterisk (*) in positions 1 and 2 of a line following the last line of program code; in positions 3–8, enter Ctdata (for compile-time data); leave position 9 blank; and, starting in position 10, enter the name of the array whose data follows.

The actual array data follows this separator line. How you enter the data at this point is up to you. You can code one element per line, two per line, three per line, and so on. The only stipulations are as follows:

- You must begin the values in the first position of each line (unlike most RPG specifications, which begin in position 6 of each line)

- You must enter the values in the order in which you want them to appear in the array.
- You must enter multiple entries per line contiguously (without spaces separating them).
- You must be consistent in the number of entries you put on each line.

The array element coding looks like this:

```
    *.. 1 ...+... 2 ...+... 3 ...+... 4 ...+... 5 ...+... 6 ...+... 7 ...+..
**Ctdata Days
Sunday   Monday   Tuesday  WednesdayThursday Friday   Saturday
```

In this example, because each day name is nine bytes long, you can code all seven days on the same line if you so desire. You can also code each day on a single line:

```
    *.. 1 ...+... 2 ...+... 3 ...+... 4 ...+... 5 ...+... 6 ...+... 7 ...+..
**Ctdata Days
Sunday
Monday
Tuesday
Wednesday
Thursday
Friday
Saturday
```

If the number of entries per line is not an even multiple of the number of total array entries, the odd number of entries goes on the last line. For example, assume that you decide to enter three day names on one line. You code two lines of three days and a final third line containing only a single day. The coding looks like this:

```
    *.. 1 ...+... 2 ...+... 3 ...+... 4 ...+... 5 ...+... 6 ...+... 7 ...+..
**Ctdata Days
Sunday   Monday   Tuesday
WednesdayThursday Friday
Saturday
```

The declaration for a compile-time array (earlier in the program) requires a **Ctdata (Compile time data)** keyword to signal that the array's compile-time data appears at the end of the program. In addition, you may need to use the **Perrcd (Per record)** keyword to indicate how the data values are entered in the source. Each program line in your source member is a record in the source file. Accordingly, if you enter seven day names per line, each record has seven array entries. Entering three day names per line means each record has three array entries. The Perrcd keyword, with the number of array entries per record, lets the system correctly obtain the data to load within the array. If you omit keyword Perrcd for a compile-time array, the system assumes you have entered the data with only one entry per record. The size of a single entry is limited to 100 bytes, and each one must be contained in a single source record.

The following code shows the declaration for the Days array as a compile-time array with seven entries per record:

```
Dcl-s Days Char(9) Dim(50) Ctdata Perrcd(7);
```

Then, at the end of the program:

```
*.. 1 ...+... 2 ...+... 3 ...+... 4 ...+... 5 ...+... 6 ...+... 7 ...+..
**Ctdata Days
Sunday    Monday    Tuesday  WednesdayThursday Friday    Saturday
```

The array data for a compile-time array is loaded into the array when you compile the program, and its elements have the same initial values each time you call the program anew. During its execution, a program can change the values of the array elements, but those changes are not retained when the program ends with *Inlr on.

Compile-time arrays can be useful for relatively small arrays whose data is unlikely to change over time. If the array data changes frequently, a programmer must go back to the source program, change the compile-time data at the end of the program, and recompile the program each time the data needs updating. You should avoid this practice, because each time you use an editor to change your source code, you run the risk of inadvertently introducing errors into the program.

Compare this compile-time array with the earlier runtime array, which defines a similar structure:

```
Dcl-ds *N;
    *N    Char(9) Inz('Sunday');
    *N    Char(9) Inz('Monday');
    *N    Char(9) Inz('Tuesday');
    *N    Char(9) Inz('Wednesday');
    *N    Char(9) Inz('Thursday');
    *N    Char(9) Inz('Friday');
                                                    Continued
```

```
   *N   Char(9) Inz('Saturday');
   Days Char(9) Dim(7) Pos(1);
End-ds;
```

With the compile-time array, the array definition can be separated from the actual array data by many pages of other code, and can be more prone to coding errors than the simpler definition for the runtime array. In a modular programming environment, it is useful to be able to keep all the related parts of a construct close together in the actual code. For this reason, many RPG programmers prefer the runtime example over the compile-time one.

11.7. Defining Related Arrays

In RPG, an array corresponds to one column of information. To represent the information in the tables illustrated at the beginning of this chapter, you must define three separate arrays:

```
Dcl-s Abbrev  Char(2)      Dim(50);
Dcl-s State   Char(14)     Dim(50);
Dcl-s Taxrate Zoned(5:5) Dim(50);
```

Or, because the arrays are related to each other, it might be convenient to group them into a data structure:

```
Dcl-ds Taxes Qualified Inz;
  Abbrev  Char(2)      Dim(50);
  State   Char(14)     Dim(50);
  Taxrate Zoned(5:5) Dim(50);
End-ds;
```

or

```
Dcl-ds Taxes Dim(50) Qualified Inz;
  Abbrev  Char(2);
  State   Char(14);
  Taxrate Zoned(5:5);
End-ds;
```

If the arrays are compile-time arrays, however, you may find it convenient to load the data for two arrays in alternating format by defining one of the arrays with the **Alt (Alternating**

format) keyword. For example, you can define the Abbrev and State arrays as a pairs of related arrays with the following definitions:

```
         Dcl-s Abbrev Char(2)  Dim(50) Ctdata;
         Dcl-s State  Char(14) Dim(50) Alt(Abbrev);
```

In this definition, Abbrev is the main array. State is the alternate array, related to Abbrev by the Alt keyword. The main array must be a compile-time array, both arrays must include the Dim keyword, and the alternate array cannot use the Ctdata or Perrcd keyword. You code the array data at the end of the program's source format:

```
     *.. 1 ...+... 2 ...+... 3 ...+... 4 ...+... 5 ...+... 6 ...+... 7 ...+..
   **CTDATA Abbrev
   AKAlaska
   ALAlabama
   ARArkansas
   AZArizona
   CACalifornia
   ...
   WYWyoming
```

The keywords on the main array definition control how to load the arrays' elements when the program starts. The program uses the compile-time data to initialize *both* arrays in alternating order—Abbrev, State, Abbrev, State, and so on—with the end result being that the pair of arrays is loaded with the related information. The Alt keyword allows you to pair only two arrays.

Recall that the %Elem (Number of elements) function returns the number of elements in an array. You can use the %Elem function with the Dim keyword in an array definition to make the dimension of the array dependent upon the dimension of another array:

```
Dcl-s Abbrev  Char(2)    Dim(50);
Dcl-s State   Char(14)   Dim(%Elem(Abbrev));
Dcl-s Taxrate Zoned(5:5) Dim(%Elem(Abbrev));
```

In this example of related arrays, the Abbrev array has 50 elements. The State and Taxrate arrays also have 50 elements each because their definitions use the %Elem function to say,

"This array has the same number of elements as the Abbrev array." The State and Taxrate arrays *inherit* the dimension of the Abbrev array.

Chapter 7 discussed the %Size (Size in bytes) function, which returns the byte size of another data element in an RPG program. You can use the %Size function similarly to the %Elem function if you want an array's dimension to be dependent upon another variable's byte size:

```
Dcl-s Custname  Char(35);
Dcl-s Custarray Char(1) Dim(%Size(Custname));
...
For X = 1 to %Size(Custname);     // Or %Elem(Custarray)
  // This code will be executed 35 times.
Endfor;
```

This code defines Custarray with 35 elements, because Custname is 35 bytes long, and executes the For loop 35 times.

11.8. Arrays and Indexing

You can directly reference and manipulate *individual* elements of an array by using an **index**, or element number. To indicate an array element in ILE RPG, you use the array name followed by a set of parentheses that contains the ordinal location of the element within the array. The index numbering starts with 1. Thus, Days(3) means the third element in the array Days, and Taxrate(10) is the tenth element in the array Taxrate. When you use an array name *without* an index (e.g., Days or Taxrate), RPG understands that you want to reference or manipulate the entire array (i.e., *all* its elements).

The index that you use to reference an element of an array does not have to be a numeric literal. Instead, you can use a variable as an index, provided you have defined the variable as numeric with zero decimal positions. Many programmers prefer to use an unsigned integer as an array index. If the index is a variable, that variable's current value determines which element of the array to reference. Thus, an Index with a value of 3 means that Days(Index) is the third element of Days. If Index's value is 7, then Days(Index) is the seventh element of the array.

The array index can also be an expression, as long as it evaluates to a positive numeric value with no decimal places. If your program refers to an array by using an index with a value that is negative, zero, or greater than the number of elements defined for the array, a runtime error (an array index error) occurs.

11.9. Calculations with Arrays

11.9.1. Simple Array Assignment

You can use arrays or their elements with assignment expressions. If you reference individual elements in the expressions, the effects are the same as if you were using standalone variables:

```
// Assignment the third element of Array_B to the first element of Array_A
Array_A(1) = Array_B(3);
```

You can also assign entire arrays, rather than just individual elements of the arrays. In this case, the expression's result must always be an array name. If all the factors involved in the operation are arrays, the assignment is performed successively on corresponding elements of the arrays until the array with the fewest number of elements has been completely processed.

When you combine nonarray values and arrays in the expression, the assignment works with corresponding elements of the arrays, along with the nonarray values in each case, and continues until all the elements in the shortest array have been processed:

```
// Store 'ABCDE' in each element of array Array_A
Array_A = 'ABCDE';
```

Here are a few examples of array assignment, using the following definitions:

```
Dcl-ds *N;
  *N      Char(12) Inz('abcdefghijkl');
  Array_A Char(3)  Dim(4) Pos(1);
End-ds;


Dcl-ds *N;
  *N      Char(10) Inz('mnopqrstuv');
  Array_B Char(2)  Dim(5) Pos(1);
End-ds;


Dcl-ds *N;
  *N      Char(10) Inz('abcdefghij');
  Array_C Char(2)  Dim(5) Pos(1);
End-ds;
```

11.9.1.1. Array Assignment Example 1

In this example, you assign Array_B to Array_A. Because Array_B has more elements (5) than Array_A, only the first four elements of Array_B are assigned to the corresponding elements of Array_A:

```
Array_A = Array_B;
```

Array_A contains

Before	abc	def	ghi	jkl
After	mnb	opb	qrb	stb

Array_A elements are padded with blanks (represented by b). Equivalent expressions are as follows:

```
Array_A(1) = Array_B(1);
Array_A(2) = Array_B(2);
Array_A(3) = Array_B(3);
Array_A(4) = Array_B(4);
```

11.9.1.2. Array Assignment Example 2

This example does the reverse of the previous one: you assign Array_A to Array_B. Now, because Array_A has fewer elements (4) than Array_B, only the first four elements of Array_B are affected by the expression:

```
Array_B = Array_A;
```

Array_B contains

Before	mn	op	qr	st	uv
After	ab	de	gh	jk	uv

In this example, Array_A elements are truncated in Array_B. Equivalent expressions are as follows:

```
Array_B(1) = Array_A(1);
Array_B(2) = Array_A(2);
Array_B(3) = Array_A(3);
Array_B(4) = Array_A(4);
```

11.9.1.3. Array Assignment Example 3

In this example, Array_B and Array_C have identical properties:

```
Array_B = Array_C;
```

Array_B contains

Before	mn	op	qr	st	uv
After	ab	cd	ef	gh	ij

Here are the equivalent expressions:

```
Array_B(1) = Array_C(1);
Array_B(2) = Array_C(2);
Array_B(3) = Array_C(3);
Array_B(4) = Array_C(4);
Array_B(5) = Array_C(5);
```

11.9.2. Using Arrays in Arithmetic Expressions

You can use any of ILE RPG's arithmetic operations with arrays or their elements. If you reference individual elements in your calculations, the effects are the same as if you were using standalone variables:

```
// Add the values of two elements and store result in a third element.
Array(12) = Array(6) + Array(3);


// Divide the third element of array Array by 60, storing the quotient
// in Quotients(3) and the remainder in Remainders(3).
Quotients(3) = %Div(Array(3):60);
Remainders(3) = %Rem(Array(3):60);
```

You can also use entire arrays, rather than just individual elements of the arrays, in calculations. In this case, the expression's target entry must always be an array name. If all the factors involved in the operation are arrays, the operation is performed successively on corresponding elements of the arrays until the array with the fewest number of elements has been completely processed.

```
// Multiply corresponding elements of Array_A and Array_B,
// storing the products in Array_C.
Eval(H) Array_C = Array_A * Array_B;


// Take the square root of each element of Array_A and store the result
// in the corresponding element of Array_B.
Array_B = %Sqrt(Array_A);
```

When you combine nonarray values and arrays in calculations, the operation works with corresponding elements of the arrays, along with the nonarray values in each case, and continues until all the elements in the shortest array have been processed:

```
// Calculate gross pay for employees who work overtime; arrays Rate and
// Hours contain employee values; array GPay stores results.
Gpay = 40 * Rate + ( (Hours-40) * 1.5 * Rate);
```

11.9.3. %Lookup (Look up an Array Element)

You can use the **%Lookup (Look up an array element)** functions to search an array for a specific elemental value. The %Lookup functions take the following form:

```
%Lookupxx(search-argument : array {:start {:elements}} )
```

Typically, you'll have a value, either a field from an input file or a program variable, that you want to find in the array. This value is the search argument, the first argument in the %Lookup function. Next, you specify the name of the array that you want to search. The search argument must match the data type of the array that you want to search (e.g., if the array has numeric elements, the search argument must be numeric), but it need not have the same length or number of decimal positions.

%Lookup returns a number representing the array index of the element that matches the search argument. If no element in the array matches the search argument's value, %Lookup returns a zero. The following five %Lookup functions each represent a different type of match:

- %Lookup searches for an exact match.
- %Lookuplt searches for an element that is closest to but less than the search argument.
- %Lookuple searches for an exact match, or for an element that is closest to but less than the search argument.

- %Lookupge searches for an exact match, or for an element that is closest to but greater than the search argument.
- %Lookupgt searches for an element that is closest to but greater than the search argument.

The most common usage is a simple %Lookup (exact match).

If you simply want to know whether a value exists as an element in an array, but you don't need to access the element or determine its location within the array, you can compare the %Lookup result to zero. In the following example, the %Lookup indicates whether an array element exists that matches Value:

```
If %Lookup(Value:Array) > 0;
   Exsr Valuefound;
Else;
   Exsr Notfound;
Endif;
```

However, to determine not only whether a value exists in the array but also its location in the array, you need to use an index variable in an assignment expression. The following %Lookup, if successful, assigns index X the value that points to the array element whose value matches Value. For an unsuccessful lookup, X is zero:

```
X = %Lookup(Value:Array);
If X > 0;
   Exsr Valuefound;
Else;
   Exsr Notfound;
Endif;
```

An index that's greater than zero following the lookup means that the value was found in the array. Moreover, index X's value points to the location of the array element that has the same value as Value. Thus, if the third element of Array has the same value as Value, the value of index X is 3 after the %Lookup. To process that element, you can refer to it as Array(X).

If you specify a third (numeric) argument, the search begins at that element of the array; otherwise, the search starts at the first element. If you specify a fourth (numeric) argument, the search continues for that number of elements; otherwise, the search continues to the end of the array.

To understand how you might use the %Lookup functions to extract data from an array, let's reconsider the three-column table of state codes, state names, and sales tax rates discussed earlier in this chapter. Assume that you have entered the three columns of data successively into your program as three individual arrays: Abbrev, State, and Taxrate. With a single %Lookup function to search the primary array (Abbrev), you can find the appropriate index to use with all three arrays. Consider the following code fragments (for ease of illustration, the example uses runtime arrays overlaying data structures, but you can use any of the array-loading methods):

```
// --------------------------------------------------- Data structures
Dcl-ds *N;
  *N      Char(30) Inz('AKALARAZCACOCTDEFLGAHIIAIDILIN');
  *N      Char(30) Inz('KSKYLAMAMDMEMIMNMOMSMTNCNDNENH');
  *N      Char(30) Inz('NJNMNVNYOHOKORPARISCSDTNTXUTVA');
  *N      Char(10) Inz('VTWAWIWVWY');
  Abbrev Char(2)  Dim(50) Pos(1);
End-ds;

Dcl-ds *N;
  *N     Char(14) Inz('Alaska');
  *N     Char(14) Inz('Alabama');
  *N     Char(14) Inz('Arkansas');
  *N     Char(14) Inz('Arizona');
  *N     Char(14) Inz('California');
  ...
  *N     Char(14) Inz('Wyoming');
  State Char(14) Dim(50) Pos(1);
End-ds;

Dcl-ds *N;
  *N      Zoned(5:5) Inz(0);              // Alaska
  *N      Zoned(5:5) Inz(.04);           // Alabama
  *N      Zoned(5:5) Inz(.065;)          // Arkansas
  *N      Zoned(5:5) Inz(.056);          // Arizona
  *N      Zoned(5:5) Inz(.075);          // California
  ...
  *N      Zoned(5:5) Inz(.04);           // Wyoming
  Taxrate Zoned(5:5) Dim(50) Pos(1);
End-ds;
```

Continued

```
// --------------------------------------------- Standalone variables
Dcl-s Saleamount Packed(11:2);
Dcl-s Statecode  Char(2);
Dcl-s Statename  Char(14);
Dcl-s Taxdue     Packed(11:2);
Dcl-s X          Uns(5);
...
// User data provides values for Statecode and Saleamount.
...
X = %Lookup(Statecode:Abbrev);

If X > 0;
   Eval(H) Taxdue = Saleamount * Taxrate(X);
   Statename = State(X);
Else;
   Taxdue = 0;
   Statename = '*Error*';
Endif;
```

In this code, if Statecode has a value of 'CA', the %Lookup function assigns a value of 5 to the variable X. You can then reuse that index with any of the related arrays to point to the corresponding element in each additional *column* (Taxrate and State in this example). If Salesamount has a value of 53.99, Taxdue is 4.05 and Statename is 'California' after processing the preceding code. If Statecode is 'BD', then X is 0, Taxdue is 0, and Statename is '*Error*' because BD is not in the Abbrev array.

11.9.3.1. Using Unequal Searches

To understand when you might use one of the unequal %Lookup functions, consider the following table of shipping charges:

Package Weight	Shipping Charge
0–1	5.00
2–5	8.50
6–10	15.00
11–20	18.00
21–40	24.00
41–70	32.00

You use this table to look up a package weight to determine the shipping charges for the package. Unlike the previous examples, in this table the weight column entries represent a range of values rather than discrete values.

How should you represent these values, and how should you perform the %Lookup? One solution is to represent this data as two arrays, storing only the upper end of the range of weights in one array and the charges in another, as follows:

```
// ------------------------------------------------------ Data structures
Dcl-ds *N;
   *N       Zoned(3:0) Inz(1);
   *N       Zoned(3:0) Inz(5);
   *N       Zoned(3:0) Inz(10);
   *N       Zoned(3:0) Inz(20);
   *N       Zoned(3:0) Inz(40);
   *N       Zoned(3:0) Inz(70);
   Weight Zoned(3:0) Dim(6) Pos(1) Ascend;
End-ds;


Dcl-ds *N;
   *N       Zoned(5:2) Inz(5.00);           //  0- 1
   *N       Zoned(5:2) Inz(8.50);           //  2- 5
   *N       Zoned(5:2) Inz(15.00);          //  6-10
   *N       Zoned(5:2) Inz(18.00);          // 11-20
   *N       Zoned(5:2) Inz(24.00);          // 21-40
   *N       Zoned(5:2) Inz(32.00);          // 41-70
   Charge Zoned(5:2) Dim(6) Pos(1);
End-ds;


// --------------------------------------------------- Standalone variables
Dcl-s Pkgcharge    Packed(5:2);
Dcl-s Pkgweight    Packed(3:0);
Dcl-s Totalcharge Packed(5:2);
Dcl-s X            Uns(5);

...
// User data provides values for Pkgweight and Pkgcharge.

...
X = %Lookupge(Pkgweight:Weight);
```

Continued

```
If X > 0;
   Totalcharge = Pkgcharge + Charge(X);
Else;
   Exsr Cannotship;
Endif;
```

The preceding declarations define Weight and Charge as arrays of six elements each. The unequal %Lookup functions require a sequence entry in the array definition, so the Weight array uses the Ascend keyword to indicate that the data is in ascending order. The lookup statement translates to "Find the first weight that is greater than or equal to the package weight." If the search is successful, the function returns a positive number to the index X, which the program then uses with the Charge array to find the correct shipping charge. Because the maximum shippable weight is 70, failure of the search indicates an input weight over the 70 pound limit. In such cases, the program executes an error routine to indicate that the package cannot be shipped.

11.9.3.2. Sorta (Sort an Array)

As mentioned, the unequal %Lookup functions require a sequence entry in the array definition. The Ascend or Descend keywords describe the sequence of the data in the array. If the array is in ascending order, for example, elements in the array start with the lowest collating value and go to the highest; elements with duplicate values are allowed. Compile-time arrays—but not runtime arrays—are checked for the correct sequence when the program starts. If an array is out of sequence at that time, an error occurs. But the program does not check runtime arrays, and it does not recheck a compile-time array's sequence once that array's data is loaded. If a program changes an element's value, that value can cause the array to be out of sequence.

Sorta (Sort an array) is a simple but useful operation that rearranges the values of the elements of an array into ascending or descending sequence. The order used depends on the sequence keyword specified within the array's definition. If the definition includes neither keyword, the Sorta operation sorts the values in ascending sequence, the default order. The specification for this operation includes just the operation and the name of the array to sort. You can add an (A) or (D) operation extender to explicitly sort the array in ascending or descending sequence, respectively. The following example sorts the Weight array from the previous code segments:

```
Sorta Weight;
```

If you specify a sequence entry—Ascend or Descend—for an array definition, always sort the array before performing a %Lookup function, even an equal %Lookup. If you do not, the %Lookup results will be unpredictable and may be incorrect. *Unsequenced* arrays need not be sorted in order for an equal %Lookup to work properly.

Note

The %Lookup function uses a technique called a binary search to improve performance for sequenced arrays. For those arrays defined without a sequence entry, %Lookup performs a sequential search of the elements.

11.9.4. %Xfoot (Sum the Elements of an Array)

The **%Xfoot (Sum the elements of an array)** function, called *crossfoot*, sums the elements of a numeric array. The function's only argument contains the name of the array whose elements are to be added together. Use an assignment expression to name the field where you want to store the answer. If you half-adjust this operation, the rounding occurs just before the final answer is stored.

Crossfooting is an accounting term meaning to sum across a row of figures to develop a total for that row. The %Xfoot function is useful in such applications, provided the figures to be added are array elements. The following example sums the elements of array Monthlysales, storing the answer in field Ytdsales:

```
Ytdsales = %Xfoot(Monthlysales);
```

11.9.5. %Subarr (Set/Get Portion of an Array)

The **%Subarr (Set/get portion of an array)** function returns a subset of an array, similar to the way the %Subst function returns a section of a character string. The %Subarr function takes the following form:

```
%Subarr(array:start {:elements})
```

The first argument is the array that you want to subset. The second argument tells %Subarr where (i.e., at which element of the array) to begin the subset. This value must be a positive whole number less than or equal to the number of elements in the array.

You can specify a third argument to represent the number of elements to include in the subset. It must be a positive whole number less than or equal to the remaining number of elements, beginning with the starting element (indicated by the second argument).

Generally, you can use %Subarr in any expression that allows an unindexed array. When used as the result of an expression, %Subarr changes (i.e., sets) the specified elements in an array. On the right side of the expression, %Subarr retrieves the specified elements from an array so that they can be assigned to another array. You can also use %Subarr with the Sorta operation and the %Xfoot function to sort or crossfoot a subset of an array. %Subarr respects the element boundaries of the arrays involved in the expression.

To see how to use the %Subarr function, consider the following definitions, also used earlier:

```
Dcl-ds *N;
  *N      Char(12) Inz('abcdefghijkl');
  Array_A Char(3)  Dim(4) Pos(1);
End-ds;

Dcl-ds *N;
  *N      Char(10) Inz('mnopqrstuv');
  Array_B Char(2)  Dim(5) Pos(1);
End-ds;

Dcl-ds *N;
  *N      Char(10) Inz('abcdefghij');
  Array_C Char(2)  Dim(5) Pos(1);
End-ds;
```

The following tables illustrate the effects of using the %Subarr function. When evaluating the effects of using %Subarr, it is sometimes useful to divide the expression into individual assignment expressions by using single array elements, as these examples show.

11.9.5.1. %Subarr Example 1

This example assigns the three elements of Array_A beginning with the second element to Array_B:

```
Array_B = %Subarr(Array_A:2:3);
```

Array_B contains

Before	mn	op	qr	st	uv
After	de	gh	jk	st	uv

Array_A elements are truncated in Array_B. The fourth and fifth elements of Array_B are unaffected. Equivalent expressions are as follows:

```
Array_B(1) = Array_A(2);
Array_B(2) = Array_A(3);
Array_B(3) = Array_A(4);
```

11.9.5.2. %Subarr Example 2

This example assigns the three elements of Array_C beginning with the second element to Array_B:

```
Array_B = %Subarr(Array_C:2:3);
```

Array_B contains

Before	mn	op	qr	st	uv
After	cd	ef	gh	st	uv

Because the elements of Array_B and Array_C are the same size, no truncation takes place. The fourth and fifth elements of Array_B are unaffected. Equivalent expressions are as follows:

```
Array_B(1) = Array_C(2);
Array_B(2) = Array_C(3);
Array_B(3) = Array_C(4);
```

11.9.5.3. %Subarr Example 3

This example assigns the elements of Array_A to Array_B beginning with the third element of Array_B:

```
%Subarr(Array_B:3) = Array_A;
```

Array_B contains

Before	mn	op	qr	st	uv
After	mn	op	ab	de	gh

Array_A elements are truncated in Array_B. Only the first three elements of Array_A are assigned to Array_B, because Array_B runs out of elements before the complete Array_A can be assigned. Equivalent expressions are as follows:

```
Array_B(3) = Array_A(1);
Array_B(4) = Array_A(2);
Array_B(5) = Array_A(3);
```

11.9.5.4. %Subarr Example 4

This example assigns the elements of Array_C to Array_B beginning with the third element of Array_B:

```
%Subarr(Array_B:3) = Array_C;
```

Array_B contains

Before	mn	op	qr	st	uv
After	mn	op	ab	cd	ef

Only the first three elements of Array_C are assigned to Array_B, because Array_B runs out of elements before the complete Array_C can be assigned. Equivalent expressions are as follows:

```
Array_B(3) = Array_C(1);
Array_B(4) = Array_C(2);
Array_B(5) = Array_C(3);
```

11.9.5.5. %Subarr Example 5

This example assigns the third and fourth elements of Array_A to the third and fourth elements of Array_B:

```
%Subarr(Array_B:3) = %Subarr(Array_A:3);
```

Array_B contains

Before	mn	op	qr	st	uv
After	mn	op	gh	jk	uv

Array_A elements are truncated in Array_B. The expression skips the first and second elements of Array_B. The fifth element is also unaffected because Array_A runs out of elements. Equivalent expressions are as follows:

```
Array_B(3) = Array_A(3);
Array_B(4) = Array_A(4);
```

11.9.5.6. %Subarr Example 6

This example assigns the third and fourth elements of Array_C to the second and third elements of Array_B:

```
%Subarr(Array_B:2) = %Subarr(Array_C:3:2);
```

Array_B contains

Before	mn	op	qr	st	uv
After	mn	ef	gh	st	uv

The remaining elements of Array_B are unaffected. Equivalent expressions are as follows:

```
Array_B(2) = Array_C(3);
Array_B(3) = Array_C(4);
```

11.10. Using Arrays with SQL

Chapter 10 discussed the use of the SQL Fetch statement to retrieve a row from a multiple-row result set into host variables or a host structure (or both). This type of Fetch is called a **single fetch**. If the host structure is an array data structure, Fetch can perform a **multiple-row fetch**, retrieving several rows with one statement and placing the result set into individual elements of the array data structure. The Fetch statement for a multiple-row fetch takes the following form:

```
Exec SQL Fetch cursor-name For number Rows Into :host-structure;
```

Because a multiple-row fetch requires only a single access to the database to retrieve many records, one multiple-row fetch of 100 records performs much better than 100 single fetches.

These code fragments illustrate how to use this variation of the Fetch statement with an SQL cursor to fetch 100 rows from a result set by using a multiple-row fetch:

```
Dcl-ds Customers Ext Dim(100) Qualified End-ds;
...
Exec SQL Declare Custcursor Cursor For
                                Select  *
                                    From  Customers
                                    Where Czip = :Czip
                                    Order by Custno;
Exec SQL Open Custcursor;
...
Exec SQL Fetch Custcursor For 100 Rows Into :Customers;
```

Assuming the Fetch statement retrieves all 100 rows from the result set, the subfields in the Customers data structure hold the value of each row in a separate element of the Customers array data structure. The first result row is the first host structure array element, the second row is the second element, and so forth. The program refers to the columns of the first row as Customers(1).Cfname, Customers(1).Clname, and so on—the second row as Customers(2). Cfname, Customers(2).Clname, and so forth, on to all the columns in all 100 rows.

It's likely that a multiple-row fetch may not always retrieve all the rows called for. In the previous example, the number of records in the result set probably will not be an even multiple of 100. In that case, the program must be able to manage an incomplete fetch. An array in the SQL Communications Area (covered in Chapter 10) returns diagnostics information to the program about how many rows were actually fetched. Following a Fetch statement, the value of Sqlerrd(3) is the number of rows actually fetched. Sqlerrd(5) contains a value of 100 if the last row in the result set was retrieved. The following code fragments illustrate how you might use the feedback information with a multiple-row fetch:

```
Dcl-c Lastrow 100;
Dcl-c Nbrrows 100;

Dcl-s X Uns(10);

Dcl-ds Customers Ext Dim(Nbrrows) Qualified End-ds;
...
Exec SQL Declare Custcursor Cursor For
                                Select  *
                                    From  Customers
                                    Where Czip = :Czip
                                    Order by Custno;
```

Continued

```
Exec SQL Open Custcursor;

...

Dou Sqlerrd(5) = Lastrow;
  Exec SQL Fetch Custcursor For :Nbrrows Rows Into :Customers;


  If Sqlerrd(3) = 0;       // No rows retrieved
    Leave;
  Endif;


  For X = 1 to Sqlerrd(3);
    // Process rows in Customers array, using X as index:
    // Customers(X).Cfname, Customers(X).Clname, ...
  Endfor;

Enddo;
```

In this example, the Nbrrows constant determines the number of elements in the host structure, the number of rows for each multiple-row fetch. The For loop processes each element of the Customers array data structure, up to the number of rows actually fetched, using each iteration's value of X as the array index. Once the SQLCA indicates that the last row has been retrieved, or if no rows were retrieved, the program exits the Dou loop.

The SQL Insert statement also has an alternative syntax that can insert multiple rows with a single statement by using an array data structure:

```
Exec SQL Insert Into table number Rows Values (:host-structure);
```

For example:

```
Dcl-ds Customers Ext Dim(100) Qualified End-ds;

...

// Loop to populate 100 elements of Customers array data structure

...

Exec SQL Insert Into Customers 100 Rows Values (:Customers);
```

The host structure must correspond to the columns in the table. The program uses a loop to populate each element of the host structure with data, and then it uses a single Insert statement to add all the rows in one statement. Following the Insert, Sqlerrd(3) contains the actual number of rows added.

Tip
To take best advantage of its performance benefits, a multiple-row Fetch or Insert should always fetch the maximum number of rows that the program can be practically expected to process. The maximum size of an RPG data structure (dimension multiplied by element length) is 16,773,104 bytes.

11.11. Array Data Structures and Multidimensional Arrays

Recall that a typical RPG array represents only one column of data, and that an array can be a data structure subfield or a data structure itself. An **array data structure** is a data structure defined with the Dim keyword. By defining an array as a subfield within an array data structure, a program can effectively define a two-dimensional array. Consider the following declarations:

```
Dcl-ds Galaxy     Dim(8) Qualified;
  Sector Char(1) Dim(8);
End-ds;
```

Conceptually, this definition creates a structure that you can visualize with rows and columns:

	Sector(1)	Sector(2)	Sector(3)	Sector(4)	Sector(5)	Sector(6)	Sector(7)	Sector(8)
Galaxy(1)								
Galaxy(2)								
Galaxy(3)								
Galaxy(4)								
Galaxy(5)								
Galaxy(6)								
Galaxy(7)								
Galaxy(8)								

Array data structures must be qualified runtime arrays. In the preceding definition, you code Galaxy(3).Sector(6) to refer to the sixth element of Sector in the third element of Galaxy.Galaxy(3).Sector refers to the entire Sector array in the third element of Galaxy. And Galaxy.Sector, without an index entry for Galaxy, is not allowed. The index can be a whole numeric literal, constant, or expression.

If a subfield in a data structure uses the Likeds keyword (discussed in Chapter 4) to inherit the characteristics of another data structure, and if that data structure includes array subfields, the inherited subfields are also arrays. You can use this feature to add even more dimensions to an array data structure, as the following declarations illustrate:

```
Dcl-ds Xtemp Template;
  Part Char(1) Dim(8);
End-ds;


Dcl-ds Warehouse        Dim(8) Qualified;
  Pallet Likeds(Xtemp) Dim(8);
End-ds;
```

In this definition, subfield Pallet is an array within the array data structure Warehouse. Because subfield Pallet uses the Likeds keyword with data structure Xtemp as its parent, it consists of subfield Part, which is also an array. To refer to the fourth element of Part, within the third element of Pallet, within the second element of Warehouse, you code Warehouse(2).Pallet(3).Part(4). To refer to the entire Part array within the third element of Pallet, within the second element of Warehouse, you code Warehouse(2).Pallet(3).Part. In the case of a complex data structure such as this, you can omit the index only for the rightmost array.

This example also uses the Template keyword in the declaration for the Xtemp structure. While not absolutely necessary in this example, Template indicates that the program need not allocate any memory at runtime for this declaration. Instead, it's used only at compile time for further Like or Likeds declarations, not any actual processing.

If a data item uses the Like or Likeds keyword to inherit the data attributes of a standalone variable or a data structure, it will *not* copy the Dim keyword—or any other array-related keywords—from the parent. (The only situation in which the child uses the Dim keyword from a parent is the one described in this example, in which the child inherits the Dim keyword from the parent's subfield.) The child must explicitly include the Dim keyword if it is to be an array. You can, however, code the Dim keyword with the %Elem function to define a child array with the same number of elements as its parent:

```
Dcl-s Parent Char(2)     Dim(50);
Dcl-s Child  Like(Parent) Dim(%Elem(Parent));
```

11.12. Array Keys

RPG allows you to search and sort an array data structure by identifying one of its subfields as a key. A **keyed array data structure** uses an asterisk (*) as its index, followed by the name of the key subfield. For example, given the following declaration

```
Dcl-ds Taxes Qualified Dim(50) Inz;
   Abbrev   Char(2);
   State    Char(14);
   Taxrate Zoned(5:5);
End-ds;
```

the program can refer to any of the subfields in Taxes by naming the subfield as a key: Taxes(*).Abbrev, Taxes(*).State, or Taxes(*).Taxrate. The key subfield cannot be an array, and only a single (*) index can be specified.

You can use keyed array data structures with the Sorta operation and the %Lookup functions. To sort the example Taxes array data structure by the Abbrev subfield, code Abbrev as the key:

```
Sorta Taxes(*).Abbrev;
```

The following code fragment uses %Lookup with the Taxes data structure:

```
Taxes(1) = 'AKAlaska        00000';
Taxes(2) = 'ALAlabama       04000';
Taxes(3) = 'ARArkansas      06500';
Taxes(4) = 'AZArizona       05600';
Taxes(5) = 'CACalifornia    07500';
...
Taxes(50) = 'WYWyoming       04000';
...
X = %Lookup(Statecode:Taxes(*).Abbrev);
```

Assume Statecode has a value of CA; X is 5. Following this lookup, X can be the index for the Taxes array to refer to the corresponding element of the State and Taxrate subfields as well as the Abbrev subfield:

- Taxes(X).Abbrev is CA
- Taxes(X).State is California
- Taxes(X).Taxrate is .075

11.13. Navigating Legacy Code

11.13.1. Lookup Operation

Earlier in this chapter, we examined the %Lookup functions to search for a particular element in an array. Fixed-format Calculation specifications also support a Lookup operation code that performs similarly in legacy RPG programs. The Lookup operation takes the following form:

```
*.. 1 ...+... 2 ...+... 3 ...+... 4 ...+... 5 ...+... 6 ...+... 7 ...+... 8
CLON01Factor1+++++++Opcode(E)+Factor2+++++++Result++++++++Len++D+HiLoEq....
C        search-arg   Lookup    array{(index)}                      GtLtEq
```

You code the search argument (comparable to the first parameter in the %Lookup function) in Factor 1 and the array name (second parameter) in Factor 2. The Lookup operation returns the array element index for a successful search if you follow the array name with a variable (in parentheses) to hold that value.

Resulting indicators (HiLoEq) specify the search criteria and reflect the result of the search. At least one resulting indicator is required. For example, an indicator in the Eq position specifies to perform an equal lookup and to set the indicator *On if the search is successful. The following resulting indicator combinations are valid:

Resulting Indicators			Lookup Operation	Equivalent Function
--	--	Eq	Searches for an exact match	%Lookup
--	Lo	--	Searches for an element that is closest to but less than the search argument	%Lookuplt
--	Lo	Eq	Searches for an exact match, or for an element that is closest to but less than the search argument	%Lookuple
Hi	--	Eq	Searches for an exact match, or for an element that is closest to but greater than the search argument	%Lookupge
Hi	--	--	Searches for an element that is closest to but greater than the search argument	%Lookupgt

Here are some examples of using Lookup:

```
*.. 1 ...+... 2 ...+... 3 ...+... 4 ...+... 5 ...+... 6 ...+... 7 ...+... 8
CLON01Factor1+++++++Opcode(E)+Factor2+++++++Result++++++++Len++D+HiLoEq....
C                    Eval      X = 1
C        Statecode   Lookup    Abbrev(X)                              90
```

Before this lookup is performed, X is set to a value of 1. This dictates that the search is to start at element 1. If the array has an exact match to the search argument, X is set to the relevant element index, and indicator 90, %Equal, and %Found are *On. If the search is unsuccessful, X is 1 (not zero), and indicator 90, %Equal, and %Found are *Off.

```
*.. 1 ...+... 2 ...+... 3 ...+... 4 ...+... 5 ...+... 6 ...+... 7 ...+... 8
CLON01Factor1+++++++Opcode(E)+Factor2+++++++Result+++++++++Len++D+HiLoEq....
C     Statecode     Lookup    Abbrev(X)                              90
```

This example does not set X to 1 before the Lookup. The search starts at the element that corresponds to the value of X. If the array has an exact match to the search argument, X is set to the relevant element index, and indicator 90, %Equal, and %Found are *On. If the search is unsuccessful, indicator 90, %Equal, and %Found are *Off, and X is reset to 1.

```
*.. 1 ...+... 2 ...+... 3 ...+... 4 ...+... 5 ...+... 6 ...+... 7 ...+... 8
CLON01Factor1+++++++Opcode(E)+Factor2+++++++Result+++++++++Len++D+HiLoEq....
C     Statecode     Lookup    Abbrev                                 90
```

This example does not use an index. If the array has an exact match to the search argument, indicator 90, %Equal, and %Found are *On. If the search is unsuccessful, these items are *Off.

```
*.. 1 ...+... 2 ...+... 3 ...+... 4 ...+... 5 ...+... 6 ...+... 7 ...+... 8
CLON01Factor1+++++++Opcode(E)+Factor2+++++++Result+++++++++Len++D+HiLoEq....
C                   Eval      X = 1
C     Pkgweight     Lookup    Weight(X)                           90 90
```

This example is similar to the unequal search shown earlier to calculate shipping charges. It translates to "Find the first weight that is greater than or equal to the package weight." The search starts with the first element. If the array has an element closest to but greater than Pkgweight, X is set to the relevant element index, and indicator 90 and %Found are *On. If the found element is an exact match, %Equal is also *On. If the search is unsuccessful, X is 1 (not zero), and indicator 90, %Equal, and %Found are *Off.

A major difference between the Lookup operation and the %Lookup functions relates to an unsuccessful search. Lookup always returns an index value of 1 for an unsuccessful search, but the %Lookup functions return a zero for that condition. If, after a Lookup operation, the index value is 1, the program must also check the state of the resulting indicator or the %Equal or %Found function to be confident of its results.

```
*.. 1 ...+... 2 ...+... 3 ...+... 4 ...+... 5 ...+... 6 ...+... 7 ...+... 8
CLON01Factor1+++++++Opcode(E)+Factor2+++++++Result+++++++++Len++D+HiLoEq....
C                   Eval      X = 1
C     Statecode     Lookup    Abbrev(X)                              90
```
Continued

```
C                 If        %Equal
C //         Or: If        *In90
C                 Eval(h)   Taxdue = Saleamount * Taxrate(X)
C                 Eval      Statename = State(X)
C                 Else
C                 Eval      Taxdue = 0
C                 Eval      Statename = '*Error*'
C                 Endif
```

11.13.2. Preruntime Arrays

We've discussed runtime arrays and compile-time arrays earlier in this chapter. Fixed-format legacy RPG also supports a third alternative for supplying array data values: store the data in a database file that is automatically loaded into the array each time the program is run. This kind of array is called a *preruntime array*, because RPG retrieves all the array data from the file before the program's procedural processing begins.

Defining a preruntime array entails the use of fixed-format Definition specifications (D-specs). Preruntime arrays require you to include the Fromfile (From file) keyword, specifying the name of the file containing the array data. The value you indicate with the Perrcd keyword should signal how many array elements are coded per record within the array file. If only one value appears per record, you can omit the Perrcd keyword.

```
*.. 1 ...+... 2 ...+... 3 ...+... 4 ...+... 5 ...+... 6 ...+... 7 ...+... 8
DName++++++++++ETDsFrom+++To/L+++IDc.Keywords+++++++++++++++++++++++++++++++++++
D Abbrev          S             2       Dim(50)
D                                       Fromfile(States)
```

Because the data for a preruntime array is obtained from a file, you must include a definition of this file with fixed-format File specifications (F-specs). The File specification for a file that contains array data differs somewhat from that of other files. The file type (position 17) is I (Input) because the program reads the data, but the file's designation (position 18) is T (Table). This entry directs the system to read all the data into an array automatically at the program's start. The array input file for a preruntime array must be program described. You code an F (for fixed format) in position 22 and include the appropriate record length in positions 23–27. The file must be processed sequentially (key access is not allowed).

```
*.. 1 ...+... 2 ...+... 3 ...+... 4 ...+... 5 ...+... 6 ...+... 7 ...+... 8
FFilename++IPEASFRlen+LKlen+AIDevice+.Keywords+++++++++++++++++++++++++++++++
FStates    IT F  2         Disk
```

To write the array back to a file at the end of program execution—perhaps because your
program changed some of the array values and you want to update the file to reflect these
changes—you need to include the Tofile (To file) keyword as part of the array's Definition
specification, specifying the name of the target file. If the Fromfile is different from the
Tofile, you need an additional File specification defining the Tofile as an output file. To write
the table data back to the same file from which it was initially read, enter the file type as C
(for combined):

```
*.. 1 ...+... 2 ...+... 3 ...+... 4 ...+... 5 ...+... 6 ...+... 7 ...+... 8
FFilename++IPEASFRlen+LKlen+AIDevice+.Keywords+++++++++++++++++++++++++++++++
DName+++++++++++ETDsFrom+++To/L+++IDc.Keywords+++++++++++++++++++++++++++++++
   // Table file of 50 state codes, with one code per record;
   // records to be rewritten at end of processing
FStates    CT F  2         Disk

   // Preruntime array of 50 state codes, entered one per record;
   // table file to be rewritten at end of processing
D Abbrev         S          2    Dim(50)
D                               Fromfile(States) Tofile(States)
```

You cannot declare preruntime arrays by using the free-format Dcl-f, Dcl-s, or Dcl-ds
instructions. Preruntime arrays must use fixed-format F-specs and D-specs. Earlier in this
chapter, we showed a technique for loading runtime arrays from a file. This method is
essentially the same concept as a preruntime array, except that a preruntime array retrieves
the data when the program loads, as part of the RPG cycle, without any explicit processing.

11.13.3. Tables

Before RPG supported arrays, it used a similar construct—tables—for many of the same
purposes. A table is a data construct much like an array in that it contains multiple elements
all defined with a common name. As with an array, each element within a table must be the
same data type with the same length and (if the elements are numeric) number of decimal
positions. As with an array, a program can search a table to find a specific value. While ILE
RPG supports tables as a mechanism for handling similar data elements, arrays are generally
more flexible, and most programmers find arrays more suitable to their needs.

You define tables in fixed-format Definition specifications or free-format Dcl-s instructions. The required entries are the same as those for arrays. In fact, only two definition differences exist between tables and arrays:

- Table names must begin with Tab.
- Tables must be loaded at compile time or preruntime (*runtime* tables are not allowed).

The following definitions describe two compile-time tables, Tababbrev and Tabstate. These tables are similar to the arrays described earlier in the chapter:

```
*.. 1 ...+... 2 ...+... 3 ...+... 4 ...+... 5 ...+... 6 ...+... 7 ...+..
   Dcl-s Tababbrev Char(2)  Dim(50) Ctdata Perrcd(25);
   Dcl-s Tabstate  Char(14) Dim(50) Ctdata;

   ...
**CTDATA Tababbrev
AKALARAZCACOCTDEFLGAHIIAIDILINKSKYLAMAMDMEMIMNMOMS
MTNCNDNENHNJNMNVNYOHOKORPARISCSDTNTXUTVAVTWAWIWVWY
**CTDATA Tabstate
Alaska
Alabama
Arkansas
Arizona
California
...
Wyoming
```

You can also define these related tables in alternating format:

```
*.. 1 ...+... 2 ...+... 3 ...+... 4 ...+... 5 ...+... 6 ...+... 7 ...+..
   Dcl-s Tababbrev Char(2)  Dim(50) Ctdata;
   Dcl-s Tabstate  Char(14) Dim(50) Alt(Tababbrev);

   ...
**CTDATA Tababbrev
AKAlaska
ALAlabama
ARArkansas
AZArizona
CACalifornia
...
WYWyoming
```

11.13.3.1. Table Lookups

You use tables for one primary purpose: to look up data values. The major difference between arrays and tables is the way RPG searches their elements. Only one element of a table is active at a time. You cannot specify an index for a table; instead, you simply refer to the currently active element by using the table's name. Rather than using the %Lookup function to search a table, you use one of the %Tlookup (Look up a Table Element) functions or the fixed-format Lookup operation. To code the %Tlookup function, use this format:

```
%Tlookupxx(search-argument :table {:alternate-table} )
```

The search argument is the first argument in the %Tlookup function. Next, you specify the name of the table that you want to search. The search argument must match the data type of the table that you want to search (e.g., if the table has numeric elements, the search argument must be numeric), but it need not have the same length or number of decimal positions.

%Tlookup returns an *On condition (not a number) if it finds a table element that matches the search argument. If no element in the table matches the search argument's value, %Tlookup returns an *Off condition. The following five variations of %Tlookup functions each represent a different type of match:

- %Tlookup searches for an exact match.
- %Tlookuplt searches for an element that is closest to but less than the search argument.
- %Tlookuple searches for an exact match, or for an element that is closest to but less than the search argument.
- %Tlookupge searches for an exact match, or for an element that is closest to but greater than the search argument.
- %Tlookupgt searches for an element that is closest to but greater than the search argument.

The most common usage is a simple %Tlookup (exact match). The following %Tlookup indicates whether or not a table element exists that matches Value:

```
If %Tlookup(Value:Table)= *On;
   Exsr Valuefound;
Else;
   Exsr Notfound;
Endif;
```

Because %Tlookup returns a logical value (*On or *Off), you can code the previous example more simply, just like an indicator:

```
If %Tlookup(Value:Table);            // Successful search
```

or

```
If Not %Tlookup(Value:Table);        // Unsuccessful search
```

When %Tlookup is successful, in addition to returning the value *On, an internal pointer is positioned at the matching table value. You can then refer to that element of the table by simply using the table's name. If the search is unsuccessful, %Tlookup returns the value *Off and does not reposition the table pointer.

Consider the following code:

```
 *.. 1 ...+... 2 ...+... 3 ...+... 4 ...+... 5 ...+... 6 ...+... 7 ...+..


    Dcl-s Statecode Char(2);
    Dcl-s X         Char(2);


    Dcl-s Tababbrev Char(2) Dim(50) Ctdata Perrcd(25);
    ...
    If %Tlookup(Statecode:Tababbrev);
      X = Tababbrev;
    Else;
      X = '**';
    Endif;
    ...
**CTDATA Tababbrev
AKALARAZCACOCTDEFLGAHIIAIDILINKSKYLAMAMDMEMIMNMOMS
MTNCNDNENHNJNMNVNYOHOKORPARISCSDTNTXUTVAVTWAWIWVWY
```

A table lookup involving a single table is useful for validating an input field's value. In the preceding code, if Statecode has a value of CA, the %Tlookup function returns an *On value (i.e., the If condition is true), and the internal table pointer points to CA in the Tababbrev table. In the next line, X is assigned a value of CA because that is the value of the current element in the table. If Statecode is BD, %Tlookup returns an *Off value because BD is not in the table, and X has a value of "**". The pointer is not repositioned, and the previous element remains the current element (before the first successful %Tlookup, the first table element is the current element). Good programming practice suggests that you always provide for the possibility of unsuccessful lookups within your code.

11.13.3.2. Using Related Tables

You can also reposition a second table with a single %Tlookup function by naming the second table as the third argument in the %Tlookup function. Only one lookup is performed, against the primary table. But if the primary lookup is successful, %Tlookup sets the internal pointer for the secondary table as well. In the following example, which uses the tables defined earlier, a successful code search causes the internal pointer to be positioned in Tabstate at the name that corresponds to the matched code in Tababbrev.

```
If %Tlookup(Codein:Tababbrev:Tabstate);
  Statename = Tabstate;
Else;
  Statename = '*Error*';
Endif;
```

The result is that Tabstate contains the desired state name, and you can print or display Tabstate or use it in any other operation for which you need the appropriate state name. An unsuccessful search of Tababbrev results in Tabstate containing the state name from the last successful lookup. In that case, this example assigns a value of *Error* to Statename.

The %Tlookup function lets you name only a primary table and one secondary table. To set additional secondary tables based on the primary lookup, you must execute multiple %Tlookup functions, as the following example illustrates:

```
    *.. 1 ...+... 2 ...+... 3 ...+... 4 ...+... 5 ...+... 6 ...+... 7 ...+..
    Dcl-s Tababbrev Char(2)    Dim(50) Ctdata;
    Dcl-s Tabstate  Char(14)   Dim(%Elem(Tababbrev)) Alt(Tababbrev);
    Dcl-s Tabrate   Zoned(5:5) Dim(%Elem(Tababbrev)) Ctdata;
    ...
    If %Tlookup(Codein:Tababbrev:Tabstate)
        And %Tlookup(Codein:Tababbrev:Tabrate);
      Statename = Tabstate;
      Eval(H) Taxdue = Amount * Tabrate;
    Else;
      Exsr Badcode;
    Endif;
    ...
**CTDATA Tababbrev
AKAlaska
                                                          Continued
```

```
ALAlabama
ARArkansas
AZArizona
CACalifornia
...
WYWyoming
**CTDATA Tabrate
00000
04000
06000
05600
06250
...
04000
```

This example presents the Tababbrev and Tabstate data in alternating format, but you can enter them as separate tables or as preruntime tables instead. Notice that the example uses two %Tlookup functions against Tababbrev. If these searches are successful, the internal pointers for all three tables are set to the appropriate elements.

11.13.3.3. Range Tables

Recall the example earlier in this chapter that used an unequal %Lookup function to determine shipping charges based upon package weight. The following example illustrates how a program can perform the same function with tables instead of arrays:

```
*.. 1 ...+... 2 ...+... 3 ...+... 4 ...+... 5 ...+... 6 ...+... 7 ...+..
   Dcl-s Tabweight Zoned(3:0) Dim(6) Ctdata Ascend;
   Dcl-s Tabcharge Zoned(5:2) Dim(%Elem(Tabweight)) Alt(Tabweight);

   Dcl-s Pkgcharge   Packed(5:2);
   Dcl-s Pkgweight   Packed(3:0);
   Dcl-s Totalcharge Packed(5:2);
   ...
   If %Tlookupge (Pkgweight:Tabweight:Tabcharge);
     Totalcharge = Pkgcharge + Tabcharge;
   Else;
     Exsr Cannotship;
   Endif;
                                                            Continued
```

```
        . . .
**CTDATA Tabweight
00100250
00500425
01000750
02000900
04001200
07001600
```

11.13.3.4. Changing Table Values

Programmers generally use tables for extracting values. It is possible, however, to change table values during program execution. Anytime you specify a table name as the result of a mathematical or an assignment operation, the value of the entry where the table is *currently* positioned changes. Failing to understand this fact can lead to inadvertent program errors.

For example, consider the shipping weight problem. Assume that in the program you want to add and print either the appropriate shipping charge or, for packages weighing more than 70 pounds, to add and print 0 to indicate that the package can't be shipped. The following incorrect solution may tempt you, but it can inadvertently change random values in Tabcharge to 0:

```
If Not %Tlookupge(Weightin:Tabweight:Tabcharge);
  Tabcharge = 0;
Endif;
Totalcharge = Pkgcharge + Tabcharge;
```

The result of this code is that each time a package weighing more than 70 pounds is processed, the lookup fails, Tabcharge is not repositioned, and the Tabcharge value of the *most recently successful* lookup is set to 0. The next time a package of that lower weight is processed, its shipping charge will be incorrectly extracted as 0. Before changing a table value, ensure that you first execute a successful %Tlookup operation to position the table correctly.

If the table data came from a file and you want to store the table with its revised values back in the file at the end of processing, you can accomplish this task simply with a few changes to the File and Definition specifications. First, designate the table file as a combined file rather than an input file. Then, include the filename with keywords Fromfile and Tofile on the Definition specification. These two changes cause the (changed) table values to be written back to the file upon program completion.

11.13.4. Multiple-Occurrence Data Structures

Before it allowed array data structures, RPG supported the concept of a multiple-occurrence data structure (MODS). A MODS is similar to an array data structure in that it defines several instances of the same data structure. But a program cannot search or sort a MODS. A program can process only one occurrence of a MODS at a time, and the program must explicitly set the current occurrence to process. An SQL multiple-row fetch can use a multiple-occurrence host structure instead of an array data structure, especially in legacy programs, to store data values from multiple rows.

To declare a MODS, use the Occurs keyword to indicate the number of occurrences:

```
Dcl-ds Customers Ext Occurs(100) End-ds;
```

The data structure can be program described or externally described as well as a qualified data structure. Legacy programs can use fixed-format Definition specifications to declare the MODS:

```
*.. 1 ...+... 2 ...+... 3 ...+... 4 ...+... 5 ...+... 6 ...+... 7 ...+... 8
DName+++++++++++ETDsFrom+++To/Len+IDc.Keywords+++++++++++++++++++++++++++++++
D Customers      E Ds                   Occurs(100)
```

Multiple-occurrence data structures do not refer to an index to indicate which instance the program is to process. Instead, the fixed-format Occur (Get/Set Occurrence of a Data Structure) operation establishes the active occurrence:

```
*.. 1 ...+... 2 ...+... 3 ...+... 4 ...+... 5 ...+... 6 ...+... 7 ...+... 8
CLON01Factor1+++++++Opcode(E)+Factor2+++++++Result++++++++Len++D+HiLoEq....
C     value          Occur     data-struc
```

For example, to activate the third occurrence, you code this:

```
*.. 1 ...+... 2 ...+... 3 ...+... 4 ...+... 5 ...+... 6 ...+... 7 ...+... 8
CLON01Factor1+++++++Opcode(E)+Factor2+++++++Result++++++++Len++D+HiLoEq....
C     3              Occur     Customers
```

You can also use the Occur operation to retrieve the current occurrence's value by specifying a result field instead of, or in addition to, Factor 1:

```
*.. 1 ...+... 2 ...+... 3 ...+... 4 ...+... 5 ...+... 6 ...+... 7 ...+... 8
CLON01Factor1+++++++Opcode(E)+Factor2+++++++Result++++++++Len++D+HiLoEq....
C                    Occur     Customers     X
```

Following the activation of an occurrence, the program refers to the data structure name to manage that occurrence. To process another instance, Occur must activate a new current occurrence.

The following example shows how SQL might use a MODS instead of an array data structure:

```
*.. 1 ...+... 2 ...+... 3 ...+... 4 ...+... 5 ...+... 6 ...+... 7 ...+... 8
DName+++++++++++ETDsFrom+++To/Len+IDc.Keywords++++++++++++++++++++++++++++++
CLON01Factor1+++++++Opcode(E)+Factor2+++++++Result++++++++Len++D+HiLoEq....
D X             S             10U 0

D Customers     E Ds                  Occurs(100) Qualified
...
C/Exec SQL Declare Custcursor Cursor For
C+                          Select *
C+                            From  Customers
C+                            Where Czip = :Czip
C+                            Order by Custno
C/End-exec
C/Exec SQL Open Custcursor
C/End-exec
...
C               Dou       Sqlerrd(5) = 100

C/Exec SQL Fetch Custcursor For 100 Rows Into :Customers
C/End-exec
```

Continued

```
C                    If        Sqlerrd(3) = 0
C                    Leave
C                    Endif

C                    For       X = 1 to Sqlerrd(3)
C         X          Occur     Customers
*                    Process rows in Customers data structure:
*                    Refer to fields Customers.Cfname, Customers.Clname, ...
C                    Endfor

C                    Enddo
```

11.14. Chapter Summary

ILE RPG uses arrays to store sets of similar elements. The Dim keyword indicates how many elements are in the array. You can explicitly reference an individual array element by using an index, or you can manipulate the array as a whole by using the array name without an index. You can use a numeric literal or field as an index to point to a specific array element.

Arrays can be standalone variables, data structure subfields, or array data structures. Array data structures can simulate multidimensional arrays. You can load arrays at compile time, from data hard-coded at the end of the source program or during runtime, or from values contained in program or file data (or both).

The %Lookup function searches an array for a specific value, returning a number representing the index of the found value. %Lookup typically searches for equal matches, but can also find unequal matches. The Sorta operation sorts an array into ascending or descending sequence, depending upon the sequence you specify in the array definition or in an operation extender. The %Xfoot function sums all the elements of a numeric array. The %Subarr function allows you to process a subset of an array instead of the entire array.

The SQL Fetch statement can retrieve several rows with one statement, and a multiple-row fetch places its result set into individual elements of an array data structure. A single multiple-row fetch performs better than several individual single fetches. The SQL Insert statement also has a multiple insert alternative syntax.

A keyed array data structure allows a subfield to be named as a key. You can use the key to search and sort the array data structure.

The following table summarizes the functions and operation codes discussed in this chapter:

Function or Operation	Description	Syntax
%Elem	Number of elements in an array, table, or multiple-occurrence data structure	**%Elem(Data-item)**
%Lookup %Lookuplt %Lookuple %Lookupge %Lookupgt	Look up element in an array	**%Lookupxx(Search-argument : Array {: Start {: Elements}})**
%Size	Size	**%Size(Data-item {: *All})**
Sorta	Sort array	**Sorta Array-name**
%Subarr	Get or set portion of an array	**%Subarr(Array-name : Start {:Elements})**
%Xfoot	Sum array expression elements	**%Xfoot(Array-expression)**

11.15 Key Terms

Alt (Alternating format)

array

array data structure

compile-time array

crossfooting

Ctdata (Compile-time data)

**Ctdata record

%Elem (Get number of elements)

Index

keyed array data structure

%Lookup (Look up an array element)

multiple-row fetch

Perrcd (Per record)

runtime array

single fetch

Sorta (Sort an array)

%Subarr (Set/get portion of an array)

%Xfoot (Sum the elements of an array)

11.16. Discussion/Review Questions

1. To describe the telephone book as a runtime array by using a data structure in ILE RPG, how many subfields would you define?
2. What factors would you employ to determine whether to use a runtime array or a compile-time array?
3. Explain the differences between a runtime array and a compile-time array. Give an example of where you would use each of them.
4. Explain how using the %Elem function to control a loop is often referred to as *soft-coding* a loop.
5. Explain the use of **Ctdata record function.
6. When defining an array, how would you use the Alt keyword?
7. When you use an index to access data in an array with ILE RPG, what difference causes problems for programmers who have written code by using other modern languages besides RPG?
8. What is a multiple-row fetch, and how is it used?
9. How are the effects of standard arithmetic operations dependent upon whether array elements or arrays are entered as factors in the calculations?

10.   What ILE RPG operations are used with arrays? Give a short description of how each operation works.

11.17. Exercises

1. You are writing an application to process orders. Records include the date ordered in *yymmdd* format, but you want to print the name of the month ordered, rather than the number of the month.

   a. Show how you would hard-code data for a two-column array relating month number to month name.

   b. Code the declarations for these compile-time arrays, matching the definitions to the way in which you've laid out your data.

   c. Write the calculations needed to look up OrdMonth (order month) in one array to extract the appropriate month name.

2. Modify your work in exercise 1 by using arrays, rather than tables. Don't require your program to do more work than necessary. (Hint: Can you think of a way to obtain the correct month name without performing a lookup?)

3. An input file contains sales records. Each record represents one week of sales, with seven sales figures, each 10 digits long with two decimal positions, in positions 20–90 of the input record. Code the declarations and the portion of the calculations needed to generate a weekly sales total and to separately accumulate sales for each day of the week as input to the file is processed.

4. Assume the IRS wants you to use the following table of data to determine how much salary to withhold for federal taxes:

If weekly salary is	Tax rate	
	Single	Married
0–$150	.18	.15
$151–$250	.25	.18
$251–$500	.28	.25
$501–$1,000	.31	.28
Over $1,000	.33	.31

For this exercise, you will use three related compile-time arrays.

   a. Define the declarations to reflect your compile-time arrays.

   b. Write the calculations necessary to assign the proper value to field Rate based on Salary (salary) and Marital status (marital status: S = single, M = married) of an employee's input record.

   c. Create a simple table containing the salary and demographic information that the preceding table shows.

d. Using the SQL examples in this chapter, code the declarations and lookups to assign the proper value to field Rate based on Salary (salary) and Marital status (marital status: S = single, M = married) of an employee's input record.

5. This exercise requires the use of runtime arrays and related arrays that this chapter covered. Review data and the structure of the table ACCTPERIOD (see "Data Files for Programming Exercises," which you can download, along with other supplemental materials for this book, at *www.mc-store.com/Programming-ILE-RPG-Fifth-Edition/dp/1583473793*).

Name	Record	Type	Length	Text
IBM - Power System: File RPGIV_5THW/ACCTPERIOD (4 Fields)				
PDPER#	ACCPEDR	Zoned Decimal	5.0	Period Number
PDBDAT	ACCPEDR	Zoned Decimal	7.0	Period Begin Date
PDEDAT	ACCPEDR	Zoned Decimal	7.0	Period End Date
PDWKDY	ACCPEDR	Zoned Decimal	2.0	Number Of Working Days

a. Declare four related arrays.

b. Using the SQL example in this chapter, load the related arrays with data.

c. Use the appropriate %Lookup function to return the accounting period (PDPER#) and the number of working days (PDWKDY) based on a date.

Notes

12

Writing Interactive Applications

12.1. Chapter Overview

In this chapter, you learn how to define display files, and how to use them to develop interactive applications.

12.2. Batch and Interactive Programs

So far, the programs you have written were designed to run in batch. In **batch processing**, once a program begins to run, it continues to execute instructions without human intervention or control. Most batch applications in the business environment involve processing one or more transaction files sequentially. The programs end when the transaction files reach end-of-file.

Interactive applications, in contrast, are user driven. As the program runs, a user at a workstation interacts with the computer—selecting options from menus, entering data, responding to prompts, and so on. The sequence of instructions the program executes is determined in part by the user; the program continues until the user signals that he or she is ready to quit.

This dialogue between the user and the computer is mediated through what IBM i calls display files, which define the screens that the program presents as it runs. Display files allow values keyed by the user in response to the screen to be input as data to the program. Thus, display files serve as the mechanism that lets the user and program interact.

Users typically interact with display files through desktop software called a **5250 emulator**. This software provides user interface functions equivalent to legacy IBM 5250 workstations (green-screen terminals) that are no longer manufactured. Although the actual 5250 hardware is rarely seen today, many IBM i interactive applications still employ the 5250-style interface. Several software vendors sell 5250 emulators; the IBM i Access Family software offering includes, among other functions, emulators that work with Web browsers and as standalone desktop applications.

Note

Some applications may incorporate Hypertext Markup Language (HTML) for their user interface instead of a 5250-based data stream. These applications use Web browsers instead of display files as their display mechanism. Chapter 18 examines how you might build Web pages by using RPG.

12.3. Display Files

Display files are device files, conceptually similar to printer files, except that they are tied to a 5250 display workstation instead of a printer. You define display files externally to the program that uses them. To create display files, you code DDS in a source member (with type DSPF) and compile the source code to create a display file object. The command to compile display file source is **CRTDSPF (Create Display File)**. IBM also provides utilities, such as Screen Design Aid (SDA) and Screen Designer, that automatically generate the DDS source code as you design and create display screens in an interactive environment.

As an introduction to DDS coding for display files, the following situation employs the Customers file used earlier. A company identifies each of its customers through a customer identifier. This field is the key to the Customers file. Figure 12.1 recaps the Customers file record layout.

Properties									
<Table> CUSTOMERS									
General									
Columns	Name	Primary ...	Domain	Data Type	Length	Scale	Not Null	Generated	Default Value/Generate ...
Relationships	CUSTNO	☑		CHAR	9		☑	☐	
Documentation	CFNAME	☐		CHAR	15		☐	☐	SYSTEM_DEFAULT
	CLNAME	☐		CHAR	20		☐	☐	SYSTEM_DEFAULT
	CADDR	☐		CHAR	30		☐	☐	SYSTEM_DEFAULT
	CZIP	☐		CHAR	5		☐	☐	SYSTEM_DEFAULT
	CPHONE	☐		CHAR	10		☑	☐	
	CEMAIL	☐		CHAR	50		☑	☐	
	CDOB	☐		DECIMAL	8	0	☑	☐	
	CGENDER	☐		CHAR	1		☑	☐	

Figure 12.1: Customers file record layout

The company wants a simple online inquiry program that lets a user enter a customer identifier and then display information about that customer. The application initially presents the input, or entry, display in Figure 12.2.

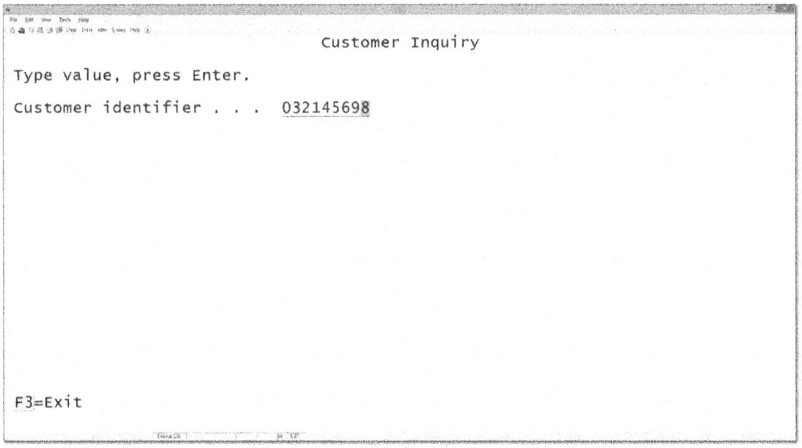

Figure 12.2: Customer selection display (CUSTSEL)

After the user enters a customer identifier on the first display, the program shows that customer's information by using the inquiry display in Figure 12.3.

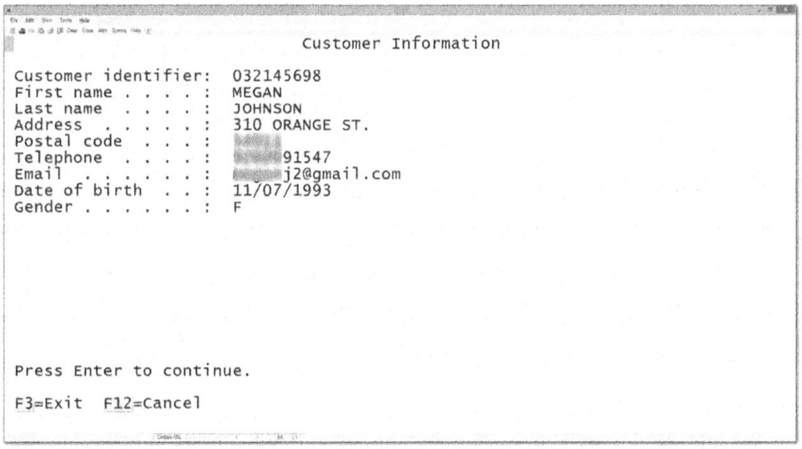

Figure 12.3: Customer inquiry display (CUSTINQ)

In the DDS code for a display file, each record format defines what is written to or read from the workstation in a single input/output (I/O) operation. On an output operation, the record can fill an entire screen with prompts or values (or both). On an input operation, the record can read several values keyed from the workstation. Unless you make special provisions, only one screen displays at a time. When a different record format is written, the first screen is erased before the second one appears. Figure 12.4 shows the DDS for the display file record formats needed to produce the screens in Figures 12.2 and 12.3.

```
CUSTINQD.DSPF          CUSTINQ.RPGLE
 Line 25        Column 38      Insert
    .....AAN01N02N03..Name++++++RLen++TDpbLinPosFunctions+++++++++++++++++++++++++++++Comments+++++++
 000100    A                                        REF(CUSTOMERS)
 000101    A                                        INDARA
 000200    A          R CUSTSEL
 000300    A                                        CA03(03 'F3=Exit')
 000400    A                                     1 33'Customer Inquiry'
 000500    A                                     3  2'Type value, press Enter.'
 000600    A                                     5  2'Customer identifier . . . .'
 000700    A            CUSTNO    R       I       5 29
 000800    A                                    23  2'F3=Exit'
 000900    A          R CUSTINQ
 001000    A                                        CA03(03 'F3=Exit')
 001100    A                                        CA12(12 'F12=Cancel')
 001200    A                                     1 31'Customer Information'
 001300    A                                     3  2'Customer identifier:'
 001400    A            CUSTNO    R       O     3 24
 001500    A                                     4  2'First name . . . . :'
 001600    A            CFNAME    R       O     4 24
 001700    A                                     5  2'Last name  . . . . :'
 001800    A            CLNAME    R       O     5 24
 001900    A                                     6  2'Address  . . . . . :'
 002000    A            CADDR     R       O     6 24
 002100    A                                     7  2'Postal code  . . . :'
 002200    A            CZIP      R       O     7 24
 002300    A                                     8  2'Telephone  . . . . :'
 002400    A            CPHONE    R       O     8 24
 002500    A                                     9  2'Email  . . . . . . :'
 002600    A            CEMAIL    R       O     9 24
 002700    A                                    10  2'Date of birth  . . :'
 002800    A            CDOB      R       O    10 24EDTCDE(Y)
 002900    A                                    11  2'Gender . . . . . . :'
 003000    A            CGENDER   R       O    11 24
 003100    A                                    21  2'Press Enter to continue.'
 003200    A                                    23  2'F3=Exit'
 003300    A                                    23 11'F12=Cancel'
 Design Source Preview
```

Figure 12.4: DDS for customer inquiry program displays

Notice that each record format begins with an identifier, an R in position 17, followed by a name—CUSTSEL and CUSTINQ—beginning in position 19 (Name++++++). Below the record format line appear all the fields and literals that are to make up the format. You must indicate the location of each literal and field on this screen by specifying the vertical screen line on which the literal or field is to appear (in positions 39–41, Lin) as well as its starting horizontal position within that line (in positions 42–44, Pos). You code the literals and enclose them in apostrophes ('), such as 'Customer Inquiry', in the Functions area, positions 45–80 of the DDS line.

Next, enter field names left-adjusted in positions 19–28. Each field needs an assigned usage, which you code in position 38 (labeled B). Usage codes include I for input, O for output, or B for both input and output. In the first record format, Custno is an input field because its value is to be entered by the user and read by (input to) the program. Its usage code is therefore I. In the second format, all the fields, including Custno, are output fields (usage code O), with no input capability.

This DDS example uses a reference file, discussed in Chapter 3. If a field is not defined in a reference file, you must specify its length in positions 30–34 (Len++), data type in position 35 (T), and for numeric fields the number of decimal positions in positions 36–37 (Dc).

Recall from Chapter 3 that column 35 (T) indicates a data type for database files. For display files, column 35 is actually more appropriately called *keyboard shift* because it allows many more possible values than are permitted for field definitions of physical files. These additional values affect the **keyboard shift attribute** of different workstations to limit what characters users can enter. Although a complete description of allowable values is beyond the scope of this text, the following table describes four commonly used values.

Keyboard shift value	Description
A (Alphanumeric shift)	Used for character fields; puts keyboard in lower shift; lets user enter any character
X (Alphabetic only)	Used for character fields; lets user enter only A–Z, commas, periods, dashes, and spaces; sends lowercase letters as uppercase
S (Signed numeric)	Used for numeric fields; lets user enter digits 0–9 but no signs; uses Field- key for entering negative values
Y (Numeric only)	Used for numeric fields; lets the user enter digits 0–9, plus or minus signs, periods, commas, and spaces

One critical distinction between keyboard shift values S and Y is that Y lets you associate edit codes and edit words with the field, but S does not.

Just like printer file definitions, display file definitions include entries at one of three levels: file, record, or field level. File-level entries appear at the very beginning of the definition and apply to all the record formats within the file. Record-level entries are associated with a single record format (usually one screen). Field-level entries are coded for specific fields or constants within a record format.

The record-level entry CA03(03 'F3=Exit') establishes a connection between the F3 key and the 03 indicator. You haven't encountered frequently used indicators previously in this text. The need for them is rapidly disappearing from ILE RPG, but an indicator is still the primary means by which a DDS display file communicates conditions with an RPG program. When you code interactive applications, indicators communicate between the screen and the program that uses the screen. Control generally returns from the screen to the program when the user presses the Enter key or a function key that has been assigned a special meaning. In this screen, for instance, the user is prompted to press F3 to exit the program. But because you cannot readily reference the function key directly within an RPG program, an indicator must serve as a mediator.

The record-level keyword CA03 accomplishes three things. First, the CA03 portion establishes F3 as a valid function key in this application; only those function keys explicitly referenced within the DDS are valid, or enabled, during program execution. Second, the 03 within the parentheses associates indicator 03 with F3 so that when F3 is pressed, indicator 03 is turned on. Although you can associate any indicator (01–99) with any function key, it makes good programming sense to associate a function key with its corresponding numeric indicator to avoid confusion. Last, by referencing the function key as CA (Command Attention) rather than CF (Command Function), the code specifies that the workstation device is to return control to the program without the input data values (if any) that the user has just entered. If you code the line as CF03(03 'F3=Exit'), control returns to the program with the input data for the program to process.

The information within apostrophes—'F3=Exit'—serves only as documentation. You can omit it, meaning code only CA03(03), without affecting how the screen functions. Good programming practice, however, suggests including such documentation. To prompt the user to press the F3 key, you must explicitly code the 'F3=Exit' literal (on line 23, in this case).

Notice that record format CUSTINQ enables the F12 key as well as F3. Generally accepted IBM i screen design standards use F12 (Cancel) to signal a return to the previous screen and F3 (Exit) to exit the entire application.

In addition to naming a reference file, the DDS in Figure 12.4 adds another file-level keyword, INDARA. **INDARA (Indicator Area)** organizes all the indicators that the display file uses into relative positions into a 99-byte data structure—indicator 03 in position 3, indicator 12 in position 12, and so on. We use this data structure in the ILE RPG program to avoid referring to numbered indicators and, instead, assign them meaningful names.

12.4. Declaring Display Files

Before examining some of the many additional features available for defining display files, let's develop the customer inquiry program to see how to use display files in interactive programs. Recall that the user wants to enter a customer identifier to request information from the Customers file. The program should display the retrieved information on the screen. The user can then enter another customer identifier or signal that he or she is finished by pressing F3.

In writing the program, you must define display file Custinqd, as with any other kind of file, in the declarations section. Display files are full procedural, externally described files. The device for display files is Workstn. Previously, you have worked with input files (I), output files (O), and update files (U). Workstation files represent a new type: combined. A **combined file**, Usage(*Input:*Output), supports both input and output, but as independent operations. You cannot update a combined file. Although you can specify Usage(*Input:*Output) for a workstation file, that is the default usage.

Finally, you code the Indds keyword, which instructs RPG to store the indicators passed to and from this display file in the data structure named Indicators (we discuss this data structure later). The following code shows the complete file declarations for the customer inquiry program.

```
Dcl-f Customers Keyed;
Dcl-f Custinqd  Workstn Indds(Indicators);
```

12.5. Performing Screen I/O

Before we examine the program code, it pays first to think through a solution's logic. Interactive programs are extremely prone to *spaghetti coding*, primarily because the flow of control is less straightforward—depending on which function key a user presses, you may need to repeat, back up, or exit early out of different routines.

The program needs to loop until the user presses F3 in response to either screen. If the user presses F12 at screen CUSTINQ to back up, that effectively is the same in this program as pressing Enter because, in both cases, the user should next see screen CUSTSEL again. A rough solution written in pseudocode looks like the following:

- While user wants to continue (no Exit)
  - Display screen CUSTSEL
  - Obtain user's response to the screen
  - If user wants to continue (no Exit)
    - » Random read Customers file to retrieve information
    - » If record found
      - – Display screen CUSTINQ
      - – Obtain user's response
    - » Endif
  - Endif
- Endwhile

You can easily develop the ILE RPG calculations from the pseudocode once you know how to send screens of data to the user and read user input. The allowable operations for screen I/O are Write, Read, and **Exfmt (Execute Format)**. All three operations require an operand to designate a record format name.

The Write operation displays a screen and returns control to the program without waiting for user input. A subsequent Read operation sends control to the currently displayed screen, waits for the end of user input (signaled by the user's pressing either Enter or any other enabled special key), and returns control to the program.

The Exfmt operation combines the features of Write and Read; it first writes a record to the screen and then waits for user input to that screen. When the user has finished, the system reads the data back from the screen and returns control to the program. Because in most screen I/O you want to display some information and then wait for a user response, Exfmt is the operation you use most frequently in your interactive programs.

The following code shows an ILE RPG implementation of the pseudocode solution to the customer inquiry problem:

```
Dow Not *In03;
  Exfmt Custsel;
  If Not *In03;
    Chain Custno Customers;
    If %Found(Customers);
      Exfmt Custinq;
    Endif;
  Endif;
Enddo;
```

In this code, indicator 03, which turns on when the user presses F3, controls the main program loop. Because the user can signal Exit at screen CUSTSEL, the calculations need an If operation following the return from the CUSTSEL screen to check for this possibility. If the user keys in a wrong section number, which causes the Chain operation to fail, the program executes the information panel, CUSTINQ, only if the Chain found a record.

12.6. Using an Indicator Data Structure

You can eliminate the somewhat obscure reference to *In03 in the preceding code by including a definition for a special data structure called an **indicator data structure**. Recall that the Indara keyword in the DDS for the display file instructed the system to organize all the display file's indicators into a 99-byte data area. In the ILE RPG program, the file declaration for the display file included the Indds keyword, which moves the indicator area from DDS into the data structure named as the keyword value. Given these two requirements (the INDARA keyword in DDS and the Indds keyword in the file declaration), you can then include a data structure that contains the indicators. The code for this data structure is as follows:

```
Dcl-ds Indicators Len(99);
  Exit   Ind Pos(3);
  Cancel Ind Pos(12);
End-ds;
```

In this definition, position 3 in the data structure corresponds to *In03, and position 12 corresponds to *In12. These positions are assigned to indicator variables named Exit and

Cancel, respectively. Note that this definition uses the Pos (Position) keyword to specify exact positions of fields within the data structure. After including this data structure, you can refer to Exit instead of *In03 in the ILE RPG code, making the program more readable:

```
Dow Not Exit;
  Exfmt Custsel;
  If Not Exit;
    Chain Custno Customers;
    If %Found(Customers);
      Exfmt Custinq;
    Endif;
  Endif;
Enddo;
```

Note

If you specify an Indds keyword in a file declaration, you can no longer refer to the indicators in that file by using the *In*xx* notation. You must use the indicator data structure to communicate the indicator state, and you must refer to the indicators by their subfield names in the data structure. If your program refers to *In03, that indicator state is not communicated with the DDS; you must use the named variable (Exit in the preceding example) to set indicator 03 in the DDS.

12.7. Basic Interactive Inquiry Program

Once you have created the required display file object, you can easily combine the previous code into a complete inquiry program:

```
// ------------------------------- Files
Dcl-f Customers Keyed;
Dcl-f Custinqd  Workstn Indds(Indicators);


// -------------- Indicator data structure
Dcl-ds Indicators Len(99);
  Exit   Ind Pos(3);        // F3=Exit
  Cancel Ind Pos(12);       // F12=Cancel
End-ds;
                                          Continued
```

```
// ----------------------- Main procedure
Dow Not Exit;
  Exfmt Custsel;
  If Not Exit;
    Chain Custno Customers;
    If %Found(Customers);
      Exfmt Custinq;
    Endif;
  Endif;
Enddo;


*Inlr = *On;
Return;
```

12.8. Additional DDS Considerations

Although the DDS definition for the previous example will work, it represents a minimalist approach to screen design—it contains no bells and whistles. More important perhaps, as the DDS is presently coded, numeric fields display without editing, and information about a possible important program event (a customer not found in the file) is not conveyed to the user. You can include these and other kinds of special effects by using additional DDS keywords.

You have already been introduced to four keywords used with display files: CAnn, CFnn, INDARA, and REF. DDS supports a long list of permissible keywords for display files to let you change a screen's appearance or the interaction between screen and user. This section discusses some of the major keywords. Refer to IBM's online documentation for more detail.

Always code keywords in positions 45–80 (the Functions area) of the DDS line. Keywords apply at a file, record, or field level. You can use some keywords with two levels and others to just one level. Where you code the keyword determines the level with which the keyword is associated.

12.8.1. File-Level Keywords

File-level keywords must always appear as the first lines in the DDS, before any record format information. If you have several file-level keywords, the order in which you code them does not matter. You have already encountered two file-level keywords: REF, which indicates a database file that contains definitions of fields in the screen, and INDARA, which organizes indicators into a 99-byte data structure.

The CAnn (Command Attention) and CFnn (Command Function) keywords, which we've already discussed, enable the use of function keys and associate the keys with program indicators. You can use as many function keys as are appropriate to your application by including a CAnn or CFnn keyword for each one.

If you code these keywords at a file level, they apply to all the record formats within the file. Alternatively, you can associate them with individual record formats, as you did in the section inquiry example. In that case, the keys are valid only during input operations for the screen or screens with which they are associated.

VLDCMDKEY (Valid Command Key) is a file- or record-level keyword that turns on an indicator when a user presses *any* valid (enabled) command key. Note that command keys include any special key, such as the Roll up key, in addition to function keys. The format for this keyword is as follows:

```
VLDCMDKEY(indicator ['text'])
```

The indicator can be any numbered indicator (01–99); the text description is optional and serves only as documentation. VLDCMDKEY is useful because it lets the program differentiate between control returned as a result of the Enter key and control returned by any other key. You often need to set up separate logic branches based on this distinction.

12.8.2. Record-Level Keywords

Record-level keywords appear on the line on which the record format is named or on lines immediately following that line (or both) preceding any field or literal definition. These kinds of keywords apply only to the screen with which they are associated. They do not carry over to or influence other record formats defined within the file.

You can use CAnn, CFnn, and VLDCMDKEY as record-level keywords as well as file-level keywords. Some other keywords are strictly record-level keywords. OVERLAY is a record-level keyword that specifies to present the record format without clearing the previous display. OVERLAY works only when the record formats involved do not overlap lines on the screen. The following DDS demonstrates the use of record-level keywords:

```
*.. 1 ...+... 2 ...+... 3 ...+... 4 ...+... 5 ...+... 6 ...+... 7 ...+... 8
AAN01N02N03T.Name++++++RLen++TDcBLinPosFunctions++++++++++++++++++++++++++++
  * Sample DDS showing record-level keywords
A           R SAMPLE                 PRINT
A                                    CA03(03 'F3=Exit')
                                                            Continued
```

```
A                                    CA12(12 'F12=Cancel')
A                                    VLDCMDKEY(25 'Any valid key')
A                                    OVERLAY
```

12.8.3. Field-Level Keywords

A **field-level keyword** applies only to the specific field with which it is associated. A field can have several keywords. The first keyword appears on the same line as the field definition or on the line immediately following the definition. You can code additional keywords on the same line (provided there is room) or on successive lines. All keywords for a field must be coded before the next field definition line.

Two field-level keywords control the format of numeric output fields on the display: **EDTCDE (Edit Code)** and **EDTWRD (Edit Word)**. Recall that you can edit only numeric fields and that the keyboard shift specification in column 35 of the DDS must be Y or blank to use editing for a displayed field.

Display file edit codes and edit words match and have the same meaning as those within ILE RPG itself. In DDS, EDTCDE's format is as follows:

```
EDTCDE(editcode {*|$})
```

The parentheses contain a valid edit code, such as 1, optionally followed by a single asterisk (*) to provide asterisk protection or a single dollar sign ($) to supply a floating dollar sign.

This is the format for EDTWRD:

```
EDTWRD('editword')
```

To review ILE RPG edit words and edit codes, see Chapter 3.

The following DDS sample shows the use of keywords EDTWRD and EDTCDE. Note that because editing is a concept related to output, the use of EDTWRD and EDTCDE is appropriate for fields defined for output usage or fields used for both input and output, but not for fields defined for use with input only.

```
*.. 1 ...+... 2 ...+... 3 ...+... 4 ...+... 5 ...+... 6 ...+... 7 ...+... 8
AANO1N02N03T.Name++++++RLen++TDcBLinPosFunctions+++++++++++++++++++++++++++++
 * Sample DDS showing the use of editing keywords
                                                              Continued
```

```
A              R SAMPLE
A                SOCSEC          9Y 00  4 10EDTWRD('   -   -      ')
A                NAME           20   0  5 10
A                BILLDATE        6Y 00  6 10EDTCDE(Y)
A                AMOUNTDUE       7Y 20  7 10EDTCDE(1 $)
```

Another field-level keyword, **DSPATR (Display Attribute)**, determines the appearance of fields on the screen. You can use DSPATR more than once for a given field, and you can include more than one attribute with the same keyword. The keyword is followed by parentheses containing the codes of the desired attributes. You can assign the following attributes to all types of fields (input, output, or both):

Attribute	Meaning
BL	Blinking field
CS	Column separator (a vertical bar separating each position within a field)
HI	High intensity
ND	Nondisplay (keyed characters don't appear on screen)
PC	Position cursor (position cursor to the first character of this field)
RI	Reverse image
UL	Underline

The following code illustrates the use of **display attributes**:

```
*.. 1 ...+... 2 ...+... 3 ...+... 4 ...+... 5 ...+... 6 ...+... 7 ...+... 8
AAN01N02N03T.Name++++++RLen++TDcBLinPosFunctions+++++++++++++++++++++++++++++
  * Sample DDS illustrating display attributes
A              R SAMPLE
A                SOCSEC          9Y 00  4 10DSPATR(ND)
A                NAME           20   0  5 10DSPATR(BL UL)
A                BILLDATE        6Y 00  6 10EDTCDE(Y)
A                                         DSPATR(PC HI BL)
```

This sample is not intended to set a style standard to follow. A screen with so many display attributes distracts the user. Generally, use such features sparingly and consistently to draw attention to specific fields on the screen or to problems the user must handle.

Another important set of field-level keywords concerns **data validation**. Every programmer should recognize the extreme importance of preventing invalid data from entering the system, as corrupt data files can cause abnormal endings or incorrect processing. Although no way exists within DDS to completely ensure that values a user enters are correct, by validating data as tightly as possible, you can eliminate some kinds of errors. The four major keywords for validating user entry are as follows:

- VALUES
- RANGE
- COMP
- CHECK

Each of these keywords lets you place restrictions on what the user can enter. Violating these restrictions causes the system to automatically display an appropriate error message on the message line and to display the field in reverse image to force the user to change the entered value.

Note
When the DDS uses these keywords, the workstation input is validated and the error message appears without passing control back to the program. Consequently, the messages are necessarily generic unless you use advanced message handling techniques beyond the scope of this text. You may prefer to pass the invalid data back to the program for more specific validation than the DDS keywords can provide.

The VALUES keyword lets you specify the exact valid values allowed for a field. The keyword format is as follows:

```
VALUES(value1 value2 . . . )
```

You can enter up to 100 values and must enclose character values within apostrophes.

The RANGE keyword lets you specify a range within which the user's entry must fall to be considered valid. The following shows the format for this keyword:

```
RANGE(lowvalue highvalue)
```

If you use RANGE with character fields, you must enclose each of the low and high values in apostrophes. The valid range includes the low and high values, so the entered value must be greater than or equal to the low value and less than or equal to the high value to be considered valid.

The **COMP keyword** lets you specify the relational comparison to make with the user's entered value to determine validity. Here is this keyword's format:

```
COMP(relational-operator value)
```

The relational operator can be one of the following:

Operator	Meaning
LT	Less than
LE	Less than or equal to
EQ	Equal to
GE	Greater than or equal to
GT	Greater than
NL	Not less than
NE	Not equal to
NG	Not greater than

CHECK is a field-level keyword that you can use for validity checking. Its format is as follows:

```
CHECK(code {...})
```

You can associate one or more validity-checking codes with a single CHECK entry. Some of these validity codes are ME (Mandatory Enter), MF (Mandatory Fill), and AB (Allow Blank). For Mandatory Enter fields, the user must enter at least one character of data (the character can be a blank); the user cannot simply bypass the field. Mandatory Fill specifies that each position in the field have a character in it. (Again, a blank is considered a character.) Allow Blank provides the user with an override option for a field that fails a validity check. For example, if a field has a VALUES keyword associated with it and the user is uncertain which value is appropriate to the record he or she is entering, the user can simply enter blanks and the value is accepted. The following DDS demonstrates the use of keywords for data validation:

```
*.. 1 ...+... 2 ...+... 3 ...+... 4 ...+... 5 ...+... 6 ...+... 7 ...+... 8
AAN01N02N03T.Name++++++RLen++TDcBLinPosFunctions++++++++++++++++++++++++++++++
 * Sample DDS illustrating the use of keywords for data validation
A          R SAMPLE
A            DEPT          3   I  4 10VALUES('CIS' 'DPR' 'MGT')
A                                   CHECK(MF AB)
A            MONTH         2Y 0I  6 10RANGE(1 12)
A            REGHOURS      3Y 1I  7 10COMP(LE 40)
```

The CHECK keyword also supports parameter values concerned with functions other than validity checking. CHECK(LC), for example, lets the user enter lowercase (as well as uppercase) letters for character fields. Without this keyword, all user-entered alphabetic characters are returned to the program as uppercase. You can use CHECK(LC) at a field, record, or file level, depending on how broadly you want to enable lowercase data entry.

One field-level keyword of major importance is ERRMSG (Error Message). When an error message is in effect for a field, the message displays on the message line of the screen, and the field the message is associated with appears on the screen in reverse image. The format for the ERRMSG keyword is as follows:

```
ERRMSG('message text' {indicator})
```

If you specify an indicator, the indicator is turned off as part of the input operation that follows the display of the error message. Error messages are useful for conveying information about program processing problems to the user's screen.

Two field-level keywords serve as built-in variables to display the date and time on the screen. TIME, entered as a keyword along with screen line and column position values, causes the system time to display in *hhmmss* format (hours, minutes, and seconds). The time appears with the default edit word '0b:bb:bb' unless you specify an alternative display format. You can display the current date by using keyword DATE along with line and column entries. DATE appears as a six-position, unedited value unless you associate an edit code or word with it.

```
*.. 1 ...+... 2 ...+... 3 ...+... 4 ...+... 5 ...+... 6 ...+... 7 ...+... 8
AAN01N02N03T.Name++++++RLen++TDcBLinPosFunctions+++++++++++++++++++++++++++++
 * Sample DDS illustrating the use of DATE and TIME keywords
A          R SAMPLE
A                                  1  5TIME
A                                  1 60DATE EDTCDE(Y)
```

12.8.4. Conditioning Indicators

So far, we've discussed field-level keywords as though they are always in effect. However, if this were the case, many would be of little value. Why, for instance, would you want to display an error message each time a field appears on the screen? In fact, you can condition most individual field-level keywords on one or more indicators. The status of these **conditioning indicators** that displays on the screen determines whether the keywords are in effect. Not only can you condition keywords, but you can also associate fields and literals with indicators to control whether the field or literal appears on the screen.

Moreover, you can use multiple indicators, in AND and in OR relationships, to condition screen events. You can include up to three indicators on a DDS line. These indicators are in an AND relationship with one another, such that all the indicators on the line must be on for the event they are conditioning to occur. If you need to use more than three indicators to control an event, you can signal an AND by coding A in position 7 of the DDS line.

To cause an event to occur when one of several indicators is on (i.e., you want to express an OR relationship), you code one indicator per line, with an o in position 7 of the second (and successive) lines. The keyword, field, or literal conditioned by these indicators should appear on the last line of the set.

```
*.. 1 ...+... 2 ...+... 3 ...+... 4 ...+... 5 ...+... 6 ...+... 7 ...+... 8
AANO1NO2NO3T.Name++++++RLen++TDcBLinPosFunctions+++++++++++++++++++++++++++++++
 * Sample DDS showing the use of indicators
A           R SAMPLE
A   10        FLDA          10   O  4 15
A N10         FLDB          12   O  4 30
A             FLDC           5   O  6  5
A   20 25                             DSPATR(HI)
A   30
AO  40                                DSPATR(UL)
A   10                          15  5'Indicator 10 is on'
```

The preceding code displays FLDA if indicator 10 is on, and FLDB displays only if indicator 10 is off (signaled by the N in position 8). FLDC always appears, but it displays in high intensity only if indicators 20 and 25 are both on; it is underlined if either indicator 30 or indicator 40 is on. The literal 'Indicator 10 is on' appears only if indicator 10 is, in fact, on.

Because you can turn indicators on or off as part of your program logic, they provide a way for program events to control screen display. For example, in the sample program, say a user enters a customer identifier that didn't exist in the Customers file. To help the user, you want to not only return the user to the first screen but also return with the erroneous customer identifier displayed in reverse video, with the message "Customer not found" appearing at the bottom of the screen and with the cursor positioned on the field. You can easily cause this to happen by making a few changes in the first screen format. First, use the ERRMSG keyword to display a message when an unsuccessful chain occurs, and then use indicator 80 to condition the ERRMSG keyword, showing it only if *In80 is on.

```
*.. 1 ...+... 2 ...+... 3 ...+... 4 ...+... 5 ...+... 6 ...+... 7 ...+... 8
AAN01N02N03T.Name++++++RLen++TDcBLinPosFunctions+++++++++++++++++++++++++++++
...
A              CUSTNO    R        B  5 24
A N80                                      DSPATR(HI UL)
A  80                                      ERRMSG('Customer not found' 80)
```

Note that one of the changes includes altering the usage of field CUSTNO to B (both) so the erroneous section number is returned to the screen. When indicator 80 is off, the field is underlined and appears in high intensity (usually white). When 80 is on, the error message displays and the field appears in reverse image.

A few simple changes to the ILE RPG program enable it to display the error message if the Chain fails. First, define position 80 in the Indicators data structure to give it a name:

```
Dcl-ds Indicators Len(99);
  Exit         Ind Pos(3);
  Cancel       Ind Pos(12);
  Custnotfound Ind Pos(80);
End-ds;
```

Then, make a simple addition to the logic to support the Custnotfound field:

```
// ----------------------- Main procedure
Dow Not Exit;
  Exfmt Custsel;
  If Not Exit;
    Chain Custno Customers;
    Custnotfound = Not %Found(Customers);
    If %Found(Customers);
      Exfmt Custinq;
    Endif;
  Endif;
Enddo;
```

Because Custnotfound is an indicator with a value of *On or *Off, you can simply use an assignment expression to move the result of the %Found function (also either *On or *Off) to Custnotfound and, consequently, to *In80.

12.9. Interactive File Maintenance

A common data processing task is **file maintenance**: adding, changing, and deleting records in a company's database files. In a typical maintenance program, the user specifies the key of a record and signals whether to add, change, or delete that record. Because businesses typically want key field values to master records to be unique (e.g., they do not want to assign the same customer identifier to two customers), a user request to add a record with a key that matches the key of a record already in the file generally is handled as an error. Similarly, it is impossible to change or delete a record that does not exist in the file.

As a result, the first tasks of an update program are to accept the user's update option request (add, delete, or change) and the key of the record to maintain, and then to check the file for the existence of a record with that key before letting the user actually enter data values.

A critical concern of interactive updates is how to detect invalid data entries to prevent corrupting the business's database files. The system offers four methods of safeguarding against invalid data:

- implementing physical file constraints
- using validation keywords within the DDS database definitions themselves, provided those fields are displayed for input and reference back to the database file
- including validation keywords within the DDS for the display file
- validating field values within the program after they are read from the screen

SQL and IBM i commands support various physical file **constraints**, rules to which the data in a file must conform. These rules are stored with the file or table itself, independent of any program code, and are enforced by the system when a change occurs. This architecture maintains database integrity regardless of the method you use to change the data. Several major types of constraints are available. For example, a unique constraint—commonly used with key fields but not restricted to them—prevents duplicate values for a field in a file. A referential constraint sets the rules for data relationships between files (e.g., preventing an order file from containing an order record for a customer who doesn't exist in the customer file). A check constraint sets restrictions on the field values in a file (e.g., restricting a gender field to values of M or F). The SQL Alter Table instruction, or the ADDPFCST (Add Physical File Constraint) command, adds constraint relationships to a file. Refer to IBM's online documentation for details; further discussion of constraints goes beyond the scope of this text.

DDS also handles some validation automatically. For example, the system prevents users from entering a nonnumeric value for a numerically defined field. Or, if the DDS specifies type X for a character field, the system permits alphabetic entries only. The use of DDS validation keywords also automatically limits what users can enter without the need for further programming on your part. For example, if you specify VALUES('A' 'C' 'D') for field

CODE, a user's attempt to enter any value other than 'A', 'C', or 'D' automatically causes an error message to appear on the bottom line of the screen and field CODE to display in reverse video.

Always validate your data as tightly as possible, given the nature of the data. For some fields (e.g., name), the best you can do is ensure that users enter some value rather than skipping the field. For other fields (e.g., gender), you can specify permissible values for the entered data. Never overlook validating data at any point where it enters the system.

To illustrate screen and program design for interactive updating, let's develop a program to maintain the Customers file. Figure 12.5 shows the first screen of the application, CUSTSEL. The user keys in a customer identifier and an action code to specify whether he or she wants to add, change, or delete the customer record. If the user tries to enter an invalid action code, an error message displays. If the user enters a customer identifier with an action code inappropriate for that customer—that is, the user tries to add a customer already in the file or tries to change or delete a customer not in the file—an appropriate error message appears on the screen.

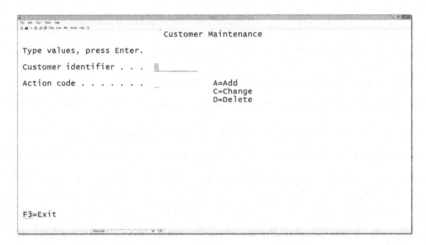

Figure 12.5: Customer Maintenance selection screen

When the user's entries are valid and appropriate, the second screen (CUSTMNT) displays, with blank fields if the user is in Add mode or with the field values from the selected record displayed if the mode is Change or Delete. In Add or Change mode, when the user presses Enter, the program performs the appropriate action and then returns the user to the first screen. To delete a record, the user must press F10. If the user presses F12 at the second screen, no maintenance occurs for that record, and the user is returned to the first screen. Pressing F3 at the second screen causes a program exit without maintenance of the last displayed data. Figures 12.6, 12.7, and 12.8 illustrate the layouts of screen CUSTMNT in Add, Change, and Delete modes.

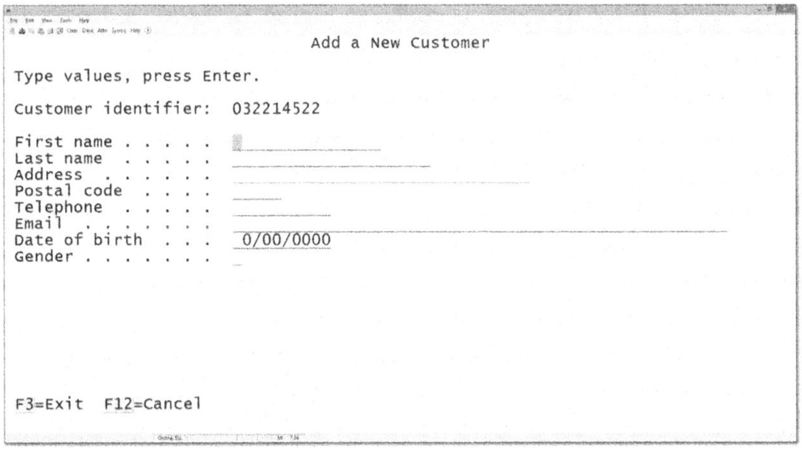

Figure 12.6: Customer maintenance: Add mode

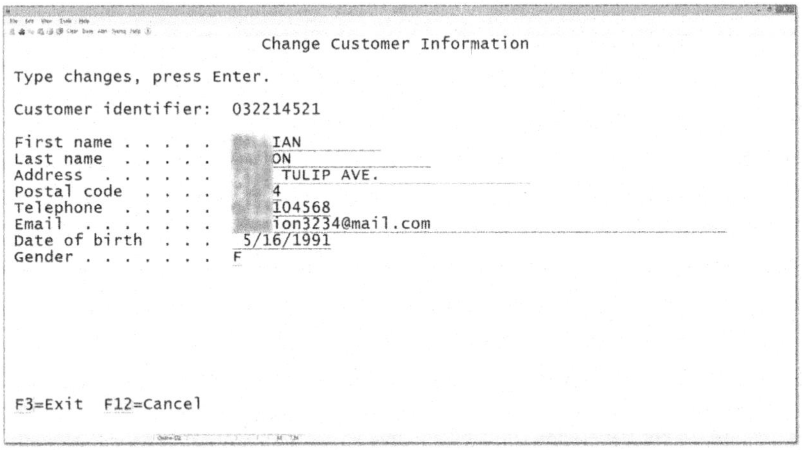

Figure 12.7: Customer maintenance: Change mode

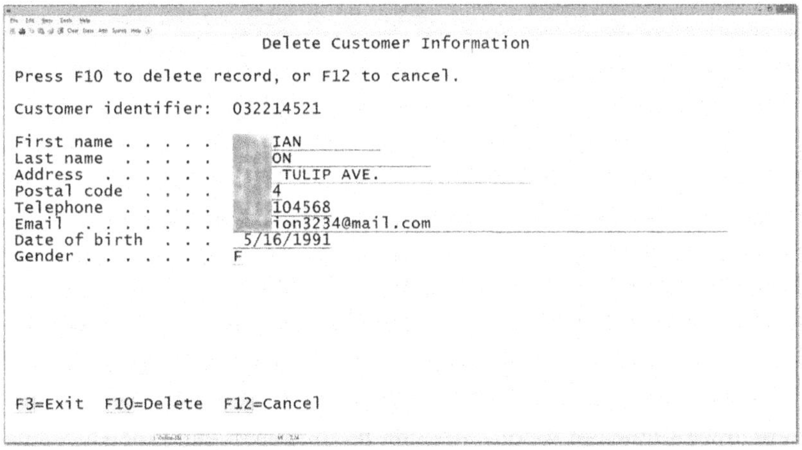

Figure 12.8: Customer maintenance: Delete mode

The DDS for the display file, Custmntd, is coded as Figure 12.9 shows. Notice that 12 lines have been omitted from the figure for presentation purposes. The missing lines (for fields Caddr, Czip, Cphone, and Cemail) are similar to the lines that precede and follow the missing lines.

```
CUSTMNTD.DSPF 
   Line 55         Column 1       Insert
        ....AAN01N02N03..Name++++++RLen++TDpBLinPosFunctions++++++++++++++++++++++++++++++
   000100      A                                      REF(CUSTOMERS)
   000101      A                                      INDARA
   000102      A                                      CA03(03 'F3=Exit')
   000103      A                                      VLDCMDKEY(25)
   000200      A            R CUSTSEL
   000400      A                                    1 31'Customer Maintenance'
   000500      A                                    3  2'Type values, press Enter.'
   000600      A                                    5  2'Customer identifier . . . .'
   000700      A              CUSTNO    R        B  5 29
   000701      A 30                                   ERRMSG('Customer already exists' 30)
   000702      A 31                                   ERRMSG('Customer not found' 31)
   000703      A 32                                   ERRMSG('Customer not found' 32)
   000705      A                                    7  2'Action code . . . . . . .'
   000706      A              ACTION    1    I    7 29VALUES('A' 'C' 'D')
   000707      A                                    7 41'A=Add'
   000708      A                                    8 41'C=Change'
   000709      A                                    9 41'D=Delete'
   000800      A                                   23  2'F3=Exit'
   000900      A            R CUSTMNT                  CA12(12 'F12=Cancel')
   001101      A 42                                    CA10(10 'F10=Delete')
   001103      A 40                                  1 32'Add a New Customer'
   001104      A 41                                  1 27'Change Customer Information'
   001105      A 42                                  1 27'Delete Customer Information'
   001106      A 40                                  3  2'Type values, press Enter.'
   001107      A 41                                  3  2'Type changes, press Enter.'
   001108      A 42                                  3  2'Press F10 to delete record, +
   001109      A                                                 or F12 to cancel.'
   001300      A                                    5  2'Customer identifier:'
   001400      A              CUSTNO    R        O  5 24
   001500      A                                    7  2'First name . . . . .'
   001600      A              CFNAME    R        B  7 24
   001601      A 42                                   DSPATR(PR)
   001700      A                                    8  2'Last name   . . . . .'
   001800      A              CLNAME    R        B  8 24
   001801      A 42                                   DSPATR(PR)
      ----- 12 lines excluded. -----
   002700      A                                   13  2'Date of birth  . . .'
   002800      A              CDOB      R        B 13 24EDTCDE(Y)
   002801      A 42                                   DSPATR(PR)
   002900      A                                   14  2'Gender . . . . . . .'
   003000      A              CGENDER   R        B 14 24
   003001      A 42                                   DSPATR(PR)
   003200      A N42                               23  2'F3=Exit  F12=Cancel'
   003301      A 42                                23  2'F3=Exit  F10=Delete  F12=Cancel'
   003400      A                                   ......  ........  ....
```
Design | Source | Preview

Figure 12.9: Customer maintenance DDS

This DDS uses conditional indicators to display error messages and to specify maintenance modes. Indicator 40 is on for Add mode, indicator 41 for Change mode, and indicator 42 for Delete mode. The DDS contains an entry you have not seen before: DSPATR(PR) protects input-capable fields (i.e., usage I or B). In this case, it prevents users from changing field values in Delete mode (indicator 42 on). In other modes, users can type values for these fields. Notice that CUSTNO is output-only in the CUSTMNT format to prevent users from modifying that field. Also, record format CUSTSEL uses indicators to display error messages differentially, depending on processing outcomes within the program.

Before examining the ILE RPG code required to implement this interactive application, let's work out the logic of what the application should do. Typically, this *think-before-acting* approach to programming leads to more structured code. The pseudocode below illustrates the logic needed for this maintenance program. Notice that the pseudocode divides the program into separate modules based on the function the code performs.

- Program Mainline
  - While user wants to continue
    » Display/read screen Custsel
    » Select
      – When user signals exit, Leave
      – When action is Add, do subroutine Addrecord
      – When action is Change, do subroutine Chgrecord
      – When action is Delete, do subroutine Dltrecord
  - End program
- Subroutine Addrecord
  - Chain to Customers file
  - If record found, set on error indicator (Adderror)
  - Else Zero and blank all record fields except customer identifier
  - Display/read screen Custmnt
  - If user presses Enter, write record to file
- Subroutine Chgrecord
  - Chain to Customers file
  - If record not found, set on error indicator (Chgerror)
  - Else display/read screen Cstmnt
  - If user presses Enter, update record
- Subroutine Dltrecord
  - Chain to Customers file
  - If record not found, set on error indicator (Dlterror)
  - Else display/read screen Custmnt
  - If user presses F10, delete record from file

Once you have the pseudocode worked out, coding the ILE RPG is relatively simple:

```
// ------------------------------------------------------------ Files
Dcl-f Customers Usage(*Update:*Output:*Delete) Keyed;
Dcl-f Custmntd  Workstn Indds(Indicators);
                                                    Continued
```

```
// ------------------------------------ Indicator data structure
Dcl-ds Indicators Len(99);
  Exit     Ind Pos(3);      // F3=Exit
  F10key   Ind Pos(10);     // F10=Delete
  Cancel   Ind Pos(12);     // F12=Cancel
  Fkey     Ind Pos(25);     // Vldcmdkey
  Adderror Ind Pos(30);     // Customer already exists (add)
  Chgerror Ind Pos(31);     // Customer not found (change)
  Dlterror Ind Pos(32);     // Customer not found (delete)
  Addmode  Ind Pos(40);     // A = Add
  Chgmode  Ind Pos(41);     // C = Change
  Dltmode  Ind Pos(42);     // D = Delete
End-ds;


// ------------------------------------------------ Main procedure
Dow Not Exit;
  Exfmt Custsel;

  Select;
    When Exit;
      Leave;
    When Action = 'A';
      Exsr Addrecord;
    When Action = 'C';
      Exsr Chgrecord;
    When Action = 'D';
      Exsr Dltrecord;
  Endsl;

Enddo;

*Inlr = *On;
Return;

// ------------------------------------------------- Addrecord
// Add a customer record
```

Continued

```
Begsr Addrecord;
  Exsr Setmode;
  Chain(n) Custno Customers;
  Adderror = %Found(Customers);


  If Not Adderror;
    Exsr Resetdata;
    Exfmt Custmnt;


    If Not Fkey;
      Write Custsrec;
      Reset Action;
      Reset Custno;
    Endif;


  Endif;
Endsr;


// ------------------------------------------------------- Chgrecord
// Change a customer record
Begsr Chgrecord;
  Exsr Setmode;
  Chain Custno Customers;
  Chgerror = Not %Found(Customers);

  If Not Chgerror;
    Exfmt Custmnt;

    If Not Fkey;
      Update Custsrec;
      Reset Action;
      Reset Custno;
    Endif;

  Endif;
Endsr;
```

Continued

```
// ------------------------------------------------------- Dltrecord
// Delete a customer record
Begsr Dltrecord;
  Exsr Setmode;
  Chain Custno Customers;
  Dlterror = Not %Found(Customers);

  If Not Dlterror;
    Exfmt Custmnt;

    If F10key;
      Reset Action;
      Delete Custsrec;
      Reset Custno;
    Endif;

  Endif;
Endsr;


// ------------------------------------------------------- Resetdata
// Reset customer data in preparation for adding a record
Begsr Resetdata;
  Reset Cfname;
  Reset Clname;
  Reset Caddr;
  Reset Czip;
  Reset Cphone;
  Reset Cemail;
  Reset Cdob;
  Reset Cgender;
Endsr;


// ------------------------------------------------------- Setmode
// Set processing action
Begsr Setmode;
  Addmode = (Action = 'A');
  Chgmode = (Action = 'C');
  Dltmode = (Action = 'D');
Endsr;
```

The preceding program not only updates records in the Customers file, but it also adds new records and deletes existing ones. The file declaration must reflect the complete usage:

```
Dcl-f Customers Usage(*Update:*Output:*Delete) Keyed;
```

Notice that conditional indicators turned on within the program to control screen display may have to be turned on or off, depending upon processing needs (subroutine Setmode). Those indicators associated with error messages in the screen are set to off automatically, and the program need not set them to off. Some of the code in the Setmode subroutine may warrant extra explanation. These lines combine a logical expression with an assignment expression. For example:

```
Addmode = (Action = 'A');
```

The logical expression—Action = 'A'—is *On or *Off, depending upon the value of Action. That *On or *Off value is then assigned to an indicator variable, Addmode. This line is essentially saying, "If Action equals 'A', set Addmode *On; otherwise, set Addmode *Off."

Also, notice the use of the **Reset** operation, which reinitializes a variable or a record format to its original initial value (subroutine Resetdata):

```
Reset Cfname;
```

This program resets each field individually, but it also can reset the entire record format (except for the Custno key field) by using the following entry:

```
Reset *Nokey *All Custsrec;
```

Finally, pay attention to the Chain operation in the Addrecord subroutine:

```
Chain(n) Custno Customers;
```

This subroutine is not expecting to find a record (i.e., an error condition). Because the subroutine does not update a record that it might find, it is appropriate to use the (N) extender to prevent the program from unnecessarily locking that record. The Chgrecord and Dltrecord subroutines, however, lock the record they find because they will make changes to the data.

Many RPG programmers believe that the fields in the display file should not be the same as the database fields. And in some applications, depending on the program design, such separate definition may in fact be necessary to prevent losing values input by the user (or read from the database). To implement this approach, simply define the display file fields independently, giving them new names. Then, in your RPG program, add two subroutines—one that assigns the screen field values to the database fields and one that does the reverse (assigns the database fields to the screen fields). Before you add or update a record, execute the subroutine that assigns the screen fields to the database fields. Before you display the data entry screen for a change or delete, execute the subroutine that assigns the database fields to the screen fields.

12.10. Screen Design and CUA

The screens illustrated in this chapter are based on a set of design standards called **Common User Access (CUA)**. IBM developed CUA as a way of standardizing user interfaces across platforms. All IBM i screens follow these standards. Under CUA, all panels have the same general layout (from top to bottom):

- a panel title centered on the first screen line
- an optional information area
- an instruction area
- a panel body area (where the menu, list, data entry fields, or informational output occurs)
- an optional command line near the bottom of the screen
- a list of available function keys
- a message line

IBM's *CUA Basic Interface Design Guide* (available online) provides specific guidelines for row and column placement of screen items, vertical alignment of screen columns, capitalization and punctuation, color, function key use, error condition handling, and so on. Although you may think such standards stifle creativity, there are two excellent reasons for standardizing the user interface.

First, a standardized interface makes it easier for users to learn new applications because the interface is consistent with other applications. If F3 is always the Exit key across applications, for instance, and F12 always backs up to the previous screen, users don't have to learn new commands counter to those they've used in other applications.

A second major reason for adopting CUA (or other) standards is that such standards can improve programmer productivity. If you adopt a set of design standards, you can easily develop a set of generic DDS descriptions that you can then simply tailor to your specific applications.

12.11. Chapter Summary

While batch applications, once started, execute without user intervention, interactive programs are guided by user input and selection. A display file, defined with DDS, is a mechanism that lets a user and a program interact. Each record screen format of a display file defines a screen. The screen format can include literals to display and fields for output or input or both. Each data item is positioned on the screen based on line and column DDS entries.

DDS relies on keywords to achieve specific desired effects. You can associate some keywords with the entire file, others with a specific record format, and yet others with specific fields. Keywords enable function keys, determine the displayed items' appearance and format, control what the user can enter as input values, and associate error messages with fields.

You can condition most keywords, as well as fields and literals, by using indicators. If the indicator is on at display time, the keyword is in effect (or the field or literal is displayed); if the indicator is off, the effect or data item with which the indicator is associated is suppressed. The indicators are turned on within a program to control screen display. On the display side, you can associate valid command keys with indicators to convey information back to the program. While DDS requires the use of numbered indicators to condition fields, RPG lets you map those indicators to an indicator data structure wherein you can name the indicators.

Today's businesses frequently use interactive applications to display database information or the results of processing data. More and more companies also use interactive applications for file maintenance. In the latter case, you should pay special attention to validating users' entries to maintain data file integrity. SQL and IBM i support several types of physical file constraints—rules to validate data. These rules reside in the files themselves, not in a program. The system enforces the rules whenever users make a database change.

An interactive program uses display files as combined (both input and output) files, coded with a Workstn device. To display a screen, the program writes a display record; to retrieve user input, the program reads the display record. The Exfmt operation combines the write and read operations into a single operation.

IBM has developed a set of screen design guidelines, called Common User Access (CUA), for standardizing interactive applications. Such screen design standards can make it easier for users to learn new applications and for programmers to develop new applications more efficiently.

The following table summarizes the functions and operation codes discussed in this chapter:

Function or Operation	Description	Syntax
Exfmt	Write then read screen	**Exfmt{(e)} format-name;**
Read	Read a screen	**Read{(e)} format-name {ds-name};**
Reset	Reset field or record format values	**Reset{(e)} {*Nokey} {*All} name;**
Write	Display a screen	**Write{(e)} format-name {ds-name};**

12.12. Key Terms

batch processing

CHECK keyword

combined file

Common User Access
  (CUA)

COMP keyword

conditioning indicator

constraint

data validation

display attributes

display files

DSPATR (Display Attribute)

EDTCDE (Edit Code)

EDTWRD (Edit Word)

Exfmt (Execute Format)

file-level keywords

file maintenance

indicator data structure

interactive application

keyboard shift attribute

record-level keywords

Reset

12.13. Discussion/Review Questions

1. Contrast batch and interactive applications.
2. What are the permissible I/O operations that you can use with record formats or display files? What are the effects of each?
3. Describe how a combined file differs from an update file.
4. What lets the system determine whether you are using a keyword at the file, record, or field level?
5. What's the difference between referring to a function key as CA (Command Attention) and CF (Command Function)? How does each affect your program?
6. Explain the meaning of each of the following display attribute codes: BL, CS, ND, HI, UL, RI, and PC.
7. Why might you want to know, in general, whether a user pressed a valid function key or a special key (i.e., enable the VLDCMDKEY keyword) when each valid key has its own indicator whose status can be checked within your program?
8. What are the relational codes used with COMP in DDS display files?
9. What's the difference between Mandatory Enter and Mandatory Fill?
10. What happens when an error message (ERRMSG) is in effect for a field? Describe the screen effects.
11. How can program events influence screen display, and how can screen input influence program flow of control?
12. Describe how a record's existence affects the validity of adding, deleting, or changing the record when maintaining a file with unique keys.
13. Discuss the pros and cons of adopting IBM's CUA standards in your screen design.
14. What impact do you think graphical user interfaces (GUIs), as typified by Microsoft's Windows environment and Internet browsers, will have on future IBM i interactive applications?
15. Research some of IBM third-party software vendor products that allow applications developed with RPG to run in a Web browser or mobile device. How will the skills that you are learning in this class transfer to Web or mobile programming?

12.14. Exercises

1. Assume that your school has a student file containing name, gender, total credits accumulated, residency code, grade point average, major (or degree program), and student classification. Write the DDS for a record format that prompts users to enter values for these fields, including as many validation keywords as are appropriate.

2. Write a DDS record format that will prompt users to enter salesperson number, date of sale, and amount of sale. Make sure that the cursor blinks, salesperson number is underlined with column separators, date of sale is displayed in high intensity, and amount of sale is in reverse image and blinking.

3. Rewrite the DDS from exercise 2 so that the salesperson number is underlined if indicators 10 *and* 12 are on, and displayed with column separators if 10 *or* 12 is on. Date of sale is to display in high intensity only if indicator 10 is on. Amount of sale must be in reverse image and blinking if 10 and 12 are on or if 14 and 16 are on.

4. Write the pseudocode for a program to allow interactive processing of received goods. The program must let users enter a product number (on Screen 1), determine whether that product number exists in the file, and either display an error message (on Screen 1) if the product number is incorrect or display a second screen (Screen 2) that prompts users to enter the quantity of the product received. The program must add the amount entered to the current quantity on hand and then update the product record. Include provisions for exiting and canceling.

5. Write the ILE RPG for the pseudocode in exercise 4. Don't code the DDS. Make up whatever file names and field names you need, and document the indicators you use.

Notes

CHAPTER **13**

Calling Programs and Passing Parameters

13.1. Chapter Overview

This chapter examines modular programming and shows you how ILE RPG programs can communicate with one another by passing data values as parameter arguments. You also learn how to define prototypes and procedure interfaces. In addition, this chapter compares two methods for passing parameters and discusses the advantages of each technique. Finally, it outlines the use of data areas to provide external data to a program, as well as to pass information to other programs without using parameters.

13.2. Modular Programming

As concern about program development and maintenance efficiencies has grown, programmers have become increasingly interested in developing small, standalone units of code (rather than monolithic programs thousands of lines long). This approach, often called **modular programming**, offers many advantages.

First, if you develop code in small, independent units, you often can reuse these units because it is common for several applications to share identical processing requirements for some parts of their logic. Furthermore, small programs are easier to test than large programs. In addition, code changes are less likely to cause unexpected—and unwanted—side effects when they are made within a small, standalone module rather than in a routine that is embedded within a massive program. Finally, because you can separately develop and test such modules, a modular approach to programming makes it easier to divide an application development project among programming team members, each with responsibilities for developing different modules.

ILE RPG provides the **Callp (Call a Prototyped Procedure or Program)** operation to let you adopt this modular approach to program development. Before examining this operation in detail, you need to understand how the call affects flow of control. When program execution reaches a call statement, control passes to the called program (which is itself a *PGM object). The called program runs until it reaches a Return statement, and then control returns to the calling program at the statement immediately following the original call. Figure 13.1 illustrates this flow of control among calling and called programs.

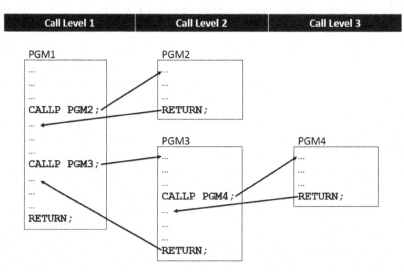

Figure 13.1: Call stack example

As you can see, the flow of control with a call is like that of an Exsr operation, except that a call invokes an external program (or a subprocedure, discussed in Chapter 14) rather than a subroutine internal to the program. The ordered list of active programs in a job is called the **call stack**. Each call stack entry (program or procedure) in the call stack has a call level that depends upon its position in the stack relative to other call stack entries. The first program has a call level of 1. That program can in turn call other programs, which are at call level 2. Should any call level 2 entry make additional calls, those are at call level 3, and so on. When a call level 3 program ends, it returns to call level 2. Similarly, when a call level 2 entry ends, it returns to call level 1. And when call level 1 ends, the job ends. The system uses the call stack to keep track of the point to which each program should return control when it ends.

Under normal circumstances, an RPG program cannot call itself or any other already active program on the call stack; that is, it cannot make a **recursive call**. For example, in Figure 13.1,

PGM4 cannot call PGM3 or PGM1 because they are both active on the call stack while PGM4 is running.

13.3. Prototyping the Call Interface

A call would be of limited value if it did not permit the called and calling programs to share data. While an ILE RPG program can normally access any variable's value from anywhere within the program, this *global* feature of variables does not extend across program boundaries. It is said that a variable's **scope** (i.e., its extent of influence) is limited to the program in which it is defined. That means if you want a called program to process some data and return the results of the processing to the calling program, you must make special provisions to let this sharing take place.

The Callp operation passes parameters to communicate values between the calling program and the called program. **Parameters**—sometimes referred to as **arguments**—are values, usually contained in variables, that a program can pass to another program. The called program can then accept the parameters and use those values to control its processing.

Before you can use Callp to call a program, you must define the **call interface** to the called program. The basic program call interface includes the name of the program to call, the number of parameters to pass, the parameters' data attributes, and the order in which to pass the parameters.

To define this interface, you define a special structure called a **prototype**. The ILE RPG compiler uses the prototype to call the program correctly and to ensure that the caller passes the correct parameters to the called program. You code a prototype in the Declarations section of the calling program. If the calling program calls more than one program, it must include a prototype for each call interface.

To code a prototype, you define a structure similar to a data structure. The prototype definition has two parts:

- the prototype definition itself (the prototype header)
- the descriptions of parameters to share between the programs

The **Dcl-pr (Declare prototype)** instruction signals the beginning of a prototyped call interface. It conforms to this format:

```
Dcl-pr name {keywords};
```

The following is an example of a prototype for a program call interface:

```
Dcl-pr Updcust Extpgm('AR002');
  Company  Char(5);
  Customer Zoned(7:0);
End-pr;
```

You must give the prototype a name, which is the name the Callp operation is to use. Code the external name of the program associated with this prototype by using the Extpgm keyword—the program is the object that the caller executes when you perform the call. The Extpgm entry is usually a literal, but it can be a named constant or a field specifying the name of the program. The Extpgm name must match the called program's actual name; it is case sensitive, which usually means that it must be in all uppercase characters. In the preceding example, performing a call to the Updcust prototype actually calls program AR002. The prototype's name need not match the external program's name, although you may find it convenient to use matching names. If the names do match, you need not name the program twice:

```
Dcl-pr AR002 Extpgm;
  Company  Char(5);
  Customer Zoned(7:0);
End-pr;
```

Describe the parameters on subsequent lines, following the Dcl-pr instruction, using coding similar to that of data structure subfields. The preceding prototype has two parameters: a five-character field and a seven-digit (zoned) numeric field with zero decimals. A prototype can list a maximum of 255 parameters for a called program.

If the parameter name duplicates the name of an RPG operation code, you must precede the parameter name with the Dcl-parm (Declare parameter) instruction:

```
Dcl-pr Mypgm Extpgm;
  Dcl-parm Return   Ind;          // Dcl-parm required
  Dcl-parm Currency Char(3);      // Dcl-parm not required, but valid
End-pr;
```

Note that you need not name the parameters. You may find it convenient to document the parameter usage by naming the parameters, but the compiler treats these names as comments. In the preceding prototype, the compiler does not define variables named Return or Currency, as they are merely comments to indicate the purpose for each of the two parameters. If the program needs those variables, you must define them separately. If you choose to not name the parameters, you can use the *N placeholder value instead:

```
Dcl-pr Mypgm Extpgm;
  *N Ind;
  *N Char(3);
End-pr;
```

When there are no parameters to pass to the called program, the prototype can consist of a single line:

```
Dcl-pr Sleep Extpgm End-pr;
```

13.4. Callp (Call a Prototyped Procedure or Program)

The **Callp** operation takes this form:

```
Callp prototype(parm1: parm2: ... parmn)
```

Callp invokes the program object (type *PGM) associated with the prototype named in the required first argument and then passes control to it. List any parameters in parentheses immediately following the prototype name:

```
Callp Updcust(Company:Custnbr);
```

When coupled with the Updcust prototype in the earlier example, the previous code calls program AR002, named in the Updcust prototype, passing fields Company (five characters) and Customer (seven digits, zoned) as parameters. Note that you define Company and Customer elsewhere in the program, and that their definitions must match those in the prototype definition. If the parameters that Callp passes do not match the number, order, and data types of the parameters in the prototype definition, the program will not compile. If there are no parameters, you must code empty parentheses instead:

```
Callp Sleep();
```

Actually coding the Callp operation is optional in the free-format specification. You can let the compiler infer the Callp operation, instead of explicitly coding it, as the following examples illustrate:

```
UpdCust(Company:CustNbr);
Sleep();
```

This code calls the programs associated with their respective prototypes, just like in the previous examples. Most programmers prefer to omit explicitly coding the Callp operation, as this abbreviated syntax matches similar call operations in other computer languages, such as C or Java.

13.5. The Procedure Interface

Recall the call stack in Figure 13.1. In the calling program (e.g., PGM1), ILE RPG uses the prototype definition to describe the list of parameters that it will pass on to the called program. The called ILE RPG program (e.g., PGM2) should also use a prototype definition to describe the corresponding list of parameters that it is to receive from the caller.

The prototypes in each program must match each other. That is, they must have the same number of parameters, and the corresponding parameters between the two programs must have the same data attributes. ILE RPG passes parameter arguments by passing the address of the storage location represented by the parameter, so in fact these corresponding parameters reference the same storage location within the computer. The data names of the parameters you use in the caller and the called program need not be the same.

To access those storage locations passed by the calling program, the called program must include a **procedure interface** definition (in addition to the prototype). Like the prototype, the procedure interface describes the parameters that the called program is to share with the caller. Unlike the prototype, however, the procedure interface defines variable names to hold the parameter values that the called program is to receive, allowing you to refer to and manipulate those parameter values.

You code the procedure interface similarly to the prototype by using the **Dcl-pi (Declare procedure interface)** instruction. The program's procedure interface must appear after the primary program prototype, called the **main procedure prototype**. Many programmers prefer to code the procedure interface immediately following the prototype and to make these two definitions the first ones in the program. The procedure interface has two parts:

- the procedure interface itself (the header)
- the definitions for parameters the called program is to receive

The following is an example of a main procedure prototype and a matching procedure interface. These definitions appear as the first definitions in program AR002 (the called program):

```
Dcl-pr AR002 Extpgm;
  *N        Char(9);
  *N        Zoned(7:0);
End-pr;

Dcl-pi AR002;
  Company  Char(5);
  Customer Zoned(7:0);
End-pi;
```

The Dcl-pi instruction signals the beginning of a prototyped call interface. You must name the procedure interface, and the name must match the name in the called program's prototype. Some programmers prefer to always give the main procedure interface a consistent name, such as Main. In that case, the Extpgm keyword must refer to the actual program name:

```
Dcl-pr Main Extpgm('AR002');
  *N        Char(9);
  *N        Zoned(7:0);
End-pr;

Dcl-pi Main;
  Company  Char(5);
  Customer Zoned(7:0);
End-pi;
```

When the call interface involves passing parameters, define the parameters on subsequent lines, following the header. You must name the parameter variable—the program uses this name to refer to the parameter. The data attributes and length of parameters in the procedure interface must match the corresponding parameter entries in the prototype. The preceding procedure interface contains two parameters: Company, a five-character variable, and Customer, a seven-digit zoned decimal variable with zero decimals.

The prototype is optional for a called program that's called only from programs written in languages other than ILE RPG. In this case, code the Extpgm keyword with the procedure interface instead of the prototype. If you omit the prototype, you need not name the procedure interface:

```
Dcl-pi Extpgm('AR002');
  Company  Char(5);
  Customer Zoned(7:0);
End-pi;
```

Though it's optional, the prototype is still recommended. The compiler uses the prototype to call the program correctly and to ensure parameter consistency between the caller and the called program. If you don't include a prototype, the compiler uses the procedure interface to implicitly generate one.

When no parameters are involved in calling a program, the called program need not have either a prototype or a procedure interface. You may still want to code each of them, however, for consistency among your programs and to promote future enhancements in the application. Regardless of any parameter-passing considerations, Callp always requires that the calling program have a prototype.

13.6. Passing Parameters and Changing Values

Prototypes provide an effective means to describe the data items to pass between programs. Once the prototype and procedure interface definitions are in place in both the calling program and the called program, the caller can pass parameters to the called program, and the called program can use the parameters during the course of its processing. Prototypes also offer some flexibility in the method the system uses to pass those parameters. ILE RPG employs two methods for passing parameters between programs:

- Pass by reference
- Pass by read-only reference

13.6.1. Passing Parameters by Reference

By default, RPG passes a parameter by passing the address of the memory storage location represented by the variable (called **passing by reference**). The called program then uses that storage address to retrieve and process the parameter value. In effect, both programs are sharing the same storage location. Because they both share the storage, if the called program changes the value of the parameter variable, the caller recognizes that change when the called program returns control to the caller. In the following example, variable Okay has a value of *Off before calling another program:

```
// Caller
Dcl-pr Nextpgm Extpgm;
  *N Ind;
End-pr;

Dcl-s Okay Ind Inz(*Off);
...
Nextpgm(Okay);      // Okay = *Off before call
...
```

As part of its processing, the called program changes the value of Flag (the first parameter):

```
// Nextpgm
Dcl-pr Nextpgm Extpgm;
  *N Ind;
End-pr;

Dcl-pi Nextpgm;
  Flag *Ind;
End-pi;
...
Flag = *On;      // Change value of Flag
*Inlr = *On;
Return;
```

Upon return to the caller, Okay now has a value of *On because Okay and Flag reference the same storage location. When a program passes a parameter by reference, the parameter's value must exist within a variable. To pass the parameter, you name the variable in parentheses following the prototype name during the Callp operation.

13.6.2. Passing Parameters by Read-only Reference

While passing by reference is the default, prototypes support an alternative method of passing parameters between programs: **read-only reference**. Passing parameters by read-only reference offers several advantages over passing parameters by reference:

- The parameter values need not be represented in a variable.
- The parameter data types need not precisely match the prototype.
- The system offers protection against the called program changing the parameter values.

On occasion, you may want to pass expressions or literals, instead of variables, to called programs. This capability gives you more flexibility in coding the Callp operation than being limited to representing the parameter value in a variable. When ILE RPG passes a parameter by read-only reference, it can first evaluate an expression or a literal and then make a temporary copy of that value before invoking the called program; the caller then passes the storage address of the temporary copy. To specify read-only reference, you code the Const keyword in the prototype:

```
Dcl-pr Updcust Extpgm('AR002');
  *N Char(9)    Const;
  *N Zoned(7:0) Const;
End-pr;
...
Updcust('BBY' : Customer);
...
```

This example calls a program, passing two parameters. The first parameter is passed as a literal ('BBY'), and the second one is passed as a variable (Customer).

You can also code an expression as the parameter when passing by read-only reference:

```
Dcl-pr Addcust Extpgm('AR001');
  *N Char(9)    Const;
  *N Zoned(7:0) Const;
End-pr;
...
Addcust('BBY' : Lastcustomer + 1);
...
```

In this example, the second parameter is an expression. You can mix passing methods in the same prototype, if necessary. When you omit the Const keyword for a parameter, the parameter is passed by reference.

The Const keyword allows you some flexibility in passing parameters of slightly different data formats than the prototype specifies. For example, you might pass an integer when a prototype calls for a packed decimal field. As long as the field's value is appropriate for the data type, the prototype can manage this minor mismatch.

When a program passes a literal or an expression as a parameter, the system uses the same rules as the Eval operation to assign the parameter value. For example, a character parameter that is longer than the character literal being passed is padded on the right with blanks; numeric parameters are aligned with the decimal point.

When a program passes a parameter by read-only reference, the called program should avoid changing the value of that parameter. Because the passed parameter may be a copy of the actual information, the calling program may not see any changes that the called program makes to that parameter value. Indeed, if the called program includes a prototype and a procedure interface, the compiler will prevent the program from changing the parameter. Assuming the previous example is in a calling program, the following example fragment for program AR001 (the called program) is not allowed to change the values of Company or Customer:

```
// Called program (AR001)
...
Dcl-pr Addcust Extpgm('AR001');
  *N Char(9)     Const;
  *N Zoned(7:0) Const;
End-pr;

Dcl-pi Addcust;
  Company  Char(5)     Const;
  Customer Zoned(7:0) Const;
End-pi;
...
// (Some processing goes here...cannot change Company or Customer)
...
*Inlr = *On;
Return;
```

If the called program lacks a PR/PI combination (e.g., the called program is written in another language that does not support prototyping, such as CL), it may be allowed to change the parameter values. But you should avoid doing so because you cannot be sure whether the calling program will recognize the change.

To improve the flexibility of your coding, and to help protect the integrity of the calling program's data, use read-only reference as the preferred method for passing parameters between programs. If the calling program needs to access any changes made by the called program, pass by reference. Or if a large number of parameters must be passed, pass by reference to improve the performance of the call.

13.7. Return and *Inlr

The system returns control to the calling program when the called program encounters a Return operation. If the LR indicator is also on when the Return is executed, the system releases any resources tied up by the called program. A subsequent call to the program causes it to start again as though for the first time. However, if LR is not on within the called program when it returns, it remains activated. As a result, a subsequent call to that program finds all its variables (except parameter variables) and indicators with the values they had at the time of the previous Return. Moreover, any files the called program used remain open as a result of the previous call. (Linear main programs, discussed in Chapter 14, do not use *Inlr.)

To illustrate this behavior, consider the following calling program:

```
Dcl-pr Samplepgm Extpgm End-pr;

Dcl-s X Uns(3);

For X = 1 To 100;
   SamplePgm();
Enddo;

*Inlr = *On;
Return;
```

The caller executes Samplepgm 100 times. Samplepgm increments a variable called Count each time it is called:

```
// Samplepgm
Dcl-s Count Uns(5);

Count += 1;
Return;
```

In this example, Samplepgm executes a Return statement without turning on LR. Samplepgm remains active, and each time the caller calls it, variable Count is incremented by 1, having retained its latest value from its latest invocation. Notice that setting *Inlr in the calling program does not affect *Inlr in Samplepgm; each program has its own copy of *Inlr. Indeed, even after the caller has ended, Samplepgm is still active because its *Inlr has not been set to *On.

If you substitute the following version of Samplepgm, in which LR is turned on before the
Return operation, the program is deactivated, and Count is initially 0 each time Samplepgm
is called:

```
// Samplepgm
Dcl-s Count Uns(5);


Count += 1;
*Inlr = *On;
Return;
```

Whether you should turn on LR before returning from a called program, then, depends on
whether you want the called program to start afresh each time the calling program invokes
it, or you want the called program to pick up where it left off on the previous call (within
a given call stack entry). Failure to correctly handle the LR indicator can cause undesired
effects in the called program.

You should ensure that a program ends with LR on after a process is finished with it. For
example, using the following Samplepgm ensures that it remains active for only 100 calls
(matching the For loop in the calling program):

```
// Samplepgm
Dcl-s Count Uns(5);


Count += 1;
*Inlr = (Count = 100);      // Set LR *On if Count = 100
Return;
```

In this version of Samplepgm, the hybrid assignment/logical expression ensures that LR
remains off until Count is equal to 100. Then, the Return operation closes the program
completely. Any files used by Samplepgm are closed as well. A subsequent call to
Samplepgm invokes it with fresh variable initialization and file opens. This example
illustrates one method for ending Samplepgm gracefully. Another common technique is for
the caller to pass a parameter to Samplepgm indicating whether it should close:

```
Dcl-pr Samplepgm Extpgm;
  *N Ind;
End-pr;
```
Continued

```
Dcl-s Shutdown Ind;
Dcl-s X        Uns(3);


For X = 1 To 100;
  Shutdown = (X = 100);      // Set Shutdown *On if X = 100
  SamplePgm(Shutdown);
Enddo;


*Inlr = *On;
Return;
```

In this example, the caller controls whether Samplepgm is to turn on *Inlr by setting the value of the Shutdown parameter, which it passes to Samplepgm. The called program then sets *Inlr on or off, depending upon the value of Shutdown:

```
// Samplepgm
Dcl-pr Samplepgm Extpgm;
  *N Ind;
End-pr;

Dcl-pi Samplepgm;
  Closepgm Ind;
End-pi;

Dcl-s Count Uns(5);

Count += 1;
*Inlr = Closepgm;
Return;
```

Notice that the parameter need not have the same name in both programs (although the names can match, if you wish).

13.8. Fitting the Pieces

Here is a summary of the requirements for having one ILE RPG program call another ILE RPG program. The calling program includes two items:

- A prototype definition to describe the parameters to pass
- The Callp operation to execute the call

The called program contains the following:

- A prototype definition to describe the parameters to receive
- A procedure interface to receive the parameters and define their variables
- The Return operation to return control to the calling program

In the following example snippets, program AR000 calls AR002, passing it three parameters: Company (with a value of 'BBY'), Customer (10487), and Okay (*Off). Study this example to understand the relationship between the programs, as well as the relationship between the prototype and the procedure interface. (Program AR000 receives no parameters, but the example includes a prototype and a procedure interface for the sake of consistency):

```
// Program AR000
// --------------------- Main procedure prototype/interface
Dcl-pr AR000 Extpgm End-pr;
Dcl-pi AR000 End-pi;


// --------------------- Prototype(s) for called program(s)
Dcl-pr Updcust Extpgm('AR002');
  *N Char(9)    Const;
  *N Zoned(7:0) Const;
  *N Ind;
End-pr;


// ---------------------------------- Standalone variables
Dcl-s Company  Char(5)    Inz('BBY');
Dcl-s Customer Packed(7:0) Inz(10487);
Dcl-s Okay     Ind        Inz(*Off);
...
Updcust(Company:Customer:Okay);


If Okay;     // If AR002 executed normally, Okay will be *On
  Exsr Process;
Endif;
...
```

Here are the relevant code segments for program AR002:

```
// Program AR002
// ---------------------- Main procedure prototype/interface
Dcl-pr AR002 Extpgm;
  *N Char(9)    Const;
  *N Zoned(7:0) Const;
  *N Ind;
End-pr;

Dcl-pi AR002;
  Company  Char(5)    Const;
  Customer Zoned(7:0) Const;
  Flag     Ind;
End-pi;

// Company = 'BBY'(Value received from first parameter)
// Customer = 10487 (Value received from second parameter)
// Flag = *Off (Valued received from third parameter)
...
Flag = *On;      // Change value of Flag
*Inlr = *On;
Return;
```

Program AR000 passes the first two parameters by ready-only reference, using the Const keyword in the prototype. Program AR002 is not allowed to change those parameter values; attempting to do so causes the compile to fail. The third parameter, though, uses the default method: pass by reference. In this case, ILE RPG passes the memory address used to store the variable. Both programs AR000 and AR002 in this example are, in effect, sharing the same storage address for the third parameter, even though they may refer to that address by different names. If program AR002 changes Flag, the value of the corresponding parameter in AR000—Okay—also changes. After AR000 calls AR002, the value of Okay will be *On.

13.9. Using a Modular Approach

You will find a wide variation in the extent to which different companies use RPG's calling features. Some companies incorporate calls within menu programs that present application choices to users. The menu programs then call the selected programs to perform the desired processing. Typically, this kind of program does not require passing data between the calling program and the programs it calls.

Another application of RPG's calling features is to access a routine that performs a specific task, without recoding the routine every time you need it. For example, you might write a routine to determine the day of the week for a given date in *ISO format. You can perform this day-of-the-week calculation within a called program. The calling program will include two parameters: one to contain the given date and one to store the calculated day of the week. The called program determines the day of the week of the value represented in the first parameter, stores the result in the second parameter, and then returns control to the calling program.

One example of a routine that many programs might call is one that converts a numeric value representing dollars and cents (e.g., 123.43) to its representation in words (e.g., one hundred twenty-three dollars and 43 cents). The logic required for such a conversion is not trivial, and companies do not want to continually reinvent that particular wheel.

Calling an external program offers an additional significant advantage over an Exsr operation: you need not create the called program from ILE RPG source. You can write a program in any high-level language (HLL) supported by IBM i, or in Control Language (CL), compile it, and then call it from an ILE RPG program. Similarly, you can call an ILE RPG program from a CL program or from one written in a different HLL supported by IBM i. The RPG program's Return statement returns control to whatever program called it.

This flexibility lets you separate a problem into logical units, write each unit in the language best suited for developing the algorithm that unit requires, and then call the units to perform their processing as needed. Use of this multilanguage approach is growing as cooperative processing and the use of graphical user interfaces (GUIs) demand more sophisticated capabilities than those RPG alone can offer. As a result, modular programming is common in IT departments that use ILE RPG.

IBM's Integrated Language Environment (ILE) encourages modular programming techniques. As more programmers adopt ILE concepts in their applications, modular programming is a natural companion technology. (Chapter 14 covers ILE in more detail.) Modular programming techniques also allow ILE RPG programs to exploit application programming interfaces, or APIs. **APIs** (discussed in Chapter 18) are programs supplied with the operating system that let you access lower-level machine functions or system data not otherwise available within an HLL program. APIs provide you with a variety of callable routines to access IBM i resources in ways not possible with RPG alone.

13.10. Data Areas

Parameters let calling and called programs share data. **Data areas** are system objects you use to share data between programs within a job or between jobs. However, one program does not have to call another to share the data if the data resides in a data area, nor does a calling program have to pass parameters to a called program to share the data. You can use data areas to store information of limited size (up to 2,000 bytes), independent of database files or programs.

The system automatically creates a **local data area (LDA)** for each job in the system. Each LDA is 1,024 positions long, with type character; initially, blanks fill the LDA. Programs within a job can share the information in that job's LDA. Other jobs have their own LDAs with their own data. When you submit a job with the CL SBMJOB (Submit Job) command, the value of your job's LDA is copied into the submitted job's LDA so that the submitted job can access any data values stored in the LDA by your initial job. When a job ends, its LDA ceases to exist.

You also can create more permanent data areas with the **CRTDTAARA (Create Data Area)** command. A data area created in this way remains an object on the system until you explicitly remove it. Any program, regardless of its job, can access such a data area.

Programmers use data areas to store small quantities of data used frequently by several programs or by the same program each time it is run. For example, they might prefer storing within a data area the next assigned order number or customer number to avoid having to retrieve that information from a database file of orders or customers. Programmers sometimes use a data area to store constant values used by several programs, such as tax rates or discounts, or to transfer the processing results of one program to another.

13.10.1. Data-Area Data Structures

As a programmer, you should understand how to access data areas from within an ILE RPG program. You can make a data area accessible to a program by defining a variable or a data structure for the data area. To identify a data structure as a **data-area data structure**, declare it with the Dtaara(*Auto) option:

```
Dcl-ds *N Dtaara(*Auto);
   Returncode Ind;
   Company    Char(5);
   Nextresnbr Zoned(7:0);
End-ds;
```

When, as in this example, you do not provide a name for a data-area data structure (i.e., if you specify *N), the data structure automatically represents the LDA.

If you want the data structure to contain data from a permanent data-area object, you must provide a name for the data structure. Usually, that name matches the external name of the data area in the system. In the following example, the RPG program uses *LIBL/RESCOUNTER to populate the data structure:

```
Dcl-ds Rescounter Dtaara(*Auto);
  Returncode Ind;
  Company    Char(5);
  Nextresnbr Zoned(7:0);
End-ds;
```

When the names do not match, or when the program is to use a data area in a specific library, you can name the data area in the Dtaara keyword:

```
Dcl-ds Nextres Dtaara(*Auto:'MYLIB/RESCOUNTER');
  Returncode Ind;
  Company    Char(5);
  Nextresnbr Zoned(7:0);
End-ds;
```

You can use a named constant or a variable to hold the name of the data area, or you can specifically name it with a literal enclosed in apostrophes. The name's value must be all uppercase.

The contents of any data area defined via a data structure, as in the previous examples, are read into the program at program initialization. The data-area object is then locked to prevent other programs from accessing it. When a program locks a data area, other programs can read the data area, but they cannot update it—this is called an **exclusive lock**. When the program ends, the system writes the contents of the data structure from the program back to the data area and removes the lock.

13.10.2. Using In, Out, and Unlock

If your program must process a data-area data structure in more detail than simply reading and locking it when the program begins and then writing/unlocking it when the program ends, three operation codes relate to data-area processing:

- In (Retrieve a Data Area)
- Out (Write a Data Area)
- Unlock (Unlock a Data Area)

These operation codes allow the program to process the data area while it is running, at times other than the beginning and the end of the program.

The **In (Retrieve a data area)** and **Out (Write a data area)** operations allow you to retrieve and write a data area in a program, as well as to control the locking or unlocking of a data area. To use them, you must declare the data-area data structure with the Dtaara(*Usrctl) option. The **Unlock (Unlock a data area)** operation unlocks a data area without updating it. To use these operations, you must declare the data area with the Dtaara(*Usrctl) option:

```
Dcl-ds Nextres Dtaara(*Auto:*Usrctl:'MYLIB/RESCOUNTER');
  Returncode Ind;
  Company    Char(5);
  Nextresnbr Zoned(7:0);
End-ds;
...
Unlock Nextres;
...
In *Lock Nextres;
Nextresnbr += 1;
Out Nextres;
...
```

In this example, the data area RESCOUNTER is unlocked near the beginning of the program so that other programs can read and update it. When the program is ready to find the value of Nextresnbr, it uses the In operation to retrieve the data area and lock it. Then, it promptly updates the data area with a new value. If the subsequent Out operation does not specify *Lock, the data area is automatically unlocked after the update. If the lock is to remain in effect, specify *Lock:

```
Out *Lock Nextres;
```

You cannot indicate *Lock for the local data area. The Unlock operation can also unlock all the data areas locked by a program:

```
Unlock *Dtaara;
```

13.11. Navigating Legacy Code

Legacy ILE RPG programs use fixed Definition specifications (D-specs) to define prototypes and procedure interfaces instead of Dcl-pr and Dcl-pi instructions. They can also use an older operation—Call (Call a Program)—in place of Callp to call external programs.

13.11.1. Fixed-Format Prototypes

To use D-specs to define a prototype, code PR in columns 24–25 (Ds):

```
*.. 1 ...+... 2 ...+... 3 ...+... 4 ...+... 5 ...+... 6 ...+... 7 ...+... 8
DName+++++++++++ETDsFrom+++To/Len+IDc.Keywords+++++++++++++++++++++++++++++++
D Updcust        PR                    Extpgm('AR002')
D   Company                   5
D   Customer                  7S 0
```

If you choose to not name the parameters, simply leave columns 7–21 (Name+++++++++++)
blank. If you do name a parameter, the entry serves as a comment:

```
*.. 1 ...+... 2 ...+... 3 ...+... 4 ...+... 5 ...+... 6 ...+... 7 ...+... 8
DName+++++++++++ETDsFrom+++To/Len+IDc.Keywords+++++++++++++++++++++++++++++++
D Updcust        PR                    Extpgm('AR002')
D                             5
D                             7S 0
```

13.11.2. Fixed-Format Procedure Interfaces

To define fixed-format procedure interfaces by using D-specs, you code a PI in columns
24–25 (Ds):

```
*.. 1 ...+... 2 ...+... 3 ...+... 4 ...+... 5 ...+... 6 ...+... 7 ...+... 8
DName+++++++++++ETDsFrom+++To/Len+IDc.Keywords+++++++++++++++++++++++++++++++
D AR002          PI                    Extpgm
D   Company                   5
D   Customer                  7S 0
```

13.11.3. Fixed-Format Calls

The fixed-format-only Call operation performs a program call in legacy programs; however,
it does not support a prototype or a procedure interface. The Call operation names the
program to call in Factor 2:

```
*.. 1 ...+... 2 ...+... 3 ...+... 4 ...+... 5 ...+... 6 ...+... 7 ...+... 8
CL0N01Factor1+++++++Opcode(E)+Factor2+++++++Result+++++++Len++D+HiLoEq....
C                 Call      'AR002'
```

The program entry can be a variable, literal, or named constant, and the value must be uppercase.

To pass parameters to the called program, list them on the immediately subsequent lines by using the fixed-format-only Parm (Identify Parameters) operation:

```
*.. 1 ...+... 2 ...+... 3 ...+... 4 ...+... 5 ...+... 6 ...+... 7 ...+... 8
CLON01Factor1+++++++Opcode(E)+Factor2+++++++Result++++++++Len++D+HiLoEq....
C                   Call      'AR002'
C                   Parm                    Company
C                   Parm                    Customer
```

You can list up to 255 parameters. Parm statements must be in the order the called program expects, and the data types must be compatible.

The Call operation does not support prototypes. You can, however, first define a parameter list and then later use that parameter list as the Result (positions 50–63) of the Call instead of listing individual parameters:

```
*.. 1 ...+... 2 ...+... 3 ...+... 4 ...+... 5 ...+... 6 ...+... 7 ...+... 8
CLON01Factor1+++++++Opcode(E)+Factor2+++++++Result++++++++Len++D+HiLoEq....
C     Updcust       Plist
C                   Parm                    Company
C                   Parm                    Customer
...
C                   Call      'AR002'       Updcust
```

A program can contain several parameter lists. Using a prototype and procedure interface definition is preferable to using the older Plist and Parm operations. The older operations do not support parameter checking at compile time and are prone to runtime errors.

The fixed-format Call operation always passes parameters by reference. To pass parameters by read-only reference, you must use a prototyped Callp operation, discussed earlier in this chapter.

13.11.4. Using an *Entry Plist

Instead of requiring a main procedure prototype and a matching procedure interface, legacy RPG programs can use a specially named parameter list, commonly called an entry parameter list or an *Entry Plist:

```
*.. 1 ...+... 2 ...+... 3 ...+... 4 ...+... 5 ...+... 6 ...+... 7 ...+... 8
CLON01Factor1+++++++Opcode(E)+Factor2+++++++Result++++++++Len++D+HiLoEq....
C     *Entry        Plist
C                   Parm                     Company
C                   Parm                     Customer
```

Only one *Entry Plist can appear in a program. The *Entry Plist serves roughly the same purpose as the main procedure interface: it allows the program to accept parameters and places those parameter values into variables. If program AR002 in the examples included the preceding *Entry Plist, you could call AR002 from another RPG program by coding one of the fixed-format calls shown earlier. You can also call it from an IBM i command line, supplying values for the parameters:

```
CALL PGM(AR002) PARM('BBY' 13579)
```

An *Entry Plist does not support parameter checking at compile time, and it is susceptible to runtime errors if the parameters passed at runtime do not match the definitions in the *Entry Plist.

13.11.5. Fixed-Format Data-Area Data Structures

Legacy programs use Definition specifications to define data-area data structures. Placing a U in position 23 (T) of the data structure definition identifies it as a data-area data structure:

```
*.. 1 ...+... 2 ...+... 3 ...+... 4 ...+... 5 ...+... 6 ...+... 7 ...+... 8
DName++++++++++ETDsFrom+++To/Len+IDc.Keywords+++++++++++++++++++++++++++++++
D                   UDS
D     Returncode             N
D     Company                5A
D     Nextresnbr             7S 0
```

When you do not provide a name for a data-area data structure, it automatically represents the local data area. You can also explicitly base a data structure on the LDA by using the Dtaara keyword:

```
*.. 1 ...+... 2 ...+... 3 ...+... 4 ...+... 5 ...+... 6 ...+... 7 ...+... 8
DName++++++++++ETDsFrom+++To/Len+IDc.Keywords+++++++++++++++++++++++++++++++
                                                             Continued
```

```
D Localdata        UDS                     Dtaara(*Lda)
D   Returncode                    N
D   Company                       5A
D   Nextresnbr                    7S 0
```

The data-area data structure (U in position 23) is automatically read and locked when the program starts, and then it's updated and released when the program ends. Because the preceding example uses the Dtaara keyword to explicitly base the data structure on the LDA, the program can also use the In and Out operations to manage the LDA contents.

D-specs can also define a data-area data structure based on a permanent data area, using concepts and keywords similar to the free-format Dcl-ds instruction:

```
*.. 1 ...+... 2 ...+... 3 ...+... 4 ...+... 5 ...+... 6 ...+... 7 ...+... 8
DName++++++++++ETDsFrom+++To/Len+IDc.Keywords++++++++++++++++++++++++++++++++++
D Nextres          UDS                     Dtaara('MYLIB/RESCOUNTER')
D   Returncode                    N
D   Company                       5A
D   Nextresnbr                    7S 0
```

13.12. Putting It All Together

To illustrate the modular programming techniques discussed in this chapter, let's divide the file maintenance program from Chapter 12 into separate programs for each maintenance function: add, change, and delete. That program isn't particularly complex, but you can see how it simplifies and focuses each function when you work with smaller, but related, components. The customer file maintenance application will consist of four programs:

- CUS00—The master *driver* program that selects a customer record to process
- CUS01—The program that adds a new customer record
- CUS02—The program that changes an existing customer record
- CUS04—The program that deletes an existing customer record

The program uses the same Customers database file and the same display file from Chapter 12. Here is the code for program CUS00:

```
// Program CUS00 - Select a customer record for maintenance


// ----------------------------------------------------------- Files
                                                               Continued
```

```
Dcl-f Customers Keyed;
Dcl-f Custmntd  Workstn Indds(Indicators);


// ------------------------------------------------------ Prototypes
Dcl-pr Addcust Extpgm('CUS01');
  Custno Char(9);
End-pr;


Dcl-pr Chgcust Extpgm('CUS02');
  Custno Char(9);
End-pr;


Dcl-pr Dltcust Extpgm('CUS04');
  Custno Char(9);
End-pr;


// ------------------------------------- Indicator data structure
Dcl-ds Indicators Len(99);
  Exit     Ind Pos(3);      // F3=Exit
  Adderror Ind Pos(30);     // Customer already exists (add)
  Chgerror Ind Pos(31);     // Customer not found (change)
  Dlterror Ind Pos(32);     // Customer not found (delete)
End-ds;


// --------------------------------------------- Main procedure
Dow Not Exit;
  Exfmt Custsel;

  Select;
    When Exit;
      Leave;
    When Action = 'A';
      Exsr Addrecord;
    When Action = 'C';
      Exsr Chgrecord;
    When Action = 'D';
      Exsr Dltrecord;
  Endsl;
```

Continued

```
Enddo;

*Inlr = *On;
Return;


// ---------------------------------------------------- Addrecord
// Add a customer record
Begsr Addrecord;
  Chain Custno Customers;
  Adderror = %Found(Customers);

  If Not Adderror;
    Addcust(Custno);
  Endif;
Endsr;


// ---------------------------------------------------- Chgrecord
// Change a customer record
Begsr Chgrecord;
  Chain Custno Customers;
  Chgerror = Not %Found(Customers);

  If Not Chgerror;
    Chgcust(Custno);
  Endif;
Endsr;


// ---------------------------------------------------- Dltrecord
// Delete a customer record
Begsr Dltrecord;
  Chain Custno Customers;
  Dlterror = Not %Found(Customers);

  If Not Dlterror;
    Dltcust(Custno);
  Endif;
Endsr;
```

Program CUS01 adds a new customer record. It is invoked by program CUS00 when a user selects an Action code of A in that program:

```
// Program CUS001 - Add a new customer record


// ----------------------------------------------------------- Files
Dcl-f Customers Usage(*Output) Keyed;
Dcl-f Custmntd  Workstn Indds(Indicators);


// -------------------------- Main procedure prototype/interface
Dcl-pr CUS01 Extpgm;
  Custno Char(9);
End-pr;


Dcl-pi CUS01;
  Custno Char(9);
End-pi;


// ------------------------------------- Indicator data structure
Dcl-ds Indicators Len(99);
  Fkey     Ind Pos(25);     // Vldcmdkey
  Addmode  Ind Pos(40);     // A = Add
End-ds;


// --------------------------------------------- Main procedure
Addmode = *On;
Exfmt Custmnt;

If Not Fkey;
  Write Custsrec;
Endif;

*Inlr = *On;
Return;
```

Program CUS02 changes a customer record. It is invoked by program CUS00 when a user selects an Action code of C in that program:

```
// Program CUS02 - Change a customer record


// ------------------------------------------------------- Files
Dcl-f Customers Usage(*Update) Keyed;
Dcl-f Custmntd  Workstn Indds(Indicators);


// -------------------------- Main procedure prototype/interface
Dcl-pr CUS02 Extpgm;
  Custno Char(9);
End-pr;


Dcl-pi CUS02;
  Custno Char(9);
End-pi;


// ----------------------------------- Indicator data structure
Dcl-ds Indicators Len(99);
  Fkey      Ind Pos(25);      // Vldcmdkey
  Chgmode  Ind Pos(41);      // C = Change
End-ds;


// --------------------------------------------- Main procedure
Chgmode = *On;
Chain Custno Customers;


If %Found(Customers);
  Exfmt Custmnt;


  If Not Fkey;
    Update Custsrec;
  Endif;


Endif;


*Inlr = *On;
Return;
```

Finally, program CUS04 deletes a customer record. It is invoked by program CUS00 when a user selects an Action code of D in that program:

```
// Program CUS04 - Delete a customer record


// ------------------------------------------------------- Files
Dcl-f Customers Usage(*Delete) Keyed;
Dcl-f Custmntd  Workstn Indds(Indicators);

// ------------------------- Main procedure prototype/interface
Dcl-pr CUS04 Extpgm;
  Custno Char(9);
End-pr;


Dcl-pi CUS04;
  Custno Char(9);
End-pi;


// ------------------------------------- Indicator data structure
Dcl-ds Indicators Len(99);
  F10key   Ind Pos(10);      // F10=Delete
  Dltmode  Ind Pos(42);      // D = Delete
End-ds;


// ------------------------------------------------ Main procedure
Dltmode = *On;
Chain Custno Customers;

If %Found(Customers);
  Exfmt Custmnt;

  If F10key;
    Delete Custsrec;
  Endif;


Endif;


*Inlr = *On;
Return;
```

This file maintenance example is necessarily small and simplified, but it serves to illustrate the concept of modular development. The integration of several smaller programs instead of one monolithic program to perform the various file maintenance functions simplifies the application, despite the introduction of several *pieces*. Each function is easier to troubleshoot, the resulting application has benefits for software quality, and it is easier to add features to individual functions by enhancing programs or adding new ones. In addition, you can more easily reuse discreet functions in other applications and use modularity to facilitate team development. As an application grows larger, more complex, and more *mission critical*, the advantages of modular design and development become obvious.

13.13. Chapter Summary

Programming experts advocate a modular approach to programming, in which you divide complex processing into separate programs or modules, each focused on accomplishing a single function. Other programs can then call these programs. If you compile and bind a routine into a separate *PGM object, you use operation Callp to invoke that program. IBM i lets you write calling and called programs in any mix of languages available on the system, including CL. The call stack is the ordered list of active programs in a job. The system uses the call stack to trace the flow of control among called and calling programs.

In ILE RPG, all variables are global within a program but local to the program. To share data between a calling and a called program, both programs use parameters to define the shared data. These parameters are described by a prototype definition and appear as arguments to a Callp operation. The procedure interface definition lets the called program accept parameter values and assign them to variables.

When you pass parameters by reference, the corresponding parameter variables in the calling and called programs share a common storage location. As a result, changes to a parameter's value in one of the programs affect the corresponding parameter's value in the other program. Using prototype definitions, you can also pass parameters by read-only-reference, a method that improves the call's flexibility and avoids problems with parameters being changed by called programs.

The LR indicator controls whether a called program will completely *shut down* when it returns to its caller. If *Inlr is off when a program returns, the program remains active. But if *Inlr is on, the program starts fresh the next time it is called. You should ensure that a program ends with *Inlr set to *On after a process is finished with it.

IBM i provides data areas (special storage areas defined on the system) for sharing values between programs. The programs do not have to call one another to access the same data area. A temporary local data area (LDA) is automatically available for each job. You also can define permanent data areas that any program can subsequently access. You access the contents of a data area within a program by defining a special data structure—a data-area data structure. Information contained in data areas is automatically retrieved at the start of a program and written back to the data area at the end of the program. The In and Out operations also provide explicit read and write functions for data areas, and the Unlock operation releases the locks on a data area.

The following table summarizes the operation codes discussed in this chapter:

Function or Operation	Description	Syntax
Callp	Call a prototyped procedure or program	{Callp} name({parm1 : parm2 : ...});
Dcl-pi	Declare procedure interface	**Dcl-pr name {keywords};**
Dcl-pr	Declare prototype	**Dcl-pr name {keywords};**
In	Retrieve a data area	**In {*Lock} data-area-name;**
Out	Write a data area	**Out {*Lock} data-area-name;**
Return	Return to caller	**Return;**
Unlock	Unlock a data area	**Unlock name;**

13.14. Key Terms

arguments
call interface
call stack
Callp (Call a Prototyped Procedure or Program)
CRTDTAARA (Create Data Area)
data-area data structure
data areas

Dcl-pi (Declare procedure interface)
Dcl-pr (Declare prototype)
exclusive lock
In (Retrieve a data area)
local data area (LDA)
main procedure prototype
modular programming
Out (Write a data area)

parameters
passing by reference
procedure interface
prototype
read-only reference
recursive call
scope
Unlock (Unlock a data area)

13.15. Discussion/Review Questions

1. What does *modular programming* mean?
2. What are the advantages of a modular approach to application development?
3. What effect does LR have on a called program?
4. What is the purpose of the prototype definition?
5. List the parts of a prototype definition.
6. List the rules that must be observed when defining a prototype.
7. What are the default data attributes for numeric and character data types?
8. When passing parameters *by reference*, why is a change in a parameter variable reflected in the called program?
9. Why would a programmer want to pass a parameter *by read-only reference*?

10. Explain the difference between the type of data that can be passed by reference and by read-only reference.
11. What is the purpose of the procedure interface?
12. Explain the difference between passing parameters by reference and by read-only reference. Why would you use one instead of the other?
13. What is an LDA?
14. Why might you use a data area rather than a database file to store values?
15. Describe how to access a data area through a data-area data structure.

13.16. Exercises

1. Write the ILE RPG code to call ProgA, ProgB, or ProgC, depending upon whether the value of field Option is 1, 2, or 3. No parameters are needed with any of the calls.

2. Write the portion of a calling program that passes a numeric data-type date in *yymmdd* format to a called program to convert the date to month-name, day, and four-digit-year format (e.g., January 1, 1993).

3. Write the entire ILE RPG program that would be called in exercise 2 to convert the date to the desired format.

4. Assume that a data area named CheckValue contains a six-position number representing the last check number used, a six-position date reflecting the most recent date on which the check-writing program was run, 10 positions containing the name of the last user running the check-writing program, and four positions signifying the number of checks written during the last program run. Code a data-area data structure to enable access to this data area.

5. Write the code to allow Prog01 to call Prog02 given the following requirements. Your code must include the prototypes, procedure interfaces, and field definitions for both programs.

Prog01 will pass four parameters.

   a. A zoned numeric constant with a length of seven and two decimals

   b. A date field constant

   c. A time field

   d. A character field with a length of 35 characters

14

Building Modular Programs with Procedures

14.1. Chapter Overview

This chapter continues coverage of modular programming techniques by discussing procedures. You learn how procedures differ from subroutines and called programs, and the advantages of using procedures. The chapter compares three different programming constructs: cycle main programs, linear main programs, and Nomain modules. It also shows how to compile modular components and bind them to callable program objects. Finally, this chapter introduces several other application development topics related to the Integrated Language Environment (ILE), including passing parameters by value and using binder language.

14.2. Dynamic Program Calls and Static Binding

Chapter 13 discussed a modular approach to programming in terms of calling separate executable program (*Pgm) objects. In this environment, the calling programs and the called programs are complete in themselves, having been individually compiled. This technique is called a **dynamic program call**. With this technique, when a program encounters the Callp operation to invoke another program, the system goes looking for the called program dynamically, during runtime, using an internal process known as **resolution**. The calling program depends upon the existence of the called program not at the time you compile it, but at the time you actually run it. The programs are never physically connected to each other, but they can execute in concert with each other at runtime.

If an application is call intensive (i.e., one program calls another program hundreds or even thousands of times), this dynamic resolution takes time and can degrade system performance—

in some instances, severely—compared with performance when the programmer handles the code in the called programs as subroutines internal to the calling program.

ILE RPG participates in the **Integrated Language Environment (ILE)**, a common runtime environment supported by several languages, including CL, COBOL, C, and of course RPG. When IBM introduced ILE to IBM i, it included the option of connecting RPG modules before runtime. This **static binding** alleviates some of the performance degradation of dynamic program calls. With static binding, the calling component and the called component are bound together into a single *PGM object. The resolution process occurs one time— when the program is first created—and has already been accomplished by the time the program runs.

14.3. Introduction to Procedures

Central to the static binding model is the concept of the procedure. An RPG **procedure** is a self-contained, identifiable collection of RPG statements, within a program, that performs a specific task and returns to the caller. Procedures are not system objects, but are a means of identifying a set of code that you can call and run within a program. Recall from Chapter 2 that ILE RPG programs consist of four main sections:

- Control options section—provides default options for the program
- Declarations section—identifies and defines the files, variables, and other data items a program will use
- Main procedure section—details the processes, calculations, and procedures the program will perform
- Subprocedure section—includes declarations and processes for optional distinct functions (subprocedures) of the program that the main procedure section or other subprocedures can execute once or many times

Previously, all the programs we have presented and discussed have contained one procedure, the main procedure. The **main procedure** is the first user-written code that executes when a program runs; it is the *driver* that ultimately controls the rest of the program. With the introduction of subprocedures, a program can now consist of a main procedure and, optionally, one or more subprocedures.

Coding multiple procedures in a program allows you to design and build programs in a modular fashion. Modular programming enhances your ability to reuse code (i.e., using a single component in several programs to reduce or eliminate duplicate code). It simplifies program maintenance and testing, and speeds compile times, by allowing you to work with smaller sections of code instead of large, monolithic programs. Modular design concepts also encourage the division of labor among several programmers on a team, enabling each to work on separate pieces of the same program, making the best use of his or her talents and knowledge.

14.3.1. The Role of Procedures in a Program

A subprocedure is like a subroutine, but with several important differences. First, the subprocedure can be created independently from the rest of the program that will process it. You can code a program's procedures in separate source members and compile them into separate modules, then bind them together when you create the program.

The second important difference between a subprocedure and a subroutine lies in the scope of the variables in the two kinds of routines. For a program containing subroutines (no subprocedures), all data definitions are **global**, meaning that all variables are equally accessible by both the main procedure and its subroutines. In contrast, procedures introduce the concept of **local variables** to RPG. Local variables are recognized only within the procedure in which they are defined. Data values are communicated from one procedure to another by passing parameters.

A third difference between subprocedures and subroutines is that subprocedures are recursive; a procedure can call itself (actually a new copy of itself). Some applications can make good use of subprocedures' recursive functionality. For example, in a manufacturing application, a complex component might contain yet other components, each of which might require identical subprocedure processing at its own level.

Another important difference between subprocedures and subroutines is the **return value.** A subprocedure (e.g., a built-in function) can return a value to its caller outside the context of any parameter variable. This capability effectively lets you incorporate user-defined functions into your programs, using your own functions as easily as you can use RPG's built-in functions. After you have created a subprocedure, if it returns a value to the calling procedure, you invoke it the same way you invoke a function.

Note
Don't be confused or overly concerned about the differences between a procedure and a subprocedure. ILE RPG simply uses the term subprocedure to distinguish a program's main procedure from other procedures in the program.

14.3.2. Coding a Procedure

A subprocedure begins with a **Dcl-proc (Declare Procedure)** instruction and ends with an End-proc instruction:

```
Dcl-proc proc-name {keywords};

...

End-proc {proc-name};
```

Between these instructions, the subprocedure can include the following:

- A procedure interface
- Declarations
- Processing statements (calculations)

To understand the basic coding requirements for a procedure, let's look at an example. The following procedure converts a Fahrenheit temperature value into its Celsius equivalent:

```
// ---------------------------------------------------
//
// Procedure - Celsius - Converts Fahrenheit to Celsius
//
// ---------------------------------------------------
Dcl-proc Celsius;

Dcl-pi *N Int(5);
  Fahrenheit Int(5);
End-pi;

Dcl-s Temperature Int(5);

Eval(H) Temperature = (5/9) * (Fahrenheit - 32);
Return Temperature;

End-proc Celsius;
```

The first declaration inside the subprocedure defines the procedure interface. Remember from Chapter 13 that the procedure interface accepts parameters and assigns their values to variables. Notice a couple of differences in this procedure interface compared with the ones the previous chapter discussed. First, you need not name the subprocedure interface. A subprocedure can have only one interface, so the example uses the *N placeholder instead of a name. In addition, the interface declaration includes the data attributes of the value the subprocedure is to pass back to its caller (i.e., its **return value**). A subprocedure can have only a single return value, which can be any supported data type as well as a data structure (using the Likeds keyword) or an array (using the Dim keyword). In this example, the Celsius procedure returns a five-digit integer value and accepts a single parameter, Fahrenheit, as a five-digit integer. The procedure interface is optional if the subprocedure has no return value and no parameters.

Following the procedure interface, the subprocedure defines Temperature, a standalone variable (with the Dcl-s instruction). In addition to standalone variables, you can code data structures, arrays, tables, and named constants within a subprocedure. The definitions described within the subprocedure have a **local scope**. In this example, variables Fahrenheit and Temperature are local—they are restricted to the subprocedure in which they are defined. No other procedure in the program will recognize that these variables exist, and they cannot be referenced or changed outside the boundaries of the Celsius subprocedure. In fact, in a program that contains several subprocedures, each one can include local variables with identical names, even if they have different data attributes.

Any local variables you define inside a subprocedure are allocated by default in **automatic storage**, which is allocated only while the subprocedure is active. Each time the subprocedure is called during a program's execution, those variables are automatically reinitialized; they do not retain their values from previous iterations of the subprocedure. On the rare occasion that a local variable must preserve its value between subprocedure calls, you can define it with the Static keyword to allocate it in **static storage**, which remains allocated while the entire program is running, even between calls to the subprocedure:

```
Dcl-s Counter Uns(5) Static;
```

The processing instructions inside the subprocedure do the actual work of the subprocedure. In this case, the subprocedure accepts the sole parameter into local variable Fahrenheit and then uses Eval to convert it to the appropriate value in local variable Temperature. Following that assignment, the Return operation immediately returns control to the main procedure. But this operation is not the simple Return that you have used before. Note that the name of the variable containing the calculated value (Temperature) is included with the Return operation to allow the subprocedure to return this value to the calling procedure.

It's important to understand that the subprocedure is not returning the Temperature variable itself but only the value of that variable. It is the calling procedure's responsibility to use that value in its proper context (e.g., assigning it to another variable or using it in an If statement). Instead of coding a variable with the Return statement, you can return the value of an expression or a literal. The following Return statement accomplishes the same end as the previous example (without the need for the Temperature variable):

```
Return(H) (5/9) * (Fahrenheit - 32);
```

The same source member that contains the subprocedure code should include a prototype for the subprocedure. The compiler uses the prototype to ensure that the caller passes the correct parameters to the subprocedure and that the subprocedure passes the correct return value to its caller. You code the prototype outside of the subprocedure. This prototype is similar to the prototypes discussed in Chapter 13:

```
Dcl-pr Celsius Int(5);
  *N Int(5);
End-pr;
```

Notice that the prototype does not include the Extpgm keyword. Because the Extpgm keyword specifies a dynamic program call, it is inappropriate for this procedure call. The prototype names the subprocedure. (If the prototype name does not match the procedure name, or if the procedure name is case sensitive, you can use the Extproc keyword to name the procedure.) Like the procedure interface, the prototype now includes the length and type of the subprocedure's return value. The prototype must exactly match the procedure interface. The data attributes of the return value and the parameters must be the same in both declarations. Any keywords in the prototype must match as well. If a mismatch occurs, the compile will fail.

14.3.3. Executing a Procedure

RPG uses two methods to call a subprocedure:

- Callp operation
- Function-like call in an expression

When the subprocedure does not return a value (or, rarely, if the program ignores the return value), use the same Callp operation discussed in Chapter 13 to execute a subprocedure:

```
Callp Updcust(Company:Custnbr);
```

Most subprocedures, however, return a value—even if only an indicator to signal whether the subprocedure was successful. In that case, the program executes the subprocedure much like a built-in function by embedding it within an expression:

```
Metrictemp = Celsius(Englishtemp);
```

Because the prototype for the Celsius subprocedure includes a return value, the main procedure can now use Celsius like a function when it needs to convert a Fahrenheit temperature to its Celsius equivalent. In this example, the program will execute the Celsius subprocedure, passing it a single parameter, Englishtemp. The return value from Celsius will be assigned to the Metrictemp variable. The expression need not be an assignment expression. Instead, the caller can use a comparison expression:

```
If Celsius(Englishtemp) > 100;
...
Endif;
```

Note

It is often useful, as well as documentary, to give the subprocedure a meaningful name that describes the return value.

14.4. Cycle Main Programs

Up to now, all the RPG programs we've discussed have been cycle main programs. A **cycle main program** has a main procedure implicitly specified in the main section of the program. In a cycle main program, the main procedure does not have a name; it is the main procedure by virtue of its location in the program code. A cycle main program includes a main source section (the main procedure), followed by zero or more subprocedure sections. The main procedure is everything before the first Dcl-proc instruction. You need not code anything special to define the main procedure. It does not begin with a Dcl-proc instruction or end with an End-proc instruction. The cycle main program is so called because the compiler automatically includes the RPG cycle to provide program initialization and termination as well as ordered processing steps for file input and output (I/O). Most traditional RPG programs are cycle main programs.

To understand the basic coding requirements for a cycle main program, let's look at an example. The following program demonstrates how to code a main procedure and include the example Celsius subprocedure within the same source, an architecture sometimes called a **local procedure**. Although the program is complete as shown, we have abbreviated it to concentrate on those lines that relate to procedures.

```
// ------------------------------------------------------
//
// Program - THISPGM - Displays Celsius temperature and
//                     corresponding water state
//
// ------------------------------------------------------
```

Continued

```
// ------------------------ Cycle main procedure PR/PI
Dcl-pr Thispgm Extpgm;
  *N Int(5);
End-pr;

Dcl-pi Thispgm;
  Englishtemp Int(5);
End-pi;


// ----------------------------------------- Prototypes
Dcl-pr Celsius Int(5);
  *N Int(5);
End-pr;


// ---------------------------------- Global variables
Dcl-s Message    Char(50);
Dcl-s Metrictemp Int(5);
Dcl-s State      Varchar(8);

// ------------------------------------ Main procedure
Metrictemp = Celsius(Englishtemp);

Select;
  When Metrictemp < 0;
    State = 'solid';
  When Metrictemp = 0;
    State = 'freezing';
  When Metrictemp = 100;
    State = 'boiling';
  When Metrictemp > 100;
    State = 'gaseous';
  Other;
    State = 'liquid';
Endsl;


Message = 'At ' + %Char(Englishtemp) + ' degrees (' +
          %Char(Metrictemp) + ' Celsius), water is ' +
          State + '.';
```

Continued

```
Dsply Message;
*Inlr = *On;
Return;


// ----------------------------------------------------
//
// Procedure - Celsius - Converts Fahrenheit to Celsius
//

Dcl-proc Celsius;

   // --------------------------- Procedure interface
   Dcl-pi *N Int(5);
     Fahrenheit Int(5);
   End-pi;


   // ------------------------------- Local variables
   Dcl-s Temperature Int(5);

   Eval(H) Temperature = (5/9) * (Fahrenheit - 32);
   Return Temperature;

End-proc Celsius;
```

Notice the declarations in this program under the *Global variables* comment for Message, Metrictemp, and State. Those variables, which you define before the main procedure, have a **global scope** and can be accessed from anywhere in the compile unit. If you have a need to do so, the Celsius subprocedure can also process any of those variables as well as the Englishtemp parameter, which is also global. The main procedure in a cycle main program cannot declare local variables or access a subprocedure's local variables.

Tip
Generally, you should define variables with the narrowest scope that will accomplish your program's goal. Instead of accessing global variables in a subprocedure, you should pass parameters to share information between the main procedure and any subprocedures. In a large program consisting of many modules, this practice helps avoid confusion and errors and makes your programs easier to maintain.

The main procedure of this program accepts one parameter, Fahrenheit, and then executes the Celsius subprocedure to convert that value to Celsius. It then assigns a (sea level) state based on the temperature and builds a message along the lines of "At 20 degrees (-7 Celsius), water is solid." Finally, the **Dsply (Display Message)** operation shows the message on the workstation that is running the program (or sends the message to the job log).

The Celsius subprocedure is coded following the main procedure. In a cycle main program, the main procedure code ends once it encounters the first subprocedure. The main procedure code should end with *Inlr set to *On to ensure proper *cleanup* after the program has completed. The cycle then automatically closes files, unlocks data areas, and frees memory used by the program.

14.5. Linear Main Programs

RPG supports a second type of program (as an alternative to cycle main programs) that does not include the RPG cycle. A **linear main program** explicitly names a procedure to be the main procedure for the program. A linear main program includes a Ctl-opt instruction with the Main keyword to name the main procedure:

```
Ctl-opt Main(proc-name);
```

You then code the main procedure just as any other subprocedure, starting with a Dcl-proc instruction and ending with an End-proc instruction. The main section in a linear main program (before the first Dcl-proc instruction) does not contain any executable code, although it can include global declarations.

The RPG compiler will not embed the RPG cycle into a linear main program. A linear main program implicitly initializes variables, locks data areas, and opens files when the program starts, but these resources are not *cleaned up* or closed when the program ends, unless the program explicitly does so, using RPG operations. A linear main program does not use *Inlr to trigger such an automatic shutdown.

To understand the basic coding requirements for a linear main program, let's modify the earlier cycle main program to now be a linear main program. Notice the highlighted differences between this program and the earlier cycle main program.

```
// ------------------------------------------------------
//
// Program - THISPGM - Displays Celsius temperature and
//                     corresponding water state
                                                    Continued
```

```
//
// --------------------------------------------------------

Ctl-opt Main(Driver);


// ------------------------------------------ Prototypes
Dcl-pr Driver Extpgm('THISPGM');
  *N Int(5);
End-pr;


Dcl-pr Celsius Int(5);
  *N Int(5);
End-pr;


// --------------------------------------------------------
//
// Main procedure
//
Dcl-proc Driver;

  // ---------------------------- Procedure interface
  Dcl-pi *N;
    Englishtemp Int(5);
  End-pi;


  // ------------------------------- Local variables
  Dcl-s Message    Char(50);
  Dcl-s Metrictemp Int(5);
  Dcl-s State      Varchar(8);

  Metrictemp = Celsius(Englishtemp);

  Select;
    When Metrictemp < 0;
      State = 'solid';
    When Metrictemp = 0;
      State = 'freezing';
```

Continued

```
      When Metrictemp = 100;
        State = 'boiling';
      When Metrictemp > 100;
        State = 'gaseous';
      Other;
        State = 'liquid';
    Endsl;

    Message = 'At ' + %Char(Englishtemp) + ' degrees (' +
              %Char(Metrictemp) + ' Celsius), water is ' +
              State + '.';
    Dsply Message;
    Return;

  End-proc Driver;

  // ---------------------------------------------------
  //
  // Procedure - Celsius - Converts Fahrenheit to Celsius
  //

  Dcl-proc Celsius;

    // ---------------------------- Procedure interface
    Dcl-pi *N Int(5);
      Fahrenheit Int(5);
    End-pi;

    // -------------------------------- Local variables
    Dcl-s Temperature Int(5);

    Eval(H) Temperature = (5/9) * (Fahrenheit - 32);
    Return Temperature;

  End-proc Celsius;
```

The first difference is the addition of the Ctl-opt instruction to name the program's main procedure, Driver (it can be any valid name). The Main keyword to name the main procedure is the key to creating the linear main program. The Driver procedure will be coded with other subprocedures, but it will be the first user-written code to execute when the program starts. You code the prototype for the Driver procedure in the global declarations section of the program. The Extpgm keyword indicates the name of the program: THISPGM.

The Driver procedure begins with a Dcl-proc instruction and ends with an End-proc instruction. The first declaration in Driver is its procedure interface. All the variables are local variables, restricted to the procedure in which they are declared. Like the main procedure in the earlier program, the Driver procedure in this program accepts a single parameter, Fahrenheit, and then executes the Celsius subprocedure to convert that value to Celsius. It then assigns a state and displays a message.

Unlike in the earlier program, the Driver main procedure does not set *Inlr to implicitly close the program; instead, the program ends when it encounters the Return operation. Note that any open files or locked data areas, without the presence of explicit Close or Unlock operations, will remain open or locked after the program ends.

The result of running this program is the same as the earlier cycle main program. But a linear main program does not include logic for the RPG cycle. While it cannot use the automatic features of the cycle, a linear main program also avoids any possible performance impact of the cycle, however minimal it may be. In addition, a linear main program is recursive. Unlike a cycle main program, a linear main program can call itself for those applications where recursive calls are necessary.

Choosing which type of program to code, cycle main or linear main, is largely a matter of style, preference, and shop standards. Most traditional programs use the cycle main model. Many newer programs (and newer programmers) tend toward the linear main model, which is similar to that of other computer languages. Unless your program requires RPG cycle features—most notably using *Inlr to close the program—the runtime differences between the two models are negligible.

14.6. Nomain Modules

The programs previously discussed are complete programs in themselves. They include a main procedure, along with all the other required subprocedures, coded within one source member, or compile unit. ILE also enhances modular programming concepts by allowing you to code a source member that consists of a segment of a program *without* a main procedure. The resulting **Nomain module** contains only subprocedures (one or more) that you can combine with other modules to create a program. By itself, a Nomain module cannot create a program object. One of the modules in a program must have a main procedure.

A Nomain module includes a Ctl-opt instruction with the Nomain keyword. To see how to code a Nomain module, let's separate the example Celsius subprocedure from the rest of the program that uses it. The highlighted code illustrates the necessary changes:

```
// --------------------------------------------------
//
// Source member: Celsius
//

Ctl-opt Nomain;


// --------------------------------------- Prototypes
Dcl-pr Celsius Int(5);
  *N Int(5);
End-pr;


// --------------------------------------------------
//
// Procedure - Celsius - Converts Fahrenheit to Celsius
//
Dcl-proc Celsius Export;

  // --------------------------- Procedure interface
  Dcl-pi *N Int(5);
    Fahrenheit Int(5);
  End-pi;


  // -------------------------------- Local variables
  Dcl-s Temperature Int(5);

  Eval(H) Temperature = (5/9) * (Fahrenheit - 32);
  Return Temperature;

End-proc Celsius;
```

The primary change in this example is the inclusion of the Nomain control option. This keyword tells the compiler that the source code does not contain a main procedure. Instead, the source consists only of global declarations and subprocedures (just one, Celsius, in this case).

The only other change in this code is the addition of the **Export** keyword on the Dcl-proc instruction. The Export keyword allows the procedure to be called from outside this module.

When you combine this module with others to create a program, procedures in those other modules can execute the Celsius procedure, even though they don't contain the code for the procedure. The calling procedures need not have any special coding to execute an exported procedure. Without Export, the Celsius procedure can only be executed from a procedure within this module. Most procedures in Nomain modules are exported to other modules and include the Export keyword.

Note

If a procedure will *not* be called from another ILE RPG module (e.g., if you omit Export), the prototype is optional, but recommended. The compiler uses the prototype to ensure the accuracy of the return value and parameters.

Nomain modules allow the ILE RPG programmer to fully exploit modular programming concepts. Code that is common to many programs can be isolated as a procedure in a Nomain module and then reused many times by any program that needs it. In addition, Nomain modules can eliminate redundant code in an application, making the application easier to maintain and more reliable than if the application had multiple copies of the same code scattered among many programs. Nomain modules also can help enforce business rules and practices in an organization by centralizing application functions in a common library of modules for use and reuse throughout the organization.

14.7. Creating Modular Programs

Up to now, you have used the CL CRTBNDRPG (Create Bound RPG Program) command to create single module RPG programs. The CRTBNDRPG command combines the two program-creation steps briefly introduced in Chapter 1:

- Compile—translate the ILE RPG source member into a machine language module (*Module) object.
- Bind—copy and organize the module to produce a program (*Pgm) object.

With the introduction of ILE, the system now allows, and sometimes requires, you to separate the compile and binding steps by using two CL commands:

- CRTRPGMOD (Create RPG Module)
- CRTPGM (Create Program)

Figure 14.1 illustrates the process.

Figure 14.1: Creating an ILE program

When you compile source code with the CRTRPGMOD command, the compiler creates a *Module object, rather than an executable program (*Pgm) object. A **module** (sometimes called a **compile unit)** contains compiled, executable code, but you cannot run a module by itself; its purpose is to be a building block for the eventual program object. To form the runnable program, you must perform a separate binding procedure, invoked through the CRTPGM command.

Because the binding step in this process physically copies the compiled code from the modules into the program object, this model of static binding is called **bind-by-copy**. The two-step method for creating an ILE program has two primary advantages over the single CRTBNDRPG process: 1) it supports subprocedures and linear main programs, and 2) it expedites creation of programs from multiple modules.

ILE programs can comprise code from many module objects. The CRTPGM command can combine one or more modules during its program creation process. Furthermore, those modules may have been written using any ILE language (e.g., ILE COBOL, ILE CL, ILE C, or ILE C++), so a portion of an ILE program might use ILE RPG while another portion might use ILE CL. Although one of the modules in a program must include a main procedure, the others can be Nomain modules, each with one or more subprocedures. Such architecture enables efficient code reuse, along with the other modular programming advantages we've discussed. In addition, it allows the programmer to exploit the advantages of one language over another or gain a greater familiarity with another language. The multiple-module program model is a key feature of ILE. Figure 14.2 illustrates the creation process for a multiple-module program.

Notice in Figure 14.2 that each ILE language has its own specific compile command. For ILE RPG, the command is CRTRPGMOD; for ILE CL, it's CRTCLMOD. However, the binding command, CRTPGM, is not language-specific. The same CRTPGM command binds modules from any ILE language.

Figure 14.3 shows the essential parameters for the prompted CRTRPGMOD command. The compiler generates a listing that you use to verify the creation of the module object or to find errors. After each required module has been created, you bind them by using the CRTPGM command (Figure 14.4).

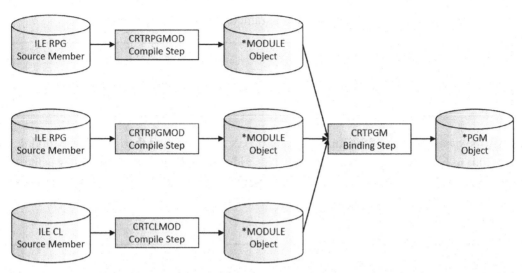

Figure 14.2: Creating a multiple-module ILE program

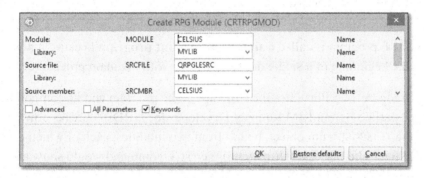

Figure 14.3: CRTRPGMOD command

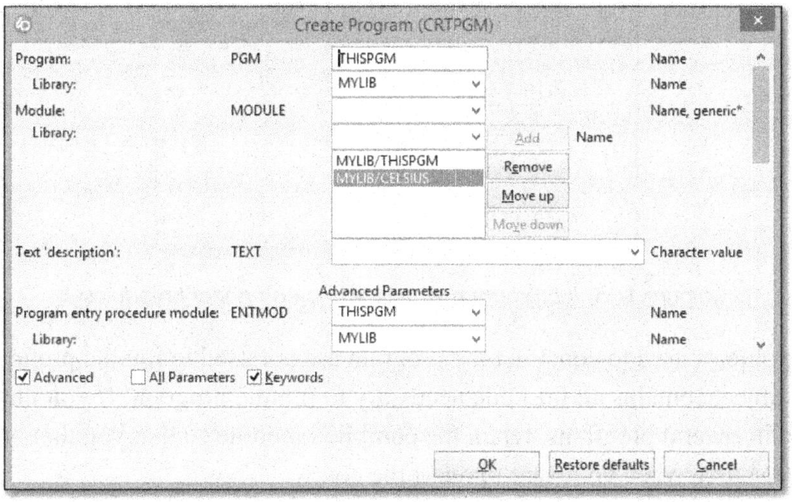

Figure 14.4: CRTPGM command

The CRTPGM command uses these essential parameters to create a program:

```
CRTPGM PGM(pgm-name)         +
       MODULE(module-list)  +
       ENTMOD(entry-module)
```

Specify the desired name of the final program object to create, and then list all the modules (up to 300) to bind to the program. You must also identify which of those modules is the entry module (i.e., the one with the program's main procedure). The command defaults to the first module in the list if you don't make an ENTMOD entry. For this example, the full command is as follows:

```
CRTPGM PGM(MYLIB/THISPGM)                      +
       MODULE(MYLIB/THISPGM  MYLIB/CELSIUS) +
       ENTMOD(MYLIB/THISPGM)
```

The resulting ILE program is called a **single entry-point program** because it always begins execution at the beginning of a single module, the one with the main procedure.

The outline in Figure 14.5 illustrates the structure of the program and its component modules. This outline—from IBM Rational Developer for i (RDi)—breaks down the structure of the THISPGM *Pgm object, bound from two modules, each of which contains a single procedure. The DSPPGM (Display program) CL command would show a similar analysis. Figure 14.5 also displays the individual *Module objects separate from the *Pgm object.

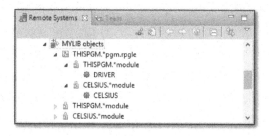

Figure 14.5: ILE program structure and component modules

The *Module objects used to construct the program are not used to run the program; the bound *Pgm object contains all the code necessary to run the program. If you intend to use a module in several programs, retain the compiled module so that you do not need to recompile the source when you want to reuse the code.

To create multiple-module programs and Nomain modules, use the two-step method (CRTRPGMOD and CRTPGM). Single-module programs can also use these commands. As an alternative for single-module programs, the CRTBNDRPG command lets you combine the compile and binding steps into one command. But the default options for the CRTBNDRPG command will cause the compile to fail if you try to use it to create a linear main program or a cycle main program with subprocedures. You can, however, make a change when you execute the CRTBNDRPG command to allow procedures. Executing the command with the Dftactgrp(*No) option permits the use of local procedures. You can specify this option when you run the command, or you can indicate it in the control options section of the ILE RPG program itself:

```
Ctl-opt Dftactgrp(*No) Actgrp(*Caller);
```

This option specifies that the program should not be forced to run in the job's default activation group. An activation group is a subdivision of a job that ILE enlists to keep track of the resources a job uses; one job can have several activation groups in use simultaneously. Programs that are forced to run in the default activation group do not strictly conform to ILE concepts and do not support procedures. When it is free to create a program to run in other activation groups, the CRTBNDRPG command supports linear main programs and cycle main programs with subprocedures. Chapter 15 discusses activation groups in more detail.

14.7.1. Using Binding Directories

When you create an ILE program with the CRTPGM command, you can list up to 300 modules to bind. Typing all 300 entries in the module list would be tedious at best, error prone at worst. A binding directory helps to relieve this difficulty. A **binding directory** is an object (type *Bnddir) that contains a list of the modules (and service programs, discussed in Chapter 15) that the CRTPGM command may need to create an ILE program. Instead of explicitly listing the modules, the CRTPGM binder command can refer to one or more binding directories to find the code necessary to complete the binding process:

```
CRTPGM PGM(pgm-name)        +
       MODULE(module-list)  +
       ENTMOD(entry-module) +
       BNDDIR(bnddir-list)
```

The binding directory does not include the actual code; it merely names the *Module objects where the binder might find the code. The compiled code remains in the modules themselves.

The CRTBNDDIR (Create Binding Directory) CL command creates a *Bnddir object. After creating the binding directory, you can use the WRKBNDDIRE (Work with Binding Directory Entries) CL command to add or remove entries in the binding directory, as in Figure 14.6.

```
                         Work with Binding Directory Entries

 Binding Directory:    MYBNDDIR         Library:

 Type options, press Enter.
   1=Add    4=Remove

                                                        -------Creation--------
 Opt    Object        Type        Library     Activation  Date         Time
        WWWDUMP       *MODULE     *LIBL                   10/27/        15:12:45
        WWWECHO       *MODULE     *LIBL                   10/27/        13:31:18
        WWWEXTRACT    *MODULE     *LIBL                   10/27/        14:31:42
        WWWGETDOC     *MODULE     *LIBL                   10/27/        13:53:58
        WWWGETENV     *MODULE     *LIBL                   10/27/        14:22:08
        WWWGETIFS     *MODULE     *LIBL                   10/28/        17:15:24
        WWWREAD       *MODULE     *LIBL                   10/27/        16:59:01
        WWWREPLACE    *MODULE     *LIBL                   10/27/        14:07:14
                                                                          Bottom
 Parameters or command
 ===>
 F3=Exit   F4=Prompt   F9=Retrieve   F5=Refresh   F12=Cancel   F17=Top
 F18=Bottom
```

Figure 14.6: Binding directory entries

To use the binding directory when creating a program, you refer to it when entering the CRTPGM CL command:

```
CRTPGM PGM(MYPGM)      +
       MODULE(MYPGM)   +
       ENTMOD(MYPGM)   +
       BNDDIR(MYBNDDIR)
```

The MODULE parameter defaults to using a module with the same name as the program, and the ENTMOD parameter defaults to using the first listed module as the entry module. So you can write the preceding command more simply:

```
CRTPGM PGM(MYPGM)      +
       BNDDIR(MYBNDDIR)
```

The binder first copies all the modules (or, as in this case, the only module) in the module list. When those modules refer to other procedures needed to create the program (i.e., exported procedures that are not in any modules in the module list), the binder attempts to find any such *unresolved imports* in the modules listed in the binding directory. When the binder finds an exported procedure in one of the modules listed in the binding directory, it binds that module by copying it to the program just as if you had explicitly listed the module. It will ignore any modules in the binding directory that it does not need. After the binder processes all the listed modules and all the binding directories, if it resolved all the procedure references, the program is created. If it cannot find all the necessary procedures, the binder will fail and will not create the program.

14.7.2. Maintaining Modular Programs

To modify the code in an ILE program, you must go through the same compile and binding steps to incorporate the changes to the program. Once you have modified the source code, recompile it with the CRTRPGMOD command, replacing the original module.

Instead of recreating the entire program anew, though, you can use the UPDPGM (Update Program) CL command to accomplish an abbreviated binding step. UPDPGM lets you list just the module (or modules) that you want to remove from the original program, replacing its code with the new version that now resides in the newly recompiled module. UPDPGM performs the same functions as CRTPGM, except that it replaces only the changed modules (i.e., those you list) in an existing program. The unchanged modules are unaffected. Figure 14.7 illustrates the prompted UPDPGM command.

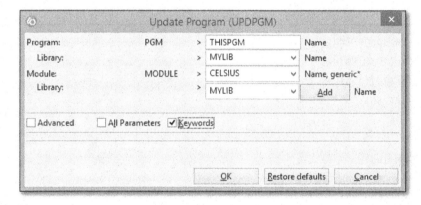

Figure 14.7: UPDPGM command

14.8. Passing Parameters by Value

Chapter 13 discussed two different methods for passing parameters between programs: pass by reference and pass by read-only reference. You can also use these two methods to pass parameters between procedures. In addition, procedures afford a third method: **pass by value**.

Passing parameters by value offers many of the same advantages as passing by read-only reference, but with a major difference. When a procedure passes a parameter by value, it does not share storage with the called procedure. Instead, the caller passes the parameter's actual value, not a storage address. It is the called procedure's responsibility to allocate its own local storage for the parameter. The called procedure can make changes to the parameter if necessary for its own processing, but the caller will never recognize those changes when it regains control. The caller's storage is absolutely protected from change when the parameter is passed by reference. To pass a parameter by value, you code the Value keyword in the prototype and procedure interface:

```
Dcl-pr Celsius Int(5);
  *N Int(5) Value;
End-pr;
...
Dcl-pi *N Int(5);
  Fahrenheit Int(5) Value;
End-pi;
```

The called procedure initializes its own local variable (Fahrenheit, in this example) with the value passed from the caller. You can code a variable, a literal, or an expression as the parameter when passing by value.

You can mix pass methods within the same call:

```
Dcl-pr Usrspace Ind;
  *N Char(10)  Value;
  *N Char(10)  Value;
  *N Char(256);
End-pr;
...
Dcl-pi *N Ind;
  Objname Char(10)  Value;
  Libname Char(10)  Value;
  Errmsg  Char(256);
End-pi;
```

This example passes the first two parameters by value, and the procedure places them into local variables Objname and Libname. The third parameter is passed by reference. If the procedure changes the value of Errmsg, the caller will recognize the change.

Generally, you should pass parameters by value when calling procedures and pass by read-only reference (Const) when calling programs. Restrict passing by reference to those instances when your application needs two-way parameter communication between the caller and the called entity. The three passing methods do have some performance considerations. Passing by reference is fastest but offers no protection against changes; passing by value is slowest but offers absolute protection against changes. It's unlikely that a user will notice the performance differences unless the program is passing a large number of parameters or very large parameters.

14.9. File I/O and Subprocedures

Traditionally, RPG programs have declared the files they use in the global declarations, before any procedures. Any procedure in the program can process globally declared files, along with their records and fields. Alternatively, you can declare externally described files within subprocedures. You can declare files in the main procedure of a linear main program in local subprocedures or in subprocedures of a Nomain module. Locally scoped files can be processed only by the procedure within which they are declared.

For globally scoped files, the compiler automatically allocates storage to hold the file data when the program reads or writes it. For locally scoped files, however, you must use a result data structure to hold the file data, and that data structure must be explicitly declared. Declare the result data structure by using the Likerec or Extname keyword

```
Dcl-f Customers;

Dcl-ds Custdata Likerec(Custsrec);

Read Customers Custdata;
```

or

```
Dcl-f Customers;

Dcl-ds Custdata Extname(Customers:Custsrec:*All);

Read Customers Custdata;
```

Declaring the data structure with Extname requires you to indicate which type of fields should be in the data structure. You will usually specify Extname(*All) to include all fields from the record format. The other allowed values, *Input and *Output, restrict the data structure to input- or output-capable fields only. If you declare the data structure with Likerec, you need only specify the record format name.

Like other data items declared in a procedure, local file declarations use automatic storage. Each time the procedure returns to its caller, it closes the file. If the file should remain open for the next time the program calls the procedure, include the Static keyword:

```
Dcl-f Customers Static;
```

14.10. Using /Copy, /Include

RPG supports a **/Copy** function that allows you to store source records in a secondary source member, sometimes called a **copybook**, and then copy that source member into the primary source member at compile time. With this capability, you can reuse a single copy of code without having to retype it in every module. A copybook is especially useful for storing prototypes, which tend to be duplicated across many programs, but it is also convenient for keeping any reusable code *snippets*.

To use a copybook for prototypes, you use an editor to store all the reusable prototype definitions in a source member (here we call it PROTOTYPES). Then in each source member that needs one or more of the prototypes in the copybook, at the point where the prototypes normally appears, instead of coding the prototypes, code the following compiler directive:

```
/Copy Mylib/Mysource,Prototypes
```

A **compiler directive** instructs the compiler to perform an action or switch processing modes. Compiler directives always begin with a slash character (/) in position 7 or later. The /Copy directive causes records from a secondary source member to be copied into the primary source member at the point where the directive occurs. In this example, the copybook member Prototypes is in source file Mysource within library Mylib. You must specify a member name. If you do not specify a library (e.g., Mylib), the /Copy function searches the library list for the copybook. And if you do not specify a source filename (e.g., Mysource), the system uses the default name QRPGLESRC.

The /Copy directive can appear anywhere in the source. It causes the compiler to include records from the copybook at the point where it encounters the /Copy. The copybook records must fit the context of the file being compiled; you cannot, for example, include copybook declarations outside the declarations section of the program. The compiler listing shows all the merged source code. The copybook can also include /Copy directives, if necessary, to merge nested copybook records as well as the original copybook. Avoid nesting so deeply that the architecture becomes difficult to understand—also take care not to have copybooks copy each other indefinitely.

Another compiler directive, **/Include**, performs the same function as /Copy:

```
/Include Mylib/Mysource,Prototypes
```

As long as your program does not include embedded SQL statements, you can use either /Copy or /Include with equal effect. If the program does include SQL, the precompiler (discussed in Chapter 10) will always process /Copy statements but will usually ignore /Include statements. IBM's online documentation for the CRTSQLRPGI CL command explains the options.

14.10.1. Defining a Template

RPG code can include variable or data structure definitions that are intended to serve as templates for the definition of other data items. Copybooks can be especially useful for defining templates. The **Template** keyword indicates that the compiler is to use a data item definition only to define other data items. The following template might be part of a copybook:

```
Dcl-ds Templ_Indicators Len(99) Template;
  Exit   Ind Pos(3);
  Cancel Ind Pos(12);
  Error  Ind Pos(50);
  Sflclr Ind Pos(90);
  Sfldsp Ind Pos(91);
  Sflend Ind Pos(92);
End-ds;
```

Other source members that use /Copy to include the copybook code can then define a data structure based on the template:

```
Dcl-ds Indicators Likeds(Templ_Indicators);
```

This definition uses the Likeds keyword to define the Indicators data structure to have the same subfields as the Templ_Indicators template. When a definition includes the Template keyword, the template can be used only with the Like keyword (for variables and subfields) or the Likeds keyword (for data structures).

14.11. Conditional Compiler Directives

Several **conditional compiler directives** let you include or omit blocks of source code when compiling the module, based upon conditions that you can set. The most commonly used conditional compiler directives are as follows:

- /Define and /Undefine to name a condition and to set it on or off
- /If, /Elseif, /Else, and /Endif to test a condition's state and to control whether to include the subsequent source in the compile process
- /Eof to direct the compiler to ignore the rest of the subsequent source

Like /Copy, these directives begin with a slash character (/) in position 7 or later and can be included anywhere in the source.

The /Define directive names a condition and adds it to a list of currently defined conditions; the /Undefine directive removes the condition from the list. The condition name can be any descriptive name you choose. It is not a program variable but exists only while the compiler is processing the source. You use the /If, /Elseif, /Else, and /Endif directives to block sections of code. They tell the compiler to include or exclude those code sections based upon whether the condition is on the list of currently active conditions. These directives are separate from the RPG If, Elseif, Else, and Endif operations.

Conditional compiler directives are useful when using copybooks. For example, if a copybook contains the prototypes for many procedures, you can eliminate unused prototypes from being included in the compile by coding a conditional directive in the copybook to create a block of code around each prototype:

```
/If Defined(Pr_Dayname)
  // ------------------------ Prototype: DayName
  Dcl-pr DayName Char(9);
    *N Date Value;
  End-pr;
/Endif


/If Defined(Pr_Dayofweek)
  // ------------------------ Prototype: DayofWeek
  Dcl-pr DayofWeek Packed(1:0);
    *N Date Value;
  End-pr;
/Endif


/If Defined(Pr_Isweekday)
  // ------------------------ Prototype: IsWeekDay
  Dcl-pr IsWeekDay Ind;
    *N Date Value;
  End-pr;
/Endif
```

Then in each program that uses the procedures, add the appropriate condition name to the compiler's list of conditions:

```
/Define Pr_Dayname
/Define Pr_IsWeekday
/Copy Mylib/Mysource,Prototypes
```

In this example, the /Copy directive includes only the prototypes for the Dayname and Isweekday procedures, skipping over the Dayofweek prototype in the copybook.

The compiler CL commands also have a DEFINE parameter to let you preset up to 32 conditions for a single execution of the compiler, without the need to define the conditions in the source. In addition, the compiler supports several predefined conditions that are automatically added to the condition list, including these commonly used ones:

- *Crtbndrpg, if the compiler is invoked by the CRTBNDRPG CL command
- *Crtrpgmod, if the compiler is invoked by the CRTRPGMOD CL command
- *V*x*R*x*M*x, to indicate which release the compiler is using (e.g., *V7R1M0 for Release 7.1 or later)

14.12. Navigating Legacy Code

14.12.1. P Specifications

In legacy ILE RPG code, the Procedure Boundary specification (P-spec) is the fixed-format equivalent of the Dcl-pr instruction. Every procedure begins with a P-spec and ends with a P-spec. As you might expect, the P-spec has a P in position 6. You name the procedure in positions 7–21 (Name++++++++++++). Placing a B in position 24 (T) marks the beginning of the procedure and an E marks the end. Keywords are also allowed, beginning in position 44:

```
*.. 1 ...+... 2 ...+... 3 ...+... 4 ...+... 5 ...+... 6 ...+... 7 ...+... 8
PName++++++++++..T.................Keywords+++++++++++++++++++++++++++++++
```

The Nomain module in the following example includes the Celsius procedure written in fixed-format code (with P-specs highlighted):

```
*   ------------------------------------------------------
*
* Source member: Celsius
*
                                                        Continued
```

```
H Nomain


 * ------------------------------------------ Prototypes
D Celsius          PR              5I 0
D                                  5I 0 Value


 * -------------------------------------------------
 *
 * Procedure - Celsius - Converts Fahrenheit to Celsius
 *
P Celsius          B                    Export


 * ------------------------------ Procedure interface
D                  PI              5I 0
D Fahrenheit                       5I 0 Value


 * ------------------------------ Local variables
D Temperature      S               5I 0

C                  Eval(H)   Temperature =
C                            (5/9) * (Fahrenheit - 32)
C                  Return    Temperature

P Celsius          E
```

14.13. Chapter Summary

ILE enhances traditional module programming techniques by supporting static procedure binding as well as dynamic program calls. Static binding involves a two-step compile-then-bind process to connect RPG modules before runtime, saving the runtime overhead of object resolution and improving performance.

A procedure is a segment of code, like a subroutine, but with many additional capabilities. Procedures support parameters and can use several parameter-passing methods: value, reference, or read-only reference. When a procedure passes parameters by value, a caller can protect its data from being inadvertently changed by the called procedure. Procedures can define their own local variables or can use global variables. Because they support a return value, you can incorporate procedures into your RPG code just like functions.

Procedures begin with a Dcl-proc instruction and end with End-proc. All the declarations and processing inside the procedure are local to the procedure. Procedures require a prototype and a procedure interface to describe the return value and any parameters they are to pass. To return a value to its caller, a procedure uses the Return operation.

You can code local procedures, which appear in the same source member as the main procedure. Or you can code procedures as independent Nomain modules and then bind the modules together when you create the callable program. The coding requirements are similar for either programming model.

To call a procedure, use a function-like call in an expression. If a procedure does not return a value, you can call it with the Callp operation.

A cycle main program has an unnamed main procedure implicitly specified in the main section of the program. A linear main program specifically names its main procedure, using the Main keyword, and does not include any RPG cycle features. Either type of program can also include subprocedures as well as the main procedure. You can also code subprocedures separately in Nomain modules, which do not have a main procedure. By itself, a Nomain module cannot create a program; instead, you must bind it along with other modules, one of which must have a main procedure. To make a procedure accessible outside its own module, use the Export keyword.

ILE programs are typically created in two steps: a compile step (CRTRPGMOD command) followed by a binding step (CRTPGM command). ILE compilers create *Module objects—not programs—and then bind those modules to form runnable program (*Pgm) objects. A single entry point ILE program can comprise one or more compiled modules. One of the modules serves as the entry module and contains the main procedure for the resulting single entry point program. This binding model is called *bind-by-copy*.

A binding directory is a list of reusable modules. You can refer to the binding directory instead of listing all the modules when you use the CRTPGM command to bind a program.

In addition to passing parameters by reference or read-only reference, procedures can pass parameters by value when you want to prevent the called procedure from changing the caller's storage. You can mix parameter passing methods in the same prototype.

If a subprocedure includes file declarations, all the file I/O operations for that local file must use a result data structure to hold the file data. The result data structure is defined by using the Likerec or Extname keyword.

Several compiler directives instruct the compiler to use special features. The /Copy and /Include directives allow the use of a copybook to store often-reused code. Conditional compiler directives—including /Define, /If, and others—let you include or omit blocks of source code depending upon conditions at compile time.

This chapter discussed the following CL commands, which compile, bind, rebind, or display ILE programs:

- CRTBNDDIR (Create Binding Directory)
- CRTBNDRPG (Create Bound RPG Program)
- CRTPGM (Create Program)
- CRTRPGMOD (Create RPG Module)
- DSPPGM (Display Program)
- UPDPGM (Update Program)
- WRKBNDDIRE (Work with Binding Directory Entries)

The following table summarizes the operation codes and functions discussed in this chapter:

Function or Operation	Description	Syntax
Callp	Call a prototyped procedure or program	{Callp} name({parm1 : parm2 : ...});
Dcl-proc	Declare a procedure	Dcl-proc proc-name {keywords};
Dsply	Display a message	Dsply message;
Return	Return to caller	Return {expression};

14.14. Key Terms

automatic storage	dynamic program call	Nomain module
bind-by-copy	Export	pass by value
binding directory	global scope	procedure
compile unit	/Include	resolution
compiler directive	Integrated Language	return value
conditional compiler	Environment (ILE)	single entry-point program
directive	linear main program	static binding
/Copy	local procedure	static storage
copybook	local variables	Template
cycle main program	main procedure	
Dcl-proc (Declare Procedure)	module	

14.15. Discussion/Review Questions

1. Explain the similarities of subprocedures and subroutines.
2. What advantages do subprocedures have over subroutines?
3. Although static binding leads to improved system performance, when might you still want to use dynamic binding to call a program?

4.   How do subprocedures improve the reusability and reliability of an application?

5.   Describe the distinction between a parameter and a return value.

6.   What is required to allow a local variable to retain its value between calls to a subprocedure?

7.   What are the benefits of multiple-module programs?

8.   List the benefits of static binding versus dynamic program calls.

9.   What is the Static keyword used for when coding modules?

10.   What is the importance of using binding directories?

11.   Why would a parameter be passed by value?

12.   Why would a prototype be stored in a copybook?

13.   Explain the differences between a cycle main program and a linear main program.

14.   What is a Nomain module?

15.   What is a binding directory, and why would a programmer use binding directories?

14.16. Exercises

1. List the steps required to compile two source members into modules and then into one runnable program object.

2. Write CL commands to create modules from source members MOD01 and MOD02. Then write the CL command to bind the two module objects into a runnable program object called MYPGM01.

3. Write the ILE RPG code to define two procedures:

a. The first procedure (DATEDIFF) will accept two parameters: StartDate and EndDate. This procedure will return the number of days between the two dates.

b. The second procedure (FUTURDATE) will accept two parameters: InDate (a date) and NbrOfDays (number of days). This procedure will add NbrOfDays to InDate and return the calculated future date.

4. Write the ILE RPG code for two modules; one module will export a variable, and the other will import the same variable.

5. Research Web Services on the Internet. How can you use ILE RPG in this technology? Write a report on what you have discovered.

Notes

CHAPTER 15

Building and Using Service Programs

15.1. Chapter Overview

In this chapter, you learn about service programs—what they are, how to create and maintain them, and when to use them. The chapter also presents the concept of service program signatures and how to control them using binder language. In addition, it explains ILE activation groups, and how the various activation group options affect the resources an application uses.

15.2. Introduction to Service Programs

Chapter 14 introduced the bind-by-copy model for creating an ILE program. Under this technique, a program includes a main procedure and optional subprocedures; all code for the program is physically copied into the program during the binding process. The resulting program (*Pgm object) is a single entry-point program. The entry module contains the main procedure, which is the first user-written code that is executed when the program is called. When many different programs use the same subprocedure, then many redundant copies of the subprocedure exist. If it is necessary to change the subprocedure, you must copy the new code into all those different programs, perhaps by using the UPDPGM CL command many times. Unless your organization has excellent documentation disciplines or change management tools, determining which programs are using any one subprocedure can be challenging.

To provide an alternative to the bind-by-copy single entry point program, ILE introduces a different kind of program, the service program (**Srvpgm** object). A **service program** is a container for subprocedures—a code *toolbox* that many programs can use without the binder having to physically copy the subprocedure code into each program. This program creation model is called **bind-by-reference.**

A service program is not a standalone executable object; it does not have a main procedure. Instead, any subprocedure in a service program can be an entry point into the service program. Thus, a service program is said to be a **multiple entry-point program**. A single entry-point ILE program—or another service program—can invoke any exported procedure in the service program. But, in the service program, only one copy of the actual subprocedure code exists, which many other programs (*clients*) share. Service programs combine some of the performance advantages of bind-by-copy static binding with the modularity and flexibility benefits of the dynamic program call.

15.3. Compiling and Binding Service Programs

Procedures that reside in a service program have no unique coding requirements. You code the procedures in a service program in Nomain modules. The procedure code uses the same syntax that we've already discussed. Although there is no main procedure, the source can still have a global declarations section. Items you declare in the global section, before any subprocedures, will be available to the procedures within the module. This section includes a prototype for each procedure, and items you declare within a procedure will be local to that procedure. After entering the source code for the module, you compile it normally by using the CRTRPGMOD command. The end result of the compile process is a *Module object.

Typically, procedures in a service program's Nomain module use the Export keyword to ensure that they are available to client programs. If, however, you want to *hide* a procedure in a service program so that only other procedures in the same module object can invoke it, omit the Export keyword.

As you might expect, you must next bind the appropriate module objects to use them. Just as with single entry-point programs, you can bind service programs from a single module or from multiple modules, and you can include modules written in different languages. Recall that the CRTPGM CL command performs the binding step for a single entry-point program. The **CRTSRVPGM (Create Service Program) command** performs the same function for a multiple entry-point service program. Figure 15.1 illustrates the prompted CRTSRVPGM command.

The CRTSRVPGM command looks much like the CRTPGM command, and it serves much the same purpose, except that it creates a service program. As with the CRTPGM command, the service program binding process requires a list of modules to copy into the *Srvpgm object. Notice, though, that CRTSRVPGM specifies no parameter to designate an entry module. Because a service program is a multiple entry-point program, there is no entry module.

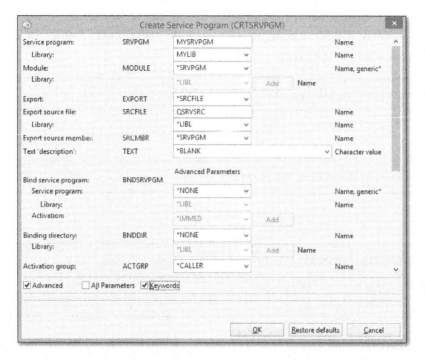

Figure 15.1: CRTSRVPGM (Create Service Program) command

When you create a service program, its procedures might refer to other procedures that reside in other service programs. The CRTSRVPGM binder can list those service programs (in the BNDSRVPGM parameter, under Advanced Parameters), which are then bound by reference to the service program you are creating. All the exported procedures from those service programs are available to your service program as well. We'll discuss binding by reference in more detail shortly.

Also notice that the CRTSRVPGM command, like the CRTPGM command, supports the use of binding directories. Recall from Chapter 13 that a binding directory—a list of reusable modules—allows the binder to find necessary modules that you may not have explicitly listed with the binder command. In addition to module entries, a binding directory can store the names of service programs that you intend to reuse among many different programs. When the binder finds the required procedure in a module entry, it binds the module by copy. When it finds the necessary procedure in a service program entry, it binds the service program (and all its procedures) by reference. Once the binder finds all the procedures it needs, the end result of a successful binding step is a *Srvpgm object.

15.4. Deploying Service Programs in an Application

A single entry-point program—or another service program—can invoke any procedure in a service program. But the calling program does not call the service program itself. Because a service program lacks a main procedure, you cannot call it. Instead, the caller invokes an individual procedure in a service program by using the same syntax that it would use if the procedure were bound to it by copy

```
Callp Updcust(Company:Custnbr);
```

or

```
Metrictemp = Celsius(Englishtemp);
```

or

```
If Celsius(Englishtemp) > 100;
...
Endif;
```

Recall that when you bind a module to a program, the binder physically copies the executable code from the module into the program—hence, the term *bind-by-copy*. When you bind a service program to an ILE program or to another service program, the binder does not physically copy the code to the client. Instead, the binder makes a reference associating the client with the service program and each of the procedures in it (i.e., *bind-by-reference*). You can think of the program as jotting a note to itself, a reminder that when it's time to load itself at runtime, it must also load any service programs that have been bound to it by reference. After the client program and any of its associated service programs have been loaded, all the procedures work together as a unit, regardless of whether they were bound by copy or by reference. If the client program cannot find all the service programs bound to it, or if a bound service program no longer exports a needed procedure, the program activation fails.

Regardless of how many clients use the procedures in a service program, only one copy of the executable code exists in the service program. When many programs use a procedure, bind-by-reference avoids the redundancy of bind-by-copy, and it can eliminate the need to update many programs when you must correct or enhance a procedure.

If the way you invoke a procedure in a module and the way you invoke it in a service program are the same, how will your program know which technique to use? The answer lies in the way that you bind the procedure to the calling program. When you use the CRTPGM command to bind a single entry-point program or the CRTSRVPGM command to bind a service program, you choose between either bind-by-copy or bind-by-reference. These commands have three parameters in common that control the binding technique:

- MODULE
- BNDSRVPGM
- BNDDIR

You have several components to consider when creating a single entry-point program or a service program. Both the CRTPGM command and the CRTSRVPGM command bind these components in order. First, all the *Module objects listed in the MODULE parameter are bound by copy. Next, all the *Srvpgm objects listed in the BNDSRVPGM parameter are bound by reference. Finally, for any unresolved exports, the binder searches entries in the binding directories listed in the BNDDIR parameter. If it finds a required procedure in a module entry, it binds that *Module by copy. The binding directory can also list service programs as well as modules (Figure 15.2). If the binder, either CRTPGM or CRTSRVPGM, finds a needed procedure in a service program entry, it binds that *Srvpgm by reference. The binder ignores all unnecessary binding directory entries to complete the binding process.

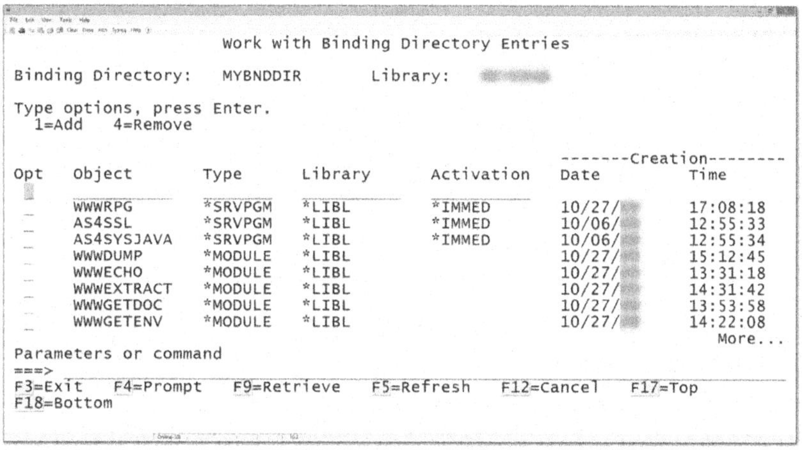

Figure 15.2: Binding directory entries

When the binding process uses a service program by reference, all the exported procedures in that service program are available to the bound program (or service program), whether or not the bound program uses all of them. You should organize service programs efficiently to avoid unnecessarily activating an excess of procedures that the client program will not use. The procedures in a single service program should be closely related to each other, a concept known as **cohesion**. Usually, when you activate a service program, most of the procedures in it should be used.

When you first activate an ILE program or service program, by default, all the service programs bound by reference are also activated. Activation allocates and initializes the storage needed to execute the program or service program. You can choose to defer activation of a particular service program until the caller invokes one of the exported procedures in the service program (i.e., until it truly uses the service program). When you specify a service program in the binder's BNDSRVPGM parameter, or you list it in a binding directory, indicate *DEFER instead of *IMMED activation (Figures 15.1 and 15.2). Deferred activation can offer a small performance improvement if the program binds many service programs but uses some of them only infrequently in actual practice.

The **DSPPGM (Display Program)** CL command lists the modules and service programs that make up a program if you specify the parameter value DETAIL(*MODULE *SRVPGM). Figures 15.3 and 15.4 illustrate the DSPPGM output. Similarly, the **DSPSRVPGM (Display Service Program)** CL command shows the modules and service programs that a service program uses. RDi's Remote Systems Explorer also offers an application diagram to help visualize the program or service program construction (Figure 15.5).

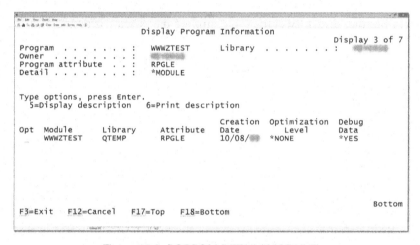

*Figure 15.3: DSPPGM DETAIL(*MODULE)*

*Figure 15.4: DSPPGM DETAIL(*SRVPGM)*

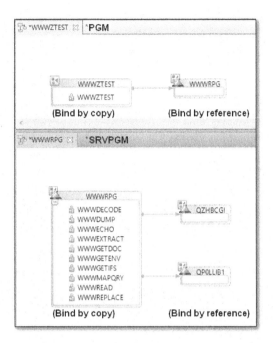

Figure 15.5: RDi application diagrams

15.5. Maintaining Service Programs

To modify the code in a service program procedure, you must go through the same compile-then-bind process to apply those changes to the service program. Instead of recreating the entire service program, though, you can use the **UPDSRVPGM (Update Service Program)** command to complete an abbreviated binding step. The UPDSRVPGM command lets you list just the module (or modules) that you want to remove from the original service program, replacing its code with the new version that now resides in the newly recompiled module. Figure 15.6 illustrates the prompted UPDSRVPGM command.

The UPDSRVPGM command performs the same functions as the CRTSRVPGM command, except that it replaces only the changed modules (i.e., those you list) in an existing service program. The unchanged modules are unaffected.

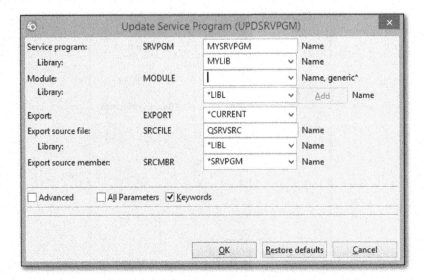

Figure 15.6: UPDSRVPGM (Update Service Program) command

15.5.1. Service Program Signatures

If you make a change to a service program that does not affect its external interface (i.e., you don't change its exported procedures, or the procedures' parameters or return value), the programs that use that service program require no action on your part to reflect the change. This advantage is key to service programs. Even though a service program may have hundreds of client programs, they may not require any maintenance to support the updated service program. Whether you must rebind those client programs depends upon the **service program signature**. The signature is a service program attribute that identifies its external interface—the exported procedures (and data items) it contains.

The signature is a property that is stored with the service program; its identity is usually a system-generated string. When you bind a service program to a client, the client makes a note of the service program's signature. At runtime when the client is loading itself and any associated service programs, it checks each service program to ensure that it still supports the signature the client is expecting. When the signatures in the client and the service program match, the client can use the service program. A mismatch, however, causes the program load to fail.

The service program has only one current signature, but it can retain many previous signatures, representing many different public interfaces. When you bind a service program to a client, the binder associates the two objects by using the current signature. But if any clients exist that know the service program by a previous signature, those programs can continue to use the service program without recompiling or rebinding. The DSPSRVPGM command (Figure 15.7) shows all of its valid signatures.

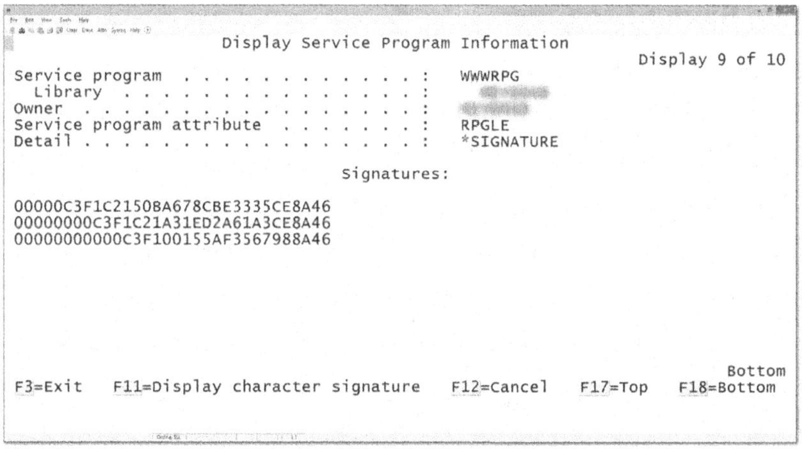

```
                    Display Service Program Information
                                                        Display 9 of 10
 Service program . . . . . . . . . . . . :   WWWRPG
   Library  . . . . . . . . . . . . . . :
 Owner  . . . . . . . . . . . . . . . . :
 Service program attribute  . . . . . . . :   RPGLE
 Detail . . . . . . . . . . . . . . . . :    *SIGNATURE

                              Signatures:

 00000C3F1C2150BA678CBE3335CE8A46
 00000000C3F1C21A31ED2A61A3CE8A46
 00000000000C3F100155AF3567988A46




                                                              Bottom
 F3=Exit    F11=Display character signature    F12=Cancel   F17=Top   F18=Bottom
```

Figure 15.7: DSPSRVPGM DETAIL(*SIGNATURE)

To understand why you might want a service program to have multiple signatures, consider a hypothetical service program, WWWRPG. When first created, the service program contained only four procedures (their functions are not relevant to this discussion):

- WWWDECODE
- WWWDUMP
- WWWECHO
- WWWEXTRACT

If this service program were in use for some time, it probably had many programs using its four exported procedures. At some point, it might be desirable to create new procedures and package them within the service program. For example, you might to add the following procedures to the service program:

- WWWGETDOC
- WWWGETENV
- WWWGETIFS

You could code this procedure in additional Nomain modules and then bind them to the WWWRPG service program. To avoid having to rebind all the existing client programs that use WWWRPG—but that do not use the new procedures—the service program needs to have two signatures. The current signature would support all seven exported procedures, but the older previous signature would support only the original four procedures. To enable this scenario, ILE allows you to manage the service program signatures by using a feature called *binder language*.

15.5.2. Using Binder Language

Binder language is a special syntax that consists of commands to describe a service program's external interface. Using an editor, you enter these commands into a source member (source type BND) and then refer to that source member when you create the service program. Although you do not compile the binder language source, the binder incorporates it into the algorithm it uses to create the service program signature. There are three binder language commands:

- STRPGMEXP (Start Program Export List)
- EXPORT (Export a Program Symbol)
- ENDPGMEXP (End Program Export List)

To understand how binder language relates to the service program signature, consider the hypothetical service program WWWRPG described earlier. When first created, the service program contained four procedures, compiled to *Module objects. Before binding the service program, you should create a new source member to store the binder language that will define the service program signature. Usually, you name the source member the same as the service program, WWWRPG in this example:

```
STRPGMEXP  PGMLVL(*CURRENT)
   EXPORT  SYMBOL(WWWDECODE)
   EXPORT  SYMBOL(WWWDUMP)
   EXPORT  SYMBOL(WWWECHO)
   EXPORT  SYMBOL(WWWEXTRACT)
ENDPGMEXP
```

The STRPGMEXP binder language statement forms the beginning of the binder language to define a service program signature. Specifying PGMLVL(*CURRENT), the default value, indicates that the signature is to be the current signature. In this example, the system automatically generates a signature identifier by default. The ENDPGMEXP statement indicates the end of the signature.

Between the beginning and the ending statements, EXPORT statements list the procedures to include in the signature. The order of the procedures in the export block affects the signature, so you should not change the order after you have created the service program. In addition, you must have created the procedures with the Export keyword in the ILE RPG source. In the rare case that the procedure names are case sensitive, you must enclose the names between apostrophes (').

You cannot compile the binder language source member. Instead, you refer to it when you create the service program:

```
CRTSRVPGM  SRVPGM(WWWRPG)                                       +
             MODULE(WWWDECODE WWWDUMP WWWECHO WWWEXTRACT) +
             EXPORT(*SRCFILE)                                   +
             SRCFILE(QSRVSRC)                                   +
             SRCMBR(WWWRPG)
```

Figures 15.1 and 15.6 illustrate the EXPORT, SRCFILE, and SRCMBR parameters. Specifying EXPORT(*SRCFILE) tells the binder that it will generate the service program signature by using binder language. The SRCFILE and SRCMBR parameters identify the location of the binder language.

After the service program is created, you can view the resulting signature by using the DSPSRVPGM (Display Service Program) command. The signature is a system-generated 16-byte string, as Figure 15.7 shows. When you bind this service program to a client program, the client also stores the current signature from the service program. When the client and the service program are loaded at runtime, their signatures must match. To view the service programs used by the client, along with their expected signatures, you can use the DSPPGM (Figure 15.4) or DSPSRVPGM command, depending upon the caller's object type.

The use of binder language goes well beyond using it to create a single signature for a service program. As you add new procedures to a service program, binder language manages not only the service program's new current signature, but it also supports its previous signatures. So, if any clients know the service program by a previous signature, those callers can continue to use the service program without recompiling or rebinding. For example, with the hypothetical WWWRPG scenario, when you want to add three new procedures to the service program, you must first make changes to the service program's binder language:

```
STRPGMEXP PGMLVL(*CURRENT)
   EXPORT  SYMBOL(WWWDECODE)
   EXPORT  SYMBOL(WWWDUMP)
   EXPORT  SYMBOL(WWWECHO)
   EXPORT  SYMBOL(WWWEXTRACT)
   EXPORT  SYMBOL(WWWGETDOC)
   EXPORT  SYMBOL(WWWGETENV)
   EXPORT  SYMBOL(WWWGETIFS)
ENDPGMEXP
```

Continued

```
STRPGMEXP PGMLVL(*PRV)
    EXPORT SYMBOL(WWWDECODE)
    EXPORT SYMBOL(WWWDUMP)
    EXPORT SYMBOL(WWWECHO)
    EXPORT SYMBOL(WWWEXTRACT)
ENDPGMEXP
```

This binder language now supports two signatures. The second signature is the original signature, but it has now been changed to be the previous signature: PGMLVL(*PRV). The new current signature is the same as the original signature, but with the three new procedures added to the end. You should not remove or rearrange entries in existing binder language export blocks. The current signature's export block must contain the same procedures in the same order as previous export blocks. You add new procedures only to the end of the block.

When you recreate the service program, it will support both signatures. Clients that know the service program by its old signature continue to run without changes. When you associate a new client with the service program, or rebind an existing client, it will use the current signature.

As you add new procedures to the service program, adding those procedures to the signature by using binder language is simple:

```
STRPGMEXP PGMLVL(*CURRENT)
    EXPORT SYMBOL(WWWDECODE)
    EXPORT SYMBOL(WWWDUMP)
    EXPORT SYMBOL(WWWECHO)
    EXPORT SYMBOL(WWWEXTRACT)
    EXPORT SYMBOL(WWWGETDOC)
    EXPORT SYMBOL(WWWGETENV)
    EXPORT SYMBOL(WWWGETIFS)
    EXPORT SYMBOL(WWWMAPQRY)
    EXPORT SYMBOL(WWWREAD)
    EXPORT SYMBOL(WWWREPLACE)
ENDPGMEXP

STRPGMEXP PGMLVL(*PRV)
    EXPORT SYMBOL(WWWDECODE)
```

Continued

```
    EXPORT  SYMBOL(WWWDUMP)
    EXPORT  SYMBOL(WWWECHO)
    EXPORT  SYMBOL(WWWEXTRACT)
    EXPORT  SYMBOL(WWWGETDOC)
    EXPORT  SYMBOL(WWWGETENV)
    EXPORT  SYMBOL(WWWGETIFS)
  ENDPGMEXP

  STRPGMEXP  PGMLVL(*PRV)
    EXPORT  SYMBOL(WWWDECODE)
    EXPORT  SYMBOL(WWWDUMP)
    EXPORT  SYMBOL(WWWECHO)
    EXPORT  SYMBOL(WWWEXTRACT)
  ENDPGMEXP
```

If, in the future, you do not want to support a previous signature, simply remove the entire signature from the binder language and update the service program (UPDSRVPGM command). Then, any clients that are still using the outdated signature will no longer run until they are rebound.

You can also explicitly name a service program signature, instead of letting the system automatically generate one. In the binder language, specify a SIGNATURE value when you start the export block:

```
STRPGMEXP  PGMLVL(*CURRENT)  SIGNATURE(WWWRPG)
```

The explicit signature should be 16 or fewer characters. If you name the signature, your binder language source needs only one export block and one signature. You can add new procedures to the end of the lone export block, and existing programs will still run.

Note

A service program signature is a means of listing the exported procedures and data items from a service program. It does not ensure that the interface to a particular procedure in the service program is valid. If you make changes to the parameters or return value in a procedure, those changes can render the procedure incompatible with existing clients, regardless of the signature. In that case, you must rebind all the clients by using CRTPGM or CRTSRVPGM.

15.5.3. Exporting Data Items

The most common use of the Export keyword is to make a subprocedure accessible outside the module in which it is coded. In a modular programming environment, you can also use Export to define a variable or a data structure whose contents are available across modules. If a data item is used across several modules, you must define it within each relevant module. But only one module actually allocates storage for that data item. In that module, specify the Export keyword when you declare the data item. In the other modules that are to reference the data item, specify the Import keyword—those modules use the data item allocated by the exporting module. You should not use data items you code with Export and Import as parameters. The module exporting the data item is responsible for any initialization of that variable.

The following example snippets illustrate the definition of such an intermodular data item in two different modules. First, a module named PRIMARY defines and allocates storage for variable Mydata. This variable can be exported from the PRIMARY module. It then calls procedure PROCA, which is coded in another module:

```
// Module: PRIMARY
Dcl-s Mydata Packed(9:2) Export Inz(200);
...
Proca();
```

The following example also declares variable Mydata in module PROCA. Because this declaration uses the Import keyword, PROCA will not allocate any storage for Mydata:

```
// Module: PROCA
Dcl-s Mydata Packed(9:2) Import;
...
```

Compiling these two modules and binding them to a program causes the primary module to allocate the storage and initialize Mydata. Both modules use the same storage for Mydata, which is a *superglobal* definition.

Usually, it is more convenient and flexible to pass parameters between procedures, rather than using Export and Import to define such intermodular data items. You may find it useful, however, to export data items from a service program and then import them into a client program that is to use that service program. Just as you can think of a service program as a procedure *toolbox*, you can also use it as a collection of data items that will cross modular boundaries. Such exported data items are included in the service program signature and should be referenced in binder language.

15.6. Understanding Activation Groups

An **activation group** is a subdivision of a job that ILE enlists to keep track of the resources a program uses; one job can have several activation groups in use simultaneously. The resources include the storage a program uses, certain error-handling routines, and temporary data management resources. Each job has its own activation groups, separate from other jobs. Within a job, a program can run in its own activation group, independent of other programs in the same job. The system uses activation groups to allow a job to create logical boundaries around applications in a job. An activation group is not an object but an attribute of a job. Think of it as a *subjob*.

For most applications, you need not concern yourself with activation group details. However, the activation group property allows an application to make private two common data management resources: file overrides and file open data paths. Activation groups also give a programmer the means to clean up storage and close files related to an application without affecting other applications in the job. After we discuss the various activation group options, we'll cover how to use them to control those two resources.

The binder (CRTPGM or CRTSRVPGM command) determines which activation group a program is to use. Each of these commands has an ACTGRP parameter to assign an activation group property to the program. There are several options:

- The default activation group (DFTACTGRP)
- A user-named ILE activation group
- A system-named (*NEW) activation group
- The caller's activation group (*CALLER)

15.6.1. The Default Activation Group

A job always includes two **default activation groups.** One is used by the operating system, and the other is used by application programs. RPG/400 (RPG III) programs have no option but to run in the default activation group. RPG/400 is known as an **Original Program Model (OPM)** language. OPM programs, which must run in the default activation group, do not support modules, procedures, service programs, or binding directories. ILE RPG/400 (RPG IV) programs, however, are ILE programs that support all the modern ILE features. Although ILE RPG programs can run in the default activation group, they should not. If you force an ILE program to run in the default activation group, it will not support modules, procedures, or service programs, among other restrictions.

The only way to force a program to run in the default activation group is to use the CRTBNDRPG *shortcut* CL command to create the program:

```
CRTBNDRPG PGM(program-name) ... DFTACTGRP(*YES)
```

This DFTACTGRP value is the default for this command. It is the *toggle* that disallows any ILE architecture in the program. It allows ILE RPG programs to behave like OPM programs.

15.6.2. User-Named ILE Activation Groups

A user-named activation group is a genuine ILE activation group. You attach the activation group name to an ILE program during program creation

```
CRTPGM PGM(program-name) ACTGRP(ag-name)
```

or

```
CRTSRVPGM PGM(program-name) ACTGRP(ag-name)
```

The name itself is not usually important. Many IBM commands use the name QILE for an ILE activation group, and you can use it as well.

A user-named activation group is created by a job when the first program that is to use that activation group starts. If subsequent programs specify an activation group of the same name, they will *plug in* to that activation group without creating a new one. The activation group remains active until the job ends or until the user explicitly reclaims the activation group. The **RCLACTGRP (Reclaim Activation Group)** command reclaims an active activation group that is not in use by any program.

The CRTBNDRPG shortcut can specify a user-named activation group if you don't force the program to use the default activation group:

```
CRTBNDRPG PGM(program-name) ... DFTACTGRP(*NO) ACTGRP(ag-name)
```

15.6.3. System-Named Activation Groups

A **system-named activation group**, also called a *NEW activation group, is also a genuine ILE activation group. Unlike a user-named activation group, however, a *NEW activation group only stays active while the program that uses it is still in the call stack. The activation group is newly created whenever the program is called and is destroyed when the program ends. The following example assigns a system-named activation group to a program:

```
CRTPGM PGM(program-name) ACTGRP(*NEW)
```

Service programs cannot use the *NEW activation group.

Using a *NEW activation group allows a program to call itself. Each time the program calls itself, the system creates a new copy of the program in a different activation group, with its own storage, its own data, and so forth. While certain applications may require this capability, you must be careful to ensure that each copy of the program will end at some point to avoid a *runaway* job. Unless your application specifically requires such *recursive* calls, you should avoid the *NEW activation group option. There is no need to reclaim a system-named activation group, as the system automatically destroys it when its program ends.

The CRTBNDRPG shortcut can specify a system-named activation group, provided you don't force the program to use the default activation group:

```
CRTBNDRPG PGM(program-name) ... DFTACTGRP(*NO) ACTGRP(*NEW)
```

15.6.4. Using the Caller's Activation Group

The most useful activation group option may be the *CALLER option. This option doesn't specify any particular activation group. With this option, the program simply runs in the same activation group as the program that called it. No new activation group is created; instead, the program uses the same resources as its caller. Unless an application specifically requires separation between the two programs, this option will usually suffice:

```
CRTPGM PGM(program-name) ACTGRP(*CALLER)
```

The caller can run in any activation group, including the default activation group. The program will support all ILE features.

This option works especially well for service programs. When a job is working with only one ILE activation group, using *CALLER for the service programs provides the fastest procedure calls. But when the job contains multiple activation groups, with several clients using the same service program, employing a separate user-named activation group for the service program allows one copy of the service program to work for several activation groups.

If you don't force the program to use the default activation group, the CRTBNDRPG shortcut can specify the *CALLER option:

```
CRTBNDRPG PGM(program-name) ... DFTACTGRP(*NO) ACTGRP(*CALLER)
```

15.6.5. Which Activation Group Is Best?

A complex activation group structure in an application environment is not usually necessary. Most applications can run in a single activation group, unless you must isolate them from other applications running in the same job. By keeping an application's activation group structure simple, you make it easier to examine a job while it's running and easier to control its resources.

Generally, the *CALLER activation group is appropriate for most single entry-point programs in an application. Of all the options, it offers the most flexibility by not imposing a specific activation group. The programs can be called from either the default activation group or any ILE activation group.

One initial program typically starts an application, maybe a menu offering options to *drill down* into the application's functions. If that initial program is an ILE program, it should use a named activation group, perhaps called QILE. All other programs in the application will *follow* the initial program into QILE. Why QILE? That is the name IBM chose for most programs if you don't choose an activation group. The default is as follows:

```
CRTPGM ... ACTGRP(*ENTMOD)
```

With this ACTGRP default, the binder examines the entry module for the program. If that module is an RPGLE module, the binder assigns QILE as the activation group. This is also the activation group that the binder automatically assigns if you use the *shortcut*:

```
CRTBNDRPG ... DFTACTGRP(*NO) ACTGRP(QILE)
```

For service programs, the *CALLER option usually works well. This option is also the default for the binder:

```
CRTSRVPGM ... ACTGRP(*CALLER)
```

Figure 15.8 illustrates this simple activation group structure within a job.

If an application does indeed require a logical boundary surrounding it within a job, updating the initial program to assign it to a different activation group is easy, as this example shows:

```
UPDPGM ... ACTGRP(PAYABLES)
```

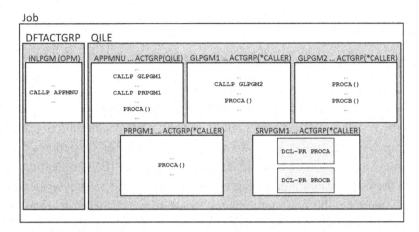

Figure 15.8: Simple activation group structure

At the same time, if several applications are to use the same service programs, you can assign those service programs to a separate named activation group:

```
UPDSRVPGM ... ACTGRP(SERVICES)
```

Figure 15.9 illustrates this more segmented activation group architecture, which provides activation group *containers* for each application as well as a separate one for service programs.

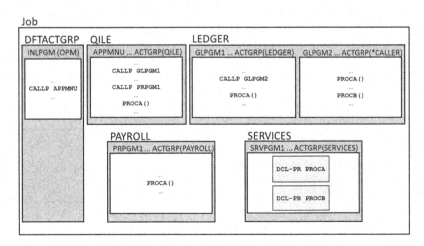

Figure 15.9: Detailed activation group structure

The initial program in an application can run in the default activation group but call programs that run in ILE activation groups. Once an application is running in an ILE activation group, however, you should avoid calling programs in the default activation group. Doing so can prevent problems in the areas of overrides, open data paths, and reclaiming program resources.

15.6.6. Activation Groups and File Overrides

Activation groups come into play most often in conjunction with file overrides. Sometimes you need to make minor changes in how a program functions without recompiling the program. Maybe it's necessary for a program to redirect a file declaration to process a file in a specific library, a file of another name, or a specific file member. Or perhaps the program must change some other attribute of a file. The method that the IBM i operating system uses to accomplish these minor modifications is called an **override**. Using overrides, you can make programs more flexible and more general in nature—and, therefore, more useful. File overrides are usually executed by a CL program to prepare a file for processing by an RPG program. Several commands can accomplish an override, but the most commonly used one is OVRDBF.

The **OVRDBF (Override with Database File)** command has two purposes: to direct a program to use a database file other than the one named in the program or to temporarily change the attributes of a file used by a program. All overrides are temporary, and they affect only the job or activation group in which the override command is executed. The OVRDBF command takes the following form (showing only the parameters used most often):

```
OVRDBF  FILE(overridden-file-name)                    +
        TOFILE(library-name/database-file-name)        +
        MBR(member-name)                               +
        SHARE(open-data-path-sharing-option)           +
        OVRSCOPE(override-scope)
```

Here is an example of an OVRDBF command that issues an override:

```
OVRDBF  FILE(CUSTOMERS)       +
        TOFILE(MYLIB/CUSTFILE) +
        OVRSCOPE(*CALLLVL)
```

This command appears in a CL program that ultimately calls an RPG program. You would have originally compiled the CL program by using a file declaration for the CUSTOMERS file. But at runtime, the program uses the CUSTFILE object in library MYLIB instead of the identically formatted CUSTOMERS file used for the compile process. This command invokes MYLIB/CUSTFILE to *play the role* of the CUSTOMERS file while the program is running.

The FILE parameter specifies the name of a file as it was declared in the program. The attributes of the named file are changed temporarily within the scope of the job, activation group, or call stack. The TOFILE parameter is optional; it enables you to replace references to the file named in the FILE parameter with the file you specify in the TOFILE parameter. You can use this parameter to change the name of the file the program is to process (so that a different file is processed at runtime) or to specify a library for the file you want to process. The MBR parameter allows a program to process a specific member, instead of the first one. The SHARE parameter, discussed in the next section, enables a program to share the file open data path for this file with other programs.

The OVRRDBF command can specify a **scope**—an extent of influence—for the override. The override is effective only for the specified scope. Three options determine the scope:

- OVRSCOPE(*ACTGRPDFN)
- OVRSCOPE(*CALLLVL)
- OVRSCOPE(*JOB)

The default value, OVRSCOPE(*ACTGRPDFN), determines the scope of the override automatically, based upon the activation group of the program in which the override is issued. If the system issues the command from the default activation group, the override is effective at the current call stack level and at any later call stack levels in the job. The override is effective as long as the call stack level that *owns* it remains active or until the program issues a **DLTOVR (Delete Override)** command. If the system issues the OVRDBF command from an ILE activation group, the scope of the override is the activation group that issued the override, regardless of call stack level. The override is effective as long as the activation group that *owns* it is active or until the override is deleted.

OVRSCOPE(*CALLLVL) explicitly calls for call-stack-level scoping of the override, as previously described. OPM programs, which must run in the default activation group, will always issue overrides with call-stack-level scoping by default. OPM and ILE programs can also scope an override to the entire job, regardless of call stack level or activation group, by using OVRSCOPE(*JOB). Use this option carefully, and be sure to delete the override when it is no longer needed. Otherwise, you run the risk of inadvertently using an override that has remained active from an earlier function.

The DLTOVR CL command deletes an override. Further discussion of overrides goes beyond the scope of this text; refer to the online IBM i documentation for more information.

15.6.7. Activation Groups and File Opens

When a program opens a database file, the system provides the program with an **open data path**, a plan for accessing the records in the file. To permit several programs within a single job to share the same open data path to a file, specify SHARE(*YES) on the OVRDBF command. This situation, in which more than one program shares a single open data path to a file, is called a **shared open**.

If you are considering open data path sharing (e.g., to improve an application's performance), be aware of its implications. An open data path includes a property called a **file cursor** that points to the next record to process. Each file's open data path has only one file cursor. Each program that shares the same open data path is responsible for positioning the file cursor to meet its own needs. If a program calls another program and the called program accesses a record in the shared file, the file cursor is repositioned. When the called program returns, the file cursor is still located at the record that was accessed last. The calling program must be able to reposition the file cursor at the record that it now wants to access.

The OVRDBF command includes an OPNSCOPE parameter that lets you closely control the extent of influence of the shared open data path:

```
OVRDBF FILE(CUSTOMERS)        +
       TOFILE(MYLIB/CUSTFILE) +
       OVRSCOPE(*CALLLVL)     +
       SHARE(*YES)            +
       OPNSCOPE(*ACTGRPDFN)
```

The two allowed values are OPNSCOPE(*ACTGRPDFN) and OPNSCOPE(*JOB). The options are similar to the ones the override scope uses.

Programmers sometimes use the **OPNDBF (Open Database File)** command as a performance technique to *preopen* files for use by other programs. This command also includes sharing and open scope parameters that control the scope of the open data path. The file remains open, sharing its data path with any other programs within its open scope. It's important to explicitly close the preopened files and delete any file overrides when your program is finished with those files. Otherwise, if the program is running in an ILE activation group, the files' open data paths might remain open even after the program has completed.

15.7. Chapter Summary

A service program (*SRVPGM) is a container for procedures that many client programs can use without copying the procedures into each client. The program creation model that service programs use is called *bind-by-reference*. A service program does not have an entry module because every procedure in the service program is an entry point. You use the CRTSRVPGM command to bind procedures to service programs.

Any ILE program—a single entry point program or another service program—can use a service program. When a client program is activated, all the service programs bound to that client are also activated by default. The client program matches its bound reference signature to a supported signature in the service program. When the signatures match, the service program activates. A service program can support multiple signatures, so a change to a service program may not require any changes to client programs. Binder language describes and manages the supported service program signatures.

In addition to procedures, a module can export data items to other modules in an ILE program. The exporting module allocates storage and initializes the data item. Other modules can import the data item, sharing its storage with the exporting module.

An activation group is a subdivision of a job that ILE uses to manage the resources an application is to use. One job can have several activation groups in use simultaneously. The binder command determines which activation group a program is to use. Original Program Model programs must run in the default activation group. ILE programs can run in the default activation group, but those programs might be restricted from using ILE features if they do. ILE activation groups (user named or *NEW) support concepts such as procedures, service programs, and multiple module programs. ILE programs can also run in their caller's activation group without creating a new one. Generally, the *CALLER option works best for most programs; the initial program that starts an application should run in a named ILE activation group.

Activation groups affect file overrides and shared file open data paths. A file override is a means of redirecting a program to use a different file than the one used by the compiler, perhaps to a specific library or member. A shared open data path allows several programs in an application to share a single open data path to a file. You can scope overrides and shared opens to the call stack, activation group, or job level. Their scope determines their extent of influence within the job.

15.8. Key Terms

activation group

bind-by-reference

binder language

cohesion

CRTSRVPGM (Create Service
    Program)

DLTOVR (Delete Override)

DSPPGM (Display Program)

DSPSRVPGM (Display
    Service Program)

default activation group

file cursor

multiple entry-point
    program

open data path

OPNDBF (Open Database
    File)

Original Program Model
    (OPM)

Override

OVRDBF (Override with
    Database File)

RCLACTGRP (Reclaim
    Activation Group)

scope

service program (*Srvpgm)

service program signature

shared open

UPDSRVPGM (Update Service
    Program)

15.9. Discussion/Review Questions

1. What is a service program, and why is it referred to as multiple entry-point program?

2. Why is the use of binder language important to the maintenance of service programs?

3. What is the significance of signatures when coding service programs?

4. What is the CL command used to display a service program's signature? What does it tell a programmer?

5. Describe the Export keyword, and explain why it is important for subprocedures.

6. What is an activation group?

7. How does the system use activation groups?

8. List the steps needed to create a service program.

9. What is the purpose of the UPDSRVPGM CL command? Explain its use.

10. What is the difference between the CRTSRVPGM and UPDSRVPGM CL commands?

15.10. Exercises

1. List five program scenarios in which a service program would be useful for a programmer.

2. Choose one of the five scenarios that you listed in the previous exercise; write the pseudocode describing the service program.

3. Write the code for the calling program and for a called service program with three procedures. Include any procedure and variable declarations, as well as procedure interfaces. The procedures need not do any processing, other than accepting the following described parameters and return values.

Here is an overview of the code requirements:
- The calling program contains the code to call the following procedures:
  - Call Procedure A—with a date, and receive an integer
  - Call Procedure B—with a 25-character string, and receive a 25-character string
  - Call procedure C—with a numeric date, and receive an internal date

Handling Errors

16.1. Chapter Overview

This chapter covers a variety of error-handling techniques that you can use to make your programs more reliable.

16.2. Capturing Operation Code Errors

Without explicit error handling within your program, runtime errors will cause the system to suspend the program and send a message to the interactive user or the system operator (when the program is running in batch). You can anticipate some errors that might arise during program execution. For those cases, most programmers prefer to practice defensive programming; that is, they handle errors internally within the program rather than letting them cause a program abend (abnormal ending). You can use any of several alternative methods to handle errors. ILE RPG supports facilities to process errors at any of three scopes:

- Errors that occur on a specific operation code
- Errors that occur in a block of code
- Errors that occur anywhere in the program

16.3. Using the (E) Extender

Many operation codes allow you to code an **(E) operation code extender**, in parentheses immediately following the operation code. The (E) extender's purpose is to permit the program to continue when an error happens on that operation code. Many, but not all, operation codes support an (E) extender. Of the operation codes we have discussed thus far in this text, the following ones support an (E) extender:

- Callp
- Chain
- Close
- Delete
- Exfmt
- Open
- Read
- Reade
- Readp
- Readpe
- Setgt
- Setll
- Unlock
- Update
- Write

When an error occurs on an operation that uses the (E) extender, the program is not suspended but instead continues as if no error had happened. It is then left up to the program to perform processing appropriate to the error. Common errors that might arise are as follows:

- Attempts to divide by zero
- Use of an invalid date/time/timestamp value
- Insufficient authority to use a data area
- Invalid array index
- Variable too small to hold result
- Decimal data error

All the file I/O operation codes support the use of the (E) extender. Some errors that might occur for a file operation include the following:

- Attempting to retrieve a locked record
- Attempting to retrieve a record from a closed file
- Attempting to open an already open file

Note that if a file I/O operation cannot find a record or reaches end-of-file, an error condition is *not* signaled. You should already be familiar with the %Found and %Eof functions, which you use to capture those conditions.

If an error happens during an operation that includes the (E) extender, the program simply continues to the next sequential instruction:

```
Read(e) Customers;

Dow Not %Eof(Customers);
  Chain(e) Zipcode Taxrates;


  If %Found(Taxrates);
    Callp(e) Calctaxes;
  Endif;


  Read(e) Customers;
Enddo;
```

Although this method prevents an abend of your program, it simply ignores the error—a potentially dangerous practice. A better method is to include an error routine that the program executes immediately upon encountering an error. You can easily use two functions to capture an error:

- %Error (Return Error Condition)
- %Status (Return File or Program Status)

16.3.1. %Error (Return Error Condition) Function

If an error occurs during an operation that includes the (E), the **%Error function** is turned on and the program continues. By checking the status of the %Error function after each operation that uses the (E) extender, your program can appropriately execute a special routine should an error arise:

```
Read(e) Customers;
  If %Error;
    Exsr Error;
  Endif;

Dow Not %Eof(Customers);
  Chain(e) Zipcode Taxrates;
    If %Error;
      Exsr Error;
    Endif;
```

Continued

```
    If %Found(Taxrates);
      Callp(e) Calctaxes;
        If %Error;
          Exsr Error;
        Endif;
    Endif;


    Read(e) Customers;
      If %Error;
        Exsr Error;
      Endif;

  Enddo;
```

Remember that the %Error function is tied to the (E) extender. Its value always pertains to the most recently executed operation code with the (E) extender—even if the appearance of %Error does not immediately follow that operation code. If an error occurs on an operation code without the (E) extender, the value of the %Error function remains unchanged.

16.3.2. %Status (Return File or Program Status) Function

The %Error function provides a generic on/off indicator if its related operation ends in error, but it gives you no indication of the specific nature of the error. ILE RPG offers more specific **status codes** that identify an error when it arises. The **%Status (Return file or program status) function** supplies the most recent status code to your program. RPG categorizes errors into two classes:

- Program errors
- File errors

The program associates file errors with a specific file, whereas program errors have a wider scope and are not necessarily related to a file. The %Status function value is set whenever the program status or file status changes, usually when an error occurs. %Status is a numeric value; it is set to 0 before any operation with an (E) extender begins. Operation codes without the (E) extender can also set the value of %Status (but not the value of %Error).

The following table lists a few common status codes. Status code values below 100 are not considered errors. Status codes between 100 and 999 are program errors, and status codes between 1000 and 9999 are file errors.

Status Code	Description
00000	No error occurred
00102	Divide by zero
00103	Variable too small to hold result
00112	Invalid date/time/timestamp value
00121	Invalid array index
00414	Insufficient authority to use a data area
00907	Decimal data error
01211	File I/O to a closed file
01215	Attempt open an already open file
01218	Record locked

Usually, you use %Status along with the (E) extender and the %Error function, as the following example shows. When coding a filename in parentheses immediately following the %Status function, you enter the most recent value for that file. But if you omit the filename, %Status will refer to the most recent change to the program or file status code.

```
Read(e) Customers;

Select;
  When %Error And %Status(Customers) = 01218;
    Exsr Lockedrec;
  When %Error;
    Exsr Fileerr;
  When %Eof(Customers);
    *Inlr = *On;
    Return;
  Other;
    Exsr Process;
Endsl;
```

Use of the (E) extender, the %Error function, and the %Status function greatly improves your program's ability to prevent runtime errors in a specific operation from ending your program abnormally. Including all these checks, however, greatly increases the length of your program and still doesn't solve the problem of errors generated by operations (such as Eval) that do not permit the use of the (E) extender. Fortunately, two alternative methods of error trapping exist. Using the Monitor and On-error operations, you can check for errors that occur within a block of code in an ILE RPG program. The Infsr and *Pssr subroutines allow you to check for errors anywhere in the program that are not otherwise handled.

16.4. Monitor and On-error Operations

Sometimes, it may be useful to provide a single error-trapping mechanism for a block of code instead of one operation. For these situations, ILE RPG supports another means of trapping errors: the **Monitor (Begin a Monitor Group)** and **On-error (On Error)** operations. These operations provide error trapping within a block of multiple code lines in a program. The concept behind Monitor and On-error is that you can isolate a block (or a line) of code to execute. If an error happens in that block, you can specify error-handling code specifically for that block. In some computer languages, this concept is called *try and catch* because the program tries to execute a block of code and catches any errors that occur in the block.

The Monitor and **Endmon (End a Monitor Group) operations** form **monitor groups**—code for which you provide error-handling routines. A monitor group consists of a monitor block, followed by one or more On-error blocks, and finally an Endmon operation. The monitor block contains the code you think might generate an error, and the On-error blocks hold the code to process any errors that arise in the monitor block:

```
Monitor;

  Dow Not %Eof(Customers);
    Chain Zipcode Taxrates;

    If %Found(Taxrates);
      Calctaxes();
    Endif;

    Read Customers;
  Enddo;

On-error 01218;
  Exsr Lockedrec;
On-error 01211:01215;
  Exsr Opensample;
On-error *File;
  Exsr Fileerr;
On-error *All;
  Exsr Generr;
  *Inlr = On;
  Return;
Endmon;
```

If an error occurs while any line (without an (E) extender) in a monitor group is being processed, control immediately passes to the first On-error block within the monitor group. Each On-error operation lists one or more errors for which it is responsible. These errors correspond to the status codes from 00100 to 09999, or you can specify *File for general file errors, *Program for general program errors, or *All for any errors. The code following an On-error operation forms an On-error block and is executed when the error that occurred matches the On error statement. Only the first matching On-error statement is processed. If no matching On-Error statements exist, none are processed. After an On-error block has been processed, or when the monitor block executes without error, control passes to the Endmon statement that ends the group; control cannot return directly to the monitor block.

In the preceding example, if the code in the Monitor block finishes without error, the program will skip the On-error blocks and pass control to the line following the Endmon operation. But if an error does arise, control will pass to the first On-error block whose status code matches the one generated by the error. After the code in the appropriate On-error block has executed, control passes to the line following the Endmon operation.

A monitor group can appear anywhere in an RPG program; you can nest monitor groups as well (innermost groups are considered first). Notice that the program no longer needs to use the (E) extender to monitor for errors. If an operation (e.g., Read or Chain) generates an error, the On-error blocks automatically take control. In fact, if the Calctaxes procedure in the previous example generates an error, the On-error groups will handle the error (unless Calctaxes also is coded with its own monitor blocks). It's a good idea to end the block with a *catch-all* On-error *All statement to handle generic errors. When the line of code that generates an error in a monitor block includes the (E) extender, then %Error and %Status is set, but the On-error blocks do not get control.

Although you primarily use the Monitor operation to process errors that occur in a block of code, Monitor can apply to an individual operation as well. Not all operation codes support an (E) extender; for example, the commonly used Eval operation does not support the (E) extender but can still generate errors. The following example, which you might use in a currency conversion program, illustrates the use of Monitor and On-error to handle errors that arise for an Eval operation:

```
Monitor;
  Eval(H) Foreign = Local / Buyrate;
On-error 00102;                        // Divide by zero
  Foreign = 0;
On-error 00103;                        // Result too small
  Foreign = 9999999.99;
Endmon;
```

In this example, if the expression encounters a divide by zero error, Foreign will be 0. If the Buyrate variable's value is so small that the expression result cannot fit into Foreign, the program will assign a value of 9999999.99 to Foreign. Notice that this example uses comments to document the conditions.

To make your program more documentary, you should assign named constants to status codes, as the following example shows:

```
Dcl-c Dividebyzero     00102;
Dcl-c Resultoverflow   00103;
Dcl-c Recordlocked     01218;
...
Monitor;
  Eval(h) Foreign = Local / Buyrate;
On-error Dividebyzero;
  Foreign = 0;
On-error Resultoverflow;
  Foreign = 9999999.99;
Endmon;

Read(e) Salesfile;
If %Status(Salesfile) = Recordlocked;
  Exsr Wait;
Endif;
```

Also consider using a copybook (discussed in Chapter 14) to store the constants that represent status codes, and then including that copybook (with the /Copy function) in any programs that are to use status codes.

16.5. Finding Data Errors

Some of the most frequent processing errors occur as a result of invalid or unexpected data values. For example, a date variable contains a nonexistent date, a numeric variable has a nonnumeric value, or a conversion function encounters problems when converting a character value to a numeric value. RPG offers several approaches to dealing with invalid data. We've already discussed how to capture these types of errors when they happen by using the %Error and %Status functions, and the Monitor and On-error operations. RPG features several options to capture these errors before they happen.

16.5.1. Decimal Data Errors

One of the most common errors is the **decimal data error**, which occurs when a program tries to process a numeric variable that contains nonnumeric information. You might encounter this situation, for example, when processing data that comes from another system or application. The decimal data error generates a status code of 00907, which you can capture in the program. Perhaps the easiest way to catch a decimal data error is to attempt a numeric expression:

```
Dcl-c Decimalerror 00907;

Monitor;
  Transamt += 0;
On-error Decimalerror;
  Transamt = 0;
Endmon;
```

In this example, the program attempts to add zero to the Transamt variable. If the Transamt variable is numeric, it remains unchanged and can be processed. If Transamt contains invalid numeric characters, the expression causes a 00907 status code, and its value is set to zero. Instead of changing the value to zero, you can code alternative processing.

For the module to detect and fix decimal data errors *before* processing any input data, the Ctl-opt instruction has a **Fixnbr** parameter that fixes invalid numeric data. Any of the following parameter combinations are valid:

```
Ctl-opt Fixnbr(*Zoned *Inputpacked);
Ctl-opt Fixnbr(*Zoned);
Ctl-opt Fixnbr(*Inputpacked);
Ctl-opt Fixnbr(*Nozoned *Noinputpacked);
Ctl-opt Fixnbr(*Nozoned);
Ctl-opt Fixnbr(*Noinputpacked);
Ctl-opt Fixnbr(*Zoned *Noinputpacked);
Ctl-opt Fixnbr(*Nozoned *Inputpacked);
```

With the Fixnbr(*Zoned *Inputpacked) option, the module will fix decimal data errors that occur in any zoned or packed numeric variables that the module uses. For zoned variables, invalid data (blanks, invalid digits) is treated as zeros; invalid signs are generally treated as positive. For packed variables, the entire variable is set to zero.

If a module has no appropriate Ctl-opt instructions to fix invalid numeric data, the compiler uses corresponding options specified with the compile commands (CRTRPGMOD or CRTBNDRPG), which also have a FIXNBR parameter—the default is FIXNBR(*NONE).

The compiler options to fix decimal data errors are not very flexible and can cause your programs to receive incorrect results. Most programmers prefer to individually check *problem* input fields rather than let the program fix them en masse.

16.5.2. Date Errors

If you try to process a date, time, or timestamp variable that contains an invalid value, the program generates error RNQ0112. The status code is 00112, which you can, of course, capture:

```
Dcl-c Dateerror 00112;

...

Monitor;
   Duedate = Invoicedate + %Days(30);
On-error Dateerror;
   Duedate = %Date() + %Days(30;
Endmon;
```

This example calculates Duedate (type Date) to be 30 days after Invoicedate (also type Date). If Invoicedate contains an invalid value, or if the expression causes Duedate to have an invalid value, Duedate will be set to 30 days from the current system date. Remember from Chapter 8 that the format you use for a date field can affect its range of valid values.

The **Test (Test date/time/timestamp)** operation can check the validity of date, time, or timestamp variables *before* you try to process them. The operation takes the following form:

```
Test(e) date-field;
```

The %Error function is turned on if the variable contains an invalid date/time value. The following example demonstrates this use of the Test operation:

```
Test(e) Today;
If %Error;
   Today = %Date();
Endif;
```

In this example, Today is a date variable. If Today lacks a valid date value, the Test operation turns on the %Error function, and subsequent lines assign the current system date to Today. When you use Test to check date, time, or timestamp variables, they can be in any valid format without any special coding.

You can also use the Test operation to check character or numeric variables *before* using them as dates, times, or timestamps. When you use it with these data types, the Test operation takes one of the following forms, depending upon data type:

```
Test(de) format field-name;
Test(te) format field-name;
Test(ze) format field-name;
```

To use Test to check character and numeric fields for valid date/time data, you must include an operation extender—(D) for date, (T) for time, (Z) for timestamp—to identify which test to perform. Be sure to include the (E) extender to support the %Error function as well. Before coding the name of the variable to test, you must also code the date/time display format (e.g., *Iso, *Mdy, *Usa) to compare to your data. Consider the following examples in which Userdate and Usertime are numeric fields.

```
Test(de) *Iso Userdate;
Test(te) *Hms Usertime;
```

When testing the date/time validity of character variables, RPG also checks whether the value contains valid separator characters. If the character value does not include separators, you can override the separator with a zero (0). Assume in the following examples that Userdate and Usertime are character fields without separators:

```
Test(de) *Iso0 Userdate;
Test(te) *Hms0 Usertime;
```

16.5.3. Data-Conversion Errors

Previously, we discussed several functions that convert a character value to a numeric value:

- %Dec (and %Dech) to convert to packed decimal
- %Int (and %Inth) to convert to integer
- %Uns (and %Unsh) to convert to unsigned integer

When you use these functions to convert a character value, the following rules apply to the character value:

- An optional sign (+ or -) can precede or follow the data value.
- A decimal point (. or ,) is optional.
- Blanks can appear anywhere in the data.
- The remaining data must include only digits (0–9).
- Floating point data is not allowed.

If one of these functions encounters invalid numeric data, it will generate a status code of 00105. Perhaps the easiest way to catch a **conversion error** is to attempt the conversion:

```
Dcl-c Numbererror 00105;
...
Monitor;
  Numfield = %Dec(Charfield:13:2);
On-error Numbererror;
  Numfield = 0;
Endmon;
```

In this example, the program converts the Charfield variable (type Char) to packed decimal format (13 digits, 2 decimal places) and places the value in the Numfield variable (type Packed). If the program cannot successfully convert the value, it will return status code 00105 and set the Numfield variable to zero.

To check the data value *before* attempting the conversion, you can use the **%Check (Check Characters)** function to see whether any invalid characters appear in Charfield:

```
If %Check(' +-.,0123456789':Charfield) = 0;
  Numfield = %Dec(Charfield:13:2);
Endif;
or
Dcl-c Numeric ' +-.,0123456789';
...
If %Check(Numeric:Charfield) = 0;
  Numfield = %Dec(Charfield:13:2);
Endif;
```

The %Check function ensures that Charfield contains only the characters that can be converted. It does not, however, guarantee that they are in the proper places. Depending upon the specific circumstances, you can use other functions (e.g., %Scan, %Subst) to validate the position of various characters.

16.6. Error Subroutines and Data Structures

Previously, we've discussed using the (E) extender to capture errors that occur with a specific operation code, and using the Monitor operation to capture errors that arise in a particular block of code. RPG also supports several error-handling mechanisms that take effect on a wider scope:

- File information data structure (Infds)
- File error subroutine (Infsr)
- Program status data structure (Psds)
- Program error subroutine (*Pssr)

16.6.1. File Information Data Structure

For each file in an ILE RPG program, you can define a **file information data structure (Infds)** to provide feedback to your program about a file's current status, along with details about any file errors that may have occurred. To name a file information data structure, use the Infds keyword when you declare the file:

```
Dcl-f Customers Infds(Custinfds);
```

Each file's information data structure must be unique to that file. You must, of course, then define the data structure; you can externally describe it, if you wish. The declaration for the file information data structure appears in the same procedure as the file declaration, usually the main procedure.

The subfields in the file information data structure are in predetermined locations, documented in IBM's online documentation. Some of the information available in the file information data structure includes the following:

- The name of the file
- The record being processed when the error occurred
- The last operation being processed when the error occurred
- The ILE RPG routine in which the error occurred
- The status (%Status) code

Some of the information and its location in the file information data structure are specific to the device you code in the file declaration. For example, if the device is a printer file, the information includes the current line number and the current page count. Information for a workstation file has a variable identifying which key has been pressed. For a database (disk) file, the information contains the current record count.

Here is an example of a file information data structure:

```
Dcl-f Customers Usage(*Update:*Delete:*Output) Keyed Infds(Custinfds);
...
Dcl-ds Custinfds Qualified;
  Filename  Char(8)     Pos(1);
  Fileopen  Char(1)     Pos(9);
  Endoffile Char(1)     Pos(10);
  Status    Zoned(5:0)  Pos(11);
  Opcode    Char(6)     Pos(16);
  Routine   Char(8)     Pos(22);
End-ds;
```

To find the correct location for other subfields, refer to IBM's online documentation. For some subfields, RPG supports predefined names, which you can use instead of locations:

```
Dcl-f Customers Usage(*Update:*Delete:*Output) Keyed Infds(Custinfds);
...
Dcl-ds Custinfds Qualified;
  Filename  *File;
  Fileopen  Char(1)     Pos(9);
  Endoffile Char(1)     Pos(10);
  Status    *Status;
  Opcode    *Opcode;
  Routine   *Routine;
End-ds;
```

In this example, *File, *Status, *Opcode, and *Routine are such predefined subfields.

The %Status function, discussed earlier in this chapter, provides the same information as the *Status subfield in the file information data structure. A program can refer to %Status without including an Infds.

Even if a file does not use a file information data structure, the program can still report the Infds information by using a formatted RPG program dump. A dump is a report that shows the details of the error, the current state of all files, and the current values of all the variables in the program. It is useful when you need to debug a problem with a running program.

The **Dump (Program Dump)** operation issues the program dump and then continues with the next line in the program. The Dump operation includes the Infds data for each file. The listing is written to a spooled file called QPPGMDMP. The operation takes this form:

```
Dump(a);
```

The (A) extender on the Dump operation ensures that the dump will always be issued, regardless of other debugging or optimization entries coded in your program.

16.6.2. Using a File Error Subroutine

You can designate a subroutine to automatically execute when a main procedure encounters a file error. This file exception/error subroutine is commonly called the **Infsr subroutine**. Infsr takes control when a file I/O operation encounters an error that is not handled by one of the other error-handling mechanisms (e.g., an (E) extender or a Monitor group). You can also explicitly execute an Infsr subroutine with the Exsr operation. One subroutine can handle errors for several files, or you can code multiple Infsr subroutines in a single program.

To add an Infsr subroutine to your program, you must include the Infsr keyword on the declaration for the files you want to associate with the subroutines. With this keyword, you name the subroutine that is to handle that file's errors. This name can be any subroutine (including the *Pssr subroutine, discussed later in this chapter).

An Infsr subroutine has no unique requirements. You can use any RPG operations, but you should avoid using Infsr to perform file I/O operations on the same file that caused the error. The subroutine might refer to subfields in the file's Infds, if any. The following example shows how you might use an Infsr subroutine:

```
Dcl-f Customers Usage(*Update:*Delete) Keyed Infsr(Custinfsr);
Dcl-f Backlog   Usage(*Output) Keyed;
...
Chain (Company:Customer) Custrec;

If %Found(Customers);
  Lasdat = %Date();
  Update Custrec %Fields(Lasdat);
Endif;
...
Begsr Custinfsr;
  Write Backrec;
```

Continued

```
   Dump(a);
   *Inlr = *On;
Endsr '*CANCL';
```

This example designates the Custinfsr subroutine as the file error subroutine for the Customers file. If an error arises for the Chain or Update operations associated with the Customers file, this subroutine will take control. The Custinfsr subroutine writes a Backrec record to the Backlog, executes a Dump operation, turns on *Inlr, and then ends.

Notice that the Endsr operation has an extra entry that you have not seen before. This optional entry indicates the **return point** for the subroutine; it is valid only with error-handling subroutines. This entry indicates what the program should do when it is finished executing the subroutine. It is usually one of the following entries:

- '*DETC' to continue the program at the top of the calculations
- '*CANCL' to cancel the program

The entry can be a literal, a constant, or a variable (six characters) with the desired value. When you do not code a return point, one of two things happens: 1) if the subroutine is executed because of a file error, the program will generate an error; 2) if the subroutine is executed as the result of an Exsr operation, control will return to the next sequential instruction (just like a normal subroutine).

Several limitations on the Infsr subroutine cause most programmers to prefer other error-handling mechanisms instead. First, the Infsr subroutine handles only file errors that occur in the main procedure of a cycle main program, not in subprocedures or in linear main programs—the Infsr must appear in the main procedure. Next, if an error happens when the program is initially opening a file, the Infsr will not get control (only errors that occur after the program is running cause the Infsr to take over). Finally, the Infsr cannot easily return to the point of the error after executing. For these reasons, most programmers use Monitor groups or the %Error and %Status functions—or the *Pssr subroutine—instead of, or along with, an Infsr subroutine.

16.6.3. Program Status Data Structure

Within an RPG program, you can define a **program status data structure (Psds)** to make program error information available to the program. These program errors contain such things as attempts to divide by zero, endeavors to use an invalid array index, or errors on a Callp operation. In addition to error information, the Psds includes other information, such as the user identifier of the current user and the job name/number. You code the program status data structure with a Psds keyword in the data structure declaration:

```
Dcl-ds *N Psds;
   Pgmstatus   Zoned(5:0) Pos(11);        // *Status
   Jobname     Char(10)   Pos(244);
   Jobuser     Char(10)   Pos(254);
   Jobnumber   Zoned(6:0) Pos(264);
   Currentuser Char(10)   Pos(358);
End-ds;
```

The Psds must be in the global declarations, and a program can have only one Psds. The subfields in the program status data structure are in predetermined locations, documented in IBM's online documentation. Some subfields, such as *Status or *Routine, are predefined and can be specified without coding a location. The *Status subfield has the same value as the %Status function and can be accessed without declaring a Psds. You can externally describe Psds or code it in a copybook.

Even if a file does not use a program status data structure, the program can still report the Psds information by using a formatted RPG program dump. The Dump operation includes the program status data structure information.

16.6.4. Using a *PSSR Subroutine

By including a subroutine named *Pssr within your program, you enable that subroutine to automatically receive control when an unhandled program error occurs anywhere in the code. The ***Pssr subroutine** provides a *last defense* against errors—to handle those errors not processed with the (E) extender, the %Error function, the %Status function, Monitor groups, or an Infsr.

The following example shows a basic *Pssr subroutine:

```
Begsr *Pssr;
   Dump(a);
   *Inlr = *On;
Endsr '*CANCL';
```

This *Pssr subroutine causes the program to issue a formatted RPG program dump and then end the program.

Like the Infsr subroutine, the *Pssr subroutine can include a return point on its Endsr operation. When you do not code a return point, one of two things happens: 1) if the subroutine is executed because of a program error, the program will generate an error; 2) if the subroutine is executed as the result of an Exsr operation, control will return to the next sequential instruction (just like a normal subroutine).

For a *Pssr subroutine that is more complex than the preceding one, be careful to avoid errors that might arise within the *Pssr subroutine itself. An unhandled error that happens in the *Pssr subroutine can cause endless reiteration of the *Pssr subroutine. You can avoid this endless recursion by defining a variable to *remember* whether the *Pssr subroutine has already executed:

```
Dcl-s Pssrdone Ind Inz(*Off);
...
Begsr *Pssr;
  If Pssrdone;
    *Inlr = *On;
    Return;
  Endif;

  Pssrdone = *On;
  Dump(a);
  // Additional error processing goes here
Endsr '*CANCL';
```

The *Pssr subroutine handles program errors that occur. To have this subroutine control file errors as well, you must explicitly designate *Pssr as the error handler for the files. This assignment is quite straightforward: simply use the Infsr keyword as part of the file definition and name *Pssr as the file error subroutine:

```
Dcl-f Customers Usage(*Update:*Delete) Keyed Infsr(*Pssr);
```

You can handle most errors in a program with a combination of the (E) extender, the %Error and %Status functions, and Monitor groups. The Infsr and *Pssr subroutines, along with the file information and program status data structures, provide more customized error handling. It is left to you, the programmer, to determine the best response to the error—perhaps ignoring the error and continuing, writing a line to an error report and continuing, or noting the error and bringing the program to a normal ending. While the optimal design of error-handling logic can be complex, as you gain more experience with the language, you will no doubt begin to incorporate these tools in your programs.

16.7. Handling SQL Errors

When an SQL statement embedded in an RPG program ends in error, the program does not stop but continues to run with the next subsequent statement. Chapter 10 discussed the SQL Communication Area, which the SQL precompiler automatically inserts into any SQLRGPLE program. To review, the SQLCA is updated every time the program executes an SQL statement. Two important subfields in this data structure, **Sqlcode** and **Sqlstate**, signal the success or failure of an SQL statement. Sqlcode values are unique to IBM i, and Sqlstate values are set by industry standards. Whenever a program executes an SQL statement, it should immediately check one of these subfields to catch any error that may have occurred.

Sqlcode will return one of the following values:

- Sqlcode = 0 means the SQL statement was successfully executed (although there may be warnings).
- Sqlcode = 100 indicates no row was found (end-of-file).
- Sqlcode > 0 (but not 100) denotes the statement was successful, but warnings were issued.
- Sqlcode < 0 means the SQL statement was unsuccessful.

Each Sqlcode value corresponds to an IBM i message, which you can research on IBM's online documentation to obtain more details. For example, Sqlcode 100 is explained in IBM i message SQL0100, Sqlcode -0313 parallels message SQL0313, and Sqlcode 23505 corresponds to message SQ23505.

Sqlstate is five characters long. The first two characters indicate a general class of conditions:

- Sqlstate beginning with 00 means the SQL statement was successfully executed, with no errors or warnings.
- Sqlstate beginning with 01 indicates the statement was successful, but warnings were issued.
- Sqlstate beginnng with 02 denotes the SQL statement found no row (end-of-file).
- Any other Sqlstate class means the SQL statement was unsuccessful.

Sqlstate values are also detailed in IBM's online documentation. Unlike Sqlcode values, Sqlstate values have no correspondence to IBM i messages.

Two additional SQLCA subfields, **Sqlwarn** and **Sqlerrd**, are arrays that contain specific diagnostic indications of warnings or exceptions that an SQL statement may have encountered. Sqlwarn is an 11-element array of warning indicators. Each element includes a nonblank value (usually a W) if SQL generated a warning, corresponding to the warnings in Figure 16.1. Sqlerrd is a six-element array that contains diagnostic information, primarily related to advanced SQL concepts, including cursors (discussed in Chapter 10). IBM's online documentation provides a more detailed explanation of Sqlwarn and Sqlerrd.

Sqlwarn Element	Meaning
Sqlwarn(1)	W = At least one warning exists
Sqlwarn(2)	W = Data column was truncated in host variable
Sqlwarn(3)	W = Null values were ignored
Sqlwarn(4)	W = More data columns than host variables
Sqlwarn(5)	W = Update or Delete is missing a Where clause
Sqlwarn(6)	1 = SQL cursor is read only 2 = SQL cursor is read/delete capable 4 = SQL cursor is read/delete/update capable
Sqlwarn(7)	W = Date arithmetic caused end-of-month adjustment
Sqlwarn(8)	(Not used)
Sqlwarn(9)	W = Character conversion contains substitution character
Sqlwarn(10)	(Not used)
Sqlwarn(11)	(Not used)

Figure 16.1: Sqlwarn values

If an error occurs while an SQL statement is being executed, the RPG program will continue to run the next statement, as if no error had happened. You should always explicitly test either Sqlcode or Sqlstate to check the consequence of executing an SQL statement. Sqlwarn and Sqlerrd can also provide details about the error. Chapter 10 illustrated the use of Sqlstate to trap errors. The following code uses Sqlcode and Sqlwarn to test for errors following an SQL statement:

```
Dcl-c Duplicatekey -803;
Dcl-c Endoffile    100;
Dcl-c Success      000';
...
Exec SQL Select  Cfname, Clname
          Into   :Cfname :NullCfname,
                 :Clname :NullClname
          From   Customers
          Where Custno = :Custno;

Select;
  When Sqlstate = Endoffile;              // Sqlcode = 100
      // End of file
  When Sqlstate = Duplicatekey;           // Sqlcode = -803
      // Insert or Update attempted duplicate key
  When Sqlcode < 0;
      // Select was unsuccessful; other error
                                                          Continued
```

```
    When Sqlwarn(1) = 'W' Or Sqlcode > 0;
        // Select generated warnings
    Other;
        // Select was successful
Endsl;
```

16.8. Navigating Legacy Code

16.8.1. Detecting Errors with Resulting Indicators

Chapter 6 introduced the use of resulting indicators in fixed-format C-specs to reflect the result of executing an operation. Many operation codes can set a resulting indicator in positions 73–74 (Lo) to signal an error. The error resulting indicator serves the same purpose as the (E) extender. When an error occurs on a line that includes an error resulting indicator, that indicator is set to *On and the program continues—in this case, the %Error function is *not* set to *On. When no error arises, the indicator is set to *Off. The following code illustrates the use of an error resulting indicator:

```
*.. 1 ...+... 2 ...+... 3 ...+... 4 ...+... 5 ...+... 6 ...+... 7 ...+... 8
CLON01Factor1+++++++Opcode(E)+Factor2+++++++Result++++++++Len++D+HiLoEq....
C                   Read      Customers                                98
C                   If        *In98
C                   Exsr      Error
C                   Endif
```

16.8.2. Program Status Data Structures and Fixed Format

Fixed-format RPG uses D-specs to define a program status data structure. Coding S in position 23 of the header identifies the data structure as the program status data structure:

```
*.. 1 ...+... 2 ...+... 3 ...+... 4 ...+... 5 ...+... 6 ...+... 7 ...+... 8
DName+++++++++++ETDsFrom+++To/Len+IDc.Keywords++++++++++++++++++++++++++++++
D                 SDs
D Pgmstatus       *Status
D Jobname             244    253
D Jobuser             254    263
D Jobnumber           264    269 0
D Currentuser         358    367
```

16.8.3. Using the SQL Whenever Statement

In addition to the Sqlcode, Sqlstate, Sqlwarn, and Sqlerrd diagnostic feedback, SQL also supports the Whenever statement to specify an action to take when an exception occurs. A Whenever statement serves as a form of monitor for an SQLRPGLE program, watching for an exception in the subsequent SQL statements and indicating the next statement to process when the exception arises. You code the Whenever statement in the program where it should begin to watch for the exception; a subsequent Whenever statement for the same condition replaces the original one. The Whenever statement watches for three types of exceptions:

- Not Found (Sqlstate = '02000' or Sqlcode = 100)
- Sqlerror (Sqlstate indicates unsuccessful execution)
- Sqlwarning (Sqlstate = '01' or 'Sqlwarn(1) = 'W')

The Whenever statement indicates the next statement to execute when one of these conditions happens. The program can either continue with the next statement after the one that caused the exception or branch to a named *tag* in the program. These examples illustrate some sample Whenever statements:

```
Exec SQL Whenever Not Found  Goto Norecord;
Exec SQL Whenever Sqlwarning Continue;
Exec SQL Whenever Sqlerror   Goto Endprog;
```

If an SQL Whenever statement instructs the program to branch to a tag, the RPG program must label a line in the program by using the fixed-format Tag operation. The Tag operation labels the line to use as the target of a Goto operation or SQL statement:

```
*.. 1 ...+... 2 ...+... 3 ...+... 4 ...+... 5 ...+... 6 ...+... 7 ...+... 8
CLON01Factor1+++++++Opcode(E)+Factor2+++++++Result++++++++Len++D+HiLoEq....
C     Endprog       Tag
```

The following abbreviated example illustrates the use of Whenever:

```
*.. 1 ...+... 2 ...+... 3 ...+... 4 ...+... 5 ...+... 6 ...+... 7 ...+... 8
CLON01Factor1+++++++Opcode(E)+Factor2+++++++Result++++++++Len++D+HiLoEq....
  Exec Sql Whenever Sqlerror Goto Sqlerr;
  ...
  Exec Sql Whenever Not Found Goto Sqleof;
  Dou Sqlcode <> 0;
                                                    Continued
```

```
      Exec Sql Fetch ... ;

      ...

      Exec Sql Update ... ;
   Enddo;
C     Sqleof        Tag
   Exec Sql Close C1;
C     Sqlerr        Tag
   *Inlr = *On;
   Return;
```

If a Whenever statement branches to a target, the Tag must appear within the same scope (i.e., in the same procedure) as the Whenever statement.

Because the SQL Whenever statement requires the use of tags, and because it mixes fixed-format code with free-format RPG, most programmers prefer to avoid Whenever. Catching errors with Sqlcode and Sqlstate offers more flexibility and control—not to mention better style—than Whenever.

16.9. Chapter Summary

ILE RPG supports facilities to process errors at a specific error code within a block of code or anywhere in the program.

The (E) extender on an operation code allows a program to continue processing if the operation generates an error. Without the (E) extender, the program is suspended while it waits for a response to an error message.

The %Error function returns a simple on/off indicator to let the program know whether an error has occurred. %Error is always associated with the last operation code that used an (E) extender. The %Status function returns a numeric value that identifies a specific error condition. Status codes from 00100 to 00999 describe program errors, and status codes from 01000 to 09999 describe file I/O errors.

The Monitor and On-error operations allow you to check for errors that happen within a block of code. You do so by creating Monitor groups that include the code to process and its error-handling instructions in a single block.

Some of the most frequent processing errors happen as a result of invalid or unexpected data values. These errors include decimal data errors, numeric conversion errors, and invalid date values. Wherever possible, you should check for these types of errors before processing the data. The Test operation checks date/time variables for valid values—you can also use this operation to validate numeric and character fields that store date values.

The Infsr and *Pssr subroutines automatically execute when a file error or a program error occurs that is not otherwise handled by another mechanism. The file information and program status data structures can also provide more information about any errors that arise.

If an SQL statement embedded in a program ends in error, the program will not stop. The automatically created Sqlcode and Sqlstate variables, as well as Sqlwarn and Sqlerrd arrays, provide diagnostic information about the execution of an SQL statement. Sqlstate contains industry-standard values, whereas Sqlcode is specific to IBM i. The program should always check these diagnostics after executing an SQL statement.

The following table summarizes the operation codes and functions discussed in this chapter:

Function or Operation	Description	Syntax
%Check	Check characters	**%Check(Check-string : Tested-field {: Start-pos});**
Dump	Program dump	**Dump{(a)};**
Endmon	End a monitor group	**Endmon;**
%Error	Error	**%Error**
Monitor	Begin a monitor group	**Monitor;**
On-error	On error	**On-error {Exception-Id1 : Exception-Id2...};**
%Status	File or program status code	**%Status{(File-Name)}**
Test	Test date/time/timestamp	**Test{(edtz)} {Format} Tested-field;**

16.10. Key Terms

abend
%Check function
conversion error
debug
decimal data error
Dump operation
(E) operation code extender
Endmon operation
%Error function

file information data
  structure (Infds)
Fixnbr
Infsr subroutine
monitor groups
Monitor operation
On-error operation
program dump
program status data structure
  (Psds)

*Pssr subroutine
return point
Sqlcode
Sqlerrd
Sqlstate
Sqlwarn
status codes
%Status function
Test operation

16.11. Discussion/Review Questions

1. Discuss different options for trapping errors (or not trapping errors) within a program, giving the pros and cons of each method.
2. Why might a programmer want to convert one data type to another in an RPG program? For example, why might you want to convert a packed decimal number to a character field? Which built-in functions would you use to perform the conversion?
3. What is the Infsr subroutine? Give an example of how (and why) you would use this.
4. What is the *Pssr subroutine, and why would you use it? Give an example.
5. Investigate the problems that writing a program not prepared to handle errors can cause. Programming professionals and your instructor are good resources for information. Write a report.
6. Summarize the rules that are applied to numeric data if the Fixnbr compile command is used when compiling a program.
7. Using IBM's online documentation, investigate the subfields available for a file information data structure. Compile a list of 10 subfields that would be beneficial in your programming efforts.
8. Using IBM's online documentation, investigate the RPG operations that set %Status. Compile a list of five operations in which the checking of %Status would be useful.

16.12. Exercises

1. Write the ILE RPG code to read a record from CSCSTP. Check for the errors you think might occur.

2. Write the ILE RPG code to check for a divide by zero error.

3. Write the ILE RPG code to check for the result of a math operation that's too large for the result field.

4. Write the ILE RPG code to monitor the conversion of character data to a packed decimal field, to an integer, and to an unsigned integer.

5. After completing question 7 in the Discussion/Review Questions section, write a file information data structure using the CSCSTP file. Using ILE RPG code, give an example of the use of each subfield.

6. Write the F-specs and the other required code to use the *Pssr subroutine. Write an example of how to use this subroutine.

7. Using the list from question 7 in the Discussion/Review Questions section, do the following:

    a. Define a data structure that includes these subfields.

b. Write the code to open the EMPLOYEE table in the FLIGHPROD schema by using the previously defined data structure.

c. Write sample code using this data structure to chain and update the EMPLOYEE table.

8. Using the list from question 8 in the Discussion/Review Questions section, write the code to use the five operations, check the value of %Status, and call an appropriately named subroutine. You do not need to actually code a subroutine.

17

Programming with Subfiles

17.1. Chapter Overview

This chapter extends your ability to write interactive list-style applications by introducing you to the concept of subfiles. It shows you how to define a subfile by using DDS, and how to use any of three methods for processing the subfile with an RPG program.

17.2. Subfiles

Chapter 12 introduced you to interactive programs. You learned how to write inquiry and maintenance programs whose logic required the display of information one record at a time. Some kinds of applications require the use of **list panels**, in which data from many records is displayed on a screen for review, selection, or update. RPG has a special feature called subfiles to handle this type of program requirement.

A **subfile** is a collection of records that is handled as a unit for screen input/output (I/O). Although subfile processing can be quite detailed, you can learn basic subfile processing techniques without great difficulty. The following problem description serves as a prelude to discussing coding requirements for subfiles.

In Chapter 12, you worked with a file of customer data and developed an interactive application to display detailed customer information based on a customer number entered by a user. Figure 17.1 repeats the record layout of that file, Customers. Now, assume that the same organization wants an application in which users can select an individual customer from a list and then display the details for that customer record. To facilitate future enhancements, the application uses a modular approach by employing two programs:

- PGM17—Customer record selection
- PGM17X—Customer detail display

Program PGM17 uses a subfile to allow users to select one or more records from a list. Program PGM17X displays the details for each selected record. Figures 17.2 and 17.3 show the desired screen layouts.

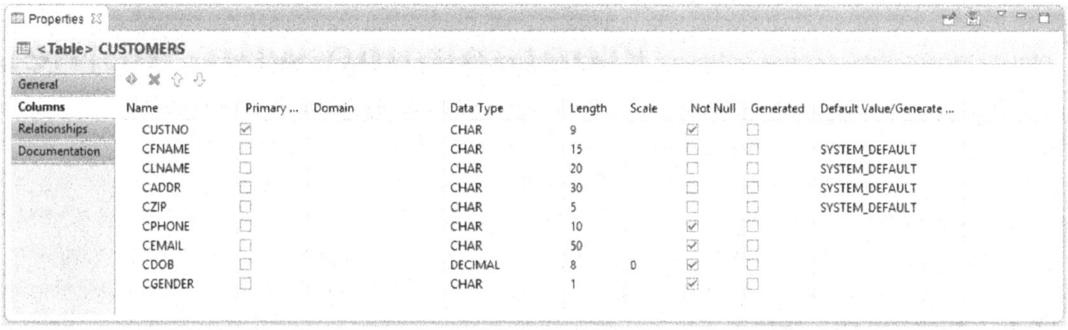

Name	Primary ...	Domain	Data Type	Length	Scale	Not Null	Generated	Default Value/Generate ...
CUSTNO	☑		CHAR	9		☑	☐	
CFNAME	☐		CHAR	15		☐	☐	SYSTEM_DEFAULT
CLNAME	☐		CHAR	20		☐	☐	SYSTEM_DEFAULT
CADDR	☐		CHAR	30		☐	☐	SYSTEM_DEFAULT
CZIP	☐		CHAR	5		☐	☐	SYSTEM_DEFAULT
CPHONE	☐		CHAR	10		☑	☐	
CEMAIL	☐		CHAR	50		☑	☐	
CDOB	☐		DECIMAL	8	0	☑	☐	
CGENDER	☐		CHAR	1		☑	☐	

Figure 17.1: Customers file layout

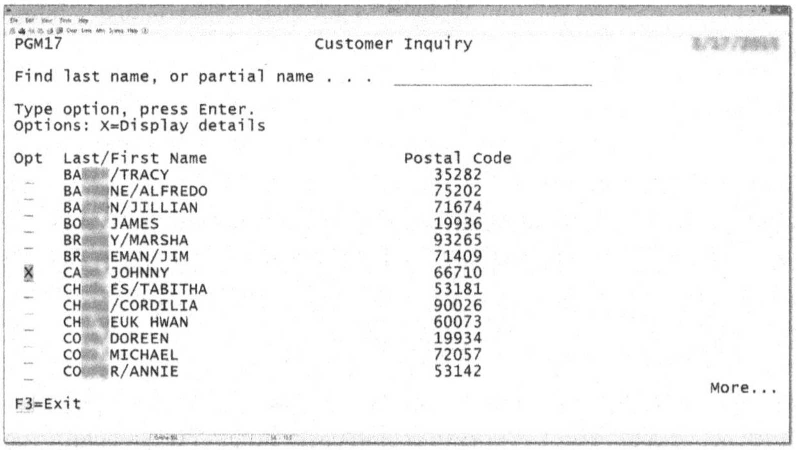

Figure 17.2: Customer selection display

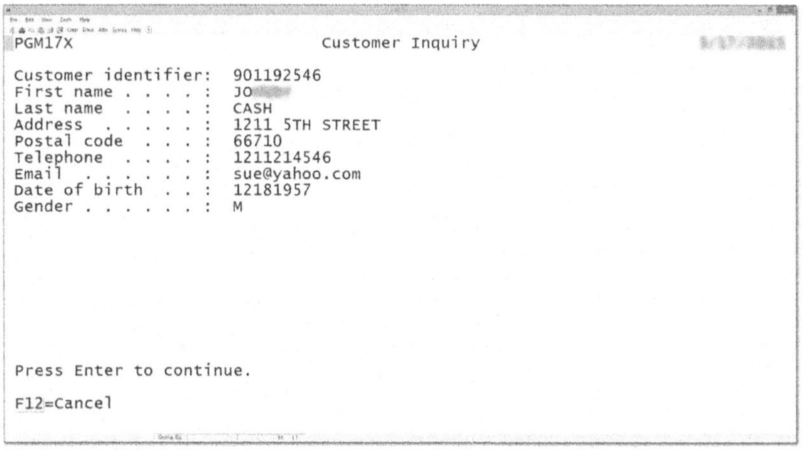

Figure 17.3: Customer details display

Your first step, before beginning the screen definition, is to create a logical file over the Customers file to access the records in order by last name and then first name. This is the file you will use to load the subfile with data in the proper order. The DDS in Figure 17.4 provides the definition for that logical file, Custf1.

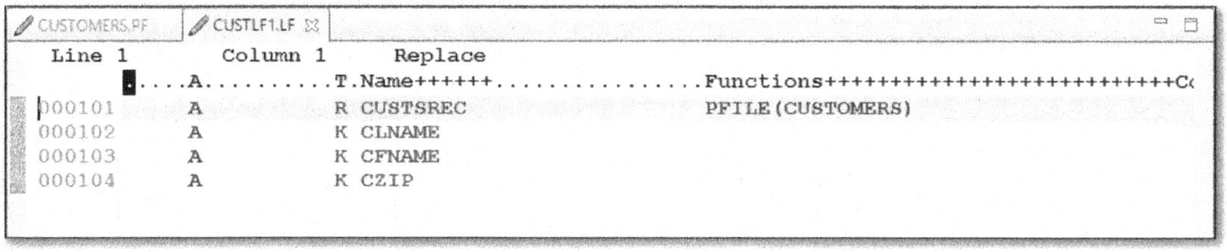

Figure 17.4: Customers logical file, keyed by last name, first name, and postal code

Now consider the DDS in Figure 17.5 for file PGM17D, the display file for the selection program PGM17. While the display file appears as a single display (Figure 17.2), it actually comprises three record formats:

- PGM17SFL—the selection list (sequence 400–800 in Figure 17.5)
- PGM17CTL—the headings (sequence 900–3700)
- PGM17BOT—the bottom function key instructions (sequence 3800–4000)

We concentrate on the first two formats, which relate to subfiles. The contents of the third format, PGM17BOT, should be familiar to you already.

```
                    PGM17D.DSPF  ⊠
  Line 5          Column 1        Replace
          .....AAN01N02N03..Name+++++RLen++TDpBLinPosFunctions++++++++++++++++++++++++++++++C
  000100    A                                          REF(CUSTOMERS)
  000200    A                                          CA03(03)
  000300    A                                          INDARA
  000400    A              R PGM17SFL                  SFL
  000500    A                OPTION          1   B  9  3DSPATR(HI)
  000600    A                NAME           36   O  9  7
  000700    A                CZIP       R       O  9 45REFFLD(CZIP)
  000800    A                CUSTNO     R       H     REFFLD(CUSTNO)
  000900    A              R PGM17CTL                  SFLCTL(PGM17SFL)
  001000    A  90                                      SFLDSP
  001100    A  91                                      SFLDSPCTL
  001200    A  92                                      SFLCLR
  001300    A  93                                      SFLEND(*MORE)
  001400    A                                          SFLPAG(13)
  001500    A                                          SFLSIZ(53)
  001600    A                                          OVERLAY
  001700    A N93                                      PAGEDOWN(94)
  001800    A                RRN            4S  OH     SFLRCDNBR
  001900    A                                       1  2'PGM17'
  002000    A                                       1 33'Customer Inquiry'
  002100    A                                          DSPATR(HI)
  002200    A                                       1 70DATE(*YY)
  002300    A                                          EDTCDE(Y)
  002400    A                                       3  2'Find last name, or partial name . +
  002500    A                                            . .'
  002600    A                FIND       R       B  3 41REFFLD(CLNAME)
  002700    A                                          DSPATR(HI)
  002800    A                                       5  2'Type option, press Enter.'
  002900    A                                          COLOR(BLU)
  003000    A                                       6  2'Options: X=Display details'
  003100    A                                          COLOR(BLU)
  003200    A                                       8  2'Opt'
  003300    A                                          DSPATR(HI)
  003400    A                                       8  7'Last/First Name'
  003500    A                                          DSPATR(HI)
  003600    A                                       8 42'Postal Code'
  003700    A                                          DSPATR(HI)
  003800    A              R PGM17BOT
  003900    A                                      23  2'F3=Exit'
  004000    A                                          COLOR(BLU)
  004100
```

Figure 17.5: DDS source for display file PGM17D (SFLSIZ > SFLPAG)

17.3. Subfile Record Formats

The **subfile record format** describes the fields that are to appear on the list. In this example, the format PGM17SFL is the subfile record format. To identify the record format as a subfile, you must use a new record-level keyword, **SFL (Subfile)**. The remaining information in the subfile record format describes the fields to display, their locations on the screen, and any editing or other special keywords desired. The row (Lin) number associated with each field represents the display row on which the first record of the subfile list is to appear. It is not necessary—or even allowed—to explicitly define subsequent rows.

The first field on the list is Option, which lets users select a list item by typing an X before a customer name. Option is both an input and an output field on the display (B in position 38). Name and Czip are output fields (o in position 38) and do not allow user entry. Finally,

Custno is a hidden field (H in position 38); it does not appear on the screen, but it is still a part of the subfile and is used to identify a customer record. Hidden fields do not include a screen location specification because, although they are part of the screen, they are not displayed. Your program can write a value to a hidden field and read the field's value, but users cannot see or change that value. Refer to Figure 17.2 to examine the list structure defined by the subfile.

17.4. Subfile Control Record Formats

The **subfile control record format** must immediately follow the subfile record format in the DDS. This record format controls the subfile records' display through the use of special record-level keywords. In addition, programmers often include the column headings for the subfile display as part of this record format. In Figure 17.5, record format PGM17CTL is the subfile control record format.

The subfile control record format requires several record-level keywords, which are as follows:

- **SFLCTL** (Subfile Control) identifies a record as the subfile control record for the subfile named within the parentheses after the keyword.
- **SFLDSP** (Subfile Display) displays the subfile itself if SFLDSP is active when an output operation is performed on the subfile control record. This keyword generally is conditioned by an indicator to control whether to display the subfile on a given output operation.
- **SFLPAG** (Subfile Page) defines how many subfile records are to appear at once on the screen. The number follows the keyword and is enclosed in parentheses. You typically determine this number by calculating the number of available screen lines, after taking into account all other lines to display along with the subfile.
- **SFLSIZ** (Subfile Size) indicates the number of records in the entire subfile. The value, enclosed in parentheses immediately after the SFLSIZ keyword, should be either equal to or greater than the SFLPAG value. If the value is greater, you can make it large enough to accommodate the maximum number of records you normally would have in the subfile. (If you underestimate, however, the system automatically extends the subfile to make room for the additional records.) A subfile cannot contain more than 9,999 records. If SFLSIZ is greater than SFLPAG, IBM i automatically handles scrolling through the subfile when a user presses the page (or roll) keys; the system then presents a plus sign (+) or a More... indicator at the bottom of the screen to indicate that some subfile records have not yet displayed.

Subfile control record-level keywords that are optional, but usually used, include the following:

- **SFLDSPCTL** (Subfile Display Control) enables the display of any output fields or constants described within the control record format. The keyword generally is conditioned with the same indicator you use for the SFLDSP keyword.

- **SFLCLR** (Subfile Clear) clears the subfile of any records if it is active when an output operation is performed on the subfile control record. This keyword requires an option indicator. The indicator often is the reverse of the one used for keywords SFLDSP and SFLDSPCTL, so you can clear the subfile in one output operation and display the subfile and the control information in a second output operation.
- **SFLEND** (Subfile End) controls the display of a plus sign (+) or a More... indicator in the lower-right corner of the list (or a graphical scroll bar to the right of the list). These elements indicate that users can use the page keys (or a mouse) to display additional list items.

Notice in Figure 17.5 that several keywords are conditioned by indicators. When *In90 is *On, the system displays the subfile list; *In91 triggers the display of the headings in the subfile control record. If *In92 is *On, the system clears the subfile list of any records. The program sets *In93 to *On when it reaches the end of the list; this DDS keyword controls the display of the More/Bottom notation at the end of the list.

Format PGM17BOT contains prompts about active function keys. This record format is necessary because the control record format (PGM17CTL) cannot reference screen lines that are both above the subfile display (i.e., the column headings) and below the subfile (the function key prompts). The control record format includes the **OVERLAY** record level keyword, so that the footer record format is not erased when the subfile is displayed.

The **PAGEDOWN** record-level keyword (sequence 1700) detects when a user presses the Page Down key; *In94 is set to *On when this occurs. The program uses this indicator to trigger loading another page of the subfile list.

Finally, the subfile control record uses the **SFLRCDNBR** field-level keyword (sequence 1800) to specify that the subfile list page to display is one with the list entry whose relative record number is in this variable (Rrn, in this case). If you do not specify a subfile record number variable, the system displays the first page of the subfile. You must enter this variable after all the record-level keywords; it must be a signed numeric variable up to four digits, no decimal places, and is usually hidden (H in position 38).

The remaining entries in the subfile control record format are the heading and instructions. The format also includes a Find variable (sequence 2400–2600), which the program uses to position the top of the list to a specific last name or partial name.

17.5. Loading the Subfile

As previously indicated, the relationship between subfile size and subfile page can vary. Programmers use several different approaches to defining this interrelationship and to loading data into the subfile. The method used depends in part on a program's anticipated processing requirements:

- Loading the subfile a page at a time
  - SFLSIZ greater than SFLPAG
  - SFLSIZ equal to SFLPAG
- Loading the entire subfile

17.5.1. Loading the Subfile a Page at a Time

When the program loads the subfile a page at a time, each page loads rapidly because the program does not have to read all the records in the file to initially build the list. The processing steps to load and display the subfile will vary, depending upon the relationship between the values of SFLSIZ and SFLPAG.

17.5.1.1. Page at a Time: Subfile Size Greater Than Page

This method of subfile handling, sometimes called the *self-extending* subfile, relies on the fact that the system will automatically expand a subfile, regardless of its stated size, as your program adds more records to it. Because this additionally allocated room is not contiguous in memory, performance degrades as the number of pages in the subfile increases. However, the technique works well when the number of records usually required within the subfile is moderate. This technique also simplifies coding a *find* function to position the list to a specific record.

This method initially loads only one page of the subfile. When a user requests an additional page by pressing the Page Down key, the program loads the next page while retaining the previous pages in memory. Paging within the already loaded subfile records is handled automatically by the operating system. When a user attempts to scroll past the last record in the subfile, however, control returns to the program, which must load an additional page (if additional appropriate records exist).

To use this method, the DDS must include three keywords in the subfile control record format. First, you must associate the PAGEDOWN keyword (or its equivalent, ROLLUP) with an indicator to let the system return control to the program when a page-down request exceeds the current limits of the subfile. You must also add the SFLEND keyword, conditioned by an indicator.

Keyword SFLEND, its associated indicator, and the Page Down key work together to determine what happens when a user tries to scroll past the current limits of the subfile. When indicator SFLEND is off, the system displays a More notation (or a + sign) and returns control to the program to load the next page. When SFLEND is on, the system shows the Bottom notation (or does not display the + sign) and does not return control to the program for additional loading. Thus, the program should turn on SFLEND when no additional records remain to place into the subfile. The system will then prohibit user attempts to scroll past the last page of records in the subfile.

The third required keyword is SFLRCDNBR field-level keyword coded along with a (usually hidden) numeric variable. The variable's value determines which page of the subfile to display when the subfile control format is written.

With the display file definition complete, let's turn to the requirements for the program that will use it. The following sample RPG program PGM17 loads the subfile a page at a time, with the SFLSIZ value greater than SFLPAG:

```
// ----------------------------------------------------------
//
// Program Pgm17 - Select customers records for processing
// Subfile processing: Page at a time, SFLSIZ > SFLPAG
//

// ---------------------------------------------------- Files
Dcl-f Cust1f1 Keyed;
Dcl-f Pgm17d  Workstn Sfile(Pgm17sfl:Rrn) Indds(Indicators);

// ------------------------------------------------ Constants
Dcl-c Sflpag 13;                     // Sflpag(13)

// ----------------------------------------------- Prototypes
Dcl-pr Pgm17x Extpgm('PGM17X');      // Display details
  *N Like(Custno);
End-pr;

// ----------------------------------------- Data structures
Dcl-ds Indicators Len(99);
  Exit       Ind Pos(03);            // F3=Exit
  Sfldsp     Ind Pos(90);            // *In90 = Sfldsp
  Sfldspctl  Ind Pos(91);            // *In91 = Sfldspctl
  Sflclr     Ind Pos(92);            // *In92 = Sflclr
  Sflend     Ind Pos(93);            // *In93 = Sflend
  Pagedown   Ind Pos(94);            // *In94 = Pagedown
End-ds;

// --------------------------------- Standalone variables
Dcl-s X Uns(5);
```

Continued

```
// ---------------------------------------------------------
//
// Main procedure
//
Clearsfl();
Loadsfl();

Dou Exit;
  Write Pgm17bot;
  Exfmt Pgm17ctl;

  Select;
    When Exit;
      Leave;
    When Pagedown;
      Loadsfl();
    When Find <> *Blanks;
      Clearsfl();
      Loadsfl();
    Other;
      Readsfl();
      Clearsfl();
      Loadsfl();
  Endsl;

Enddo;

*Inlr = *On;
Return;

// ---------------------------------------------------------
//
// Procedure Clearsfl - Clear subfile for new list
//
Dcl-proc Clearsfl;
  Sfldsp = *Off;
```

Continued

```
    Sfldspctl = *Off;
    Sflend = *Off;
    Sflclr = *On;
    Write Pgm17ctl;
    Sflclr = *Off;
    Rrn = 0;
    Setll Find Custlf1;
    Find = *Blanks;
  End-proc;


  // -----------------------------------------------------------
  //
  // Procedure Loadsfl - Load next subfile page
  //
  Dcl-proc Loadsfl;

    For X = 1 to Sflpag;
      Read Custlf1;

      If %Eof(Custlf1);
        Sflend = *On;
        Leave;
      Endif;

      Rrn += 1;
      Option = *Blanks;
      Name = %Trim(Clname) + '/' + %Trim(Cfname);
      Write Pgm17sfl;
    Endfor;

    Sfldsp = (Rrn > 0);
    Sfldspctl = *On;
  End-proc;


  // -----------------------------------------------------------
  //
  // Procedure Readsfl - Process selected records from subfile
```

Continued

```
//
Dcl-proc Readsfl;

  Dou %Eof;
    Readc Pgm17sfl;

    Select;
      When %Eof;
        Leave;
      When Option = 'X';
        Pgm17x(Custno);                // X = Display details
    Endsl;

  Enddo;

End-proc;
```

This program's structure should be familiar to you by now, but we'll highlight those sections that specifically process the subfile.

First, for all subfile applications, RPG requires you to identify a subfile within the display file's declaration with which you want to associate that subfile. In addition, as part of the display file's declaration, you need to identify a field that your program is to use to represent a subfile record's relative record number. **Relative record number** simply means the position of the record within the subfile (e.g., first subfile record, second subfile record). This field is necessary because RPG writes records to a subfile (and retrieves records from a subfile) based on the value of the relative record number. You associate the subfile and relative record number field with a workstation file by using the **Sfile (Subfile)** keyword. The subfile record format name and the field to use to store the relative record number appear within parentheses following the keyword:

```
Dcl-f Pgm17d Workstn Sfile(Pgm17sfl:Rrn);
```

In addition to the main procedure, the cycle-main program consists of three subprocedures:

- Clearsfl resets the list and positions the customer file to begin with the last name, if any, in the Find variable.
- Loadsfl loads the next page of the subfile list.
- Readsfl processes selected records from the subfile list.

The main procedure begins by doing some housekeeping, initially setting up the first page of the list:

```
Clearsfl();
Loadsfl();
```

Then it enters a loop, showing all three formats in the display file as one:

```
Write Pgm17bot;
Exfmt Pgm17ctl;
```

The subfile list (PGM17SFL) is implicitly displayed as a result of the subfile control format (PGM17CTL) being displayed. Because the subfile control format uses the OVERLAY keyword, the footer record (PGM17BOT) remains on the display when the program executes the subfile control format.

The subsequent Select group processes each of the possibilities when the program regains control:

- The program leaves the loop and returns to its caller when a user presses the F3=Exit key.
- The program loads the next page of the subfile when a user presses the Page Down key.
- The program resets the list beginning with the *found* record when a user enters a Find value.
- Otherwise, the program processes the selected records from the list, then resets the list.

```
When Exit;
  Leave;
When Pagedown;
  Loadsfl();
When Find <> *Blanks;
  Clearsfl();
  Loadsfl();
Other;
  Readsfl();
  Clearsfl();
  Loadsfl();
```

The subprocedures include details for each of these functions.

The Clearsfl procedure resets the subfile list. First, it sets *Off for all the subfile-related indicators except Sflclr, which it sets to *On. The subfile indicators are each named in the Indicators data structure. For convenience and documentary purposes, they are named the same as the keywords in the display file DDS. (To review the use of the indicator data structure, see Chapter 12.) Next, by writing the PGM17CTL format with the Sflclr indicator *On, the program enables the procedure to clear the list of any existing entries and then set Sflclr to *Off. The procedure also resets the Rrn variable so that program will load the list with new records. Finally, the Clearsfl procedure positions the Custlf1 file to locate the appropriate Find record, or at the beginning of the file if Find is blank.

The Loadsfl procedure loads a page of the subfile list. In a loop, it reads the correct number of records from the Custlf1 file. The Sflpag constant determines the number of records and corresponds to the Sflpag keyword in the DDS. If the procedure encounters end-of-file, it sets Sflend to *On and leaves the loop. For each record read, the procedure increments the Rrn variable and builds each variable to show on the list. The subfile is loaded by writing records to the subfile record format based on the relative record number. Following the loop, the procedure checks whether Rrn is greater than zero; if it is, then the subfile list contains records to display, so the Sfldsp indicator is set to *On. Also, the Sfldspctl indicator is set to *On so that the headings display as well.

When the Loadsfl procedure ends and the main procedure redisplays the formats, the new page appears. The program displays the subfile by executing the subfile control record format. The program uses Write, rather than Exfmt, to display the Footer format because a user response to that display is not required. Each time control returns to the program from the screen, if the page key triggered the return, the program must load the next page of the subfile and return control to the screen.

The Readsfl procedure processes all selected records from the list. This procedure executes when a user presses the Enter key (not a page key). The Option field in the subfile list is input capable (B in position 38 of the DDS in Figure 17.5). Typing an X to the left of one or more records in the list enables the program to detect those changes in the list. Generally used within a loop and only with subfiles, the **Readc (Read Next Changed Record)** operation reads just those subfile records that were changed during a prior Exfmt operation. The Readc operation takes this form:

```
Readc{(e)} record-name {data-structure};
```

Readc reads the next changed record from the subfile. When no changed subfile records remain to be read, %Eof is turned on. Users can make as many changes as necessary to the subfile before the program regains control; all these changes are then processed when control is returned to the program. By specifying a result data structure, you enable the Read operation to transfer data directly from the record to the data structure. In the example program PGM17, the Readsfl procedure reads a changed record. If Option is X for that record, the program calls another program PGM17X, passing that record's Custno as a single parameter to PGM17X. Any other entry for Option is ignored.

Program PGM17X is a simple program that displays the selected record's details (Figure 17.3). Figure 17.6 shows the DDS for display file PGM17XD. The RPG program itself follows:

```
// ------------------------------------------------------------
//
// Program Pgm17x - Display customer details
//


// ------------------------------------------------------- Files
Dcl-f Customers Keyed;
Dcl-f Pgm17xd  Workstn Indds(Indicators);

// ------------------------------ Main Prototype/Interface
Dcl-pr Pgm17x Extpgm;
  *N Like(Custno);
End-pr;


Dcl-pi Pgm17x;
  Incust Like(Custno);
End-pi;


// ------------------------------------------ Data structures
Dcl-ds Indicators Len(99);
  Cancel Ind Pos(12);          // F12=Cancel
End-ds;


// ------------------------------------------------------------
//
// Main procedure
//
Chain Incust Customers;
```

Continued

```
If %Found(Customers);
  Exfmt Pgm17x1;
Endif;


*Inlr = *On;
Return;
```

```
PGM17D.DSPF        PGM17XD.DSPF

 Line 1           Column 1      Replace
     .....AAN01N02N03..........................Functions++++++++++++++++++++++++++++Co
000100      A                                        REF(CUSTOMERS)
000101      A                                        INDARA
000103      A                                        CA12(12)
000900      A           R PGM17X1
000901      A                                   1  2'PGM17X'
000902      A                                   1 33'Customer Inquiry'
000903      A                                        DSPATR(HI)
000904      A                                   1 70DATE(*YY)
000905      A                                        EDTCDE(Y)
001300      A                                   3  2'Customer identifier:'
001400      A           CUSTNO    R        O    3 24
001500      A                                   4  2'First name . . . . :'
001600      A           CFNAME    R        O    4 24
001700      A                                   5  2'Last name  . . . . :'
001800      A           CLNAME    R        O    5 24
001900      A                                   6  2'Address  . . . . . :'
002000      A           CADDR     R        O    6 24
002100      A                                   7  2'Postal code  . . . :'
002200      A           CZIP      R        O    7 24
002300      A                                   8  2'Telephone  . . . . :'
002400      A           CPHONE    R        O    8 24
002500      A                                   9  2'Email  . . . . . . :'
002600      A           CEMAIL    R        O    9 24
002700      A                                  10  2'Date of birth  . . :'
002800      A           CDOB      R        O   10 24
002900      A                                  11  2'Gender . . . . . . :'
003000      A           CGENDER   R        O   11 24
003100      A                                  21  2'Press Enter to continue.'
003101      A                                        COLOR(BLU)
003300      A                                  23  2'F12=Cancel'
003301      A                                        COLOR(BLU)


Design Source Preview
```

Figure 17.6: DDS source for display file PGM17XD

By coding this basic application in a modular fashion, using called programs and subprocedures, you can easily enhance it with additional functions, such as adding, changing, and deleting records. Loading the subfile a page at a time, with SFLSIZ greater than SFLPAG, ensures consistent performance while paging and facilitates easy coding of a Find function. One possible disadvantage, though, is that it is more difficult to program a feature to allow users to scroll backward (Page Up) to a page before the beginning of the list without repositioning it. If your application requires that feature, one of the other options for loading the subfile may be more appropriate.

17.5.1.2. Page at a Time: Subfile Size Equals Page

Setting SFLSIZ equal to SFLPAG is most appropriate when users are likely to want to scroll through a large number of records. Response time is consistent, regardless of the number of records viewed.

With this method, the subfile stores only one page of records at a time. Scrolling forward requires replacing the existing page with the next page to be loaded; scrolling backward requires replacing the existing page by reloading the previous page. The program must explicitly handle scrolling in either direction. The program logic that this technique needs is therefore more complicated than that of the other methods. Moreover, the method of backward scrolling the program uses may depend on whether you are accessing records by unique keys, non-unique keys, partial keys, or relative record numbers.

The DDS for this implementation is similar to that when subfile size is greater than subfile page, except that SFLSIZ equals SFLPAG and keyword SFLRCDNBR is not used. (Because the subfile is only one page long, positioning the subfile upon redisplay is not an issue with this technique.) Figure 17.7 illustrates the changes to the subfile control format only; no changes to other formats are necessary. Note that the control record format includes keywords PAGEUP, PAGEDOWN, and SFLEND.

```
PGM17D.DSPF
  Line 9          Column 1        Insert
         .....A..........T.Name++++++..............Functions++++++++++++++++++++++++++++++C
         ----- 8 lines excluded. -----
  000900     A            R PGM17CTL              SFLCTL(PGM17SFL)
  001000     A   90                               SFLDSP
  001100     A   91                               SFLDSPCTL
  001200     A   92                               SFLCLR
  001300     A   93                               SFLEND(*MORE)
  001400     A                                    SFLPAG(13)
  001500     A                                    SFLSIZ(13)
  001600     A                                    OVERLAY
```

Figure 17.7: DDS source for display file PGM17D (SFLSIZ = SFLPAG)

Although the needed DDS changes are minimal, this method requires some significant modifications to the ILE RPG program. First, each time the program loads a subfile page, it must clear the subfile because the new records should completely replace those previously displayed. Second, the program must check the page key indicator to determine whether to put the next or previous set of customer records into the subfile.

Additionally, the program must include processing to *crawl back* through the database file so that it can scroll backward when a user presses the Page Up key. In the following program, the Crawlback procedure uses the Readp operation to move backward through Custlf1 until it is properly positioned to load a new page, using Loadsfl. The Crawlback procedure executes when a user presses Page Up.

```
// ----------------------------------------------------------
//
// Program Pgm17 - Select customers records for processing
// Subfile processing: Page at a time, SFLSIZ = SFLPAG
//


// ------------------------------------------------- Files
Dcl-f Custlf1 Keyed;
Dcl-f Pgm17d  Workstn Sfile(Pgm17sfl:Rrn) Indds(Indicators);


// ----------------------------------------------- Constants
Dcl-c Sflpag 13;                    // Sflpag(13)


// ----------------------------------------------- Prototypes
Dcl-pr Pgm17x Extpgm('PGM17X');     // Display details
  *N Like(Custno);
End-pr;


// ---------------------------------------- Data structures
Dcl-ds Indicators Len(99);
  Exit       Ind Pos(03);           // F3=Exit
  Sfldsp     Ind Pos(90);           // *In90 = Sfldsp
  Sfldspctl  Ind Pos(91);           // *In91 = Sfldspctl
  Sflclr     Ind Pos(92);           // *In92 = Sflclr
  Sflend     Ind Pos(93);           // *In93 = Sflend
  Pagedown   Ind Pos(94);           // *In94 = Pagedown
  Pageup     Ind Pos(95);           // *In95 = Pageup
End-ds;


// ------------------------------------- Standalone variables
Dcl-s Rrn Zoned(4:0);
Dcl-s X   Uns(5);


// ----------------------------------------------------------
//
// Main procedure
//
```

Continued

```
Loadsfl();

Dou Exit;
  Write Pgm17bot;
  Exfmt Pgm17ctl;

  Select;
    When Exit;
      Leave;
    When Pageup;
      Crawlback();
      Loadsfl();
    When Pagedown;
      Loadsfl();
    When Find <> *Blanks;
      Setll Find Custlf1;
      Find = *Blanks;
      Loadsfl();
    Other;
      Readsfl();
      Setll *Loval Custlf1;
      Loadsfl();
  Endsl;

Enddo;

*Inlr = *On;
Return;

// -----------------------------------------------------------
//
// Procedure Clearsfl - Clear subfile for new list
//
Dcl-proc Clearsfl;
  Sfldsp = *Off;
  Sfldspctl = *Off;
  Sflend = *Off;
  Sflclr = *On;
```

Continued

```
    Write Pgm17ctl;
    Sflclr = *Off;
    Rrn = 0;
  End-proc;


  // ----------------------------------------------------------
  //
  // Procedure Crawlback - Reset database file on Pageup
  //
  Dcl-proc Crawlback;

    If Sflend;                        // Reposition if %Eof
      Setgt *Hival Custlf1;
      Rrn += 1;
    Endif;


    For X = 1 to (Rrn + Sflpag);    // Back up X records
      Readp Custlf1;

      If %Eof(Custlf1);               // Reached beginning of file
        Setll *Loval Custlf1;
        Leave;
      Endif;


    Endfor;

  End-proc;


  // ----------------------------------------------------------
  //
  // Procedure Loadsfl - Load next subfile page
  //
  Dcl-proc Loadsfl;
    Clearsfl();

    For X = 1 to Sflpag;
      Read Custlf1;
```

Continued

```
     If %Eof(Custlf1);
       Sflend = *On;
       Leave;
     Endif;

     Rrn = X;
     Option = *Blanks;
     Name = %Trim(Clname) + '/' + %Trim(Cfname);
     Write Pgm17sfl;
   Endfor;

   Sfldsp = (Rrn > 0);
   Sfldspctl = *On;

End-proc;

// ----------------------------------------------------------
//
// Procedure Readsfl - Process selected records from subfile
//
Dcl-proc Readsfl;

   Dou %Eof;
     Readc Pgm17sfl;

     Select;
       When %Eof;
         Leave;
       When Option = 'X';
         Pgm17x(Custno);
     Endsl;

   Enddo;

End-proc;
```

17.5.2. Loading the Entire Subfile

This method involves defining the subfile size to hold the maximum expected number of records and then loading all the appropriate data into the subfile before the program displays

Chapter 17   Programming with Subfiles • **539**

the list. Although this method is the easiest to code, it results in the slowest initial response time. Once display begins, however, paging through the subfile is fast because the system handles all paging functions. Using this technique is appropriate when the entire list is relatively small, especially if users may want to see most of the list; it is least appropriate when a large number of records must be loaded and users are unlikely to want to see most of those records.

Figure 17.8 shows the DDS changes for the subfile control record. You should set the subfile size to a number you would reasonably expect to appear in the entire subfile. The paging keywords and the SFLRCDNBR keyword are not necessary when you are loading the entire subfile.

```
PGM17D.DSPF
  Line 16        Column 1       Replace
        .....AAN01N02N03.........................Functions++++++++++++++++++++++++++++++
           ----- 8 lines excluded. -----
  000900      A            R PGM17CTL              SFLCTL(PGM17SFL)
  001000      A  90                                SFLDSP
  001100      A  91                                SFLDSPCTL
  001200      A  92                                SFLCLR
  001300      A  93                                SFLEND(*MORE)
  001400      A                                    SFLPAG(13)
  001500      A                                    SFLSIZ(53)
  001600      A                                    OVERLAY
           ----- 31 lines excluded. -----

Design Source Preview
```

Figure 17.8: DDS source for display file PGM17D (Load Entire Subfile)

The following code illustrates the RPG implementation of loading the entire subfile:

```
// ----------------------------------------------------------
//
// Program Pgm17 - Select customers records for processing
// Subfile processing: Load entire subfile
//
// ----------------------------------------------- Files
Dcl-f Custlf1 Keyed;
Dcl-f Pgm17d  Workstn Sfile(Pgm17sfl:Rrn) Indds(Indicators);


// ----------------------------------------- Prototypes
Dcl-pr Pgm17x Extpgm('PGM17X');     // Dislay details
  *N Like(Custno);
End-pr;
                                              Continued
```

```
// ----------------------------------------- Data structures
Dcl-ds Indicators Len(99);
  Exit       Ind Pos(03);              // F3=Exit
  Sfldsp     Ind Pos(90);              // *In90 = Sfldsp
  Sfldspctl  Ind Pos(91);              // *In91 = Sfldspctl
  Sflclr     Ind Pos(92);              // *In92 = Sflclr
  Sflend     Ind Pos(93);              // *In93 = Sflend
End-ds;


// --------------------------------- Standalone variables
Dcl-s Rrn Zoned(4:0);
Dcl-s X   Uns(5);


// ----------------------------------------------------------
//
// Main procedure
//
Loadsfl();

Dou Exit;
  Write Pgm17bot;
  Exfmt Pgm17ctl;

  Select;
    When Exit;
      Leave;
    When Find <> *Blanks;
      Setll Find Custlf1;
      Find = *Blanks;
      Loadsfl();
    Other;
      Readsfl();
      Setll *Loval Custlf1;
      Loadsfl();
  Endsl;

Enddo;
```

Continued

```
*Inlr = *On;
Return;


// ------------------------------------------------------------
//
// Procedure Clearsfl - Clear subfile for new list
//
Dcl-proc Clearsfl;
  Sfldsp = *Off;
  Sfldspctl = *Off;
  Sflend = *Off;
  Sflclr = *On;
  Write Pgm17ctl;
  Sflclr = *Off;
  Rrn = 0;
End-proc;


// ------------------------------------------------------------
//
// Procedure Loadsfl - Load next subfile page
//
Dcl-proc Loadsfl;
  Clearsfl();

  Dou %Eof(Custlf1);
    Read Custlf1;

    If %Eof(Custlf1);
      Sflend = *On;
      Leave;
    Endif;

    Rrn += 1;
    Option = *Blanks;
    Name = %Trim(Clname) + '/' + %Trim(Cfname);
    Write Pgm17sfl;
  Enddo;
```

Continued

```
  Sfldsp = (Rrn > 0);
  Sfldspctl = *On;

End-proc;


// ------------------------------------------------------------
//
// Procedure Readsfl - Process selected records from subfile
//
Dcl-proc Readsfl;

  Dou %Eof;
    Readc Pgm17sfl;

    Select;
      When %Eof;
        Leave;
      When Option = 'X';
        Pgm17x(Custno);
    Endsl;

  Enddo;

End-proc;
```

In this implementation of the subfile application, subfile size is greater than subfile page, and the size is large enough to handle the maximum number of records that the subfile normally is expected to hold. The program stores all relevant database records in the subfile before any display. With this approach, IBM i automatically enables the page keys and signals that more subfile records are available for viewing. From a programmer's viewpoint, this technique is the simplest to code. Unfortunately, it can result in poor response time when the application is used.

The cause of the slow system response is that this technique requires the system to access all records that meet the selection criterion and store them in the subfile before displaying the first page of the subfile. Performance is satisfactory when the subfile size is small, but as the subfile size increases—say, to hundreds of records—response time degrades noticeably. In that case, especially if the user typically does not scroll much throughout the subfile, consider building the subfile a page at a time as the user requests additional pages.

17.6. Chapter Summary

Subfiles let users work with more than one database record at a time in an interactive application. Records stored in a subfile are displayed in a single output operation to the workstation file. Changes made to subfile records are returned to the program in one input operation.

Defining subfiles within DDS requires two kinds of record formats: one that defines the fields within the subfile and describes the field locations within a screen line, and a second, called a *subfile control record format*, that manages the displaying of the subfile information.

You use several required DDS keywords with subfiles. Record-level keyword SFL identifies a record format as a subfile record, and record-level keyword SFLCTL specifies a format as a subfile control record format. Additional required keywords determine how many records appear on the screen at once, how much total storage the system allocates to the subfile, and when to display the subfile and its control record.

Several different techniques exist for loading and displaying subfiles. These methods differ in the relationship they establish between subfile page and subfile size and in when they write records to the subfile relative to when the subfile display begins. Regardless of the technique you use, all applications involving subfiles require additional entries on the File specifications for the workstation files using the subfiles. You perform all input to and output from a subfile through relative record numbers. The Readc operation lets your application program process only those subfile records that a user has changed.

The following table summarizes the operation codes discussed in this chapter:

Function or Operation	Description	Syntax
Readc	Read next changed record	**Readc{(e)} record-name {data-structure};**

17.7. Key Terms

list panels	SFL	SFLRCDNBR
OVERLAY	SFLCLR	SFLSIZ
PAGEDOWN	SFLCTL	subfile
PAGEUP	SFLDSPCTL	subfile control record format
Readc operation	SFLEND	subfile record format
relative record number	SFLDSP	
Sfile	SFLPAG	

17.8. Discussion/Review Questions

1. What is a subfile?
2. What are the functions of a subfile record format and a subfile control record format in a display file?

3. Describe the meanings of the following display file keywords and which record format each is used with: SFL, SFLCTL, SFLPAG, SFLSIZ, SFLDSP, SFLCLR, and SFLDSPCTL.

4. In subfile processing, how are column headings for the subfile and screen footings (i.e., information to display below the subfile) generally handled?

5. What is a hidden field?

6. When do you need to use the keyword SFLRCDNBR?

7. Discuss the relative merits of different approaches to subfile definition and loading.

8. Discuss page-key control and action regarding the different approaches to subfile definition and loading.

9. How does the Readc operation differ from the other read operations of ILE RPG?

10. In using subfiles for updating, why do you need to use fields for subfiles that are different from the fields of the database file you are updating?

11. Explain the differences between the various ways to load subfiles. What are the benefits of one approach over the other?

12. Using IBM's online documentation, research the WINDOW (Window) keyword for display files. What benefit would this keyword have for an RPG programmer?

17.9. Exercises

1. Design the screens and write the DDS for an interactive application that lets users enter a zip code to list the names of all a company's customers residing within that zip code. Create whatever fields you may need, and make the subfile size much greater than the page.

2. Write the ILE RPG code for exercise 1. Make up whatever filenames and field names you need, but be consistent with the definitions used in exercise 1. Use the technique of loading the entire subfile prior to display.

3. Revise the DDS from exercise 1 to make the subfile size and page equal. Modify the ILE RPG code from exercise 2 to suit this change.

4. Write the pseudocode for an interactive application that displays a list of all a company's product numbers and their descriptions, and that lets users place an X in front of those products for which they want more information. The program must then display a screen of detailed product information—quantity on hand, cost, selling price, reorder point, and reorder quantity—for each product the user selects.

5. Write the generic pseudocode required to use subfiles for data entry (i.e., for adding large numbers of records to a file).

6. Write the pseudocode and flow chart for Chapter 17 program assignment 5 (download the assignments at mc-store.com/Programming-ILE-RPG-Fifth-Edition/dp/1583473793).

18

Working with APIs

18.1. Chapter Overview

This chapter introduces the concept of calling application program interfaces (APIs) from within an RPG program to access low-level machine functions or system data not otherwise available within an HLL program. In this chapter, you learn about the role of user spaces and wrapper procedures when using APIs, as well as using APIs to create HTML code for Web pages.

18.2. Popular APIs

You have learned how an RPG program can call another program written in RPG (or any other HLL) by using Callp. You can also use Callp to access **application programming interfaces**, or APIs. APIs are programs, or service program procedures, supplied with the operating system that let you access lower-level machine functions or system data not otherwise available within an HLL program. Some APIs provide functions similar to those available with CL commands; for others, no comparable CL command exists. An API generally performs better than a corresponding CL command and may provide features not available in a CL command.

Many different APIs exist, and each provides a different, specific capability. For example, API QUSLSPL (List Spooled Files) builds a list of spooled files (i.e., reports) from an output queue. A related API, QUSRSPLA (Retrieve Spooled File Attributes), retrieves this data into a program. You can use APIs to obtain information about a job, a database file, a library, or any other kind of object on the system.

Almost all APIs have a required, specific set of parameters that pass values from your program or return values to your program, or both. This parameter interface to an API usually remains constant from one IBM i release to another to maintain compatibility while still allowing updates to the operating system and its applications. IBM's online documentation thoroughly documents APIs, their purposes, and their parameter interfaces. Although a complete discussion of APIs is beyond the scope of this chapter, it examines a few often-used APIs to give you a sense of how you might use APIs within your RPG programs.

18.2.1. QUSCMDLN (Display Command Line Window)

The first API to consider is **QUSCMDLN** (Display Command Line Window). This API presents an IBM i system command line as a pop-up window within your program. Say, for example, that you are writing an interactive application in which you want to give users access to the system command line so they can check the status of a spooled file, send a message to another user, or perform another task. Figure 18.1 shows an example of using such a command-line window.

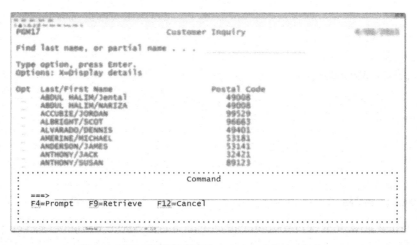

Figure 18.1: QUSCMDLN command-line window

To use this API in your display file, you enable a function key (e.g., F21, mapped via an indicator data structure to field Fkey21) to signal the user's request for a command line. Then, within your RPG program upon return from the display, you check the status of the indicator associated with that function key. If the indicator's value indicates that the user has pressed the function key, your program calls API QUSCMDLN to pop up the command line on the current screen:

```
Dcl-pr Showcmdline Extpgm('QUSCMDLN') End-pr;

Dcl-ds Indicators Len(99);
  Fkey21 Ind Pos(21);
```

Continued

```
End-ds;
...
Exfmt Screen1;
Select;
...
  When Fkey21;
    Showcmdline();
...
Ends1;
...
```

When the user finishes with the command line and exits from it, control returns to your program, which resumes processing from the point of the call. Notice that QUSCMDLN, unlike most APIs, uses no parameters.

18.2.2. QCMDEXC (Execute Command)

The next API, **QCMDEXC** (Execute Command), is more typical in its format. What does QCMDEXC do? Occasionally within an RPG program, you want to communicate directly with the operating system to issue a CL command. You might, for example, want to override one database file with another or send a message reporting on the program's progress to the user. QCMDEXC lets you execute such a CL command from within an HLL program.

Any program can call QCMDEXC. The API normally expects to receive arguments for two parameters: the first parameter should contain the command the system is to execute, and the second should contain the command's length. (You must define the variable representing this length as a numeric field with 15 positions, five of which are decimal positions.) The following example uses an expression to build a command and then uses the implied Callp to execute it:

```
Dcl-pr Runcmd Extpgm('QCMDEXC');
 *N Char(3000)   Const Options(*Varsize);   // Command string
 *N Packed(15:5) Const;                      // Length of command string
End-pr;

Dcl-s Cmd  Varchar(3000);
Dcl-s User Char(10) Inz(*User);
...
Cmd = 'WRKSPLF SELECT(' + User + ')';
Runcmd(Cmd:%Len(Cmd));
```

In this example, an interactive RPG program executes the WRKSPLF (Work with Spooled Files) CL command for a user. The prototype specifies passing by read-only reference (using the Const keyword); this option allows you to embed an expression as a parameter in the call (e.g., %Len(Cmd)). Using variable-length field Cmd simplifies the string expression used to construct the command, and using Options(*Varsize) in the prototype allows the program to pass less data than the prototype specifies.

18.3. User Space APIs

Many APIs require a special kind of storage area, called a **user space**, to receive their output or to supply their input. User spaces are objects (type *USRSPC) similar to data areas (covered in Chapter 13). But a user space can be much larger, up to 16 MB. Generally, APIs require a user space to store lists of objects. Most list APIs return a series of entries in documented formats, and your program can process each entry in the list as a data structure. For example, the **QUSLMBR** (List Database File Members) API lists all of a file's members in a user space.

Before you can use such a list API, you must create a user space. API **QUSCRTUS** (Create User Space) creates a user space for other APIs to use. Here's an example of using QUSCRTUS to create a user space named MYUSRSPC in library QTEMP:

```
Dcl-pr Quscrtus Extpgm('QUSCRTUS');
  *N Char(20) Const;                   // Qualified user space name
  *N Char(10) Const;                   // Extended attribute
  *N Uns(10)  Const;                   // Initial size
  *N Char(1)  Const;                   // Initial value
  *N Char(10) Const;                   // Public authority
  *N Char(50) Const;                   // Text
  *N Char(10) Const Options(*Nopass);  // Replace?
  *N Like(Apierr)   Options(*Nopass);  // Error code
End-pr;

Dcl-ds Apierr Len(16);
  Errmsg Char(7) Pos(9);
End-ds;
...
Quscrtus('MYUSRSPC  QTEMP     ' : 'APILIST' : 4096 : X'00' :
         '*ALL' : *BLANKS : '*YES' : Apierr);
```

Like most APIs, QUSCRTUS requires several parameters. In this example, the first six are required. The prototype comments describe the parameters—the first parameter is the qualified name of the user space to be created. APIs process qualified object names by using

20-byte character variables. The first 10 bytes are the object name, and the second 10 bytes are the library name. In this case, the user space to create will be QTEMP/MYUSRSPC. Next is the extended attribute of the user space. This parameter describes the object in more detail than simply being a *USRSPC object. You can use any valid name value; this example uses APILIST.

The third parameter indicates the initial size of the user space in bytes. If the API requires more space, the API expands the user space. QUSCRTUS initializes the user space with a character value you specify in the fourth parameter, X'00' (nulls) in this case. The public authority for this user space (fifth parameter) is *ALL to ensure that the program is allowed to perform all operations on the user space. Because this is a temporary object, you will not assign text to it (sixth parameter). The remaining two parameters are an optional group—indicated by Options(*Nopass)—but are useful in most instances. To have the API replace an existing object, specify *YES for the seventh parameter; otherwise, *NO is the default. Finally, the prototype indicates that the API should return error information to the Apierr data structure. The actual error message identifier is in the Errmsg subfield.

After the program has created the user space, it can execute the API to fill the user space with appropriate data. The following example uses the QUSLMBR API to list all of a file's members in a user space:

```
Dcl-pr Quslmbr Extpgm('QUSLMBR');
   *N Char(20) Const;                  // Qualified user space name
   *N Char(8)  Const;                  // Return format name
   *N Char(20) Const;                  // Qualified database filename
   *N Char(10) Const;                  // Member name, or generic name
   *N Char(1)  Const;                  // Process overrides?
   *N Like(Apierr) Options(*Nopass);   // Error code
End-pr;
...
Quslmbr('MYUSRSPC  QTEMP     ' : 'MBRL0100' :
        'MYFILE    *LIBL     ' : '*ALL' : '0' : Apierr);
```

In this example, QUSLMBR places member names into a list in the QTEMP/MYUSRSPC user space (first parameter). The second parameter indicates the format of the returned information. Each API formats its return information to fit a predictable data structure. In this case, you are requesting format MBRL0100, one of five formats explained in the online IBM documentation. The MBRL0100 format contains only the member name; the other formats have more detail. The third parameter (*LIBL/MYFILE) holds the qualified name of the database file whose members' names should be listed. The fourth parameter names a specific member name to list, or a generic member name (e.g., MBR* to list all members starting with

MBR), or the special value *ALL to list all members. The fifth parameter tells the API whether it should consider file overrides when locating the database file—'0' means no, '1' means yes. Finally, the optional sixth parameter accepts an error code, similar to the QUSCRTUS example.

After the API populates the user space, your program must retrieve the list from the user space. As you might expect, there's an API for that—**QUSPTRUS** (Retrieve Pointer to a User Space):

```
Dcl-pr Qusptrus Extpgm('QUSPTRUS');
  *N Char(20) Const;                    // Qualified user space name
  *N Like(Spcptr);                      // Pointer to user space
  *N Like(Apierr) Options(*Nopass);   // Error code
End-pr;
...
Dcl-s  Spcptr Pointer;
...
Qusptrus('MYUSRSPC  QTEMP      ' : Spcptr : Apierr);
```

The first and third parameters in this prototype should be familiar to you by now. They represent the qualified name of the user space and the optional error variable. The second parameter represents a new data type: a pointer. This API uses a pointer to direct your program to the memory location where the user space data is stored.

A **pointer** is a variable that contains the memory address of another variable, an object, or a procedure. The pointer tells your program where an object is kept, but not the contents of the object. The object's contents reflect the values at the address referenced by the pointer. You can **base** a variable upon the pointer address, which the program can manipulate by using simple arithmetic; the variable's value depends upon the pointer's address.

When QUSPRTUS executes, it places the QTEMP/MYUSRSPC object's address into variable Spcptr, which will then be pointing to the beginning of the user space's contents. List APIs have a consistent format. They put a data structure at the beginning of the user space—a header—which, among other things, informs the program where the list starts, how many entries are in the list, and the size of each entry. Following the header is the actual list. In the following example, the Apiheader data structure uses Spcptr to determine these values:

```
Dcl-ds Apiheader Based(Spcptr);
  Listoffset Uns(10) Pos(125);
  Nbrentries Uns(10) Pos(133);
  Entrysize  Uns(10) Pos(137);
End-ds;
```

Once you know the list's location in the user space, processing each entry is easy:

```
Dcl-s Listptr Pointer;
Dcl-ds Mbr10100 Based(Listptr);
  Mbrname Char(10);
End-ds;


Dcl-s X Uns(10);
...
Listptr = Spcptr + Listoffset;        // Point to beginning of list

For X = 1 to Nbrentries;
  ...
  // Process subfield Mbrname here
  ...
  If X < Nbrentries;
    Listptr += Entrysize;             // Point to next list item
  Else;
    Listptr = Spcptr + Listoffset;    // Reset Listptr when done
  Endif;
Endfor;
```

This example uses another pointer, Listptr, to position the Mbr10100 data structure to an entry in the list. This data structure has only one subfield, as documented in the online documentation. But other APIs or other formats are likely more complex. By adding the number of bytes in Listoffset to Spcptr, the program will point to the first list entry. After that, each time the program processes a list entry, it adds the number of bytes in Entrysize to Listptr so that it will point to the next list entry. This code also resets Listptr to the beginning of the list when the final list entry has been processed to avoid potential problems with the pointer having an invalid value.

When you combine all the pieces, processing the user space that a list API uses becomes pretty simple. The following code, while not a complete program, serves as a blueprint for the required steps:

```
// --------------------------------------------------------- Prototypes
Dcl-pr Quscrtus Extpgm('QUSCRTUS');   // Create user space
  *N Char(20) Const;                  // Qualified user space name
                                                          Continued
```

```
  *N Char(10) Const;                        // Extended attribute
  *N Uns(10)  Const;                        // Initial size
  *N Char(1)  Const;                        // Initial value
  *N Char(10) Const;                        // Public authority
  *N Char(50) Const;                        // Text
  *N Char(10) Const Options(*Nopass);       // Replace?
  *N Like(Apierr)   Options(*Nopass);       // Error code
End-pr;

Dcl-pr Quslmbr Extpgm('QUSLMBR');          // List file members
  *N Char(20) Const;                        // Qualified user space name
  *N Char(8)  Const;                        // Return format name
  *N Char(20) Const;                        // Qualified database filename
  *N Char(10) Const;                        // Member name, or generic name
  *N Char(1)  Const;                        // Process overrides?
  *N Like(Apierr) Options(*Nopass);         // Error code
End-pr;

Dcl-pr Qusptrus Extpgm('QUSPTRUS');        // Get pointer to user space
  *N Char(20) Const;                        // Qualified user space name
  *N Like(Spcptr);                          // Pointer to user space
  *N Like(Apierr) Options(*Nopass);         // Error code
End-pr;

// ---------------------------------------------------- Data structures
Dcl-ds Apierr Len(16);                      // API errors
  Errmsg Char(7) Pos(9);
End-ds;

Dcl-s  Spcptr Pointer;                      // API header format
Dcl-ds Apiheader Based(Spcptr);
  Listoffset Uns(10) Pos(125);
  Nbrentries Uns(10) Pos(133);
  Entrysize  Uns(10) Pos(137);
End-ds;

Dcl-s Listptr Pointer;                      // List entry format
```

Continued

```
Dcl-ds Mbrl0100 Based(Listptr);
  Mbrname Char(10);
End-ds;


// ----------------------------------------------- Standalone variables
Dcl-s X Uns(10);
...
// ------------------------------ Execute APIs, get pointer to list
Quscrtus('MYUSRSPC  QTEMP     ' : 'APILIST' : 4096 : X'00' :
         '*ALL' : *BLANKS : '*YES' : Apierr);      // Create user space


Quslmbr('MYUSRSPC  QTEMP     ' : 'MBRL0100' :
         'MYFILE    *LIBL    ' : '*ALL' :
         '0' : Apierr);                    // List file members to user space


Qusptrus('MYUSRSPC  QTEMP     ' : Spcptr :
          Apierr);                         // Get pointer to user space


Listptr = Spcptr + Listoffset;             // Point to beginning of list
...
// ----------------------------------------------- Process list entries
For X = 1 to Nbrentries;
  ...
  // Process Mbrl0100 data structure subfields here

  ...
  If X < Nbrentries;
    Listptr += Entrysize;              // Point to next list item
  Else;
    Listptr = Spcptr + Listoffset;     // Reset Listptr when done
  Endif;
Endfor;
...
```

Note
Take advantage of the /Copy compiler directive, discussed in Chapter 14, to store API prototypes and data structures in a single copybook. By doing so, you can reuse the same code *snippets* in many programs.

18.4. Creating API Wrapper Procedures

You can package commonly used APIs in a procedure called a **wrapper procedure**. A wrapper simply *hides* complex code in a procedure; in this case, a wrapper contains the details of calling the API. A wrapper procedure can simplify API coding. Instead of calling an API directly, a program or procedure can call the wrapper. A wrapper can eliminate seldom-used parameters, rearrange parameters to a convenient order, simplify complex parameters, and provide standardized error handling for APIs. A wrapper procedure can provide a return value capability to APIs, giving you more flexibility in coding the API call. You can also package wrappers in service programs to improve application reliability, maintainability, and performance.

The following example code shows a procedure that wraps the QUSCRTUS API discussed earlier:

```
Ctl-opt Nomain;

Dcl-pr Crtusrspc;                          // Create user space wrapper
  *N Char(10) Value;                       // User space name
  *N Char(10) Value Options(*Nopass);      // Library name
  *N Char(8)  Value Options(*Nopass);      // Object attribute
  *N Char(7)  Options(*Nopass);            // Errmsg
End-pr;

Dcl-pr Quscrtus Extpgm('QUSCRTUS');        // Create user space API
  *N Char(20) Const;                       // Qualified user space name
  *N Char(10) Const;                       // Extended attribute
  *N Uns(10)  Const;                       // Initial size
  *N Char(1)  Const;                       // Initial value
  *N Char(10) Const;                       // Public authority
  *N Char(50) Const;                       // Text
  *N Char(10) Const Options(*Nopass);      // Replace?
  *N Like(Apierr)   Options(*Nopass);      // Error code
End-pr;

Dcl-ds Apierr Len(16);                     // API errors
  Errmsg Char(7) Pos(9);
End-ds;

                                                          Continued
```

```
// ----------------------------------------- Create user space wrapper
Dcl-proc Crtusrspc Export;

  Dcl-pi *N;
    Spcname Char(10) Value;                     // User space name
    Spclib  Char(10) Value Options(*Nopass);    // Library name
    Spcattr Char(8)  Value Options(*Nopass);    // Object attribute
    Errmsg  Char(7)  Options(*Nopass);          // Errmsg
  End-pi;

  Select;
  When %Parms = 1;
    Quscrtus(Spcname + 'QTEMP' : *Blanks : 4096 : X'00' :
             '*ALL' : *BLANKS : '*YES' : Apierr);
  When %Parms = 2;
    Quscrtus(Spcname + Spclib : *Blanks : 4096 : X'00' :
             '*ALL' : *BLANKS : '*YES' : Apierr);
  Other;
    Quscrtus(Spcname + Spclib : Spcattr : 4096 : X'00' :
             '*ALL' : *BLANKS : '*YES' : Apierr);
  Endsl;

End-proc;
```

This example, which you would package as a service program procedure, wraps the QUSCRTUS API inside the CRTUSRSPC procedure. Prototypes describe both the wrapper procedure and the API. Notice that the wrapper procedure separates the qualified user space name into two separate components: the space name and the library. This technique makes the wrapper more flexible by allowing it to be called with or without a library name. If you omit the library, the wrapper uses QTEMP as a default. To count the number of parameters passed to it, the wrapper employs the **%Parms (Return number of parameters)** function. Any procedure that needs to create a user space can use the wrapper, calling it with any of the following instructions:

```
Crtusrspc('MYUSRSPC');
Crtusrspc('MYUSRSPC' : 'MYLIB')
Crtusrspc('MYUSRSPC' : 'MYLIB' : 'APILIST');
Crtusrspc('MYUSRSPC' : 'MYLIB' : 'APILIST' : Error);
```

The calling procedure requires a prototype (preferably stored in a copybook) for the wrapper, but it does not need to include other API-related code.

A wrapper procedure can also provide a return value from an API. For example, you can use the following wrapper with the QUSPRTUS API discussed earlier:

```
Ctl-opt Nomain;

Dcl-pr Usrspcptr Pointer;           // Return user space pointer wrapper
  *N Char(10) Value;                     // User space name
  *N Char(10) Value Options(*Nopass);    // Library name
  *N Char(7)  Options(*Nopass);          // Errmsg
End-pr;


Dcl-pr Qusptrus Extpgm('QUSPTRUS');      // Get pointer to user space
  *N Char(20) Const;                     // Qualified user space name
  *N Like(Spcptr);                       // Pointer to user space
  *N Like(Apierr) Options(*Nopass);      // Error code
End-pr;


Dcl-ds Apierr Len(16);                   // API errors
  Errmsg Char(7) Pos(9);
End-ds;


Dcl-s  Spcptr Pointer;                   // User space pointer


// ----------------------------- Return user space pointer wrapper
Dcl-proc Usrspcptr Export;

  Dcl-pi *N Pointer;
    *N Char(10) Value;                     // User space name
    *N Char(10) Value Options(*Nopass);    // Library name
    *N Char(7)  Options(*Nopass);          // Errmsg
  End-pi;


  Select:
    When %Parms = 1;
```

Continued

```
       Qusptrus(Spcnam + '*LIBL' : Spcptr : Apierr);
    Other;
       Qusptrus(Spcnam + Spclib : Spcptr : Apierr);
  Endsl;


  Return Spcptr;


End-proc;
```

This example uses the USRSPCPTR wrapper to return the pointer to a user space. The calling procedure can call it with any of the following instructions:

```
Spcptr = Usrspcptr('MYUSRSPC');
Spcptr = Usrspcptr('MYUSRSPC' : 'MYLIB')
Spcptr = Usrspcptr('MYUSRSPC' : 'MYLIB' : Error);
```

By using wrappers to call the user space APIs, and by packing them in a service program, you can simplify the earlier member list example (especially if a copybook includes the prototypes and API-related data structures, indicated here with a ~~strikethrough font~~):

```
// ------------------------------------------------------- Prototypes
Dcl-pr Quslmbr Extpgm('QUSLMBR');       // List file members
   *N Char(20) Const;                   // Qualified user space name
   *N Char(8)  Const;                   // Return format name
   *N Char(20) Const;                   // Qualified database filename
   *N Char(10) Const;                   // Member name, or generic name
   *N Char(1)  Const;                   // Process overrides?
   *N Like(Apierr) Options(*Nopass);    // Error code
End-pr;


Dcl-pr Crtusrspc;                       // Create user space
   *N Char(10) Value;                   // User space name
   *N Char(10) Value Options(*Nopass);  // Library name
   *N Char(8)  Value Options(*Nopass);  // Object attribute
   *N Char(7)  Options(*Nopass);        // Errmsg
End-pr;
```
Continued—

```
Dcl-pr Usrspcptr Pointer;                        // Return user space pointer
  *N Char(10) Value;                             // User space name
  *N Char(10) Value Options(*Nopass);   // Library name
  *N Char(7)  Options(*Nopass);                  // Errmsg
End-pr;


// ------------------------------------------------------ Data structures
Dcl-ds Apierr Len(16);                     // API errors
  Errmsg Char(7) Pos(9);
End-ds;


Dcl-s  Spcptr Pointer;                        // API header format
Dcl-ds Apiheader Based(Spcptr);
  Listoffset Uns(10) Pos(125);
  Nbrentries Uns(10) Pos(133);
  Entrysize  Uns(10) Pos(137);
End-ds;


Dcl-s Listptr Pointer;                        // List entry format
Dcl-ds Mbrl0100 Based(Listptr);
  Mbrname Char(10);
End-ds;


// --------------------------------------------- Standalone variables
Dcl-s X Uns(10);
...
// -------------------------------- Execute APIs, get pointer to list
Crtusrspc('MYUSRSPC') ;                                   // Create user space

Quslmbr('MYUSRSPC  QTEMP     ' : 'MBRL0100' :
        'MYFILE    *LIBL     ' : '*ALL' :
        '0' : Apierr);                    // List file members to user space


Spcptr = Usrspcptr('MYUSRSPC')
Listptr = Spcptr + Listoffset;                            // Point to list
...
```

Continued

```
// ------------------------------------------------- Process list entries
For X = 1 to Nbrentries;

  ...
  // Process Mbrl0100 data structure subfields here

  ...
  If X < Nbrentries;
    Listptr += Entrysize;                 // Point to next list item
  Else;
    Listptr = Spcptr + Listoffset;        // Reset Listptr when done
  Endif;
Endfor;
...
```

18.5. Creating Web Pages with HTTP APIs

APIs and wrapper procedures facilitate RPG programs' participation in Web-based applications by interacting with the **HTTP Server** for IBM i. The HTTP Server is a licensed program that communicates between the server and a Web browser to support Web pages. Many APIs provide access to an Internet standard called **Common Gateway Interface (CGI)** to pass information between an RPG program and the HTTP Server and then, in turn, to a browser. Here are some commonly used CGI-related APIs:

- QtmhWrStout (Write to stdout)
- QtmhRdStin (Read from stdin)
- QtmhPutEnv (Put environment variable)
- QtmhGetEnv (Get environment variable)
- QtmhCvtDb (Convert CGI input to DDS-formatted buffer)
- QzhbCgiParse (Parse QUERY_STRING)

To introduce the concept of using these APIs and building wrappers around them, we'll build a wrapper for the QtmhWrStout API, used to write data to a browser. Once you understand how that wrapper uses the API to build a Web page with dynamic content, you can refer to the online IBM Knowledge Center to learn how to use the other APIs.

The term **stdout** refers to the data output stream to which a CGI program sends data to the HTTP Server. The term **stdin** refers to the data input stream the HTTP Server provides to the CGI program. A CGI program can write an HTML data stream to stdout, read user input from stdin, process the data, and then write an HTML response back to stdout. A program that can read from stdin and write to stdout can interact with the browser. A full discussion of HTML and CGI goes beyond the scope of this text, but a few basic principles will get you started.

These CGI APIs, along with others, are packaged as bindable procedures in service program QHTTPSVR/QZHBCGI. You must bind this service program to an RPG program that will use the CGI APIs. To facilitate the binding process, use a CL command to list the service program in a binding directory that binds Web-related RPG programs, for example:

```
ADDBNDDIRE  MYLIB/WWWBNDDIR  OBJ((QHTTPSVR/QZHBCGI))
```

The **QtmhWrStout** (Write to stdout) API writes HTML data to stdout. The following prototype describes QtmhWrStout:

```
// --------------------------------- QtmhWrStout (Write to stdout) API
Dcl-pr QtmhWrStout Extproc('QtmhWrStout');
  *N Char(65535) Const Options(*Varsize);            // Data string
  *N Int(10)     Const;                              // Data length
  *N Char(16)    Options(*Varsize);                  // Error structure
End-pr;
```

The first parameter identifies the variable containing the data to write to stdout, and the second variable provides the length of the data. The third parameter is the standard API error data structure used in earlier examples.

The following example procedure, WWWEcho, is a wrapper for the QtmhWrStout API that makes it easier to use:

```
Ctl-opt Nomain;

// ------------------------------------------------------- Procedure WWWEcho
Dcl-pr WWWEcho;
  *N Char(65535) Value;                              // Data string
End-pr;

// --------------------------------- QtmhWrStout (Write to stdout) API
Dcl-pr QtmhWrStout Extproc('QtmhWrStout');
  *N Char(65535) Const Options(*Varsize);            // Data string
  *N Int(10)     Const;                              // Data length
  *N Char(16)    Options(*Varsize);                  // Error structure
End-pr;

                                                                Continued
```

```
// ---------------------------------------------------- Procedure WWWEcho
Dcl-proc WWWEcho Export;

  Dcl-pi *N;
    Browserdata Char(65535) Value;
  End-pi;

  Dcl-s Errorcode Char(16);

  QtmhWrStout(%Trim(Browserdata) : %Len(%Trim(Browserdata)) : Errorcode);
  Return;

End-proc;
```

After you have compiled and bound the wrapper to a service program, WWWEcho simplifies the API by allowing a program to write to the browser using a single parameter:

```
WWWEcho('Hello, world!' + LF);
```

(LF represents a line-feed character to move to the next line of the CGI script.) For example, the following program displays the browser screen in Figure 18.2:

```
/If Defined(*Crtbndrpg)
Ctl-opt Dftactgrp(*No) Actgrp(*New) Bnddir('WWWBNDDIR');
/Endif


// ------------------------------------------------------------Constants
Dcl-c HeaderHTML 'Content-type: text/html';
Dcl-c LF        X'15';                            // Line feed


// ----------------------------------------------------------- Prototypes
Dcl-pr WWWEcho;                                  // WWWEcho procedure
  *N Char(65535) Value;                          // Data string
End-pr;


// ----------------------------------------------------------- Variables
Dcl-s Browserdata Char(65535);


                                                          Continued
```

```
// -------------------------------------------------- Main procedure
Browserdata = HeaderHTML + LF + LF;                 // Echo CGI header
WWWEcho(Browserdata);


Browserdata = 'Hello world!<br />' + LF;
WWWEcho(Browserdata);
Browserdata = 'This is <strong>formatted</strong> text.' + LF;
WWWEcho(Browserdata);


*Inlr = *On;
Return;
```

Before sending content to stdout, the program must first issue a **CGI header**, information that describes the subsequent data to be sent to the browser. In this example, the HeaderHTML constant contains that header information, followed by two line-feed characters (hexadecimal character X'15'). This header identifies the subsequent lines as HTML data. Following the CGI header, the program can *echo* HTML data to the client browser.

When the HTTP Server is appropriately configured and started, the browser can request the program by using a Web address (URL). For example, the following URL might execute the example program, CGI02, and show the display in Figure 18.2:

```
http://myserver.com:4801/cgi-bin/cgi02.pgm
```

Figure 18.2: Browser rendering of CGI program

The actual URL would differ from this example depending upon the HTTP Server's configuration. To configure the HTTP Server, you use the IBM Web Administration for i browser interface. A full discussion of the HTTP Server configuration goes beyond the scope of this text; refer to the online IBM Knowledge Center for details.

Tip

Open-source CGI software, consisting primarily of CGI-related API wrappers, is available for download from the Internet. One popular package is a development kit called CGIDEV2, available from easy400.net.

18.6. Chapter Summary

Application program interfaces are programs or procedures that let you access lower-level machine functions or system data otherwise unavailable to an HLL program. APIs have a specific documented parameter interface, which is usually consistent as the operating system is updated. API documentation is part of the online IBM Knowledge Center.

The QUSCMDLN API displays a command-line window. QCMDEXC lets a program build a CL command string and execute it.

Many APIs require the use of a user space (*USRSPC) object to store their results. The QUSCRTUS API creates a user space, and the QUSPTRUS API retrieves a pointer to a user space. A pointer is a variable that contains the memory address of another item—a variable, an object, or a procedure. The contents of the item correspond to the address referenced by the pointer. You can base a program data item, such as a data structure, upon the pointer address, which the program can manipulate to change the data item's contents.

APIs can be executed from wrapper procedures, which facilitate and simplify the API parameter interface. Wrappers can also enable the API to provide a return value.

A group of procedures called the HTTP APIs allow an RPG program to participate in Web-based applications, using an Internet standard called Common Gateway Interface (CGI). CGI programs can create Web pages with dynamic content and read user input from a browser. CGI programs use the terms stdin and stdout to refer to the data stream passed between the server and the client browser. The CGI-related APIs are packaged as procedures in service program QHTTPSVR/QZHBCGI.

The following table summarizes the functions discussed in this chapter:

Function or Operation	Description	Syntax
%Parms	Return number of parameters	**%Parms**

18.7. Key Terms

application program	%Parms	QUSLMBR
interfaces (APIs)	pointer	QUSPTRUS
CGI header	QCMDEXC	stdin
Common Gateway Interface	QtmhWrStout	stdout
(CGI)	QUSCMDLN	user space
HTTP Server	QUSCRTUS	wrapper procedure

18.8. Discussion/Review Questions

1. What is an API? Why is it an important tool for programmers?
2. Give a short definition of the QUSCMDLN API. Why would an RPG programmer want to use this API? Give an example of its use.
3. Give a short definition of the QCMDEXC API. Why would an RPG programmer want to use this API? Give an example of its use.
4. Using IBM's online documentation, research the APIs that are available to programmers, select and list three of these APIs, and explain how you might use them.
5. This chapter briefly discussed using RPG to write Web applications. Many software vendors develop robust prepackaged software that an organization can use instead of writing programs in-house. Investigate the IBM third-party software vendors, choose three of them, and write a short report comparing the products offered.
6. Why would a company decide to develop modern interfaces for their enterprise software instead of buying and implementing completely new software?

18.9. Exercises

1. Investigate the SBMJOB command. You have a program named MYPROG01, which resides in a library called MYLIB. Using the QCMDEXC API, write the code to submit this job to the batch subsystem. Your code should include the variables and command declarations.

2. An ILE RPG program needs to delete a database file. Investigate the DLTF (Delete File) CL command. The name of the file to delete is contained in a field named FileName, a 10-position character field. Write the code to accomplish this using the QCMDEXC API.

3. After submitting an RPG program, the user needs to view the status of this job. Investigate the WRKSBMJOB (Work with Submitted Jobs) CL command, and write the code to accomplish this task using the QCMDEXC API.

4. A screen must allow a user to view the active jobs in the QBATCH subsystem. Investigate the WRKACTJOB (Work with Active Jobs) CL command, and write the code to accomplish this task using the QCMDEXC API.

ILE RPG Summary

Summary

This appendix lists ILE RPG language elements: statements, operation codes, keywords, and built-in functions. It also serves as a glossary for common ILE RPG terms. The information is current for Release 7.2 of the ILE RPG/400 compiler; earlier releases may not support some of the entries in this appendix. Further details for any of these entries are available in IBM's online documentation.

Arguments separated by vertical bars (|) indicate that several options are allowed. Generally, you can enter only one of the shown values for the argument, although in some cases, more than one value may be listed. For example, in the following syntax

```
DFTACTGRP(*NO|*YES)
```

either of the following entries are valid:

```
DFTACTGRP(*NO)
DFTACTGRP(*YES)
```

Arguments enclosed in curly braces ({}) are optional arguments. For instance, in the following syntax

```
%KDS(data-structure-name {: num-keys})
```

either of the following entries are valid:

```
%KDS(MYDS)
%KDS(MYKDS : 2)
```

Keywords associated with particular specifications are so noted. In these notes, the term Dcl-*xx* refers to multiple declaration instructions (e.g., Dcl-s, Dcl-ds, Dcl-subf, Dcl-parm).

Obsolete entries are so mentioned along with suggested alternatives. You'll notice that some code examples wrap to multiple lines, which enables them to fit on the printed page.

A

%Abs()

Function. Get absolute value of expression.

Usage: %ABS(numeric-expression)

Acq

Operation code. Acquire device.

Usage: ACQ{(e)} device-name workstn-file;

Add

Operation code. Add factors. Obsolete; use + or += operator.

Adddur

Operation code. Add duration. Obsolete; use + operator, date functions.

Actgrp

Keyword (Ctl-opt). Activation group to use.

Usage: ACTGRP(*STGMDL|*NEW|*CALLER| 'act-grp-name')

Activation Group

A job substructure in which ILE programs and service programs are activated. Contains the resources necessary to run the program, including static and global program variables, dynamic storage, temporary data management resources, certain types of exception handlers, and ending procedures.

%Addr()

Function. Get storage address of variable.

Usage: %ADDR(variable:*DATA)

Alias

Keyword (Dcl-f, Dcl-ds). Use alternative field names for data structure subfields (applies to LIKEREC or externally described data structure).

Usage: ALIAS

Align

Keyword (Dcl-ds). Align integer, unsigned and float subfields.

Usage: ALIGN

%Alloc()

Function. Allocate storage, get pointer.

Usage: %ALLOC(length)

Alloc

Keyword (Ctl-opt). Controls storage module for %Alloc, %Realloc, Dealloc.

Usage: ALLOC(*STGMDL|*TERASPACE| *SNGLVL)

Alloc

Operation code. Allocate storage. Obsolete; use %Alloc.

Alt

Keyword (Dcl-s). Alternating array or table.

Usage: ALT(main-array-name)

Alternating Arrays

Two arrays that are loaded together.

Alternating Tables

Two tables that are loaded together.

Altseq

Keyword (Ctl-opt, Dcl-*xx*). Alternate collating sequence.

Usage (Ctl-opt): ALTSEQ{*NONE|*SRC|*EXT}

Usage (Dcl-*xx*): ALTSEQ(*NONE)

Alwnull

Keyword (Ctl-opt). Allow null-capable fields.

Usage: ALWNULL{*NO|*INPUTONLY|*USRCTL}

Andxx

Operation code. And. Obsolete; use And connector.

Array

Series of elements with like characteristics; can be searched for a uniquely identified element, and elements can be accessed by their position in the array.

Array File

Input file containing array elements.

Array Index

Actual number of an element in an array, or the field containing the number or relative position of an element in an array.

Ascend

Keyword (Dcl-*xx*). Sort sequence.

Usage: ASCEND

Aut

Keyword (Ctl-opt). Authority.

Usage: AUT(*LIBRCRTAUT|*ALL|*CHANGE| *USE|*EXCLUDE|'auth-list-name')

B

Based

Keyword (Dcl-*xx*). Basing pointer.

Usage: BASED(pointer-name)

Begsr

Operation code. Begin subroutine.

Usage: BEGSR subroutine-name;

Bind

To create a callable program by combining one or more ILE modules.

Binder

The system process that creates a bound program by packaging ILE modules and resolving symbols passed between those modules.

Binder Language

Set of commands (STRPGMEXP, EXPORT, and ENDPGMEXP) to define the signature for a service program. These commands (source type BND) are not executable.

Binding

The process of creating a callable program by packaging ILE modules and resolving symbols passed between those modules.

Binding Directory

An object that contains a list of names of modules and service programs that the binder may need when creating an ILE program or service program. A binding directory is not a repository of the modules and service programs; instead, it allows the binder to refer to them by name and type.

%Bitand()

Function. Bitwise AND operation.

Usage: %BITAND(expression:expression {:expression...})

%Bitnot()

Function. Invert bits.

Usage: %BITNOT(expression)

Bitoff

Operation code. Set bits off. Obsolete; use %Bitand, %Bitnot.

Biton

Operation code. Set bits on. Obsolete; use %Bitor.

%Bitor()

Function. Bitwise OR operation.

Usage: %BITOR(expression:expression {:expression...})

%Bitxor()

Function. Bitwise exclusive OR operation.

Usage: %BITXOR(expression:expression)

Block

Keyword (Dcl-f). Record blocking.

Usage: BLOCK(*YES|*NO)

Bnddir

Keyword (Ctl-opt). Binding directories to use.

Usage: BNDDIR('bnd-dir-name' {:'bnd-dir-name'...})

Bound program

A callable object that combines one or more modules created by an ILE compiler.

C

Cabxx

Operation code. Compare and branch. Obsolete; use logical expressions.

Calculation Specifications (C-Specs)

Section of an RPG program that describes the processing the program is to perform.

Obsolete. Use free-format operation codes.

Call

Operation code. Call program. Obsolete; use Callp.

Callb

Operation code. Call bound procedure. Obsolete; use Callp.

Callp

Operation code. Call prototyped procedure or program.

Usage: {CALLP{(emr)}} name({parm1:parm2...});

Casxx

Operation code. Conditionally invoke subroutine. Obsolete; use Select, When, Other.

Cat

Operation code. Concatenate two strings. Obsolete; use + operator.

Ccsid

Keyword (Ctl-opt). Default graphic or UCS-2 character set identifier.

Usage: CCSID(*GRAPH:*IGNORE|*SRC|number)

Usage: CCSID(*UCS2:number)

Usage: CCSID(number|*DFT)

Chain

Operation code. Random file retrieval.

Usage: CHAIN{(enhmr)} search-arg name data-structure;

%Char()

Function. Convert to character data.

Usage: %CHAR(expression {:format})

%Check()

Function. Check characters.

Usage: %CHECK(comparator:string {:start})

Check

Operation code. Check characters. Obsolete; use %Check.

%Checkr()

Function. Check characters reverse.

Usage: %CHECKR(comparator:string {:start})

Checkr

Operation code. Check characters reverse. Obsolete; use %Checkr.

Class

Keyword (D-spec). Class. Obsolete; use Object keyword.

Clear

Operation code. Clear data item value.

Usage: CLEAR {*NOKEY} {*ALL} name;

Close

Operation code. Close file.

Usage: CLOSE{(e)} file-name;

Combined File

Data file that is used as both an input and output file.

Commit

Operation code. Commit file changes.

Usage: COMMIT{(e)} {boundary};

Keyword (Dcl-f). Use commitment control.

Usage: COMMIT{(rpg-name)}

Comp

Operation code. Compare factors. Obsolete; use logical expressions.

Compile

To translate source statements into modules, which can then be bound into programs or service programs.

Compile-Time Array

Array that is compiled with the program and becomes a permanent part of the program.

Compile-Time Table

Table that is compiled with the program and becomes a permanent part of the program.

Compiler Directive

Instruction that controls a compile listing or that causes source records to be included (e.g., /COPY, /INCLUDE, /DEFINE).

Conditioning Indicator

Obsolete. Indicator that specifies when to do calculations or which characteristics apply to a record format or field.

Const

Keyword (Dcl-parm). Read-only parameter.

Usage: CONST

Keyword (Dcl-c). Constant value.

Usage: CONST(value)

Constant

Data that has an unchanging, predefined value for use in processing. A constant does not change during the running of a program, but the contents of a field or variable can.

Control Boundary

Call stack entry to which control is transferred when an unmonitored error occurs.

Control Break

Change in the contents of a control field that indicates all records from a particular control group were read and a new control group is starting.

Control Field

One or more fields that are compared from record to record to detect a control break.

Control Specifications (H-Specs)

Section of an RPG program that provides information about program generation and defaults. Obsolete. Use Ctl-opt instruction.

/Copy

Compiler directive. Copy records from another source member into the current compile process.

Usage: /COPY {{library/}file},member

Copynest

Keyword (Ctl-opt). Maximum /Copy nesting level.

Usage: COPYNEST(0-2048)

Copyright

Keyword (Ctl-opt). Copyright string.

Usage: COPYRIGHT('string')

Ctdata

Keyword (Dcl-ds). Compile-time array or table.

Usage: CTDATA

Ctl-opt

Instruction. Provides information about program generation and defaults. Replaces H-spec.

Usage: CTL-OPT {Keywords};

Cursym

Keyword (Ctl-opt). Currency symbol.

Usage: CURSYM('symbol')

Cvtopt

Keyword (Ctl-opt). Data-type conversion options.

Usage: CVTOPT({*DATETIME|*NODATETIME}
 {*GRAPHIC|*NOGRAPHIC}
 {*VARCHAR|*NOVARCHAR}
 {*VARGRAPHIC|*NOVARGRAPHIC})

Cycle Main Program

Program in which the main procedure is implicitly specified in the main source section, without being specifically named. Variables are automatically initialized and files are automatically opened when the program starts. Storage is freed and files are closed when the program ends with *Inlr on.

D

Definition Specifications (D-Specs)

Section of an RPG program that defines data items, such as standalone fields, named constants, data structures, prototypes, and procedure interfaces. Obsolete; use Dcl-c, Dcl-ds, Dcl-pi, Dcl-pr, Dcl-s.

%Date()

Function. Convert to date.

Usage: %DATE({expression {:format}})

Datedit

Keyword (Ctl-opt). Date edit (Y edit code).

Usage: DATEDIT(format{-and-separator})

Datfmt

Keyword (Ctl-opt, Dcl-f-, Dcl-*xx*). Date format.

Usage: DATFMT(format{-and-separator})

%Days()

Function. Convert to number of days.

Usage: %DAYS(numeric-expression)

Dcl-c

Instruction. Declares a named constant. Replaces D-spec for named constants.

Usage: DCL-C name value;

Dcl-ds

Instruction. Declares a data structure; used with Dcl-subf, End-ds. Replaces D-spec for data structures.

Usage: DCL-DS name|*N {PSDS}
 {EXT|EXTNAME('file'} {Dcl-ds-keywords};

Dcl-f

Instruction. Identifies and describes file used by the program. Replaces F-spec.

Usage (Externally described):
DCL-F filename {device|LIKEFILE(parent)}
 {USAGE(*INPUT|*UPDATE|*DELETE|*OUTPUT)}
 {KEYED} {Dcl-f-keywords};

Usage (Program described): DCL-F filename
 {device(record-length)|LIKEFILE(parent)}
 {USAGE(*INPUT|*UPDATE|*DELETE|
 *OUTPUT)} {KEYED(*CHAR:key-length)
 KEYLOC(key-location)} {Dcl-f-keywords};

Notes: USAGE(*INPUT) is the default for DISK, SEQ, and SPECIAL files. USAGE(*OUTPUT) is the default for PRINTER files. USAGE(*INPUT:*OUTPUT) is the default for WORKSTN files.

Dcl-parm

Instruction. Declares a parameter; used with Dcl-pr, Dcl-pi. Replaces D-spec for parameters.

Usage: {DCL-PARM} name|*N datatype|
 LIKE(parent{:adjustment})
 {Dcl-parm-keywords};

Note: Supported data type entries are as follows:

```
CHAR(length),
    VARCHAR(length{:varying-size})
PACKED(digits{:decimals}),
    ZONED(digits{:decimals})
INT(digits), UNS(digits)
IND
DATE{(format)}
TIME{(format)}
TIMESTAMP
POINTER{(*PROC)}
BINDEC(digits{:decimals})
FLOAT(bytes)
OBJECT{(*JAVA:class)}
UCS2(length),
    VARUCS2(length{:varying-size})
GRAPH(length),
    VARGRAPH(length{:varying-size})
```

Dcl-pi

Instruction. Declares a procedure interface; used with Dcl-parm, End-pi. Replaces D-spec for prototypes.

Usage: DCL-PI name|*N datatype|
  LIKE(parent{:adjustment}) {D-spec-keywords};

Note: Supported data type entries are as follows:

```
CHAR(length),
    VARCHAR(length{:varying-size})
PACKED(digits{:decimals}),
    ZONED(digits{:decimals})
INT(digits), UNS(digits)
IND
DATE{(format)}
TIME{(format)}
TIMESTAMP
POINTER{(*PROC)}
BINDEC(digits{:decimals})
FLOAT(bytes)
OBJECT{(*JAVA:class)}
UCS2(length),
    VARUCS2(length{:varying-size})
GRAPH(length),
    VARGRAPH(length{:varying-size})
```

Dcl-pr

Instruction. Declares a prototype; used with Dcl-parm, End-pr. Replaces D-spec for prototypes.

Usage: DCL-PR name {datatype|
  LIKE(parent{:adjustment})} {D-spec-keywords};

Note: Supported data type entries are as follows:

```
CHAR(length),
    VARCHAR(length{:varying-size})
PACKED(digits{:decimals}),
    ZONED(digits{:decimals})
                        Continued
```

```
INT(digits), UNS(digits)
IND
DATE{(format)}
TIME{(format)}
TIMESTAMP
POINTER{(*PROC)}
BINDEC(digits{:decimals})
FLOAT(bytes)
OBJECT{(*JAVA:class)}
UCS2(length),
    VARUCS2(length{:varying-size})
GRAPH(length),
    VARGRAPH(length{:varying-size})
```

Dcl-proc

Instruction. Declares the beginning of a procedure; used with End-proc. Replaces P-spec.

Usage: DCL-PROC {name} {Dcl-proc-keywords};

Dcl-s

Instruction. Declares a standalone variable. Replaces D-spec for standalone variable.

Usage: DCL-S name datatype|
  LIKE(parent{:adjustment}) {D-spec-keywords};

Note: Supported data type entries are as follows:

```
CHAR(length),
    VARCHAR(length{:varying-size})
PACKED(digits{:decimals}),
    ZONED(digits{:decimals})
INT(digits), UNS(digits)
IND
DATE{(format)}
                        Continued
```

```
TIME{(format)}
TIMESTAMP
POINTER{(*PROC)}
BINDEC(digits{:decimals})
FLOAT(bytes)
OBJECT{(*JAVA:class)}
UCS2(length),
    VARUCS2(length{:varying-size})
GRAPH(length),
    VARGRAPH(length{:varying-size})
```

Dcl-subf

Instruction. Declares a data structure subfield; used with Dcl-ds. Replaces D-spec for data structures.

Usage: {DCL-SUBF} name|*N datatype|
  LIKE(parent{:adjustment}) {D-spec-keywords};

Note: Supported data type entries are as follows:

```
CHAR(length),
    VARCHAR(length{:varying-size})
PACKED(digits{:decimals}),
    ZONED(digits{:decimals})
INT(digits), UNS(digits)
IND
DATE{(format)}
TIME{(format)}
TIMESTAMP
POINTER{(*PROC)}
BINDEC(digits{:decimals})
FLOAT(bytes)
OBJECT{(*JAVA:class)}
UCS2(length),
    VARUCS2(length{:varying-size})
GRAPH(length),
    VARGRAPH(length{:varying-size})
```

Dealloc

Operation code. Free storage.

Usage: DEALLOC{(en)} pointer-name;

Debug

Keyword (Ctl-opt). Debug options.

Usage: DEBUG{(*DUMP *INPUT *XMLSAX)}

Usage: DEBUG{(*NO|*YES)}

%Dec()

Function. Convert to packed decimal.

Usage: %DEC(expression{:digits{:decimals}})

Usage: %DEC(date-expression{:format})

Decedit

Keyword (Ctl-opt). Decimal notation.

Usage: DECEDIT(*JOBRUN|'value')

%Dech()

Function. Convert to packed decimal with half-adjust.

Usage: %DECH(expression:digits:decimals)

%Decpos()

Function. Get number of decimal positions.

Usage: %DECPOS(numeric-expression)

Decprec

Keyword (Ctl-opt). Decimal precision.

Usage: DECPREC(30|31)

Define

Operation code. Define field. Obsolete; use D-specs with Like.

Delete

Operation code. Delete record.

Usage: DELETE{(ehmr)} {search-arg} name;

Descend

Keyword (Dcl-*xx*). Array or table in descending collating sequence.

Usage: DESCEND

Devid

Keyword (Dcl-f). Program device for SPECIAL file.

Usage: DEVID(field-name)

Dftactgrp

Keyword (Ctl-opt). Compile unit to use default activation group.

Usage: DFTACTGRP(*YES|*NO)

Dftname

Keyword (Ctl-opt). Default name for compile unit.

Usage: DFTNAME(name)

%Diff()

Function. Get difference between dates, times, timestamps.

Usage: %DIFF(date1:date2:duration)

Dim

Keyword (Dcl-*xx*). Number of elements in table or array (1-16773104).

Usage: DIM(numeric-constant)

%Div()

Function. Get integer portion of quotient.

Usage: %DIV(dividend:divisor)

Div

Operation code. Divide. Obsolete; use / operator or %Div.

Do

Operation code. Do. Obsolete; use For.

Dou

Operation code. Do until.

Usage: DOU{(mr)} logical-expression;

Douxx

Operation code. Do until. Obsolete; use Dou.

Dow

Operation code. Do while.

Usage: DOW{(mr)} logical-expression;

Dowxx

Operation code. Do while. Obsolete; use Dow.

Dsply

Operation code. Display message.

Usage: DSPLY{(e)} {message} {output-queue}
   {response};

Dtaara

Keyword (Dcl-ds). Data area name.

Usage: DTAARA({*VAR}:data-area-name)

Dump

Operation code. Dump program.

Usage: DUMP{(a)} {identifier};

E

%Editc()

Function. Edit value using edit code.

Usage: %EDITC(numeric-expression:editcode
  {:fill-symbol})

%Editflt()

Function. Convert to floating point external representation.

Usage: %EDITFLT(numeric-expression)

%Editw()

Function. Edit value using edit word.

Usage: %EDITW(numeric-expression:editword)

/Eject

Compiler directive. Skip to next page of compiler listing.

Usage: /EJECT

%Elem()

Function. Get number of elements.

Usage: %ELEM(data-item)

Else

Operation code. Else.

Usage: ELSE;

/Else

Compiler directive. Select source block to include if previous /If or /Elseif failed (conditional compilation). Used with /Define, /If, /Elseif, /Endif.

Usage: /ELSE

Elseif

Operation code. Else if.

Usage: ELSEIF{(mr)} logical-expression;

/Elseif

Compiler directive. Test conditional expression within an /If or /Elseif group (conditional compilation). Used with /Define, /Else, /If, /Endif.

Usage: /ELSEIF {NOT} DEFINED(condition|
  *CRTBNDRPG|*CRTRPGMOD|*VxRxMx|
  COMPILE_WINDOWS|COMPILE_JAVA)

Enbpfrcol

Keyword (Ctl-opt). Enable performance collection.

Usage: ENBPFRCOL(*PEP|*ENTRYEXIT|*FULL)

End-ds

Instruction. Ends a data structure definition; used with Dcl-ds.

Usage: END-DS {name};

Enddo

Operation code. End Dou or Dow block.

Usage: ENDDO;

/End-exec

Compiler directive. End of embedded SQL statement. Obsolete; use semicolon (;).

Endfor

Operation code. End For block.

Usage: ENDFOR;

/End-free

Compiler directive. End a free-format calculation block.

Obsolete; no longer required.

Endif

Operation code. End If block.

Usage: ENDIF;

/Endif

Compiler directive. End an /If source code block (conditional compilation). Used with /Define, /If, /Elseif, /Endif.

Usage: /ENDIF

Endmon

Operation code. End Monitor block.

Usage: ENDMON;

End-pi

Instruction. Ends a procedure interface definition; used with Dcl-pi.

Usage: END-DS {name};

End-pr

Instruction. Ends a prototype definition; used with Dcl-pr.

Usage: END-DS {name};

End-proc

Instruction. Ends a procedure. Replaces P-spec.

Usage: END-PROC {name};

Endsl

Operation code. End Select group.

Usage: ENDSL;

Endsr

Operation code. End subroutine.

Usage: ENDSR {return-point};

%Eof()

Function. Get end-of-file status.

Usage: %EOF(file-name)

/Eof

Compiler directive. End of file for current source file.

Usage: /EOF

%Equal()

Function. Get exact match status for Setll operation.

Usage: %EQUAL{(file-name)}

%Error

Function. Get error status.

Usage: %ERROR

Eval

Operation code. Evaluate expression.

Usage: {EVAL{(hmr)}} assignment-expression;

Evalr

Operation code. Evaluate expression, right-adjust.

Usage: EVALR(mr) assignment-expression;

Eval-corr

Operation code. Assign corresponding subfields from one data structure to another.

Usage: EVAL-CORR{(hmr)} ds1 = ds2;

Except

Operation code. Perform calculation time output.

Usage: EXCEPT except-name;

Exec Sql

Compiler directive. Execute an embedded SQL statement.

Usage: EXEC SQL sql-statement;

Exfmt

Operation code. Write, then read format.

Usage: EXFMT{(e)} format-name
  {data-structure};

Export

Keyword (Dcl-*xx*, Dcl-proc). Data item or procedure can be exported (i.e., used by another module).

Usage: EXPORT{(external-name)}

Expropts

Keyword (Ctl-opt). Expression evaluation options.

Usage: EXPROPTS(*MAXDIGITS|*RESDECPOS)

Exsr

Operation code. Invoke subroutine.

Usage: EXSR subroutine-name;

Extbinint

Keyword (Ctl-opt). Use integer format for externally described binary fields.

Usage: EXTBININT(*NO|*YES)

Extdesc

Keyword (Dcl-f). External name of file to use at compile time.

Usage: EXTDESC(file-name)

External Indicator

Indicator (U1–U8) that another program can set before a program is run or that another program can change while the program is running.

Extfile

Keyword (Dcl-f). External name of file to open.

Usage: EXTFILE(file-name|*EXTDESC)

Extfld

Keyword (Dcl-subf). Rename externally described subfield.

Usage: EXTFLD(field-name)

Extfmt

Keyword (Dcl-*xx*). External data type.

Usage: EXTFMT(B|C|F|I|L|P|R|S|U)

Extind

Keyword (Dcl-f). External indicator.

Usage: EXTIND(*INU1-*INU8)

Extmbr

Keyword (Dcl-f). File member to open.

Usage: EXTMBR(member-name)

Extname

Keyword (Dcl-ds). External file with field descriptions.

Usage: EXTNAME(file-name{:format-name} {:*ALL|*INPUT|*OUTPUT|*KEY})

Extpgm

Keyword (Dcl-pr). External program name.

Usage: EXTPGM(pgm-name)

Extproc

Keyword (Dcl-pr). External procedure name.

Usage: EXTPROC{(proc-name)}

Usage: EXTPROC(*CL|*CWIDEN|*CNOWIDEN| *JAVA:class-name{:proc-name})

Extrct

Operation code. Extract from date, time, timestamp. Obsolete; use %Subdt.

F

Feod

Operation code. Force end of data.

Usage: FEOD{(en)} file-name;

%Fields()

Function. List of fields to update.

Usage: %FIELDS(name1{:name2...})

Figurative Constant

Reserved literal that represents a value; the word can be used instead of a literal to represent the value (e.g., *BLANKS, *ZEROS, *HIVAL, *LOVAL, *ON, *OFF).

File Information Data Structure

Data structure that makes file exception or error information available to the program. Must be unique for each file.

File Specifications (F-Specs)

Section of an RPG program that identifies and describes files used by the program.

Obsolete. Use Dcl-f.

Fixnbr

Keyword (Ctl-opt). Fix invalid decimal data option.

Usage: FIXNBR({*ZONED|*NOZONED}
{:*INPUTPACKED|*NOINPUTPACKED})

%Float()

Function. Convert to floating point data.

Usage: %FLOAT(expression)

Fltdiv

Keyword (H-spec). Floating point division option.

Usage: FLTDIV(*NO|*YES)

For

Operation code. For.

Usage: FOR{(mr)} index {= start}
{BY increment} {TO|DOWNTO limit};

Force

Operation code. Force file to be read next cycle.

Usage: FORCE file-name;

Formlen

Keyword (Dcl-f). Form length of printer file.

Usage: FORMLEN(length)

Formofl

Keyword (Dcl-f). Form overflow line number.

Usage: FORMOFL(line)

Formsalign

Keyword (Ctl-opt). Forms alignment.

Usage: FORMSALIGN(*NO|*YES)

%Found()

Function. Get record found status for Chain, Delete, Setgt, Setll operation.

Usage: %FOUND{(file-name)}

/Free

Compiler directive. Begin a free-format calculation block. Used with /End-free.

Obsolete; no longer required.

Fromfile

Keyword (Dcl-*xx*). Name of file from which to load preruntime array or table.

Usage: FROMFILE(file-name)

Ftrans

Keyword (Ctl-opt). File translation.

Usage: FTRANS(*NONE|*SRC)

Full Procedural File

File that uses input operations controlled by operation codes instead of by the program cycle.

G

Genlvl

Keyword (Ctl-opt). Generation level.

Usage: GENLVL(0-20)

Goto

Operation code. Go to tag. Obsolete; use structured techniques.

%Graph()

Function. Convert to graphic value.

Usage: %GRAPH(expression{:ccsid})

H

H-Specs (Control Specifications)

Section of an RPG program that provides information about program generation and defaults. Obsolete; use Ctl-opt instruction.

Halt Indicator

Indicator (H1–H9) that stops the program when an unacceptable condition occurs.

%Handler()

Function. Identify procedure to handle XML document events. Used with XML-SAX and XML-INTO operations.

Usage: %HANDLER(procedure:comm-area)

%Hours()

Function. Convert to number of hours.

Usage: %HOURS(numeric-expression)

I

If

Operation code. If.

Usage: IF{(mr)} logical-expression;

/If

Compiler directive. Test conditional expression for conditional compilation. Used with /Define, /Else, /Elseif, /Endif.

Usage: /IF {NOT} DEFINED(condition| *CRTBNDRPG|*CRTRPGMOD|*VxRxMx| COMPILE_WINDOWS|COMPILE_JAVA)

Ifxx

Operation code. If. Obsolete; use If.

Ignore

Keyword (Dcl-f). Ignore record format.

Usage: IGNORE(format-name1 {:formatname2...})

ILE

Integrated Language Environment.

Import

Keyword (Dcl-*xx*). Field is imported (i.e., defined in another module).

Usage: IMPORT{(external-name)}

In

Operation code. Retrieve a data area.

Usage: IN{(e)} {*LOCK} data-area-name;

Include

Keyword (Dcl-f). Include record format.

Usage: INCLUDE(format-name1 {:formatname2...})

/Include

Compiler directive. Copy records from another source member into the current compile process.

Usage: /INCLUDE {{library/}file},member

Indds

Keyword (Dcl-f). Map indicators to a data structure.

Usage: INDDS(ds-name)

Indent

Keyword (Ctl-opt). Indent source listing.

Usage: INDENT(*NONE|'character-value')

Infds

Keyword (Dcl-f). File feedback data structure.

Usage: INFDS(ds-name)

Infsr

Keyword (Dcl-f). File exception/error subroutine.

Usage: INFSR(subr-name)

Input Specifications (I-Specs)

Section of an RPG program that describes input records and their fields or that adds functions to an externally described input file.

%Int()

Function. Convert to integer format.

Usage: %INT(expression)

Integrated Language Environment

ILE. A common runtime environment for all ILE-conforming high-level languages, including RPG IV.

%Inth()

Function. Convert to integer format with half-adjust.

Usage: %INTH(expression)

Intprec

Keyword (Ctl-opt). Integer precision.

Usage: INTPREC(10|20)

Inz

Keyword (Dcl-*xx*). Initialize data.

Usage: INZ{constant|*EXTDFT|*LIKEDS| *NULL|*USER|*JOB |*SYS}

Iter

Operation code. Iterate.

Usage: ITER;

J

(No entries)

K

%Kds()

Function. Use data structure as search argument.

Usage: %KDS(data-structure {:number-of-keys})

Keyloc

Keyword (Dcl-f). Key field location for program described file processed by key.

Usage: KEYLOC(number)

Kfld

Operation code. Define a key field. Obsolete; use %Kds data structure.

Klist

Operation code. Define a composite key list. Obsolete; use %Kds data structure.

L

Langid

Keyword (Ctl-opt). Language identifier.

Usage: LANGID(*JOBRUN|*JOB| 'language-identifier')

Last Record Indicator (LR)

Indicator that signals when the last record (LR) is processed; can then condition calculation and output operations to be done at the end of the program.

Leave

Operation code. Leave Do/For group.

Usage: LEAVE;

Leavesr

Operation code. Leave subroutine.

Usage: LEAVESR;

Len

Keyword (Dcl-xx).Length of data structure or character data item (1–16773104).

Usage: LEN(length)

%Len()

Function. Get/set length.

Usage: %LEN(expression{:*MAX})

Like

Keyword (Dcl-xx). Define a field like another.

Usage: LIKE(field-name)

Likeds

Keyword (Dcl-xx). Define a data structure like another.

Usage: LIKEDS(ds-name)

Likefile

Keyword (Dcl-f, Dcl-parm). Define a file specification or parameter like another F-spec.

Usage: LIKEFILE(file-name)

Likerec

Keyword (Dcl-xx). Define a data structure like a record format.

Usage: LIKEREC(format-name{:*ALL|*INPUT| *OUTPUT|*KEY})

Linear Main Program

Program in which the main procedure is explicitly named, identified by the Ctl-opt Main keyword. Variables and files are automatically initialized or opened when the program starts, but are never implicitly closed. Files in a linear main program must be explicitly closed using the Close operation. Linear main programs do not use *Inlr to close files and free storage.

%Lookup()

Function. Look up array element.

Usage: %LOOKUP(search-arg:
  array{:start{:number-elements}})

Usage: %LOOKUPLT(search-arg:
  array{:start{:number-elements}})

Usage: %LOOKUPLE(search-arg:
  array{:start{:number-elements}})

Usage: %LOOKUPGE(search-arg:
  array{:start{:number-elements}})

Usage: %LOOKUPGT(search-arg:
  array{:start{:number-elements}})

Lookup

Operation code. Look up an array or table element. Obsolete; use %Lookup or %Tlookup.

M

Main

Keyword (H-spec). Main procedure name for program.

Usage: MAIN(procedure-name)

Maxdev

Keyword (F-spec). Maximum number of WORKSTN devices.

Usage: MAXDEV(*ONLY|*FILE)

Mhhzo

Operation code. Move high to high zone. Obsolete; use %Bitand, %Bitor.

Mhlzo

Operation code. Move high to low zone. Obsolete; use %Bitand, %Bitor.

%Minutes()

Function. Convert to number of minutes.

Usage: %MINUTES(numeric-expression)

Mlhzo

Operation code. Move low to high zone. Obsolete; use %Bitand, %Bitor.

Mllzo

Operation code. Move low to low zone. Obsolete; use %Bitand, %Bitor.

Module

Object (*MODULE) that results from compiling source code. A module cannot be called until it is first bound into a program.

Monitor

Operation code. Begin Monitor group.

Usage: MONITOR;

%Months()

Function. Convert to number of months.

Usage: %MONTHS(numeric-expression)

Move

Operation code. Move. Obsolete; use Eval, Evalr, %Subst, conversion functions.

Movea

Operation code. Move array. Obsolete; use Eval, Evalr, %Subarr, %Subst, conversion functions.

Movel

Operation code. Move left. Obsolete; use Evalr Eval, %Subst, conversion functions.

%Mseconds()

Function. Convert to number of microseconds.

Usage: %MSECONDS(numeric-expression)

Mult

Operation code. Multiply. Obsolete; use * operator.

Mvr

Operation code. Move remainder. Obsolete; use %Rem.

N

Named Constant

Data item (defined with Dcl-c instruction) that represents a specific value that does not change during the running of the program. Name can be used instead of a literal to represent the value.

Next

Operation code. Force next input from a device.

Usage: NEXT{(e)} program-device file-name;

Nomain

Keyword (Ctl-opt). Compile ILE module without a main procedure. The module will contain only subprocedures and cannot be the entry module for a program.

Usage: NOMAIN

Noopt

Keyword (Dcl-*xx*). Do not optimize data item.

Usage: NOOPT

%Nullind()

Function. Get/Set Null indicator value.

Usage: %NULLIND(field-name)

O

%Occur()

Function. Get/set data structure occurrence. Obsolete; use array data structure.

Occur

Operation code. Get/set data structure occurrence. Obsolete; use array data structure.

Occurs

Keyword (Dcl-ds). Number of occurrences in a multiple-occurrence data structure (1–16773104). Obsolete; use array data structure.

Oflind

Keyword (Dcl-f). Overflow indicator for PRINTER file.

Usage: OFLIND(*INOA-*INOG|*INOV|
*IN01-*IN99|name)

On-error

Operation code. On-error.

Usage: ON-ERROR exception-id1
{:exception-id2...};

Opdesc

Keyword (Dcl-parm). Pass operational
descriptor.

Usage: OPDESC

%Open()

Function. Get file open status.

Usage: %OPEN(file-name)

Open

Operation code. Open file for processing.

Usage: OPEN{(e)} file-name;

Openopt

Keyword (Ctl-opt). Open printer file option.

Usage: OPENOPT(*NOINZOFL|*INZOFL)

OPM

Original Program Model.

Optimize

Keyword (Ctl-opt). Compile unit
optimization level.

Usage: OPTIMIZE(*NONE|*BASIC|*FULL)

Option

Keyword (Ctl-opt). Compiler options.

Usage: OPTION({*NOXREF|*XREF}
{*NOGEN|*GEN} {*NOSECLVL|*SECLVL}
{*NOSHOWCOPY|*SHOWCOPY}
{*NOEXPDDS|*EXPDDS}
{*NOEXT|*EXT}
{*NOSHOWSKP|*SHOWSKP}
{*NOSRCSTMT|*SRCSTMT}
{*NODEBUGIO|*DEBUGIO}
{*UNREF|*NOUNREF})

Options

Keyword (Dcl-parm). Parameter-passing
options for prototyped parameters.

Usage: OPTIONS({*NOPASS} {*NULLIND}
{*OMIT} {*RIGHTADJ} {*STRING}
{*TRIM} {*VARSIZE})

Orxx

Operation code. Or. Obsolete; use Or
connector.

Original Program Model

OPM. The set of functions for compiling
source code and creating programs before
the Integrated Language Environment (ILE)
model was introduced.

Other

Operation code. Otherwise Select.

Usage: OTHER;

Out

Operation code. Write data area.

Usage: OUT{(e)} {*LOCK} data-area-name;

Output Specifications (O-Specs)

Section of an RPG program that describes output records and their fields or that adds functions to an externally described output file.

Overlay

Keyword (Dcl-subf). Overlay data structure subfield.

Usage: OVERLAY(subfield-name{:position| *NEXT})

Overflow Indicator

Indicator that signals when the overflow line on a page has been printed or passed; can be used to specify which lines are to be printed on the next page.

P

Packeven

Keyword (Dcl-*xx*). Fix high-order digit for packed field with an even number of digits.

Usage: PACKEVEN

%Paddr()

Function. Get pointer to procedure address.

Usage: %PADDR(procedure)

Parm

Operation code. Identify parameters. Obsolete; use Dcl-pr, Dc-pi definitions.

%Parmnum

Function. Get ordinal position of named parameter in parameter list.

Usage: %PARMNUM(parm-name)

%Parms

Function. Get number of parameters.

Usage: %PARMS

Pass

Keyword (Dcl-f). Do not pass indicators.

Usage: PASS(*NOIND)

Perrcd

Keyword (Dcl-ds). Number of compile-time array or table elements per record.

Usage: PERRCD(numeric-constant)

Pgminfo

Keyword (Ctl-opt). Place program information directly into compiled module.

Usage: PGMINFO(*NO|*PCML:*MODULE)

Pgmname

Keyword (Dcl-f). Program to process SPECIAL device file.

Usage: PGMNAME(pgm-name)

Plist

Keyword (Dcl-f). Parameter list to be passed to SPECIAL file program.

Usage: PLIST(plist-name)

Operation code. Identify a parameter list. Obsolete; use Dcl-pr, Dcl-pi.

Post

Operation code. Post information to INFDS.

Usage: POST{(e)} {program-device} file-name;

Prefix

Keyword (Dcl-f, Dcl-ds). Add or replace a prefix to externally described fields (rename).

Usage: PREFIX(prefix-string{:number})

Usage: PREFIX('':number)

Preruntime Array

Array loaded at the same time as the program, before the program begins to run.

Preruntime Table

Table loaded at the same time as the program, before the program begins to run.

Prfdta

Keyword (Dcl-f). Collect profiling data.

Usage: PRFDTA(*NOCOL|*COL)

Primary File

If specified, the first file from which the program reads a record.

Procedure

Set of self-contained statements, in a module, that performs a task and returns to its caller.

Procedure Boundary Specifications (P-Specs)

Specifications in an RPG program that define the beginning and ending boundaries of a procedure. Obsolete. Use Dcl-proc, End-proc.

Procptr

Keyword (Dcl-*xx*). Field is a procedure pointer.

Usage: PROCPTR

Program

Callable object (*PGM) consisting of a set of executable instructions in machine-readable form. The result of binding modules together.

Program Entry Procedure (PEP)

Procedure provided by the compiler that is the entry point for a program. Also called a user entry procedure.

Prtctl

Keyword (Dcl-f). Dynamic printer control.

Usage: PRTCTL(ds-name{:COMPAT})

Public Interface

The names of procedures and data items, exported from a service program, that other ILE programs or service programs can access.

Q

Qualified

Keyword (Dcl-f, Dcl-ds). Force qualified names for record formats or subfields.

Usage: QUALIFIED

R

Rafdata

Keyword (Dcl-f). Name of date file for record address file.

Usage: RAFDATA(file-name)

Read

Operation code. Read a record.

Usage: READ{(en)} name {data-structure};

Readc

Operation code. Read next changed record.

Usage: READC{(e)} record-name
{data-structure};

Reade

Operation code. Read equal key.

Usage: READE{(enhmr)} search-arg name
{data-structure};

Readp

Operation code. Read prior record.

Usage: READP{(en)} name {data-structure};

Readpe

Operation code. Read prior equal key.

Usage: READPE{(enhmr)} search-arg name
{data-structure};

%Realloc()

Function. Reallocate storage with new length.

Usage: %REALLOC(pointer:length)

Realloc

Operation code. Reallocate storage with new length. Obsolete; use %Realloc.

Recno

Keyword (Dcl-f). Field name for relative record number processing.

Usage: RECNO(field-name)

Record Address File

Input file that indicates which records are to be read from another file and the order in which the records are to be read.

Rel

Operation code. Release device.

Usage: REL{(e)} program-device file-name;

%Rem()

Function. Get integer remainder (modulus).

Usage: %REM(dividend:divisor)

Rename

Keyword (Dcl-f). Rename record format from externally described file.

Usage: RENAME(external-fmt-name:
internal-fmt-name)

%Replace()

Function. Replace character string.

Usage: %REPLACE(replacement:string
{:start{:length}})

Reset

Operation code. Reset data item value.

Usage: RESET{(e)} {*NOKEY} {*ALL} name;

Resulting Indicator

Indicator that signals the result of a calculation. Obsolete: use %Found, %Error, %Eof, %Equal.

Return

Operation code. Return to caller.

Usage: RETURN{(hmr)} {expression};

Rolbk

Operation code. Roll back file changes.

Usage: ROLBK{(e)};

Rtnparm

Keyword (Dcl-pr). Handles procedure return value as hidden parameter.

Usage: RTNPARM

Runtime Array

An array that is loaded after the program starts to run.

Runtime Table

A table that is loaded after the program starts to run.

S

Saveds

Keyword (Dcl-f). Save data structure.

Usage: SAVEDS(ds-name)

Saveind

Keyword (Dcl-f). Save indicators.

Usage: SAVEIND(number)

SAX

Simple API for XML. SAX provides a mechanism for reading data from an XML document. RPG supports SAX with the XML-SAX operation.

%Scan()

Function. Scan string for characters and get position.

Usage: %SCAN(search-arg:string{:start})

Scan

Operation code. Scan string for characters. Obsolete; use %Scan.

%Scanrpl()

Function. Scan string for all appearances of search argument and replace with another value.

Usage: %SCANRPL(search-arg:replacement: string{:start{:length}})

Secondary File

Any input file other than the primary file, if specified.

%Seconds()

Function. Convert to number of seconds.

Usage: %SECONDS(numeric-expression)

Select

Operation code. Begin Select group.

Usage: SELECT;

Serialize

Keyword (Dcl-proc). Procedure can be run by only one thread at a time.

Usage: SERIALIZE

Service Program

Bound program object (*SRVPGM) containing utility procedures that other bound programs can call.

Setgt

Operation code. Set greater than.

Usage: SETGT{(ehmr)} search-arg name;

Setll

Operation code. Set lower limit.

Usage: SETLL{(ehmr)} search-arg name;

Setoff

Operation code. Set indicators off. Obsolete; use assignment expressions.

Seton

Operation code. Set indicators on. Obsolete; use assignment expressions.

Sfile

Keyword (Dcl-f). Subfile parameters.

Usage: SFILE(format-name:rrn-field)

%Shtdn

Function. Get shutdown request status.

Usage: %SHTDN

Shtdn

Operation code. Check for shutdown request. Obsolete; use %Shtdn.

%Size()

Function. Get byte size.

Usage: %SIZE(data-item{:*ALL})

Sln

Keyword (Dcl-f). Starting line for WORKSTN file.

Usage: SLN(number)

Sorta

Operation code. Sort array.

Usage: SORTA{(a|d)} array-name;

Usage: SORTA{(a|d)} %Subarr(array-name {:start{:number-of-elements});

/Space

Compiler directive. Compiler listing line spacing.

Usage: /SPACE nbr

%Sqrt()

Function. Get square root of expression.

Usage: %SQRT(numeric-expression)

Sqrt

Operation code. Square root. Obsolete; use %Sqrt.

Srtseq

Keyword (Ctl-opt). Sort sequence table.

Usage: SRTSEQ(*HEX|*JOB|*JOBRUN| *LANGIDUNQ|*LANGIDSHR|'sort-table-name')

Static

Keyword (Dcl-f, Dcl-*xx*). Local file or data item uses static storage, or Java method is static.

Usage: STATIC{(*ALLTHREAD)}

%Status()

Function. Get status code.

Usage: %STATUS{(file-name)}

Stgmdl

Keyword (Ctl-opt). Controls storage model of module or program.

Usage: STGMDL(*INHERIT|*TERASPACE| *SNGLVL)

%Str()

Function. Get/set null-terminated string.

Usage: %STR(pointer{:length{:position}})

Sub

Operation code. Subtract. Obsolete; use - operator.

%Subarr()

Function. Get/set portion of array.

Usage: %SUBARR(array: start{:number-of-elements})

Subdur

Operation code. Subtract duration. Obsolete; use - operator, %DIFF, date functions.

%Subdt()

Function. Extract portion of date, time, timestamp.

Usage: %SUBDT(value:duration)

%Subst()

Function. Get/set character substring.

Usage: %SUBST(string:start{:length})

Subst

Operation code. Substring. Obsolete; use %Subst.

T

Table

Series of elements with like characteristics; can be searched for a uniquely identified element, but elements in a table cannot be accessed by their position relative to other elements.

Table File

Input file that contains a table.

Tag

Operation code. Tag. Obsolete.

Template

Keyword (Dcl-f, Dcl-*xx*). File is used only as template for LIKEFILE; data item is used only as template for LIKE or LIKEDS.

Usage: TEMPLATE

Test

Operation code. Test date, time, timestamp.

Usage: TEST{(edtz)} {dtz-format} field-name;

Testb

Operation code. Test bit. Obsolete; use %Bitand.

Testn

Operation code. Test numeric. Obsolete; use Monitor, On-error.

Testz

Operation code. Test zone. Obsolete; use %Bitand.

Text

Keyword (Ctl-opt). Compile unit descriptive text.

Usage: TEXT(*SRCMBRTXT|*BLANK|
   'description')

%This

Function. Get class instance for native method.

Usage: %THIS

Thread

Keyword (Ctl-opt). Multithread environment.

Usage: THREAD(*SERIALIZE|*CONCURRENT)

%Time()

Function. Convert to time.

Usage: %TIME({expression{:format}})

Time

Operation code. Get time and date. Obsolete; use %Date, %Time, %Timestamp.

%Timestamp()

Function. Convert to timestamp.

Usage: %TIMESTAMP({expression{:format}})

Timfmt

Keyword (Ctl-opt , Dcl-f, Dcl-*xx*). Time format.

Usage: TIMFMT(format{and-separator})

/Title

Compiler directive. Specify heading information for compiler listing.

Usage: /TITLE text

%Tlookup()

Function. Look up table element.

Usage: %TLOOKUP(search-arg:
   table{:alt-table})

Usage: %TLOOKUPLT(search-arg:
   table{:alt-table})

Usage: %TLOOKUPLE(search-arg:
table{:alt-table})

Usage: %TLOOKUPGE(search-arg:
table{:alt-table})

Usage: %TLOOKUPGT(search-arg:
table{:alt-table})

Tofile

Keyword (Dcl-ds). Name of file in which
to save preruntime array or table at end of
program.

Usage: TOFILE(file-name)

%Trim()

Function. Trim leading and /or trailing
characters.

Usage: %TRIM(string{:characters})

Usage: %TRIML(string{:characters})

Usage: %TRIMR(string{:characters})

Truncnbr

Keyword (Ctl-opt). Truncate numeric values.

Usage: TRUNCNBR(*YES|*NO)

U

%Ucs2()

Function. Convert to UCS-2 value.

Usage: %UCS2(value{:ccsid})

/Undefine

Compiler directive. Remove condition
defined by /Define conditional compilation
directive.

Usage: /UNDEFINE condition-name

Unlock

Operation code. Unlock data area or release
record.

Usage: UNLOCK{(e)} name;

%Uns()

Function. Convert to unsigned integer
format.

Usage: %UNS(expression)

%Unsh()

Function. Convert to unsigned integer
format with half-adjust.

Usage: %UNSH(expression)

Update

Operation code. Modify existing record.

Usage: UPDATE{(e)} name {data-structure|
%FIELDS(name1{:name2...})};

Update File

File from which a program reads a record,
changes data fields in the record, then writes
the record back to the location from which it
came.

User Entry Procedure (UEP)

Procedure provided by the compiler that is
the entry point for a program. Also called a
program entry procedure.

Usropn

Keyword (Dcl-f). User-controlled open/close
of file.

Usage: USROPN

Usrprf

Keyword (Ctl-opt). User profile.

Usage: USRPRF(*USER|*OWNER)

V

Value

Keyword (Dcl-parm). Pass prototyped parameter by value.

Usage: VALUE

Varying

Keyword (Dcl-s). Variable-length character or graphic field.

Usage: VARYING{(2|4)}

W

When

Operation code. When true, then select.

Usage: WHEN(mr) logical-expression;

Whenxx

Operation code. When true, then select. Obsolete; use When.

Write

Operation code. Create new record.

Usage: WRITE{(e)} name {data-structure};

X

%Xfoot()

Function. Get sum of array expression elements.

Usage: %XFOOT(array-expression)

Xfoot

Operation code. Sum the elements of an array. Obsolete; use %xFOOT.

%Xlate()

Function. Translate characters.

Usage: %XLATE(from:to:string{:start})

Xlate

Operation code. Translate characters. Obsolete; use %Xlate.

XML

Extensible Markup Language. Set of standards for encoding documents electronically; widely used to represent data structures.

%Xml()

Function. Specifies XML document name and parsing options. Used with XML-SAX and XML-INTO.

Usage: %XML(document{:'option1=value1 option2=value2 ...'})

Xml-Into

Operation code. Read data from XML document directly into a variable or into an array parameter that is passed to a %HANDLER procedure.

Usage: XML-INTO{(eh)} receiver
%XML(document{:'option1=value1
option2=value2 ...'});

Usage: XML-INTO{(eh)}
%HANDLER(procedure:comm-area)
%XML(document{:'option1=value1
option2=value2 ...'});

Xml-Sax

Operation code. Initiate SAX parse for an XML document.

Usage: XML-SAX{(e)}
%HANDLER(procedure:comm-area)
%XML(document{:'option1=value1
option2=value2 ...'});

Y

%Years()

Function. Convert to number of years.

Usage: %YEARS(numeric-expression)

Z

Z-add

Operation code. Zero and add. Obsolete; use assignment expression.

Z-sub

Operation code. Zero and subtract. Obsolete; use assignment expression.

APPENDIX **B**

Program Development Tools

Overview

This appendix introduces the tools you need to develop programs—to edit program source, compile it, bind the resulting module, and finally run the program. There are two primary toolsets available for program development:

- IBM Rational Developer for i (RDi)
- Programming Development Manager (PDM)

RDi is a Windows client program, based on the open-source Eclipse platform. PDM consists of application development tools for use in a green-screen workstation environment.

Program Development Objects

Before examining these tools, let's review the IBM i object-based architecture. IBM i libraries are container objects (type *LIB) that organize other objects. A library is analogous to a PC directory. The IBM i server stores many kinds of objects: data files (*FILE), commands (*CMD), modules (*MODULE), programs (*PGM), and so on. The type associated with an object is analogous to the extension of a PC file. It determines the kinds of actions you can perform on the object. All object types begin with an asterisk (*).

During the program development cycle, you primarily work with three kinds of objects: *MODULE, *PGM, and *FILE. Recall that *MODULE objects result from successfully compiling a source member and contain the machine-language version of your source code. A program object (type *PGM) comprises one or more *MODULE objects bound together. When you call a *PGM object, you are telling the computer to perform the instructions contained in the object.

Objects with type *FILE are files. Files are further differentiated by attributes, which categorize the nature of the file. The attribute PF-SRC indicates that a file is a source physical file that contains source code. Attribute PF-DTA signifies that an object is a physical database file, and attribute LF signals that an object is a logical database file.

The contents of all database files, regardless of attribute, can be structured into members. A member is a subdivision of a file. A file must exist before you can add members to it. Each program that you edit will be stored as a member within a source physical file. Compiling that source member creates a *MODULE object, usually with the same name as the member.

Most installations use a source file named QRPGLESRC to store ILE RPG source code (although you can name the source file anything). While most installations store the source code and the object (executable) code in the same library, it is not unusual to store source code in libraries separate from their object (executable) code. Your installation's standards and practices will dictate the source filename and the library name wherein you will be working.

IBM i Development Tools

Traditionally, IBM i developers have used a toolset called Application Development Toolset (ADTS). ADTS consists of server-based tools such as Programming Development Manager (PDM) for organizing objects, Source Entry Utility (SEU) for editing source code, and Screen Design Aid (SDA) for designing screens. Developers primarily use the ADTS tools with traditional green-screen workstations. PDM and its associated programs are still available on most IBM i servers, but IBM has no plans to enhance this toolset in the future.

The current development environment is a program called Rational Developer for i (RDi). This tool is based on the industry-standard Eclipse platform (*www.eclipse.org*). RDi is a Windows-based program and includes such tools as Remote Systems Explorer (RSE) for organizing objects, a Live Parsing and Extensible editor (LPEX) for editing source code, and a DDS Designer tool for designing screens and reports. Developers are moving away from the traditional server-based development toolset in favor of RDi.

The utilities in RDi perform many of the same functions as the traditional tools, but in a graphical Windows environment, offloading the bulk of application development work from the server and onto Windows clients. RDi offers many well-known Windows features unavailable with the server's character-based interface. Instead of PDM's *Work with* screens, RDi uses familiar Explorer-like windows to help you organize libraries, objects, and members. In addition, RDi uses its own more robust graphical LPEX editor as opposed to SEU. And rather than SDA, RDi offers the DDS Designer.

Rational Developer for i provides links to the full set of IBM i language compilers; for example, ILE RPG/400, Control Language (CL), COBOL, Java, and C. You can also install the product with Web development tools for creating Internet Web applications. The platform is designed so that a developer must learn only one development environment. If a developer needs to write in a different language or for a different platform, RDi supports the installation of plug-ins to allow development for that language or platform. Still, other plug-ins enable software vendors to enhance RDi functions. These tools and more combine to make RDi a feature-filled application toolkit.

Rational Developer for i (RDi)

The primary RDi component for program development is RSE. Figure B.1 shows the initial screen that opens when you start RDi for the first time. This screen, which presents a window titled "IBM i Remote System Explorer Getting Started," guides you through all the steps required to connect to your IBM i, edit and compile a member, and then run your first program. You can open this window at any time by selecting **Help** > **IBMi RSE Getting Started** on the top menu.

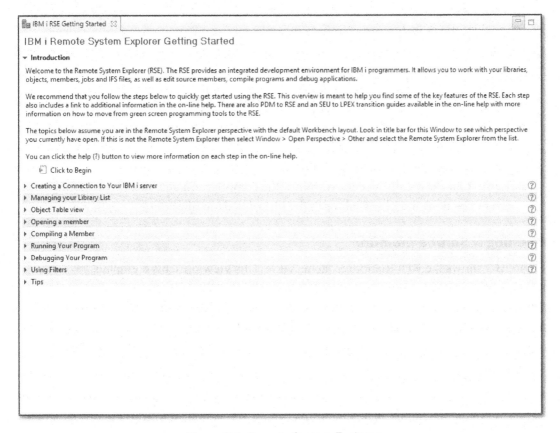

Figure B.1: Remote System Explorer

Although there's a learning curve for RDi, once you spend a little time with it, you'll find it's comfortable and familiar. With the following important steps, you can begin the program development cycle:

- Opening a source member
- Editing a source member
- Compiling a source member
- Running a program

Figure B.2 highlights five views that RDi uses for organizing, editing, and compiling programs:

- **Remote System Explorer** lets you navigate the system that you are logged on to. When you use this view, compare to it using Windows Explorer. You can copy, cut, paste, and delete objects. Double-clicking a member opens it in the LPEX editor.
- **LPEX editor** is where you edit the source member. The LPEX editor includes many traditional editor features and has some features in common with SEU. It additionally provides many features (e.g., copy, cut, and paste) modern graphical editors have.
- **Outline** provides a complete organizational outline of the source code you are editing. It shows all the files and variables and where they are in the program. It also outlines subroutines and procedures. Clicking any portion of the outline moves the LPEX editor to that area of the source code.
- **Commands Log** is similar to displaying your job log. Submitting any command to the system presents the results here. For example, when you submit a program to be compiled, those results display in this view.
- **Error List** shows all errors or warnings the compiler found. Clicking one of these errors positions the LPEX editor to the line of code in question.

Opening a Source Member

Figure B.3 shows the RDi Remote Systems view. This view presents a graphic representation of the system to which you are connected. Clicking the symbol to the left of the Library List icon (i.e., expanding it) displays the libraries in your library list as if you had used the DSPLIBL (Display Library List) command on a command line. If you aren't logged on to the system, a login window will open; enter your IBM i user ID and password, and then click OK.

When you expand the Library List icon, all the libraries in your library list appear. The next step is to expand the library that contains the source file you want to edit. Finally, expand the source file and double-click the appropriate member (or right-click the member and select Open with Remote Systems LPEX Editor). Figure B.3 illustrates the process.

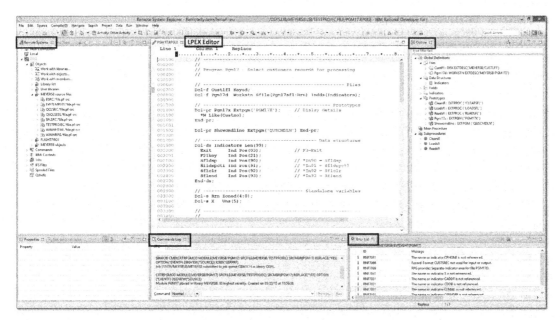

Figure B.2: RDi views

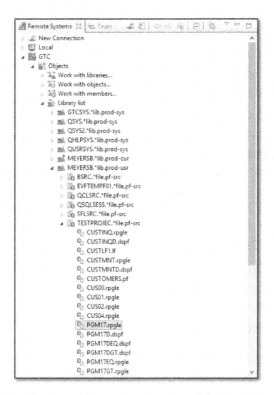

Figure B.3: Opening a source member from Remote Systems view

Editing a Source Member

The source member is now open in the LPEX editor view (Figure B.4), where you can edit the source member much like a typical document. With the LPEX editor, you can easily copy within the member or between members, just as you would within a document.

The LPEX editor can provide you with prompts for code entry as well. If you are editing a source line and press F4, RDi opens a separate view that prompts you for each component of the line. Context-sensitive help is also available from the prompter by pressing F1.

You can access some LPEX functions by typing sequence commands over the sequence number for the appropriate source lines and then pressing the Enter key. Here are some common sequence commands:

- I to insert a new line below the current line
- D to delete the current line
- DD to delete a block of lines (type DD over the sequence numbers of the first and last lines in the block)
- C to copy the current line (to indicate the desired location, type either A [after] or B [before] over the sequence number of the target line)
- CC to copy a block of lines (type CC on the first and last lines of the block, then A or B at the desired target location)
- M to move the current line (to indicate the desired location, type either A or B over the sequence number of the target line)
- MM to move a block of lines (type MM on the first and last lines of the block, then A or B at the desired target location)
- RP to repeat the current line on the next line
- RPP to repeat a block of lines (type RPP on the first and last lines of the block)

The LPEX editor offers many other useful editing features, including search/replace and source line filters. The list of additional features is beyond the scope of this book, but the RDi Help documentation provides that information.

After making changes to the member, you can the save the member by clicking the Save button, as Figure B.5 shows, or by pressing the Crtl+S keys.

Compiling a Source Member

Once you have saved the source member, the next step is to compile it into a module or a program object. Right-click the source member and navigate to the Compile option (Figure B.6). At this point, you can choose to use the CRTBNDRPG command or the CRTRPGMOD command to compile the source member. When you select a compile command, the source member is compiled in batch on the server.

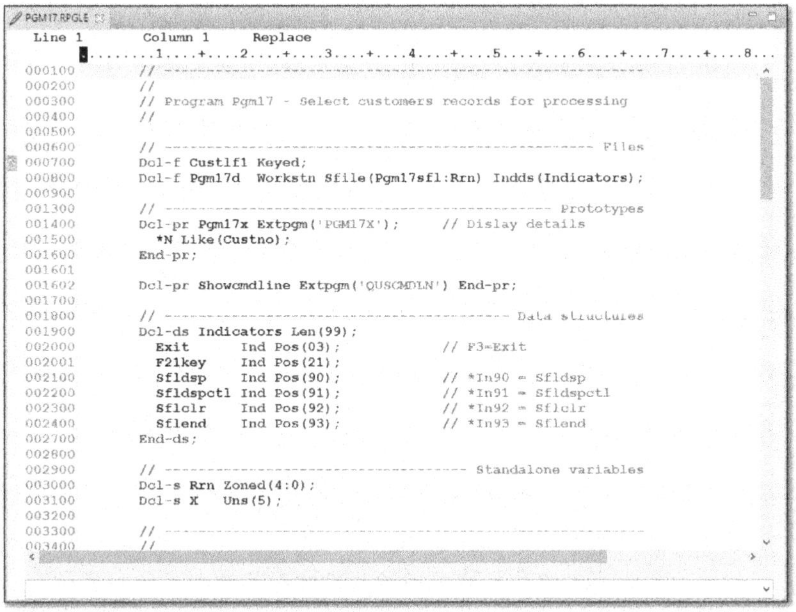

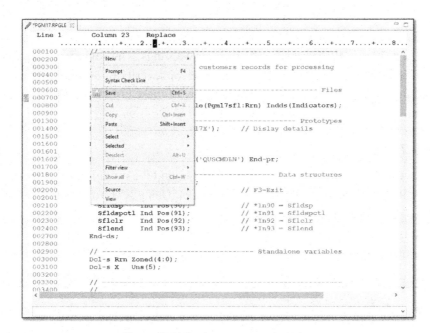

Figure B.4: Editing a source member with the LPEX Editor

Figure B.5: Saving a source member

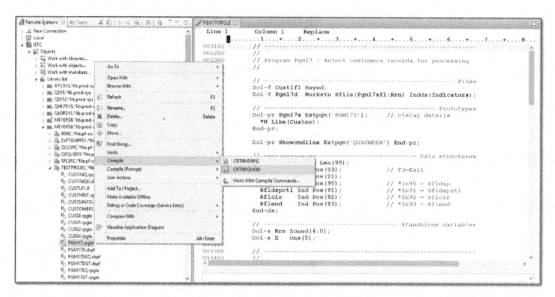

Figure B.6: Compiling a source member

You can use either of the following views to show the results of the compile job:

- Commands Log (Figure B.7) displays executed commands and the results of batch submissions.
- Error List (Figure B.8) presents all errors or warnings. The severity of the error is indicated by a number 00–99. Typically, an error severity of 30 or higher prevents a job from compiling successfully. Clicking any of these errors will move the LPEX editor to the line that caused the error.

Running a Program

After you have compiled the source member—and bound the module to a program, if necessary—the next step is to run the program object. Using RSE to navigate to the newly compiled program object (Figure B.9), right-click and select Run As. Usually, you will select the option to run the program in batch unless the program is an interactive program, in which case you'll run the program from a workstation emulation program.

Note

To run a program, you must navigate to the compiled program object itself, not the source member. You may need to refresh the RSE view by highlighting it and pressing F5.

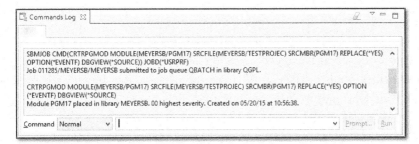

Figure B.7: Commands Log showing successful compilation

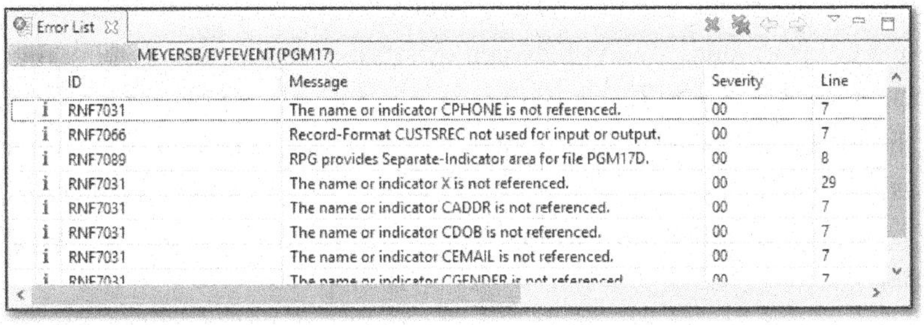

ID	Message	Severity	Line
RNF7031	The name or indicator CPHONE is not referenced.	00	7
RNF7066	Record-Format CUSTSREC not used for input or output.	00	7
RNF7089	RPG provides Separate-Indicator area for file PGM17D.	00	8
RNF7031	The name or indicator X is not referenced.	00	29
RNF7031	The name or indicator CADDR is not referenced.	00	7
RNF7031	The name or indicator CDOB is not referenced.	00	7
RNF7031	The name or indicator CEMAIL is not referenced.	00	7
RNF7031	The name or indicator CGENDER is not referenced	00	7

Figure B.8: Error List displaying errors and severity

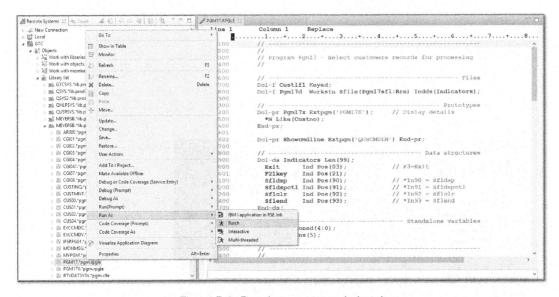

Figure B.9: Running a program in batch

Screen Designer and Print Designer

You can use RDi's LPEX editor to edit source code for DDS source members (e.g., to edit the source for display files and printer files). But it might be more convenient to use a WYSIWYG (What you see is what you get) graphical tool to design and create these objects. Two RDi tools, Screen Designer and Report Designer, provide this function.

Screen Designer and Report Designer are integrated into RDi. By right-clicking a DDS source member (member type DSPF or PRTF) and selecting either Open with Screen Designer or Open with Print Designer, you can modify the DDS source member by using the WYSIWYG tool as well as the LPEX editor.

The way these tools work differs slightly. You place fields on the design window, moving them into their desired positions. Double-clicking a field opens a window to maintain the field's properties. Refer to the product's Help documentation for additional information. You can easily move fields around, switch between different records, and display the generated DDS source code. Figure B.10 illustrates the use of Screen Designer with a display file, and Figure B.11 shows the use of Report Designer with a printer file. Both tools include a Source tab that allows you to use the LPEX editor to fine-tune the generated DDS code, if necessary (Figure B.12). Screen Designer also features a Preview tab (Figure B.13) to preview the resulting display.

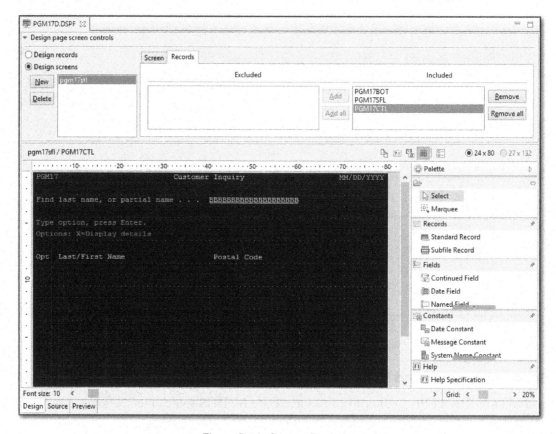

Figure B.10: Screen Designer

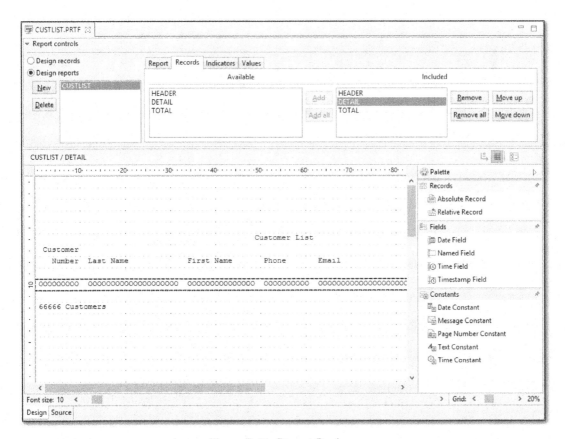

Figure B.11: Report Designer

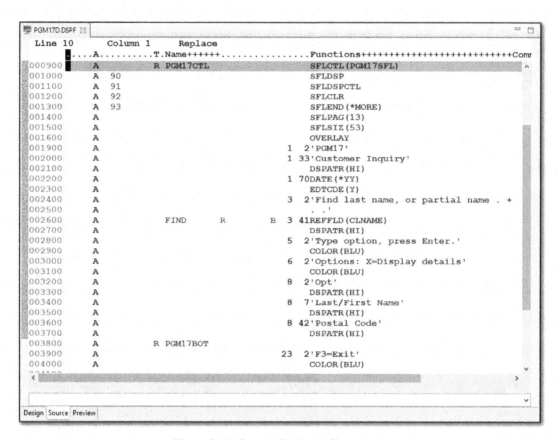

Figure B.12: Screen Designer Source tab

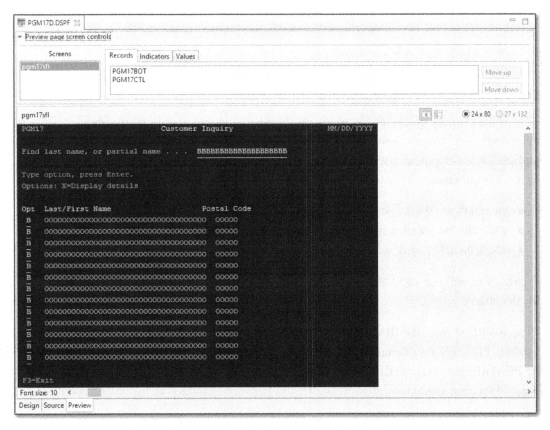

Figure B.13: Screen Designer Preview tab

After you have used Screen Designer or Report Designer to design a display or report, the tool will store the generated DDS in a source member. You can then compile it, similar to the way you compile RPG source members.

Programming Development Manager (PDM)

PDM is the primary character-based means for accessing and manipulating libraries, objects, and members. If you are using a green-screen workstation or emulation program for your application development, use PDM instead of RDi. You can launch PDM from any of three main CL commands:

- WRKLIBPDM (Work with Libraries Using PDM)
- WRKOBJPDM (Work with Objects Using PDM)
- WRKMBRPDM (Work with Members Using PDM)

Usually, you will use WRKMBRPDM to organize, edit, and compile members in a source physical file.

To access PDM from the IBM i Main menu, first select option 5, Programming. Then, at the resulting Programming menu, select option 2, Programming Development Manager to open the PDM menu in Figure B.14. You can also display this menu by executing the STRPDM (Start PDM) command.

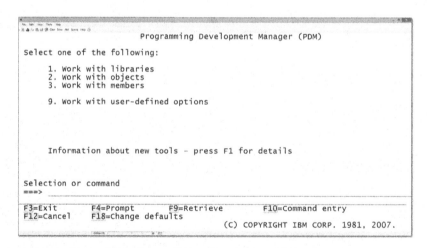

Figure B.14: Programming Development Manager menu

Enter and Edit a Source Member

To open a source member for editing, select option 3, Work with members, from the PDM menu, or prompt the WRKMBRPDM command. Figure B.15 shows the resulting prompt, which you use to select the source file containing the members you want to edit. You can either enter the desired source file or position your cursor on the file prompt and press F4 to see a list of the possible files.

```
File Edit View Tools Help
                                 Specify Members to Work With

Type choices, press Enter.

    File  . . . . . . . . . .    TESTPROJEC   Name, F4 for list

       Library . . . . . . .        MEYERSB     *LIBL, *CURLIB, name

    Member:
       Name  . . . . . . . . .    *ALL        *ALL, name, *generic*
       Type  . . . . . . . . .    *ALL        *ALL, type, *generic*, *BLANK






F3=Exit      F4=Prompt     F5=Refresh      F12=Cancel
```

Figure B.15: Selecting a source file to edit

Once you have entered or selected the desired file, the system displays all the members of that file, as Figure B.16 shows. From this screen, select a source member to edit, print, or compile by keying a 2, 6, 14, or 15, respectively, next to the member with which you want to work. Note that options 14 and 15 may not appear on the initial screen; pressing F23 (More options) reveals this and additional options for working with members. However, an option does not have to appear on the screen to be used—provided it is a valid option.

```
File Edit View Tools Help
                                 Work with Members Using PDM

File  . . . . . .    TESTPROJEC
   Library . . . .      MEYERSB                Position to  . . . . .

Type options, press Enter.
   2=Edit          3=Copy   4=Delete 5=Display      6=Print    7=Rename
   8=Display description  9=Save 13=Change text  14=Compile  15=Create module...

Opt  Member        Type       Text
     CUS02         RPGLE
     CUS04         RPGLE
2    PGM17         RPGLE
     PGM17D        DSPF
     PGM17DEQ      DSPF
     PGM17DGT      DSPF
     PGM17EQ       RPGLE
     PGM17GT       RPGLE
                                                                    More...
Parameters or command
===>
F3=Exit          F4=Prompt           F5=Refresh         F6=Create
F9=Retrieve      F10=Command entry   F23=More options   F24=More keys
```

Figure B.16: Work with Members Using PDM display

To edit an existing member, enter a 2 to the left of the member name to open that member in Source Entry Utility (SEU) and continue work on it. If you are creating a new member, press F6=Create to go to the Start SEU screen. Here, you enter the source filename, the member name, and the type.

Figure B.17 illustrates the SEU editor. The editor options in SEU are not as robust as those in the LPEX editor, but the two editors share many of the same functions. For example, SEU supports the sequence commands discussed earlier.

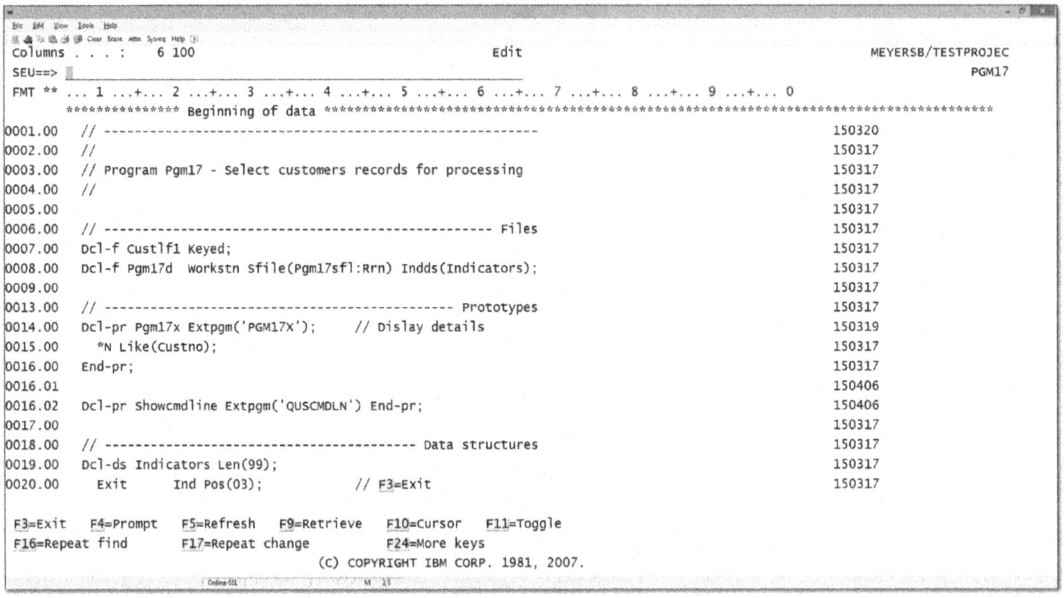

Figure B.17: Source Entry Utility

In addition, you may find the following function keys useful when editing a source member:

- F3 to exit SEU
- F4 to invoke a prompt function (similar to RDi's prompter) for the current line
- F5 to refresh the display (if you haven't yet pressed Enter)
- F13 (Shift+F1) to change the SEU defaults for the current session (e.g., to enable or disable a lowercase alphabetic entry)
- F14 (Shift+F2) to search/replace characters in the source member
- F15 (Shift+F3) to browse a second member or compiled output while working in your source code; this function key also lets you copy code from one member into another
- F16 (Shift+F4) to search for the next instance of a character string
- F17 (Shift+F5) to replace the next instance of a character string
- F23 (Shift+F11) to display all possible prompt formats and select the one you want to activate

SEU also supports a command line at the top of the display. You can use this line to enter SEU commands during the editing session. To position the cursor on the SEU command line, press F10. Here are some commands you may find useful (many of these commands also work with the LPEX editor):

- SAVE to save the member without exiting SEU
- CANCEL to leave SEU without saving and return to the previous menu
- TOP or T to move to the top of the source member
- BOTTOM or B to move to the bottom of the source member
- FIND or F to search for a string of characters in the source member
- CHANGE or C to change a string of characters to some other string

Compiling a Source Member

After editing, enter a compile option to the left of the name of the member you want to compile and bind. The compile option for the CRTBNDRPG command is 14; the option for the CRTRPGMOD command is 15. If the compiled object (either a *MODULE or *PGM) already exists, a Confirm Compile of Member screen appears; you must respond Y (Yes) to the *Delete existing object* option.

If the member is eligible to be compiled using the CRTBNDRPG command, you can use option 14 to compile it and create a *PGM object. Otherwise, you must use option 15 to compile the member and create a *MODULE object. Then to bind the modules to a *PGM object, enter the CRTPGM (Create Program) CL command on the PDM command line.

When the system returns a message indicating that the processing has completed successfully, your program is then ready to run. To display messages, type DSPMSG (Display Messages) on the command line and press Enter; or in most installations, type a *dm* shortcut in any option column of your current screen. If the message says that the processing ended abnormally, you must correct program errors and then reselect the compile option.

To correct errors, you may need to refer to the compiler listing for the source member. On many systems, you can type *sp* in any option column on any of PDM's screens to obtain a list of your spooled files. Alternatively, you can use the WRKSPLF (Work with Spooled Files) command on any command line. >From here, you can either print or view the compiler listing. Using the F15 key within SEU lets you find and view the compiler listing as well.

Run a Program

After compiling and binding a program, you can run it from within PDM. Select option 2, Work with Objects, from the PDM menu, or prompt the WRKOBJPDM (Work with Objects Using PDM) command. On the resulting display in Figure B.18, enter option 16 (Run) in the Opt column of the program object you want to run. Note that although 16 does not appear as an initial option, pressing F23 reveals it (and other options as well). Alternatively, you can enter the CALL command on any command line:

```
CALL program-name
```

If the program requires input parameters, press F4 to prompt option 16 or the CALL command, and then enter the necessary parameter values.

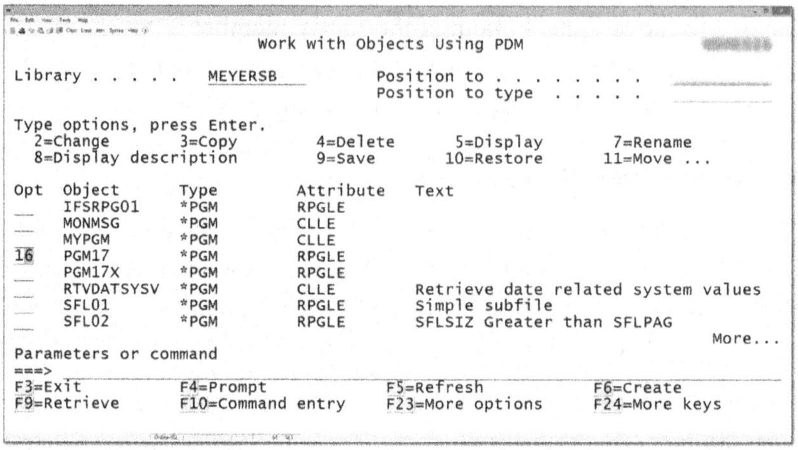

Figure B.18: Work with Objects Using PDM display

C

Program Testing and Debugging

Overview

This appendix discusses program testing issues and offers tips for solving problems that can occur when compiling or running RPG programs. It also covers the RDi Debug perspective, a tool that offers robust features for finding errors in a program.

A major part of a programmer's time is spent ensuring that the programs he or she has written are, in fact, accurately producing the desired results. This procedure involves carefully checking each program's correctness and fixing all errors this checking uncovers—a process often referred to as debugging. Program errors fall into one of two broad categories: syntax errors and logic errors.

Syntax Errors

Syntax errors stem from your use of the programming language. Because the system points out these kinds of errors for you, they are simple to find and easy to correct, once you have mastered the rules of the language in which you are programming.

The source editor you use (e.g., SEU or LPEX) detects some kinds of syntax errors as you enter program statements. For example, if you fail to make a required entry within a specification line or include an invalid value, the editor highlights the missing or erroneous entry with an accompanying error message. You may need to press the Reset key before the system lets you proceed. Typically, until you correct the error, the error message will remain as a reminder of a problem.

After you have completely entered your program and have eliminated all syntax errors detected by the editor, your next step is to compile and bind the program. Compiling is the process that translates a source member's statements into machine code instructions and stores them in a module object. The binding step copies one or more modules into a program object that the computer can then execute.

In attempting to complete the translation process, the ILE RPG/400 compiler often discovers additional syntax or contextual errors the editor failed to notice. If your program contains compile errors, the system sends you a message that your job ended abnormally. You can find the cause (or causes) of the difficulties by checking the RDi Error List view, or by printing or displaying the compile listing, a report of the compilation generated by the compiler. A compile listing includes a listing of your program. The compiler numbers the program statements sequentially in increments of 100 and indicates the date on which each statement was entered (or modified).

RDi also includes an Outline view to help you diagnose organizational problems in your program source. In addition, the compiler provides a cross-reference listing of all variables and indicators used in your program; it logs every program statement within which each of the fields or indicators occurs. Both the Outline view and the cross-reference listing show each variable and list each statement where it is used. The statement defining the variable is annotated with a D (for define), and any statement that changes the variable's or indicator's value is annotated with an M (for modify). You can use this listing to quickly locate field and indicator use within your program listing.

If your program contains syntax errors, the compiler notes the errors in the Error List view. When you select an error in the Error List view, the LPEX editor jumps to the line in the source that contains the error so that you can edit it. Problems vary in severity. A message with a severity of 00 is an informational message indicating a condition that will not prevent the program from being compiled; errors with severity of 10 or higher must be corrected before the program can be compiled normally. The compiler listing also notes errors, inserting an asterisk (*) and a numeric error code either under the line in error or within the cross-reference listing. The error message may also include an alphabetic marker (e.g., aaa, bbb) to help you correlate the error message with the location of the error on the specification line. This feature is especially useful when several errors occur on a single line.

After you have obtained a *clean compile*—that is, once the system has successfully translated your program into machine language and bound the resulting *MODULE object into a *PGM object—you can begin to check for logic errors in your program.

As a beginning programmer, you may feel frustrated at times by your inability to locate the cause of program errors. With practice, however, you'll begin to recognize what kinds of logic errors cause certain output errors, and, as a result, you'll be able to correct your programs with increasing ease. The sign of an excellent programmer is the ability to detect such problems as they occur. But remember, even seasoned programmers make logic mistakes.

Logic Errors

Faulty program design causes logic errors. You detect these kinds of errors by having the computer execute your program and then carefully checking the results of the execution. The two broad classes of logic errors are runtime errors and output errors.

Runtime Errors

Runtime errors prevent your program from reaching a normal end. These errors are simple to detect: either the program abruptly stops in the middle (an abend, or abnormal ending), or it runs continually until finally you or the operator intervenes. (The latter problem signals an infinite loop.) Although detecting the presence of a runtime error is usually easy, discovering the cause of the error can sometimes be difficult. Moreover, the kinds of logic problems that cause abends are different from those that cause infinite loops.

Diagnosing Abends

When your program ends abnormally, the system issues an error message indicating the cause of the problem and where the problem occurred within your program. Sometimes these error messages are unclear. By putting your cursor on the message and pressing the Help key, you can obtain additional information about the problem. You can also examine the job log (DSPJOBLOG or WRKJOB command) to find the cause of a problem. Typical causes of such runtime problems include trying to divide by zero, attempting to perform a numeric operation on a field that contains non-numeric data, trying to reference an array element beyond the array's defined limits (or size), attempting to read past end-of-file, and trying to update a record before you have read it.

After locating the problem statement and determining the nature of the problem, you must often trace through your program logic to determine how your program allowed that problem to occur. For example, if the program statement

```
C = A/B;
```

causes an abnormal ending because of an attempt to divide by zero, you need to determine why variable B has a value of 0 at the time the system is attempting the division operation. Is B an input variable? If so, did you forget to read a record before the division? If B is a work variable, did you neglect to assign it a nonzero value before the division? Or did you inadvertently assign 0 to B at the wrong time in your program?

When you can anticipate the problem before the program runs, and when you have a process in place that the program can execute when it encounters the error, you can use some of the error-handling techniques discussed in Chapter 16. When you cannot locate the cause of the problem, you may find it useful to run the program in debug mode, a topic discussed later in this appendix.

Diagnosing Infinite Loops

If you must cancel your job to prevent it from running forever, you know that you have an infinite loop within your program. An infinite loop is a faulty logic structure that causes the computer to repeat the same set of instructions over and over again. The following code shows two obvious infinite loops:

```
Read Customers;
Dou %Eof(Customers);
  Count += 1;
Enddo;


Dou Flag <> Flag;
  Count += 1;
Enddo;
```

The causes of the infinite loops here are simple to detect. In the first case, no statement exists within the loop to set the value of the %Eof function to *On—the condition needed to end the loop. In the second example, the value of Flag will always be equal to itself, so the loop will never end. (Actually, in these examples, at some point during the execution of the program, the size of Count will be too small to hold its value, causing the program to eventually abend.)

Generally, the cause of an infinite loop within a real program is less obvious than it is in these examples. When trying to diagnose your problem, realize that you can narrow your focus to the iterative operations in your program: Dou, Dow, and For. Also realize that somehow the condition that specifies when the looping should stop is not occurring. For example, forgetting to include a Read operation within a loop that continues until end-of-file is reached will potentially result in an infinite loop.

Output Errors

The most insidious kinds of logic errors are not those that cause abnormal program endings or infinite loops, but those that simply result in incorrect output. Some of these errors are obvious—neglecting to print heading lines on reports, for instance, or omitting an output entry that causes an entire column of information to be missing from a report. Other output errors are harder to detect and require careful manual checking to discover. You are unlikely to notice errors in complex calculations, for example, if you simply scan the output visually.

Detecting Output Errors

Carefully checking output that the computer generates against the results of your hand calculations is called *desk checking*. How much desk checking is required depends on the complexity of the logic that the program expresses. Generally, you should examine enough sets of data to test each logic branch within your program at least once. If, for example, you have written a payroll program that processes workers with overtime hours differently from workers without overtime, you should desk check the output for at least one worker with overtime hours and one without. The more conditional the logic within your program, the more desk checking you must do to ensure that your program is processing each case correctly.

Also remember to check the accuracy of subtotals and grand totals. For reports that have many columns with totals, you generally do not have to manually calculate the total for all columns. When you are doing all your accumulation in the same place within your program and have all the calculations set up the same way, if one column's total is correct, the rest should be correct as well—provided you are using the right fields in the calculations and referencing the right accumulators in your output.

In addition to using typical data, you should desk check your program logic at its extreme boundary values (i.e., verify that the logic works with the smallest and largest possible variable values). Remember to check the logic with zero values and negative numeric values if the data might include them.

The final step in checking output is to rigorously compare the computer-generated output with design documents to ensure that your output is exactly like the requested format. Are the column headings appropriately centered over the columns? Are the literals spelled correctly (e.g., Quantity, not Quanity)? Does the report's vertical alignment match that of the printer spacing chart? Did you edit the output correctly? The programmer's job is to give the designer exactly what he or she requested. Although concern with such formatting details may seem picky, careful attention to detail is one facet of the preciseness expected of first-rate programmers.

Correcting Output Errors

After you discover an output error, your next job is to find the cause of the error so you can correct it. A good programmer never makes changes within a program without having a specific reason for doing so. You should locate a problem's precise cause and fix it; in other words, do not base your changes on hunches or trial and error.

To find the cause of an error, work backward: focus your attention initially on those calculations specifically involved in generating the incorrect output. After carefully checking these program statements, if you still have not found an incorrect statement, broaden your search to those portions of the program that may be influencing the output more remotely.

It is impossible to be aware of every possible cause of erroneous output, but be alert to a number of common errors, many of which are described below, when you are working to debug a program.

Problems with Variables

Incorrectly defined variables cause overflow (or sometimes truncation), a problem most likely to occur with fields used as accumulators or fields that are the result of complex calculations. Another common field-related problem is a failure to appropriately initialize or reinitialize fields. Forgetting to reset an indicator, counter, or flag variable during repetitive processing is a frequent cause of erroneous output.

Loops

Off-by-one errors, resulting in a count-controlled loop repeating one too few or one too many times, occur frequently in programs. This kind of error happens when you incorrectly establish the conditional test to end the looping process. It often is related to an incorrect initialization of the counter field that controls the looping. For example, both of the following examples, designed to add all the numbers between 1 and 100, are erroneous. The first example sums the numbers 1 through 101, and the second adds the values 1 through 99.

```
I = 0;
Sum = 0;
Dow I < 101;
  I += 1;
    Sum += I;
Enddo;


I = 1;
Sum = 0;
Dow I < 100;
  I += 1;
    Sum += I;
Enddo;
```

Another common loop problem is a failure to enter the loop. When you use a looping operator that tests the condition before executing the steps within the loop—for example, when you want the system to read a file sequentially until it locates a desired code value within a record, process that record, and then resume reading until it finds the next record with that same code value—your program may fail to enter the loop. The following code correctly detects the first record containing the desired code but continues to process the first record infinitely:

```
Dow Not %Eof(File);
  Dow Code <> Value and Not %Eof(File);
    Read File;
  Enddo;
  Code = Value;
Enddo;
```

The first appropriate record that is located contains the code field with the desired value. As a result, the test of the inner loop will always be false and the inner loop will not be executed; no additional records will be read.

IF Logic

Sometimes, incorrectly nested If operations cause output errors. Know how the system matches If, Else, and Endif operations, and check the compiler listing's notation to make sure the system is interpreting your nested If statements the way you intended. In particular, desk check the code to ensure each If statement in a nested If group is properly closed with an Endif statement.

Another common If problem is incorrectly used ANDs, ORs, or NOTs in compound If tests. NOTs particularly are prone to errors. For example, to validate a code field that should have a value of S, H, or R, the following code falsely signals valid values as errors:

```
If Code Not = 'S' Or Code Not = 'H' Or Code Not = 'R';
     Exsr Error;
Endif;
```

Calculations

Sometimes, programmers do not execute steps in complex calculations in the correct order. Also, they occasionally overlook the possibility that a calculation can result in a negative value. This can be a difficult problem to locate because DDS prints or displays all values as absolute (unsigned) values unless field editing includes a provision for a negative sign (however, negative values are handled as negative values during calculation).

For example, when figuring income tax withholding, you often need to subtract a dependent allowance from gross earnings before applying the withholding tax percentage. The relationship between gross earnings and the number of dependents may be such that this subtraction returns a negative value. If you fail to anticipate this scenario, the tax is added to gross earnings (subtracting a negative number), and the same negative tax liability appears as a positive value on the payroll register report unless you edit the tax field with a code specifying to print negative signs.

Debugging Overview

Rational Developer for i includes a Debug perspective that is relatively easy to use and is indispensable to the programming professional. You can avoid the frustration of *poking and hoping* while trying to fix problems by learning how to use this tool. Stepping through your program and verifying that it is processing a file in the manner you anticipate, and that the variables in your program contain the values you think they do, can save hours of frustration.

Like the rest of RDi, the Debug perspective is based upon the open-source Eclipse platform. If you have used Eclipse to debug programs in other languages, you do not need to relearn the interface to debug RPG programs. This tool's client/server design allows you to debug programs running remotely on your IBM i system while using a graphical tool on your workstation. You can set breakpoints and monitors, step line by line through a program while it is running, and examine or change variables.

Figure C.1 shows the Debug perspective. When debugging a program, RDi automatically switches from the Remote System Explorer perspective to the Debug perspective and stops program execution at the first line of code. Figure C.1 highlights some of the more important views that you will regularly use when debugging a program.

The Source view and the Outline view should look familiar to you. The Source view allows you to watch your program source code as the program is being debugged. The Outline view displays a structured outline of the currently open program source. Using the Outline view, you can quickly navigate your program or easily find where variables are used.

The Debug view allows you to manage program debugging. This view displays the call stack and processes associated with the program you are debugging. It also provides several icons that let you control the debugging process. From this view, you can suspend the program, restart it, end the debug session, or *step through* the program line by line.

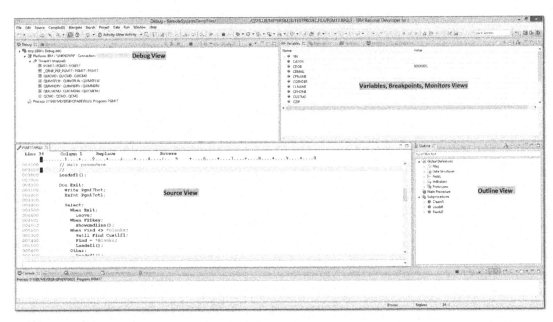

Figure C.1: Debug perspective

The remaining highlighted views in Figure C.1 primarily relate to variables, monitors, and breakpoints. With the Variables view, you can see the current values of variables in the program as it progresses. The Breakpoints view enables you to edit, disable, or remove breakpoints. Finally, the Monitors view lets you monitor changes and modify variables, registers, or expressions.

Service Entry Points

The most effective way to start a debugging session is to set a program attribute called a Service Entry Point (SEP). When an SEP is set in a program, and the program is executed by the same profile that set the SEP, the program is suspended and the debugger automatically connects to the job. When this occurs, RDi switches to the Debug perspective, and you can then begin debugging the program. To set an SEP, right-click the program object to debug, and select **Debug (Service Entry) > Set Service Entry Point** (Figure C.2) to display the SEP in the Service Entry Points view. You can also modify the SEP (e.g., you can change the user associated with it).

After recompiling/rebinding a program, you must refresh the SEP by right-clicking it in the Service Entry Points view and selecting Refresh to associate the SEP with the new program object (Figure C.3). When you are done debugging your program, be sure to remove the SEP by right-clicking it and selecting Remove. The SEP is a systemwide attribute set on the program object, and every time the program is executed, the system will attempt to start a debug session.

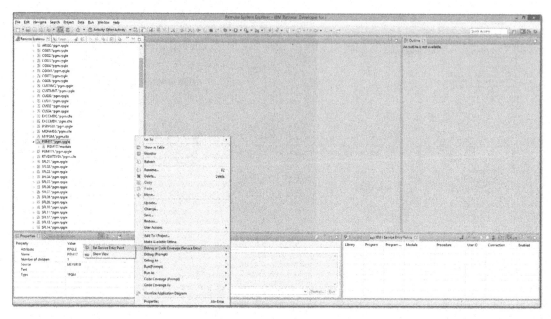

Figure C.2: Setting a Service Entry Point

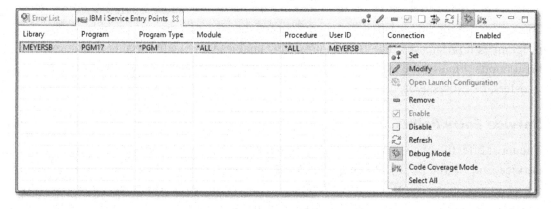

Figure C.3: Service Entry Points view

Starting a Debug Session

After you set an SEP for a program, you can start debugging the program simply by executing it. You can submit it from an RSE or workstation command line or execute it interactively from a workstation session. Once the program is loaded, RDi automatically shows the Debug perspective.

The first order of business is to set a breakpoint in the program. Breakpoints allow the debugger to suspend the program at certain points during its execution. When a breakpoint is reached, the program stops and lets you analyze its condition at that line of code, just before it executes that code. Beyond seeing which statement the program will execute next, you can also examine the current value of any variables in the program. Another useful feature is that you can change the value of a variable (or variables) to determine how your program executes when processing that value.

To set a breakpoint, right-click a line of code in the Source view and select Add/Remove Breakpoint (Figure C.4). Setting a breakpoint causes it to appear in the Breakpoints view. From here you can manage the breakpoints for this debug session (e.g., you can remove the breakpoint or temporarily disable it when you no longer want the debugger to stop at that line).

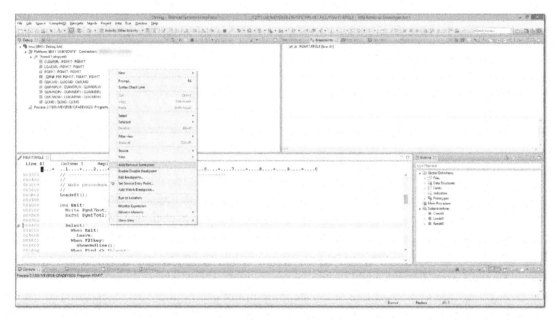

Figure C.4: Setting a breakpoint

The Variables view displays the current value of the variables in your RPG program. You can also create monitors to watch values of variables or expressions. To do so, highlight a variable or expression, right-click, and select Monitor Expression from the resulting menu, as Figure C.5 shows. The monitor then appears in the Monitors view, where you can view or modify its value.

The Debug view allows you to trace the flow of statement execution by using a feature called *stepping*, wherein the system executes all or part of your program one line at a time, stopping after each operation so you can examine the logic flow and program variables. The debugger supports several varieties of step mode, including Step Over and Step Into. In many cases, the difference between the two may be negligible. But if the program you are debugging calls another program or a procedure, these variations will differ.

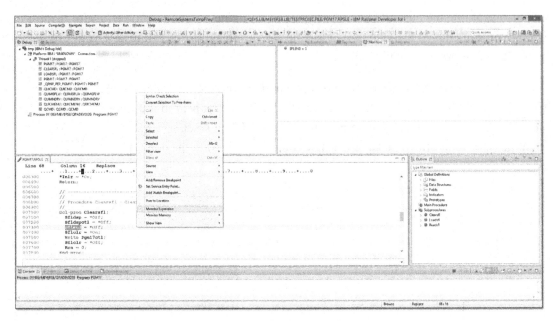

Figure C.5: Creating a Monitor

In Step Over mode, the debugger treats the call as a single line of code, executing the entire program or procedure before stopping. In Step Into mode, the debugger handles each line in the called program or procedure as a separate line, stopping at each one. While you are stepping through the program, the debugger will stop at each line in the Source view, highlighting the line that is about to be executed. As each line is processed, you can trace the execution path, view variables and monitors, and manage them. Right-clicking a process in the Debug view lets you select one of the stepping options in Figure C.6—Step Into (which you can also initiate with the F5 key) or Step Over (F6).

This brief explanation of the RDi Debug perspective covers only the highlights of its features. Be sure to read the Help documentation associated with the debugger to learn its many capabilities. Mastering this tool will save you many hours of frustration.

Debugging with STRDBG

The traditional green-screen application development environment also includes a debugger, which you initiate with the STRDBG (Start Debug) command. This debugger has fewer features than the RDi Debug perspective, but it shares many of the same concepts — breakpoints, step mode, and so forth. Before you can debug a program in this environment, you must place the program into debug mode; an SEP is not required. The STRDBG command names the program (or programs) you want to debug by using the following syntax:

```
STRDBG PGM(program-name program-name ... )
```

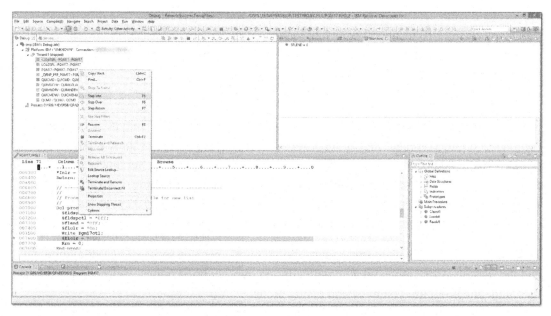

Figure C.6: Stepping through a program

A display similar to the one in Figure C.7 will appear, showing the source for the entry module of the program you are debugging. The programs remain in debug mode until you issue the ENDDBG (End Debug) command.

```
                          Display Module Source

Program:   PGM17          Library:   MEYERSB        Module:   PGM17
     31        // --------------------------------------------------------
     32        //
     33        // Main procedure
     34        //
     35        Loadsfl();
     36
     37        Dou Exit;
     38          Write Pgm17bot;
     39          Exfmt Pgm17ctl;
     40
     41          Select;
     42            When Exit;
     43              Leave;
     44            When F21key;
     45              Showcmdline();
                                                                     More...
Debug . . .

F3=End program    F6=Add/Clear breakpoint    F10=Step    F11=Display variable
F12=Resume        F17=Watch variable    F18=Work with watch    F24=More keys
```

Figure C.7: Debugging with STRDBG

Once in debug mode, you can specify at least one breakpoint by positioning the cursor on the desired line and pressing F6. Pressing F12 resumes operation, running the program until it encounters the first breakpoint. The debug display then reappears, positioned to the breakpoint.

The debug display lets you set other breakpoints (using F6) and execute the program in step mode (using F10 to step over or F22 to step into). To show a variable's current value, position the cursor on the variable and press F11. The information appears on the message line at the bottom of the display. If the information exceeds a single line, a separate display opens so you can view all the variable details.

In addition to using the function keys to debug a program, you can also type debugging commands on the command line at the bottom of the display. Some of these commands mimic the function of the function keys; other commands expand on the function keys. For example, you can use the Eval debugging command to change the value of a variable or variables while the program is running. Use the Help function (the F1 key) to learn how to use these debugging commands, as well as other commands and function keys.

Once you are finished with a debugging session, remember to issue the ENDDBG command to end the session. This command automatically removes all breakpoints. Before you edit and recompile the program, you must end debug mode.

Specifying a Debug View

Before you can use any debugger with a program, you must provide one or more debug views for the modules that make up the program. The debug view is a module attribute that specifies the type of debug data you want stored with the module when you compile it. The debug views are as follows:

- compile listing view (*LIST)
- root source view (*SOURCE)
- copy source view (*COPY)
- statement view (*STMT)

Each view offers a different level of source detail.

You choose the debug view when you compile the module (e.g., with the CRTRPGMOD command). Specify the debug view in the compile command's DBGVIEW parameter. For example, you can build a compile listing view by specifying this command:

```
CRTRPGMOD ... DBGVIEW(*LIST)
```

The DBGVIEW parameter values also include *ALL (to build all debug views) and *NONE (to omit debugging information from the compiled module).

The compile listing view (*LIST) stores within the module a representation of the actual compile listing, which includes /COPY member text and descriptions for externally described files. Of all the debug view options, the compile listing view offers the most detail and is the most reliable view if the source changes after the module is compiled. The *SOURCE and *COPY views store references to the source at compile time and are not as dependable as the *LIST view. Unlike the *SOURCE and *COPY views, the *LIST view is not tied to the original source member, so you can change, move, or rename the source member without affecting this debug view.

The statement (*STMT) view stores debug information by statement number but does not save a representation of the source. Consequently, you can't display the source when debugging a program with the statement view. This view is most useful when you want to distribute debuggable program code but don't want others to be able to see your source. To completely prevent the ability to debug a module, specify DBGVIEW(*NONE).

To debug your program, you need to compile it with the appropriate debug view to instruct the compiler to generate debug information in the object files. If you compile the program by using RDi, it creates a debug view. But if you use PDM or a workstation command to compile, you must specify the debug detail that you want to use.

Index

Boldface text or page numbers indicate illustrations.

Embedded SQL Host Language
statements in, 58
error management and, 302–303,
511–513
example code using, 314–317
Exec SQL directive for, 294–295
Execute, 310–311, 318
Execute Immediate in, 311–312,
319
Fetch, 306–307, 368
Fetch, with arrays, 350–353
formatting scripts/code in, 61
host structures in, 297–298
host variables in, 295–296, 318
IBM Data Studio client for, **60**
IBM i terminology vs., 57
indexes in, 57, 75
INSERT in. See INSERT
Interactive SQL facility for, 59
legacy code and, 317–318
naming conventions and, 64
null values in, 62–63, 298–300
Open, 306
parameter values in, 308
positioned updates in, 308
precompiler in, 313–314
Prepare, 309–310
qualified names in, 64
RDi development environment
and, 60
record format names in, with
RCDFMT, 63–64
return codes in, 300–303
rows in, 57
Run SQL Statements
(RUNSQLSTM) command in,
59, **60**
schema (collections) in, 57, 64–65
Select Into, with host variable,
296–297
SELECT in. See SELECT
semicolon (;) delimiter in, 59
Set Option in, 312–313
SQL Communication Area
(SQLCA) data structure in,
300, 318, 511–513
SQL naming convention in, 64
SQL Procedural Language (SPL)
statements in, 58
Sqlcode in, 301–302, 511–513
Sqlerrd in, 511–513
SQLRPGLE programs in,
313–314, 319
Sqlstate in, 301–303, 511–513
Sqlwarn in, 511–513
Start SQL Interactive Session
(STRSQL) in, 59, **59**
system naming convention in, 64

table creation in, with CREATE
TABLE, 61
table naming in, 61–62
tables in, 57
UPDATE in. See UPDATE
Values clause in, 292
views in, 57, 73–75
Whenever statement in, 514–515
Where clause in, 293, 318–319
Xfields function in, 293
SQL Communication Area (SQLCA),
300, 318, 511–513
SQL Procedural Language (SPL)
statements, 58
SQLCA, 300, 318, 511–513
Sqlcode, 301–302, 511–513
Sqlerrd, 511–513
SQLRPGLE programs, 313–314, 319
Sqlstate, 301–303, 511–513
Sqlwarn, 511–513
SQRT, 195
Square root (%Sqrt), 192, 198
Standalone variables, 30–32, 50
*arrays as, 324, 368. See also
Arrays*
data item name in, 118
data types in, 119–122
date, time, timestamp in, 122,
235–236
declarations and, 107, 118–122,
142
declaring, 30–32, 118
indicators and, 120
Like, Likeds, Likerec keywords in,
132–135, 142
packed data types in, 120–121
unsigned integers in, 121
zoned data types in, 120–121
Start Program Export List
(STRPGMEXP), 478–481
Statements, 24
semicolon terminator for, 24, 42
Static binding, 438
Status of file or program (%Status),
496–497
STRPGMEXP, 478–481
STRSQL, 59, 59
Structured design, 3–4, 145–146
Structured Query Language. See SQL
SUB, 195
Subfields, 124, 125–126
character data and, Eva-corr and,
203–205
date/time data and, 235–236
externally described, 129–131
initializing, 126–127
Like, Likeds, Likerec keywords in,
132–135, 142

overlapping, 127–129
qualified data structures and,
131–132
Subfile programming, 519–544
control record formats for,
523–524
entire subfile at once loading,
538–542
example of, 519–521, **520, 521,
522**
keywords for, 523–524
list panels and, 519
loading, 524–542
page at a time loading of, 525–538
record formats for, 522–523
Submit Job (SBMJOB), 422
Subprocedures, 23, 438, 441
file I/O and, 459–460, 465
Subroutines, 162–164, 167, 177, 395
automatic execution of, with
INZSR, 164
Begin subroutine (Begsr) for, 162,
178
End subroutine (Endsr) for, 162,
178
error management and, 505,
507–508
Execute subroutine (Exsr) for,
163, 178
INZSR, 164
Leave subroutine (Leavesr) for,
163–164, 178
PSSR, for error control, 509–510
recursion and, 163
Substrings, 211–212
Subtract duration (subdur), 252,
253–254
Subtraction, 182–183
sizing results for, 186–187
Sum elements of array (%Xfoot), 346,
369
Superglobal definition, 482
Syntax/syntax errors, 16–17, 19, 28
System naming convention, 64
System/3 computer, 3
System/38 minicomputers, 3
System-named activation groups,
484–485
System i, 5

T

Tables, 57, 323–324
arrays and, 323–324, 359–365
changing values in, using arrays,
365
creating, with CREATE TABLE,
61